Computer Supported Cooperative Work

Series editor
Richard Harper, Cambridge, United Kingdom

The CSCW series examines the dynamic interface of human nature, culture, and technology. Technology to support groups, once largely confined to workplaces, today affects all aspects of life. Analyses of "Collaboration, Sociality, Computation, and the Web" draw on social, computer and information sciences, aesthetics, and values. Each volume in the series provides a perspective on current knowledge and discussion for one topic, in monographs, edited collections, and textbooks appropriate for those studying, designing, or engaging with sociotechnical systems and artifacts.

Titles published within the Computer Supported Cooperative Work series are included within Thomson Reuters' Book Citation Index.

More information about this series at http://www.springer.com/series/2861

Volker Wulf • Kjeld Schmidt • David Randall
Editors

Designing Socially Embedded Technologies in the Real-World

Editors
Volker Wulf
School of Media and Information
University of Siegen
Siegen, Germany

Fraunhofer FIT
St. Augustin, Germany

David Randall
School of Media and Information
University of Siegen
Siegen, Germany

Kjeld Schmidt
Department of Organization
Copenhagen Business School
Frederiksberg, Denmark

School of Media and Information
University of Siegen
Siegen, Germany

ISSN 1431-1496
Computer Supported Cooperative Work
ISBN 978-1-4471-7115-7   ISBN 978-1-4471-6720-4   (eBook)
DOI 10.1007/978-1-4471-6720-4

Contents

Contributors

Mark S. Ackerman School of Information, University of Michigan, Ann Arbor, MI, USA

Jörg Beringer Splunk Inc., San Francisco, CA, USA

Olav W. Bertelsen Aarhus University, Denmark

Pernille Bjørn Technologies in Practice Research Group, IT University of Copenhagen, Copenhagen, Denmark

Johan Bolmsten World Maritime University, Malmö, Sweden

Nina Boulus-Rødje Technologies in Practice Research Group, IT University of Copenhagen, Copenhagen, Denmark

Roland Buchner Centre for Human-Computer Interaction, Department of Computer Sciences, University of Salzburg, Salzburg, Austria

Federico Cabitza Dipartimento di Informatica, Sistemistica e Comunicazione, Universitá degli Studi di Milano-Bicocca, Milan, Italy

Lars R. Christensen IT University of Copenhagen, Copenhagen, Denmark

Giorgio De Michelis DISCo, University of Milano – Bicocca, Milan, Italy

Yvonne Dittrich Software and System Section, IT University of Copenhagen, Copenhagen, Denmark

Gerhard Fischer University of Colorado, Boulder, CO, USA

Geraldine Fitzpatrick Vienna University of Technology, TUWIEN, Vienna, Austria

Y. Hara Hitachi Design Division, Tokyo, Japan

Dave Harley Brighton University, Brighton, UK

Thomas Herrmann University of Bochum, Bochum, Germany

Alina Huldtgren TU Delft, Delft, The Netherlands

Wijnand Ijsselsteijn TU Eindhoven, Eindhoven, The Netherlands

N. Ikeya Keio University, Tokyo, Japan

K. Kashimura Hitachi Design Division, Tokyo, Japan

Elizabeth Kaziunas School of Information, University of Michigan, Ann Arbor, MI, USA

Patricia M. Kluckner Centre for Human-Computer Interaction, Department of Computer Sciences, University of Salzburg, Salzburg, Austria

Arno Laminger Centre for Human-Computer Interaction, Department of Computer Sciences, University of Salzburg, Salzburg, Austria

Markus Latzina SAP SE, Walldorf (Baden), Germany

Myriam Lewkowicz UMR CNRS 6281 – Tech-CICO, Troyes University of Technology, Troyes, France

Lone Malmborg IT University of Copenhagen, Copenhagen, Denmark

Alexander Meschtscherjakov Centre for Human-Computer Interaction, Department of Computer Sciences, University of Salzburg, Salzburg, Austria

Nicole Mirnig Centre for Human-Computer Interaction, Department of Computer Sciences, University of Salzburg, Salzburg, Austria

Claudia Müller University of Siegen, Siegen, Germany

Sebastian Osswald Centre for Human-Computer Interaction, Department of Computer Sciences, University of Salzburg, Salzburg, Austria

Nicole Perterer Centre for Human-Computer Interaction, Department of Computer Sciences, University of Salzburg, Salzburg, Austria

Volkmar Pipek School of Media and Information, University of Siegen, Siegen, Germany

David Randall School of Media and Information, University of Siegen, Siegen, Germany

Markus Rohde School of Media and Information, University of Siegen, Siegen, Germany

Pascal Salembier UMR CNRS 6281 – Tech-CICO, Troyes University of Technology, Troyes, France

Kjeld Schmidt Department of Organization, Copenhagen Business School, Frederiksberg, Denmark

Carla Simone Dipartimento di Informatica, Sistemistica e Comunicazione, Universitá degli Studi di Milano-Bicocca, Milan, Italy

Gunnar Stevens School of Media and Information, University of Siegen, Siegen, Germany

Ewald Strasser Centre for Human-Computer Interaction, Department of Computer Sciences, University of Salzburg, Salzburg, Austria

Petra Sundstroem Centre for Human-Computer Interaction, Department of Computer Sciences, University of Salzburg, Salzburg, Austria

Manfred Tscheligi Centre for Human-Computer Interaction, Department of Computer Sciences, University of Salzburg, Salzburg, Austria

Astrid Weiss Centre for Human-Computer Interaction, Department of Computer Sciences, University of Salzburg, Salzburg, Austria

David Wilfinger Centre for Human-Computer Interaction, Department of Computer Sciences, University of Salzburg, Salzburg, Austria

Volker Wulf School of Media and Information, University of Siegen, Siegen, Germany

Fraunhofer FIT, St. Augustin, Germany

Chapter 1
Introduction: Meeting the Challenge of Change

Volker Wulf, Kjeld Schmidt, and David Randall

There is little doubt that insights gleaned from the turn to the 'social' (whatever that might mean) have had a profound impact on the development of information and communication technologies (ICTs). As was reported many years ago by Bannon (1991), there was a major epistemological shift away from the 'human factors' approach which privileged 'usability' issues towards problems which seemed, at first glance, more intractable. These included, for brief mention, the problem of how ICTs might fit, or otherwise, into complex organisational contexts (see, e.g. Grudin 1990), how they might support interaction between different individuals and groups who might not be co-located and how coordinative and cooperative functions of various kinds might be supported. A range of by-now familiar (even classic) literature addressed various issues that attended on this shift, including how best to conceptualise the field (Schmidt 1991; Schmidt and Bannon 1992), what perspectives might prove fruitful for analysis (see, e.g. Hughes et al 1992, 1993; Heath and Luff 1991; Dourish 2001), what methodologies might be usefully deployed (see, e.g. Randall et al. 2007), what a developing corpus of studies might reveal (Heath et al. 2000) and what the consequences overall for our picture of information systems might be (see, e.g. Lamb and Kling 2003). It is not unreasonable to

V. Wulf (✉)
School of Media and Information, University of Siegen, Siegen, Germany

Fraunhofer FIT, St. Augustin, Germany
e-mail: volker.wulf@unisiegen.de

K. Schmidt
Department of Organization, Copenhagen Business School, Kilevej 14A, Frederiksberg, Denmark

School of Media and Information, University of Siegen, Siegen, Germany
e-mail: schmidt@cscw.d

D. Randall
School of Media and Information, University of Siegen, Siegen, Germany
e-mail: D.Randall@mmu.ac.uk

© Springer-Verlag London 2015
V. Wulf et al. (eds.), *Designing Socially Embedded Technologies in the Real-World*,
Computer Supported Cooperative Work, DOI 10.1007/978-1-4471-6720-4_1

suggest that these insights, insights which were largely promoted within the field of computer-supported cooperative work (CSCW), have had an influence in many different contexts. One only has to look at, for instance, the way in which 'ethnographic' approaches have become commonplace in any number of design- related areas. Having said that, these largely academic changes have not been accompanied by wholesale acceptance in the commercial and industrial world. Moreover, the greatly accelerating pace of change means that as fast as we reconceptualise our analytic problems, we are confronted with new ones. Few of us dealing with the way new technology had organisational and interactional consequences foresaw the development of, and huge consequences of, the World Wide Web. The various chapters in this book, therefore, constitute attempts to grapple with these themes.

Firstly, although the last 25 years or so have seen a paradigm shift in the *academic* computing field, one which increasingly anchors technology design in social practice, this shift has not for the most part been translated into an equal shift in emphasis in the commercial/industrial world. More specifically, how to deal with the problem of situated study with large and complex settings in relation to commercial interests remains arguably under-examined. Organisational interests, regardless of this shift, largely remain vested in engineering or 'scientific' models of computing and the production of generic software applications. This incompatibility of agendas is substantially a result of two related factors. We have an incomplete understanding of the real-world problems entailed in marrying academic and organisational interests. We need to understand and implement processes which see the real needs of industry, commerce, 3rd sector interests and the academy merged in realistic and fruitful ways, especially in a context where rapidly evolving technical and social changes will further problematise our assumptions.

Secondly, the 'situated' approaches to computing that CSCW treats as foundational have yet to generate realistic solutions to the problems of comparison and generalisability. We take the view that most work in this area remains top-down and theoretically abstract. It ought to be a source of concern that after 25 years of work, there remains no consensus over the relative merits of, for instance, activity theory, ANT, distributed cognition, ethnomethodology and so on, in relation to real-world design. There is a demonstrable lack of any systematic approach to the problem of *adequate generalisation* and of an approach which integrates notions of practice with wider concerns. That is, how we best move from the single, situated, case study towards an empirically founded conceptual framework that serves real-world design needs remains a pressing problem.

Thirdly, these issues become more pressing in a context now compounded by the sheer pervasiveness of IT artefacts such that they touch on every aspect of our work, organisational and social lives. Technological developments such as the rise of digital media, mobile technology, cloud computing, open source, Web 2.0, mash-ups, collaborative environments, massive multiplayer gaming systems, recommender systems and the rapid dissemination and take-up of social software sites such as YouTube, Facebook, Twitter, Snapchat and WhatsApp have accelerated the trend towards complexity. Despite this, IT design, development and evaluation remain bedevilled by a lack of consensus as to appropriate mechanisms for understanding how best to situate new hardware and software in rapidly changing socio-digital ecologies. We need to make some progress towards new architectures and new philosophies which might underpin them.

Fourthly, there has been a developing recognition that the 'engineering' paradigm mentioned above is singularly ill equipped to deal with the progressive move of design interests into a world saturated with interests, values, preferences, hetero-geneous worldviews and so on. The notion of the 'value centred' (e.g. Friedman et al. 2006; LeDantec et al. 2009) and how best to incorporate ethical positions into the design process itself has, of course, exercised researchers since the very early days of participatory design (PD). Exactly how this incorporation is supposed to take place, given the other changes rehearsed above, however, remains an obdurate problem. Associated with this is the problem of the long term. Academic research does not always deal in long-term or sustainable outcomes. Of course, we do not wish to tar all academic work with the same brush, but most practitioners would recognise that 'end of project' decision-making can have a profound effect on the people we work with and – if honest with ourselves – we would accept that we have not always found a means to act in a fully responsible way.

The various chapters in this book therefore elaborate on a design-oriented research agenda which tries to close the gap between organisationally mandated approaches to technical development on the one hand and 'social impact' studies on the other, recognising the huge social and ethical impact that new technology can have and asking how we can best deal with this. The book consists of three main parts. The first part consists of contribution representatives from industrial and commercial partners such as SAP and Hitachi, who are interested in, and see a need for, a better articulation of the themes we mention above and suggest ways in which they are dealing with them. As Beringer and Latzina (Chap. 1) argue, there is a need for an 'extended and systematic' response to industry's demands. They suggest that the design of IT artefacts has been focused for the past 50 years on a design rationale which implies that a 'perfect' and generic design solution for supporting a given set of use cases exists. With the emergence of mobile technology, Web 2.0 networked solutions and semantic technology, this simple design equation, they argue, has been challenged. The design of next-generation products will need to take into consideration the interaction of the IT artefact with the entire context of use including social life and society. This notion of social embeddedness implies a bidirectional interaction model forming a symbiosis between IT artefact and its context of use. To reach this level of immersion and adaptivity, the design of the IT artefact has to reflect the elastic and flexible uses that will evolve over time. Their chapter, then, discusses some of the ways in which large information service providers are meeting these challenges. In Chap. 2, the same authors exemplify their insights with a discussion of the design of enterprise resource planning (ERP) systems. These 'one-size-fits-all' applications are, as they say, 'increasingly challenged by small fit-to-purpose productivity applications that are designed for very specific use cases'. ERP content, as it becomes increasingly pervasive, will necessitate significantly more adaptability of functionality and content. They propose an approach to the design of interfaces for business applications which they term 'elastic'. Elasticity means that applications must be seamless in supporting the user across both routine and knowledge-intensive working modes.

Chapter 3, by Kashimura et al. of Hitachi, deals with empirical cases and how best to approach the problem of generalisation from them in a context where real-world pressures necessitate the use of some 'shorthand' devices. The pressures include the fact that the design life cycle is now much shorter, that 'design' has become an increasingly polymorphous concept (with product, system and 'future concept' designers in this organisation working together with ethnographers) and that ethnographers require a level of training and expertise that is not always easy to find at short notice. They draw on Christopher Alexander's notion of patterns in an attempt to do two things. Firstly, to provide a language for doing comparative work across different settings in similar domains. They use maintenance and adaptive engineering as an example that enables designers, firstly, to grasp the specificities of engineering contexts and the more generic issues that are to be found and, secondly, to provide a framework that new and inexperienced ethnographers can readily adapt to.

The second part of the book reflects on the challenge of change and more specifically on how we might deal with complex environments in transformational conditions. In Chap. 4, therefore, Giorgio De Michelis examines the way in which the 'paradigm shift' towards a concept of practice affects our understanding of how IT artefacts should function. He argues that today such artefacts are largely task oriented despite the fact that practices have to be understood contextually. The fact of increasingly knowledge-intensive work makes this especially pressing. Socially embedded applications cannot be solely based on functions and features; rather, they need to be based on the new paradigm of 'situated computing', one which integrates task and sociality. This paradigm will necessitate support for identity work, continuity of purpose and the mechanics of sociality. It implies granting to users opportunities for 'radical (disruptive) innovation' and at the same time providing for 'maximum continuity'.

Thomas Herrman and Gerhard Fischer, in Chap. 5, further develop their notion of 'meta-design'. Meta-design concerns the way in which the interests and purposes of various stakeholders need to be aligned in such a way that they can participate in the design process – to act as designers. The chapter examines five different principles that need to be explored/addressed if this is to be successfully done. The principles they discuss are (1) cultures of participation, (2) empowerment for adaptation and evolution, (3) seeding and evolutionary growth, (4) under-design of models of socio-technical processes and (5) structuring of communication. They use the example of service integration and coordination for elderly people to illustrate their points.

Wulf et al. (Chap. 6) suggest design case studies 'as a method to examine similar complexities'. Comparing a set of design case studies, they elaborate on the concept and develop methodological insights. The authors, along with other contributors, are also concerned with the problem of transferability and how it is to be managed through qualitative approaches to data collection, analysis and design. They argue that design case studies, on their own, are very specific and unique in respect of socio-technical setting, time and project communication. They propose an approach to conceptualisation that reflects similarities and differences in organisational environments and elsewhere, but which is specifically contrasted to what they term 'large-scale' theoretical claims.

Christensen and Bertelsen take a slightly different view in Chap. 7. They make the point that the kinds of rhetoric associated with CSCW and its interest in contextuality are challenged by more scientific understandings of the design process, such as those emanating from design science. In order to enter into dialogue with such practices, they suggest the reintroduction of some notion of causality into CSCW thinking. They further argue that this has the merit of placing an emphasis on the material aspects of the socio-technical, something which is often under-examined. The importance of this argument, they suggest, is that the influence of the social sciences has provided us with a series of micro-studies but no way of challenging the scientific/engineering discourses. They draw on the concept of manipulability, first proposed by von Wright, in order to demonstrate their argument that this provides a basis for adequate generalisation.

Chapter 8 is by Lewkowitz and Salembier from the University of Technology of Troyes in France who are again concerned with complexity, but a complexity which comes both from the domains under examination and from the different disciplinary interests which are brought to bear. Their point is that multidisciplinarity has often been honoured in the breach. They recount their ten-year experience of team-based enquiry predicated on the analysis, modelling and design of cooperative ensembles in a wide span of settings in what they argue is a genuinely integrative, multidisciplinary approach. They describe processes of understanding, translation and testing which together form a systematic approach to design and evaluation.

Part III specifically concerns design issues. De Michelis, in Chap. 9, reflects on the experience of designing 'itsme', an operating system concept where users are people with a well-defined profile. He argues that new concepts which might replace the venerable 'desktop' metaphor are necessary in order to cope with new and innovative practices. The business of searching, sorting and otherwise organising work is now more, rather than less, difficult. Developing and implementing new metaphors, however, is not straightforward. The chapter reflects on the design of a socially embedded operating system for workstations which aimed to exploit the potential of cyberspace for work and business. The aim was and is to provide users with easy and intuitive ways to deal with the problems people encounter while managing their actions and interactions, but involves breaking the boundaries between developers and users in new, industry-focused ways.

In Chap. 10, Federico Cabitza and Carla Simone argue that there is still a gap between users' practices and the affordances of the ICT technology. Field studies, they say, continue to demonstrate that the procedures and methods that work in specific domains have evolved without any serious reflection on the relevance of these studies to wider practice. They argue that neither engineering metaphors nor 'post-engineering' approaches, like 'user-centred design', 'participatory design' and the like, guarantee design. In a radical take on the relationship between what are historically viewed as the distinct categories of 'user' and 'designer', they argue for a more or less complete collapse of that distinction and, allied to this, careful reflection on the relationship between methodologies for the investigation of the patterns of use, on the requirements elicitation and on the technical features of the applications themselves and the technological infrastructure on which they are based.

Weiss et al. describe the methodological challenges faced when researching non-traditional and 'challenging' environments (Chap. 11). Specifically, observational practices of the kind typified by 'ethnographic' work, they suggest, are not easy to carry out in certain environments, and hence, some rethinking of the way in which data is collected and analysed is necessary. They focus on two such environments: the highly context-dependent automotive environment and the complex context of a semiconductor factory. They outline general challenges posed for exploratory research, such as environmental constraints (e.g. clean room conditions in the factory and limited space in the car) which imply the need for new and sophisticated methods to support interaction design.

Geraldine Fitzpatrick looks at Ambient Assisted Living (AAL) and telehealth contexts which are receiving increasing industry and research attention and which take advantage of maturing and increasingly ubiquitous wireless, mobile and sensor-based technologies. She argues for a conceptual rethink in these areas. In Chap. 13 she shows that 'utopian' visions of support for assisted living and healthcare in general are largely driven by technological visions which have relatively little to do with understanding how such technologies come to be situated in everyday life and healthcare practice and what their potential is for enhancing new ways of living into older age. She outlines ways in which these new technological possibilities both challenge and provide new opportunities to redefine some fundamental notions: of patients and clinicians, of home and hospital caring and of growing old and living with chronic disease.

Part IV – Social and Organisational Complexity – further examines issues of organisational complexity visible already in some of the work described. Chapter 14 describes how, in the context of healthcare and elsewhere, it is possible to develop an approach to practice-based research which examines the nature of intervention and the various roles that are performed in that process. It is argued here that the nature of intervention and the ethical issues it poses are not fully understood, theoretically or empirically. Interventions are typically conceptualised differently in different disciplines. The main argument is that 'interventions' cannot be viewed as fixed and static packages to be picked off the shelf and used in any context. Rather, research interventions are socially embedded and context dependent.

Chapter 15 by Ackerman et al., from the University of Michigan, draw on a case study of Flint in Michigan, an impoverished and depressed economic location. They examine how health programs in communities are deeply embedded in their social context and in local practices and hence how, in order to create useful informational or technical programs, one must understand the ecologies of community members' practices, members' beliefs, medical and institutional structures surrounding their practices, as well as the disease itself. The case study focuses on diabetes and depression treatment/management in the area and emphasises how social conditions play an important role in defining assumptions about medical treatment.

In the final chapter, Bolmsten and Dittrich argue that the progressive inter-weaving of technology and everyday shop-floor practice has to allow for 'use in design' and 'design in use'. This puts considerable onus on IT management in the organisation as it attempts the business of integrating the two. They argue for a 'compatible' IT management at the organisational level which can capitalise on the creativity and innovative capacity of employees working on the shop floor. This is necessary if design of technical support anchored with employees' practices is to become sustainable in organisations. The chapter reports on a long-term action research study of how an organisation can leverage the capabilities of shop-floor IT development on the organisational arena.

All of the chapters in the book reflect a recognition that increasing organisational, technological and social complexity, allied to the sheer pace of change, requires us to rethink some of our dearest assumptions when dealing with situations in these arenas. The agenda we support here is one which moves us away from the 'small scale'. While all the editors are supporters of the use of detailed qualitative enquiries of one kind or another in order to understand better how work practices and technological development are necessarily interwoven, they all agree that our ability to adjust to new conditions, to defend our position against other robust formulations of the design problem and to recognise the real-world interests in cost reduction changes management as being a relevant backdrop to our concerns.

Acknowledgements This book emerged in the context of founding the European Society of Socially Embedded Technologies (EUSSET). At the occasion of the 50th birthday party of one of the editors, founding members of EUSSET met at Fraunhofer FIT and the University of Siegen for a research colloquium. Over quite some time and rounds of mutual reviewing, the book developed its current shape.

We are highly indebted to Juri Dachtera, whose current academic work centres on under-standing and supporting the EUSSET community. His engagement offered invaluable input for this book. We also wish to thank Andrea Bernards and Kathrin Zimmermann for perfectly organising the very pleasurable events in St. Augustin and Siegen. Marietta Krenzer-Gräb and Rachel Schneider supported the editing process and provided us with a well-working organisational environment. Without their continuous support, this endeavour would have hardly been possible.

References

Bannon, L. (1991). From human factors to human actors: The role of psychology and human-computer interaction studies in system design. In J. Greenbaum & M. Kyng (Eds.), *Design at work: Cooperative design of computer systems* (pp. 25–44). Hillsdale: Lawrence Erlbaum.

Friedman, B., Kahn, P., Borning, A., & Huldtgren, A. (2006). Value sensitive design and information systems. In P. Zhang & D. Galletta (Eds.), *Human-computer interaction and management information systems: Foundations advances in management information systems* (Advances in management information systems, Vol. 5, pp. 348–372). Armonk: M.E. Sharpe.

Dourish, P. (2001). *Where the action is: The foundations of embodied interaction.* Cambridge: MIT Press.

Grudin, J. (1990). The computer reaches out: The historical continuity of interface design. In *CHI'90 proceedings of the SIGCHI conference on human factors in computing systems* (pp. 261–268). New York: ACM.

Heath, C., Hindmarsh, J., & Luff, P. (2000). *Workplace studies: Recovering work practice and informing system design*. Cambridge: Cambridge University Press.

Heath, C., & Luff, P. (1991, September 24–27). Collaborative activity and technological design: Task coordination in London Underground control rooms. In L. Bannon, M. Robinson, & K. Schmidt (Eds.), *ECSCW'91. Proceedings of the second European Conference on Computer-Supported Cooperative Work*, Amsterdam (pp. 65–80). Dordrecht: Kluwer Academic Publishers.

Hughes, J. A., Randall, D., & Shapiro, D. (1992). Faltering from ethnography to design. In J. Turner & R. Kraut (Eds.), *Proceedings of CSCW'92 conference on computer-supported cooperative work* (pp. 115–122). Toronto: ACM Press.

Hughes, J. A., Randall, D., & Shapiro, D. (1993). Designing with ethnography: Making work visible. *Interacting with Computers, 5*, 239–253.

Lamb, R., & Kling, R. (2003). Reconceptualising users as social actors in information systems research. *MIS Quarterly, 27*(2), 197–235.

Ledantec, C., Poole, E., & Wyche, S. (2009). Values as lived experience: Evolving value sensitive design in support of value discovery. *Proceedings of CHI'09*. Boston: ACM Press.

Schmidt, K. (1991). Riding a tiger, or computer supported cooperative work. In *Proceedings of the 2nd European conference on CSCW*. Dordrecht: Kluwer.

Schmidt, K., & Bannon, L. (1992). Taking CSCW seriously: Supporting articulation work, Computer Supported Cooperative Work (CSCW). *An International Journal, 1*(1–2), 7–40.

Part I
The Business Perspective

Chapter 2
Socially Embedded Technology: The Pathway to Sustainable Product Development

Jörg Beringer and Markus Latzina

2.1 Introduction

The design of IT artifacts has been focused for the past 50 years on delivering products that serve the needs of a particular set of end users. User-centered design methods relating to the design of IT artifacts have evolved in both the academic context, in fields such as HCI, and in the commercial context. Both share a common commitment to the analysis and understanding of stakeholder requirements. The underlying rationale of such methods was that there exists a "perfect" design solution for supporting a given set of use cases and that the shipped design should reflect this as much as possible to guarantee product success.

However, with the emergence of mobile technology, Web 2.0 networked solutions, and semantic technology, this simple design equation has been problematized. Today's consumer applications actively connect users and their knowledge in order to seed highly engaged user communities and leverage the wisdom of the crowd. Such social applications are not stable by definition and require continuous adjustments and improvements to stay in sync with their respective communities. The design focus of these next-generation products goes well beyond designing for a single user interacting with a single system.

This paradigm shift also penetrates into large enterprises in terms of new demands for running their business. Besides high productivity and efficiency, enterprises must also pay attention to their agility to implement change and to respond to novel market opportunities or disruptive technologies by adapting

J. Beringer (✉)
Splunk Inc., 250 Brannan Street, San Francisco, CA, USA
e-mail: jberinger@splunk.com

M. Latzina
SAP SE, Dietmar-Hopp-Allee 16, 69190 Walldorf (Baden), Germany
e-mail: markus.latzina@sap.com

© Springer-Verlag London 2015
V. Wulf et al. (eds.), *Designing Socially Embedded Technologies in the Real-World*,
Computer Supported Cooperative Work, DOI 10.1007/978-1-4471-6720-4_2

Fig. 2.1 Business process
modeling vs socially
embedded solutions (inspired
by Schrage 2005)

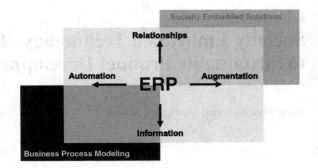

business processes or changing entire business models. While service-oriented
software architecture is an important enabler for quickly reorganizing the technical
support of business processes (Dörner et al. 2009), the most dramatic change
happens on the side of the end user. IT departments, previously specializing in
automating business processes with the help of standard ERP software, are now
aiming to provision knowledge workers with modern consumer-grade productivity
tools which are conducive to decision making in the concrete contexts of particular
business situations. Fundamentally, this extends the charter of IT departments
in large enterprises from enabling and automating business processes to also
augmenting people's work (Schrage 2005) (Fig. 2.1).

The ERP market is drifting from a monolithic process enablement approach
to a hybrid approach which involves empowering a network of users to accom-
plish collaborative business tasks. This shift from a mechanical-object ethos to
an organic-system ethos (Dubberly 2008) forces ERP vendors to enable new
consumption patterns and channels in order to allow users to contextually access
relevant business information and share outcomes with other colleagues. This in turn
forces IT departments to adopt a more user-centric approach to adapting standard
software since the system design must be tailored to the situational needs of the end
user and not just the functional requirements of a user-agnostic business process
model. This is a fundamental change and in line what Dubberly describes as the shift
from an expert-driven approach to a more user-centric approach, which in case of
generative tools becomes a participatory design approach aiming at enabling users
rather than canonically imposing a standard solution (Sanders 2008).

This notion of social embeddedness implies a bidirectional interaction model
forming a symbiosis between the IT artifact and its context of use. To reach this
level of immersiveness and adaptivity, the design of the IT artifact cannot anymore
be considered to remain static after deployment; rather, it needs to be conceived as
elastic and flexible to evolve over time during its use. This notion of sociotechnical
information systems (Taylor 1998) and design for appropriation and continuous
change (Fischer and Giaccardi 2006) has been—of course—the focus of many
academic publications and involves various research streams, design theories, and
case studies. However, this eclecticism of method and theory makes it difficult to
apply to industrial product design (Wulf and Rohde 1995).

The mission of the newly founded European Society for Socially Embedded Technologies (EUSSET) is to bring together research streams that inform the design of such sociotechnical systems and help to understand the dynamics of adopting and using IT artifacts beyond the simple interaction with a static user interface. As such, EUSSET is a catalyst for existing research results, but also aims to drive new research topics focusing explicitly on the design of socially embedded technology (Wulf et al. 2011).

2.2 Products That Transform Life

In the end, all products are socially embedded since they are used by one or several people. The analysis of social context is already the "best practice" of most user-centered design methods. Spearheaded by Contextual Design, the modeling of stakeholder networks (the role model) and socially defined motivational factors (the cultural model) became industry standard for understanding task domains (Beyer and Holtzblatt 1998). So, what is EUSSET adding to the equation?

EUSSET is the response to the extended and systematic demand in the IT industry to understand thoroughly the context of use of its products. There are a number of industry trends that all demand a deeper understanding of the interaction of IT software solutions with larger social systems and they are as follows:

Extended reach: With new cloud technology and the extended functionalities of mobile devices, virtually all users in all contexts can be reached at all times. Software vendors can inject IT artifacts into private life at home, at work, and in public. Software vendors try to invent products that quickly become part of daily practices in an increasingly ubiquitous way. The pressure to innovate and penetrate into those contexts requires the industry to think about how to address IT artifacts that support existing practices or even seed new practices. Many times, those practices are interwoven with social networks. In private life, these networks normally implicate family members, friends, and partners. At work, in contrast, solutions have to address social processes within formal and informal team structures and the dynamics of communities. Designing for one user alone feels outdated.

Ubiquitous computing: With more processing capabilities and the ability to seamlessly adjust to environmental conditions, IT artifacts can be fully integrated into everyday environments and activities. This level of integration is only possible if the functionality is coherent with the situation of use. Often such IT artifacts are equipped with sensors and machine learning algorithms to learn over time and automatically adjust to idiosyncratic preferences and patterns of use.

Viral spreading: Since Web 2.0 demonstrated how products can seed and serve large social networks, the identification of principles that facilitate the viral spreading of applications has been the focus of a number of case studies. As viral spreading takes place within the social context of the product use, the analysis of this context and the instrumentation of social relationships becomes an important accelerator for product adoption. Optimizing the "coolness factor" turns out to be a profitable design goal to improve product attractiveness and user acceptance (Holtzblatt 2011). As coolness is a subjective quality that is primarily defined by the social value system of users, it becomes obvious that the design focus extends from the user interface to the overall product performance within a larger social context.

Mass adoption: Taking successful Web 2.0 solutions as the reference, many software vendors aim for mass adoption of their product with high degree of "stickiness" and significant network effect. The product must resonate quickly with users and create a demand pull due to coolness and/or relevance. As such, the product experience and go-to-market approach must be optimized to resonate with users and allow for quick and risk-free adoption in various contexts.

Social entrepreneurship: With the trend to social responsibility and sustainability, the success of products is not only measured by their profit and market performance but by social and environmental goals. The recognition of a social problem and the achievement of social change are the ultimate goals. The IT artifact is only a tool to achieve this overarching goal and as such becomes a technical design component within a larger sociotechnical environment.

Behavioral change: While traditionally information systems are designed to support a given number of use cases relevant to an application domain or user persona, a new breed of applications emerges which attempt to change the behavior of a user for the purpose of education (how to save money), compliance (drug prescription), social responsibility (saving energy), or becoming a better sales person. This product aspiration inverts the design rationale of the system from passively supporting a fixed number of use cases to iteratively influencing the user's behavior by capturing knowledge about the user context, including social network information.

From those examples, it becomes obvious that the understanding of the interaction between IT artifact and the user and the larger social context is more relevant than ever. Understanding how a software solution fits into the social context of the target persona is essential, and the impact on the user's social environment is now often the primary design objective. This extends the design focus both in scope and in time since the adoption of the product and the appropriation to its context of use become important aspects of product performance (Fig. 2.2).

With the design focus being the interaction between context of use and the embedded IT artifact, understanding of the interplay between the two becomes important. Yet, information and knowledge about social systems is surprisingly fragmented across many academic communities like CSCW, intelligent user interfaces, MobileHCI, social computing, ubiquitous computing, and Web 2.0 conferences. This makes it difficult to gain understanding of how to design for social acceptance, ubiquitous use, and a mutual learning relationship between user and the IT artifact.

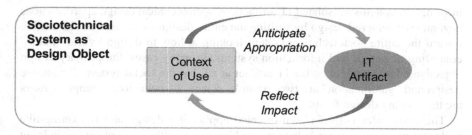

Fig. 2.2 Extending design focus in scope and time

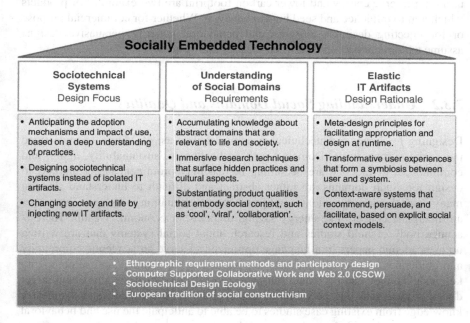

Fig. 2.3 Pillars of European Society for Socially Embedded Technologies

2.3 Pillars of Innovation

We believe that innovation socially embedded on technology and products is centered around three pillars (cf., Fig. 2.3).

2.3.1 Explicit Design Focus on Sociotechnical System

Built on the European tradition of social constructivism and participatory design, the policy focuses on designing for sociotechnical systems instead of conceiving of information systems as isolated IT artifacts. A sociotechnical design approach goes beyond user-centered design by shifting the entire design focus from the IT artifact toward the entire sociotechnical system looking at how to design hybrid systems consisting of people and information systems. In many cases, the primary design objective might even not be the IT artifact at all, but the social system. Persuasive design and "gamification" are two examples where the behavioral change of users are the primary design focus.

The boundaries between goal-oriented application design and marketing-like tools that propagate certain behaviors are blurring. Healthcare applications helping users to be compliant to prescriptions or diets and sustainability solutions helping users to preserve energy and lower carbon footprint are two examples of products which aim to influence and seed human behavior. Whether for commercial purpose or for injecting desirable attitudes and behavioral patterns, persuasive designs assume a bidirectional force between the user and system.

2.3.2 Understanding Social Domains and Qualities

Designing for larger sociotechnical systems requires us, of course, to understand the social system itself. Domains such as healthcare, sustainability, aging, and communities of practice are becoming increasingly prominent target markets to design for. Such domains are rather abstract and difficult to understand since in many cases the design context is not just a concrete situation or use case, but rather an intangible concept like energy saving, diabetes, or economic wealth. There is a huge body of field studies and research about social systems that are written up as academic papers in a language optimized to serve an academic community and guidelines of scientific journals. By extracting key findings and summarizing key insights, they can become a reusable set of foundational insights about target domains. One task we need to set ourselves is to accumulate and synthesize knowledge from existing case studies to be able to anticipate the use and behavioral impact of new designs for a given social domain.

Designing for large social systems and working with abstract concepts that are difficult to observe and to operationalize mean that the suitability of research methods themselves become an interesting research topic in its own. Methods like participatory design and ethnographic field research seem to be essential for studying large sociotechnical systems. But their applicability and feasibility must be critically reviewed. For socially embedded technology, the monitoring of actual adoption and *use beyond the moment of first design* are important additional information resources for understanding the sociotechnical system. IT artifacts must be recalibrated if necessary to reach the right level of adoption or for the intended impact on the user or society. From community research we know that it is unrealistic to assume that a sociotechnical system can be designed and shipped. It rather has to be seeded and continuously adjusted in order to grow and become pervasive.

When designing for social embeddedness, the optimization of product qualities that relate to social adoption and use within social networks becomes a key design goal. Designing for coolness (Holtzblatt 2011) or viral adoption (Michael Weiksner et al. 2008) is an example of product characteristics which go beyond the traditional understanding of usability or user experience. A systematic approach can help us to better understand such social product qualities and to identify repeatable design principles. For example, the "gamification" of products to motivate users to engage and participate to user communities is such a product characteristic which can be potentially applied to any domain.

2.3.3 New Design Rationale

The ability of an IT artifact of continuously adapting to its own context of use as an intrinsic product capability is one of the most important innovation aspects of socially embedded technology. While traditional HCI assumes that design takes place upfront before shipping a product, newer constructivist design approaches such as meta-design and end user development suggest a distribution of power in the design process between design time and use time to support a continuous adaptation of the IT artifact to its actual context of use (Lieberman et al. 2006). The IT artifact is able to recalibrate itself to adjust to context of use.

While the empowerment of the end user to customize IT artifacts is one step toward this flexibility (Fischer et al. 2004), the challenging question is: how can we design IT artifacts that are intrinsically elastic with respect to their user interface and functionality? One of these examples is the transformational user experience paradigm which enables user interfaces to reflect situational user needs by allowing users to establish context and content at runtime in a fluid way (Latzina and Beringer 2012).

The process of continuous adaptation can be further supported by intelligent IT artifacts that are aware of the social aspect of their context of use and are able to learn from previous use. This requires the translation of sociotechnical systems into machine-executable models and the definition of external sensor information that helps the IT artifact to adjust to situational needs.

All three pillars of innovation are on top of existing foundational disciplines, but our aim is to bring together those various principles and enablers to converge to a product design approach that aims for elasticity and social impact in addition to task-centric feature coherence.

References

Beyer, H., & Holtzblatt, K. (1998). *Contextual design: Defining customer-centered systems*. San Francisco: Morgan Kaufmann Publishers. ISBN 1558604111.
Dörner, C., Draxler, S., Pipek, V., & Wulf, V. (2009). End users at the bazaar: Designing next-generation enterprise resource planning systems. *IEEE Software, 26*(5), 45–51.

Dubberly, H. (2002, September + October 2008). ON MODELING. Design in the age of biology: Shifting from a mechanical-object ethos to an organic-systems ethos. *Interactions, 15*(5). doi:10.1145/1390085.1390092.

Fischer, G., & Giaccardi, E. (2006). Meta-design: A framework for the future of end-user development. In H. Lieberman, F. Paternò, & V. Wulf (Eds.), *End user development: Empowering people to flexibly employ advanced information and communication technology* (pp. 421–452). Dordrecht: Kluwer Academic Publisher.

Fischer, G., Giaccardi, E., Ye, Y., Sutcliffe, A. G., & Mehandjiev, N. (2004). Meta-design: A manifesto for end-user development. *Communications of the ACM, 47* (9, September), 33–37. doi:10.1145/1015864.1015884.

Holtzblatt, K. (2011). What makes things cool?: Intentional design for innovation. *Interactions, 18*(6, November), 40–47. doi:10.1145/2029976.2029988.

Latzina, M., & Beringer, J. (2012). Transformative user experience: Beyond packaged design. *Interactions, 19*(2, March), 30–33. doi:10.1145/2090150.2090159.

Lieberman, H., Paterno, F., & Wulf, V. (Eds.). (2006). *End user development*. Dordrecht: Kluwer Publishers.

Michael Weiksner, G., Fogg, B. J., & Xingxin Liu (2008, June 4–6). Six patterns for persuasion in online social networks. *Proceedings of the 3rd international conference on persuasive technology*, Oulu, Finland. doi:10.1007/978-3-540-68504-3_14.

Sanders, L. (2008). ON MODELING: An evolving map of design practice and design research. *Interactions, 15*(6, November), 13–17. doi:10.1145/1409040.1409043, http://doi.acm.org/10.1145/1409040.1409043

Schrage, M. (2005, May). *Automation, augmentation and innovation: Redefining the future of delegation in the new world of work*. Cambridge, MA: MIT White Paper.

Taylor, J. C. (1998). Participative design: Linking BPR and SAP with an STS approach, *Journal of Organizational Change Management*, 11(3), 233–245. doi:10.1108/09534819810216265.

Wulf, V., & Rohde, M. (1995). Towards an integrated organization and technology development. In G. Olson, & S. Schuon (Eds.), *Symposium on designing interactive systems* (Processes, practices, methods & techniques) (pp. 55–65). New York: ACM Press.

Wulf, V., Rohde, M., Pipek, V., & Stevens, G. (2011). Engaging with practices: Design case studies as a research framework in CSCW. In *Proceedings of the ACM 2011 conference on Computer Supported Cooperative Work (CSCW'11)* (pp. 505–512). New York: ACM Press.

Chapter 3
Elastic Workplace Design

Jörg Beringer and Markus Latzina

With the consumerization of IT, rugged, process-centric enterprise resource planning (ERP) systems are increasingly challenged by small fit-to-purpose productivity applications that are designed for very specific use cases. ERP content, which used to reside in transactional database applications, suddenly becomes accessible on mobile devices and blends into personal knowledge management applications. This increasing pervasiveness of information systems in work and private contexts demands, we argue, more situational adaptability of functionality and content.

The need for adaptability of ERP systems to organizational and personal workflows has been described in many papers (Henderson and Kyng 1991; Wulf et al. 2008). To improve the tailorability of information systems, the end-user development (EUD) body of research (Lieberman et al. 2006) suggests the offering of composition functionality during runtime in order to empower end users to adjust systems to situational task needs. While the "design time at use time" approach became one of the cornerstones of end-user empowerment, the antagonism of design vs. runtime remains significant since such a tailorability at runtime is still conceived of as an adaptation of an IT artifact for future use. While empowering end users to apply ad hoc changes at use time minimizes the tension between design and actual use, the general notion of a static IT artifact that needs to be designed (see Cabitza and Simone 2015) is still largely unchallenged.

To overcome this dualism between design and use time, we proposed a new design rationale which holds the promise of helping create transformative user experiences. This design rationale also aims at surpassing the enablement of specific

J. Beringer (✉)
Splunk Inc., 250 Brannan Street, San Francisco, CA, USA
e-mail: jberinger@splunk.com

M. Latzina
SAP SE, Dietmar-Hopp-Allee 16, 69190 Walldorf (Baden), Germany
e-mail: markus.latzina@sap.com

© Springer-Verlag London 2015   19
V. Wulf et al. (eds.), *Designing Socially Embedded Technologies in the Real-World*,
Computer Supported Cooperative Work, DOI 10.1007/978-1-4471-6720-4_3

use cases and it avoids rigid application boundaries between packaged applications. The user interface of a next-generation business application must be able to seamlessly support the user in all stages of task accomplishment and in switching back and forth between routine and knowledge-intensive working modes. We call this quality of user interfaces that intrinsically adapt to the current task needs at use time, *elasticity*.

The difference between tailorability which is based on building blocks and endowing user interfaces with an intrinsic elasticity is like comparing ice cubes and water. While ice cubes must be explicitly composed or shuffled to fit to a certain form, water adapts intrinsically to the environment due to its free-form characteristic. To build a transformative user interface, the system must be able to adapt the form and behavior of system objects to the current situation in a natural and organic way while ensuring continuity regarding the user and task objects.

A good example of transformative UX are today's GPS applications which allow users to look up a point of interest (POI) and then get directions on how to get there. A user may, for instance, search for a restaurant with a specific cuisine or price level and the application brings up a short list of restaurants that match the criteria. In this context, the presented information is that of a restaurant which has a name, phone number, reviews, and a location. Once the user decides on one of the restaurants, the same entity transforms into a route map incorporating the destination and expected time of arrival. This elasticity of transitioning from a restaurant to a destination and seamlessly switching from a search application to a GPS application is what creates a transformative user experience. The user moves from one task context to the next without being disturbed by application boundaries and having to reenter the same object identity twice.

While this example of transformative user experience holds true for a specific application, our goal is to establish this level of elasticity as a new *generic* quality of use. As a consequence, the traditional design of business applications which largely follows a *packaged design* rationale needs to be redefined. We introduced *transformative user experience* (*TUX*) (Latzina and Beringer 2012) as a design approach in order to dissolve the boundaries between applications and to transform aspects of appropriation (Dix 2007; Dourish 2003) into an intrinsic capability of the infrastructure rather than a post-design phenomenon inferred from observing how users interacted with the system. We acknowledge the existence of control and expertise outside of the system but aim to support the transitions of context of use inside the system.

One way to achieve this flexibility is to underspecify the user interface of an application to allow users to impose different meanings and usages on the said IT artifact at use time. MS® Excel™, for example, is underspecified in terms of what the purpose and usage of a specific spreadsheet should be. It can be used for capturing meeting minutes, for planning budget, or as an address book. In contrast, a small application for managing meeting minutes from an app store might be optimized and promoted for this particular use case, motivated by the business goal of attracting consumers to purchase and download this product. To scale for future and to some extent unexpected use, Meta-Design (Fischer and

Giaccardi 2006) stresses the importance of designing products which offer spaces of interaction potential rather than shipping applications packaged around a fixed number of use cases. While Meta-Design describes the need for such open systems that accommodate significant end-user-driven modifications of a product to serve task-centric user needs (Fischer 2009), it offers not much practical guidance on how to achieve this in a particular case (Maceli 2011).

The limitation of underspecified products is that the appropriation is taking place outside of the system in a somewhat unmanaged manner. Designers can, that is, only retrospectively observe this phenomenon instead of being able to design for it. Usually, any system awareness of such unexpected use cases is lacking. With a transformative user experience approach, we can overcome this concept of (unexpected) adaptation and foresee ostensive usages by enabling transitions from one meaning to another in the system environment.

In a corporate work environment, those transitions happen most typically between process-oriented back ends and task-oriented front ends. In common approaches to software engineering, even if usage requirements are taken very seriously, the exposure of documents designed for business processes does not match the semantic of objects consumed by users in a specific task context. This is similar to our GPS example, where a POI transforms from a restaurant to a destination. At the workplace, users move across various task contexts and along self-determined transformative vectors to achieve a work goal (Fischer and Giaccardi 2006). During those threads of interaction, task contexts may evolve, change over time, and shift between business context and more personal related task context like investigating or decision making. De Michelis (2015) reflects on previous concepts of *situated computing* and proposes to use *discursive threads* as an integrative perspective for enabling users to seamlessly pursue their tasks across a variety of contexts, in terms of an *augmented workplace*. We share this aspiration to provision users with flexible constellations of task objects in shifting contexts to support open-ended navigation.

With TUX, we attempt to bring forward this new concept of elasticity of IT artifacts by introducing novel system behavior. Thus we aim at building systems that intrinsically establish an understanding of user-managed environments for the creation of elastic task contexts at runtime. This approach is fundamentally different from the concept of tailorability (Table 3.1).

Table 3.1 Comparing characteristics of tailorability and elasticity

	Tailorability as ad hoc adaptation to identified user requirements	Elasticity as direct appropriation to situational task needs
User activities	Designing vs. using	Engaging in situational context
Rationale of flexibility	UI or functional building blocks	Elastic objects and context
Design time	Explicit	Implicit
Locality of appropriation	External	Internal

The user interface emerges at runtime in the very interplay between user intents and actual information, in other terms, ostensively (Campbell 2000; Arafat 2007). The actual task context will exceed one individual application and enable content to be transformed across applications and to be consumed on multiple devices.

We believe that those new qualities are radically changing the rationale of designing future workplaces and will contribute to overcoming the disconnect between rather static business process models and entities, on the one hand, and the situational needs for consuming this information, on the other. This high degree of runtime flexibility requires the decoupling of content and technical container as we know it from cloud and mobile technologies, respectively. Today, content sources are virtualized and can be consumed vie web APIs in any other application. Content is no longer bound to one specific technical container (e.g., the application window or the device). This trend toward transformative user interfaces requires new standards for interchangeable content, as well as for the modeling of task contexts – since both will no longer come as fixed ingredients of traditionally designed applications.

The core idea of TUX toward establishing respective design principles is to allow users to move content and contextualize it semantically across multiple containers. But we also envision containers to be elastic on their own by changing their exact meaning at runtime, depending on content and user interaction. In TUX, the appropriation to any task context takes place in the system and not only outside. The ability to adapt contexts in ways that match situational task conditions results in a new quality in which the system inherently follows users' task flow. By achieving this level of elasticity, we implicitly overcome the juxtaposition of design and runtime since the system is fluidly adapting to the social context it is embedded in.

3.1   Foundations of *Transformative User Experience*

We propose a foundational framework for a novel system architecture which intrinsically enables transformative user experience. For this purpose, we state some key principles of how to achieve situational contextualization of content at runtime in order to support task life cycles in a much more fluid way as compared to conventional approaches. The principles are based on the two basic concepts "task context" and "task object":

A *container* which is hosting and displaying task objects

A *task object* which acts as a proxy to a system object and provides functionality for the hosting container to contextualize its appearance and behavior to match the local semantics of the container

Containers model the situational context. Although an embodiment of containers corresponds often to visuospatial concepts like windows, collaboration spaces, displays, or devices, we refer to it in terms of a programming model in which the

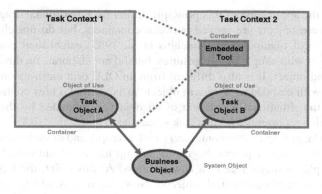

Fig. 3.1 Task object and task context

container class is a storage container for loosely coupled content and functions. Contextual appropriation of system objects is realized by allowing containers to adjust system objects to task objects reflecting the local semantics of use (cf., Fig. 3.1).

The difference between system object and task object (aka object of use) is described by Dourish (2003) in relation to paperless documents. For example, a generic document is a system object, potentially owned by a text processing application, but the use of a document in an actual context might be meeting minutes, patent application, or contract. Unlike Dourish, who describes this semantic adaptation as an appropriation between system functionality and the user's unexpected use, we see the need for appropriation primarily by moving objects along a task context which may fluidly change and evolve at runtime. Our goal is to prepare the system design to be elastic and adaptive to task contexts rather than building IT artifacts in terms of packaged designs, thus leaving task appropriation unmanaged and in conflict with the system design.

With TUX, we see the appropriation taking place in the system by contextualizing system objects to a situational semantics or task context which is represented by a technical container. This contextualization can affect an object in two ways:

A task object can adjust its posture (Cooper et al. 2007).
A task object can be abstracted or casted to change its behavior.

With these mechanisms in place, we can adapt system objects to become task objects that reflect the meaning of an object to the specific context of a container. Since this container-mediated adoption is handled in the system, the appropriation takes place within the system rather than being imposed by its users from the outside. By articulating this assumption in terms of an explicit design principle, we can actively use it in design considerations as compared to treating it solely as an implicit option:

A container model context that is used to impose situational semantics on system objects by casting them into local task objects with local appearance and behavior

Note that the application of this principle differs from traditional drag-and-drop scenarios where objects are moved between containers, but do not change their semantics. Direct manipulation (Hutchins et al. 1985) established principles of moving objects with simple mouse gestures, but did not elaborate on the interaction of context and object. It is also different from an OLE or a mesh-up environment which deals with embedding a system object "as is" within a host container. TUX is all about the situational adaptation of an object as mediated by the technical container which represents a certain task semantics.

Imagine a large display (the container) which is empty and as such is contextually nonspecific. A group of people begins to pull up names of individual managers who should play a major role in a new business. At this point, the large display is just a collection of people (task objects). Now, one user is adding a tool which provides functionality to build an organizational chart. This tool is a specialized container that is designed to display cost center hierarchies for the purpose of building organizational structures:

A container may come with a priori defined context and act as a purposed tool that has a predefined task meaning.

Because this additional container is added to the large display as an org chart planning tool, the entire display now turns into a planning environment and the context becomes that of an organizational structure with managers being the candidates for cost centers. We can capture this incremental specification of a purpose or task context as another TUX principle:

A context can change its semantics at runtime, typically becoming more specific by embedding purposed containers or by binding concrete content to the context.

Further along in the exercise, several users start to create different variants of the org chart which triggers a discussion about pros and cons of the different org structures. We still have the managers' names as task objects and the org chart itself, but now each org chart proposal becomes a decision option (task object) within a decision-making context. This transition of a task container (the org chart) to a task object (decision option) can be captured as another principle:

A context can become a task object within another context depending on focus.

Today, we have no formal way to describe the principles of designing for such an organic, open-ended interaction. We believe that with TUX, we cannot only formulate guiding design principles but also derive technical requirements to enable such transformative interfaces natively within the system. The ability of task objects being moved across contexts and the ability of adjusting the form and behavior of system objects to reflect the context-dependent semantics of task objects opens up new ways of building generative runtimes. End users can transform the design space simply by instantiating contexts and moving content across contexts. In the example above, the users transformed the large display into an org chart discussion and a decision-making context. They did this by adding and moving managers as content items around and by adding an org chart builder as an additional tool context.

In this new approach, we combine cognitive theories of action planning and task accomplishment with semantic approaches that introduce semantic frames to express situational semantics. With the transformative user experience approach, we try to mimic exactly the same interaction with the technical container constituting the frame and the task object constituting the local object of use.

The approach covers intrinsically many if not all of the user experience qualities described by Dix and Dourish (Dix 2007; Dourish 2003) and Meta-Design (Fischer and Giaccardi 2006) by allowing contexts to be underspecified (open for interpretation), by supporting aspects of direct manipulation with respect to task objects (provide visibility and immediate effect of action), and by empowering users not only to interact with a set of predefined applications but to define the purpose of a context incrementally (support – not control, expose intentions).

TUX adds one important principle, which is the *elasticity* of the system itself. The usage of the large display is an example of such an elastic technical container which underwent a transition from being an empty container to being an org chart planning environment. As we will see, most goal-oriented user task flows are subject to such transitions.

3.1.1   Elasticity as a Core Quality of Transformative User Experience

In the previous section, we focused on describing how to move task objects between containers to reflect changing object semantics due to contextual shifts and letting contexts evolve at runtime to reflect situational task semantics. In this section, we want to describe how these principles can be used to realize elastic user interfaces.

Elasticity is an important characteristic of an IT artifact if we want the artifact to be able to adapt to its social environment and form a socio-technical symbiosis. Software applications often lack elasticity because they are designed for specific tasks thus failing to adjust to new contexts. But in reality, task contexts are often not mechanistic but grow organically as needed in a given situation (cf., Dubberly 2008). We, therefore, see a need for designing IT artifacts that are to some extent elastic with respect to their meaning and user interface. Let us illustrate this new quality with an example from the enterprise resource planning (ERP) domain, in which the gap between packaged application design and situational appropriation of system functionality becomes obvious:

Let us assume, a business user is searching for suppliers who are qualified to satisfy a specific demand. When searching for suppliers who fulfill those criteria, suppliers will be listed as result items within a result list. In TUX terms, the supplier is the system object and the search/match list is a task-specific container with result items being the task objects. In this context, the user expects the result items to display information sufficient to inspect, refine, and select them as a potential match. The content is still a supplier object, but users would expect system abilities to compare, inspect, and collect each item. This functionality is motivated by the task context "search and collect potential candidates". When selecting several suppliers as prospects, the result items become members of a shortlist of candidates. Those members now inherit the behaviors of decision options which need to be evaluated

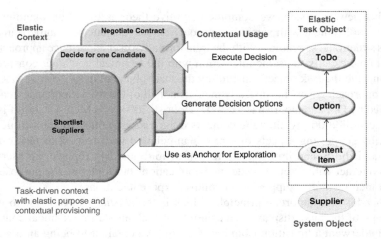

Fig. 3.2 Contextual consumption of business entities

and prioritized. The shortlist is a new container representing the activity of "short listing" which should reflect the current preferences and ranking. The fact that each item is a supplier is now less prominent, but users rather annotate and vote each item for facilitating the decision making. For the most promising candidates, in-depth due diligence might be planned, by moving the top suppliers into a To-do list. Each supplier now becomes an action item (task object) within the To-do list (container). After a final decision has been made, the decision has to be signed off by a stakeholder, in which case the preferred supplier may be forwarded by e-mail as a decision item which requires formal approval and agreement. This approval functionality is not represented by the ERP business object "supplier", but by the framing task context.

During this scenario, it is only of peripheral interest that the supplier is originally an ERP object. The supplier is rather used as an anchor for searching, as a decision option for picking the right accounts, and as an action item for the strategic purchaser. As Fig. 3.2 illustrates, the *system object* "supplier" actually is transformed into different *objects of use* depending on the task context.

With TUX, the user is able to move the supplier from one task context to the next, with the system being always aware of the identity of a supplier instance and the ability to contextually support the local meaning of the supplier within a given task setting. The context itself changed from being an unspecific empty workspace to an anchored exploration task, a decision-making task, and a work assignment task environment. Those transitions between contexts are not rigid, predesigned workflows between discrete packaged services but evolve naturally by activating methods and services and moving the suppliers as task objects from one context to the other.

With this transformative framework in place, containers can cast system objects to local semantics without losing the system identity and choose between several appearances supported by the objects. The following sections list in more detail the examples of supporting this transformative behavior of objects and containers.

3.1.2   Elasticity of Task Objects

TUX decouples the identity of an object from its usage within a given task context. A context can influence the posture of an object and add specific behaviors to it to create task objects which are tailored to this particular task context. In contrast to system or UI objects, we speak of task objects to emphasize that, in the course of user interaction, they can gain various meanings which are reflective of the current user goals and the particular task context in which they are embedded (cf., Dourish 2003). Task objects are indicative of the principle of *contextual polymorphism* since they can adapt semantically in various ways to their respective context. Practically, referring to the above example, the supplier as a system object is casted to a task object by inheriting semantics which are specific to the particular task context in which this object is used in. The binding of the task object to the actual system object – in this case the supplier within the ERP system – is always preserved; it can be used to navigate to services specific to the system object.

The creation of task objects requires different mechanisms of adapting objects to containers.

3.1.3   Contextual Casting

A system object can be casted to another class which models the behavior of a task object instead of the original system object. The new semantics is specific and local to the container which represents the task context. In order to enable the casting and hosting of system objects, the TUX framework must support the abstraction of system objects, i.e., provide a generic task object class that provides a handle to its identity and some generic interfaces to access common behaviors.

3.1.4   Contextual Postures

There must also be a solution for how to render the object by default because we cannot assume that the task container knows the object in detail. We need to find a way to adjust the appearance (phenotype) of an object despite the fact that the hosting context does not know the object type. This is achieved by provisioning the abstract task object with a set of contextual postures (appearances) which the hosting container can choose from when rendering an object. Within the TUX framework, there exist a number of standard postures which can be requested by the context and have to be provided by the object. Examples for such archetypical postures at the object level are data point, list item, table row, business card, or fact sheet. While the hosting container is responsible for the actual rendering, the object is sending the information in form of name-value pairs. For example, when the purchaser (a user) drags a supplier (an object) from a search container into a short list tool, the posture of the supplier might change from being a list item to being displayed as a business card. When the purchaser lays out the suppliers on a map, the posture might be reduced to being a data point.

Note that this approach is extending the concept of *postures of application* to *postures of objects*. As Alan Cooper pointed out, a good designer chooses always a "proper" posture for an application depending on its importance, richness, and usage mode. Similarly, we postulate a limited number of postures for objects. This contextualization of system objects corresponds to the concept of late binding, where task objects are added at runtime to the container and the container can adapt them and manipulate them by inspecting the task object. Of course, there are limitations. As soon as the user needs all details, only the original parent application can provide a domain-specific object inspector.

3.1.5   Contextual Volatility

Volatility refers to the concept of snapshotting vs. live view of an object. While the binding of the task object to the actual system object is always given, it is sometimes more appropriate to freeze the object at the time it is added to the container and thus turn it into an archival artifact instead of live data.

This difference can be quite important if task objects are expected to be tangible artifacts local to a context instead of being references to external living things. Imagine a purchaser adding an analytical chart to the short list for making an argument about the low performance of a supplier. This chart must not change over time but rather reflect the observation that was used when adding the supplier to the context as evidence for this insight.

Frozen task objects still point to their parent application, so that users can open a snapshot for editing or for deriving new versions.

3.1.6   Elasticity of Containers

The container is the technical object with which to model the task context. When users move task objects from one container to the next, they implicitly or explicitly create task contexts that are represented as the combination of the container semantics and embedded task objects.

While task models play an important role in requirements engineering and inform the design directions, they get usually lost when creating the actual system. What typically materializes within the application is only a set of core data objects, some application logic, and many static screens that have been designed to match the mental model of a prospective user. This leaves the task model as an implicit property of the application which cannot be leveraged as an explicit model at runtime.

To compensate for this loss of explicit task semantics in traditional application design, we propose to allow the container to represent semantics in a very elastic way to facilitate the creation of a proper task context at runtime under the direction of the user.

3.1.6.1 Elastic Purpose

A system is elastic if the context of use is underspecified. The less the context is defined, the more the user has freedom in projecting a specific purpose into the software application. Such designs are most appropriate for generic tools not constrained by any vertical application domain. Many Web 2.0 services are designed along such principles. For example, Wiki environments are used for multiple purposes such as the publication of facts or collaboration spaces to coordinate project work. The underspecification of design is one of the secret sources for achieving mass adoption. They are designed for very abstract needs but agnostic to any specific content. As Dix (2007) pointed out, the design has to be open for interpretation to allow appropriation to specific situations and usages. Only by filling content in, the user is incrementally developing a purposed environment.

There is obviously a trade-off between underspecification and affordance. If there is no specific purpose communicated by the design, the generic function as such must be compelling enough. For example, Wikis are popular because of the convenience of authoring and publishing self-generated content. But users are adopting this technology for various purposes ranging from intranet publishing to project coordination.

While the transition from unspecific to specific purpose is often simply done by adding content, in other cases, the transition is achieved by adding tools to an existing container to extend its purpose (e.g., SAP® StreamWork™). For example, in the large display scenario, the adding of the org chart container turned the entire display into an org chart planning environment.

3.1.6.2 Elastic Collaboration

Today, collaboration services tend to be specialized on one specific use case or technical service such as communication, online sharing, or team coordination which forces users to make a priori decisions about appropriate technology to use in their subsequent task flow. Such strict boundaries often force users to reestablish a task context within a collaboration environment simply to be able to share it with others.

The problem with such rigid design solutions is that collaboration is not a predictable process step but often evolves over time while working on a task. This problem also surfaces when constructing user stories as part of the requirements definition: "... and now John is calling Mary to discuss the reliability of supplier XYZ. They decide to create a collaboration space to share the latest KPIs and invite other stakeholders." While such stories may point to the general need for supporting breakouts into collaborative mode, they are by no means a mandatory task flow. With the exception of policy-motivated approvals and collaboration, the need for collaboration evolves primarily out of the situation and cannot be defined a priori at design time.

Users should be able to push content in terms of task objects from a non-collaborative environment into a collaboration space, or the system should be able to transform a personal context into a shared context without the need to re-instantiate the content. The collaboration service itself can also be considered as an elastic container which may transition from an ephemeral chat to a more persistent activity stream. Often the need to collaborate originates from conversations or e-mails which then cause the user to create a dedicated new task context.

3.1.6.3 Elastic Practices

Task flows in reality do not always follow the typical task life cycle but also alternate between nonroutine and routine situations. Depending on the familiarity and complexity of a particular task, the task context is more or less well defined and users will choose different strategies to cope with it (Rasmussen et al. 1994). In a nonroutine case, the system will offer rather generic functions which enable the user to define their intents and action plans in the course of interacting with the system. In a rather more well-defined task context, there will be a set of exclusive functions which represent common practices or which are reflective of user preferences.

As those needs are situational by nature and cannot be pre-modeled in terms of a workflow or standard operational procedures, the elasticity of the system environment is an important design quality for these one-time processes. To support this situational task complexity, a system environment must support the user in switching between different levels of ad hoc problem solving, for example, identifying suitable approaches to tackle a difficult problem vs. accomplishing a well-defined task within the same environment.

This flexibility, as we have shown, cannot be achieved with a packaged design that offers a number of predefined paths and breakout points to follow some prethought workflows. Containers need not only be flexible in representing task-related content but in modeling constraints and practices that may be leveraged as procedural guidance. By taking advantage of this transformative quality, the user can create new task contexts that evolve from unspecified to specified situations (Bernstein 2000).

3.2   Conclusions

While building on concepts from *design for appropriation* and *Meta-Design*, TUX proposes a fluid navigation between different task contexts via direct manipulation and contextual transformation of task objects. We combine this basic design rationale with an elastic container model that explicitly represents task semantics and can impose new usage semantics on its content (i.e., task objects). We believe that the combination of elastic object and context semantics enables not only an unprecedented natural and fluid user experience but also establishes a new design rationale for building modern interactive systems that form a symbiosis with users' activities (Winograd and Flores 1986; Suchman 1987).

With the concept of elasticity, we are able to articulate principles for how system environments can transform themselves to match the user's intention. Many of those intentions are easily identified and can be used for system design, but they are unpredictable with respect to the order, relevance, or concrete materialization within one particular situation (Dourish 2003). We believe that the combination of elastic object and context semantics enables not only an unprecedented natural and fluid user experience but also establishes a new design rationale for building modern interactive systems that form a symbiosis with users' activities (Winograd and Flores 1986; Suchman 1987; for considerations of the TUX rationale toward some design examples, cf., Werner et al. 2011; Ardito et al. 2012, 2014, 2015a, b; Costabile and Buono 2013; Latzina 2015).

The elasticity of TUX can help to establish a continuum between generic and purposed application contexts to fill the gap between operating systems and applications or generic transactional ERP applications and fit-to-purpose applications. TUX can help to bring together reusable platform components with application layers that are designed for more specific purposes in a very organic way to reflect typical task needs of knowledge workers or improve the immersiveness of an IT artifact in general.

TUX challenges common notions of system, application, and interaction design; it bears the promise of shaping novel ways of practicing design, thus potentially leading toward emergent design practices which aim at augmenting knowledge work by allowing users to interact with content in an ostensive manner. With users actively creating task contexts and the user interface not being restricted to a priori packaged applications, the difference between use time and design time vanishes (Fischer and Giaccardi 2006). Content can be composed and shaped in an ad hoc manner (Campbell 2000; Arafat 2007; Dourish 2003; Perlin and Meyer 1999). System design along these lines explicitly acknowledges the existence of control and expertise outside of systems, but at the same time, it enables systems to evolve at runtime in symbiosis with their use.

References

Arafat, S. (2007). *Foundations research in information retrieval inspired by quantum theory*. Ph.D. thesis. University of Glasgow. http://theses.gla.ac.uk/181/01/2007arafatphd.pdf. Accessed 2 Apr 2012.

Ardito, C., Costabile, M. F., Desolda, G., Latzina, M., & Matera, M. (2015a). Making mashups actionable through elastic design principles. In P. Díaz, V. Pipek, C. Ardito, C. Jensen, I. Aedo, & A. Boden (Eds.), *End-user development* (pp. 236–241). Springer International Publishing.cf. http://www.springer.com/gp/book/9783319184241

Ardito, C., Costabile, M. F., Desolda, G., Latzina, M., & Matera, M. (2015b). Hands-on actionable mashups. In P. Díaz, V. Pipek, C. Ardito, C. Jensen, I. Aedo, & A. Boden (Eds.), *End-User Development* (pp. 295–298). Springer International Publishing.

Ardito, C., Costabile, M. F., Matera, M., Piccinno, A., Desolda, G., & Picozzi, M. (2012). Composition of situational interactive spaces by end users. In *NordiCHI 2012: Proceedings of the 7th nordic conference on human-computer interaction: Making sense through design*, October 14th–17th, Copenhagen, Denmark: ACM Press.

Ardito, C., Costabile, M. F., Lanzilotti, G. D. R., Matera, M., Piccinno, A., Picozzi, M. (2014). User-driven visual composition of service-based interactive spaces. *Journal of Visual Languages & Computing, 25*(4), 278–296. http://dx.doi.org/10.1016/j.jvlc.2014.01.003.

Bernstein, A. (2000). *How can cooperative work tools support dynamic group processes? Bridging the specificity frontier*. Philadelphia: CSCW, ACM Press.

Cabitza, F., & Simone, C. (2015). Building socially embedded technologies: Implications about design. In V. Wulf, K. Schmidt & D. Randall (Eds.), *Designing socially embedded technologies in the real-world* (pp. 217–270). London: Springer.

Campbell, I. (2000). *The ostensive model of developing information needs*. Ph.D. dissertation. Department of Computer Science, University of Glasgow.

Costabile, M. F., & Buono, P. (2013). Principles for human-centred design of IR interfaces. In *Information retrieval meets information visualization* (pp. 28–47). Berlin/Heidelberg: Springer.

Cooper, A., Reimann, R., & Cronin, D. (2007). *About Face 3: The essentials of interaction design*. Indianapolis, IN: John Wiley & Sons.

De Michelis, G. (2015). Situated computing. In V. Wulf, K. Schmidt & D. Randall (Eds.), *Designing socially embedded technologies in the real-world* (pp. 65–77). London: Springer.

Dix, A. (2007). Designing for appropriation. In *Proceedings of the 21st British HCI Group annual conference on people and computers: HCI . . . but not as we know it – Vol. 2 (BCS-HCI '07)* (pp. 27–30). Swinton: British Computer Society.

Dourish, P. (2003). The appropriation of interactive technologies: Some lessons from placeless documents. *Computer Supported Cooperative Work (CSCW) – The Journal of Collaborative Computing, 12*(4), 465–490.

Dubberly, H. (2008). On modeling. Design in the age of biology: Shifting from a mechanical-object ethos to an organic-systems ethos. *Interactions 15*(5), 35–41. doi:10.1145/1390085.1390092

Fischer, G. (2009). Democratizing design: New challenges and opportunities for computer-supported collaborative learning. In C. O'Malley, D. Suthers, P. Reimann, & A. Dimitracopoulou (Eds.), *Proceedings of the 9th International Conf. on Computer-supported Collaborative Learning (CSCL'09), Vol. 1.* (pp. 282–286). International Society of the Learning Sciences. Rhodes, Greece: International Society of the Learning Sciences.

Fischer, G., & Giaccardi, E. (2006). Meta-design: A framework for the future of end user development. In H. Lieberman, F. Paternò, & V. Wulf (Eds.), *End user development* (pp. 427–457). Dordrecht: Kluwer Academic.

Henderson, A., & Kyng, M. (1991). There's no place like home: Continuing design in use. In J. Greenbaum, M. Kyng (Eds.), *Design at work – Cooperative design of computer artifacts* (pp. 219–240). Hillsdale, NJ: Lawrence Erlbaum Associates.

Hutchins, E. L., Hollan, J. D., & Norman, D. A. (1985). Direct manipulation interfaces. *Human-Computer Interaction, 1*(4), 311–338.

Latzina, M. (2015). Searching in a playful manner. In P. Díaz, V. Pipek, C. Ardito, C. Jensen, I. Aedo, & A. Boden (Eds.), *End-user development* (pp. 279–282). Springer International Publishing.

Latzina, M., & Beringer, J. (2012). Transformative user experience: Beyond packaged design. *Interactions 19*(2), 30–33. doi: 10.1145/2090150.2090159

Lieberman, H., Paternò, F., & Wulf, V. (Eds.). (2006). *End user development*. Dordrecht: Springer.

Maceli, M. G. (2011). Bridging the design time – Use time divide: Towards a future of designing in use. In *Proceedings of the 8th ACM conference on Creativity and cognition (C&C '11)* (pp. 461–462). New York: ACM. doi:10.1145/2069618.2069751. http://doi.acm.org/10.1145/2069618.2069751

Perlin, K., & Meyer, J. (1999). Nested user interface components. In *Proceedings of the 12th annual ACM symposium on user interface software and technology (UIST '99)* (pp. 11–18). New York: ACM.

Rasmussen, J., Pejtersen, A. M., & Goodstein, L. P. (1994). *Cognitive systems engineering*. New York: Wiley.

Suchman, L. A. (1987). *Plans and situated actions: The problem of human-machine communication*. New York: Cambridge University Press.

Werner, H., Latzina, M., & Brade, M. (2011). Symbik – A new medium for collaborative knowledge-intensive work. In *Proceedings of the international conference on education, informatics, and cybernetics* (Orlando, Florida, Nov 29–Dec 2, 2011). icEIC 2011. Winter Garden, Florida: International Institute of Informatics and Systemics (IIIS). Available: http://www.iiis.org/CDs2011/CD2011IDI/ICEIC_2011/PapersPdf/EI924DD.pdf

Winograd, T., & Flores, F. (1986). *Understanding computers and cognition: A new foundation for design*. Norwood: Ablex.

Wulf, V., Pipek, V., & Won, M. (2008). Component-based tailorability: Enabling highly flexible software applications. *International Journal on Human-Computer Studies (IJHCS), 66(1)*, 1–22.

Chapter 4
Patterns of Work: A Pragmatic Approach

K. Kashimura, Y. Hara, N. Ikeya, and David Randall

4.1 Introduction

As was suggested in Chap. 1, we need to '... accumulate and synthesize knowledge about such social domains from case studies to be able to anticipate the use and behavioral impact of new designs'. In turn, Beringer suggests, we need to go about, 'extracting key findings and summarizing key insights [so that] they can become a reusable set of foundational insights about target domains'. How we might do this, however, is a somewhat intractable problem. The past 20 years and more has, without question, seen a significant shift in the way in which data relating to design problems is collected and analysed. One of the most significant aspects of this has been the 'turn to the social' often associated with the deployment of ethnographic practices for design-related purposes.

Despite the undoubted gains that come from this move away from the 'formalities' of business processes towards a 'real world, real time' analysis, we have, as yet, little insight into the way ethnographic practices and design work get mobilised in commercial practice in a timely and generalisable way. A 'turn' which incorporates a view of the subtle, interactive processes by which work actually gets done and the contextual character of breakdown and repair work has not as yet been shown to translate conveniently into general design features. That is, there are few studies which show how ethnographic studies might be used and deployed by design teams

K. Kashimura • Y. Hara
Hitachi Design Division, Tokyo, Japan

N. Ikeya
Keio University, Tokyo, Japan

D. Randall (✉)
School of Media and Information, University of Siegen, Siegen, Germany
e-mail: D.Randall@mmu.ac.uk

© Springer-Verlag London 2015   35
V. Wulf et al. (eds.), *Designing Socially Embedded Technologies in the Real-World*,
Computer Supported Cooperative Work, DOI 10.1007/978-1-4471-6720-4_4

(although we should acknowledge that there are systematic attempts to specify the relation, for instance, Beyer and Holzblatt 1998), how their value is constructed and what problems with the record need to be dealt with. In addition, as we will argue below, since it is by no means clear that the highly detailed and radically contextual view implicated in (some) ethnographic work might be made to fit with some level of 'generic' design, some examination of how a design team might deal with this would be useful. This chapter examines the on-going work of a team of researchers and designers in the UX group at the Hitachi Design Division based in Tokyo, Japan. The Hitachi team has used ethnographic techniques for a significant period of time now, largely in the study of 'infrastructural' projects of one kind or another mining, power plants, train repair and maintenance and so on. Whilst considering ethnographic investigation to be valuable, the team believes that results can be made even more useful through a process of comparison. In this chapter, we consider how, in the first year of a 2-year project, this has been done. To be clear, there is a substantial existing literature on the relationship between ethnography and design (see Crabtree et al. 2012 for a recent example) which has covered a range of themes including the issues of participation and co-creation. In addition, there is an existing literature on theoretical devices which might help in the analysis of ethnographic work (see, e.g., Hutchins 1995; Kaptelinen and Nardi 2006 in the context of CSCW and other technology research; Glaser and Strauss 1967; Strauss and Corbin 1997; Charmaz 2006 in a more general context). The problem we describe, however, is somewhat different. Where Strauss and Corbin, for instance, describe the constant comparative method as a means to provide for comparisons across settings but within a domain and where the theoretical positions we mention provide frameworks for analysing any and all settings, albeit at a high level, our concern lies in comparisons across different settings and domains, but in which we may nevertheless find points of comparison and moreover comparisons which might have a design relevance.

4.2   The Setting

The design team's work has, for some years, been substantially ethnographic in its orientation, and studies have been conducted in a large variety of domains. Nevertheless, as the company has refocused its efforts towards 'quality of service' issues in complex organisational and inter-organisational settings, we have identified various kinds of maintenance work as a core topic. The group has largely oriented over a period of time to some version of 'contextual design' (Beyer and Holzblatt, ibid). Despite this, the group has expressed certain concerns about this mode of operation, in the main a function of the sheer number of enquiries being undertaken and, at the same time, the range of design possibilities under consideration. Put simply, at any one time there might be between 6 and 12 people doing ethnographic work in different areas (normally in ones and twos) and reporting to a moveable feast in respect of design teams. Fieldworkers can be, and are, deployed at relatively short notice into domains of which they may have no prior knowledge. They typically have had little background in ethnographic research, although a number have a background in 'usability' testing of one kind or another. The concerns of the group have effectively centred on three related difficulties. Firstly, and it will come as no surprise to experienced ethnographers, there are doubts about the capacity of designers to deal with significant amounts of ethnographic data either in relation to written records or in meetings. Although there will be more than one reason for this, in our case this mainly had to do with the structuring of data so as to reflect what designers might construe as their most significant problems. Secondly, and given the large amount of work being done in different domains, there was a concern for consistency and focus in respect of reporting. That is, how reporting might be done in such a way that ethnographic reports have a recognisable character from one setting to another was seen to be a problem, in that designers wanted ethnographic data to take a typical and consistent form and one, moreover, which might lead to relatively clear problem statements. Thirdly, there was a concern for time taken in the conduct of ethnographic enquiry. Designers, as is well known, cannot wait whilst long-term studies are completed. In the 'real world', there are also difficulties with the concurrent model described by Hughes et al. (1992, 1993). We should perhaps stress here what they are, because it has important consequences for the way in which our work progressed. The way in which ethnographic results might feed into design has important commercial implications. The team needs to demonstrate that it can provide useful and significant results both within and across a number of settings and, moreover, represent those results to a heterogeneous group of designers. Design scenarios might include, for instance, information system design, work and procedural design, augmented reality, mobile devices, video conferencing and data sharing, distributed database provision and so on. The large number of people involved at one time or another means that long-term and 'personal' collaborations of the kind often found in academic environments are difficult to pursue. Although there is a preference for face-to-face meetings between ethnographers and designers, this is not always possible. When it is, marshalling the vast range of data that ethnographers have collected and translating it into a language that is relevant and useful for design have proven less than straightforward. The ethnographic record itself, in the unstructured form that social scientists are used to, has proven unpopular. Various 'storyboarding' efforts have been undertaken, with limited success. We should point out here that, although this is not the topic of this chapter, a series of interviews with system designers of one kind or another (who described themselves variously as 'product', 'system' or 'future' designers) were conducted whilst the work was progressing, with a view to establishing what their informational and representational needs might be. One of the outcomes of these interviews was the recognition that a simplified and relatively standardised way of representing results was required if they were to derive the kinds of problem statement they felt they needed.

As a result, and in recognition of the need to develop some kind of reporting structure, a small group along with academics from Japan and Europe were convened to examine ways of dealing with the somewhat vaguely glimpsed problems mentioned above. At the outset, and in the first instance done largely through email and Skype communications, an attempt was made to discuss initial moves before contracts were signed and analytic work began. A number of Skype meetings took place in which discussions predicated on the possibility of using 'patterns' as an analytic device for producing a standard presentation format were the main focus, followed by the first of two intensive workshops, each lasting 5 days, one at the beginning of the project year (September 2012) and one towards the end (March 2013). Regular Skype calls involving the whole group took place about once every two weeks, and others involving the academic partners alone were also a regular feature. The outcome, as we shall see, was that a version of 'patterns' was developed which was significantly different from what has been produced previously. Notably, an initial decision was that 'patterns' were most likely to prove useful, at least in the first instance, if they were adapted from existing data in a circumscribed group of settings. The decision was made, reflecting on-going work by the design team, that the settings in question would be limited to those involving some form of (loosely defined) maintenance and construction engineering context.

4.3 Construction and Maintenance Engineering

If some form of 'generalised' findings were to be an outcome of the work, it was important to gain an understanding of what the existing literature had to say and how problems in our chosen domain were typically framed. Our discussion of the literature is framed around some specific matters which have to do with the inevitability of failure and attempts to minimise its impact, the desire to enhance control so that failure rates are reduced or kept to a minimum and the recognised need to embed solutions within the actual work of maintenance. Problems, of course (and as all ethnographers can attest), can be seen to be at least partly characterised by the specific domains within which they unfold. This would seem to present a challenge regarding what lessons might be appropriately learnt from investigations in other areas of construction and maintenance. This does not preclude an examination of those features with a view to establishing what might prove to be relevant and valuable for design-related purposes. Our review took us through a variety of domains encompassing, inter alia, software maintenance, general ICT maintenance in education, manufacturing systems maintenance, software maintenance, industrial systems maintenance, aircraft maintenance, railway maintenance, ship maintenance, vehicle maintenance, road construction and maintenance, photocopier and printer repair maintenance, network equipment maintenance and home device assembly and maintenance work. Now, of course, such domains are heterogeneous. The purpose of this review of the literature was to provide an initial, high-level, view of common problems (if any could be found) and subsequently to identify a subset of domains which would constitute a manageable resource for comparative work. We were able to identify certain domain features which, if not universally shared, at least could be found in more than one setting. Thus and for instance, the literature on software maintenance points to problems such as the need to keep systems running whilst maintenance takes place. As Swanson (1976) argues:

> The amount of time spent by an organization on software maintenance places a constraint on the effort that may be put into new system development. Further, where programming resources are cut back due to economic pressures, new development is likely to suffer all the more since first priority must be given to keeping current systems 'up and running'. (p. 492)

Swanson refers firstly to 'corrective maintenance', which mainly involves diagnosis procedures in relation to failure, and secondly to 'adaptive maintenance', which is done in anticipation of environmental change. Thirdly, there is 'perfective maintenance' which, in contrast, refers to performance enhancement (e.g., cost-effectiveness). The latter, he suggests, is not well understood but is at least as important as the first two since it is 'directed toward keeping a programme up and running at less expense, or up and running so as to serve the needs of its users [and customers]' (p. 493). Tan and Gable (1998) – also in the context of software engineering – demonstrate how there are radical differences between the attitudes of management and those of 'maintainers' and how this 'knowledge gap' also concerned what problems maintainers faced and how managers interacted with maintainers. Perhaps more importantly, from our point of view, there has been a developing recognition in the area of software maintenance that, along with attention to the above factors, we need to pay attention to local patterns of work. Bendifallah and Scacchi (1987) were amongst the first to recognise variation in local patterns of work. They argue (in a comparative study of two organisations) that we need:

> ... to understand the ways local circumstances in the workplace affect how and why people perform software maintenance tasks, and conversely, how maintenance work affects workplace arrangements. Local circumstances include the incentives and constraints for why people alter their software systems, and indicate when people act to maintain their systems. The workplace specifies where maintenance work is performed and the ways it is organized. How people order and perform their maintenance work also entails who does this work, and what kind of maintenance activity is performed. (p. 311)

Interestingly, the idea of 'beacons' or recurring patterns is occasionally referenced in this literature (see Boehm-Davis et al. 1996; Crosby et al. 2002). Ko et al. (2005) draw attention to the need for detailed studies of the way in which maintenance tasks are actually accomplished when Java programmers are using Eclipse, with a view to designing tools which might support their work. We might also briefly mention the work of Kemerer and Slaughter (1997) in this context, because they point explicitly to the gap between technical and managerial knowledge in maintenance work. They draw on the notion of patterns to argue that managerial information can be made more robust if these patterns can be identified. Hence:

> Software maintenance is a task that is difficult to manage effectively. In part, this is because software managers have very little knowledge about the types of maintenance work that are likely to occur. If managers could forecast changes to software systems, they could more effectively plan, allocate workforce and manage change requests. But, the ability to forecast software modifications depends on whether there are predictable patterns in maintenance

> work. We posit that there are patterns in maintenance work and that certain characteristics
> of software modules are associated with these patterns. (p. 1)

We then looked at maintenance in manufacturing industries. Bateman (1995) describes three basic forms of maintenance in relation to manufacturing. The first is *reactive*, such that equipment is allowed to run until it fails and then firefighting techniques are implemented. Gits (1992) calls this failure-based maintenance. The second is *preventive* (sometimes called use-based maintenance) and is obviously more proactive. Preventive maintenance usually involves maintenance work at particular and scheduled times. The third is *predictive maintenance* or is sometimes called condition-based maintenance. This relies on reporting about the condition of equipment and depends on new forms of diagnostic technique (measuring, for instance, vibration, noise, lubrication and corrosion). Laura Swanson (2001) introduces a fourth form, which she terms *aggressive maintenance*. She argues this is typical of strategies such as total productive maintenance (TPM) and which have been introduced as a result of global competition and enhanced technological capability. It is predicated on the view that small teams can create cooperative relationships by integrating production and maintenance functions. This, of course, implicates the raising of skill levels through constant communication and cooperation. Much of the literature is of a technical nature and focuses on such matters as optimization problems, replacement models and so on (examples are Nakagawa (2005) and Smith and Mobley (2008)). Other work focuses more on maintenance *management*. Here, the main interest is in best practice. Wireman (2004), for instance, notes that the failure to introduce proper policy and procedure is commonplace. He suggests that this is because maintenance is viewed by most organisations as a necessary evil and hence their main interest tends to be cost control. One of his observations is that, roughly, only half of time at work by maintenance workers is actually spent doing hands-on maintenance. He sees the main failures as having to do with job planning (better planning, he argues, leads to a cost ratio of 1:5 against poor planning) and with poor work order systems. Only 10 % of organisations, he maintains, have any form of performance monitoring or failure analysis. He further argues that much more maintenance work is reactive than it should be (evidenced by high levels of overtime). Frequently, the cause of these failures lies in under-skilling, lack of coordination between operations and maintenance, poor communication and poor use of materials (which are typically 40–60 % of all costs). One feature of this is overstocking and poor inventory control. Maintenance costs are also poorly assessed, since they seldom include the cost of 'downtime'. Such emphases have led to a concern with 'lean maintenance' (see Smith and Hawkins 2004).

A third area where maintenance work has been theorised is in safety critical systems. Here, and unsurprisingly, measures of risk are paramount. The literature here is highly technical, although there are some studies based on managerial and 'cultural' perspectives (see, for instance, McDonald et al. 2000) where interviews and documentary analysis are used to understand how organisational cultures affect safety. The main thrust of their work is to show that professional subcultures mediate the rules and procedures mandated by organisations. The fact that failure in safety critical systems can be catastrophic means that standard 'trial and error' approaches cannot be relied on. More importantly, there is a limited literature of a more sociological or social psychological kind which looks at the way in which groups in such contexts deal with problems. This includes some classic literature such as work by James Reason and Jens Rasmussen, work on 'high reliability' organisations by Laporte and Consolini (see, e.g., Laporte 1996; Laporte and Consolini, 1991, 1998a, b), work on aircraft cockpit errors by Charlotte Lind, more general theoretical work by Charles Perrow and – to a certain extent – work by the Lancaster school (Hughes et al. 1992; Randall et al. 1993) and others on air traffic control. Variously, such studies show cultural factors of one kind or another produce 'error tolerance'. Cultures, in this literature, either guarantee that errors are less likely to be made, are more likely to be seen or are less likely to be consequential. The exception is Perrow (1999) who argues that two factors – 'interactive complexity' and 'tight coupling' – mean that, in some contexts, accidents are more or less inevitable. 'Tight coupling' refers to the strong causal link between actions or events, whilst 'interactive complexity' refers, fairly obviously, to the many and varied ways in which people and systems can interact in complex organisations. Perrow is particularly interesting insofar as, when he points to failure, he identifies several individual factors which are relevant, including human error, mechanical failure, the environment, design of the system and the procedures used. Perrow is nevertheless insistent that catastrophic failure is never produced by any one of these factors but by the interaction of them all.

What became clear from our review of these and other domains was that there are some fundamental perspectival differences in play. Maintenance problems can be seen in a variety of ways and one of them we might call 'managerial/technical'. Maintenance has increasingly been seen through the organisational lens and associated with this as a management issue. Maintenance management, in other words, has become a quite distinctive approach, characterised as:

> All the activities of the management that determine the maintenance objectives or priorities (defined as targets assigned and accepted by the management and maintenance department), strategies (defined as a management method in order to achieve maintenance objectives), and responsibilities and implement them by means such as maintenance planning, maintenance control and supervision, and several improving methods including economical aspects in the organization. (Marquez 2007, p. 3)

The above demonstrates a view of maintenance which is, in the main, top-down. In other words, even though domains vary, the general perspective is that defined goals, along with procedures which are consistently implemented by managerial teams, define 'best practice'. There is, even so, an extensive literature which argues that best practice is not easily achieved. Various barriers need to be overcome (see, e.g., Raouf and Ben-Daya 1995). Cooke (2000) argues that certain organisational barriers are consistently found and they include political, financial, departmental and inter-occupational barriers.

In recent years, much of this work has been conceptualised in terms of trust and dependability. Avizienis et al. (2001) characterise dependability in the following way (much of what they say relates to computer systems, but there are some overlaps):

> *"A systematic exposition of the concepts of dependability consists of three parts: the **threats** to, the **attributes** of, and the **means** by which dependability is attained"*, and argues that fault prevention, tolerance, removal and forecasting are the critical issues. The threats to dependability, unremarkably, consist in faults, errors and failures. Nakagawa (2005) also emphasises reliability in maintenance and argues that the basic attributes required are availability (readiness of service), reliability (continuity of service), safety, confidentiality, integrity (absence of improper system state alterations) and maintainability.

In contrast, there is an approach we can think of as broadly ethnographic. An acknowledged classic in this area is Julian Orr's (1996) study of photocopier repair. Orr makes a number of related points, many of which are still under-examined by the more 'managerialist' literature. They include the fact that *work is heterogeneous*, meaning that problems are much more varied and unpredictable than we might assume. He further identifies, along with other ethnographers, the *social distribution of expertise* (he does not call it this; see Randall et al. 2007) meaning that we cannot assume that all are equally skilled. He suggests that not all maintenance work is done in the same way. It can be done in order to provide a minimum level of serviceability – i.e., doing the bare minimum – or it can be aimed at actually providing a solution to problems. He makes the point that decisions of this kind are made because of a variety of pressures including time available. Probably most importantly, he identifies the fact that this work is done collaboratively, even if maintenance is being done by one person at any given moment. They do this in large part by informal knowledge sharing, for instance, by meeting up for breakfast. Orr makes the point that much of this talk is generated by the sheer unpredictability of their work. Each machine behaves differently. Problems as described sometimes turn out not to be the problem at all. What is important here is the fact that much of the knowledge and skill is not formally codified but depends on experience and practice. Technicians become familiar over time with the characteristics and weaknesses of particular models of machinery. Technicians in this field have values concerning 'being good at your job' which include thoughtfulness, attention to detail, freedom from panic and resourcefulness when the documentation does not provide the answers (p. 34). Orr also reflects on the codification of expertise, pointing out that such codification is seldom entirely satisfactory. It seems that, in this context, documentation did not point adequately to solutions. In a similar vein, Carstensen (1999) has pointed to difficulties inherent in codifying processes when perspectives, practices and terminology are different from work group to work group. For a critique of the whole approach, see Schmidt (2012). Schmidt uses an example from the manufacture of diesel engines for ships:

> ... diesel engines for large ships are not produced for inventory, in the hope of somebody filing an order sometime in the future: marine propulsion plants are far too costly and take up far too much space for that to be a viable business model. Thus, many months may pass between orders for an engine of any particular model are received. Consequently, it was likely to be difficult for whoever was tasked with a given assembly job to remember how exactly to assemble the particular model requested in the given purchase order. So, although at least some of the workers would know how to assemble the model in question,

each of them would not necessarily be able to assemble it efficiently and correctly. They therefore strove to maintain their collective capabilities by documenting the sequential order and key operations of the procedure and by thus offering means for each other (or for future colleagues) to maintain (or acquire) their individual ability to do so efficiently and correctly.

Schmidt's work, inter alia, draws attention to timeliness, to 'competent readership' and to practical matters of one kind or another. Pipek and Wulf (2003) provide a critical review of the problem of knowledge sharing in maintenance work in relation to what is sometimes called 'organisational memory'. This describes the problem of retaining the expertise and experiences of skilled members. Pipek and Wulf draw on the work of Mark Ackermann who identified a number of issues in relation to the informalities of work and the difficulty of knowledge sharing. These variables include the complexity of the knowledge domain, the interactive nature of the problem-solving process, technological infrastructure, the existence or not of a common body of knowledge (shared expertise) and how dynamic changes in the body of knowledge are. Pipek and Wulf describe difficulties in maintenance work in a steel mill which have some similarity to those described by Orr, mainly in relation to documentation of various kinds and how accurately it describes the real state of play. They point to some typical issues around the nature of the documents (paper and electronic), which include that a large number of documents are not classified or are classified in such a way they cannot easily be found, that many are old or of poor quality, that search functions are inadequate, that some knowledge resources are 'private' and so on.

None of this is to argue that codification is impossible, only difficult. Indeed, work at Xerox following on from Julian Orr's study involved precisely the design of knowledge-sharing systems for photocopier repair across international sites. The work on this (see Bobrow and Whalen 2002; Yamauchi et al. 2003) is interesting because it discusses the organisational barriers to getting ethnographic work accepted and also provides examples of cost and productivity benefits that resulted.

Our review of the literature indicated a number of things to us. Firstly, managerialist and technical approaches, whilst pointing to the need for actions at the strategic level, for instance, in relation to the 'the acquisition of the requisite skills and technologies' or to 'the correct assignment of maintenance resources (skills, materials, test equipment, etc. to fulfil the maintenance plan). (Marquez 2007) say little about how such things might be achieved in practice. Similarly, technical approaches focus in the main on metrics and tools for the measurement of known criteria. Both, we feel, produce generalised levels of argumentation that are insufficient for dealing with the specific requirements identifiable in any given setting. The 'ethnographic' approach, and readers would be familiar with this argument, tends instead to emphasise local contingency, the gap between formal rules and procedures and actual practice and so on. A significant 'background' assumption here is that the kinds of problem – as well as the practical management of solutions – that occur are specific to the setting under investigation and are best understood by close investigation of the cooperative elements of work. However, and as we have already indicated, the practical management of ethnographic enquiry is problematic. A number of different individuals, remember, may be working in a number of different settings and – sometimes at least – taking a considerable period of time to 'gear in' to those settings (which are frequently of a highly technical nature). They in turn are reporting back to a large and disparate group of designers who sometimes struggle to understand the results. The task the group set itself, then, was firstly to find a means to provide a manageable level of generalisation, one which both indicated what kinds of commonality might exist across a range of broadly similar settings but at the same time retained a sensitivity to local contingency. Secondly, an aim was to find a language which allowed for a common means of expression, such that both ethnographers and designers might find it easier to interrogate their own and others' work.

4.4 Patterns

The idea of the pattern language originates with Christopher Alexander (1979) but was quickly taken up within software engineering communities. Alexander was offering an approach to the design of buildings which reflected patterns of use and as such was critical of 'heroic', modernist conceptions of architecture which rather ignored user needs in favour of abstract notions of 'function'. In 'a pattern language', Alexander claimed to have identified 253 basic patterns which recur in architecture. Patterns have particular attributes, which he characterised as follows:

> Name: A name to identify the pattern.
> Context: The situation(s) where the pattern is relevant.
> Forces (problems): The forces present which may constrain or suggest alternative solutions. When these forces are in tension with one another, the problem is harder to solve and a compromise may be necessary.
> Solution: A solution which resolves, as far as possible, the various forces.

For Alexander, these patterns had to be validated in some way (including observation) and were prescriptive. That is, they instruct us what to do about certain things. We should not forget that these patterns were also invariant. In other words, they are to be found across settings (see Dearden and Finlay 2006, who also provide a useful summary of the way patterns are used in a variety of contexts). They can be distinguished from other forms of generalisation, they argue, in the following ways:

> 1. the level of abstraction at which guidance is offered;
> 2. the grounding of patterns in existing design examples, or "capture of practice";
> 3. the statement of the problem addressed by a pattern;
> 4. the discussion of the context in which a pattern should be applied;
> 5. the provision of a supporting rationale for the pattern;
> 6. the organisation of patterns into pattern languages; and
> 7. the embedding of ethics or values in the selection and organisation of patterns. (Dearden and Finlay 2006, p. 21)

There has been a significant uptake of 'patterns' in computer science (see, e.g., Gamma et al. 1993; Gabriel 1996; Rising 1998; Denef 2012), but here the idea of 'pattern *language*' became much more significant. According to Erickson (2000), patterns are particularly interesting for object-oriented programming because they embody concrete prototypes, are grounded in the social and express values. Patterns of code are easy to identify, but connecting them into more complex frameworks requires a language which consists of connective rules. Salingaros (2000) gives some examples:

> One pattern contains or generalizes another smaller-scale pattern.
> Two patterns are complementary and one needs the other for completeness.
> Two patterns solve different problems that overlap and coexist on the same level.
> Two patterns solve the same problem in alternative, equally valid ways.
> Distinct patterns share a similar structure, thus implying a higher-level connection.

Patterns, then, have a formalising quality, involve connections and levels and further involve selections as to what is and is not relevant. It has been pointed out that one of the main values of the pattern approach is that it documents or codifies these relevant factors. Put simply, they have a systematic quality. If patterns can be systematically connected through the use of a common language, then, they should in principle provide us with a framework to anchor design. Nevertheless, for the reasons given above, they cannot determine design. There is an obvious analogy here between software engineering approaches which rely on formal models of organisational 'need' and those which orient to user behaviours, since understanding patterns clearly entails understanding behaviour (as well as functionality) in a systematic way. Having said that, the idea of a 'pattern' is a rather vague one and can mean many things. The notion of 'patterns' has also been subjected to extensive critique (see Dovey 1990) insofar as it is clear that patterns cannot provide complete design solutions (the reasons for this have to do with their putative inability to encompass economic, policy and construction or implementation issues). They can, in other words, only be seen as one tool in the toolbox. One of the evident difficulties in the application of patterns to human behaviour lies in the different perspectives on 'relevance' that are brought to the table. By this, we mean that patterns are sometimes applied within disciplinary boundaries but might be better understood as a communication device for interdisciplinary work. Denef (ibid), for instance, deploys patterns in an attempt to integrate the perspectives of ethnographers and designers in relation to firefighting. Mahemoff and Johnston focus on patterns of *usability*. Their patterns are structured at the level of task, user, user interface and 'entire systems'. In a different vein, and of more immediate relevance for our purposes, Martin and Sommerville draw extensively on existing ethnomethodological work to draw attention to recurrent topics. These, for ethnomethodologists, might include:

1. Sequentiality and temporality
2. The working division of labour (egological-alteriological principles)
3. Plans and procedures (representations)
4. Routines, rhythms and patterns (orderliness in self-organising systems)
5. (Distributed) coordination
6. Awareness of work
7. Ecology and affordances

What Martin and Sommerville try to do is use these 'topics' as a resource for generating patterns in more specific circumstances and then exemplifying the patterns through data. They argue:

> Patterns are intended to be a resource that is a structured collection of findings from field studies of work and technology. As such, reading through them should provide a good background understanding of some of the social design issues that arise out of these ethnomethodologically-informed studies.

Now, Martin and Sommerville accept the Alexandrian principle that patterns are independent of context and can be deployed across a range of different settings. Our position evolved differently. Partly as a result of the work that had already been done in various settings by the design team and partly because of the similarities and differences we glimpsed during the literature review process, we were concerned to circumscribe our generation of patterns by limiting them to settings where we were confident we had sufficient knowledge and which were, on some level, similar.

Equally important is the discussion of the way in which patterns can be integrated into approaches to observation, intervention, participation and learning, and communication. There is a certain amount of work on the relationship between pattern languages and participatory design (PD) (this includes, for instance, Borchers (2001); Lin and Landay (2002)) and for interaction design (see, e.g., van Welie and van der Veer 2003). Other work, like that of Goodyear (2005), orients to education. For our purposes, this is a critical feature. It was and is a fundamental feature of our enquiries that they should aid the communication process – ethnographer to ethnographer and ethnographer to designer (and vice versa). For our purposes, there were nevertheless decisions to be made.

4.5   Developing 'Patterns of Work'

Our strategy was to identify some high-level, domain-independent questions which could then be decomposed and translated into a domain-relevant set of questions. We make no claim to originality here. The questions are similar to those in Martin and Sommerville (2004), to those posed by Randall et al. (2007), to Checkland's CATWOE analysis and so on. They were evolved by the academic partners and were delivered with some rough sub-questions which were intended to be illustrative of the range of issues. It is important to recognise that these high-level questions have no theoretical status – they are simply orienting devices. They were in no sense intended to direct enquiry but were rather geared to the assumption that the evolution of our patterns would be an iterative process and one which ethnographic data would feed into. That is, ethnographic findings and evolving patterns would be mutually elaborated. Indeed, they were posed as questions precisely for this reason. The 'nine questions', as they became referred to, are laid out below, exactly as they were posed to the project group.

1. *What actors are involved?* Of course this raises a number of important sub-questions, especially in the light of the fact that work is increasingly complex, mobile and Internet reliant. Do we include only immediate workers in our studies, or should we be looking at a wider organisational context? When knowledge is shared, is it only shared locally? How heterogeneous are the groups that share a working environment?
2. *What are they doing?* Again, we need to make decisions about granularity, and this depends on how we decide on what is interesting. For some purposes, it is obvious that we need to pay attention to the sequentiality of work in some detail (in what order do people actually do things?). Video analysis is an obvious way of doing this. For other purposes, less detailed observations may be possible, and for others interviews are likely to elicit information that observation will not ('Why did you do that? Why not do it another way?' What was the problem there?').
3. *Why are they doing it?* This speaks to the goals of management and the organisation, to 'accountability' issues and so on.
4. *Why are they doing it this way?* In much the same way, there may in principle be any number of different ways of performing tasks. If things are typically done in one fashion, then we can ask why. Are there constraints caused by material resources? How rule governed are the activities? Are there problems with skill levels? Is this the most elegant and effective way things can be done given various constraints?
5. *What materials, resources and spaces do they deploy and in what order?* The point of this is obvious, but we need to remember that ALL material resources are relevant. Scraps of paper like Post-it notes, scribbled bits of information, reminders and other more human resources (e.g., asking questions) are important.
6. *What knowledge and skill do they demonstrate?* This is possibly the most difficult thing to uncover, not least because it often means the ethnographer has to understand technical terminologies. It also means one has to pay attention to a series of quite mundane skills – who seems to know most and what is it that they know (sometimes called the social distribution of expertise).
7. *What (if anything) needs to be changed?* It is often easy to identify bottlenecks, problems and so on. It is not quite so easy to see how to correct them. An example is the idea of redundancy. In one sense, if processes are redundant, it means they are being duplicated for no good reason. It does, however, mean that we have to be sure there is no good reason. It could be, for instance, that redundancy is how mistakes are identified and corrected.
8. *How do we go about justifying and making changes?* Whatever problems we identify, there is still the important issue of persuasion. Management is often reluctant to accept that the themes the ethnographer has identified are real (I have personal experience of this). Workers sometimes have a vested interest in preserving current work patterns.
9. *How do we evaluate the effects of intervention and over what period of time?* One of the classic ethnographic problems is that of evaluation of change. Over what period of time should we be looking at practices and the changes that are taking place?

Following literature reviews and the generation of the 'nine questions', the group met at a workshop to interrogate existing data with a view to establishing what general areas of interest in the field sites might be identified and hence what the focus of subsequent patterns might be. It was agreed that the project, which was to last 2 years, would be divided into two fairly distinct phases, and only the first six questions above would be dealt with in year 1. That is, the first phase of the project was regarded as largely descriptive/analytic, whilst the second phase was to be representational/interventionist. As pointed out above, an early decision had to do with the practical possibilities inherent in making comparisons from field research conducted by the team allied to published literature. It was felt that too much heterogeneity might result in generalisations that were of little practical use, and so settings which could loosely be termed as 'engineering maintenance' or 'construction' were chosen. Following this and again done by pulling out some identifiable features from data we already had (based both on ethnographic studies which were under way or, in one case, completed and on the literature we had examined), we cautiously isolated five themes which formed the basis for the development of the patterns. During this workshop, members of the group described the work they were doing in various settings, including train maintenance, power plant construction, an Australian mining camp and an international software collaboration. From this we tentatively outlined five potential patterns:

(a) Finding tools and materials
(b) Sequencing technical activities
(c) Coupling work activities
(d) Sharing knowledge
(e) Scheduling for contingencies

These general patterns were not clearly demarcated, at least to begin with, but reflected a common-sense approach to the kinds of issue that we saw as typically arising in the settings under investigation. 'Finding tools and materials' is fairly self-explanatory and refers to the fact that tools and materials are not always easily identified, can go missing and are sometimes used by more than one individual or group and that, as a consequence, work can sometimes be held up. 'Sequencing technical activities' reflects a classic ethnomethodological concern, the detailed description of how activities are organised on the basis of an egological orientation. It deals, that is, with the 'what do I do next' questions rehearsed in Randall et al. (2007). 'Coupling work activities' deals with the fact of coordination 'down the line'. That is, how the activities of one group of workers cascade down consequentially to those of another. 'Sharing knowledge' was an attempt to specify the skills, expertises, local knowledges and so on that might be possessed by one group but not necessarily shared with others with a view to understanding how consequential that might be. Finally, 'scheduling for contingencies' reflected the well-known fact that the standard ordering of work schedules was sometimes disrupted by contingencies, by new priorities and so on.

It needs to be stressed here that data collection from various sites was continuing. Additional data was analysed and fed into the evolution of the patterns. Space precludes a detailed analysis of the data from the several studies that fed into our decision-making, and in any case the provision of detail is not the primary function of the chapter. We can, however, at least give some examples of the way in which ethnographic data fed into the refinement of our comparative patterns. Below, we give an outline of two. Again, we need to be clear that the purpose of this chapter is not to rehearse ethnographic data in any detail, and we do not do so. Our purpose is to do with representing ethnographic data in such a way that it can be seen to 'fit' with evolving schema.

Example 1 One of the areas that Hitachi fieldworkers had been studying was train maintenance in the UK. Maintenance work of this kind is done in a depot and, at the site in question, on five tracks in the depot. Five teams of operatives work in parallel, each consisting of about 15 maintainers. Most of the work done on site (though not all) is routine and scheduled, and, typically, a manual of rules and procedures is used to identify the stages of specific operations, and work completed is recorded on an application running on a laptop. In presenting the work, fieldworkers drew attention to the fact that work was frequently held up as a result of the fact that various tools and materials were not always 'to hand'. There were a number of different reasons for this, including the fact that manuals did not provide exhaustive lists of tools required for the completion of particular jobs which meant pauses whilst the requisite tools were obtained, the fact that the stock management system was not easy to use and inventory checking was cumbersome and that tools which were supposed to be located on workbenches often went missing. Now, in comparing this site to others, we observed that 'finding tools and materials' was a generic problem, though one which took on specific characteristics in different circumstances. Thus and for instance, a range of fairly typical dimensions seemed to be implicated. These included such issues as whether the same people who organised resources also used them, whether adequate catalogues of resources were maintained, where equipment was kept, whether more than one person or team used the equipment and so on. After a process of iteration, the following pattern was evolved, with the issues that seemed to be salient highlighted:

Now, what we describe here is not a pattern in the sense that it was used by Alexander. It is not prescriptive and it does not seek to describe universalities. Indeed, the questions are designed to elicit the dimensions of variation. The pattern itself, however, is not the point. We should remind ourselves that the purpose of the 'patterning' process is to make complex data from individual sites available to both other ethnographers and to designers in a form which enables them to 'read' the data in a usable form. To this end and having said that data feeds into pattern construction, ethnographic data is also progressively being structured in a way which is consistent with the patterns. The process, in other words and as already stated, is mutually elaborative. An example is given below (Tables 4.1 and 4.2).

We should remember here that it is the ethnographic data that provides for the specific rendering of the problems experienced at work in this context as well as, of course, descriptions and analyses of the ordinary routines. The patterns do not, and cannot, replace the insights the ethnography provides. The pattern, that is, represents

Table 4.1 Maintenance engineering: finding tools and materials

The questions	*The pattern*-maintenance work-finding tools and materials	Comments
What actors are involved?	1.1 How are maintenance teams constructed?	
	1.2 What is the division of labour?	1.2.1 Do they deal with planned work or exceptions?
		1.2.2 How are tasks allocated?
	1.3 How is authority formally distributed?	
	1.4 How are responsibilities actually organised?	
	1.5 What aspects of the work involve fixed positions and/or mobility?	1.5.1 Do they work in confined spaces?
		1.5.2 Do they need to cover large distances?
2. What are they doing?	2.1 What different kinds of equipment are used?	2.1a How specialised is the equipment and does it take specialised knowledge to use it?
		2.1b Are the same people responsible for the organisation of resources as the people who use them?
	2.2 How is equipment organised?	2.2.1 Is equipment kept in a centralised position?
		2.2.2 Is a catalogue of the equipment used?
		2.2.2a Is the catalogue easy to use?
		2.2.3 Who maintains the catalogue and is it done accurately?
		2.2.4 Is the catalogue digital or physical in form?
		2.2.5 Who allocates equipment?
		2.2.6 Who is responsible for its return?
		2.2.7 How often does equipment go missing or get lost?
		2.2.8 Is equipment used by others?
		2.2.9 How long does searching for equipment take?

Why are they doing it?		
Why are they doing it this way?	3.1 How adequate is the equipment they use?	3.1.1 Is equipment up to date? If not, why not?
	3.2 How clear are instructions for using it?	3.2.1 Do people have difficulty working with the equipment?
	3.3 Is there anyone with specialised skills to use the equipment?	3.3.1 Are the members of the team adequately skilled for equipment use?
	4.1a Are there health and safety concerns?	4.1.1 What restrictions are there on the way equipment can be used?
	4.1b Are there external reasons for organising this way? (e.g., do contracts specify what equipment or information resources will be used?)	4.1.2 Are these restrictions imposed by the government, the organisation or trade unions?
What materials, resources and spaces do they deploy?	5.1a Are equipment and materials standardised?	5.1.1 Do workers carry personal tools or materials with them?
	5.1b Do workers ever use 'unofficial' equipment?	5.1.2 Do workers carry personal information with them?
	5.1c Is the equipment always available? If not, why?	5.1.3 Are documents in standard formats?
	5.1d Are information resources/documents used?	5.1.4 Is documentation in physical or digital form? Why?
	5.1e Are there any overheads to using this equipment or information?	5.1.5 Does it slow the work up?
What knowledge and skills do they demonstrate?	6.1a What kind of training is needed to use the equipment?	6.1.1 Are the specialists on site?
	6.1b Are there specialists?	6.1.2 Are there enough of them?
		6.1.3 Do they have adequate knowledge of local conditions?

Table 4.2 Finding tools and materials: train maintenance

Case 1	Source	UK train maintenance
	1.2.3 How are tasks allocated?	Maintenance teams are mainly concerned with scheduled, routine, maintenance, although they have to deal with breakdowns as well.
	2.1b Are the same people responsible for the organization of resources as the people who use them?	There is a central storage area, but tools are only returned once a day. There are other storage areas located at different places in the shed. There is no clear responsibility as to who should return tools to the designated areas.
	2.2.1 Is equipment kept in a centralised position?	Equipment is kept in a variety of places and it is sometimes time-consuming to walk around trying to find tools. Necessary tools/ materials are often missing in the storage area. Expendables like cans are sometimes placed in the office or work bench, not in the designated storage area.
	2.2.2 Is a catalogue of the equipment used?	Yes
	2.2.2.a Is the catalogue easy to use?	It is difficult to use. Workers do not use the same language to describe tools and equipment as is used in the e-catalogue. It can be very difficult to trace what new equipment is needed.
	2.2.4 Is the catalogue digital or physical in form?	Digital
	2.2.5 and 2.2.6 Who allocates equipment and who is responsible for its return?	The store manager at the beginning of the day, otherwise, individual workers as needed. No-one has a specific responsibility for return
	2.2.7 How often does equipment go missing or get lost?	Frequently
	2.2.8 Is equipment used by others?	Yes, all the time. Teams are working in parallel and often borrow equipment from other teams. Some equipment is in short supply
	2.2.9 How long does searching for equipment take?	It depends, but we have seen examples of 2 h

a means to represent problems in a particular way, using a consistent language and thus affording an easy and convenient means to compare.

Example 2 A second theme, which we evolved by drawing on existing data, was that of 'coupling work activities'. This was intended to describe situations where the work of one individual or team affects the work of another individual or team. The degree of 'coupling' of work activities is scarcely a new insight (see, e.g., Weick 1976; Orton and Weick 1990), but our purpose, we remind ourselves, is pragmatic. That is, we set out to establish what the conditions which in practice affect the flow of work from one group to another might be. Again, we drew on data from published (and some unpublished) work conducted by others and also on fieldwork data collected by the design team. The questions that we evolved, again iteratively, as new data became available, are listed in Table 4.3. An example of the data which informed the construction of the pattern comes from analysis of construction and maintenance work in a power plant. Here, members of a warehouse management group make preparations in response to requests for receiving (from a subcontractor) and delivering (to the construction site) materials (two people for incoming materials and three in charge of delivery). The materials in question include pipe lengths of varying and non-standard sizes and shapes which need to be stored in a physical location. The amount of space available for the storage of these pipes is limited. The pipes are ordered from a subcontractor some 3 months in advance of need. Having said that, changes in construction schedules mean that pipes are often stored for longer than that. The locations at which pipes are stored are registered using a GPS system. Problems occur, however, when the warehouse team unexpectedly receives materials from the subcontractor which do not correspond to digital delivery slips. They have to be inspected against load manifests, recorded and then stored somewhere. Having said that and to compound the problem, the pipes that are delivered will not always correspond accurately with descriptions on the manifest. That is, they will often not be needed at that moment because work schedules have been changed. Thus, they need to be stored, often for months. The pipes are too big to be handled entirely by hand and a range of moving equipment is used. Moreover, because they are often of unusual shapes and sizes, they sometimes cannot be placed in spaces originally allocated for them. There is a limited amount of space on site for the storage of these pipes and, because they are often stored for months on end, there is a tendency for them to be moved around as workers search for pipes that are needed in the near future. Limited time means that the location of pipes is not always accurately recorded.

In theory, pipe delivery to the construction site is organised three days before fitting specialists pick them up. At the same time, pipe fitters sometimes make unexpected demands because of changes to their work schedules. These sudden and unexpected requests mean that preparation is sometimes hurried and, more consequentially, that pipe fitters from the construction site collect pipes themselves (often displacing other pipes whilst they search for what they need, making it difficult for the warehouse group to control the location of inventory). Here, then, the practices of one group (pipe fitters, suppliers) have a significant effect on the efficiency of another (warehouse management) (Figs. 4.1 and 4.2).

Here, then, ethnographic data can be described in relation to the highlighted features in the pattern. That is, the data is examined to see what the salient questions might be, as below:

In a similar vein, then, the problems that could be identified across the different sites involved in this work (most of which are not reported here) are revealed by detailed ethnographic analysis. The pattern, once again, is used as a device for producing results in a format that allows for comparison.

Table 4.3 Coupling work activities: pipe delivery and collection

The questions	The *pattern*-maintenance work-coupling work activities	Comments
1. What actors are involved?	1.1 How are maintenance teams constructed?	1.1. 1 Here, we want to know about the numbers of people in teams
	1.2 What is the division of labour?	1.2. 1 What jobs are people formally required to do? What are their job descriptions? Do they actually do more than that?
	1.3 How is authority formally distributed? 1.4 How are responsibilities actually organised?	1.3.1 and 1.4.1 The kind of thing we are interested in here is whether members of the team work strictly to orders or whether they themselves have discretion in what they do. Can they, for instance, change the order of work if they think it is efficient to do so without asking anyone else?
	1.5 What aspects of the work involve fixed positions and/or mobility?	1.5.1 Do they work in confined spaces?
		1.5.2 The literature indicates that geographical mobility creates a different set of problems than working in fixed locations, and we have found the same thing. Some problems can be caused by having only a small amount of space to work in, others by having to work a long way from other people
2. What are they doing?	2.1 What order is the work done in?	2.1.1 Here we are specifically interested in sequentiality-detailed description of the way work is done and if possible the reasons why people decide to do it like this. Video and pictures are often used to get a good sense of this
		2.1.2 Is there a difference between expected workflow and actual flow of work?
	2.2 How rule based is it?	2.2.1 How much discretion is there in the way people do their work, or are they tightly controlled?
	2.3 How coupled with other work is it?	2.3.1 Do changes cascade through to other work? Do stoppages in one place cause stoppages in another?
	2.4 How is it coordinated?	2.4.1 How are problems communicated to other work groups, if at all? How are changes in work plans communicated, if at all?

(continued)

Table 4.3 (continued)

The questions	*The pattern*-maintenance work-coupling work activities	Comments
	2.5 What is difficult?	2.5.1 What things actually cause plans to be altered?
		2.5.2 How often do they occur?
	2.6 What is unexpected?	2.6.1 We make a difference between 'normal natural troubles', the things which regularly occur which affect the flow of work, and the 'unexpected', more serious, perhaps more rare, events
3. Why are they doing it?	3.1 What does the organisation demand of them (workload)?	3.1.1 What time and resource allocations are made?
	3.2 How clear are the instructions?	3.2.1 What is the role of manuals and other instructions? Do workers pay attention to them? It is well known that workers often find it difficult to identify what the problem is in a manual (or where to find the answers) and often find other solutions
	3.3 Who instructs them?	3.3.1 What is the structure of authority and who, in practice, decides what should be done next?
	3.4 How are roles actually distributed?	3.4.1 Is there any difference between formally described roles and what people actually do?
	3.5 How formal/informal is the distribution of tasks?	3.5 Do managers or supervisors change the order of work, or do they stick rigidly to planned schedules?
4. Why are they doing it this way?	4.1 What determines the order they do things in?	4.1.1 Why are there sometimes delays?
	4.2 How easy is it to organise and coordinate?	4.2.1 What don't they know that they need to know?
	4.3 How well does resource management fit the flow of work?	4.3.1 Are there resource problems because no one in management knows what is needed?
	4.4 How economic is it? Is there waste or redundancy?	4.4.1 Can we tell the difference between unnecessary duplication and useful checking?
	4.5 What disrupts the work, how long for and who is affected?	4.5.1 What are the factors that create 'normal natural troubles'?
	4.6 What external factors govern the work?	4.6.1 Work activities are often constrained by factors such as contract obligations, health and safety regulations, legislation and other background conditions and external scheduling

(continued)

Table 4.3 (continued)

The questions	The *pattern*-maintenance work-coupling work activities	Comments
5. What materials, resources and spaces do they deploy?	5.1 What limits the pace of work?	5.1.1 Here, we are mainly thinking of technical limitations – are the tools they use adequate?
6. What knowledge and skills do they demonstrate?	6.1 What do workers need to know and how are they trained?	6.1.1 To what extent is the training on the job?
		6.1.2 Is it regularly updated? How is skill maintained?
	6.2 When are these skills obvious?	6.2.1 When can you tell that workers need high levels of skill and when does it matter less?
	6.3 How technical is the work?	6.3.1 How difficult is it for the ethnographer to understand what the skills are?
		6.3.2 Are the skills social as well as technical?
	6.4 How easy is the skill to acquire?	6.4.1 How much training is needed?
		6.4.2 Do people pick up the skills by informal methods?
	6.5 How much of it needs to be shared?	6.5.1 Is it enough that there is one person who has the skill and can tell others what to do, or is it important that everyone has it?
	6.6 What is the distribution of skill?	6.6.1 Is everyone equally good at the work, or are some people obviously more expert than others?
	6.7 How is information maintained and by whom?	6.7.1 Does a knowledge base need to be maintained, and if so, how is it done?
1.5.1 and 1.5.2	Storage space available is limited. The problem is made more difficult by the fact that pipes are of many different shapes and sizes. These are often non-standard which means they cannot easily be stored in a defined order	
2.3.1 Do changes cascade through to other work? Do stoppages in one place cause stoppages in another?	The problems cascade across three locations. They start in the subcontractor's, where pipes are supposed to be made in accordance with work schedules but unexpected, and urgent, requests are quite common. In turn, this means that pipes are delivered to the storage site in a somewhat unpredictable way and sometimes have to be stored for long periods. Their non-standard shape and size means they are difficult to organise and other pipes have to be moved to accommodate them	
	When pipes are to be delivered to the construction site, they are often difficult to find because they have been moved, which causes delays in construction	

(continued)

Table 4.3 (continued)

The questions	The *pattern*-maintenance work-coupling work activities	Comments
2.4.1 How are problems communicated to other work groups, if at all? How are changes in work plans	There is very little communication across different workgroups, except through documentation. Changes in storage location as pipes get moved around are not communicated at all	
2.5.1 What things actually cause plans to be altered?	Changes to work schedules at the construction site cause most problems	
	The contingencies which arise on the construction site mean that the order in which the pipes are manufactured is not the same as the order in which they are needed, meaning that pipes have to be stored often for long periods	
2.5.2 How often do they occur?	Frequently. It is quite common for work to be delayed because the right pipes or materials cannot be found	
2.6.1 We make a difference between 'normal natural troubles', the things which regularly occur which affect the flow of work, and the 'unexpected', more serious, perhaps more rare, events	Most of what happens can be described as normal, natural troubles	
4.1.1 Why are there sometimes delays?	The delays are almost entirely caused by the different problems associated with storage	
4.2.1 What don't they know that they need to know?	There is very little communication between one group and the next, other than through documentation	
4.3.1 Are there resource problems because no one in management knows what is needed?	The biggest resource problem is lack of space at the site	
4.6.1 Work activities are often constrained by factors such as contract obligations, health and safety regulations, legislation and other background conditions and external scheduling	The various delays are caused by differences between schedules, which are established months in advance, and the immediate needs of the construction site	

4.6 Conclusion

The work we report above was conducted, as indicated, with some pragmatic ends in view. It was intended to provide, as we have intimated, a common set of questions which could be decomposed to address specific themes relevant to the setting in question but phrased in a way which was generic enough that comparisons with other settings could be made. It was done with the approximate aim of achieving

Fig. 4.1 Storing and
retrieving pipes

Fig. 4.2 Storing and retrieving pipes

certain quite pragmatic objectives. These included shortening the time taken to do ethnographic work by sensitising fieldworkers to 'what they might find'; addressing the concerns of designers who had difficulty understanding what the lessons of fieldwork data might be; and perhaps most importantly providing a focus on problems of similarity and difference. Design work in the plant construction case, for instance, is further forward than in the train maintenance case and has focused initially on using an iPod touch for video conferencing and for the sharing of visual images. Visual imagery, in the context of non-standard sizes, seems to be a great deal more effective than any other form of description. Medium term design is orienting towards an augmented reality system which will dovetail with a system intended for use in construction sites themselves and which will feature point and tag functionality such that visual images of locations are overlaid with other data. The point here, of course, is that it would be naïve to imagine that envisaged systems will be used in one setting only. As far as possible, for sound economic reasons, they will be deployed in a range of settings where similar issues are described. The patterns, as we have remarked, are intended to outline the lines along which similarity and difference can be identified. Whilst we are not the first to remark on the tensions between the provision of detail inherent in case studies and the comparative work, we do believe that few efforts have been made to examine these issues *across cases*. What we have described above is an on-going attempt to do so. A significant part of the work has been concerned with finding cases at an appropriate level of generality, such that useful comparison can be made. Although the conceptual issue of what exactly we might mean when we talk about 'domains' and 'settings' was not a part of our deliberations, the selection of cases which were 'similar enough' clearly was a relevant and problematic matter. We continue to examine the patterns in the light of data from new cases. A recent effort has been the examination of a railway control room.

Having said this, the patterns undergo constant refinement. The design team finds them useful but, at the same time, expresses certain reservations. To some extent, this is because we have not always had a clear, shared, understanding of exactly what benefits might accrue from the work. For instance, it became progressively more clear over the year that one implied (but initially unexpressed) need was to enable inexperienced workers to go into the field armed with something more than an 'ethnography and how to do it' literature, something which the patterns were never intended to do. Equally, the patterns were perceived to overlap such that it was sometimes difficult to identify which pattern asks pertinent questions about which situation. Even so, fieldworkers involved in the business of representing their work to designers report that they feel more confident in their efforts to do so. As one of them said, 'at last, I feel I have a language I can use to them'. Regardless, how best to represent these evolving structures such that both requisite detail and necessary generality are encompassed remains an issue. Representing those similarities and differences and aligning them with detailed case data are something we are embarking on at the time of writing.

References

Alexander, C. (1979). *The timeless way of building*. New York: Oxford University Press.

Alexander, C., Ishikawa, S., Silverstein, M., Jacobson, M., Fiksdahl-King, I., & Angel, S. (1977). *A pattern language*. New York: Oxford University Press.

Avizienis, A., Laprie, J. C., & Randell, B. (2001). *Fundamental concepts of dependability*. Computing Science: University of Newcastle upon Tyne.

Bateman, J. (1995). Preventive maintenance: Stand alone manufacturing compared with cellular manufacturing. *Industrial Management, 37*(1), 19.

Bendifallah, S. A., & Scacchi, W. (1987). Understanding software maintenance work. *IEEE Transactions on Software Engineering, SE-13*(3), 311–323.

Beyer, H., & Holzblatt, K. (1998). *Contextual design: Defining customer-centred systems*. San Francisco: Morgan Kaufmann Publishers. ISBN 1558604111.

Bobrow, D. G., & Whalen, J. (2002). Community knowledge sharing in practice. *Reflections, 4*(2), 47–59.

Boehm-Davis, D. A., Fox, J. E., & Philips, B. H. (1996). Techniques for exploring program comprehension, empirical studies of programmers (pp. 3–37). Washington, DC: Ablex.

Borchers, J. (2001). A pattern approach to interaction design. *AI & Society, 15*, 359–376 (*Human Computer Interaction, 21*(1), January 2001).

Carstensen, P. (1999). Here is the knowledge-where should I put it? Findings from a study of how knowledge spaces are used within a support group. In IEEE 8th International Workshops on Enabling Technologies: Infrastructure for Collaborative Enterprises (WET ICE '99) Proceedings.

Charmaz, K. (2006). *Constructing grounded theory: A practical guide through qualitative analysis.* London: Sage.

Cooke, F. L. (2000). Implementing TPM in plant maintenance: Some organisational barriers. *International Journal of Quality & Reliability Management, 17*(9), 1003–1016.

Crabtree, A., Rouncefield, M., & Tolmie, P. (2012). *Doing design ethnography.* London: Springer.

Crosby, M. E., Scholtz, J., & Widenbeck, S. (2002). The roles beacons play in comprehension for novice and expert programmers. In *14th Workshop of the Psychology of Programming Interest `Group, Brunel University* (pp. 58–78).

Dearden, A. M., & Finlay, J. (2006). Pattern languages in HCI: a critical review. *Human Computer Interaction, 21*(1), 49–102.

Denef, S. (2012). A pattern language of firefighting frontline practice to inform the design of ubiquitous computing. *Communications in Computer and Information Science, 277*, 308–312.

Dovey, K. (1990). The pattern language and its enemies. *Design Studies, 11*, 3–9.

Erickson, T. (2000). Lingua Francas for design: Sacred places and pattern languages DIS '00. In *Proceedings of the 3rd conference on designing interactive systems: Processes, practices, methods, and techniques* (pp. 357–368). New York: ACM.

Gabriel, R. (1996). *Patterns of software.* New York: Oxford University Press.

Gamma, E., Helm, R., Johnson, R., & Vlissides, J. (1993). *Design patterns: Abstraction and reuse of object-oriented design* (Lecture notes in computer science, Vol. 707, pp. 406–431). Berlin: Springer.

Gits, C. W. (1992). Design of maintenance concepts. *International Journal of Production Economics, 24*, 217–226.

Glaser, B. G., & Strauss, A. L. (1967). *The discovery of grounded theory: Strategies for qualitative research.* Chicago: Aldine.

Goodyear, P. (2005). Patterns, educational design and networked learning: Patterns, pattern languages and design practice. *Australasian Journal of Educational Technology, 21*(1), 82–101.

Hughes, J. A., Randall, D., & Shapiro, D. (1992). From ethnographic record to system design. In *Computer supported cooperative work* (Vol. 1, pp. 123–141).

Hughes, J. A., Randall, D., & Shapiro, D. (1993). Designing with ethnography: Making work visible. *Interacting with Computers, 5*(2), 239–253.

Hughes, J., King, V., Rodden, T., & Anderson, H. (1994). Moving out of the control room: Ethnography in system design. In *Proceedings of the ACM conference on computer supported cooperative work, Chapel Hill, North Carolina* (pp. 429–438). New York: ACM Press.

Hutchins, E. (1995). *Cognition in the wild.* Cambridge, MA: MIT Press.

Kaptelinen, V., & Nardi, B. (2006). *Acting with technology: Activity theory and interaction design.* Cambridge: MIT Press.

Kemerer, C., & Slaughter, S. (1997). Determinants of software maintenance profiles: An empirical investigation. *Software Maintenance: Research and Practice, 9*, 235–251.

Ko, A. J., Aung, H. H., & Myers, B. A. (2005). Eliciting design requirements for maintenance-oriented IDE's: A detailed study of corrective and perfective maintenance tasks. Human-Computer Interaction Institute, Paper 179.

Laporte, T. (1996). High reliability organizations: Unlikely, demanding and at risk. *Journal of Contingencies and Crisis Management, 4*, 60–71.

Laporte, T. R., & Consolini, P. M. (1991). Working in practice but not in theory. *Journal of Public Administration Research and Theory, 1*(1), 19–47.

Laporte, T., & Consolini, P. (1998a). Theoretical and operational challenges of "high-reliability organizations": Air-traffic control and aircraft carriers. *International Journal of Public Administration, 21*(6-8), 847–852.

Laporte, T., & Consolini, P. (1998b). Working in practice but not in theory: Theoretical challenges of "high-reliability organizations". *Journal of Public Administration Research and Theory, 1*(1), 19–48.

Lin, J., & Landay, J. A. (2002). Damask: A tool for early-stage design and prototyping of multi-device user interfaces. In *Proceedings of the 8th international conference on distributed multimedia systems (2002 international workshop on visual computing), San Francisco, CA, September 26–28, 2002* (pp. 573–580).

Marquez, A. C. (2007). *The maintenance management framework: models and methods for complex systems maintenance*. Berlin: Springer.

Martin, D., & Sommerville, I. (2004). Patterns of cooperative interaction: Linking ethnomethodology and design. *ACM Transactions on Computer-Human Interaction, 11*(1), March (the patterns archive is available at http://polo.lancs.ac.uk/patterns/)

McDonald, N., Corrigan, S., Daly, C., & Cromie, S. (2000). Safety management systems and safety culture in aircraft maintenance organisations. *Safety Science, 34*, 151–176.

Nakagawa, T. (2005). *Maintenance theory of reliability*. Berlin: Springer.

Orr, J. (1996). *Talking about machines: An ethnography of a modern job*. Ithaca: Cornell University Press.

Orton, J. D., & Weick, K. (1990). Loosely coupled systems: A reconceptualization. *Academy of Management Review, 15*, 203.

Perrow, C. (1999). *Normal accidents: Living with high-risk technologies*. Princeton: Princeton University Press.

Pipek, V., & Wulf, V. (2003). Pruning the answer garden: Knowledge sharing in maintenance engineering. In Proceedings of the 6th European Conference on Computer Supported Cooperative Work, 14–18 September, Helsinki, Finland.

Randall, D., Harper, R., & Rouncefield, M. (2007). *Fieldwork for design*. London: Springer.

Randall, D., Hughes, J., & Shapiro, D. (1993). Systems development – the fourth dimension: Perspectives on the social organization of work. In P. Quintas (Ed.), *Social dimensions of systems engineering: People, processes, policies and software development* (pp. 197–214). Hemel Hempstead: Ellis Horwood.

Raouf, A., & Ben-Daya, M. (1995). Total maintenance management: A systematic approach. *Journal of Quality in Maintenance Engineering, 1*(1), 6–14.

Rising, L. (1998). *The patterns handbook: Techniques, strategies, and applications*. Cambridge: Cambridge University Press.

Salingaros, N. (2000). The structure of pattern languages. *Architectural Research Quarterly, 4*, 149–162.

Schmidt, K. (2012). The trouble with 'tacit knowledge'. *International Journal of Computer Supported Cooperative Work, 21*(2–3), 163–225.

Smith, R., & Hawkins, B. (2004). *Lean maintenance*. Oxford: Elsevier.

Smith, R., & Mobley, R. K. (2008). *Rules of thumb for maintenance and reliability engineers*. Oxford: Elsevier.

Strauss, A., & Corbin, J. (1997). *Grounded theory in practice*. London: Sage.

Swanson, L. (2001). Linking maintenance strategies to performance. *International Journal of Production Economics, 70*, 237–244.

Swanson, E. B. (1976). The dimensions of maintenance. In *ICSE '76 Proceedings of the 2nd international conference on software engineering* (pp. 492–497). New York: ACM Press.

Tan, W.-G., & Gable, G. (1998). Attitudes of maintenance personnel towards maintenance work: A comparative analysis. *Journal of Software Maintenance: Research and Practice, 10*(1), 59–74.

van Welie, M., & van der Veer, G. (2003). *Pattern languages in interaction design: Structure and Organization Human-Computer Interaction – INTERACT'03M* (Rauterberg, M., Menozzi, M., & Wesson, J., Eds., pp. 527–534). Amsterdam: IOS Press.

Weick, K. (1976). Educational organizations as loosely coupled systems. *Administrative Science Quarterly, 21*(1), 1–19.

Wireman, T. (2004). *Benchmarking best practices in maintenance management*. New York: Industrial Press.

Yamauchi, Y., Whalen, J., & Bobrow, D. (2003). Information use of service technicians in difficult cases. In 2003 Proceeding CHI '03: Proceedings of the SIGCHI conference on Human factors in computing systems.

Part II
The Challenge of Change

Chapter 5
Situated Computing

Giorgio De Michelis

5.1 Introduction

Some members of EUSSET (European Society for Socially Embedded Technologies), the European professional association dedicated to the development of technological tools and infrastructures that incorporate a human-centred design perspective, presented at one of the workshops accompanying the development of the new R&D programme of the European Union, Horizon, a position paper (Bannon et al. 2012) where situated computing is proposed as a new paradigm engaged with design and development of technologies from a perspective of evolving social practices.

The position paper is not the right place where to fully develop the argumentation supporting a new user-oriented technological paradigm. Moreover, the position paper is well grounded on the European research on CSCW and related topics, regarding the characterization of the human/social side of the issue, but is opening a new front at the technology level that is not typical of a human-centred design community.

As a coauthor of the above-mentioned position paper, I am willing to stress the novelty of this move inside technology, offering some arguments to a discussion inside and outside EUSSET.

The paper grounds 'situated computing' on the change that has happened on how ICT technology is used, today. Then it recalls the situated action paradigm, as the viewpoint that has been able to recognize and conceptualize the above change. Situated computing is presented as the natural counterpart of situated action and it is surveyed how the concept has been formulated in the last ten years. Finally,

G. De Michelis (✉)
DISCo, University of Milano – Bicocca, Milan, Italy
e-mail: gdemich@disco.unimib.it

I propose my view on situated computing and I introduce some features situated computing systems should have.

5.2 A Change in Use

To shorten our historical account, let us go back to the decade between mid-1980s and mid-1990s: in 1984, Apple launched Macintosh, and in 1992 SAP presented its Sap R/3 system, later named SAP ERP.

Why are these dates important? Because Macintosh, at the personal computing level, and Sap R/3, at the organizational computing level, fix, from the user interaction viewpoint, the standards that characterize, in their domains, all the systems that are proposed to the market up to current days. It is not by chance in fact that all operating systems for personal computers resemble each other, sharing the desktop metaphor, invented by Alan Kay at Xerox PARC in the late 1970s (Kay 1977) and made popular by Macintosh, and that the same is true for ERPs, adopted by the majority of medium and large companies all around the world (Kumar and Hillergersberg 2000).

Despite the evolution that both operating systems for workstations and ERPs have had in these 20 and more years, due to the combined effect of continuously growing memories, better communication channels, the web, etc., both remain, structurally and from human interaction viewpoint, the same.

When they conquer the markets, both are in essence multifunction devices supporting users in a growing variety of tasks. Their success depends on their capability to solve the problems affecting the diffusion of ICT within work environments: the simple and highly usable interface of Macintosh and imitators allows everyone to use it, and the strong integration of ERP systems gives to enterprises the possibility of planning, managing, and controlling their operations in a smooth way.

Until people use them for doing their tasks, in fact, their support is effective, even if the number of tasks and the amount of stored data and/or documents grow. Accessing data and files is considered one function among the others and what matters is being able to find a document (in the workstations) and to process data (in the ERPs).

But changes of ICT have induced unexpected changes in the way its applications are used: some users, in particular, have slowly but irreducibly changed the role they attribute to ICT. Let us look closely at those for whom reading and writing documents, searching and elaborating information, and collecting, interpreting and calculating data constitute the texture connecting all their activities. They have in the digital world (directly in the workstation or in the web or, finally, in the information system of the organizations with which they are collaborating) almost all what they need both in terms of content and functions (from an organizational science viewpoint, they are called knowledge workers; see, e.g., Blackler et al. 1993; Drucker 1999; Mosco and McKercher 2007). These people have progressively ceased to approach their PC (and what there is behind it) when they have to perform a task, but rather, always more frequently, they have it always on, and whatever they are doing, they switch to it to find and/or do what may help them to act and interact effectively. In other words, when the number of tasks they are executing with the support of ICT has become so large and, mainly, when the amount of their digital data and documents has become so big that they are almost always interacting with a digital device, it happens that ICT systems progressively change, from tools for executing tasks to relational extensions of their capability to act and interact. The workstation (or, in other circumstances, the tablet and/or the smartphone) is always on, because it plays a crucial role, in any situation, allowing the user to act and/or interact effectively: sometimes it is an extension of his/her memory, sometimes it is a powerful communication channel, and sometimes it is necessary for executing tasks like writing and/or calculating and the like. But what is required is that, in any situation, contents, communication channels, and productivity tools are filtered so that all and only what may be useful is accessible.

While, as tools for executing tasks, current ICT-based systems are user-friendly and effective, as companions to act and interact effectively, they appear always more cumbersome and inefficient (the literature on this issue is rich; see, e.g., Kaptelinin and Czerwinski 2007; Eppler and Mengis 2006; Monsell et al. 2000; Oulasvirta 2008; Yeung et al. 2006). For accompanying users in any situation they may encounter during their (working) day, in fact, it is not sufficient that tools are user-friendly; what is also and mainly needed is that, in any moment, all and only what the user needs for acting and interacting (data, documents, messages, information resources, tools, communication channels, people) is ready at his/her hands. But this is not the case, because both workstations and ERPs are multitasking systems and are not capable to provide help depending on the situation of the user.

Let me repeat one thing, to avoid misunderstandings: I am not critiquing the design of the Macintosh and/or of SAP R/3; rather, I am only claiming that they were designed for a time when machines and the way of using them were different and that they, today, have become inadequate. The desktop, emulated by operating systems for personal computers and workstations, is not well designed neither from the point of view of keeping all the things a user needs altogether (it is well known that, while documents created by the user are in the folders of the file system where he/she has stored them, messages are inside the mail system, their attachments are in a special folder of the file system and documents from the web are memorized as URLs in a list) nor from the viewpoint of collecting them in separate spaces. The problem of putting together things related with the same user issue is left to his/her goodwill of creating and updating dedicated folders fighting with the obstacles its organization opposes to him/her. In the same vein, ERP systems are highly integrated monolithic systems that are quite efficient at integrating data with respect to routine or expected tasks, but, conversely, they are quite rigid with respect to free access and unexpected processing.

5.3   Situatedness

The issue, here, is understanding how things are correlated with respect to users, what should be ready at their hands whenever they need to interact with their system. Research on CSCW and related topics in the last 30 years has deeply investigated it, bringing forth several hints on human practice in different work contexts and situations. Situated action (Suchman 1987), language action perspective (Winograd and Flores 1986), and embodied interaction (Dourish 2001) are some of the headings that have been formulated in the effort to characterize what is constitutive of human practice and relevant for the design of ICT-based systems supporting it. Altogether, they underline that human practice is intrinsically social, that it is situated, and that what people say is strictly and bidirectionally linked with what they do.

These three hints on human practice recall that the effectiveness of human beings strongly depends on the awareness they have of their situation, i.e. of the context where they are situated. From what we have said above, a question emerges with big evidence: in the frame of the discourse that we are carrying on, what is the context that people should be aware of? The answer is not as immediate as anyone could think at first moment: there are, in fact, different dimensions of the context where a person acts and interacts (see e.g. Kishore et al. 2004).

First, we can assert that it is not the spatial context: the place where a person is (with the various things and people populating it) strongly affects what she can do and what she cannot do and being aware of it is important, but we cannot say that it reflects the social dimension of human experience.

Second, we can also assert that it is not the temporal context: in different days, at different times of the same day as well as of any day, what she can do and not do changes, as well as what she should and should not do, but social experience evolves in a way that goes beyond strict temporality.

Beyond spatial and temporal contexts, there is a 'social context' that, in some sense, includes both of them: with whom is the person engaged while acting and interacting? What are they doing together and what is the aim of their interactions? What have they already done and what are they mutually committed to do? Whatever a person is doing, this is part of an experience she is living with some other people, with whom she exchanges documents and other things, she shares information and knowledge, and she has mutual commitments. All what participants do during a social experience intertwines language and action, so that, at the same time, things are created, imported, and/or modified and knowledge is created and shared.

The thread of events constituting a social experience creates also the language (game; this implicit reference to Wittgenstein (1953) is not casual) and the knowledge shared by its participants, and for this reason, being aware of the context in which she is acting and interacting is, for a person, necessary in order to be effective in it. We call this thread a 'story', to underline its sense-making role for its participants. All events of what we have called a story are, naturally, situated in space and their thread develops in time: on the one hand, a story, taking place in a space, where its actors live their common experience, transforms that space in its place (Harrison and Dourish 1996); on the other hand, any story has a duration, during which it evolves reacting to the events involving its actors and to the mutual commitments they have established.

Social context is of paramount importance, in particular, for those people who are involved in many different stories, because whichever is the story she is acting and interacting and what is happening in others is, both, disturbing (creating noise and confusion in it) and enriching (opening it to new knowledge) it.

For our target users, i.e. the knowledge workers, whose work is woven of what they read and write, the issue is not if they are using the word processor, the spreadsheet or the mail, but which is the story in which they are engaged so that they can act effectively in it.

5.4   Situated Computing

Systems supporting human practice should therefore be able to improve context awareness of their users, so that they can act and interact effectively in any situation of their life. Researchers in CSCW and related areas have become aware of this fact from many years, as the emergence of a new heading 'situated computing' shows with great evidence.

The term 'situated computing', in fact, is not new and it may be useful to survey its history. For what I know, it is in the second half of the 1990s (1997) that it was used for the first time, by three researchers of the HP Laboratories, R. Hull, P. Neaves, and J. Bedford-Roberts, in a paper they presented at the First International Symposium on Wearable Computers (ISWC '97): 'Towards situated computing'. In the abstract, they wrote: 'Situated computing concerns the ability of computing devices to detect, interpret and respond to aspects of the user's local environment' (Hull et al. 1997). Using the terminology we introduced in the previous section, the authors make reference to spatial context. From 1997 to present days, several other authors have revived the term proposing their view on it.

Let us survey some of the contributions appearing in the literature and some of the initiatives launched under this heading.

In 2001, Masahito Hirakawa and K. Priyantha Hewagamage published 'Situated computing: A paradigm for the mobile user-interaction with multimedia sources' in the *Annals of Software Engineering*. In the abstract they wrote: 'Situated computing is a new paradigm for mobile computer users based on their physical context and activities carried out as a part of their working business. It provides the mechanism to have a mobile computer as a utility to satisfy the user's real world requirements as well as an infrastructure for the situated interaction using applications' (Hirakawa and Hewagamage 2001). Here the authors are again narrowing their use of the term for mobile systems, focusing on spatial context.

One year later, Kevin L. Mills and Jean Scholtz published 'Situated computing: The next frontier for HCI research' in a book edited by J. M. Carroll, *HCI in the New Millennium*. In the paper it is written: 'An impressionist painting emerges of nomadic workers with collections of small, specialized devices roaming among islands of wireless connectivity within a global sea of wired networks. Each wireless island defines a context of available services, embedded devices, and task-specific information. As nomadic workers roam the landscape the context in which they are working continuously changes. As workers move onto wireless islands of connectivity, their context is merged with the context of the island to automatically compose a computational environment to support their needs. At other times, when not connected, an array of portable devices provides each nomad with a local context for computing. This painting, which relies heavily on Weiser's (1991) concept of ubiquitous computing and on Suchman's (1987), notion of situated computing, suggests a future where information and people connect directly and work together across a range of contexts'. (Mills and Scholtz 2001). Even if here 'situated computing' assumes a visionary character for becoming the label of what could be the future of computing, it has to be remarked that while the relationship between space and mobile devices is well developed, the same cannot be said about the 'user's context'.

It goes in the same direction when, in 2005, John S. Gero presented 'Virtual Environments Using Situated Computing Can Change What We Design' at Virtual Concept, a conference held in Biarritz (France). This paper considers situated computing as a new design paradigm. Its abstract says: 'This paper presents the foundational concepts of situated computing: first-person interaction, constructive memory and situations. It then describes two classes of situated design that differ from other forms of designing: situated interaction design and situated artifact design' (Gero 2005). The social nature of situated action is not considered, and in some sense we can consider situatedness as a combination of individual memory and spatial context.

In 2009, the call for the 15th International Conference on Distributed Multimedia Systems claims: 'DMS conference is an international conference series, which covers a wide spectrum of paper presentations, technical discussions and demonstrations in the fields of distributed multimedia computing. ... The main themes of the DMS2009 conference are: network and systems, emergency management and security, *situated computing*, multimedia software engineering, and multimedia information retrieval, mining and fusion'; the term has become a label for describing one of the themes of a conference focusing on distributed multimedia computing.

In 2011, Inderscience started publishing a new *International Journal of Space-Based and Situated Computing*. Its aim is extending 'the pervasive computing vision of everyday objects communicating and collaborating to provide intelligent and context-aware information and services to users in larger geographical spaces. The ultimate goal is to build context-aware global smart space and location-based service applications that integrate information from independent systems (such as sensors, actuators or mobile information systems), which autonomously and securely support human activities. *IJSSC* provides a fully refereed international forum for publishing the latest research into space-based and situated computing'. The term has found its place in the scientific community, but again, its focus has been narrowed to spatial contexts.

But, from the very beginning, there are contributions that go in a direction echoing in a stricter sense than what we have discussed in the previous section.

In 1999, A. V. Gershman, J. F. McCarthy, and A. E. Fano presented 'Situated Computing: Bridging the Gap between Intention and Action' at the 3rd International Symposium on Wearable Computers. In the abstract, they wrote: 'Situated computing represents a new class of computing applications that bridges the gap between people's intentions and the actions they can take to achieve those intentions. These applications are contextually embedded in real-world situations, and are enabled by the proliferation of new kinds of computing devices, expanding communication capabilities and new kinds of digital content. Three types of discontinuities give rise to intention/action gaps and provide opportunities for situated computing applications: physical discontinuities, information discontinuities and awareness discontinuities' (Gershman et al. 1999). Here the authors make reference to a broader view of context, where its social dimension is taken into account.

In 2000, Michel Beaudouin-Lafon and Wendy E. Mackay organize at CHI2000 a workshop on situated computing. In the presentation of the workshop, it is written: 'The term *situated computing* describes socio-technical systems in which situations of use and context play a central role in the use of computers. Since most computing is arguably situated computing, we need to reflect on our current understanding of context, establish a common language for discussion and define processes for developing *systems-in-use*' (Beaudouin-Lafon and Mackay 2000). Among the contributors to the workshop, there is Paul Dourish (A Foundational Framework for Situated Computing; 2000) who, in his position paper, wrote: 'One starting point for this exploration is a conundrum which was, interestingly, raised for me by the call for this workshop. The call coins the term "situated computing" to refer to the set of technologies and usage experiences that make up the burgeoning area of contextually informed system design. The term I use myself is "Embodied Interaction" (for reasons that will become clear. However, I think "situated computing" is an excellent term, because it captures two distinct elements of the area. First, it captures its technological foundations, and the relationship to other, related technological explorations such as the Ubiquitous Computing work spearheaded at PARC in the early 1990s. Weiser (1991) set out a vision of a world in which technology supported us more intimately by retreating into the background, one in which the world around us was imbued with computational power that could be called upon intrinsically as part of everyday activity. At the same time, the word "situated" evokes the "situated action" perspective that has played a dominant role in the sociological foundations of Computer-Supported Cooperative Work. Suchman (1987), drawing on the ethno-methodology of Harold Garfinkel [5], radically revised cognitivist accounts of natural activity to turn attention to the improvised and contingent nature of the sequential organization of activity – its situated character'.

With this workshop, the proponents underline that situated computing should not focus on a particular class of systems, since it refers to a feature that is relevant for a very large variety of the ICT-based systems already in use, but, maybe, because the debate is still restricted in a small group of specialists within the CSCW/HCI research community, it is not clear which situated computing systems do the participants have in mind.

Concluding this historical survey, it may be useful to recall that 'situated computing' with the attention it calls for the coupling between situatedness and ICT-based systems has given rise to the term 'situated software' (Balasubramaniam et al. 2008) and, more recently, has been used by Carlo Ghezzi and co-workers for characterizing the change in perspective they propose in software engineering, taking into account that most software development is contextualized, since it aims to modify existing running systems (Salvaneschi et al. 2012).

I do not pretend that my survey is complete, but, I think, it suffices for showing that situated computing has become a popular header and that it is used with different meanings, moving from the identifier of the emerging class of mobile location-aware computing systems to the label for a new paradigm for the design of information systems and services. Even from this radical viewpoint, however, it has not yet opened its eyes towards the systems already in use, neither to evaluate them from a viewpoint going beyond task-oriented use nor to figure out how they can be redesigned.

5.5 A New Definition of Situated Computing

As said above, situatedness recalls the existence of contexts, and designing systems for it requires to characterize the latter in a way suitable for understanding what computing systems may do to help user situation in them. Contexts, we have recalled, are, intrinsically, multidimensional: they are spatial, since in any moment a person is situated in a portion of space that can be, sometimes, a place she inhabits; they are temporal, where we intend time with all its facets – the absolute one, when we consider the current date and hour, or the relative one, when we consider the current part of the day (morning, afternoon, etc.); they are social, when we consider the social relations in which our actions and interactions are immersed. Making a drastic schematization, we can claim that the social dimension embodies the other ones, since social relations develop in space and time and play a major role in configuring the sense-making vector of any action or interaction. What a person is doing gets, in fact, its sense from the actor network (Latour 2005) which she is part of, from its past events and from its events and mutual commitments scheduled in the future. Summarizing shortly, a social context is generated by a thread of past and future events involving an actor network within which its participants create their common place and knowledge for sense making and effective action and interaction. Its complexity has two orthogonal dimensions: on the one hand, sharing an experience is never definitive – even if and when we live together, we cannot share what we feel; on the other hand, we are generally engaged in several different social experiences: this gives us the capability to enrich any experience in which we participate and, conversely, may distract us from contributing effectively to any one of them.

Situated computing has to do, therefore, with supporting people in the threads in which they participate. This may require the design of new applications but, mainly, it needs a strong help from the applications a person is already using: first, the workstation she uses as the principal terminal for organizing her augmented workplace so that she is kept aware of her threads; second, the information resources of the net and the information produced within the organizations which she is part of that may be necessary for performing in those threads. But, as they are now, neither the operating system for workstations is capable to support user participation in her threads nor information resources (both in the net and in the information systems of the organizations) are offering effective support; instead, they are making always more complex for users situating themselves in the context where they are operating.

Situated computing calls for systems which are designed to take into account the situatedness of human action. It challenges ICT scholars and professionals to redesign the most diffused ICT applications, like operating systems of personal computers and other mobile devices, on the one hand, ERPs and other organizational computing systems, on the other.

5.6 Some Hints on Possible Situated Computing Systems

The generic definition I gave above may leave many readers unsatisfied. Therefore, I add to it some preliminary hints on how situated computing systems can be designed and how I am doing some work in this line. I underline the adjective 'preliminary', I have used in the lines above, because I cannot make any strong assertion on the subject and I do not think that it would be serious to make strong assertions on it. Being specific with respect to 'situated computing' is not possible because we are speaking about not yet existing systems and we do not have any real experience with them, so that we cannot evaluate the qualities of the software inspired by it, without people experimenting it.

I will dedicate two separate subsections to (1) systems for end users (front ends) and (2) big data repositories and systems for managing organizational information (back ends), like in any client–server architecture. The front end needs to adhere directly to the needs and desires of the user, while back ends need to be open to what front ends may require for serving their users.

At front end side, it is necessary that systems (from personal computer operating systems to web-based services for mentioning the two most important classes of systems that are characterized by their front ends) are designed so that the context of usage is accessible without noise and confusion. This requires that front ends are designed keeping together the events constituting threads. We have designed both an operating system for personal computers (De Michelis et al. 2009; De Michelis 2015) and a platform for web services (De Michelis 2014) on the basis of a new metaphor, called 'stories and venues', considering the life of human beings as the intertwining of several different stories and considering for each story the venue where participants find all that is relevant in it. Stories, as sets of threads, are not objective phenomena; rather, they are quite subjective – different people may group in a story different threads – but they are not arbitrary, because threads are, in our approach, the new atomic elements of human experience. How can a story be captured/reflected in a digital application? Organizing the user workspace so that she can access, for each story, to all and only what characterizes it and she can move among her stories. The apparent contrast between *multiplicity* (of stories) and their *openness* can be solved putting at their boundaries the resources needed to grant *continuity* (Brown and Duguid 1994; De Michelis 1998, 2003).

At back end side, the question is quite different: the problem is making any system supporting services or containing data and/or information that users may need to be as open and accessible as possible. Disregarding, here, web-based systems making public large amount of information, for whom the perspective of open linked data promises the needed developments, let us to discuss here, briefly, systems containing the information of organizational systems like ERPs, because, as they are today, they are quite far from what situatedness requires (Dörner et al. 2009).

ERPs and the likes owe their large popularity and diffusion to the fact that they were able to integrate the different information generated by an organization (logistics and accounting, marketing and production, etc.) creating a unique database reflecting a well-defined organizational model that serves all the functions of the organization. This choice has determined a strong standardization of the architecture of information systems (whose efficiency in the routinary tasks is quite high), as well as of the ways to build them (building an ERP is a well-defined task that can be completed in less than 1 year), but, conversely, has made any information processing that is not defined in accordance with the standards characterizing the system difficult (generally a 'mining' activity is needed in this case). The growing relevance that business intelligence and strategic planning have within organization tells us that unforeseen processing of organizational information is becoming a frequent and non-exceptional need: how can we couple the efficiency of existing ERPs with flexibility?

Can ERP systems be redesigned so that innovation and changes to information processing can be possible despite the strong integration of applications they imply?

As a blueprint for this objective, I shortly indicate what follows. First, we can redesign ERP systems as modular systems made of small modules separating functions and data (a similar proposal can be found in Dorner et al. 2009). This means that users will build their system in a bricolage-like style (Ciborra 1999) selecting their components in a large library of modules and linking them in accordance with the business intelligence governing the organization. It has to be underlined that designing the new generation of ERP systems sketched above is possible today, thanks to some ICT technology that has appeared today.

First, cloud computing (Armbrust et al. 2010), among other potential advantages deriving from its capability to support a pay per use policy, offers a strongly homogenous platform simplifying the construction of modular systems; second, mashup technology allows a flexible merging of several APIs needed for interacting with different organizational systems and websites in the front end of user worksta-tions; third, ontologies, supporting an effective tagging of software objects, allow to substitute the vertical integration typical of traditional ERPs with the light coupling you can get through metadata.

It may be useful to underline, here, that modularity has been for long time a concept that scholars and practitioners considered capable to increase the quality of systems, but it has been obstructed, up to now, for its difficult feasibility in heterogeneous computing environments. Cloud computing, with its homogeneous hardware and software platform, together with mashup and ontologies, dissolves the obstacles modular systems have encountered up to now.

5.7   Conclusion

All the new systems we can design and build along the 'situated computing' perspective constitute a great challenge for the community of CSCW and related area researchers, since all of them will strongly influence our engagement with the development of ICT technology.

It is a challenge that they can accept, because the features characterizing 'situated computing' systems emerge from an interaction design (Telier 2011) approach. Their further characterization is not possible without the adoption of the same approach that those disciplines dedicate to new and emergent applications like Web 2.0, collaboration systems, and the likes, for mature systems that have conquered a solid and permanent position in organizations.

But the solidity and duration of existing ICT technologies on the desktops and in the inner parts of organizations tells us that innovation in that field requires a great cure in managing the transition from existing to new systems. The migration from an ERP to its modular replacement is a complex process, both at the human (organizational) and technological levels, requiring that new systems are designed for supporting this migration.

Even more difficult is the transition from operating systems based on the desktop metaphor to the new ones that can be designed along the situated computing perspective, since, here, we deal with human behaviour and expectations. It is well known that innovative systems may fail, because users refuse to pay the price to abandon their system (which is transparent to them, even when ineffective) for adopting the new one (which requires an extra cognitive effort for being used). This means that the design of a new operating system for workstation must couple its innovativeness with the highest degree of continuity with the systems it wants to substitute. It seems a strange paradox, but it indicates the critical quality supporting the adoption of innovation in areas where technology is already present.

Acknowledgments As recalled in Introduction, this paper is an extension of my contribution to the position paper Liam Bannon, Pernille Bjørn, Fabio Paternó, Dave Randall, Kjeld Schmidt, Ina

Wagner, and Volker Wulf and myself presented to the 2nd FIA Research Roadmap Workshop 'Looking to the Horizon – Future Internet Assembly Research Roadmap for Horizon 2020' (Bannon et al. 2012). Before that occasion I had several occasions to discuss situated computing in Italy and abroad. It has been quite relevant for me the panel on this theme at CTS2011, with Steve Benford, John Carroll, Elizabeth Churchill, and Prasun Dewan, where my first formulation of a situated computing manifesto has been deeply and constructively critiqued. Federico Cabitza and Carla Simone are currently engaged with me in a book project on situated computing where my views are enlarging under the inspiration of their viewpoints, theorizations, and experiences. I thank also the reviewers and the editors of this book for the valuable comments on its first version that helped me to try to improve its readability and effectiveness.

References

Armbrust, M., Fox, A., Griffith, R., Joseph, A. D., Katz, R., Konwinski, A., Lee, G., et al. (2010). A view of cloud computing. *Communications of the ACM, 53*(4), 50–58.

Balasubramaniam, S., Lewis, G. A., Simanta, S., & Smith, D. B. (2008). Situated software: Concepts, motivation, technology, and the future. *IEEE Software, 25*(6), 50–55.

Bannon, L., Bjørn, P., De Michelis, G., Paternó, F., Randall, D., Schmidt, K., Wagner, I., & Wulf, V. (2012). *Building a socially embedded future internet*. Paper presented at 2nd FIA research roadmap workshop – Looking to the horizon, future internet assembly research roadmap for horizon 2020, 2012. Germany: University of Siegen.

Beaudouin-Lafon, M., & Mackay, W. E., (Organizers). (2000). Workshop on research directions in situated computing, at the *ACM conference on human factors in computing systems CHI 2000*, Position papers. Netherlands: The Hague.

Blackler, F., Reed, M., & Whitaker, A. (1993). Editorial introduction: Knowledge workers and contemporary organizations. *Journal of Management Studies, 30*(6), 851–862.

Brown, J. S., & Duguid, P. (1994). Borderline resources: Social and material aspects of design. *Human–Computer Interaction, 9*(1), 3–36.

Ciborra, C. (1999). A theory of information systems based on improvisation. In W. Currie & R. Galliers (Eds.), *Rethinking management information systems: An interdisciplinary perspective* (pp. 136–155). Oxford: Oxford University Press.

De Michelis, G. (1998). *Aperto, molteplice, continuo*. Milano: Dunod Italia.

De Michelis, G. (2003). The Swiss Pattada: Designing the ultimate tool, (with original drawings by Marco Susani). *Interactions, 10*(3), 44–53.

De Michelis, G. (2014). *Open social services* (manuscript), available from the author.

De Michelis, G. (2015). Interaction design at itsme. In V. Wulf (Ed.), *Designing socially embedded technologies in the real-world* (pp. 193–215). London: Springer.

De Michelis, G., Loregian, M., & Moderini, C. (2009). Itsme: Interaction design innovating workstations. *Knowledge, Technology & Policy, 22*, 71–78.

Dorner, C., Draxler, S., Pipek, V., & Wulf, V. (2009). End-users at the bazaar: Designing next generation enterprise resource planning systems. *IEEE Software, 26*(5), 45–51.

Dourish, P. (2000). *A foundational framework for situated computing*. Mackay: Beaudouin-Lafon.

Dourish, P. (2001). *Where the action is: The foundations of embodied interaction*. Cambridge, MA: MIT Press.

Drucker, P. F. (1999). Knowledge-worker productivity: The biggest challenge. *California Management Review, 41*(2), 79–94.

Eppler, M. J., & Mengis, J. (2006). The concept of information overload: A review of literature from organization science, accounting, marketing, MIS, and related disciplines. *The Information Society, 20*(5), 325–344.

Gero, J. (2005). Virtual environments using situated computing. In X. Fischer & D. Coutellier (Eds.), *Proceedings of virtual concept 2005*.

Gershman, A. V., Mccarthy, J., & Fano, A. (1999). Situated computing: Bridging the gap between intention and action. In *Proceedings of the 3rd international symposium on wearable computers* (pp. 3–9). San Francisco: IEEE.

Harrison, S., Dourish. P. (1996). Re-place-ing space: The role of place and space in collaborative systems. In: *Proceedings of the 1996 ACM conference on computer supported cooperative work* (pp. 67–76). New York: ACM Press.

Hirakawa, M., & Priyantha Hewagamage, M. (2001). Situated computing: A paradigm for the mobile user-interaction with multimedia sources. *Annals of Software Engineering, 12*(1), 213–239.

Hull, R., Neaves, P., & Bedford-Roberts, J. (1997). Towards situated computing. In *First international symposium on wearable computers (ISWC '97)*. Cambridge, MA: IEEE.

Kaptelinin, V., & Czerwinski, M. (Eds.). (2007). *Beyond the desktop metaphor*. Cambridge, MA: MIT Press.

Kay, A. (1977). Microelectronics and the personal computer. *Scientific American, 237*(3), 230–244.

Kishore, R., Sharman, R., & Ramesh, R. (2004). Computational ontologies and information systems: I. Foundations. *Communications of the Association for Information Systems, 14*, 158–183.

Kumar, K., & Hillergersberg, J. (2000). ERP experiences and evolution. *Communications of the ACM, 43*(4), 23–26.

Latour, B. (2005). *Reassembling the social – An introduction to actor-network-theory*. Oxford: Oxford University Press.

Mills, K. L., & Scholtz, J. (2001). Situated computing: The next frontier for HCI research. In J. M. Carroll (Ed.), *HCI in the new millennium*. New York: Addison Wesley.

Monsell, S., Yeung, N., & Azuma, R. (2000). Reconfiguration of task-set: Is it easier to switch to the weaker task? *Psychological Research, 63*(3-4), 250–264.

Mosco, V., & McKercher, C. (2007). Introduction: Theorizing knowledge labor and the information society. In *Knowledge workers in the information society* (pp. vii–xxiv). Lanham: Lexington Books.

Oulasvirta, A. (2008). Feature when users "do" the ubicomp. *Interactions, 15*(2), 6–9.

Salvaneschi, G., Ghezzi, C., & Pradella, M. (2012). Context-oriented programming: A software engineering perspective. *Journal of Systems and Software, 85*(8), 1801–1817.

Suchman, L. (1987). *Plans and situated actions*. New York: Cambridge University Press.

Telier, A. (Binder, T., De Michelis, G., Ehn, P., Jacucci, G., Linde, P., Wagner, I.). (2011). *Design things*. Cambridge, MA: MIT Press.

Weiser, M. (1991). The computer for the 21st century. *Scientific American, 251*(11), 94–104.

Winograd, T., & Flores, C. F. (1986). *Understanding computers and cognition. A new foundation for design*. Wilmington: Intellect Books.

Wittgenstein, L. (1953). *Philosophical investigations*. Oxford: Blackwell.

Yeung, N., Nystrom, L. E., Aronson, J. A., & Cohen, J. D. (2006). Between-task competition and cognitive control in task switching. *The Journal of Neuroscience, 26*(5), 1429–1438.

Chapter 6
Meta-design: Transforming and Enriching the Design and Use of Socio-technical Systems

Gerhard Fischer and Thomas Herrmann

The meta-design of socio-technical systems (STSs) is an approach which complies with the need of integrating two different types of structures and processes: *technical systems* which are engineered to provide anticipatable and reliable interactions between users and systems and *social systems* which are contingent in their interactions and a subject of evolution. Meta-design is focused on objectives, techniques, and processes to allow users to act as designers. In doing so, it does not provide fixed solutions but a framework within which *all stakeholders* (designers and users) can contribute to the development of technical functionality and the evolution of the social side such as organizational change, knowledge construction, and continuous learning.

This paper describes the possibilities of transforming and enriching the design and use of STSs grounded in the conceptual framework of meta-design. It explores cultures of participation, seeding, evolutionary growth and reseeding, and under-design as specific components of the framework. Two specific examples of meta-designed STSs illustrate the conceptual framework, and findings derived from the assessment of these developments in practice are briefly discussed. Based on the combination of conceptual and methodological consideration, initial guidelines for the meta-design of STSs are derived.

G. Fischer (✉)
University of Colorado, Boulder, CO, USA
e-mail: gerhard@colorado.edu

T. Herrmann
University of Bochum, Bochum, Germany
e-mail: thomas.herrmann@rub.de

© Springer-Verlag London 2015
V. Wulf et al. (eds.), *Designing Socially Embedded Technologies in the Real-World*,
Computer Supported Cooperative Work, DOI 10.1007/978-1-4471-6720-4_6

6.1   Introduction

New technologies and new media are important driving forces and prerequisites to address the complex and systemic problems our societies face today. But technology alone does not improve social structures and human behavior, making the design of *socio-technical systems (STSs)* (Herrmann 2003; Mumford 2000; Trist 1981) a necessity rather than a luxury.

A unique challenge faced in focusing on STSs is that they combine two types of fundamentally different systems:

- *Technical systems* that are produced and continuously adapted to provide a reliable, anticipatable relationship between user input and the system's output. This relationship is engineered to serve the needs of users and is preplanned.
- *Social systems* that are the result of continuous evolution including emergent changes and behavior. The development of their characteristics cannot be planned and controlled with respect to the final outcome; the changes within STSs are a matter of *contingency* (Luhmann 1995). They can only—if ever—be understood afterward and not in advance; social systems mainly serve their own needs and not those of others.

The strength of STSs is that they integrate these different phenomena so that they increase their performance reciprocally. Even more important, the integration of technical and social systems helps them to develop and to constitute each other, for example, the interaction among community members is supported by technical infrastructure, and the members themselves can contribute to the development of the infrastructure (as it is, e.g., demonstrated by open-source communities). However, the relationships between the development of the social and the technical are not deterministic but contingent. For example, developing software for specific organizations does not deterministically change them but only influences the evolution of their social structures. Software designers can be reflective with respect to the impact of a software system on its social context, and they can make their assumptions about the expected evolution of the social system explicit and a matter of discourse, but they cannot control the organizational change.

One emerging unique opportunity to make a systematic and reflected contribution to the evolution of social structures in STSs is *meta-design* (Fischer and Giaccardi 2006), representing a design methodology supporting the evolution of systems that have contingent characteristics. Whereas many design activities aim to develop concrete technical solutions, meta-design provides a *framework* within which STSs can be developed. Focusing meta-design on the development and evolution of STSs gives the opportunity for a more detailed reflection of methodological implications and guidelines. Meta-design of STSs leads to new considerations that complement traditional participatory design, end-user programming, or previous principles for the design of STSs.

The paper discusses our understanding of STSs and meta-design. In our analysis, we draw on a body of literature and on a variety of concepts that stem from an interdisciplinary background, such as the interdependence between technology and organization (Orlikowski 1992), sociological systems theory (Luhmann 1995), wicked problems (Rittel and Webber 1984), participatory design (Kensing and Blomberg 1998), and end-user development (Lieberman et al. 2006).

We describe several different theoretical approaches (cultures of participation, the SER model, and the underdesign methodology) being relevant for the integration of STSs and meta-design. These theoretical considerations are complemented with insights derived from concrete examples that we have developed in our research. Based on the theoretical analysis and the reflection of practical cases, we provide a short list of guidelines for transforming and enriching the design and use of socio-technical systems with meta-design. The concluding section summarizes the reasons for a meta-design approach in the context of socio-technical systems.

The paper represents a condensed (in some parts) and extended (in other parts) version of a paper entitled "Socio-Technical Systems: A Meta-Design Perspective" published earlier by the two authors (Fischer and Herrmann 2011).

6.2 Socio-technical Systems (STSs)

6.2.1 Characteristics of STSs

Socio-technical systems can be understood as the systematic integration of two kinds of phenomena that have very diverging, partially contradictive characteristics. STSs are composed *both* of computers, networks, and software *and* of people, procedures, policies, laws, and many other aspects. STSs therefore require the *codesign* of social and technical systems (Herrmann 2009).

Whereas *technical systems* are purposeful artifacts that can reliably and repeatedly be used to support human needs and to enhance human capabilities, *social systems* are dedicated to purposes that lay within themselves and are a matter of continuous change and evolution, which makes their behavior difficult to anticipate. Social structures can be identified on several levels: communicative interaction between people or in small groups such as families or teams, organizations or organizational units, communities, or social networks. The reactions of social systems to their environment are contingent—they are not independent from external stimuli, but they also are not determined by them. As opposed to necessity, universality, constancy, and certainty, *contingency* (Pedersen 2000):

- Refers to variability, particularity, mutability, and uncertainty
- Implies that the system creates its own necessity in its pattern of reactions toward events
- Provides a basis for continuous evolution, including opportunities for emergent changes

How new phenomena will emerge in social systems cannot be predicted or made the result of a well-planned, algorithmically organized procedure; they depend on coincidences and are context related in the sense of *situatedness* (Suchman 1987). Technical systems may also react contingently toward their users, but the more mature a technical system has become, the more one will expect that it is reliable for the users, predictable, and noncontingent. Obviously, the socio-technical perspective covers more aspects than the viewpoint of human-computer interaction (HCI): it is about the relationship between technical infrastructure as a whole and structures of social interaction, which cover organizational and coordination issues, sensemaking, and common ground as a basis for communication, power relations, negotiation, building of conventions, and so forth.

It is not unlikely that formal communication, anticipatable procedures, scripts, and prescriptions may be empirically observable within in social systems. For example, workflow management systems (Herrmann and Hoffmann 2005) demonstrate the managerial attempt to implement scripts and institutionalize plan-oriented behavior in the context of organizations. However, it is a social system's dominant characteristic that rules and routines can be revised and become subjects of negotiation, and it cannot be predicted whether and when anticipatable behavior is no longer sustained but becomes a subject of evolutionary or emergent change.

By contrast to those researchers who assume that complex human activities can also be assigned to technical systems (Latour 1999), we suggest that the crucial characteristics of social versus technical systems point in two opposite directions (Table 6.1). The strength of socio-technical systems results of the *integration* of these two kinds of different phenomena.

Table 6.1 Main characteristics of technical and social systems

	Technical systems	Social systems
Origins	Are a product of human activity, can be designed from outside	Are the result of evolution, cannot be designed but only *influenced* from outside
Control	Are designed to be controllable with respect to prespecified performance parameters	Always have the potential to challenge control
Situatedness	Low: preprogrammed learning and interaction with the environment	High: includes the potential of improvisation and non-anticipatable adaptation of behavior patterns
Changes	Are either preprogrammed so that changes can be autonomously conducted but are anticipatable or are a result of interventions from outside (so that a new version is established)	Evolutionary: gradual accumulation of small, incremental changes, which can lead to emergent changes (which, however, are not anticipatable). There is no social system that can simulate the changes of another social system
Contingency	Are designed to avoid contingency; the more mature a version is the less its reactions appear as contingent	The potential for change and evolution is based on contingency
Criteria	Correctness, reliability, unexpected, unsolicited events are interpreted as malfunction	Personal interest, motivation; in the case of unsolicited events, intentional malpractice may be the case
Modeling	Can be modeled by describing how input is processed and leads to a certain output	Models can only approximate the real behavior and have continue to be adapted

6.2.2   Beyond Coincidental Connectedness: The Need for Systematic Integration

STSs are more than a coincidental connectedness of technical components and people. STS research is not just applying sociological principles to technical effects, but it explores how social and technical aspects integrate into a higher-level system with emergent properties.

The synergy between technical and social systems can be achieved only if both parts are closely integrated. One of the important theoretical challenges with respect to STSs is to explain how this integration can happen, by which factors it is influenced, and how it can be observed. Sociologists such as Luhmann (1995) and Habermas (1984) identify *communication*, among all kinds of human activities, as the most relevant constituent of social systems. Our research emphasizes the role of communication when we try to understand the integration between social and technical structures. The degree of integration between social and technical structures increases with the extent of the following factors:

- Communication that uses the *technical systems as a medium* helps to convey communicational acts and shapes them.
- Communication *about the technical system* includes how it is used, how it has to be maintained, how it could be adapted to the needs of an organization and its users, how its effects can be compared with other technical systems, and so forth. This kind of communication leads to what we can call the appropriation of the technical system by the social system. The communication mirrors the organization's understanding of the technical structures.
- Content or social structures (e.g., responsibilities or access rights) *regulating communication* are being represented within the technical system as well as the social structures.
- Self-description describes and constitutes the characteristics of the STSs and can be found in the oral communication and in the documents of the social system as well as in the technical system's content and structures (Herrmann et al. 2007).

Within the large set of areas where socio-technical integration takes place, this paper focuses on the design of technical systems that are related to information processing and software development. To determine a clear focus with respect to the social structures into which technical systems are integrated proves difficult. The classical socio-technical literature (Trist 1981) usually addresses the meso-level, concerning such organizations as companies, administrations, and nongovernment organizations (NGOs) or their subunits. However, with the emergence of the web, and in particular Web 2.0 and social software, phenomena have to be taken into account such as virtual communities, which form larger units between the middle- and the macro-level where individuals and/or several companies are interacting within new social structures that became possible only by new types of technical infrastructure. The new phenomena that emerged in the context of the web and Web 2.0 also gave new reasons for intensifying socio-technical analyses and approaches. It also became obvious that socio-technical phenomena cannot always be appropriately described by the concept of "closed system" as it is defined by Maturana and Varela (1980). By contrast, it can be more adequate to focus the analysis on *socio-technical environments* (Carmien and Fischer 2008) within which the integration of technical and social structures can develop. Such a socio-technical environment is less the result of engineering or design activities and more a context within which design takes place and is intertwined with the evolutionary growth of social structures.

With respect to their evolution, socio-technical systems integrate two characteristics: on the one hand, they are the result of such human activities as design, engineering, managing, communication, learning, and continuous improvement; on the other hand, they serve on a higher level as the environment or framework within which these kind of human activities take place. Therefore we argue that the concept of "meta-design" is more appropriate to describe how socio-technical systems are developed and do develop.

6.3   Meta-Design: Enriching the Ecology of Design Methodologies

6.3.1   Established Design Methodologies

In all design processes two basic stages can be differentiated: *design time* and *use time*. The established design methodologies are primarily related to design time: system developers (with or without user participation) create environments and tools for the world as *imagined* by them to anticipate users' needs and objectives. They engage in formal and intentional design activities targeted toward the creation of artifacts or systems as imagined. They engage in planning activities guided by the predicted needs of future user populations.

At *use time*, users will use the system. Their activities are shaped by a world as *experienced*, they are able to deal with a world as experienced, and planning is enriched by situated actions. But because their needs, objectives, and situational contexts can only be anticipated at design time, the system often requires modification to fit the users' needs (Henderson and Kyng 1991).

The need to empower users as designers and active contributors is not a luxury but a necessity: computational systems modeling some particular "world" are never complete; they must evolve over time because (1) the world changes and new requirements emerge, and (2) skilled domain professionals change their work practices over time—their understanding and use of a system will be very different after a month and certainly after several years. If systems cannot be modified to support new practices, users will be locked into existing patterns of use.

The following established *design methodologies* (Ye and Fischer 2007) can be differentiated (with respect to: which stakeholders are present at design and use time, which information do they take into account, and which activities do they carry out):

- *Professional Design.* Early digital artifacts were developed by professionals without too much concerns about users. This was an adequate design methodology at the time, because the users were computer professionals and the designers lived in the same "world" as the users.
- *User-Centered Design.* As digital artifacts became more ubiquitous and users were not only computer professionals but came from all disciplines, *user-centered design* (Norman and Draper 1986) complemented professional design. Designers (with the help of ethnographers) studied use community and derived design criteria characterizing the world of different use communities.
- *Participatory design* approaches (Kensing and Blomberg 1998; Schuler and Namioka 1993) seek to involve users (or user representatives) more deeply in the process as co-designers at design time by empowering them to propose and generate design alternatives themselves (see Fig. 6.1). Participatory design (characterized as *design for use before use* in Binder et al. (2011)) supports diverse ways of thinking, planning, and acting by making work, technologies, and social institutions more responsive to human needs. It requires the social inclusion and active participation of the users. Participatory design has focused on system development at design time by bringing developers and users together to envision the contexts of use.

The three design methodologies described above focused primarily on activities and processes taking place at design time in the systems' original development and have given little emphasis and provided few mechanisms to support systems as living entities that can be evolved by their users.

But despite the best efforts at design time, systems need to be evolvable to fit new needs, account for changing tasks, deal with subjects and contexts that increasingly

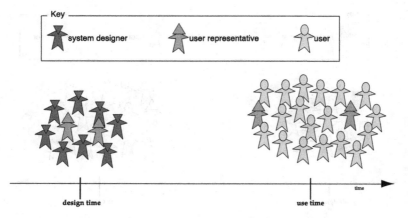

Fig. 6.1 Design and use time—roles and involvements in participatory design

blur professional and private life, couple with the socio-technical environment in which they are embedded, and incorporate new technologies (Henderson and Kyng 1991).

6.3.2 Meta-design

Meta-design (Fischer and Giaccardi 2006) provides the enabling conditions for putting owners of problems in charge by defining the technical and social conditions for broad participation in design activities. It addresses the challenges of fostering new mind-sets, new sources of creativity, and cultural changes to create foundations for innovative societies.

Meta-design is an emerging conceptual framework aimed at defining and creating socio-technical systems or environments and at understanding both as living entities. It extends existing design methodologies focused on the development of a system at design time by allowing users to become co-designers at use time. Meta-design (see Fig. 6.2), characterized as *design for design after design* in Binder et al. (2011), is grounded in the basic assumption that future uses and problems cannot be completely anticipated at design time, when a system is developed (Suchman 1987; Winograd and Flores 1986). At use time, users will discover mismatches between their needs and the support that an existing system can provide for them. Meta-design *extends boundaries* by supporting users as active contributors ("users as designers") who can transcend the functionality and content of existing systems. By facilitating these possibilities, *control* is distributed among all stakeholders in the design process.

Meta-design integrates approaches, which comprise objectives, techniques, representations of concepts, boundary objects, and processes for creating new media

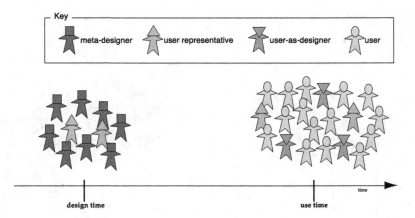

Fig. 6.2 Design and use time—roles and involvements in meta-design

and environments that allow "owners of problems" as members of a social system to act as *designers*. A fundamental objective of meta-design is to establish a basis for the creation of STSs that empower all relevant stakeholders of groups, communities of practice, communities of interest, and organizations to engage actively in the *continuous development* of a concrete socio-technical solution rather than being restricted to a prescribed way of interacting with the technical system or with its users.

The crucial aspect of meta-design, which leads to its name, is that of *designing design* (Fischer and Giaccardi 2006). This refers to the concept of higher-order design and the possibility of a malleability and modifiability of structures and processes as provided, supported, or influenced by computational media. It is a design approach that focuses on a framework of general structures and processes, rather than on fixed objects and contents, and rules.

The meta-design objective of "designing design" supports IT developers to overcome the following dilemma: on the one hand, a successful usage of software does not only rely on its technical features but also on the development of appropriate organizational processes and structures representing the context of the software's application. Therefore, meta-designers should not solely focus on technology but also support managers and those who are in charge with organizational development. On the other hand, organizational structures and processes evolve by the activities, routines, and decisions of people and are not a subject of design methods which are usually focused on artifacts. However, meta-designers can develop a framework (in participatory design efforts with domain experts) that allows its users to intertwine the design of technical systems and the development of appropriate organizational structures and procedures to integrate them into a socio-technical system. Typical examples for this objective are features that support the specification of rules for accessing data or documents. On the basis of those features, users can develop their own organizational rules for accessing information and implement them with the help of support mechanisms provided by the meta-designers. "Designing design" does therefore not only support technical modifications but also provides a framework for the development of additional organizational features.

6.4   Components of the Conceptual Framework

6.4.1   Cultures of Participation

Cultures are defined in part by their media and their tools for thinking, working, learning, and collaborating. In the past, the design of most media emphasized a clear distinction between producers and consumers (Benkler 2006). In a similar manner, our current educational institutions often treat learners as consumers, fostering a mind-set in students of "consumerism" rather than "ownership of problems" for the rest of their lives. As a result, learners, workers, and citizens often feel left out of decisions by teachers, managers, and policymakers, denying them opportunities to take active roles.

The rise in *social computing* (based on social production and mass collaboration) has facilitated a shift from *consumer cultures* (specialized in producing finished artifacts to be consumed passively) to *cultures of participation* (in which all people are provided with the means to participate and to contribute actively in personally meaningful problems) (Fischer 2011). These developments represent unique and fundamental opportunities, challenges, and transformative changes for innovative research and practice in socio-technical systems as we move away from a world in which a small number of people define rules, create artifacts, and make decisions for many consumers toward a world in which meta-design environments support everyone to actively participate.

Our research is exploring *theoretical foundations* and *system developments* for understanding, fostering, and supporting *cultures of participation* grounded in the basic assumption that innovative technological developments are *necessary* for cultures of participation, but they are *not sufficient*. Socio-technical environments are needed because cultures of participation are not dictated by technology: they are the result of changes in human behavior and social organization in which active contributors engage in innovative design, adoption, and adaptation of technologies to their needs and in collaborative knowledge construction. While cultures of participation are dependent on interactive technologies, they are also different: interactivity is a property of the technology, while participation is a property of culture. A sole focus on expanding access to new technologies is limited if we do not also foster the skills and cultural knowledge necessary to deploy those tools toward our own ends.

Meta-design supports and requires cultures of participation by allowing people with different competencies (in application domains, in media) to contribute to socio-technical solutions. *Cultures of participation* are facilitated and supported by a variety of different technological environments (such as the participatory Web ("Web 2.0") (O'Reilly 2005), tabletop computing, and domain-oriented design environments), all of them contributing in different ways to the aims of engaging diverse audiences, enhancing creativity, sharing information, and fostering the collaboration among users acting as active contributors and designers. They democratize design and innovation (von Hippel 2005) by shifting power and control toward users, supporting them to act as both designers and consumers ("prosumers") (Tapscott and Williams 2006) and allowing systems to be shaped through real-time use. Meta-design supports the inclusion of user-generated content in cultures of participation, in which "content" is broadly defined as (a) creating artifacts with existing tools or (b) changing the tools. In specific environments, such as open-source software, the content is subject to the additional requirement of being computationally interpretable.

6.4.2   Seeding, Evolutionary Growth, and Reseeding (SER) Model

The SER model (Fischer and Ostwald 2002) (see Fig. 6.3) was developed as a descriptive and prescriptive model for creating systems that best fit an emerging and evolving context. In the past, large and complex systems were built as complete artifacts through the large efforts of a small number of people. Instead of attempting to build complete systems, the SER model advocates building seeds that change and grow and can evolve over time through the small contributions of a large number of people. The seeds play the role of *boundary objects* (Star 1989), to which the communication between involved people can refer. SER postulates that systems that evolve over a sustained time span must continually alternate between periods of planned activity and unplanned evolution and periods of deliberate (re)structuring and enhancement.

The SER model encourages designers to conceptualize their activity as meta-design, thereby aiming to support users as active contributors. The applicability, feasibility, and usefulness of the SER model have been demonstrated in the context of several STSs (including the two described in Sect. 6.5).

Meta-design provides methods and practices that support seeding and evolution-ary growth. SER works only in the context of the other principles of meta-design such as participation, underdesign, and empowerment for adaptation. Similar to action research (Avison et al. 1999) or the behavior of reflective practitioners (Schön 1983), phases of experimenting and practicing have to alternate with phases of reflection during the evolutionary growth. Transferring the SER model to STSs implies that seeds are built not only for technical features but also for social structures and interactions. The growth of the seeds (for both the technical and social dimensions) cannot be anticipated at design time. How seeds will evolve or are used is situated in future uses at use time and cannot be sufficiently planned at design time.

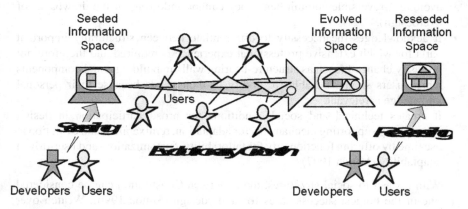

Fig. 6.3 The seeding, evolutionary growth, and reseeding (SER) model

Developments conceptualized with the SER model see the "unfinished" as an opportunity rather than as an obstacle or as something to be avoided. It is grounded in the basic assumption that for most real-world systems "design time" and "use time" should not be totally separated and suggests a more complex relationship between these different phases.

6.4.3 Underdesign

To accommodate unexpected issues at use time, systems need to be underdesigned at design time. *Underdesign* (Brand 1995; Habraken 1972) in this context does not mean less work and fewer demands for the design team, but it is fundamentally different from creating complete systems. The primary challenge of underdesign is to develop not solutions but environments that allow the *owners of problems* (Fischer 2002) to create the solutions themselves at use time. This can be done by providing a context and a background against which situated cases, coming up during use time, can be interpreted. Underdesign is a defining activity for meta-design aimed at creating design spaces for others. It assumes that the meaning, functionality, and content of a system are not fully defined by designers and user representatives alone at design time but are socially constructed throughout the entire design, deployment, and use cycles of the system. Underdesign is based on the following design principles and mechanisms:

- It is grounded in the need for "loose fit" in designing artifacts at design time so that unexpected uses of the artifact can be accommodated at use time; it does so by creating contexts and content-creation tools rather than focusing on content alone.
- It avoids design decisions being made in the start of the design process, when everyone knows the least of what is needed.
- It offers users (acting as designers at use time) as many alternatives as possible, avoiding irreversible commitments they cannot undo (one of the drawbacks of overdesign).
- It acknowledges the necessity to differentiate between structurally important parts for which extensive professional experience is required and therefore not be easily changed (such as structure-bearing walls in buildings) and components which users should be able to modify to their needs because their personal knowledge is relevant.
- It creates technical and social conditions for broad participation in design activities by supporting mechanisms for adaptation, remixability, and evolution at use time by offering functionality for tailorability, customization, and user-driven adaptability (Morch 1997).

With respect to social structures, the American Constitution can be considered as one of the biggest success cases for underdesign (Simon 1996). Written over

200 years ago and updated by only a small number of amendments, it still serves as a foundation for the United States of America in a world that has changed dramatically.

Underdesign in the context of STS not only refers to hardware and software but also to the plans that describe how the technology will be used and how the collaboration of the users is coordinated. The most prominent examples of representing this kind of plan are process models. They can be overdesigned, as in the case of models that are developed to implement organizational prescriptions by programming workflow management engines. Preprogrammed workflow management systems force the users into inflexibility, which causes problems in handling exceptions or improvising a solution, for example. Conversely, it is not reasonable to go without explicit process models because they help people within an STS explain the need for changes to others, introduce newcomers to the STS, or document changes that have taken place so that evolutionary growth is supported (Smith 1997). The solution pursued by our research team is the *modeling method SeeMe* (Herrmann et al. 2004) supporting underdesign with flexible degrees of incompleteness and impreciseness.

SeeMe was developed to support the drafting of organizational plans that mix prescriptions with space for free decisions (Fischer and Herrmann 2011). The following examples can frequently be observed in practical cases:

- There is a mix of two types of decisions in the course of tasks: (1) the first type can be freely made by users who are carrying out the tasks, and (2) the second type is made by others such as superiors or quality management representatives. With increasing experience the control by others becomes more and more irrelevant and is often only a subject of formal execution. Flexible planning allows the organization to react on the increase of competencies. For example, in the case of collaboratories (see Sect. 6.5.1), users who did not dare to modify the features without the help of others will start to do this after a period of growing confidence.
- Activities can either be carried out in a prescribed sequence or in a sequence that is specified by those who carry out the work. In many cases sequences are prescribed although they do not represent the most efficient procedures. Similarly, organizational planning requires in many cases that a certain task is completed before the next one can start despite the fact that this requirement is very often unnecessarily inflexible.
- Adaptation of a plan at use time can be an activity that is part of the plan developed at design time. The meta-designers can specify when and under which conditions such a replanning should take place.

Another approach toward underdesign is environments for *open systems* and *open design spaces* (Budweg et al. 2009), which are systems focused on the "unfinished" and take into account that design problems have no stopping rule and need to remain open and fluid to accommodate ongoing change and for which "continuous beta" becomes a desirable rather than a to-be-avoided attribute.

6.5 Examples of Meta-designed STSs

As indicated in Sect. 3.3.2, the principles of meta-design have been applied in numerous projects. The two projects described in this section illustrate the meta-design of STSs in two different domains: decision-making environments for urban planning and support system for cognitively disabled persons.

6.5.1 The Envisionment and Discovery Collaboratory (EDC)

The EDC (Arias et al. 2001) is a long-term research platform that explores conceptual frameworks for new paradigms of learning in the context of design problems. It represents an STS supporting reflective communities by incorporating a number of innovative technologies, including tabletop computing environments, the integration of physical and computational components supporting new interaction techniques, the support of reflection in action as a problem-solving approach (Schön 1983), and an open architecture supporting meta-design activities.

The EDC serves as an immersive social context in which a community of stakeholders can create, integrate, and disseminate information relevant to their lives and the problems they face. The exchange of information is encouraged by providing stakeholders with tools to express their own opinions, requiring an open system that evolves by accommodating new information. The information is presented and handled in a way that it can be used as boundary objects. For example, city planners contribute formal information (such as the detailed planning data found in Geographic Information Systems), whereas citizens may use less formal techniques (such as sketching) to describe a situation from their points of view. Figure 6.4 shows the EDC in use, illustrating the following features:

- The pane at the bottom shows a tabletop computing environment that serves as the *action space*: the stakeholders engage in determining land use patterns as a collective design activity in the context of an urban planning problem; this can be easily done, e.g., by moving around tangible blocks.
- The left pane at the top is the associated *reflection space* in which quantitative data (derived dynamically from the design moves in the action space) is displayed.
- The right pane at the top *visualizes the impact* of the height of new buildings (sketched by the stakeholders in the action space) on the environment by using Google Earth.

The EDC brings together participants from different domains who have different knowledge from various backgrounds to collaborate in resolving design problems. The contexts explored in the EDC (e.g., urban planning, emergency management, and building design) are all examples of ill-defined, open-ended design problems (Rittel and Webber 1984).

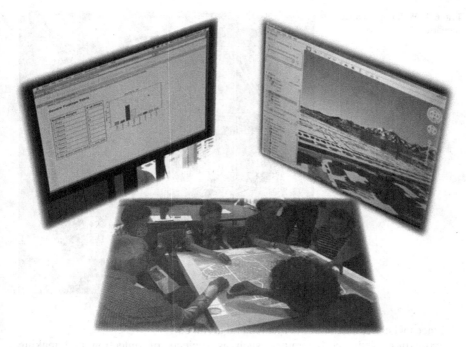

Fig. 6.4 The envisionment and discovery collaboratory (EDC)

The following example illustrates how the stakeholders gathered around the tabletop computing environment explore one of these ill-defined, open-ended design problems: the community has designed a new bus route and tries to decide where the bus stops should be placed. As shown in Fig. 6.5, stakeholders identify where they live by placing a house on the table, and they indicate how far they are willing to walk in good weather (large circles around the houses) and in bad weather (small circles around the houses). After specifying this information, colored circles appear around their house icons, indicating the range of area in which they might be willing to walk to catch a bus. As the participants all specify their information, the display shows emerging, overlapping patterns of areas that might be suitable for bus stops, providing information and perspectives that no individual had in their head prior to the exercise.

The EDC is a *collaboratory* (Finholt and Olson 1997) where people come together to work on such tasks such as design, planning, developing visions, and solving concrete problems and are willing to collaborate, to learn from each other, and to reflect and improve the tools and methods they use. The constituents of a collaboratory are not only the technical infrastructure; they also include:

- People who dynamically share various roles and tasks as well as their social interaction; they are users of the collaboratory.

Fig. 6.5 Walking-distance
scenario

- Places where results are documented and archived.
- Properties of the collaboratory, such as subjects of reflection and making proposals for improvement.
- Some people who prepare sessions in the collaboratory and maintain it, some who have the task to develop visions of how the collaboratory can evolve, and some who work on adapting the technology and contributing to incremental improvement.

Collaboratories are places where heterogeneous perspectives are melted, transdisciplinary collaboration takes place, and learning is continuously going on (Fischer 2001). They are special but typical examples of STSs, and their properties and constellation are very flexible and include a wide range of possibilities for further development so that they can be considered as the typical outcome of metadesign.

6.5.2 The Memory Aiding Prompting System (MAPS)

Individuals with cognitive disabilities are often unable to live independently due to their inability to perform activities of daily living, such as cooking, housework, or shopping. By being provided with *socio-technical environments* to extend their abilities and thereby their independence, these individuals can lead lives less dependent on others.

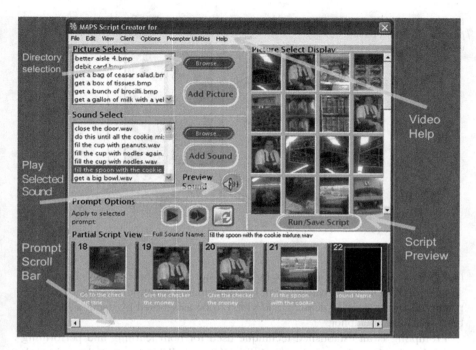

Fig. 6.6 The MAPS design environment (MAPS-DE) for creating scripts

MAPS (Carmien 2006) provides an environment in which caregivers (such as relatives, professionals, voluntary helpers) can create scripts that can be used by people with cognitive disabilities ("clients") to support them in carrying out tasks that they would not be able to achieve by themselves.

MAPS consists of two major subsystems that present different affordances for the two sets of users: (1) the *MAPS design environment (MAPS-DE)* for caregivers employs web-based script and template repositories that allow content to be created and shared by caregivers of different abilities and experiences, and (2) the *MAPS prompter (MAPS-PR)* for clients provides external scripts that reduce the cognitive demands for the clients by changing the task. The specific tasks that we studied and supported with MAPS included: using public transportation systems (Carmien et al. 2005), folding clothes in a secondhand store, and going shopping with a list of images rather than textual descriptions of objects (see Fig. 6.6).

To effectively support users, the scripts created with MAPS-DE are specific for particular tasks, creating the requirement that the people who know about the clients and the tasks (i.e., the local caregivers rather than a technologist far removed from the action) must be able to develop scripts. Caregivers generally have no specific professional technology training nor are they interested in becoming computer programmers. This creates the need for STSs complying with meta-design guidelines

Fig. 6.7 The MAPS prompter (MAPS-PR) for using scripts

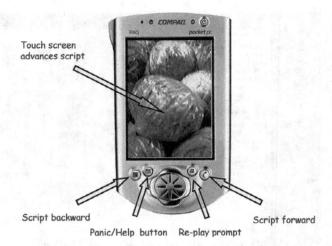

Touch screen advances script

Script backward   Script forward

Panic/Help button   Re-play prompt

(see Sect. 6.7) to allow caregivers to create, store, and share scripts. Figure 6.6 shows MAPS-DE for creating complex multimodal prompting sequences. The prototype allows sound, pictures, and video to be assembled by using a filmstrip-based scripting metaphor.

Prompting is an established technique used for both learning and performing a task by people with cognitive disabilities by verbally instructing them through each step, until it has been internalized by the promptee, such that he/she could successfully perform the task unaided. Prompting has been historically part of instructional techniques for persons with cognitive disabilities: being prompted through tasks in a rehearsal mode and then using the memorized instructions at use time. A prompting script is a sequential set of prompts that when followed perform a task.

MAPS-PR presents to clients the multimedia scripts that support the task to be accomplished. Its function is to display the prompt and its accompanying verbal instruction. MAPS-PR has a few simple controls (see Fig. 6.7): (1) the touch screen advances the script forward one prompt and (2) the four hardware buttons on the bottom, which are mapped to (i) back up one prompt, (ii) replay the verbal prompt, (iii) advance one prompt, and (iv) activate panic/help status. The mapping of the buttons to functions is configurable to account for the needs of individual users and tasks.

MAPS supports the off-loading of the memorization and decision-making elements of the task to the device and the system that supported it. Our research in this context (Carmien and Fischer 2008) explored meta-design, cultures of participation, and underdesign by supporting mobile device customization, personalization, and configuration by caregivers and effective use by clients.

6.6 Findings and Assessment of the Conceptual Framework in Practice

Our conceptual framework of meta-design (Sect. 6.3) and its components (Sect. 6.4) has served as the design methodology in the development of the two case studies EDC and MAPS (Sect. 6.5). This section reports some of the findings and assessments that we have gathered by employing the EDC and MAPS in *practice* (a closely related approach linking case studies with a conceptual framework for CSCW is described in Wulf et al. (2011)).

6.6.1 The Envisionment and Discovery Collaboratory (EDC)

6.6.1.1 Beyond the Information Given

One original design objective of the EDC was to create an end-user modifiable version of SimCity (http://en.wikipedia.org/wiki/SimCity_4) that transcended the modification possibility provided by the game designers (e.g., using a bitmap editor to change the appearance of objects). A specific example that guided us in our approach is as follows: if players in SimCity notices that there is too much crime in their city, they can fight crime by increasing the police force—but there is no support to reduce crime by increasing social service. The designers did not anticipate at design time that players wanted to explore this option.

While we have not directly solved this specific issue, we have included mechanisms within the EDC to allow participants to inject content into the simulations and adapt the environment to new scenarios by creating ways to link to existing data and tools so that participants can draw on information from their own areas of expertise to contribute to the emerging, shared model. These mechanisms support that the design activities complement guidelines, rules, and procedures with *exceptions, negotiations, and work-arounds* to complement and integrate accredited and expert knowledge with informal, practice-based, and situated knowledge (Orr 1996; Suchman 1987; Winograd and Flores 1986).

6.6.1.2 Cultures of Participation

Urban planning (one of the major application domains for the EDC) can be undertaken as a professionally dominated activity in which experts (city planners, administrators, transportation developers) act as decision makers and citizens are consumers. The EDC involves citizens as active participants and supports a culture of participation as all stakeholders gather around a shared environment provided by a tabletop computing environment (see Fig. 6.4).

6.6.1.3 Who Are the Meta-designers and What Do They Do

The meta-designers use their own creativity to create socio-technical environments in which other people can be creative. They must create the social conditions for broad participation in design activities which is as important as creating the artifact itself. Furthermore, they encourage and facilitate the objective to develop maximum participation by activating as much knowledge as possible. The main activity of meta-designers shifts from determining the meaning, functionality, and content of a system to encouraging and supporting users to engage in these activities. Meta-designers must be willing to share control of how systems will be used, which content will be contained, and which functionality will be supported.

6.6.1.4 Support of Meta-design with Collaborative Work Practices

Early studies (Nardi 1993) already identified that meta-design is more successful if supported by collaborative work practices rather than focusing on individuals. The studies observed the emergence of "gardeners" and "local developers" who are technically interested and sophisticated enough to perform system modifications that are needed by a community of users, but other end users are not able or inclined to perform. The EDC supports *mutual development* (Andersen and Mørch 2009) as a model for how professional developers and users contribute to development in both design and use. For example, during the urban planning sessions, developers supported users in overcoming problems with the technical environment; in doing so, they interacted with users and became immediately aware of further needs for technical improvements.

Meta-design promotes the quality that the set and the characteristics of the involved roles are highly dynamic: new roles emerge such as power users or codevelopers (Nardi 1993), and the traditional roles can continuously achieve and lose competencies that are needed to contribute to the development of their tools. Meta-design promotes a rich *ecology of participation* (Fischer et al. 2008; Preece and Shneiderman 2009), which includes a broad variety of roles with varying characteristics.

6.6.1.5 Technical Infrastructures and Social Interactions of Various Roles Are Intertwined

An early technical realization of the EDC required that the participants take turns (e.g., in the scenario represented by Fig. 6.5). Consequently, participants had to wait until one person has completed the moving around of a toy block before they could go ahead with their own contributions. Experimental design sessions clearly indicated that this was a restriction at odds with the social interactions that the participants preferred. A newer hardware environment eliminated this limitation and supported more flexible and fluent interactions. However, it has to be considered whether the possibility to act simultaneously might reduce the awareness of what others are doing. Design trade-offs of this kind provide further evidence for the reciprocal shaping between technical features and social interactions.

6.6.1.6   Collaboratories Evolve in Cultures of Participation with a Variety of Participants in Various Roles

The EDC environment (similarly to other cultures of participation such as open-source systems (Fischer et al. 2008)) supports a rich ecology of roles and the migration between them. The particular roles that emerged in the EDC environment are:

- *Project leaders*, who are responsible for the overall design and the usage of the collaboratory
- *Chief designers*, who acted as meta-designers
- *Users* (being knowledgeable in different domains), who owned (e.g., being residents in neighborhoods) parts of the problem to be investigated (e.g., the design of a new bus line and where the bus stops should be placed)
- *Scientists*, who use the collaboratory as members of research teams.
- *Students and teachers*, who use the collaboratory for learning and knowledge construction

In traditional design environments, it would have been a goal that the competencies and roles of the involved stakeholders are clearly defined, and the responsibility and authority of individuals are visible for all participants. By contrast, in an evolving culture of participation, the tasks, activities, and competencies of these roles can overlap: the technical infrastructure can be considered as a domain itself, and problems of this domain are discussed and partially solved by everybody in the collaboratories; the experts of other domains (e.g., urban planners) can contribute with proposals for technical improvement (e.g., color-coding various risk zones with respect to flooding); thus, users become codevelopers and vice versa, and developers become co-users (by contributing data which supports urban planning).

6.6.1.7   Adaptation of the Technical Infrastructure Is User Driven

In his book *Democratizing Innovation* (von Hippel 2005), the author provides evidence for the following claim (page 1): *Users that innovate can develop exactly what they want, rather than relying on manufacturers to act as their (often very imperfect) agents. Moreover, individual users do not have to develop everything they need on their own: they can benefit from innovations developed and freely shared by others.* Interesting evidence is provided from a variety of different areas: new mountain bikes, new surfboards, and new application software are envisioned and *designed primarily by lead users rather than by manufacturers.* We observed the same developments in the EDC: innovative ideas for new developments originated with the needs of users. Some prominent examples of design requirements originated from users are as follows: (1) the need for a virtual EDC (possibly implemented in an environment such as Second Life) to support the collaboration of design teams in Boulder and in San Jose, Costa Rica; (2) the integration of the EDC with geographical information systems to greatly reduce the overhead to apply urban planning situations to different locations; and (3) the linkage with Google Earth to easily create visualizations of new buildings from different perspectives.

In the course of this collaboration, not only the technical infrastructure was adapted but also the social system. Newcomers brought in new perspectives and ideas of how the EDC could be enhanced and used. From the perspective of meta-design, collaboratories are self-referential socio-technical systems: they are designed to evolve, they are the place where this evolution takes place, they provide the infrastructure that supports this evolution, and they provide the context that represents the common ground on which this evolution is driven by the communication between problem owners.

6.6.2 The Memory Aiding Prompting System (MAPS)

6.6.2.1 Caregivers as End-User Designers

A unique challenge of meta-design in the domain of cognitive disabilities is that the clients themselves cannot act as designers, but the caregivers must accept this role. Caregivers, who have the most intimate knowledge of the client, need to become the end-user designers. They mediate between the contribution of MAPS designers (the meta-designers) and the needs of clients by developing situationally adapted scripts (see Fig. 6.8).

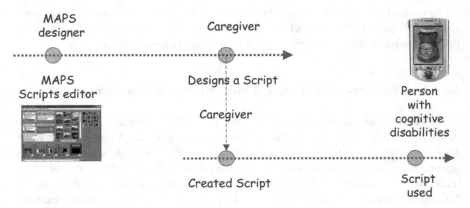

Fig. 6.8 Empowering caregivers to act as user designers

Caregivers generally have no specific professional technology training nor are they interested in becoming computer programmers. This creates the need that meta-design provides extensive end-user support to allow caregivers to create, store, and share scripts. To identify requirements for meta-design, the following studies were conducted:

- Discovering and learning about the client's and caregiver's world and their interactions
- Observing and analyzing how tasks and learning of tasks were currently conducted
- Understanding and explicating the process of creating and updating scripts
- Comprehending and analyzing the process of using the scripts with a real task
- Gaining an understanding of the role of meta-design in the dynamics of MAPS adoption and use

6.6.2.2 Underdesign: An Approach Coping with the *Universe of One* Problem

People with cognitive disabilities represent a *universe of one*: a solution for one person will rarely work for another. The *universe of one* conceptualization is based on the empirical finding that (1) *unexpected islands of abilities* exist (clients can have unexpected skills and abilities that can be leveraged to ensure a better possibility of task accomplishment) and (2) *unexpected deficits of abilities* exist. Accessing and addressing these unexpected variations in skills and needs require an intimate knowledge of the client that *only caregivers* can provide. The scripts needed to effectively support users are specific for particular tasks and contexts, implying the requirement that the people who know about the clients and their needs (i.e., the local caregivers rather than a technologist far removed from the action) must be able to develop scripts. The meta-design environment (developed in this case by us) needs to be underdesigned (we being the technologists far removed from the action) allowing the caregivers as user designers to create the situationally informed specific developments in accordance with the clients' varying needs and to implement them in dynamically changing social contexts.

Currently, a substantial portion of all assistive technology is abandoned after initial purchase and use resulting in that the very population that could most benefit from technology is paying for expensive devices that end up in the back of closets after a short time.

By designing MAPS as a meta-design environment, caregivers were able to create an environment that matched the unique needs of an individual with cognitive disabilities (Carmien and Fischer 2008). MAPS represents an example for democratizing design by supporting meta-design, embedding new technologies into socio-technical environments, and helping people with cognitive disabilities, and their caregivers have more interesting and more rewarding lives by empowering caregivers to provide a situated and tailored STS, the needs of the persons with cognitive disabilities, thereby allowing them to do things that they could not have done with the empowerment provided by MAPS.

6.6.2.3   Design over Time: Instantiating the SER Model

The design of MAPS was grounded in the conceptual framework of meta-design and contributed to its extension. The theme of design over time was illustrated in both MAPS-DE with the addition of a multi-script modality and in MAPS-PR with the reuse of script sequences. By designing the MAPS environment to enable script redesign and reuse, caregivers were able to create precisely fitting solutions for the user with cognitive disabilities. MAPS represents an important example for democratizing design by supporting meta-design, embedding new technologies into socio-technical environments, and helping people with cognitive disabilities and their caregivers have more interesting and more rewarding interactions.

6.6.3   *Potential Drawbacks of Meta-design*

It has to be clearly stated that the goal of meta-design is not to let people with little or no experience develop and evolve sophisticated software systems but to put *owners of problems* in charge. Meta-design does not eliminate expertise but recognizes the multifaceted aspects of expertise (e.g., in architecture, inhabitants should be free to arrange their office furniture, but they should not be able to move the structure-bearing wall between their and their neighbors' offices).

6.6.3.1   The Tension Between Standardization and Improvisation

Meta-design creates inherent tensions, for example, between standardization and improvisation. The SAP Info (July 2003, page 33) argues to reduce the number of customer modifications ((Fischer and Giaccardi 2006), p. 446): *every customer modification implies costs because it has to be maintained by the customer. Each time a support package is imported there is a risk that the customer modification may have to be adjusted or re-implemented. To reduce the costs of such on-going maintenance of customer-specific changes, one of the key targets during an upgrade should be to return to the SAP standard wherever this is possible.* Finding the right balance between *standardization* (which can suppress innovation and creativity) and *improvisation* (which can lead to a Babel of different and incompatible versions) has been noted as a challenge in open-source environments, in which forking has often led developers in different directions.

6.6.3.2 Participation Overload

Meta-design (and specifically the required active engagement in cultures of participation) opens up unique new opportunities for mass collaboration and social production (Benkler 2006), but they are not without drawbacks. One such drawback is that humans may be forced to cope with the burden of being active contributors in *personally irrelevant activities* leading to a *participation overload*. "Do-it-yourself" societies empower humans with powerful tools; however, they force them to perform many tasks themselves that were done previously by skilled domain workers serving as agents and intermediaries. Although this shift provides power, freedom, and control to customers, it also has urged people to act as contributors in contexts for which they lack the experience that professionals have at their disposal (Hess et al. 2013).

More experience and assessment are required to determine the design trade-offs for specific contexts and application domains in which the *advantages* of cultures of participation (such as extensive coverage of information, creation of large numbers of artifacts, creative chaos by making all voices heard, reduced authority of expert opinions, and shared experience of social creativity) will outweigh the *disadvantages* (accumulation of irrelevant information, wasting human resources in large information spaces, and lack of coherent voices). The following research questions need to be further explored (Fischer 2011):

- If more and more people can contribute, how do we assess the *quality and reliability* of the resulting artifacts? How can curator networks effectively increase the quality and reliability?
- What is the role of trust, empathy, altruism, and reciprocity in such an environment, and how will these factors affect cultures of participation?

6.7 Guidelines for the Meta-design of STSs

This section describes *guidelines* (Fischer et al. 2009) derived from our conceptual considerations (see the sections on meta-design and practical experiences) with the development of STSs.

6.7.1 Construction Kits

From a technical point of view, a meta-design framework should include components and building blocks for the creation of content and modifications of the system. The users as designers of an STS should be empowered to combine, customize, and improve these components with a reasonable effort or ask power users or local developers to do so (Nardi 1993). The building blocks will have the role of a seed that inspire the evolutionary growth of a new assembly of components that fits into the STS. Meta-design must be continuously aware of new technological trends, and the meta-designed framework must be flexible enough to integrate these trends by providing new building blocks.

6.7.2 Underdesign for Emergent Behavior

STSs need to be *underdesigned* so that they can be viewed as *continuous beta* that are open to facilitate and incorporate emergent design behavior during use. Underdesign is not less design but different design: it allows all stakeholders with various and varying competencies to collaboratively design socio-technical solutions. Underdesign explores the most promising ground between (1) providing a powerful seed without reinventing the wheel or violating constraints such as legal norms, ethical restrictions, and the like and (2) allowing the users as designers to transcend the information given and functionality provided. It shares many objectives with *libertarian paternalism* (Thaler and Sunstein 2009): the paternalism part being grounded in the objective that it is important, legitimate, and supportive that meta-designers (called "choice architects" in the *Nudge* book) provide seeds and support environments for users and the libertarian part allowing users to be free to do what they like and create the functionality that they need.

6.7.3 Foster and Support Cultures of Participation

People should be enabled and attracted to bring their competencies and perspectives into the development of STSs requiring transparent policies and procedures to incorporate user contributions. To motivate more users to become developers, meta-design must offer "gentle slopes" of progressive difficulty and incremental extension of the included design aspects so that newcomers can start to participate peripherally and move on gradually to take charge of more difficult tasks (Fischer et al. 2008). Rewarding and recognizing contributions is an essential prerequisite of fostering intrinsic motivation. Roles and their rights and duties must not be fixed for the period of an STS's evolution but should be part of this evolution so that domain experts can become co-designers, new roles can be integrated, and control can be shifted in accordance with increased competencies (Preece and Shneiderman 2009).

6.7.4 Additional Discourses

While meta-design changes design activities from developers and users, it has a fundamental impact on the following aspects of human behavior (Benkler and Nissenbaum 2006):

- *Motivation*: Human beings are diversely motivated beings acting not only for material gain but for psychological well-being, social integration, connectedness, social capital, recognition, and improving their standing in a reputation economy. The motivation for going the extra step to engage in cultures of participation is based on the overwhelming evidence of the IKEA effect (Ariely 2010) that people are more likely to like a solution if they have been involved in its generation, even though it might not make sense otherwise. Creating something personal (such as hand-knitted sweaters and socks, home-cooked meals), even of moderate quality, has a different kind of appeal than consuming something of possible higher quality made by others.
- *Control*: Meta-design supports users as active contributors who can transcend the functionality and content of existing technical systems. By facilitating these possibilities, control is distributed among all stakeholders in the design process. Meta-design erodes monopoly positions held by professions, educational institutions, experts, and high-tech scribes (Fischer 2002). Empirical evidence gathered in the context of the different design activities (Ariely 2010) indicates that projects are less successful when users are brought into the process late (thereby denying them ownership) and when they are "misused" to fix problems and to address weaknesses of systems that the developers did not fix themselves.
- *Changing human behavior*: Technology alone does not determine social structure nor does it change human behavior; it creates feasibility spaces for new social practices (Benkler 2006), and it can persuade and motivate changes at the individual, group, and community level. Meta-design can change people's lives (1) by making it easier for people to do things, (2) by allowing people to explore cause-and-effect relationships, and (3) by providing value that cannot be accounted for in monetary terms. Research in behavioral psychology (Thaler and Sunstein 2009) has shown that providing feedback, goal setting, and tailored information are useful in motivating people to change their behavior.

6.7.5   Promote Mutual Learning and Support of Knowledge Exchange

Users have different and varying levels of skill and knowledge about systems. To get involved in contributing to the system's evolution or using the system, they need to learn many things. Peer users are important learning resources. A meta-designed STS should be flexible enough to address the skill differences and support knowledge-sharing mechanisms that encourage users to learn from each other. Knowledge management infrastructures should be integrated into STSs as important components that support their evolution.

6.8 Summary

New media and new technology provide new possibilities to rethink learning, working, and collaborating. In this article, we argued that new media and new technology on their own cannot support and transform these activities to meet the demands of the future but that they have to be integrated into STSs.

Our research is anchored in the basic assumption that STSs cannot be designed anticipating all future demands and uses and that meta-design supporting users as designers is not a luxury but a necessity to address the challenge of dynamically changing needs and conditions. We discussed meta-design as a conceptual framework which complements other more established approaches, and we described essential components of this framework: cultures of participation, seeding, evolutionary growth and reseeding, and underdesign. Two case studies of specific STSs illustrated how meta-design has served as the foundation of these development efforts, and we discussed some of the findings derived from our assessments about the conceptual framework.

Socio-technical phenomena are self-referential: on the one hand, they are the outcome of design and evolution, and on the other hand, they have the potential to support their own evolution. The strengths of STSs result from the integration of deterministic structures and processes and the contingency of social systems. Meta-design supports this integration.

Acknowledgments The authors thank the members of the Center for LifeLong Learning & Design at the University of Colorado (specifically Hal Eden, the main developer of the EDC, and Stefan Carmien who developed MAPS as part of his PhD) and the team of the Information and Technology Management group at the University of Bochum, Germany, who have made major contributions to the ideas described in this paper.

The research at CU Boulder was supported in part by:

- Grants from the National Science Foundation, including (a) IIS-0613638 *A Meta-Design Framework for Participative Software Systems*, (b) IIS-0709304 *A New Generation Wiki for Supporting a Research Community in 'Creativity and IT,'* and (c) IIS-0843720 *Increasing Participation and Sustaining a Research Community in 'Creativity and IT'*
- Google research award *Motivating and Empowering Users to Become Active Contributors: Supporting the Learning of High-Functionality Environments*
- SAP research project *Giving All Stakeholders a Voice: Understanding and Supporting the Creativity and Innovation of Communities Using and Evolving Software Products*

The research at the University of Bochum was funded by the Federal Ministry of Education and Research, including:

- SPIW: Logistics agencies in the web – 01 HT 0143
- Service4home: Coordination of services for elderly people by micro-systems technology input devices – 01 FC08008

The first author was supported in part for this work by a fellowship of the Hanse-Wissenschaftskolleg (an Institute for Advanced Study) in Delmenhorst, Germany.

References

Andersen, R., & Mørch, A. (2009). Mutual development: A case study in customer-initiated software product development. In V. Pipek, M. B. Rossen, B. de Ruyter, & V. Wulf (Eds.), *End-user development* (pp. 31–49). Heidelberg: Springer.

Arias, E. G., Eden, H., Fischer, G., Gorman, A., & Scharff, E. (2001). Transcending the individual human mind—Creating shared understanding through collaborative design. In J. M. Carroll (Ed.), *Human-computer interaction in the new millennium* (pp. 347–372). New York: ACM Press.

Ariely, D. (2010). *The upside of irrationality—The unexpected benefits of defying logic at work and at home*. New York: HarperCollins.

Avison, D. E., Lau, F., Myers, M. D., & Nielsen, P. A. (1999). Action research. *Communications of the ACM, 42*(1), 94–97.

Benkler, Y. (2006). *The wealth of networks: How social production transforms markets and freedom*. New Haven: Yale University Press.

Benkler, Y., & Nissenbaum, H. (2006). Commons-based peer production and virtue. *Political Philosophy, 14*(4), 394–419.

Binder, T., DeMichelis, G., Ehn, P., Jacucci, G., Linde, P., & Wagner, I. (2011). *Design things*. Cambridge, MA: MIT Press.

Brand, S. (1995). *How buildings learn: What happens after they're built*. New York: Penguin.

Budweg, S., Draxler, S., Lohmann, S., Rashid, A., & Stevens, G. (2009). Open design spaces supporting user innovation. In *Proceedings of the international workshop on open design spaces; international reports on socio-informatics, 6*(2). Available at http://www.iisi.de/fileadmin/IISI/upload/IRSI/IRSIV6I2.pdf.

Carmien, S. (2006). *Socio-technical environments supporting distributed cognition for persons with cognitive disabilities*. Phd thesis, Computer Science Department, University of Colorado, Boulder. Available at http://www.scarmien.com/papers/dissertation_sm.pdf.

Carmien, S., Dawe, M., Fischer, G., Gorman, A., Kintsch, A., & Sullivan, J. F. (2005). Socio-technical environments supporting people with cognitive disabilities using public transportation. *Transactions on Human-Computer Interaction (ToCHI), 12*(2), 233–262.

Carmien, S. P., & Fischer, G. (2008). Design, adoption, and assessment of a socio-technical environment supporting independence for persons with cognitive disabilities. In *Proceedings of CHI 2008* (pp. 597–607). Florence: ACM Press.

Finholt, T., & Olson, G. M. (1997). From laboratories to collaboratories: A new organizational form for scientific collaboration. *Psychological Science, 8*, 28–36.

Fischer, G. (2001). Communities of interest: Learning through the interaction of multiple knowledge systems. In *24th annual information systems research seminar in Scandinavia (IRIS'24)* (pp. 1–14). Ulvik, Norway.

Fischer, G. (2002). Beyond 'couch potatoes': From consumers to designers and active contributors, in Firstmonday. *Peer-Reviewed Journal on the Internet*. Available at http://firstmonday.org/issues/issue7_12/fischer/

Fischer, G. (2011, May + June). Understanding, fostering, and supporting cultures of participation. *ACM Interactions, XVIII*(3), 42–53.

Fischer, G., & Giaccardi, E. (2006). Meta-design: A framework for the future of end user development. In H. Lieberman, F. Paternò, & V. Wulf (Eds.), *End user development* (pp. 427–457). Dordrecht: Kluwer Academic Publishers.

Fischer, G., & Herrmann, T. (2011). Socio-technical systems: A meta-design perspective. *International Journal of Sociotechnology and Knowledge Development, 3*(1), 1–33.

Fischer, G., Nakakoji, K., & Ye, Y. (2009, September/October). Meta-design: Guidelines for supporting domain experts in software development. *IEEE Software, 26*, 37–44.

Fischer, G., & Ostwald, J. (2002). Seeding, evolutionary growth, and reseeding: Enriching participatory design with informed participation. In *Proceedings of the participatory design conference (PDC'02)* (pp. 135–143). Sweden: Malmö University.

Fischer, G., Piccinno, A., & Ye, Y. (2008). The ecology of participants in co-evolving socio-technical environments. In P. Forbrig & F. Paternò (Eds.), *Engineering interactive systems (Proceedings of 2nd conference on human-centered software engineering)* (Vol. LNCS 5247, pp. 279–286). Heidelberg: Springer.

Habermas, J. (1984). *The theory of communicative action: Reason and the rationalization of society*. Boston: Beacon.

Habraken, N. J. (1972). *Supports: An alternative to mass housing*. London: Architectural Press.

Henderson, A., & Kyng, M. (1991). There's no place like home: Continuing design in use. In J. Greenbaum & M. Kyng (Eds.), *Design at work: Cooperative design of computer systems* (pp. 219–240). Hillsdale: Lawrence Erlbaum Associates, Inc.

Herrmann, T. (2003). Learning and teaching in socio-technical environments. In T. J. V. Weert & R. K. Munro (Eds.), *Informatics and the digital society: Social, ethical and cognitive issues* (Proceedings of Seciii 2002, pp. 59–72). Kluwer: Boston.

Herrmann, T. (2009). Systems design with the sociotechnical walkthrough. In A. Whitworth & B. de Moore (Eds.), *Handbook of research on socio-technical design and social networking systems* (pp. 336–351). Hershey: Idea Group Publishing.

Herrmann, T., & Hoffmann, M. (2005). The metamorphoses of workflow projects in their early stages. *Computer Supported Cooperative Work, 14*(5), 399–432.

Herrmann, T., Hoffmann, M., Kunau, G., & Loser, K. (2004). A modeling method for the development of groupware applications as socio-technical systems. *Behaviour & Information Technology, 23*(2), 119–135.

Herrmann, T., Kunau, G., & Loser, K.-U. (2007). Socio-technical self-description as a means for projects of introducing computer supported cooperation. In *Electronically published;40th Annual Hawaii International Conference on Systems Sciences (HICCS 2007)*: Available at http://www.hicss.hawaii.edu/diglib.htm

Hess, J., Randall, D., Pipek, V., & Wulf, V. (2013). Involving users in the wild—Participatory product development in and with online communities. *International Journal of Human-Computer Studies, 71*(5), 570–589.

Kensing, F., & Blomberg, J. (1998). Participatory design: Issues and concerns. *Computer Supported Cooperative Work, 7*(3), 167–185.

Latour, B. (1999). *Pandora's hope: Essays on the reality of science studies*. Cambridge, MA: Harvard University Press.

Lieberman, H., Paterno, F., & Wulf, V. (Eds.). (2006). *End user development*. Dordrecht: Kluwer Publishers.

Luhmann, N. (1995). *Social systems*. Stanford: Stanford University Press.

Maturana, H. R., & Varela, F. J. (1980). *Autopoiesis and cognition: The realization of the living*. Dordrecht: Kluwer Publishers.

Morch, A. (1997). Three levels of end-user tailoring: Customization, integration, and extension. In M. Kyng & L. Mathiassen (Eds.), *Computers and design in context* (pp. 51–76). Cambridge, MA: MIT Press.

Mumford, E. (2000). A socio-technical approach to systems design. *Requirements Engineering, 5*(2), 125–133, Springer.

Nardi, B. A. (1993). *A small matter of programming*. Cambridge, MA: The MIT Press.

Norman, D. A., Norman, D. A., & Draper, S. W. (Eds.). (1986). *User-centered system design, new perspectives on human-computer interaction*. Hillsdale: Lawrence Erlbaum Associates, Inc.

O'Reilly, T. (2005) *What is Web 2.0 – Design patterns and business models for the next generation of software*. Available at http://www.oreillynet.com/pub/a/oreilly/tim/news/2005/09/30/what-is-web-20.html

Orlikowski, W. (1992). The duality of technology: Rethinking the concept of technology in organizations. *Organization Science, 3*(3), 398–427.

Orr, J. (1996). *Talking about machines—An ethnography of a modern job.* Ithaca: ILR Press/Cornell University Press.

Pedersen, P. P. (2000). Our present: Postmodern? In H. Andersen & L. B. Kaspersen (Eds.), *Classical and modern social theory* (pp. 412–431). Oxford: Blackwell Publishers.

Preece, J., & Shneiderman, B. (2009). The reader-to-leader framework: Motivating technology-mediated social participation. *AIS Transactions on Human-Computer Interaction, 1*(1), 13–32.

Rittel, H., & Webber, M. M. (1984). Planning problems are wicked problems. In N. Cross (Ed.), *Developments in design methodology* (pp. 135–144). New York: Wiley.

Schön, D. A. (1983). *The reflective practitioner: How professionals think in action.* New York: Basic Books.

Schuler, D., & Namioka, A. (Eds.). (1993). *Participatory design: Principles and practices.* Hillsdale: Lawrence Erlbaum Associates.

Simon, H. A. (1996). *The sciences of the artificial* (3rd ed.). Cambridge, MA: MIT Press.

Smith, K. (1997). Of maps and scripts. The status of formal constructs in cooperative work. *Information and Software Technology, 6*(41), 319–329.

Star, S. L. (1989). The structure of ill-structured solutions: Boundary objects and heterogeneous distributed problem solving. In L. Gasser & M. N. Huhns (Eds.), *Distributed artificial intelligence* (Vol. II, pp. 37–54). San Mateo: Morgan Kaufmann Publishers Inc.

Suchman, L. A. (1987). *Plans and situated actions.* Cambridge: Cambridge University Press.

Tapscott, D., & Williams, A. D. (2006). *Wikinomics: How mass collaboration changes everything.* New York: Portofolio, Penguin Group.

Thaler, R. H., & Sunstein, C. R. (2009). *Nudge—Improving decisions about health, wealth, an happiness.* London: Penguin.

Trist, E. L. (1981). The sociotechnical perspective: The evolution of sociotechnical systems as a conceptual framework and as an action research program. In A. H. VanDe Ven & W. F. Joyce (Eds.), *Perspectives on organization design and behavior.* New York: Wiley.

von Hippel, E. (2005). *Democratizing innovation.* Cambridge, MA: MIT Press.

Winograd, T., & Flores, F. (1986). *Understanding computers and cognition: A new foundation for design.* Norwood: Ablex Publishing Corporation.

Wulf, V., Rohde, M., Pipek, V., & Stevens, G. (2011). Engaging with practices: Design case studies as a research framework in CSCW. In *Proceedings of the ACM 2011 conference on computer supported cooperative work, Hangzhou, China* (pp. 505–512). Hangzhou: ACM Press.

Ye, Y., & Fischer, G. (2007) *Converging on a "science of design" through the synthesis of design methodologies* (Chi'2007 workshop). Available at http://swiki.cs.colorado.edu:3232/CHI07Design/3

Chapter 7
Practice-Based Computing: Empirically Grounded Conceptualizations Derived from Design Case Studies

Volker Wulf, Claudia Müller, Volkmar Pipek, David Randall, Markus Rohde, and Gunnar Stevens

7.1 Introduction

The introduction of IT has changed the way we live in many ways. Historically, it can even be argued that socially embedded applications of information technology challenge and change practices to an extent rarely seen before with any other type of technological artifacts. If these IT artifacts have strong and recurrent impacts on people's lives, we need to reconsider design practice artifacts which allow for anticipating use practices and bring together inspirational creativity with evaluative methods.

Approaches such as participatory design (Greenbaum and Kyng 1991) and user-driven innovation (von Hippel 2005) have already significantly increased the level of involvement of users and their fields of practice into IT development and have strengthened the role of ethnographic methods as well as the importance of methods providing direct user feedback. But even a strong component of domain analysis or user participation does not warrant an accurate anticipation of the changes in social practices resulting from new technological artifacts or infrastructures. Moreover, the immaterial nature of software contributes to its application beyond the originally

V. Wulf (✉)
School of Media and Information, University of Siegen, Siegen, Germany

Fraunhofer FIT, St. Augustin, Germany
e-mail: volker.wulf@unisiegen.de

C. Müller
University of Siegen, Siegen, Germany

V. Pipek • D. Randall • M. Rohde • G. Stevens
School of Media and Information, University of Siegen, Siegen, Germany
e-mail: D.Randall@mmu.ac.uk

© Springer-Verlag London 2015   111
V. Wulf et al. (eds.), *Designing Socially Embedded Technologies in the Real-World*,
Computer Supported Cooperative Work, DOI 10.1007/978-1-4471-6720-4_7

intended context. The material and social foundations of IT usage have significantly changed over the past two decades. Technologically, the standardization of communication interfaces, the increase of bandwidth and speed of Internet connections, and their ubiquitous availability have connected more and more devices with each other. At a social level, this has also created stronger connections between professional and private domains and practices, offering new room to adapt these practices and renegotiate their relations and compositions. These developments have made us now look at ecosystems (Draxler et al. 2015) or infrastructures (Star and Ruhleder 1996) of technology-based practices.

With regard to methods, EUSSET's research agenda would benefit from a convergence of a broadly defined research program which looks at technology development as well as scenarios of usage and accumulates results in various ways, bridging the gap between a simple "technology-in-practice" perspective and a "technology-based practice change" perspective. We need to consider how to carefully transfer emerging design concepts, IT artifacts, and pattern of appropriation derived in a specific context to other fields of application. We also need to better understand how to transfer findings gained with the design and appropriation of one artifact toward that of another, related one.

In this paper, we will outline a research program, called practice-based computing, which suggests collecting a corpus of highly contextualized design case studies and supports the transferability of insights by comparative concept building on top of these cases.

7.2   State of the Art: Conceptions of Social Practices

In social science, various theories of social practice have been developed as interpretation patterns that serve to provide an explanation for human interaction. Some of the most important contributors to social theories elaborating on practice include Bourdieu (1977, 1990), Giddens (1979, 1984), Garfinkel (1967), and Latour (1993). These approaches turn against rationalistic or structurally deterministic interpretations of human action and interaction as well as interpretations which neglect historical imprint, sociality, and reflexivity of human interaction.

Reckwitz (2002) attempted to elaborate on the various practice theoretical approaches by identifying core assumptions shared by the different theoreticians. According to him, these schools of thinking understand practices as the smallest unit in the analysis of social phenomena. Within the bounds of practice, a pattern is understood as being a considerably routinized, subsiding human action, an action which is not only encompassed by mental and physical forms of activity but that is also greatly imprinted by objects, especially by tools, media, and their usage. A practice generated by human actors is structured by background knowledge that is not entirely explicit but contains emotional and motivational elements. Examples of practices depict a certain manner in which work, research, cooking, or even playing soccer is to be conducted.

With concrete relationships as their contexts, practices represent collective patterns of interaction that are reproduced by human actors. While the interaction patterns may be routinized, the repetitive and tangible acts of execution take place context-specifically. The reproduction of practices goes hand in hand with certain world views, a related normative stance, and use of specific language. Human actors typically belong to different practice systems and mediate among them.

In contrast to other cultural-theoretical positions, practice theoreticians emphasize in particular the social efforts expended in reproducing common routines, the close connection between bodily and mental activities, and the importance of (technical) artifacts for the constitution of practices. In this respect, they offer interesting conceptions for design-oriented research (Wulf 2009; Wulf et al. 2011; Kuutti and Bannon 2014). Regarding the academic discussion in the field of human-centered computing, certain conceptions have already been used by individual authors (cf. Orlikowski 1992; Hanseth et al. 1996; Walsham 2006; Huysman and Wulf 2004, 2006). However, conceptualizations of IT-related social practices have not yet been systematically explored with regard to a methodological grounding for design research.

7.3 State of the Art: The Interplay of Practice and Design

An understanding of social entities that is grounded in an analysis of social practices offers interesting implications. If IT artifacts are not aimed at complete automatization, but rather keep the human actors in the loop by focusing on the support of their collective activities, then these artifacts need to be appropriated within the social practices of their specific fields of application.

The field of human-centered computing has seen different approaches to deal with the interrelation between social practices and IT artifacts. The research can be broadly classified into four lines of thinking: (1) one which grounds the design of innovative IT artifacts in ethnographical studies of one – or a few – specific instance(s) of their domain of application, (2) one in which the appropriation of (innovative) technical artifacts is investigated empirically over a longer period of time, (3) one in which designers engage with practitioners in exploring the design of innovative IT artifacts in situ in a participatory manner, and (4) one that reflects design research on and within design practices.

7.3.1 Grounding Design by Means of Ethnographical Field Studies

At the emergence of the CSCW community, Lancaster University was one of the first places to systematically explore the role of ethnographic field studies for the design of IT artifacts. Ethnographic studies on work practices in air traffic control, still seminal in the field, informed computer scientists to develop innovative IT artifacts (Bentley et al. 1992). The reference between the work context and IT designers' activities was mainly created by the ethnographers' account. This account became an important element in design activities. Hughes et al. (1992) have classified different roles an ethnographical case description can play in the design process.

Emerging from similar epistemological roots, Dourish (2006) even suggested keeping the linkage between ethnographic (pre-)study and the construction of technical artifacts on a less enforced level. He strongly suggested abandoning the requirement for ethnographers to conclude their studies with a section on implications for design.

On a more fundamental level, Schmidt (2011) sees the role of ethnographers in analyzing complex cooperative work practices. From such empirical analysis, he argues, computer scientists will be able to deduce software architectures and applications which are sufficiently generic or tailorable to be appropriated in different fields of applications.

While the Lancaster school opened the way for the fertilization of design practices by ethnographic accounts, the linkage between designers and users was still a rather mediated one, mediated by ethnographers' documentation of practices. Dourish (2006) contributed to the clarification of this linkage. Overall, in these schools of thinking, there is little interest in rolling the IT artifacts out in the wild; an investigation into their appropriation in practice was not a crucial part in the research endeavor. Schmidt (2011) anticipated context-specific appropriation activities and a need to technically support them. Moreover, he assumed that their range could sufficiently well be anticipated in an ethnographic study. Brödner et al. (2015) proposed an approach of grounded design (GD) as a praxeological research perspective for information systems research, specifying an ethnologically informed set of GD principles and according research process guidelines.

7.3.2   Studies on Supporting the Appropriation of IT Artifacts

There are numerous studies on the adoption of information technology available in the field of information systems, leading up to theories that systematize studies of adoption processes (e.g., the Adaptive Structuration Theory (DeSanctis and Poole 1994) or the diverse versions of the Technology Acceptance Model (TAM) (Davis 1989; Venkatesh and Davis 2000) and epistemologically similar approaches (Venkatesh et al. 2003)). Although TAM has proven useful in understanding behavioral intentions of use, it remained difficult to identify drivers, crucial moments, and activities that lead to a successful technology usage (Turner et al. 2010).

We interpret the appropriation of information technology not as an abstract phenomenon that somehow happens once a software application is in its "application field," but as a network of activities that users perform in order to make a software "work" in the new work environment. Existing practices evolve and result in new practices that may also include software usages that go beyond what was envisioned by the designers of the software application (Pipek 2005). Appropriation work is a specific part of an IT artifact's usage, but it also remains linked (through the artifact's materiality) with its design process and the designer's work environments. This work has to be studied empirically.

Several early case studies have investigated appropriation work of IT artifacts in a long-term perspective (Karsten and Jones 1998; Ngwenyama 1998; Orlikowski 1996a; Pipek and Wulf 1999, 2003; Törpel et al. 2003; Wulf 1999; Hinrichs et al. 2005; Draxler et al. 2015). They offer empirical insights into appropriation activities and the resulting changes in work practices, and they also show that a significant part of the work being done to make software applications work is collaborative by nature and that it spans from simple sense-making efforts to detailed configuration efforts to make a new technology fit an existing practice.

Pipek (2005) aimed at turning these activities into a seed for new types of functionality to support appropriation work within the technology that is being appropriated: articulation support (support for technology-related articulations – real and online), historicity support (visualizing appropriation as a process of emerging technologies and usages, e.g., by documenting earlier configuration decisions, providing retrievable storage of configuration and usage descriptions), decision support (in a collaborative appropriation activity, providing voting, polling, etc.), demonstration support (providing communication channels to demonstrate usages from one user or group to another user or group), observation support (supporting the visualization of – accumulated, anonymized – information on the use of tools and functions in an organizational context), simulation/exploration support (showing the effects of possible usages in an exemplified or actual organizational setting, maybe allowing configuration manipulations in a sandbox; see also Wulf (2000)), explanation support (explaining the reasons for application behavior, automated vs. communication with experts), delegation support (supporting delegation patterns within configuration activities), and support for (re-)design support (feedback to designers on the appropriation processes). This list focuses on user-user collaboration, and most support ideas still remain as challenges that have to be met with appropriate technological support.

7.3.3 Participatory Design

The Scandinavian tradition of participatory design (PD) was the first to involve practitioners from selected domains of application in the design of IT artifacts (Floyd et al. 1989). As an example of the still seminal work, in the Utopia project, new tools were designed together with employees of the printing industry which was on the verge of digitalization. Over the course of several years, the participatory design community developed and evaluated a variety of techniques of user participation in software development practices (Greenbaum and Kyng 1991). In its traditional mainstream, fieldwork was not considered necessary since its findings could conflict with the self-expressions of the workers' needs (for notable exceptions, see Blomberg et al. (1996) and Kensing et al. (1998)).

With their empirical analyses, (participatory) designers can however contribute to the reflection processes of practitioners. Some authors discussed the relationship between ethnographic studies and participatory design activities, mainly in using ethnographic data from "rapid" or "quick and dirty" pre-studies to inform PD sessions (Crabtree 1998; Hughes et al. 1995; Millen 2000). As a consequence, Crabtree (1998, p. 93) suggested putting more emphasis on an ethnographic pre-study to gather solid information about the organization in order to avoid "the danger of 'tunnel vision' and thus, of coming up with perfect technological solutions to the wrong set of work problems" in PD workshops. In a long-term analysis on their PD work in office settings, Suchman et al. (1999) summarize the PD activities of critical analyses of technical discourses, ethnographic work at the workplace, and design interventions as a program of reconstructing existing and emerging social practices in the field as well as reconstructing the methodological practices of designers as researchers. The authors do not draw strong methodological consequences but rather demand increased sensitivity toward these two levels of reflection. Suchman (2002) later gave a more detailed account of technology development and its structural problems that result from the existing structures of professional specialization, however focusing more on a lack of continuous interaction between practitioners and technology specialists.

Several more recent reflections try to move away from the product focus (e.g., Ehn 2008; Karasti 2001; Karasti and Syrjänen 2004) and the process focus (e.g., Pipek and Wulf 2009; Di Salvo et al. 2012; Dittrich 2014) that is inherent to technology design efforts (even with "participation"). However, it remains difficult to find clear methodological advice about organizing these efforts in a way that satisfies the needs of all stakeholders involved.

7.3.4   Research Through Design and Design Science

In a more deliberate manner, the "research through design" school of thinking has developed techniques to understand social practices for supporting the design of IT artifacts (Gaver 2012; Forlizzi 2008; Stolterman 2008; Zimmerman et al. 2010). Emerging from a traditional design stance, the output of their works takes the form, primarily, of artifacts and systems, sometimes with associated accounts of how these are used in field tests (Gaver 2012). The main concern of this perspective is on the exploration of new design spaces for IT artifacts. As a consequence, analyses of the existing practice and related empirical (predesign) studies play a lesser role. The immediate reaction to the designed artifact is in the focus, and long-term issues of appropriation work are rarely explored, partly because the artifacts are only at a prototype level. Nevertheless, most projects engage with real practice, not with experimental settings.

Referring back to Herbert Simon's work (1996), Hevner et al. (2004) and Hevner and Chatterjee (2010) have postulated a design science approach to the field of information systems. They argue in favor of a three-step process in which the artifact design needs to be grounded in an important and relevant business problem. Moreover, the utility, quality, and efficacy of the design artifact must be rigorously demonstrated via well-executed evaluation methods. However, Hevner's work suffers from a mechanistic understanding of design and lacks a systematic grounding in social practices (Rohde et al. 2009).

Inspired by the participatory design tradition, Scandinavian researchers in IS have developed design approaches which intervene in real-world organizations (Braa and Vidgen 1999; Mathiassen 2002; Sein et al. 2012). However, they typically pay little attention to the long-term appropriation of IT artifacts (Braa and Vidgen 1999; Mathiassen 2002) or classify their cases in a too schematic manner (Sein et al. 2012).

7.3.5 On the Issue of Transferability

In the field of human-centered computing, there are different understandings with regard to the generality and transferability of research findings. A positivist stance underlying, for instance, the design science approach of Hevner et al. (2004) follows a theory-building paradigm derived from the sciences. It assumes that models and theories can be generated which describe the interaction of humans and IT artifacts in a reproducible, design-oriented manner. In such an understanding, models and theories do not refer specifically to the context of their origin – since they claim general applicability within the limits of their scope of validity (cf. Chi et al. 2011).

Most other schools of practice-oriented design do not follow the positivist stance and raise epistemological concerns whether the generalization of findings is possible in such a context-independent manner. Findings are usually presented together with a description of the context from which they emerged. However, this school of thinking has not yet come up with coherent guidance on how to transfer knowledge beyond individual design cases. Empirical work in the information systems community, e.g., Orlikowski (1996a), thrives on the elaboration of widely applicable concepts and descriptions dealing with appropriation activities. In the participatory design community, the attitude is held traditionally that results should not be transferred from one case to others since the workers should determine their work and codevelop their tools and local knowledge.

When dealing with transferability, the ethnographically grounded design community rather looks upon the transfer of insights as being mediated by the resulting IT artifact that would be designed for the appropriation in different social settings. Such an understanding is close to Gaver's (2012) perspective on a potential epistemological grounding of the "research through design" community. He suggests collecting a set of examples of (well-)designed IT artifacts and annotating such a portfolio with conceptual considerations ("the role of theory should be to annotate those examples rather than replace them"). This position has been contested by others in the "research through design" community who claim that theory building should be at the core of its academic activities (Zimmerman et al. 2010).

7.3.6 Gap in the State of the Art

The relations between a design process, a design product, and the related fields of practice have been discussed from many angles. The contributions range from philosophical reflections (e.g., Ehn 2008) over case study collections (e.g., Di Salvo et al. 2012) to comprehensive theories (e.g., Hevner et al. 2004). The challenge is – in our eyes – not a lack of attention and discourse, but the lack of a discourse structure that allows a comparison of different practical experiences from different design projects. The quality of IT design can only be determined by looking at the changes in social practices resulting from appropriation activities. We need a conception of how to document design cases in a holistic manner spanning the different phases of a practice-oriented design process: the status of technology and activity systems as well as ongoing sense-making activities that provide orientation for possible further developments of a practice that precede any decision of practitioners to engage in design activities, the (possibly participatory) conceptualization of a new technology aiming at improving a practice as the actual design process, and the appropriation of the new technology that results in a changed social practice. Roughly, this reflects a participatory action research perspective (Whyte 1991), but we need to be more specific with regard to the relations between technology design and practice reflection to allow better comparisons.

The different schools of practice-related design thinking have not yet come up with a convincing understanding as to what extent and how transferability across different contexts could be achieved. Theory building across different examples is mostly dismissed, looked upon with great suspicion, or limited to the generation of concepts to describe only the new phenomena emerging in the case at hand. Claiming the context dependency of the findings, it lacks a convincing model of how to transfer design-relevant findings from one context to the next. The core mechanism of concept building seems to be the comparison of case studies with earlier findings – be they other case studies or theoretical concepts. There is little progress toward establishing what we could call a "corpus" of studies. There is no coherent model of comparative analysis. So it would appear to be the reader of a case study rather than its author who is responsible for transferring findings to a new context.

In the following, we suggest "design case studies" as an action research methodology, and we argue that a repository of design case studies and their comparative analysis can help us in concept building and increasing the level of transferability (cf. Brödner et al. 2015).

7.4   Design Case Studies

In the following, we want to propose design case studies to be an appropriate element in a practice-based research program. To design, we need to better understand the relationship between specific instances of social practices and the design space for IT artifacts in their support. The design of IT artifacts needs to take the given social practices, including the already existing IT infrastructures, into account. However, when these artifacts are rolled out "in the wild," these practices undergo changes during the appropriation process. We need to understand the interaction between the IT design and the appropriation activities over a longer period of time (Pipek and Wulf 1999; Rohde et al. 2009; Wulf et al. 2011).

These changes in practices can occur on different societal levels. The introduction of IT artifacts often connects social practices that were previously unconnected. Because social practices cannot be changed in some random way, due to issues of embodiment and routinization, we need to grapple with the expansive repertoire of practices one encounters in various fields of practice. We also need to gain an understanding concerning the possibilities of change in the context of the introduction of IT artifacts.

Design case studies ideally consist of three phases:

1. Empirical pre-study: This should offer microlevel descriptions of the social practices before any intervention takes place. An analysis should particularly describe already existing tools, media, and their usage. It should also capture the development seen by horizon practitioners from a technological, organizational, and social perspective. Such documentation can be typically formulated in a certain problem or need statement when setting up the research agenda. This documentation may be already available in documents in the fields of practice, or it needs to be collected in an ethnographic endeavor that helps practitioners in reflecting upon their situation.
2. Prototyping/(participatory) IT design: Design case studies should describe the innovative IT artifact from a product as well as from a process perspective. This includes a description of the specific design process, the involved stakeholders, the applied design methods, and the emerging design concepts. A focus should lie on the documentation of what changes in social practices the stakeholders anticipate and aim for and how these considerations have influenced the design of the IT artifact.
3. Evaluation/appropriation study: Design case studies should document the introduction, appropriation, and potential redesign of the IT artifact in its respective domain of practice. Such documentation allows the transformative impact of certain functions and design options realized within the IT artifact to be analyzed. At this point, it is also necessary to document the distribution patterns of the new technology in the field of practice. The work in all phases is always a collaboration between researchers/designers and practitioners. Although there is a natural order of starting points of the phases, we do not understand the phases as being strictly consecutive, but as continuing: once an analysis of

existing practices has started, it does not make sense to stop reflecting upon the momentum of the existing practice; rather, it continues throughout the design and the study of the appropriation. Once the design has started, it may be continued in several iterations, although the technology has already been introduced to potential future users. In the late phase of a design case study, the "phases" should rather be perceived as perspectives.

One other important point to be described is the reflection upon limitations in the researchers' practices. To a certain extent, the funding structures of research define the time and the amount of resources that researchers may be able to invest, particularly in very time-consuming tasks such as participatory observations. Additionally, side agendas (of the researchers as well as practitioners) may influence the dedication of stakeholders. In comparing cases, it is not the exact quantification of these issues that is important, but rather the reflection of the relations between researchers and practitioner's practices.

The whole idea about design case studies aims at informing the aggregation of cases. Typically, a "case" is a "natural" unit to look at: it is one set of connected activities of researchers and practitioners in one field of practice. There may be, however, difficulties of different types that make it impossible to maintain collaboration over the necessary time span of a design case study. There are basically two ways to deal with such a situation:

1. Design case studies may shift over time from one field of practice to a related one. For instance, the pre-study may have been conducted in one field of practice, while the appropriation can only be observed in a similar, but different, field of practice. In this case, we speak about an *aggregated* design case study.
2. Design case studies may need to be disrupted at a certain point of time without covering design or appropriation phases. For instance, we may end up with only a pre-study. However, this empirical study has been conducted in a manner to explore design opportunities. In this case, we speak about a *partial* design case study.

In both cases, it is the research practice that defines the design case study. The necessity to work with aggregated or partial design case studies may result from the practice under observation (e.g., the practice of organizing a conference, Saeed et al. 2011, or the practice of crisis management, Ley et al. 2012). But it may also result from the resource structure of researchers. Again, the point is to comment on the consequences of these restrictions in the design case study itself (Fig. 7.1).

In the following, we discuss the details of our approach against case studies we have conducted. All examples have already been published elsewhere. Starting with a procedural description of our research practice, we continue by referring to those aspects of the individual cases relevant to discuss our approach. We will later also use a fifth example of consecutive case studies to illustrate the concept of partial design case studies.

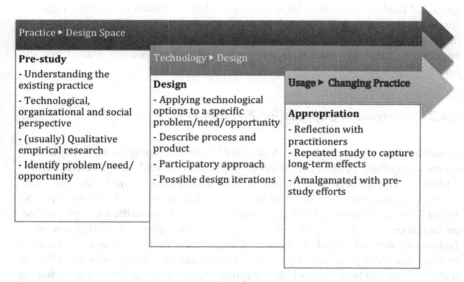

Fig. 7.1 Schematic display of the structure of a design case study

7.4.1   Expert Finder in a Networked Organization

An early example of a design case study is the development of the *Expert Finder*, a recommender system to foster expertise sharing among workers within an industrial association (NIA) and its member companies (Reichling and Veith 2005; Reichling et al. 2007; Reichling and Wulf 2009). The lack of visibility and accessibility of expertise is a recurrent problem in larger organizations and organizational networks. The project was initiated by a fraction of the association's management and was partly funded by the German Federal Ministry of Economic Affairs within a funding scheme on knowledge management. In the first phase, the field of application was investigated empirically by observational studies, an analysis of the IT infrastructure, and 16 semi-structured interviews. The study focused on one operating section of the industrial association, some central units, and their relationship with selected member companies. The study looked at collaborative work with a specific emphasis on knowledge exchange needs and practices. Based on these findings, the design of *Expert Finder* was developed. The development was based on already existing software components, the ExpertFinding framework (Reichling et al. 2005). Specifically, the functionality of selecting documents from the users' ordinary file system, the configuration of the matching according to the specific types of text, and the concepts to protect workers' privacy were stimulated by the findings of the pre-study (Reichling et al. 2007). Finally, the *Expert Finder* was rolled out for a period of 9 months, mainly in those parts of the association which had participated in the pre-study and one member company. The somewhat restricted field of application impacted the evaluation results concerning expertise sharing practices because many of the actors knew each other rather well. However, the study provided interesting insights with regard to the self-representation of employees within the recommender system and their sensitivity toward privacy-oriented features.

7.4.2 Navigation Support for Firefighters

A second design case study was conducted when developing *Landmarke,* a ubiquitous computing platform to support firefighters in navigating inside burning buildings. The project was funded in two consecutive projects by the European Commission and the German Ministry of Research. The EU-funded project WearIT@work focused on bringing wearable technologies to different types of blue-collar workers. Working with the Paris firefighters, the rather basic design concept of *Landmarke* was developed. At its core, it suggested a navigation support system to leverage the social practices of the firefighters on reconnaissance missions in finding routes by themselves, instead of compiling maps automatically and providing computer-generated guidance. A consecutive project, called *Landmarke* (German term for "landmark"), was funded by the German Ministry of Education and Research (BMBF) to explore and implement the platform for navigation support. In *Landmarke,* we worked closely with the Fire Brigade of Cologne and with the Firefighting Institute of the German State of North Rhine-Westphalia (IdF).

Since it was impossible to observe firefighters and to deploy prototypes in burning buildings, we mainly used training sessions constructed according to realistic firefighting conditions in training centers such as at the Firefighting Institute. The Institute offers buildings in which different architectonical settings are realized, like different apartments, a restaurant, an underground parking lot, and a laboratory. At the beginning of the project, we had little insight into the subtle navigation practices of firefighters. From the very beginning, we therefore followed a participatory design in which intended users have a significant amount of control in design decisions. Video recordings and observations while prototyping, rather than traditional ethnographies, were the driving technique to explore given navigation practices and to bridge between the present and the future in navigation. Prototypes of different levels of sophistication were built and explored in the training center. The Arduino toolset proved to be very helpful in constructing prototypes of medium complexity (Ramirez et al. 2012). Finally, we built our own ubiquitous device which we integrated into doorstoppers: artifacts the firefighters were carrying with them anyway (Ramirez 2012). These devices were used in specifically laid out training scenarios in the Institute's buildings. Due to the danger to life involved when entering burning buildings and the related safety regulations, we were not able to explore the landmarks in real firefighting practice. However, the training sections indicated that the landmarks augmented already existing navigation skills. Specific advantages could be seen when withdrawing from the building and when handing over to a second troop of firefighters.

7.4.3 Location Tracker for Dementia Patients and Their Caregivers

A third design case study is an aggregated one and deals with the development of a GPS service for caregivers of individuals suffering from Alzheimer's disease with a disposition toward wandering behavior. The study was funded by the German Ministry of Economics in a technology transfer funding scheme, supporting a software company in bringing such a product to market. This Alzheimer disposition is very problematic for patients since it fosters anxiety and disorientation and can even lead to life-threatening situations. Caregivers react to these threads by strategies which may reduce the patients' freedom to move. In the first phase of the study, we conducted 21 semi-structured interviews with six family caregivers who live at home with their relatives suffering from dementia and 15 professional caregivers working in retirement homes. We investigated caregivers' practices and uncovered their attitudes toward monitoring systems, which revealed two value-laden dilemmas in the design of location trackers: "awareness vs. privacy" and in particular "safety vs. autonomy" (Müller et al. 2010, 2013). The next step was to implement two location tracker clients, one mobile and the other stationary, which indicated the position of the patient on a map. Certain movements in areas near the patient's home could be excluded from being tracked. Over a period of 4 months, we introduced the system into three fields of application: a family and two different care homes. After the appropriation of the application, we saw a considerable change in the practices of dealing with dementia patients suffering from the wandering symptom (Müller et al. 2013). However, the fields of application where we tested the location tracker were not exactly the same as the ones in which we conducted the pre-study. This was due to two aspects: firstly, there was a deterioration in the health of the patients whose caregivers had first participated in the pre-study to the extent that they could no longer walk on their own anymore; secondly, we had to find evaluation environments in which the system would be embedded in real practices but with a high safety level and risk control as we could not guarantee full 24/7 performance of the prototype (Wan et al. 2014).

7.4.4 Social Display

Social Display is a project located in a residential care home aiming to research the question whether IT can be an appropriate means to support quality of life of persons of advanced age (aged on average between 80 and 90) (Müller et al. 2012). When the project started, the home did not offer public Internet access; few (if any) residents had computers; and only a very small number had any experience at all in using IT. In a similar way, the caregivers only very rarely use new media and the Internet in their work with the residents, and most of them only use the PC for their administrative work (such as documentation, digital records) and had minimal interest in IT, even in their private lives.

The project started in 2009 with an interview pre-study and several participatory workshops to elicit applications for a large-screen display which would be of interest to the elderly residents as well as to the caregivers in their work with the residents. Initially, we undertook 13 interviews with residents and caregivers and 30 h of participant observation in order to study their routines, their wishes, and demands. Based on these findings, we developed design ideas for the display. The pre-study provided insights in the elderly's self-concepts and revealed a high degree of passivity to which an alignment of design ideas looked rather impossible. On the other hand, previous research had consistently shown that the appropriation of specific IT applications may offer significant benefits for the elderly and even for very old people living in residential settings (Piper et al. 2010). We therefore believed we had good grounds for pursuing methods for engaging this potential user population. In recognizing that the residents were familiar with and willing to participate in organized activities, we established "Internet Days." During the Internet Days, we presented different online services at five stations, four with computers on large monitors and one with a Wi-Fi device connected to a large-screen television. It transpired that the Internet Days provided a fruitful setting for mutual learning and common engagement with IT and Internet applications.

Based on these experiences, we built the first version of the social display offering four functionalities: local news, national news, a photo album, and short films presented on a large-screen display. As an input device, we chose a PlayStation buzzer with five colored buttons, each of four buttons representing one functionality. For the more technically affine caregivers, an Internet browser accessed by keyboard and mouse was available to support collaborative Internet sessions, mostly for biographic work. The first stable version, introduced in 2010, has been slightly improved over time according to the results from the ongoing fieldwork. Manifold appropriation processes could be observed; for instance, residents started new forms of interaction in front of the display, while – in the pre-study – we had experienced that the residents found it problematic to get in touch with each other. The staff started to use the display for biography work sessions with both single residents and groups. In the same way, nonresidents, who were regular lunch guests in the home, also started to use the system and came into contact with the residents, something which had hardly ever happened before. In recent years, many additional initiatives associated with the display have been introduced by student groups from our university with the aim of developing additional hard- and software pertinent to the display. Additionally, we developed a training concept for the staff. The work is still ongoing and is nowadays (in January 2015) mainly based on regular meetings with interested residents and staff members to document the appropriation and elicit further design options.

7.5 Characteristics of Design Case Studies

Design case studies represent an idealized model for conducting design research in practice. They provide a clear orientation for the design process. However, as a result of the contingences of a practice-oriented research approach, the concrete methods to be applied in each of the different phases of a case study will be distinct. Also, the duration and the depth of the activities of each of the three phases may differ. Phases will interleave as well. We want to discuss the variability of design case studies according to the different phases.

7.5.1 Setting Things Up

Design case studies first attain thematic and institutional positioning in the course of their establishment. Developers of innovative technologies need to come together with actors who are willing to explore the potentials of such technology in their daily practices. There may be other stakeholders to be involved in the design process, such as representatives of marketing divisions of the IT companies or higher management and workers' representatives on the side of the user organization. The actors involved in the project establishment define the vision of the research project and should be selected with great care. The experiences and the mind-set of the developers, the selection of the application partners and their individual actors, as well as the mode of cooperation among designers and stakeholders shape the emerging IT artifact. For instance, in the *Location Tracker* project, we decided to involve family caregivers as well as those in residential homes. The resulting IT design reflected the broader variety of different practices rather than just the involvement of one field of application.

These actors contribute their specific interests and perspectives which are not always in line with the issues on the researchers' agendas. For instance, initial access to the home was via the manager. At the outset, his intentions were marketing driven. He asked us to develop a large-screen display for advertising rather than for care purposes. For this reason, it was supposed to be located in the entrance hall. However, we were more interested in large-screen displays in the care context of very old residents, and we finally convinced the manager to open up the project with a stronger care focus while the displays were still visible from the entrance hall. The project setup often requires negotiations to align problem perceptions in practice with an academic positioning of the work.

In the European context, design case studies are often funded by research agencies which either take technological innovation to be a driver in societal innovation and international competition or want to explore the potential of innovative technologies in tackling certain social problems. These governmental agencies fund research institutions and IT industries, and in addition there are often also partners who plan to apply these technologies in their social practices. In most of the design case studies mentioned above, the institutional setting was defined by the project proposal receiving government funding. In the case of the *Location Tracker*, the application partners were not defined by the research proposal, and the *Social Display* project was not funded by any government agency. Institutional divides on the side of the technology developers can impact the course of design case studies considerably (see Dachtera et al. (2014) for the case of the *Landmarke* project).

7.5.2   Pre-study

To ground the design process, the empirical pre-study allows the given social practices in the envisioned field of application to be better understood. The methods are empirical, consisting typically of interviews, observations, video and document analysis, as well as an investigation of already existing IT artifacts and their appropriation, which can include log-file analysis. The configuration of the empirical methods depends on the nature of the given practice, the researchers' already existing knowledge, and how the practices can best be accessed and understood. Certain practices can be better described verbally, while others need to be observed in detail, e.g., the subtle navigation moves of firefighters.

In one extreme, there can be design case studies in which the actual practice, before conducting the design interventions, is so well understood that the researchers may abstain from an explicit pre-study. A good understanding of existing practices and related problems which should possibly be supported by future prototypes is often based on a preexisting problem perception and analysis by the application partners and their ability to articulate and reflect in terms of possible technical solutions.

When working with elderly and non-technology-affine people, there was often no such common ground. This points at other elements the pre-study has to encompass too. For the case at hand, the pre-study target was divided into two parts: gaining insights into current everyday practices and the problem perception of the target groups. However, the pre-study may include measures to help the actors become familiar with ideas of possible IT support.

In *Expert Finder* we mainly worked with semi-structured interviews, while in the *Landmarke* study the firefighters were mainly observed while conducting navigation tasks. The navigation practices we observed were partly made even more challenging by the introduction of specific conditions, such as blindfolding the firefighters' eyes. In the *Location Tracker* project, in addition to semi-structured interviews, we accomplished several days of participant observations in institutions of dementia care. In the *Social Display* project, it was quite a challenge to gain access to the elderly residents in the realm of the pre-study based on a qualitative interview approach. This was due to specific psychological and social issues of the target group. Thus, we enhanced the interview study with interventions such as the Internet Days. Off-the-shelf technology was brought into the residential home for residents and care workers alike to explore Internet content such as Google Earth, which enabled the elderly residents to see their birthplace or where they used to live or work, and YouTube to access music and films, or news sites. In the interview sessions, it had not been possible to find out what the elderly would class as fun since the triggers for chatting about these things had been missing.

The focus of the pre-study is somehow directed by the anticipations – often still blurred – of the design concept to be addressed; it uncovers elements of current social practices and their problematic aspects. For instance, *Expert Finder*'s pre-study indicated severe organizational barriers in knowledge sharing within the industrial association NIA and its member organizations – related to the fact that people working on similar topics did not know each other.

Based on these findings, the pre-study provides hints at how to design IT artifacts as incentives for the development of the practices investigated. Compared to social science research endeavors which require empirical depth for a profound understanding of the site, the pre-study phase can be a bit fractal since it is the first step of a potentially ongoing engagement. The design case study approach allows the correction of misperceptions during the subsequent participatory design activities and investigations into the appropriation of the IT artifact.

Activities in the realm of the pre-study also aim to build up trustful relationships between users and design team which are essential for further engagement. In addition, measures have to be taken up which help to build a common notional realm of possibilities and also to help the target group to become familiar with ideas of possible IT usages. This may include measures to help the target group reflect and talk about their everyday life and to be able to start thinking about possible IT support for their practices. In the *Social Display* project, the Internet Days created a fruitful environment for prototyping and appropriation. These interventions opened up a common frame of reference and a learning environment which made residents, care staff, and even researchers eager to engage in the next sessions.

The results of the empirical pre-study are, like those of a whole design case study, typically partial in the sense that they only cover a certain, often small, part of the IT artifact's potential field of application. When planning a pre-study, one has to balance depth against breadth under the temporal restrictions resulting from the design process. To envision the appropriate set of stakeholders requires a certain anticipation of the IT artifact. Moreover, a broader variety of different practices and resulting design concepts may contribute to the implementation of a higher level of technical flexibility. It may therefore make sense to involve more potential users and user organizations' perspectives in the pre-study than can be involved in the design process later on. However, the limiting factors are (a) obtaining the required empirical depth in analyzing relevant practices and (b) coming up with relevant results timely enough to influence the design phase. In the case of *Expert Finder* and *Location Tracker*, the empirical pre-studies took between 4 and 6 months and partly interleaved with the following design phase. The selection of the users involved in the early stage of the design case study contributes to the definition of the artifact's scope of validity.

As the *Location Tracker* project focused on both practice areas, familial and residential, we aimed at contacting interview partners in both fields. Obtaining contact to professional caregivers in residential care homes was rather easy because most of them were interested in these new technologies and were eager to learn more about them. In contrast to this, we learned that the "moral universe" in families where a family member suffers from dementia can be very complex and often inhibits them from talking freely about related problems and sorrows. It was often only with the help of a self-help organization that we could gain access to the families. However, some families and institutions read about our project in the newspaper and contacted us to learn more about the project.

The results of the pre-study revealed partly extremely controversial attitudes toward possible GPS-based IT support. We learned that the field of practice is based upon very different and individual approaches to dementia care, depending on the level of care theory knowledge, the familial relationships, and organizational issues such as work load, risk perceptions and risk management, as well as individual IT expertise.

7.5.3 (Participatory) Design

The design phase of the case study builds on the findings and commitments derived from the empirical pre-study. It takes the descriptions of the social practices and their inherent problems and developmental needs as input for the design process. However, the results of the pre-study do not determine the outcome of the design process. Descriptions of given practices do not determine how to support them in the future by means of innovative IT artifacts. Design is a sophisticated activity best conducted by specialists. It requires the anticipation of technological as well as social futures. However, we enrich the design process by input derived from the relevant fields of practice. This includes engaging practitioners, preferably those already involved in the pre-study, in the design process. While empirical findings of the pre-study play an important role in grounding the process, there are other important factors such as the given practices of the design team, its creative potential, its interaction with the stakeholders and potential users, already existing design concepts, and technical infrastructure, such as software repositories at hand, which influence the final outcome considerably.

The four different design case studies deviated quite considerably in their concrete design approach. In *Landmarke*, the firefighters' navigation practices had not yet been perfectly analyzed after the pre-study activities – also the non-design-oriented literature did not offer sufficient insights. Even after a broad design concept emerged, it remained unclear how to support navigation practices in detail. Moreover, there was not yet any technical framework to build the design on. Therefore, the design process was most extensive, including a wide set of participatory design activities (Ramirez et al. 2012).

In *Expert Finder*, the pre-study described problems in knowledge-intense work in quite some detail. The design process was grounded on the assumption that some of the problems which cropped up in the empirical pre-study could be tackled by means of an already existing software framework. In this sense, the pre-study rather hinted at the need to refine an already existing design approach, e.g., by integrating private folder hierarchies and dealing with resulting privacy concerns.

In *Social Display*, the residents' reaction to the Internet Days offered a valuable input. To operationalize the study's results into design features and functionalities, we chose to cooperate with the manager of the home and some of the care staff who showed a degree of technical interest. We chose this design approach because we learned in the pre-study that concrete design aspects would overwhelm the residents.

When including stakeholders in the design phase, we apply a wide spectrum of techniques developed by the participatory design community (Floyd et al. 1991; Greenbaum and Kyng 1991). However, the design phase always has the goal to come up with a running system version whose appropriation will become the subject of investigation. Beyond issues of traditional usability, technical criteria of software quality play an important role in our development process. If an innovative artifact is performing badly algorithmically or does not run stably enough, we cannot seriously investigate its appropriation.

Since our implementation capacities are somewhat restricted, we tend to build our development efforts on top of already existing software frameworks. In the *Expert Finder* project, we implemented on top of our own software framework. In *Location Tracker*, our industrial partner used the open-source framework Liferay in combination with OpenStreetMap to display positioning data. Off-the-shelf GPS trackers were purchased. *Social Display* also drew on existing content on the Internet, e.g., local and national news sites as well as YouTube and standard technologies, such as the photo album and the PlayStation buzzer.

Even in *Landmarke*, a project in which we prototyped in a very substantial manner, we applied the Arduino framework to build some of the prototypes. As a consequence, the availability of given hardware and software frameworks may impact the outcome of the design phase.

7.5.4 Appropriation

The appropriation phase of the design case study takes the IT artifact, rolls it out into one or more fields of application, and observes its usage empirically over a longer period of time. The goal is to understand how the usage of the innovative artifact is changing social practices. The investigation into this phenomenon requires a long-term perspective (Orlikowski 1996a; Pipek and Wulf 1999, 2009).

Ideally, we would like to roll the artifact out into the same fields of application where we conducted the empirical pre-study. This would allow the changes in social practices to be detected in detail. Unfortunately, this is not always possible. We do not always reach the appropriation phase with all our research efforts. Smaller or larger shifts in the project setting or the fields of application may require switching the site to investigate the IT artifact's appropriation. If such a switch takes place, more intense observations to detect differences in practice are needed.

In the case of the *Expert Finder*, the resulting software was basically rolled out in those parts of the organization with which we had conducted the field study. In the second stage of the rollout, we included one of NIA's member companies which had not participated in the pre-study. In *Landmarke*, the pre-study was basically conducted with Paris firefighters, while the participatory design process and the appropriation study were conducted with firefighters of the city of Cologne. However, in *Location Tracker*, we were no longer able to work with the families and care institutions who had participated in the pre-study and, partly, in the design process. The physical condition of those patients we had worked with in the pre-study had deteriorated so badly that they were no longer able to run away anymore. The care institutions participating in the pre-study did not have appropriate patients at the time of our rollout. To investigate the location tracker's appropriation, we had to find elderly people with wandering syndrome whose institutional or family care setting could compensate for a potential failure of the system.

In the *Social Display* project, pre-study and evaluation took place in the same residential home. However, we could not work with the same people during the whole process. Although many of the elderly and the care workers involved from the beginning used the first prototype, we were confronted with the sudden death of some of the residents working with us in the earlier phase. So there is a variety of practical reasons why the continuity in the field of application is not always given throughout the course of a design case study.

There are other challenges we experienced when trying to investigate into the appropriation of IT artifacts. Some IT artifacts require a critical mass of users to study the appropriation of its whole functionality. For instance, the evaluation of the *Expert Finder* suffered from the problem that most of the initial users knew each other quite well since they were from the same organizational subunit of NIA. For this reason, our empirical study concentrated more on the self-presentation functionality rather than on the one-on-one people search.

A rollout in practice can also be problematic, if the required technological infrastructure is not yet there. For instance, Dörner (2010) developed an interesting toolset allowing end users to find and assemble software services to tailor ERP applications. However, we did not find any ERP ecosystems in organizational practice which would have allowed us to evaluate this application. We were therefore restricted to a lab study for evaluation purposes.

We experienced a different type of problem with the technical infrastructure when evaluating the location tracker. While the system requires a state-of-the-art browser, one of the care institutions provided the nurses only with a set of outdated Internet tools, which meant that our system could not run on the house's infrastructure. For this reason, we had to provide the nurses with an iPad with mobile Internet access via SIM card instead of letting them use the desktop PCs for tracking.

In *Social Display*, the research team built up a fully new technical infrastructure and even acted as counselors to the manager of the residential home in building up a sustainable IT environment. Here, prototyping and investigation into the appropriation directly led to a long-term usage scenario.

When trying to understand how our ubiquitous computing application supported the navigation practices of firefighters, we experienced another problem. Due to the highly risky nature of their work, it was not possible to roll out the IT artifacts in actual firefighting practice. However, even if the firefighters had used the markers inside burning buildings, we would not have been able to observe their practices easily. In this case, therefore, our investigations into IT appropriation remained on the level of training practices.

While the investigation of an IT artifact's appropriation in practice is a real challenge, it is the final proof of the validity of an IT artifact's quality.

7.5.5   *Discussion*

Design case studies represent an idealized model of our research approach. As a result of the contingences of the practice orientation, one may not be able to conduct all suggested phases – at least not to their full extent. Specifically, the appropriation phase requires the researchers to deliver a high standard of software technical perfection, with regard to performance, stability, and usability. Moreover, the field of application needs to provide an appropriate technological infrastructure to roll out the newly designed artifacts. The practitioners need to be willing to engage with the technological opportunities.

However, the presented instances of design case studies also indicate potential limitations for the ongoing participation of practitioners. For instance, the fact that the elderly participants in the *Location Tracker* and *Social Display* projects were not capable of expressing their perspectives in an ongoing manner poses a serious challenge to our design approach. In these cases, other stakeholders and the designers play a dominant role which poses the danger of paternalizing the elderly. In these cases, the pre-study phase is of specific importance.

In terms of setting up appropriate environments for investigation into the appropriation, both the firefighting domain and the aging domain pose special challenges. With the firefighters, the prototype had to be tested in a training center where researchers were allowed to participate and observe. However, neither the researchers' participation nor the usage of the prototype was possible in a real fire emergency. There are strict standards in that domain in order to avoid endangering the firefighters (and their observers). Thus, the evaluation of a prototype whose stability and functionality are not certified is not possible in a real fire.

The safety aspect was similarly important in the *Location Tracker* project when allowing patients to wander outside the well-protected care settings. We need to find a viable trade-off in an environment which is as close as possible to real practice while avoiding putting users at risk by relying on prototypes which might not operate stably. A proper balance has to be worked out together with the relevant stakeholders.

The projects differ in the degree to which different fields of practice were covered in the individual phases. The breadth of the coverage was typically influenced by the institutional setup and the available (financial) resources. In the European context, the requirements of the funding agency play an important role in shaping the institutional setting. In the *Expert Finder* project, the application partner was a predefined part of the publicly funded project setup. The design case study *Landmarke* involved two different firefighting organizations – in two publicly funded projects following up on each other. The *Location Tracker* project did not predefine application partners because in this scheme there was no funding available for any application partners. In *Social Display*, the project was set up in a single residential home by a PhD student who had a university grant to pursue his thesis. Whether the integration of more application partners would have enhanced the understanding of relevant practices is an interesting question. Given the limited

research resources, one has to typically trade off breadth against depth with regard
to the involvement of practitioners (see above).

Public funding schemes considerably influence the domains of practice being
addressed and seem to act as an incentive for the participation of (well-known)
institutions in domains considered by the funding agencies to be socioeconomically
important. This sheds light on the institutional conditions which typically frame
research interest and outcome. Without external funding for application partners,
the researchers are quite free in their theoretical sampling and can add application
partners whenever it seems meaningful. Projects in which the application partner is
defined during the project setup can restrict the researcher's opportunities to orient
the project and can dictate that a certain practice be employed. However, a lack of
funding can limit the practitioners' commitment and level of involvement. Beyond
money, the researchers have to typically come up with additional stimuli to motivate
the practitioners during long-term cooperation. Such incentives are related to their
personal perspectives and ambitions.

Another important issue is sustainability beyond a (funded) design research
activity. When we examine the appropriation of IT, we must take the post-research
phase into consideration. When people start integrating the technology in their
everyday life to leverage specific problems, the technology can become an important
part of their social practices (Ogonowski et al. 2013). A sudden withdrawal could
disrupt and challenge the newly established practices (cf. Pipek and Wulf 1999,
2009). Therefore, researchers have to carefully consider the sustainability of their
interventions in practice.

In the case of *Social Display*, sustainability is given by the strong collaboration
with the residential home from the beginning and the manager's motivation to keep
the system running. He understands it to be his task to make sure that the application
is to be maintained. The other design case studies followed a different path. We had
agreed with the application partners to test the prototypes over a defined period
of time. However, in the *Location Tracker* case, one family appropriated the IT
support to such an extent that they wished to keep it permanently – a service we
were not able to provide. In this case, we helped to find an application with less
functionality but already available on the market and economically affordable for
the family (which is not always the case). Affordability of the resulting artifacts
and the accompanying business models thus present another issue which has to be
considered in the project setup – beyond traditional plans of transferability of results.

7.6 Concept Building Grounded in a Corpus of Design Case Studies

Our research approach documents design case studies (or parts of them) in different
application domains. Based on a growing corpus of design case studies, we
try to identify intersecting themes, compare the context-specific findings, build

terminology, and try to develop abstractions. These abstractions should facilitate the transferability of findings while still staying related to their context of emergence. They can be seen as elements of a theory of practice-based computing.

With regard to the role of abstractions, our work follows a similar epistemological stance as that of Herbert Blumer when he speaks about sensitizing concepts: "[A sensitizing concept] gives the user a general sense of reference and guidance in approaching empirical instances. Whereas definite concepts provide prescriptions of what to see, sensitizing concepts merely suggest directions along which to look" (Blumer 1954: 7). Following Blumer (1954), we are able to question taken-for-granted concepts in the given literature and enrich them with empirical phenomena found in our design case studies.

Concepts, in this sense, can deal with:

1. Specific features of social practices: Prominent examples of abstractions dealing with aspects of social practices are the concepts of *awareness*, as suggested by Heath and Luff (1991), or on a more abstract level the concept of *situated action* (cf. Suchman 1986).
2. Principles for the design of IT artifacts: Examples of such principles are the architectural model of an *awareness pipeline* (Fuchs et al. 1996; Fuchs 1998) and *mechanism for handling conflicts* when activating groupware functions (Wulf 1997; Wulf and Rohde 1996; Wulf et al. 2001). On a more general level, the concept of *tailorability* is another example (Henderson and Kyng 1991; Wulf et al. 2008).
3. Specific features characterizing the appropriation of IT artifacts and the resulting changes of social practices: The concept of *over the shoulder learning* (Twidale 2005) is an example of such a category. At a higher level, the concepts of *anticipated, emergent, and opportunistic organizational changes* following the introduction of groupware fall into this category (Orlikowski and Hofman 1997; Stiemerling et al. 1998; Pipek and Wulf 1999). Overall, this category seems to be less developed so far.

Concepts can also deal with methods covering the individual steps of a design case study or research practices providing a perspective for a whole case study. The concepts of *integrated organization and technology development* (Wulf and Rohde 1995; Rohde 2007) or *infrastructuring* (Pipek and Wulf 2009) are examples for the last type of abstractions.

Concept building can also be grounded in partial design case studies, e.g., just containing a design-oriented empirical study of social practices and/or a study on the appropriation of an IT artifact. Indeed, many of the abovementioned conceptualizations were developed based on a partial design case study. However, we argue that full-fledged design case studies offer a more profound insight into the complex interaction of innovative IT artifacts and the supported social practices.

Based on a repository of design case studies, there is a vast variety of different perspectives for classifying, grouping, and comparing. As already stated, resulting abstractions can be built on different levels. In the following, we want to explore

comparative concept building on a more detailed level. In Sect. 7.6.1, we elaborate
on two concepts which have emerged from the complete design case studies *Location Tracker* and *Social Display*, conducted in the elderly domain. In Sect. 7.6.2,
we look in the domain of office work and elaborate on practice-oriented design of
access control mechanism. The concept building in Sect. 7.6.2 is based on partial
design case studies.

7.6.1   Concept Building in the AAL Domain

In the following, we first introduce two concepts which we think may help to better
understand specific aspects of the design space in the AAL domain. Then we will
reflect upon the concepts' emergence from a practically grounded perspective.

We suggested the first concept, (a) Grown and Constructed Autonomies, as
an abstract term to sensitize for a better understanding of specific features of
social practices in the AAL domain. We coined the second concept (b) Procedural
Interaction Design with which we would like to describe a principle for the IT design
for elderly people.

7.6.1.1   Grown and Constructed Autonomies

When we started our research, the provision and preservation of elderly peoples'
autonomy was considered a major goal, at least in government-funded European
research projects following the AAL agenda (Malanowski et al. 2008). In this
perspective, autonomy is basically understood as the ability to lead one's everyday
life as independently as possible. Technologies developed in this realm should serve
this target, and an autonomous appropriation of these technologies is taken for
granted. Autonomy then, one would assume, is a well-defined concept in directing
AAL research. However, when looking at elderly people with special cognitive
or physical needs, our design case studies have argued for differentiation of this
understanding.

Our research work in the field of dementia care showed a more nuanced picture
of autonomy-related thinking and acting. The handling of the topic in practice has
many more facets than seen so far in public discourses. This variety of facets
influences IT appropriation which is supposed to foster autonomy and lead to a
multitude of emerging practices.

Our initial approach to the field of dementia care was in the context of the
Location Tracker project. The project proposal had a strong focus on caregivers
in familial and institutional contexts rather than on the people with dementia
themselves because the caregivers were seen as the ones actually appropriating
the application. However, our interviews and participant observations directed our
view at a very early stage to the caregivers' value trade-offs between "autonomy
and privacy" and "autonomy and safety." These trade-offs found their instantiation

in relationship-based problems at microlevel, but were also interwoven in broader organizational, ethical, and legal problem spheres.

Autonomy was thus reflected and enacted differently in the various application contexts (cf. Wan et al. 2014). The situated enactment of the legal concept of "freedom-depriving measures" is a good example for our argument. In the nursing institutions interviewed, "freedom-depriving measures" were mentioned frequently by both the managers and the ward nurses as measures to be avoided. In Germany, such measures are forbidden by law; their initiation requires the ruling of a judge. However, what would count as such a measure was not always well defined. The participants in our study agreed on some core principles, such as not fixating residents to a chair or their beds without a court ruling or the fact that entrance doors to nursing homes must always be kept open. However, workloads on wards in some cases lead to practices which in effect had freedom-depriving effects but would not be easy to prosecute legally – such as heavy doors which could not be opened by a weak elderly person. Other institutions put, e.g., curtains on the doors to distract the wandering residents from finding the door.

The analysis of the interviews with family caregivers – husbands, wives, sons, and daughters – offers very different perspectives on the concept of autonomy of wandering patients. The differences range from one extreme to the other. In one case, where care took place in the home, the husband reported that he allowed very little freedom of movement to his wife, who is a dementia patient. When in their home, he would not allow her to be alone on another story for fear that she might hurt herself. Being a retired engineer himself, he developed coping mechanisms for their everyday life: he "engineered" her eating, sleeping, and bathroom habits by means of medication. In his understanding, autonomy was not a relevant issue to his wife as she was "no longer here" with her mind.

At the other extreme, the daughter of a woman suffering from the early stages of dementia has built a social network to collaboratively take care of her mother. Her mother was able to live independently in her own home and conduct everyday tasks – even go to the city – on her own. For the daughter, it is vital that her mother feels she is autonomous – and she has adopted many measures to "artificially" achieve this, such as asking shop assistants and bank clerks to give the mother what she wants, but only within reason. Sometimes the daughter "shadows" her mother on her way to town. From the daughter's perspective, her mother's ability to maintain a public and independent "face" is of primary importance.

In another case, a husband with dementia was taken care of by his wife and daughter at home. The women reported that the father had always had a dominant role in the family and a strongly independent attitude. Despite the onset of dementia, he continued to assert this dominance. He still took long walks on his own, leaving his family in a self-confessed position of helplessness. This, we discovered, is not uncommon in situations where female relatives have to cope with male dementia. This treatment of autonomy is quite different from the case of the husband who "engineered" the behavior of his dementia-suffering wife. His preexisting and continuing dominance in the family had actually helped him manage his wife's life with less resistance.

In the home context, we learned, families tailor care strategies to fit local conditions and needs. Each family has its own habitual familial pattern, such as structure, hierarchy, balancing between genders, and children vs. parent roles. Our empirical analysis indicated that preexisting life practices lead to completely different effects on the care concept when dementia occurs.

For many of the relatives, the classic value trade-off between safety and autonomy is of minor relevance in their decision-making, especially when the disease advances. Many relatives report primarily about the overwhelming burden of safety concerns with regard to family members who are dementia patients. So for them, keeping the patient safe is much more important than preserving the patient's autonomy. As Alzheimer's disease progresses, the patient's mental existence is often perceived as "fading away," and autonomy thus becomes less and less important for caregivers who put the symptoms of the disease at forefront.

It is a feature of such relationships that they engender a great deal of reflexive concern, contingently negotiated – which means autonomy is far from being a universal discourse to be used for organizing people's actions and behaviors (O'Connor and Purves 2009). In addition, current approaches in AAL research often neglect the social and interpersonal contexts in which actions and reflections on autonomy-related decisions occur.

What the studies strikingly have shown is that the term "autonomy" – and how this is used to talk about care practices for elderly persons – is manifold in its appearance in the practical context. It has implications on different levels, whether at a political, social, or practical level in the everyday work of caregivers (Müller et al. 2010). To stress interdependencies between increasing physical and cognitive decline of elderly persons and the respective needs for help of caregivers, Fitzpatrick et al. (2010) suggest the concept "dependable autonomies." This, however, seems to imply that autonomy might be conceptualized in stages or steps, which need a related adaptation of care measures when a disease progresses. From a practical perspective, this seems to be a helpful approach at an operational level. Our research, however, wishes to contribute to a better understanding of autonomy-related care situations from a more deconstructing perspective in questioning the rationales being used in care relationships toward concepts of personhood and how they are positioned in the related sociocultural contexts of families, care homes, etc. From this conceptual perspective, the deconstruction of autonomy in decision-making processes may open up new areas for improvement (O'Connor and Purves 2009). The analysis of our case studies makes visible the multiple and sometimes contradictory meanings the different measures and decisions taken by caregivers in dementia care imply. And they are rooted in personal value systems, in historic and habitualized developments of the patient-caregiver relationships, and in micro-political contexts, such as care home politics, or situated aspects, such as the actual health statuses of the patients. In addition, decisions in caregiving for an institutional patient or a relative at home can be consciously reflected, but also stem from habitualized activity and value patterns. This also implies that we need to better understand how situated care experiences are shaped by and embedded in broader societal contexts.

Authors in gerontology or care sciences point at the need to move beyond the focus on the individual to examine collective experiences and interrelational aspects in dementia care and to take up a more critical lens in order to implement new ways of thinking "about the place of autonomy (and arguably cognition) both within our society, but especially in the lives of persons with dementia" (O'Connor and Purves 2009: 206). For them, the task of deconstructing autonomy is a major first step toward envisioning personhood and for providing a useful framework for ethical decision-making. This is far more important for IT development, and our concept aims at challenging taken-for-granted assumptions of design teams and guiding their attention to a more holistic and deconstructive stance.

The *Social Display* design case study revealed yet another reference to how autonomy and self-determination are being negotiated and enacted, both by the elderly care home residents themselves and by the care staff. As reported above, the initial interview and observational studies in the care home showed a huge passivity on the residents' behalf and thus a great reluctance to engage in a common project with us. This was equally mirrored by many of the social workers who often told us that they did not think that many residents would be interested. That is the reason why we initially had to strongly convince the staff that the Internet Days might indeed be interesting for people who were mainly perceived as passive. In the end, all the social workers were extremely surprised that residents formerly perceived as passive started to engage so actively in the workshops. On the residents' side, the pre-study revealed their behavior and the way they thought of themselves as being strongly self-positioned at the margin of society, expressing sentiments such as "people do not care about old people like us, but that is just how it is." Thus, we were confronted with their self-image of being marginalized but also their huge acceptance of this issue.

Here, we furthermore learned that the caregivers' perceptions of what the residents would be able to do or in which topics they would be interested influenced the process at first. However, by dint of the Internet Day interventions, not only did the interests and motivations of the residents open up, but also those of the caregivers.

All in all, we see that the term "Grown and Constructed Autonomies" aids a better understanding of the design space in the analysis phase as well as in guiding actual design research methods.

In the *Location Tracker* case, the issue of stakeholder constructions of autonomy (and by this the evaluation of what a person with dementia should or should not be allowed in daily practice) points to the need of providing a communication area in the system in which collaborative caregiving and negotiation would be allowed to align individual views and to develop a more human viewpoint to the affected persons' everyday practice and needs. Various stakeholders with diverse backgrounds often have to align their approaches of thinking what good management of "wanderers" should be in regard of their conception of autonomy. That is why the IT system should enable mutual learning and negotiation around this issue – at system level, support must be provided for negotiation space on how functionalities should be adapted to manage the wandering of an individual person.

7.6.1.2 Procedural Interaction Design

We coined this term to highlight several issues which come to the foreground when designing with the very target group. The concept is relevant for the design phase as well as for the empirical work in the context of pre-studies and studies on appropriation.

The first aspect of the "procedural" is devoted to the target of building up a common design space with the partners of the very target group. The elderly people themselves with whom we worked as well as their caring social networks at home and in caregiving institutions can be described as not affine to new technologies and the Internet in most cases. There is also a lack of ability in articulating problems of their social practices in which design ideas are usually grounded. We therefore tried to find "anchor points" in the people's social practices which can serve as "tickets to talk" (Svensson and Sokoler 2008) to start a deeper conversation about issues of everyday life.

In the *Social Display* project, we organized workshops which helped the target group to develop a sense of how technology could be meaningful for their lives and for the caregivers' work with the elderly. Bringing in off-the-shelf technology in a very early phase turned out to be very helpful for two reasons: firstly, the collaborative search for interesting media content on the Internet could easily be linked to the elderly person's former or current experiences in a broad sense. For example, showing a music show from the 1960s was met with joy and excitement and could serve as a starting point for a further journey through the Internet to other anchor points bringing enjoyment to the elderly person. Secondly, the technology used at the Internet Days also served immediately as an experience-based example of what the residents might be able to achieve with modern technology, and it also afforded them hands-on experience. The mutual learning processes between the elderly, the staff, and the design team initiated by these interventions revealed anchors to former and current aspects of life practices which could be explored more deeply and from which meaningful design ideas could be derived.

In the *Location Tracker* project, we used a similar early intervention – however this time mainly with the caregivers. We discussed with them examples of off-the-shelf technologies and elaborated on their concerns to find their specific "anchor points."

For the design phase, another "procedural" element became important. We were confronted with problems of reminiscence in the care home. We therefore attempted to install a performing prototype as soon as possible in order to keep the residents on track and interested in our project. We rolled out the display offering only very simple functionality and reduced content to help the elderly become acquainted with the system. The first prototype version included a very simple color-coding system and reduced selection options. By doing this, we could lower the barrier to technology appropriation and were able to increase complexity in successive versions of the application. In addition, the technology and the media content during the workshop/Internet sessions as well as in the first functional prototype were kept similar in order to support the residents' ability of recognition and reminiscence.

7.6.2   Computer-Supported Access Control: Building Concepts by Comparing Cases

We have worked for a longer period of time on access control in cooperative work. When we started our research, the discourse on access control was merely framed by a technical perspective. The given concepts suggested how to design access control in the sense of a technical functionality (Lampson 1974; Shen and Dewan 1992).

We conducted empirical research investigating how access to data was controlled across three different organizational settings: a state representative body, a federal ministry, and an editorial office (Stiemerling and Wulf 2000). In the first two cases, we observed access control practice dealing with a groupware application; in the third case, we observed access control to paper documents. Comparing the three empirical cases, we could identify three factors which were relevant elements of the observed practices of controlling access:

1. The control of access could be delegated to an actor who was not the owner of the data to be accessed (third person).
2. Actors who accessed the protected item could be tracked and made accountable (awareness).
3. The legitimacy of a certain attempt to access the groupware application was negotiated among those who wanted to have access and those who granted access (negotiation).

In the first two cases, the observed elements of practice had to be realized in circumventing the implemented access control functionality. An analysis of the state of the art indicated that these elements of practices were not yet supported by technical functionality. As inspiration to design access control functionality in an innovative manner, we related back to earlier work on conflict management when activating groupware functions (Wulf 1997; Wulf et al. 2001). Considering access to data to be a potentially contested activation of a function, we transferred and adapted design concepts to this particular case. Based on these concepts, we implemented a prototype which supported negotiating over access to data by means of a semi-structured communication protocol (Stiemerling and Wulf 2000). This design case study remained fractal since it fell short of an evaluation in practice.

In a fourth case study, we investigated access to a steel mill's central drawings archive. The steel mill was maintained cooperatively by an internal work unit and external engineering offices. The drawings were stored on paper, on fiches, and, partly digitally, in a central archive and its database. We investigated empirically how the external engineers' access was controlled, considering the existence of different media and a historically grown classification scheme. Controlling access appeared to be a highly situated activity which was not well enough supported technically, specifically for granting permission remotely to the external offices.

Looking more systematically at the temporal structure when access permissions were granted, we were able to differentiate between three cases:

- Ex ante control: if permission has been defined before the access takes place
- Uno tempore control: if permission is defined at the moment of access
- Ex post control: if permission is checked after access has taken place

Based on the empirical findings, we built a prototypical access control system in extending the steel mill's database. To support different access control strategies, the application was built using software components which could be (re-)assembled by users during runtime. We involved the different internal and external engineers in both lining out the set of components and defining suitable access control functionality. However, this design case study fell short of a long-term evaluation in practice.

In a final journal paper, we elaborated more fundamentally on the four fragments of design case studies. The first step was to suggest the conceptual differentiation between the social practice of controlling access to data/resources ("computer-supported access control (CSAC)") and the IT functionality which supports this social practice ("CSAC system"). This distinction enables us to discuss in a more differentiated manner how to complement practices by IT design. In our earlier publications, the design approaches were based on the assumption that given CSAC practices were insufficiently supported because (1) awareness is only possible in physical proximity; a technical substitute would be needed in a more distributed setting; (2) negotiations happened either face to face or by means of external media, such as telephone; and an integration of a (semi-structured) communication channel into the CSAC system would better enable the direct implementation of the negotiation's outcome (Stevens and Wulf 2009).

Comparing the four cases with regard to the different design approaches, we were able to describe the design space for CSAC in a more systematic manner. A two-dimensional matrix classified the different approaches according (a) to the temporal relationship between the legitimation of access and the access attempt taken from Stevens and Wulf (2002) and (b) to the mode of interaction, specifically awareness, protection, and negotiation. The second dimension was an elaboration of the classification scheme emerging from Wulf et al. (2001) and Stiemerling and Wulf (2000). Based on these two dimensions, the given technical mechanisms could be classified. By comparing different implementations of CSAC systems, we were able to extract further design requirements – specifically with regard to modularization of their implementation.

7.6.3   Discussion: Concept Building in an Environment of Competing Claims

We have presented two domains in which we have explicated sensitizing concepts based on a comparison of different design case studies. Following Blumer (1954), we understand these concepts as suggestions to consider a certain perspective on design in practice. In this sense, they can be seen as condensates of practice-based research.

The sensitizing concepts cover quite different aspects of a design case study. In Sect. 7.6.1, we elaborated on the concept of Grown and Constructed Autonomies to frame a certain perspective on practices in care settings. The concept of Procedural Interaction Design describes the procedural experiences we gathered when working for and with the elderly. For the development of a first working prototype, we also were able to describe specific aspects in actual design. In Sect. 7.6.2, our first conceptualizations dealt with recurrent elements of access practices. While exploring design opportunities for unsupported elements of these practices, we were able to describe the design space for technical implementations of access control in a new and systematic manner. Finally, a practice-based analysis of the fractal design case studies allowed us to reflect upon the relationship between access practices and technical control mechanisms. We labeled such a research perspective "computer-supported access control."

The very nature of the data generated in design case studies positions concept building into a certain epistemological tradition. This tradition is often at odds with prevalent styles of concept building. Our research approach is strongest where it offers empirical data or design-oriented insights which contradict or extend the findings of given research traditions. The conceptual work in the domain of access control is a good example of how our research tradition can help to develop design concepts beyond the mainstream understanding in computer science; see the extension of the Lampson matrix in Stevens and Wulf (2009).

When pursuing design in certain domains, we are occasionally confronted with the fact that the academic discourse has not yet dealt with it at all or, at least, not in a design-relevant manner. For instance, we could not identify any academic work which had described or conceptualized the navigation practices of firefighters in burning buildings in a manner suitable to ground design. In the gerontology domain, we found care and aging theories which were mainly quantitative in method and context unspecific regarding its findings. At this level, we found competing theories which came to contradictory conclusions, e.g., in analyzing the wandering symptom of early Alzheimer patients. While the gerontological discourse postulated that person-centered care would be the standard approach in Germany, detailed descriptions of caring practices were rather scarce. Our design-oriented studies revealed a much more nuanced view on caring practice. In the mainstream of design-oriented research, a profound level of interdisciplinary cooperation was missing.

However, the state of the art still plays a central role in our work in generating sensitizing concepts. The state of the art in epistemologically related fields shapes our thinking and allows us to identify concepts from our design-oriented work. For instance, when postulating the concept of "computer-supported access control," we drew on two decades of work in the CSCW community.

Pursuing academic innovation in a nonmainstream paradigm can also lead to complications in practice. The world view of the practitioners we work with is often framed by a mainstream understanding often shaped by professional and educational institutions. We observed these phenomena in the aging domain. The prevalent concepts there do not match up with a practice-based perspective on the analysis of the existent and the design for the future. For instance, the gerontological mainstream has not dealt much with computer support in engaging people of an advanced age in residential homes. The few studies which do exist consider IT to be either not necessary or not successful in these contexts. The caregivers were therefore quite skeptical when they began to work with us. Yet our design-oriented explorations revealed a rather considerable potential in improving the residents' quality of life.

We still have little experience regarding how our approach to concept building supports the transfer of design-relevant issues and insights. We believe that the sensitizing concepts need to be understood as linked to the design case studies they are derived from.

7.7 Discussion

The work with sensitizing concepts is an important bottom-up strategy to develop relevant themes from different design case studies (DCS). For each of the studies above, we were able to derive domain theories that helped to analyze the practices observed and informed design. One of the main perspectives for establishing DCS as an empirical tool is to devote more attention to the emergence of new/changed practices in connection with innovative information technology. The appropriation of a new technology is often a very complex process that is not only influenced by the characteristics of the new technology and the landscape of experiences and needs that lead to the initiative of becoming involved with this new technology and to the requirements that informed the development process. That landscape may have changed significantly during the development phase and during/after the technology introduction, and alternative technological or non-technological solutions may have surfaced along the way – with unforeseeable consequences. The art of conducting a DCS is to be able to capture this richness of relevant developments, although one may have had an initial (technological) idea to follow and although much effort may have gone into making this idea a new software artifact. As these developments may take their time, the appropriation phase cannot be considered finished at a certain point; it merely merges into the "normal" emerging practice of the field. For a design case study, it may even make sense to revisit a field a decade after the technology was introduced and to look for the traces that the then new technology and the discourses around it left behind and to reconsider the level of "success" that can be associated with this technology development project.

It is obvious that if we want to consider and acknowledge the various contributions that led to this level of "success," we can not only look at the actors and activities that contributed to the final shape of the technology product at hand; we further want to look at the actors and activities that contributed to the shape of the technology usages that emerged. If we consider the narrower environment of the technology development process, we are likely to be able to come up with rather well-structured descriptions of actors, their roles, and their activities, as these may already be suggested by the technology development methods that have been used (e.g., the Rational Unified Process, Agile Software Development methods, etc.). This is much more difficult with the wider field of actors and activities. Even participatory design methodologies that are already more sensitive toward contributions from the field of practice often remain focused on the product (as a design result) and the project (the planned process that guided the mutual exchanges between technology developers and existing/future users) and cannot guide good descriptions outside this scope.

7.7.1 Tensions Between Research-/Development-Based and Practice-Based Thinking

Orlikowski (1996b) started a discourse on practice-based research that focused on the events and actions that made a particular practice emerge. She made explicit that a further development of technology-based practices ("organizational change") is far from being the plannable, organized process that development process models usually assume when they talk about "introduction" as a final phase of development. In research-/development-oriented thinking, a defined, structured process is necessary to organize the work around creating an IT artifact, and this is what process models in software engineering and information systems design do. "Organizational change" is often a spontaneous, challenge-based, or opportunity-based phenomenon that does not align well with the structuring perspectives of these technology development methods, with the time frames to consider being the maybe most obvious asynchronicity: development and research projects having a fixed time frame in which the resources of researchers and programmers are allocated, practice as an evolving phenomenon emerges at speed, and a resource investment that strictly follows practice-internal needs and considerations. Although there have been tendencies to overcome the project/product focus (e.g., Dittrich 2014 looks beyond the project as an entity of activity in software engineering, Hanseth and Lundberg 2001 argue in favor of speaking about "infrastructure improvement" rather than of "information systems design"), we would argue the necessity of establishing a level playing field for describing the various actors, roles, and activities with a similar level of detail for those parts of a study that are concerned with the professionalized field of technology development and its related domain models, as well as those parts of the study that are concerned with the emerging/changing practices in the field. Earlier, we (Pipek and Wulf 2009) suggested a theoretical framework of "infrastructuring" for this purpose.

7.7.2 Infrastructural Breakdowns and the Point of Infrastructure

The term "infrastructuring" has been used occasionally earlier, but a consistent description of its potential has only been provided by Star and Bowker (2002), and it was first used in that sense by Karasti and Baker (2004).

Project-based thinking usually assumes that the project goal is so important that all stakeholders are involved with a level of attention that matches their project role. With "infrastructural" thinking, practice emerges along discrete events that bring infrastructural issues into the focus of attention of the stakeholders affected. From their perspective, Star labeled these events "breakdowns." We wanted to have a broader and deeper understanding of the attention economy around technological infrastructures and called that event the "point of infrastructure" (POI) (Pipek and Wulf 2009).

On these occasions, the invisibility/transparency that infrastructures usually have during use ends and issues concerning the extension or reconfiguration of an infrastructure come to the fore. These are the occasions when practitioners are "by nature" able and willing to engage in a discourse about the future developments of an infrastructure and about the associated reconfigurations that lead to a changed practice.

Within the context of DCS, these concepts are important to consider on three occasions:

- When relevant practitioners decide to engage in a design case study, the researchers may assume that there have already been several "points of infrastructure" that lead to relevant insights and attitudes. During a pre-study, this element of the practices' historicity should be captured and acknowledged.
- During the pre-study, it makes sense to actively look for potential discrepancies between what the work infrastructure provides and what is perceived as necessary or interesting by the workers. These are potentials for "points of infrastructure" to be explored during the design case study. During the course of the study, more "points of infrastructure" may occur that need to be acknowledged to inspire and inform good design.
- The introduction of a new technology that results from the (participatory) design activities is an additional "point of infrastructure."

On these occasions, empirical work within the framework could take "points of infrastructure" as a sensitizing concept to reflect upon the infrastructure development that practitioners engage in.

7.8 Conclusion

Design case studies can be understood to be empirical investigations into interventions which explore the potentials of an innovatively designed IT artifact. The direction of the empirical pre-study is broadly defined by a technological potential available but not yet explored in (this) context. Therefore, design case study-based research is driven by new technologies as much as by societal problems and potentials. They are a means to understanding the opportunities in encouraging social innovation by introducing appropriately designed IT applications (cf. Pipek and Wulf 2009). Thus, they allow the understanding of the quality of design by its effects in practice. To reach such an understanding, a long-term engagement with the relevant domains of social practice is important. It is required to gain sufficient commitment from the practitioners in the design process and to allow for the investigation into changing practices during IT appropriation. The findings of such a single design case study are highly specific to the social context they take place in. Their results do not allow for simple generalizations; their transferability into other contexts needs to be considered with care. We, therefore, suggest building a corpus of well-documented design case studies. We hope that the contextualized description of the social practices, the IT design, and its appropriation, together with a link to the authors of the study, may enable other researchers and practitioners to transfer findings to their own contexts. The transferability of findings is supported by the creation of sensitizing concepts which are grounded in individual case studies. Following Blumer's (1954) tradition, these concepts do not claim general validity. We understand sensitizing concepts rather to be an offer to the reader to be aware of condensed insights and a pointer to more contextualized results – documented in the original case studies. We believe that the discourse on "infrastructuring" (Bowker and Star 1999; Pipek and Wulf 2009) provides interesting perspectives to conduct, document, and compare different design case studies. Rather than pruning the research questions and methodology poorly according to technological design opportunities, we would like a case study to be a unit whose coherence in presentation is mainly shaped by the practices undergoing investigation. Our research approach needs to find an often delicate balance between relevance defined from the practitioners' point of view with relevance and rigor emerging from the researchers' academic practice.

We are still at the beginning of the research program outlined in this paper. Its viability still has to be proven empirically.

References

Bentley, R., Hughes, J. A., Randall, D., Rodden, T., Sawyer, P., Shapiro, D., & Somerville, I. (1992). Ethnographically-informed systems design for air traffic control. In *Proceedings of CSCW '92: sharing perspectives (November 2–4, Toronto, Canada)* (pp. 123–129). New York: ACM Press.
Blomberg, J., Suchman, L., & Trigg, R. (1996). Reflections on a work-oriented design project. *Human-Computer Interaction, 11*(3), 237–265.
Blumer, H. (1954). What's wrong with social theory? *American Sociological Review, 1954*, 3–10.
Bourdieu, P. (1977). *Outline of a theory of practice.* Cambridge: Cambridge University Press.
Bourdieu, P. (1990). *The logic of practice.* Cambridge: Polity Press.

Bowker, G., & Star, S. L. (1999). *Sorting things out*. Cambridge, MA: MIT Press.

Braa, K., & Vidgen, R. (1999). Interpretation, intervention, and reduction in the organizational laboratory: A framework for in-context information system research. *Accounting, Management and Information Technologies, 9*, 25–47.

Brödner, P., Rohde, M., Stevens, G., Betz, M., & Wulf, V. (2015). Grounded design – A praxeological IS research perspective (Submitted for publication).

Chi, E., Czerwinski, M., Millen, D., Randall, D., Stevens, G., Wulf, V., & Zimmermann, J. (2011). *Transferability of research findings: Context-dependent or model-driven. CHI extended abstracts* (pp. 651–654). New York: ACM Press.

Crabtree, A. (1998). Ethnography in participatory design. In *Proceedings of the PDC'98* (pp. 93–105). New York: ACM Press.

Dachtera, J., Randall, D., & Wulf, V. (2014). Research on research: Design research at the margins: Academia, industry and end-users. In *Proceedings of ACM conference on computer human interaction (CHI 2014)* (pp. 713–722). New York: ACM Press.

Davis, F. D. (1989). Perceived usefulness, perceived ease of use, and user acceptance of information technology. *MIS Quarterly, 13*, 319–340. doi:10.2307/249008.

DeSanctis, G., & Poole, M. S. (1994). Capturing the complexity in advanced technology use: Adaptive structuration theory. *Organization Science, 5*(2), 121–147.

Disalvo, C., Clement, A., & Pipek, V. (2012). Communities: Participatory design for, with, and by communities. In J. Simonsen & T. Robertson (Eds.), *International handbook of participatory design* (pp. 182–209). Oxford: Routledge.

Dittrich, Y. (2014). Software engineering beyond the project – Sustaining software ecosystems. *Information and Software Technology, 56*, 1436–1456. doi:10.1016/j.infsof.2014.02.012.

Dörner, C. (2010). *Tailoring software infrastructures: Integration of end-user development and service-oriented architectures*. Eul: Josef Eul Verlag GmbH.

Dourish, P. (2006). Implications for design. In *Proceedings of ACM conference human factors in computing systems CHI 2006 (Montreal, Canada)* (pp. 541–550). New York: ACM Press.

Draxler, S., Stevens, G., & Boden, A. (2015). Keeping the development environment up to date – A study of the situated practices of appropriating the eclipse IDE. In *IEEE Transactions on Software Engineering*. IEEE explore (online resource).

Ehn, P. (2008, October 01–04). Participation in design things. In *Proceedings of the tenth anniversary conference on participatory design 2008* (pp. 92–101). Bloomington/Indianapolis: Indiana University.

Fitzpatrick, G., Balaam, M., Axelrod, L., Harris, E., McAllister, G., et al. (2010). Designing for Rehabilitation at Home. In *Proceedings of workshop on Interactive Systems in Healthcare, Atlanta April (2010)* (pp. 49–52). Workshop Paper.

Floyd, C., Reisin F.-M., & Schmidt G. (1989). STEPS to software development with users. In *2nd European conference on software engineering (ESEC'89)*, Coventry, UK.

Floyd, C., Mehl, W.-M., Resin, F.-M., Schmidt, G., & Wolf, G. (1991). Out of Scandinavia: Alternative approaches to software design and system development. *Human–Computer Interaction, 4*(4), 253–350.

Forlizzi, J. (2008). The product ecology: Understanding social product use and supporting design culture. *International Journal of Design, 2*(1), 11–20.

Fuchs, L. (1998). Situation-oriented support of group awareness in CSCW systems. PhD Thesis, Department of Mathematics and Computer Science, University of Essen, Germany.

Fuchs, L., Sohlenkamp, M., Genau, A., Pfeifer, A., Kahler, H., & Wulf, V. (1996). Transparenz in kooperativen Prozessen – Der Ereignisdienst in POLITeam. In H. Krcmar, H. Lewe, G. Schwabe (Hrsg.) *Herausforderung Telekooperation (Proceedings der DCSCW'96, 30.9. – 2.10.1996 in Stuttgart-Hohenheim)* (pp. 3–16). Berlin: Springer.

Garfinkel, H. (1967). *Studies in ethnomethodology*. Englewood Cliffs: Prentice Hall.

Gaver, W. (2012). What should we expect from research through design? In *Proceedings of ACM conference on computer human interaction (CHI 2012)* (pp. 937–946). New York: ACM Press.
Giddens, A. (1979). *Central problems in social theory*. London: Macmillan.
Giddens, A. (1984). *The constitution of society. Outline of the theory of structuration*. Cambridge: Polity Press.
Greenbaum, J., & Kyng, M. (Eds.). (1991). *Design at work – Cooperative design of computer systems*. Hillsdale: Lawrence Erlbaum.
Hanseth, O., & Lundberg, N. (2001). Designing work oriented infrastructures. *Computer Supported Cooperative Work: The Journal of Collaborative Computing, 10*(3–4), 347–372.
Hanseth, O., Monteiro, E., & Hatling, M. (1996). Developing information infrastructure: The tension between standardization and flexibility. *Science, Technology & Human Values, 21*(4), 407–426.
Heath, C., & Luff, P. (1991). Collaborative activity and technological design: Task coordination in London underground control rooms. In *Proceedings of the second European conference on computer supported cooperative work (ECSCW 1991)* (pp. 65–80). Dordrecht: Kluwer.
Henderson, A., & Kyng, M. (1991). There's no place like home: Continuing design in use. In J. Greenbaum & M. Kyng (Eds.), *Design at work – Cooperative design of computer artifacts* (pp. 219–240). Hillsdale: Lawrence Erlbaum Associates.
Hevner, A., & Chatterjee, S. (2010). *Design research in information systems*. New York: Springer.
Hevner, A. R., March, S. G., Park, J., & Ram, S. (2004). Design science in: Information systems research. *MIS Quarterly, 28*(1), 75–105.
Hinrichs, J., Pipek, V., & Wulf, V. (2005). Context grabbing: Assigning metadata in large document collections. In *Proceedings of the ninth European conference on computer supported cooperative work (ECSCW 2005)* (pp. 367–386). Dordrecht: Springer.
Hughes, J. A., Randall, D., & Shapiro, D. (1992). Faltering from ethnography to design. In *Proceedings of CSCW '92: sharing perspectives (November 2–4, Toronto, Canada)* (pp. 115–122). New York: ACM Press.
Hughes, J., King, V., Rodden, T., & Anderson, H. (1995). The role of ethnography in interactive systems design. *Interactions, 2*(2), 56–65.
Huysman, M., & Wulf, V. (Eds.). (2004). *Social capital and information technology*. Cambridge, MA: MIT-Press.
Huysman, M., & Wulf, V. (2006). IT to support knowledge sharing in communities: Towards a social capital analysis. *Journal of Information Technology (JIT), 21*(1), 40–51.
Karasti, H. (2001). Bridging work practice and system design: Integrating systemic analysis, appreciative intervention and practitioner participation. *Computer Supported Cooperative Work (CSCW), 10*(2), 211–246. doi:10.1023/A:1011239126617.
Karasti, H., & Baker, K. S. (2004). Infrastructuring for the long-term: Ecological information management. In *Proceedings of the 37th annual Hawaii international conference on system sciences, 2004*. doi:10.1109/HICSS.2004.1265077.
Karasti, H., & Syrjänen, A.-L. (2004). Artful infrastructuring in two cases of community PD. In *Proceedings of the eighth conference on participatory design: Artful integration: Interweaving media, materials and practices* (pp. 20–30). doi:10.1145/1011870.1011874.
Karsten, H., & Jones, M. (1998). The long and winding road: Collaborative IT and organisational change. In *International conference on computer supported work (CSCW'98)*. New York: ACM Press.
Kensing, F., Simonsen, J., & Bodker, K. (1998). MUST: A method for participatory design. *Human–Computer Interaction, 13*(2), 167–198.
Kuutti, K., & Bannon, L. J. (2014). The turn to practice in HCI: Towards a research agenda. In *Proceedings of CHI '14* (pp. 3543–3552). Berlin: Springer.
Lampson, B. (1974). Protection. *ACM Operating Systems Review, 8*, 18–24.
Latour, B. (1993). *We have never been modern*. Cambridge: Harvard University Press.
Ley, B., Pipek, V., Reuter, C., & Wiedenhoefer, T. (2012). Supporting improvisation work in inter-organizational crisis management. In *Proceedings of ACM conference on computer human interaction (CHI 2012)* (pp. 1529–1538). New York: ACM Press.

Malanowski, N., Özcivelek, R., & Cabrera, M. (2008). *Active ageing and independent living services: The role of information and communication technology. JRC41496*. Luxembourg: Office for Official Publications of the European Communities.

Mathiassen, L. (2002). Collaborative practice research. *Information Technology & People, 15*(4), 321–345.

Millen, D. R. (2000). Rapid ethnography: Time deepening strategies for HCI field research. In *Proceedings of the DIS '00* (pp. 280–286). New York: ACM Press.

Müller, C., Wan, L., & Hrg, D. (2010). Dealing with wandering: A case study on caregivers' attitudes towards privacy and autonomy when reflecting the use of LBS. In *Proceedings of GROUP conference 2010, November 7–10*, Sanibel Island, Florida, USA.

Müller, C., Neufeldt, C., Randall, D., & Wulf, V. (2012, May 05–10). ICT-Development in residential care settings: Sensitizing design to the life circumstances of the residents of a care home. In *Proceedings of ACM-CHI 2012*. Austin: ACM Press.

Müller, C., Wan, L., & Wulf, V. (2013, May 5–8). Dealing with wandering in institutional care: Exploring the field. In *7th international conference on pervasive computing technologies for healthcare (PervasiveHealth 2013)* (pp. 101–104), Venice, Italy. Venice: EAI Publications.

Ngwenyama, O. K. (1998). Groupware, social action and organizational emergence: On the process dynamics of computer mediated distributed work. *Accounting, Management and Information Technologies, 8*(4), 123–143.

O'Connor, D., & Purves, B. (2009). *Decision-making, personhood and dementia: Exploring the interface*. London: Jessica Kingsley Publishers.

Ogonowski, C., Ley, B., Hess, J., Wan, L., & Wulf, V. (2013). Designing for the living room: Long-term user involvement in a living lab. In *Proceedings of ACM conference on computer human interaction (CHI 2013)* (pp. 1539–1548). New York: ACM Press.

Orlikowski, W. J. (1992). The duality of technology: Rethinking the concept of technology in organizations. *Organization Science, 3*(3), 398–427.

Orlikowski, W. J. (1996a). Evolving with notes: Organizational change around groupware technology. In C. Ciborra (Ed.), *Groupware & teamwork* (pp. 23–60). Chichester et al.: Wiley.

Orlikowski, W. J. (1996b). Improvising organizational transformation over time: A situated change perspective. *Information Systems Research, 7*(1), 63–92.

Orlikowski, W. J., & Hofman, J. D. (1997). An improvisational model for change management: The case of groupware technology. *Sloan Management Review*, (Winter), Cambridge, MIT, 11–21.

Pipek, V. (2005). From tailoring to appropriation support: Negotiating groupware usage. Oulu: Faculty of Science, Department of Information Processing Science, University of Oulu.

Pipek, V., & Wulf, V. (1999). A groupware's life. In *Proceedings of the sixth European conference on computer supported cooperative work (ECSCW '99)*. Dordrecht: Kluwer.

Pipek, V., & Wulf, V. (2003). Pruning the answer garden: Knowledge sharing in maintenance engineering. In *Proceedings of the eighth European conference on computer supported cooperative work (ECSCW 2003)* (pp. 1–20). Dordrecht: Kluwer.

Pipek, V., & Wulf, V. (2009, May). Infrastructuring: Towards an integrated perspective on the design and use of information technology. *Journal of the Association of Information System (JAIS), 10*(5), 306–332.

Piper, A. M., Campbell, R., & Hollan, J. D. (2010). Exploring the accessibility and appeal of surface computing for older adult health care support. In *Proceeding of CHI 2010* (pp. 907–916). New York: ACM Press.

Ramírez, L. (2012). *Practice-centered support for indoor navigation: Design of a ubicomp platform for firefighters*, PhD thesis, Fakultät III Wirtschaftswissenschaften, Wirtschaftsinformatik und Wirtschaftsrecht, University of Siegen.

Ramirez, L., Betz, M., Dyrks, T., Scholz, M., Gerwinski, J., & Wulf, V. (2012). Landmarke – An ad hoc deployable ubicomp infrastructure to support indoor navigation of firefighters. *Personal and Ubiquitous Computing (PUC), 16*(8), 1025–1038.

Reckwitz, A. (2002). Toward a theory of social practices: A development in culturalist theorizing. *European Journal of Social Theory, 5*(2), 243–263.

Reichling, T., & Veith, M. (2005). Expertise sharing in a heterogeneous organizational environment. In *Proceedings of the ninth European conference on computer supported cooperative work* (pp. 325–345). Dordrecht: Springer.

Reichling, T., & Wulf, V. (2009). Expert recommender systems in practice: Evaluating semi-automatic profile generation. In *Proceedings of ACM conference on computer human interaction (CHI 2009)* (pp. 59–68). New York: ACM Press.

Reichling, T., Schubert, K., & Wulf, V. (2005). Matching human actors based on their texts: Design and evaluation of an instance of the expert finding framework. In *Proceedings of GROUP 2005* (pp. 61–70). New York: ACM Press.

Reichling, T., Veith, M., & Wulf, V. (2007). Expert recommender: Designing for a network organization. *Computer Supported Cooperative Work: The Journal of Collaborative Computing (JCSCW), 16*(4–5), 431–465.

Rohde, M. (2007). *Integrated organization and technology development (OTD) and the impact of socio-cultural concepts – A CSCW perspective*. Datalogiske skrifter, University of Roskilde.

Rohde, M., Stevens, G., Brödner, P., & Wulf, V. (2009). Towards a paradigmatic shift in IS: Designing for social practice. In *Proceedings of the 4th international conference on design science research in information systems and technology (DESRIST 2009)*. New York: ACM Press, Article 15.

Saeed, S., Rohde, M., & Wulf, V. (2011). Analyzing political activists' organization practices: Findings from a long term case study of the European social forum. *Computer Supported Cooperative Work: The Journal of Collaborative Computing (JCSCW), 20*(4–5), 265–304.

Schmidt, K. (2011). *Cooperative work and coordinative practices*. Contributions to the Conceptual Foundations of Computer-Supported Cooperative Work (CSCW), London u.a.

Sein, M. K., Henfridsson, O., Purao, S., Rossi, M., & Lindgren, R. (2012). Action design research. *MIS Quarterly, 35*(1), 37–56.

Shen, H., & Dewan, P. (1992). Access control for collaborative environments. In *Proceedings of the ACM conference on computer-supported cooperative work (CSCW 2002)* (pp. 51–58). New York: ACM Press.

Simon, H. A. (1996). *The sciences of the artificial* (3rd ed.). Cambridge, MA: MIT Press.

Star, S. L., & Bowker, G. C. (2002). How to infrastructure. In L. A. Lievrouw & S. Livingstone (Eds.), *Handbook of new media – Social shaping and consequences of ICTs* (pp. 151–162). London: Sage.

Star, S. L., & Ruhleder, K. (1996). Steps towards an ecology of infrastructure: Design and access for large information spaces. *Information Systems Research, 7*(1), 111–134.

Stevens, G., & Wulf, V. (2002). A new dimension in access control: Studying maintenance engineering across organizational boundaries. In *Proceedings of ACM conference on computer supported cooperative work (CSCW 2002)* (pp. 196–205). New York: ACM Press.

Stevens, G., & Wulf, V. (2009). Computer-supported access control. *ACM Transactions on Computer Human Interaction (ToCHI), 16*(3), Article 12.

Stiemerling, O., & Wulf, V. (2000). Beyond "Yes and No" – Extending access control in groupware with awareness and negotiation. *Group Decision and Negotiation, 9*(2000), 221–235.

Stiemerling, O., Wulf, V., & Rohde, M. (1998). Integrated organization and technology development – The case of the OrgTech-Project. In: *Proceedings of concurrent engineering (CE 98)* (181–187), July, 13–15, Tokyo.

Stolterman, E. (2008). The nature of design practice and implications for interaction design research. *International Journal of Design, 2*(1), 55–65.

Suchman, L. (1986). *Plans and situated action: The problem of human-machine communication*. Cambridge: Cambridge University Press.

Suchman, L. (2002). Located accountabilities in technology production. *Scandinavian Journal of Information Systems, 14*(2), 91–105.

Suchman, L., Blomberg, J., Orr, J. E., & Trigg, R. (1999). Reconstructing technologies as social practice. *American Behavioral Scientist, 43*(3), 392–408. doi:10.1177/00027649921955335.

Svensson, M. S., & Sokoler, T. (2008). Ticket-to-talk-television: Designing for the circumstantial nature of everyday social interaction. In *Proceedings of NordiCHI 2008* (pp. S. 334–S. 343). New York: ACM Press.

Törpel, B., Pipek, V., & Rittenbruch, M. (2003). Creating heterogeneity – Evolving use of groupware in a network of freelancers. Special issue on evolving use of froupware. *Computer Supported Cooperative Work: The Journal of Collaborative Computing (JCSCW), 12*(1–2), 381–409.

Turner, M., Kitchenham, B., Brereton, P., Charters, S., & Budgen, D. (2010). Does the technology acceptance model predict actual use? A systematic literature review. *Information and Software Technology, 52*(5), 463–479. doi:http://dx.doi.org/10.1016/j.infsof.2009.11.005.

Twidale, M. B. (2005). Over the shoulder learning: Supporting brief informal learning. *Computer Supported Cooperative Work, 14*(6), 505–547.

Venkatesh, V., & Davis, F. D. (2000). A theoretical extension of the technology acceptance model: Four longitudinal field studies. *Management Science*. doi:10.1287/mnsc.46.2.186.11926.

Venkatesh, V., Morris, M., Davis, G., & Davis, F. (2003). User acceptance of information technology: Toward a unified view. *MIS Quarterly, 27*, 425–478. doi:10.2307/30036540.

von Hippel, E. (2005). *Democratizing innovation*. Cambridge, MA: MIT Press.

Walsham, G. (2006). Doing interpretive research. *European Journal of Information Systems, 15*, 320–330.

Wan, L., Müller, C., Wulf, V., & Randall, D. (2014). Addressing the subtleties in dementia care: Pre-study & evaluation of a GPS monitoring system. In *Proceedings of ACM conference on computer human interaction (CHI 2014)* (pp. 3987–3996). New York: ACM Press.

Whyte, W. F. (1991). *Participatory action research*. Newbury Park: Sage.

Wulf, V. (1997). Konfliktmanagement bei Groupware, Vieweg, Braunschweig und Wiesbaden 1997, Zugleich: Dissertation Universität Dortmund 1996.

Wulf, V. (1999). Evolving cooperation when introducing groupware – A self-organization perspective. *Cybernetics and Human Knowing, 6*(2), 55–75.

Wulf, V. (2000). Exploration Environments: Supporting Users to Learn Groupware Functions. *Interacting with Computers, 13*(2), 265–299.

Wulf, V. (2009). Theorien sozialer Praktiken als zur Elemente zur Fundierung der Wirtschaftsinformatik. In J. Becker, H. Krcmar, & B. Niehaves (Hrsg.), *Wissenschaftstheorie und Gestaltungsorientierte Wirtschaftsinformatik* (pp. 211–224). Berlin: Springer.

Wulf, V., & Rohde, M. (1995). Towards an integrated organization and technology development. In *Proceedings DIS '95, symposium on designing interactive systems: Processes, practices, methods, and techniques* (pp. 55–65). New York: ACM Press.

Wulf, V., & Rohde, M. (1996). Reducing conflicts in Groupware: Metafunctions and their empirical evaluation. *International Journal on Behaviour and Information Technology, 15*(6), 339–351.

Wulf, V., Pipek, P., & Pfeifer, A. (2001). Resolving function-based conflicts in groupware systems. *AI and Society, 15*, 233–262.

Wulf, V., Pipek, V., & Won, M. (2008). Component-based tailorability: Towards highly flexible software applications. *International Journal on Human-Computer Studies (IJHCS), 66*(1), 1–22.

Wulf, V., Rohde, M., Pipek, V., & Stevens, G. (2011). Engaging with practices: Design case studies as a research framework in CSCW. In *Proceedings of ACM conference on computer supported cooperative work (CSCW 2011)* (pp. 505–512). New York: ACM Press.

Zimmerman, J., Stolterman, E., & Forlizzi, J. (2010). An analysis and critique of research through design: Toward a formalization of a research approach. In *ACMDIS 2010* (pp. 310–319). New York: ACM Press.

Chapter 8
A View of Causation for CSCW: Manipulation and Control in the Material Field of Work

Lars R. Christensen and Olav W. Bertelsen

In this chapter, we attempt to achieve a better understanding of how cooperative work is partly accomplished by virtue of the actors' manipulation and control of causal relationships central to their material field of work. Previous CSCW studies have *not* focused extensively on causation in cooperative work (e.g. see Schmidt and Bannon 2013). Consequently, it is a challenge to find a conception of causation appropriate for the study of cooperative work. This chapter addresses this challenge.

Inspired by manipulability conceptions of causation (e.g. Gasking 1955; Pearl 2009; von Wright 1971; Woodward 2003), we focus on causal relationships in the material field of work that are potentially exploitable for purposes of manipulation and control by the cooperative actors. This is a practical approach to causations with human agency at the centre – often we find that cooperative actors are focused on causation in order to change some feature of their world.

Our empirical data originate from two studies of cooperative work, namely, a study of chemotherapy and a study of the building process. The first study shows that in chemotherapy the actors are manipulating and controlling the causal relationship between drugs and cancer cells. The second study of causation shows that actors in the building process are engaged in understanding and manipulating the causal relationships between the building in the making and the forces of nature. Combined, the two studies point to the centrality of causation in cooperative work. More precisely, the cases show that the cooperative actors are systematically engaged in understanding, manipulating and controlling causal relationships making up their material field of work.

L.R. Christensen (✉)
IT University of Copenhagen, Copenhagen, Denmark
e-mail: lrc@itu.dk

O.W. Bertelsen
Aarhus University, Denmark

© Springer-Verlag London 2015
V. Wulf et al. (eds.), *Designing Socially Embedded Technologies in the Real-World*,
Computer Supported Cooperative Work, DOI 10.1007/978-1-4471-6720-4_8

Broadly speaking, the chapter may be said to address the elusive yet core CSCW problem of characterising the actors' engagement with *materiality* in cooperative work. Analysing how actors manipulate and control causal relationships central to the material field of work is part of this.

We will proceed in the following manner. First, we will discuss causation theory with the purpose of substantiating an approach appropriate for CSCW. Second, we will analyse causation in, respectively, chemotherapy and the building process. Finally, we will discuss our findings and their perspectives for CSCW.

8.1 A View of Causation for CSCW: Manipulation and Control

According to Cartwright (2007), causation is not one monolithic concept, nor is there one single phenomenon – the 'causal relation' – that underpins the correct use of that concept. There are a variety of different kinds of relations pointed to by the abstract term 'causes' and a variety of different – correct – uses of the term for a variety of different purposes. The variety of theories of causation provides one of the major reasons in favour of this plurality view. Each theory or approach seems good for one sort of examples or phenomenon and not others, each theory seems to be good at illustrating the phenomenon selected, but each has counterexamples and problems (Cartwright 2007, p. 44).

Here are some of the key contemporary theories and their major proponents[1] (the list is adapted from Cartwright 2007, p. 43):

1. *Probabilistic theory of causality* designates a group of theories that aim to characterise the relationship between cause and effect using the tools of probability theory. Interpreting causation as a deterministic relation means that if A causes B, then A must always be followed by B. In this sense, war does not cause deaths, nor does smoking cause cancer. As a result, many turn to a notion of probabilistic causation. Informally, A probabilistically causes B if A's occurrence increases the probability of B (e.g. see Spirtes, Glymour and Scheines 1993; Suppes 1970).
2. *Process theories of causation* are based on a distinction between causal processes and noncausal processes. Crudely put, these approaches often distinguish between a process and a pseudo-process. As an example, a ball moving through the air (a process) is contrasted with the motion of a shadow (a pseudo-process). The former is causal in nature, while the latter is not according to this view (e.g. see Dowe 2000; Salmon 1984).
3. *Counterfactual accounts of causation* harbour the basic idea that the meaning of causal claims can be explained in terms of counterfactual conditionals of the form 'if A had not occurred, B would not have occurred' (e.g. see Hendry 2009; Holland and Rubin 1988; Lewis 1973).

---

[1]It is beyond the scope of this chapter to review these theories in full; please see, for example, Cartwright (2007) for an excellent treatment of the subject.

4. *Manipulability notions of causation* focus on causal relationships that are potentially exploitable for purposes of manipulation and control: roughly, if A is a cause of B, then if I can manipulate A in the right way, this should be a way of manipulating or changing B. This is a practical approach to causations with human agency at the centre, since often we ask causal questions in order to change some feature of our world (e.g. Gasking 1955; Von Wright 1971; Woodward 2003; Pearl 2009).

If we accept Cartwright's (2007) plurality view of causation theories[2], then it becomes pressing to find the theory or view of causation most promising for the enterprise of CSCW, namely, to understand cooperative work in order to be able to better computer support it (Schmidt and Bannon 1992). That is, given the variety of characterisations of the notion of causal explanation, some regimentation of the usage is pertinent in order for our enterprise to move forward. We suggest that for the purposes of CSCW, the distinguishing feature of causal explanation must be that they furnish information that is potentially relevant for manipulation and control (e.g. of entities in the material field of work such as technologies): they tell us that if we change one or more variables, we could change the value of other variables and potentially the outcome of an operation or action. We suggest that causal explanations are informed by our interests as practical agents in changing our world. In particular, we hold that it is useful to think of causal relationships as relationships that are potentially exploitable for manipulation and control. This idea is stressed in manipulability notions of causation such as those developed by Gasking (1955), Von Wright (1971), Woodward (2003) and Pearl (2009).

On this view, our interest in causal explanation represents a sort of extension of an interest in the manipulation and control of material artefacts, including technologies across various settings and situations. Von Wright (1974, p. 51) argues that the concept of cause presupposes that of (human) action. If man 'stood quite passive' against nature, if he did not possess the notion that *he* or *she* can do things, manipulate materiality, make a difference in the world, then there would be no notion of causality. Dummett (1964) makes a similar argument in saying that if we had been unable to manipulate nature, if we had been, in his example, intelligent trees capable only of passive observation, then it is reasonable to conjecture that we would never have developed the notion of causal explanation and the practices associated with it.

Relatedly, the manipulability conception of causal explanation plays an important role in how scientists think. Weinberg (1985) draws a distinction between descriptive and explanatory science in a paper on recent developments in molecular biology. Weinberg informs us that 'biology has traditionally been a descriptive

---

[2]In a review of Nancy Cartwright's (2007) book *Hunting Causes and Using Them*, Kevin Hoover (2009) finds that sometimes Cartwright treats the various accounts of causation as if they were so different that it is not clear why they should be the subject of a single book. The critique goes on to say that she fails to explain what they have in common, if, as she apparently believes, they do not have a common essence. In fact Cartwright (2007, p. 44) does state that she finds that the various theories of causation seem to have 'little of substantial content in common'. Do they have a Wittgensteinian family resemblance?

science' that has now moved to provide 'explanations' and identify 'causal mechanisms' primarily due to recent advances in instrumentation and experimental techniques. Note the contrast between description and causal explanation. Weinberg links the ability of molecular biology to provide causal explanations with the practical activity of manipulating and controlling substances – causal explanations inform manipulation and control. In Weinberg's (1985) account, new experimental and instrumental techniques have played a decisive role in developing the field of molecular biology into a science concerned with making causal explanations. New techniques make it possible to manipulate and control biological systems and to observe results in a way that was previously not possible – moving it from description towards intervention, manipulation and control (see also Woodward 2003). According to Weinberg (1985, p. 48), 'the invisible sub-microscopic agents they study can explain, at one essential level, the complexity of life' as manipulating these agents makes it possible now 'to change critical elements in the biological blueprint at will'.[3]

This passage illustrates the underlying idea of the manipulability account of causal explanation: causal explanations (ought to) involve insights that are relevant to manipulating, controlling and changing our world. Take for example computer technology. Computer programs, or subsections hereof, are executed on the computer in an invariant and predictable manner. We are in a position to explain when we have insights that are relevant to manipulating, controlling and changing the computer technology. Or put the other way around, being able to explain the workings of the computer application (to some extend) puts us in a position to potentially manipulate and control the technology. Causal explanations, however partial and incomplete, are part of what makes us able to use (and design) computer applications. It is important to emphasise that when we are talking of causal explanations enabling the manipulation and control of technology, we are aware that these explanations need not be more complete, extensive or consistent than required by the practical demands of the situation. That is, any causal explanation for the purpose of manipulation and control, of, for example, computer technology, is a situational property. This general phenomenon relates to what Schutz (1970) refers to as 'the problem of relevance' and what Bourdieu (1992) has called the 'economy of logic'.

---

[3]Since we raise the relevance of the manipulability conception of causation for scientific work, it may be appropriate to distinguish our arguments and interests from existing science and technology studies (STS) and sociology of scientific knowledge (SSK) literature. Briefly told, proponents of STS (e.g. Barad, Keller and Tchalakov) and SSK (e.g. Bloor, Collins and Yearly) are primarily interested in how social, political and cultural values influence scientific research and technological innovation and how these, in turn, affect society, politics and culture. In comparison, we are in this chapter, from the starting point of causal plurality, primarily interested in identifying and in turn employing a conception of causation relevant and useful for the enterprise of CSCW. Our evolving argument is that the manipulability conception of causation may be useful for CSCW, and we will as advertised attempt to show that in the following pages of analytical work in relation to two cases of cooperative work. In this manner our interest in this chapter differs somewhat from those of STS and SSK.

Relatedly, there is an important dimension along which causal claims may differ. Consider the following claim: *clicking on the printer icon in my Word application on my computer causes my printer to print out the document in focus.* Assuming that my computer system is functioning normally, the manipulationist view that we are advocating – following in the footsteps of Gasking (1955), Von Wright (1971) and Woodward (2003) – holds that this is a true causal claim and one to which we might appeal to explaining why my computer system has printed out a document on some particular occasion. However, some might say that there is an obvious sense in which it is explanatory 'shallow' compared to the sort of explanation that would account for the internal workings of the computer system that might be provided by a computer scientist or engineer – complete with explanations of Turing machines, Boolean algebra, Shannon's symbolic analysis of switching circuits and more. Some might say that we don't have a very 'deep' understanding of the computer system if we only know that *clicking on the printer icon in my Word application on my computer causes my printer to print out the document in focus.* Some might say that this example illustrates that causal explanations may differ in depth of understanding. But keep in mind that causal explanations are situational properties. It seems that the binary opposition shallow/deep is misleading when talking about causal explanations. Does the computer user need to know more than the claim mentioned above in order to print? Probably not, in most situations that is sufficient causal insight for the situation at hand involving the action of printing a document. So, instead of talking about depth of understanding or the lack of it, we should talk about the usefulness or adequacy of a causal explanation in relation to a particular situation or context.

Note that although manipulability theories of causation have been criticised on two primary grounds, none of these criticisms are pertinent for our enterprise. Let us elaborate. First, critics complain that these accounts are circular. According to the critics, any plausible version of a manipulability theory must make use of the notion of an intervention and that this must be characterised in causal terms. That is, attempting to link causal claims to manipulation requires that manipulation is more basic than causal interaction. But describing manipulations in noncausal terms has provided a substantial difficulty – causal talk refers to more causal talk – hence the circularity. Attempts to defend manipulability theories from this critique are recent accounts that don't claim to reduce causality to manipulation. These accounts, e.g. Pearl (2009) and Woodward (2003) used in this chapter, use manipulation as a sign or feature in causation without claiming that manipulation is more fundamental than causation and in this manner address the circularity critique.[4]

The second criticism centres on concerns that causal relationships exist in many places where human manipulation and control is not readily possible (an example being the surface of the sun). In this sense, the critics points out, manipulability accounts of causation makes humans (overly) central. In response to this criticism,

---

[4]For a more in-depth discussion of the 'circularity' issue and its implications, see Woodward (2013).

we may rely on Pearl (2009) to point out that 'cause' does not make sense divorced from manipulability *when the purpose of the analysis is to understand human practice or to furnish information relevant to human practice (the enterprise of this chapter)*. Pearl (2009, p. 407) makes the observation that knowing 'what causes what' makes a big difference in how we act. Let us give you a deceptively simple example. Drawing on Pearl (2009), what if we told you that the rooster's crow makes the sun rise? If that was true the implication would be that waking up the rooster earlier and making him crow would make the night shorter. But this is *not* so, and we act accordingly. Making this type of a distinction is relevant and has implication for how we act. This is true even when we are dealing with relationships that we cannot readily control. For example, we have no practical way of controlling celestial motion (or what goes on at the surface of the sun), and still knowledge of celestial motion is relevant to us. We can, for instance, predict the tide of the seas as a consequence of our understanding of the gravitational pull exerted on the seas by the moon, and just as important this understanding also provides us with assurance that the manipulation of earthly things will *not* control the tide. The point is that not being able to directly manipulate causal relationships does not necessarily mean that knowledge of this relationship is irrelevant to human practice (Pearl 2009).

If we accept the manipulability conception of causality, including the notion of causal explanation as a situational property, then it becomes relevant for us in CSCW to understand causation in various situations, in various work practices. In the following, causation in two cases of cooperative work, namely, chemotherapy and the building process, will be explored and analysed in order to open up the phenomenon for CSCW research.

We shall start by considering causation in chemotherapy and subsequently turn to the building process.

8.2 Causation in Work Practice: Chemotherapy

We shall start by briefly considering the methods and setting of the study before moving on to the analysis of causation in chemotherapy.

8.2.1 Methods and Setting

The study of causation in chemotherapy is based on data generated through 7 weeks of ethnographic fieldwork on oncology departments. The fieldwork included interviews and observations as well as the collection of documents used and produced by the actors.

One of the departments studied consists of an outpatient clinic, a day clinic with room for 12 patients and a ward with 33 beds. In addition, the department has a centre for patient information as well as a centre for cancer research. Approximately

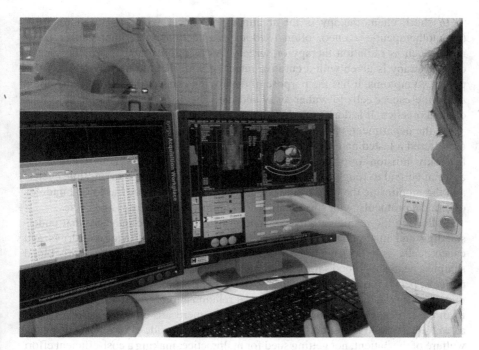

Fig. 8.1 Medical technologist at work scanning the body of a cancer patient

400 healthcare professionals with expertise in cancer treatment, care and research are associated with the department. The department offers radiation therapy as well as chemotherapy. There are approximately 4,400 new referrals to the departments per year and 3,600 admissions. On a yearly basis the department administers 56,000 sessions of radiation therapy as well as 27,000 sessions of chemotherapy. The hospital's surgical department performs tumour surgery in collaboration with the department. Although the department is highly specialised and devoted to chemotherapy and radiation therapy, oncology is highly interdisciplinary. The department needs to cooperate with other clinical specialties, such as the department of surgery, urology and gynaecology, with the laboratory as well as with the pharmacy (Fig. 8.1).

The staff at the department is organised in teams with each team focusing on a particular kind of cancer such as lung cancer, breast cancer, prostate cancer or colon cancer (our focus).

8.2.2   Causation in Chemotherapy

In chemotherapy, understanding and manipulating the causal relationship between cytotoxic drugs and cancer cells (as well as the wider human body) is central to the work practice.

In short, chemotherapy is the treatment of cancer with one or more drugs (chemotherapeutic agents), often used in conjunction with other cancer treatments such as radiation therapy or surgery. As mentioned above, whether or not chemotherapy is given with a curative intent or with the aim to prolong life or to palliate symptoms, it has the purpose of destroying cancer cells. That is, the drugs *cause* the cancer cells to wither away and die. This is the central rationale of this clinical practice. It is done with this aim in mind.

At the department, patients with a particular kind of metastasised colon cancer are offered a tested and tried protocol of carefully regimented chemotherapy with biweekly infusions of cytotoxic drugs that affect rapidly dividing cells. Chemotherapy can be said to roughly consist in the administering of drugs, in multiple cycles, and the monitoring the state of the patient. Chemotherapies are based on hundreds of clinical protocols, with specifications of combinations of drugs and cycles.

Following the manipulability conception of causation, we may say that understanding and manipulating the causal relationship between cytotoxic drugs and cancer cells is (very) central to the practice. As we shall see, taking blood samples, analysing blood samples, administering drugs, regulating doses, observing patients, performing PET/CT scans and doing the documentation are (partly) about understanding and manipulating the causal relationship between drugs and tumour in order to destroy the cancer cells. Of course there are other concerns or aims as well intertwined in chemotherapy such as minimising side effects, optimising the welfare of the patient, not getting sued for malpractice, making a cost-efficient effort and so on. However, it remains accurate to say that one relationship very central to this *clinical* practice is understanding and manipulating the causal relationship between drugs and tumour. Without this causal relationship chemotherapy would not be chemotherapy.

We are *not* trying to reduce the varied and complex practice of chemotherapy to a matter of controlling and manipulating one causal relationship – there are many such relationships in chemotherapy not to mention oncology as a whole – but we are pointing out that the causal relationship between drugs and tumour is central to chemotherapy.

It is worthwhile to consider how causal relationships in chemotherapy intersect in practice and must be balanced by the actors. The premise of this balancing act is that in chemotherapy it is relatively easy to kill all cancer cells with highly toxic drugs, but relatively hard to do so without also killing the patient. This is the reason for the monitoring of not only the causal relationship between the drugs and the tumour but also the relationship between the therapy and the patient's body as a whole. That is, we may say that there is a myopic view or interest in the causal relationship between drugs and cancer cells. For example, are the drugs destroying the cancer cell? Can we see the tumour shrinking when we are comparing PET/CT scans of the tumour over time? In addition, there is the interest in the causal relationship between the chemotherapy (as a whole) and the patient's body (as a whole). For example, what are the side effects of the treatment? How is the patient's performance status effected by the treatment? Can the patient's body tolerate the doses?

The organising principle for chemotherapy in relation to, for example, colon cancer is as indicated the concept of 'series'. Each cycle or series involves the infusion of drugs at the 14th day of each series,[5] as well as control in terms of the establishment of performance status, blood values, side effects and tumour size at the 7th day of any given series.[6] In this manner each series of treatment and examination amounts to the manipulation and control of the causal relationships mentioned above between (1) drugs and cancer cells and (2) the chemotherapy (as a whole) and the patient's body (as a whole).

In practice, these two causal relationships are as indicated represented and monitored in different ways. While the causal relationship between drugs and tumour is monitored primarily via PET/CT scans, the causal relationship between therapy and the patient's body (as a whole) is recorded as side effects on a form according to a grading system (from 0 to 4 where 4 is most severe). Let us elaborate.

PET/CT scans are the primary means of evaluating the causal relationship between drugs and tumour. PET/CT imaging combines nuclear medicine techniques with special x-ray equipment to produce multiple images of the inside of the body that many be compared over time. These cross-sectional images of the area being studied can then be examined on a computer monitor or printed. PET/CT scans of tumours reveal more details than regular x-ray exams. The objective is to identify when tumours in cancer patients improve ('respond'), stay the same ('stabilise') or worsen ('progress') during chemotherapy. These criteria are specifically *not* meant to determine whether patients have improved or not *per se*, as these are tumour-centric, not patient-centric, criteria.

The causal relationship between the therapy as a whole and the patient body (as a whole) are considered in terms of side effects. That is, a nurse interviewing and observing the patient makes use of a side-effect form in order to quantify, in accord with WHO standards, the performance status as well as fatigue level and level of pain experienced by the patient after each chemotherapy session. This is done according to a grading system (from 0 to 4 where 4 is most severe). This is a process that relies on the expressions and observations of feelings of pain and discomfort as relayed by the patient to the nurse.

When the two causal relationships, between drugs and tumour on the one hand and on the other hand between therapy and the patient's body (as a whole), intersect in practice, a causal nexus emerges that must be handled by the physician. For example, in a situation where the patient is suffering third-degree side effects such as severe diarrhoea, the treatment of the patient is postponed by the physician until the side effect has been reduced to at least grade 1 and thereafter only continued with 75 % of the original drug dose. This is done routinely according to the protocol described in a dose-modification guideline set up to handle this balancing act. In this manner two causal relationships very central to chemotherapy may be represented, intersected and balanced by the actors.

---

[5]This is from series 3 and onwards once the preliminaries such as establishing a baseline have been completed.

[6]There are 53 series of examination and treatment in total in this protocol of chemotherapy.

Again, we are *not* trying to reduce the varied and complex practice of chemotherapy to a matter of merely controlling and manipulating one set of causal relationships – there are obviously much more to oncology as a whole – but we are pointing out that there are causal relationships central to chemotherapy.

Generally speaking, in work practice actors are often manipulating a set of fundamental causal relationships. We have considered chemotherapy and the relationship between drugs and the patient's body – let us now turn to consider a different practice, i.e. the construction of a building.

8.3   Causation in Work Practice: The Building Process

Before moving on to an analysis of causation in the building process, we shall first consider the methods and setting of the study.

8.3.1   Methods and Setting

The study of causation in the building process is based on data generated through ethnographic fieldwork carried out in the course of fourteen months in architectural offices and on building sites (see also Christensen 2013). One of the building projects studied was the development of the new domicile for a publishing house, a multistorey building in glass, steel and concrete constructed at the city of Copenhagen's waterfront.

It is a relatively large building of 18,000 m^2 distributed across eight floors (see Fig. 8.2). A combination of observation and interviews was used. The fieldwork also included collecting (scanning, taking screenshots or photographs of) artefacts used and produced by the actors engaged in the building projects.

8.3.2   Causation in the Building Process

One fundamental causal relationship in a construction project is between the building in the making and the forces of nature including gravity. There will be no building if we cannot adequately manipulate and control the materiality of the building in the making in order to secure its stability (see also Christensen 2013). Arguably, for example, aesthetics and financial concerns are subservient to the matter of harnessing the causal relationship between building in the making and the forces of nature. We could, for example, have a beautiful design or a very low-cost building project, but if the finished building cannot stand, it is in the context of the building industry considered a failure.

Fig. 8.2 One of the building projects studied, a domicile for a publishing house

The actor's ability to adequately understand, control and manipulate causal relationships is fundamental to the building process and evident (1) in the design of the building by way of static calculation and design, (2) in the choice of building materials and (3) in the sequential order of construction work. We shall start with statics engineering, move on to consider causation related to the choice of building materials and finally consider how causal relationships influence the order of construction work on the building site.

8.3.2.1   Causation: Statics Calculation and Design

In a building project, it is very rare for the architects to vouch for the stability of the building themselves. Although the architects may select and design the general appearance of the load bearing elements, it is the engineers that craft a set of static plans for the building project, placing particular emphasis on statically relevant elements (Fig. 8.3). Statics describe the distributed forces in a system such as a building at rest. Buildings and parts of building are usually motionless (if we disregard wind-induced movement), and all the effective forces are calculated to balance each other out for the benefit of the stability of the building. Static calculations may include determining the assumed loads involved, calculating the forces that affect a particular structural element and the forces that it transmits to others, calculating the forces within structural elements themselves, determining the stability of the planned construction, etc.

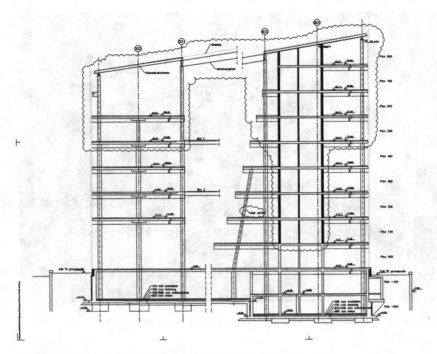

Fig. 8.3 Plan pertaining to the load bearing 'skeleton' of the domicile

The load bearing structure of the, for example, the domicile building (our building project in focus), is a so-called skeleton construction made up of bar-shaped elements forming a structure like scaffolding. Exterior façade panels and interior walls are then added to this structure. The load bearing structure and the elements that create the interior spaces are, in effect, two separate systems.

Fundamentally, the skeleton structure of the domicile is made up of three kinds of structural elements: the columns and the decks that absorb vertical loads and the walls in the kernels that absorb horizontal forces. All the vertical forces from the floor slabs (decks) are transferred into the columns, and this means that the point of transition from columns to floor is very heavily loaded. There is a risk of the column punching through the floor. To avoid this, the columns must be evenly spread and appropriately dimensioned. The structural engineer distributes these structural elements appropriately as he or she designs the load bearing structure.

Of course, there are various approaches and options available in a building project when considering and planning for the structural integrity of the building. However, the reality that structural integrity is called for is probably not debatable considering the ubiquitous presence of the forces of nature, including not least gravity. We could suggest that some form of load bearing structure is a necessity in a large and complex building project.

Structural engineers craft a set of static plans for the building project, placing particular emphasis on statically relevant elements (Fig. 8.3). Here, it is also important to establish which structural elements load with others. For example, the roofing is not just supported by the roof structure but also affects the beams, decks and columns, right down to the foundations. It must be established which structural elements absorb the loads of the upper storeys.

In addition, there are numerous other cases that we could mention in passing where causal phenomena are evident and may be anticipated in design. For example, the anticipation of temperature fluctuations may be related to the design of heating and cooling systems, the anticipation of the build-up of air contamination may be related to the design of the ventilation system, the anticipation of wet weather conditions may be related to the design of the exterior of the building (i.e. roof, façade, windows and so on), etc.

Perhaps it is evident by now that designing a building such as the domicile for the publishing house – a large and complex eight-storey building – involves understanding, manipulation and planning for the casual relationship between the building in the making and the forces of nature (i.e. gravity, weather, temperature, etc.). Perhaps we could assert that such design practice is conditioned by 'natural necessity'. In order to give ourselves the opportunity to properly asses this assertion, perhaps we ought to take a closer look at one of the central concepts used, namely, that of 'natural necessity'.

Harré and Madden (1975) coined the expression 'natural necessity' in their seminal work on causal powers. The notion captures the host of complex connections, actions and reactions that stem from the causal relationships inherent to not least to our natural world (Harré and Madden's 1975). In the context of describing the building process, using the notion of natural necessity may make us receptive to the assertion that in the building process, there is no known option but to act in accord with nature by anticipating the forces of nature – hence the expression natural necessity.

8.3.2.2 Causation: Choosing Building Materials

Furthermore, the notion of natural necessity may also be relevant in regard to the discussion of other types of design choices not least the choice of building materials. That is, perhaps the choice of some building materials is conditioned by natural necessity. Let us take a closer look.

According to Harré and Madden (1975, p. 11), the notions 'natural necessity' and 'power' are intimately interwoven. Moreover, Harré and Madden (1975, p. 85) report that under the influence of Ryle (1949) and others, a particular way of handling the ascription of power to material entities has become widespread. Ryle and others recommend that we treat power ascriptions not as the assertions of the presence of qualities but analyse them as hypothetical or conditional statements. For example, the meaning of 'It is brittle' is supposed to mean 'If maltreated, it will break'. In a similar spirit, 'It is poisonous' is held to be identical with 'If taken, it will kill or make ill', and 'It can crush a car' is taken to mean 'If it presses a car, the car will be reduced to the size of a suitcase'. Following this approach, 'It is strong' may mean 'If placed under great pressure, it will hold'.

However, according to Harré and Madden (1975, p. 86), the problem of what the ascription of a property or power to a thing means when it is not exercised is not really solved in this approach. To hold, for example, that to assert that a particular slab of concrete is strong is to make a prediction about how it would behave, if certain conditions of pressure were fulfilled is only part of it. That is, conditional statements are not enough when ascribing powers to things or materials. Things and materials have powers even when they are not exercising them, and this is a current fact about them manifest in our language about them, a way in which they are currently differentiated from other things or materials that lack these powers. Indeed, the reason why we believe that a certain disposition can be asserted of a thing or material is that we think or indeed know that it currently has such and such powers.

One of our reasons as actors, and sometimes our only reason, for believing that if certain conditions are met, then a material or individual thing will behave in a certain way, is that the thing or material now has the power to behave in that way should the conditions obtain. The difference between something that has the power to behave in a certain way and something that does not have that power is a difference in what they themselves are now as material entities, rather than solely a difference between what they will do under certain conditions, since it is contingently or circumstantially the case that their powers are, in fact, ever manifested. It is a difference that may be ascribed to intrinsic nature, rather than only to extrinsic circumstances (Harré and Madden 1975). In this manner Harré and Madden refuse to base their characterisation of the powers of material entities solely on conditional circumstances, and in addition to these relational parameters, they retain the notion of powers as internal or intrinsic to the particular thing or (composite) material such as the reinforced concrete used for the domicile.

Harré and Madden's position can be understood in the context of a particular tradition of language philosophy concerned with the everyday or common use of language (e.g. Wittgenstein, Austin, Searle and Ryle). Arguably, it is in this tradition that Harré and Madden are asserting that when we talk about the powers of things and materials, we routinely ascribe intrinsic powers to them as well as extrinsic conditions. 'In a sense the ascription of power is a schema for an explanation of the manifestation of the power' (Harré and Madden 1975, p. 87). That is, in explaining the powers of material entities, both extrinsic conditions and intrinsic qualities may be invoked or referenced. This view may be corroborated if we consider, for example, how Hegger et al. (2007) describes the (compound) material concrete with reference to both intrinsic qualities and extrinsic conditions:

> The mixture of cement, aggregates and water determines the properties of concrete. The cement acts as the binder, the water is present so that it can set, and the aggregates cut down the amount of cement needed and determine density, strength, thermal conductivity and heat storage capacity. Typical concrete has a high gross density, great surface hardness and great strength. The usual aggregate is gravel. The structure of large and small granules

is calculated to create as few cavities as possible. The gravel will be completely enveloped by the cement and bound to it non-positively. The smaller granule sizes help the concrete to flow more easily. The properties of the concrete are determined by the aggregates. Normal concrete has high thermal conductivity and heat storage capacities. Thermal conductivity can be significantly reduced by changing the aggregates, for example by using expanded clay, particularly porous clay balls or wood chips. Thermal conductivity can be reduced further by introducing air pores as an insulation device. This is done by means of blowing agents, which make the concrete rise like a cake. The result is called aerated concrete. Chemical substances can also be added to make the fresh concrete easier to work; or colour pigments to dye the concrete. (Hegger et al. 2007, p. 42).

In this paragraph Hegger and associates seem mostly to describe concrete with reference to what Harré and Madden (1975) call the intrinsic qualities of the material (e.g. '[. . .] concrete has a high gross density, great surface hardness and great strength'). However, they also refer to extrinsic conditions:

As a simple mixture, concrete has little tensile strength, so if it is used structurally it will always be reinforced concrete. Reinforcing steel is introduced into the concrete at the points where loads have to be absorbed. (Hegger et al. 2007, p. 43).

In this paragraph Hegger and associates (2007) seem in part to refer to what Harré and Madden (1975) describe as extrinsic conditions (e.g. '[. . .] if it is used structurally').

It is not uncommon, then, to explain the choice of building materials such as (reinforced) concrete with reference to the intrinsic nature of the compound, i.e. 'concrete has great strength', as well as by conditional statements such as 'if used structurally steel reinforced concrete will hold'. In a similar spirit, we could suggest that 'glass is transparent and wind breaking' and this makes it suitable, 'if used in windows or even sections of a roof'. Note how this allows for making a distinction between changes in the material itself and changes in extrinsic circumstances. We could argue that if a strict relational or conditional view were maintained as argued for by Ryle and others, changes in the material itself would be hard to express or speak of.

While on the subject of materials, we could briefly return to the load bearing structure of the domicile. In principle, any material that has the properties of being both compression and tension resistant can be used for the load bearing skeleton structures, for example, timber, steel or concrete. Each of these has its own construction methods with a particular set of problems arising from the material and the methods used for joining it (we won't go into the details of this). The material chosen mainly for the domicile's skeleton structure is concrete or, more precisely, the compound steel reinforced concrete. We may note, then, that a strong rather than a brittle material is chosen for the load bearing structure of the domicile, a compound material that if placed under great pressure will hold rather than crumble. In this manner the designers anticipate the forces of nature in their choices of building materials. That is, choices are made partly out of natural necessity (and partly out of concerns for cost, aesthetics, etc.).

8.3.2.3 Causation: The Order of Construction Work

As mentioned above, the ability to understand, control and manipulate the causal relationship between the building in the making and forces of nature also influences the order of construction work. The construction of the building follows what is known as 'the load bearing path'.[7] This means that the building elements that are capable of bearing the load of other elements are built before the latter are. One obvious example is that the foundation is built before the walls and the walls are built before the roof. This is the general order of construction work. An example at another level of granularity is that the concrete decks must be cast before the ventilation ducts or electrical cables are fitted or hung underneath them. This may be described as a matter of natural necessity considering that forces of gravity have a large part to play.

What this implies, then, is that natural necessity in part necessitates certain sequences of work, a certain ordering of the construction tasks. In combination with the specialised division of labour found among the network of actors, natural necessity influences the ordering of the construction tasks. For example, the concrete crew necessarily must perform the work of constructing the foundation and load-bearing superstructure of the building before the carpenters can do their part on the interior of the building. This implies that the carpenters (as well as electricians, plumbers and painters) must rely on the concrete crew and associated actors to literally lay the foundation for their subsequent work. Note that there is nothing arbitrary about this specific ordering of the cooperative work tasks in this case. For example, the work on the foundation must according to natural necessity be completed before any subsequent task literally resting on this can be performed.

This discussion implies that when designing or constructing a building, the cooperative work ensemble must out of natural necessity manipulate and control the causal relationship between the building in the making and the forces of nature, and this is manifested in static calculation and design, in the choice of building materials and in the order of construction work. All this may be verging on the trivial; however, one point is perhaps worth making: if they ignore or fail to do so at a critical juncture, the building simply will not rise let alone stand. This may be a trivial observation; however, it does underpin the building process. Let us now turn to discuss our findings.

8.4 Discussion

Does it make analytical sense to talk of *central causal relationships* when trying to understand cooperative work practices such as chemotherapy or the building process? Let us discuss.

---

[7]This is a member's concept, i.e. an expression used by the actors on the building site.

In chemotherapy, for example, we found the manipulation of the casual relationship between drugs and cancer cells to be very fundamental to the practice. Could it be *the central causal relationship* of the practice? Chemotherapy would not be chemotherapy, as we know it, without the control and manipulation of this causal relationship. In a similar manner, in the building process, we also found a significant causal relationship. That is, we found the manipulation and control of the relationship between the forces of nature and the building in the making to be literally very fundamental to the practice. Paraphrasing our conclusion on chemotherapy, the building process would not be the building process without the actor's manipulation and control of this causal relationship.

We are probably able to identify a *central causal relationship* (or set of relationships) in many other practices too.

Having a research interest in causal relationships in work practice may help us understand something very fundamental, namely, what are the actors doing? What are the basic causal relationships co-constitutive of a given practice? Arguably, this goes beyond the explanatory power of common sense ideas like 'skilful tool use' as it has the potential to analyse the constitutive elements of complex work practices. Focusing on causal phenomenon may help us as we have seen in relation to understanding both chemotherapy and the building process. However, can we always expect to be able to identify *central* causal relationships in any given cooperative work practice?

It is probably possible to identify causal relationships in most work practices both in technical domains and on other occasions. But the question of whether or not these relationships are to be deemed *central* to the practice is an empirical question entirely. Above we have seen how manipulating and controlling causal relationships are *central* to both chemotherapy and the building process. We have argued that it is a defining feature of these practices. However, we cannot take it for granted that the manipulation and control of causal relationships in the material field of work is *central* to *all* work practices. It is an empirical question.

Relatedly, if we turn to the use of computers in general, then at first hand the picture becomes perhaps a bit murkier as it can be hard to identify any one causal relationship to be 'very' fundamental or central, and all talk of a 'causal base' may evaporate. Computers are hardware machines (CPU, motherboard, ram and much more) running software machines (OS, applications, Internet services and much more) with multiple countless interconnected causal relationships crisscrossing. If we wish to say something about computer technology and causation, then we have to be very specific about the use of the technology. Again, it is an empirical question. The point being that computers are used in many practices, and as such central causal relationships, to the extent than they can be identified, will vary. Perhaps we may even say that what may differentiate one practice from another practice is precisely differences in regard to what can be considered to be 'central causal relationships' – to the extent that they can be identified and identified as central. That may serve as a way to differentiate between practices in a relatively consistent way, and that may be helpful when we are asking questions such as 'what are the actors doing' or 'what fundamental causal relationship (or set of relationships) is the cooperative actors involved in manipulating and controlling, and how do we computer support this practice?'

8.5 Conclusion and Perspectives

In this chapter the manipulative account of causation has been brought forward as a conceptual framework for the understanding and analysis of causal relationships central to cooperative work practice. Causal relationships central to, respectively, chemotherapy and the building process have been described and analysed.

In chemotherapy, we found that it is a central part of work practice to understand, manipulate and control the causal relationships between drugs and cancer cells in an effort to destroy the latter. Furthermore, it is also part of chemotherapy to monitor and manipulate the causal relationship between the therapy (as a whole) and the patient's body (as a whole) in order to safeguard the wellbeing of the patient. In practice these two relationships form a causal nexus intertwined in an intractable manner yet handled routinely by the actors in the clinic.

The study of causation in the building process showed that the cooperative actors are engaged in manipulating and controlling the causal relationship between the building in the making and the forces of nature. This is evident in the design of the building by way of static calculation and design, in the choice of building materials and in the sequential order of construction work.

In terms of perspectives for CSCW, we may say that studying causation may also address the elusive question of how to deal with the actor's engagement with materiality in the study of cooperative work. That is, in this chapter the analysis of materiality in cooperative work has been cast as the study of the actor's manipulation and control of key causal processes in the material field of work. This is a path that could be explored further in future studies of cooperative work that has an emphasis on the materiality of the work setting.

Acknowledgements We would like to express our sincere gratitude to the practitioners in both oncology and the building process for access to their work. Furthermore, we would like to thank Volker Wulf and Dave Randall for encouraging us to write this chapter and for providing invaluable comments and critique.

References

Bourdieu, P. (1992). *The logic of practice*. Cambridge: Polity Press.
Cartwright, N. (2007). *Hunting causes and using them*. Cambridge: Cambridge University Press.
Christensen, L. R. (2013). *Coordinative practices in the building process: An ethnographic perspective*. London: Springer.
Dowe, P. (2000). *Physical causation*. Cambridge: Cambridge University Press.
Dummett, M. (1964). Bringing about the past. *Philosophical Review, 73*, 338–359.

Gasking, D. (1955). Causation and recipes. *Mind, 64*, 479–487.

Harré, R., & Madden, E. H. (1975). *Causal powers: A theory of natural necessity.* Oxford: Blackwell.

Hegger, M., Drexler, H., & Zeumer, M. (2007). *Materials.* Basel: Birkhäuser.

Hendry, D. F. (2009). *Causality and exogeneity in non-stationary economic time series* (Vol. 269). Technical Report 18/04. London: London School of Economics.

Holland, P. W., & Rubin, D. B. (1988). Causal inference in retrospective studies. *Evaluation Review, 12*(3), 203–231.

Hoover, K. D. (2009, December 9). Causal pluralism and the limits of causal analysis: A review of Nancy Cartwright's hunting causes and using them. In *Approaches in Philosophy and Economics.* Available at: SSRN: http://ssrn.com/abstract=1562262 or http://dx.doi.org/10.2139/ssrn.1562262

Lewis, D. (1973). Causation. *Journal of Philosophy, 70*, 556–567.

Pearl, J. (2009). *Causality: Models, reasoning and inference.* Cambridge: Cambridge University Press.

Ryle, G. H. (1949). *The concept of mind.* Chicago: University of Chicago Press.

Salmon, W. C. (1984). *Scientific explanation and the causal structure of the world.* Princeton: Princeton University Press.

Schmidt, K., & Bannon, L. (1992). Taking CSCW seriously: Supporting articulation work. *Computer Supported Cooperative Work (CSCW). An International Journal, 1*(1–2), 7–40.

Schmidt, K., & Bannon, L. (2013). Constructing CSCW: The first quarter century. *Computer Supported Cooperative Work (CSCW), 22*(4-6), 345–372.

Schutz, A. (1970). *Reflections on the problem of relevance.* New York: Pegasus.

Spirtes, P., Glymour, C., & Scheines, R. (1993). *Causation, prediction and search.* New York: Springer.

Suppes, P. (1970). *A probabilistic theory of causation.* Amsterdam: North Holland.

von Wright, G. (1971). *Explanation and understanding.* Ithaca: Cornell University Press.

von Wright, G. (1974). *Causality and determinism.* New York: Columbia University Press.

Weinberg, R. (1985). The molecules of life. *Scientific American, 253*(4), 48–57.

Woodward, J. (2003). *Making things happen – A theory of causal explanation.* Oxford: Oxford University Press.

Woodward, J. (2013). Causation and manipulability. In E. N. Zalta (Ed.), *The Stanford encyclopedia of philosophy* (Winter 2013 Edition). Stanford: Stanford University.

Chapter 9
Analysing and Supporting Cooperative Practices: An Interdisciplinary Approach

Myriam Lewkowicz and Pascal Salembier

In this chapter we present an approach that aims at the development of a research program that entails a theoretical-empirical and a technological dimension simultaneously. The objective is both to contribute to the understanding of the socio-cognitive phenomena that underpin cooperation and collaboration in context and to contribute to the sustainable development of society by designing services that fulfil societal needs in a selected set of domains (e.g. risk and crisis management, social support for the disabled and the elderly, ecological sustainability and energy savings). One of the distinctive points of our approach is that it involves a set of researchers coming from different disciplines and working in a single team on the same empirical-theoretical and technological objects: mediated communication, cooperative practices and cooperative technologies. This approach has different but complementary faces: the naturalistic analysis of cooperative practices in different contexts, the design of services to support cooperative practices and the design of technological models, architectures and platforms that provide an infrastructure to support the cooperative services.

9.1 Introduction

Like others, we have been involved for many years now in interdisciplinary projects that put at the forefront of their agenda the development of design solutions which are both practical and socially relevant by taking into account the user as a socio-cognitive agent, embedded in a cultural and historical context and in a field of situated practices (professional, educative, domestic). One of the distinctive points

M. Lewkowicz (✉) • P. Salembier
UMR CNRS 6281 – Tech-CICO, Troyes University of Technology, Troyes, France
e-mail: myriam.lewkowicz@utt.fr

© Springer-Verlag London 2015
V. Wulf et al. (eds.), *Designing Socially Embedded Technologies in the Real-World*,
Computer Supported Cooperative Work, DOI 10.1007/978-1-4471-6720-4_9

in our own approach (which is the reason why we use the term 'interdisciplinary') is that it involves a set of researchers coming from different disciplines and working in a single team (named Tech-CICO[1]) on the same empirical-theoretical and technological objects: mediated cooperative practices and the technologies to support them.

The most exciting but sometimes difficult aspect of this endeavour is to manage how to handle the articulation of different disciplinary fields which have different traditions of research, various methodological orientations and sometimes conflicting, even contradictory, theoretical statements. On the other hand, it offers a unique opportunity to confront ideas, insights and design options and to mutually discuss and enrich both the different theoretical frames of reference and the design process of new situations of interaction and cooperation.

Ultimately, we are more concerned with designing services that support critical societal challenges (social support, autonomy of the elderly, crisis and risk management, sustainable development) than with designing the interface of the next generation of mobile phones or massively distributed games.[2] This focus is partially determined by contingent factors[3] but also by personal or collective ethical engagement in a field of activity of societal value.

In this chapter, we will start by situating our position in the context of the EUSSET manifesto (see introduction) and by giving a general overview of our approach. We will then present our interdisciplinary research program in detail and will illustrate it by one project example before concluding on issues coming from reflection on the implementation of our research framework.

9.2 Positioning

9.2.1 A Syncretic View of the Adopted Interdisciplinary Approach

When we – the Tech-CICO team – are conducting interdisciplinary design-oriented projects, our collective positioning can be characterised as follows:

It is *transformative* in essence since it aims at (re)designing situations. Obviously this aspect is claimed by disciplinary fields represented in the team that encompass a

---

[1] *Technologies pour la Coopération, l'Interaction et les Connaissances dans les collectifs* (Technologies for Cooperation, Interaction and Knowledge in Collective).

[2] We have no problem with such research, but it is not the topic of this chapter. Some of our recent projects are actually related to the design of participative serious games and social software for smartphones.

[3] It is fair here to face the reality: in a context where public funding gets lower and lower, it has become critical to be able to find external resources, and this can lead to the opening of new studies in fields of application of societal concerns related to current trends in funding policies (see, e.g. Wulf et al. 2011) for a similar reflection).

technological commitment, namely, informatics and ergonomics. But the very idea of mutual shaping as constituent of the relationship between humans and technology is at the core of the general project of our team and is shared by all its members. We are strongly committed to the view that thinking that introducing a new artefact will solely have an augmentative/linear effect on users and their field of practices is an unrealistic and naïve view.

It is *prescriptive* by necessity as it aims at process improvement by (re)designing situations where the importance of procedures, rules and good practices – be it made explicit as scripts that guide action or embodied in the constraints imposed on activities by the logics of a technological artefact or process – is significant. For us, it is therefore clear that designing is prescribing. This prescriptive approach seems, on the face of it, to sit uncomfortably with the informal, situated, emergent dimension of work activities (e.g. francophone tradition of ergonomics and work psychology and unorthodox trends in management sciences) (de Montmollin 1984). We disagree. Prescribing is inherent to any engineering of situations of human activities; the critical point here is not prescription per se, but the way it is informed by empirical evidences and integrated in a participative approach that takes into account the current practices as well as the capabilities of actors appropriate of these implemented prescriptions in the field of work.

Finally, it has a *direct concern with contemporary societal challenges*. That is why our scope of interest and action is now mainly focused on a restricted set of application domains of significant social value: risk and crisis management (Matta et al. 2012), social support and autonomy (Tixier and Lewkowicz 2011), collaborative sustainability (Cahier 2009), arrangement of informational and knowledge layers in urban spaces (Cahier et al. 2011; Soulier et al. 2011, 2012).

This global approach takes different but complementary faces:

- *The naturalistic analysis of cooperative practices in different contexts.* These are mainly real situations, but occasionally experimental studies in ecologically sound situations too, especially when there is a need to perform limited evaluation of technology-mediated cooperation.
- *The design of services to support cooperative practices.* This idea is to 'translate' the results of the analysis and interpretation of outcomes from empirical studies.
- *The design of technological models, architectures and platforms* that provide an infrastructure to support the design of cooperative services.

The building of this collective project has different implications. First, it requires adhesion to a set of shared principles and values (see above) as a prerequisite for team working. Second, it has a direct effect on the composition which, we argue, must be intentionally heterogeneous. Comprehensive studies of practices in complex settings at different levels of analysis require the intervention of different competencies from human and social sciences (sociology, psychology, linguistics, management science). Conversely, the instrumental dimension of the project requires competencies in computer science and engineering (knowledge engineering, web design, software engineering, etc.). Finally, taking critical societal challenges seriously leads to the building of long-term relations with the different actors involved in the field of practice (associations, hospitals, etc.). This relation of mutual trust is of course necessary to develop relevant technological support, services and organisational solutions. It is also necessary when one wishes to be able to perform an empirically informed follow-up and appraisal of the effects of the introduction of an innovation in the field of activities. This is especially critical when the analyst has to enter, for instance, the intimacy of a family (Budweg et al. 2012; Tixier et al. 2009), a community (Gaglio and Foli 2011) or a group of co-workers in a tricky context (Palaci et al. 2012) over a long period of time.

9.2.2 General Context: The EUSSET Manifesto and the ECSCW Community

The EUSSET Situated Computing manifesto (EUSSET 2012) provides a set of analytic policies intended for promoting a new field of research that will be distinctively identified and institutionally recognised in the years to come. Needless to say, we embrace most of the statements expressed in this manifesto with a special emphasis on the following points which resonate with our own practices:

– First, the manifesto stresses the need 'to close the gap between purely technical development on the one hand and "social impact" studies on the other'. From the beginning we have attempted to overcome this limitation by associating human and social scientists, computer scientists and engineers within joint projects where each disciplinary community can develop its own research activity as long as its members keep in mind that they are committed to the more global objective of providing thinking, concepts, frameworks, methods, empirical data and technical realisations (mock-ups, prototypes, simulation tools) to feed the design process and the implementation of artefacts (technical and organisational) with the aim of supporting human practices in the real world.
– Subsequently, we have attempted, since the birth of Tech-CICO, to simultaneously conduct a theoretical/empirical research program and a technological research program (design-oriented effort). This implies, consistent with other contributions to this book, interwoven breakthroughs in the design of new computational environments and a scientific attempt to understanding the instrumentality of artefacts, informed by 'in-depth analysis of complex practices'.
– The radical extension of the domain of activities under the scrutiny of CSCW researchers has become more and more obvious for some years now (see, e.g. the panel on the future of CSCW organised during the 2010 edition of the COOP conference). As a matter of fact, historically devoted to the study of cooperation in professional settings and to the design of systems (groupware, workflow, etc.) that support those activities, CSCW has moved more and more outside of its original domain of work so as to encompass such fields as the coordination of activities at home, group education, collective cultural and leisure activities, non-professional social interactions and communities of interest. Our involvement

in fields like social support (Tixier et al. 2010), mobile social interaction (Zouinar et al. 2010), creative and artistic thinking (Salembier and Legout 2012), mediated interaction in diaspora communities (Atifi and Marcoccia 2003) and sustainability (Cahier et al. 2008; Salembier et al. 2009) makes this enlargement of CSCW's initial scope a natural move for us.

– Finally, one of the major contributions of the EUSSET manifesto is its emphasis on informal, highly distributed mechanisms that support the capture of context and meaning as opposed to formal and mechanical models of semantic search. This idea of keeping tracks of contextual features that embed manifest cooperation and interaction finds an illustration in the works we have been doing for many years now in the domains of semiotic ontologies (Zacklad 2005), multi-viewpoint models (Cahier and Zacklad 2001), participative annotation of shared resources (Merle et al. 2012), narrative account of project memories (Soulier and Caussanel 2002) and collaborative translation (Lacour et al. 2013).

We believe these commitments to be emblematic of a joint set of interests evidenced in what we will call the situated computing/ECSCW community (although we do not mean to imply they are not found elsewhere). They all share a common twofold objective: (1) *understanding* (what we call theoretical-empirical dimension of a research program), labelled as 'intellectual project' (Vienna University of Technology, Multidisciplinary Design Group), 'theoretical and epistemological concerns' (IT University of Copenhagen, GIRI) or 'research challenge' (University of Siegen), and (2) *designing* technological and organisational artefacts for the support of cooperative activities (what we refer as the technological dimension of a research program).

Second, these approaches generally follow an *action-research* perspective which highlights the interest of translating academic research into community problem-solving strategies (Stokols 2006).[4] The idea behind action research here is to promote sustained collaboration between different stakeholders (researchers, community members, policy makers) focused on a similar object of concern that entails a scientific interest and societal issues and where actors integrate expertise drawn from different disciplines and field experiences.

Third, they tend to restrict their scope of intervention to a limited more or less select set of application domains of societal relevance: health care, community support, social and ecological sustainability, ageing society, cross-cultural communication and gender studies to name a few.

---

[4]But in our opinion, this cannot be reduced to a mere 'applied science' perspective where outcomes from academic research could be transferred and applied so as to manage problems of societal concern in an uncritical way. Quite the opposite: it is the prerogative of the field to question findings from scientific disciplines, giving new, sometimes unexpected, impetus to the study of phenomena of theoretical and practical interest.

9.3   An Interdisciplinary Research Program

9.3.1   A General Position: Cooperation as Participation and Contribution

CSCW at large has been involved over many years with (1) the design and evaluation of computing systems that can be seen as a technological reification of prescriptive organisational artefacts (norms, procedures, scripts, good practices, etc.) such as ERP and workflows or (2) the design and evaluation of systems that support coordination by providing mutual awareness, shared context and alignment of representations between actors and workers, and most of our research effort can be labelled as an attempt to investigate the notion of cooperation from the 'participation' or 'contribution' point of view. That is, it provides a coherent and principled conceptual approach to the problem of effective transformation.

The late modern world contains growing sets of situations in which different actors, identified or unidentified, ratified or not, distributed in space and time, contribute to a sometimes ill-defined collective goal, using most of the time low-overhead web-based technologies. A prototypical example of this kind of situation is the multiple Internet forums in which people exchange information, advice and comment on various (and sometimes critical) concerns such as social support, personal experience of disease, cultural interest, practical know-how in domestic daily practices, professional wisdom and tricks, etc. Doing so, people participate to a collective design that aims (more or less intentionally and in a more or less controlled manner) at generating a bunch of perpetually dynamic collective knowledge (and decisions) submitted to discussion, negotiation and sometimes dismissal.

This endeavour finds a field of application in a variety of different professional settings, for example, programming language communities. This relatively new phenomena gave rise to a convergence between professional networks with restricted access (intranets) and widely open social networks. In the context of the CSCW community, this convergence has been studied recently in different domains, for example, crisis management (Reuter et al. 2012) and software engineering communities (Bourguin et al. 2013).

This propensity to consider cooperation as a collective effort to contribute to design led us to adopt structural or conjectural standpoints at the ontological, epistemological and instrumental (design) levels.

9.3.2   Underlying Statements

9.3.2.1   Ethical and Ontological Levels

This orientation to a collaborative/contributive approach is partly determined by contingent factors (commitment to particular fields of activities) and partly by ethical considerations that orient to relevant theoretical objects (social support, presence, responsibility). Of course, a history of attention to the collaboration per se can partly explain this orientation. For example, the delivery of patient-centred care at home is made possible by the ability of caregivers (including professionals from different disciplines and family members) to collaborate (Tixier et al. 2010). Similarly, in the domain of sustainable development, the participation of citizens in the debate related to ecological degradations is a critical point for escalating demand for natural resources, energy consumption and so on (Cahier 2009). At the same time, personal concerns and collective engagements in favour of the development of collaborative policies and participative attitudes in the management of societal issues have led many of us to choose to address these issues in their professional activities as researchers and designers.[5]

Ontological should be understood in a modest or 'weak' sense. The purpose is not to address the question of the very nature of cooperation[6] but to make explicit that we put the emphasis on a particular dimension of cooperative activities. One might say that the focus is more on the collaborative than on the coordinative facet of cooperative practices, even though we do not dismiss the critical role played by coordinative mechanisms. We are especially interested in the informal dimension of coordination mechanisms, based on the building and continuous updating of a mutual awareness, for example, and by the regulation mechanisms of mediated conversations. For instance, in a forum, the intervention of an actor may have a direct impact on the thread of a discussion seen as a jointly managed process, and it may consequently require the intervention of other actors so as to regulate interventions that threaten the more or less explicitly and mutually ratified desirable state of affair.

9.3.2.2 Epistemological Level

At a general level, our perspective is concerned with how communication, joint actions and knowledge are collaboratively constructed, understood, negotiated and maintained in a particular context of practice. Thus, following the traditional doxa of normative epistemology, this general perspective must be refined and made more explicit: it is necessary to define a set of relevant methods and analytic approaches for empirically accounting for the theoretical objects and statements formulated at the ontological level.

This multilevel frame can be divided in several layers of theoretical-empirical analysis:

– At the micro level, fine-grained analysis of sequences of interaction is performed according to the tradition of conversational analysis and interactionism. It enables

---

[5]Let us remind a trivial point: the relation between ethics and theory is always present in the definition of a research program. It is not just a question of selecting or rejecting more or less amenable fields of application: ethics orients (or should orient) the choice of theoretical objects offered to the scrutiny of the researcher.

[6]See, for example Schmidt (2011).

us, for example, to identify sequential structures and organisation of speech acts that permit the achievement of a successful exchange in the context of a cooperative episode. It makes it possible to identify informal, sometimes non-explicit, rules of communication observed by actors (e.g. ad hoc communicative contact). Similarly and when the constraints of the setting make it possible, an emphasis is put on the phenomenological experience of the actor's own activity. This level of analysis gives us an opportunity to have an access to the fine-grained detail of the pre-reflective thinking which might reveal dimensions of activity such as emotion and the nature of experience (trust, well-being, stress) (Cahour and Salembier 2012; Février et al. 2011; Lewkowicz et al. 2008).

- At an intermediate (meso) level, the activity of individuals is observed, recorded and analysed in order to recompose the organisation of collective practices ('individual-collective' approach). The basic idea here, in the tradition of francophone ergonomics (Salembier 2013; Schmidt et al. 2011) and partially in micro-sociology of activity, is to give account to what is actually done by the human agents, sometimes in reference/opposition/tension to what should be done according to the organisational artefacts (rules, procedures), sometimes for its own content (thus more and more activities are independent of any organisational prescription). The emphasis put on these dimensions of activity and the importance given to the meaning ascribed by the actor to his/her own activity have a direct influence on the range of methods used by the analyst. Besides the traditional approach, francophone work psychology and ergonomics have developed a method that aims at articulating the manifest expression of activity and retrospective verbal reports. This method, sometimes quoted as 'self-confrontation interviews' (Cahour et al. 2005), aims at showing a subject a recording of his/her own activity in order to put him/her in the context of or to re-enact a past experience. The goal is to collect verbal reports that may be factual descriptions of the actions performed by the actor or general comments that allow the analyst to give meaning to what has been done.
- At a more macro level, different relevant concepts (standards, rules, procedures, processes, organisational routines, cultural communities, end-to-end management, institutional and public policies, etc.) may be evoked in order to provide a better understanding of higher-level organisational, social and cultural factors that may shape the organisation and dynamics of collective practices in a particular field of activities. This approach may be used at the level of a group, a community or a network of actors.

9.3.2.3 Design Level

The technological side of our research program aims at making concrete realisations of theoretical thinking and empirical data built together at the different epistemological levels. The different perspectives/levels of analysis of the different disciplines involved allow us to design from a rich and eclectic characterisation of the activity to be instrumented. Combining methods coming from conversational analysis, psychology and sociology permits us to merge interviews with potential end users and observations of both face-to-face and online practices (through email or social media), helping us to get a deep analysis of existing cooperative situations from which we can start designing and implementing pertinent services.

This implementation can serve different purposes:

- First, as expected in any user-centred approach, the results of the empirical studies and theoretical/speculative thinking are expected to feed the design process and to influence the designer's decisions (depending on the level of granularity of the empirical material; see above). Ultimately, the traditional minimal objective is to design a service, an artefact or a device that hopefully will be of some practical utility to a group or community of potential users in the context of a societally relevant field of activity. But what we strive towards here is to adopt a more integrative approach that aims at proposing an articulated solution that includes technological media, a content and a set of organisational principles compatible with the field of activities. The general idea is one of what we call 'engineering of situations[7] of activities'. These situations can be of different nature: from co-located dyadic interaction to large-scale sociotechnical systems.
- Second, the objective is also to inform the organisation of the design process (Dubois et al. 2006; Alaoui and Lewkowicz 2013), by providing intermediary objects that are used as resources for promoting exchanges between the actors (designers, users, stakeholders) involved in the project.
- Third, mock-ups and prototypes can be used as 'heuristic probes'. The artefacts provide opportunity for the academics to test theoretical hypothesis of interest in the context of their own field of research in a semi-realistic way. For example, an experimental forum can be used to study the effect of different factors on the organisation of communication and the emergence of patterns of interaction.
- Fourth, the work done at the ontological and empirical levels is used to help developing, enhancing or modifying a software infrastructure dedicated to the collaborative representation and manipulation of data, contents and knowledge (Cahier et al. 2013). Taking a biologically inspired metaphor, the idea here is that design concerns should reflect ontological and epistemological statements not only at the 'phenotypic' (services and interfaces) level but also at the 'genotypic' (infrastructure and architecture) level. This idea, according to which the adoption of a specified underlying computing paradigm should lead to the implementation and use of a dedicated infrastructure, is illustrated, for example, by the GIRI initiative (Bardram et al. 2011) and by the ITSME project (DeMichelis and Loregian 2009).

---

[7]Theureau characterised this orientation as 'methodological situationism' in order to contrast it with 'methodological collectivism' and 'methodological individualism' as research strategies for studying cognition in real-world settings (Theureau 2006).

9.3.3 Usage, Services and Architecture

During the past 15 years, we have conducted empirical studies in a wide range of professional and non-professional situations. These studies were opportunities to apply, in a more or less integrated way, the elements of the frame described above. Each project includes an empirical dimension where the analysis of a group of actors' current practices is performed using different methods: ethnographic observations, activity analysis, free interviews and retrospective verbal reporting based on different traces (writings, sketches, notes, automatic acquisition of actions on a computer system and audio and video recordings). Similarly, these methods are applied to the assessment of 'situations of activity' engineered in the project. This empirical phase is an occasion for collective reflexive thinking on the nature of the theoretical objects, concepts, descriptive and analytical categories and behavioural markers tackled in the context of the study.

The outcomes of the data analysis are then used to inform the design of services that are supposed to offer a solution to an aspect of a broader societal challenge. As a recent evolution in our work, the design of these services is not 'simply'[8] seen as a purely applied enterprise of reifying empirically inspired elements into technological and organisational artefacts. The notion of service here is considered as an object of conceptual thinking that goes beyond its instrumental status (i.e. as an integrated bunch of artefacts that fulfils a particular need and supports a specific activity). From this point of view, service is an instrument of task and social shaping but may also be considered as an interdisciplinary effort aiming at gathering and organising a set of practical and theoretical knowledge, empirical methods and case studies in order to enhance the performance of the service business and to extend the capabilities of innovation.

Even though we manage to avoid the design of services as a repeated one-shot process by considering service as an object worthy of conceptual thinking, the capitalisation of experience gained on each design project remains a critical problem. One solution to soften this possible limitation, and in the same time a way to embed the general principles listed in the research program in a material substrate, is to propose a software architecture or platform that can be used as an infrastructure in every new project which aims at designing collaborative supports. Different studies conducted at Tech-CICO since 2000 in the domain of collaborative knowledge engineering gave birth to the notion of 'socio-semantic web' (Caussanel et al. 2002) and to the hypertopic model (Zhou et al. 2006), seen as a semiformal alternative to the formal approach of semantics promoted by the semantic web. It aims at fostering participation among knowledge workers (Zhou et al. 2006). Hypertopic was notably designed to overcome the limits of topic maps by enabling the expression of different viewpoints on shared items. It was first implemented in agorae, a 'marketplace' where different professions can describe a given catalogue

---

[8] As everyone involved in this sort of translation knows, this is far from being simple.

depending on their viewpoints. At the same time, a similar model was implemented in Porphyry, a digital library system in which scholars could annotate documents and confront their interpretations. Comparing both systems helped in defining a protocol that could be used by these tools, by a core service (Argos), and by other add-on utilities (Cassandre, LaSuli, Steatite). Hypertopic was successfully used to manage multi-viewpoint catalogues built by citizens (sustainable development projects, open-source software), educators and students (open courseware), managers (telecom and aeronautics), mechanical engineers and researchers (social scientists, open archive, UNESCO diaspora knowledge network).

9.4 An Illustration: Developing Online Social Support Services

9.4.1 Context: The MISS Project

Social support involves giving advice, information and emotional, psychological or material support to people experiencing difficult situations (disease, stress, loss of work, etc.). It is often provided by relatives, friends, the family or trained professionals (such as psychologists or social workers). However, a new trend has been developing on the Internet during the last few years: social support is now being provided by peers, who are neither relatives nor professionals, mostly on Internet forums. In view of this emerging trend, it was proposed to define and apply new principles for developing innovative online services to meet the current social demand which has arisen.

The challenge here was to succeed in understanding and implementing an activity (social support) which is difficult to describe. We started off by analysing the specific needs of a group of people, the family caregivers of patients with memory disorders (Alzheimer's disease in most of the cases) in the Aube region (N–E of France), where a dedicated health-care network named 'Réseau Pôle Mémoire' (RPM) was launched in 2001. It was therefore proposed to design a tool for family caregivers that would be as intuitive as possible. It was assumed that the more we keep in mind actual social support practices in designing our platform, the more intuitive and user-friendly it will be for caregivers.

For this purpose, we carried out an 'action-research' approach in which several analyses (conducted by researchers in sociology, conversational analysis and psychology) were combined in order to design services and to define the appropriate infrastructure to run these services.

9.4.2 The Interdisciplinary Design of Situations of Activity

We started by studying online social support practices to understand the factors making online social support exchanges work. It led us to identify the efficient patterns of interaction and therefore to define the main episodes of which online social support exchanges should consist, along with the corresponding functionalities, which will form the core of the platform. For instance, the initial results of the conversational analysis suggested that 'asking a question' and 'sharing experience' are important components. These results also showed that reciprocity is a key to successful online social support exchanges and that information seeking and the assessment of this information are an important feature.

In addition, to obtain detailed information about the actual social support practices and the expectations of the group for whom we were designing the platform, we observed face-to-face social practices while attending RPM support groups for family caregivers.

To supplement these findings and ideas, we conducted semi-directive interviews with the family caregivers participating in the support group meetings, facilitating understanding of their day-to-day practices outside the monthly support group meetings. Their description of the way they cope with their ailing relatives and the burden they often feel is key to understanding their needs, which can be either clearly expressed or more latent.

Observation and interviews confirmed some of the findings we had made on analysing online social support exchanges and brought to light some new findings: first, experience sharing is also identified as a key point by the caregivers themselves. What links the members of the support group together is their experience of Alzheimer's disease from the caregiver's point of view, especially as they feel no one else can understand what this experience is like unless they have been in a similar situation; 'If you have not been through it yourself, you cannot understand what it involves' was an expression which cropped up frequently in the interviews. Second, the need for information was expressed very strongly. In fact, most of the needs clearly expressed by the caregivers we met were related to information seeking and information management. For instance, they were interested in tips and advice, they would like to learn about the side effects of the patients' medicine and how to improve the patients' well-being, and they would like to be given some help with the paperwork they have to deal with. This gave rise to the idea that the social support platform should include a section for exchanging documents and information, structured in line with the categories of information listed above (medicine, well-being and paperwork). Finally, reciprocity was again identified as a key factor in social support; the caregivers clearly stated that they came to the support group to talk about themselves as well as with other people.

These findings were used to inspire the design of the social support platform. This does not mean that the results were translated directly one by one into functionalities, as functionalities are complex combinations, and the models and data on which they are based are often complex too. However, the results of our analyses (e.g. the need for reciprocity) determined several design options, from which we take four examples to illustrate our approach:

1. *Reciprocity as a key to successful social support*: This led the informatics researchers to think about how to encourage reciprocity among the users of the platform. This cannot be achieved by simply using a single 'reciprocity function-

ality' nor is it possible to compel users to act in a reciprocal way. The idea was to make people aware of each other's contributions (messages) in order to multiply the opportunities for reciprocity. By highlighting the number of requests that have received few or no messages of support on the homepage and at the top of each section, we can hope to encourage reciprocity. Providing users with 'mail alert' features that signal any messages they receive is another functionality which may serve this purpose (it also helps people to stay in touch with the platform). In addition, the platform provides a weekly and monthly digest, a kind of newsletter helping members to be aware of the activity of the group.

2. *The central role of informational support*: What we learned by observing real-life support groups, such as the fact that caregivers go there to learn more about diseases and how to deal with patients' day-to-day care and the fact that requests for information are prominent on social support websites that led the informatics researchers to include sections dedicated to exchanging information. The first section is dedicated to document sharing and to online discussion facilities. Users can read and upload interesting file documents or website links and have the ability to organise documents around topics through keywords. The section is bootstrapped with some of the domain literature like, for instance, patients' associations and respite care services websites, socio-demographic studies about family caregivers and document about memory disorders. The 'discussions' sidebar, which has its proper instance for each document, enables users to comment, share their opinion and discuss the contents. The second section, which is dedicated to questions and responses (Q&A), is based on a metaphorical situation where users can ask other people questions via a one-line question text field followed by a larger text field for giving details. The rules and norms found to apply in situations involving the exchange of social support show how relevant this choice of metaphor and these technical features are, since our users are familiar with real-life situations of this kind, as compared with more abstract metaphors such as those on which forums and chat rooms are often based.

3. *The central role of experience sharing*: The importance of accounts on personal experience and stories in social support exchange has been emphasised both in the online social support analysis (i.e. description or narration of the problem, presentation of its negative consequences) and in the field analysis (i.e. caregivers come to the support group to talk with other people but also to talk about themselves). This led the informatics researchers to create a 'story and experience sharing' section where a user can post a new topic and share his/her story. Other users are enabled to post their personal stories under the same topic. The 'story sharing' form has also been designed keeping in mind the reciprocity factor, since it enables users to invite other people to share their experience on one topic through email alerts. Inside a topic, stories are sorted by authors, and each of them has a dedicated page to underline the personal dimension of such content. Discussions on the topic can be performed through the discussions sidebar.

4. *Tips and advice*: The interviews with caregivers and the observation of the support group meetings showed how important it is for family caregivers to be able to exchange tips and advice. The relevance of encouraging the exchange

of good daily caregiving practices is based not only on the participants' own practices but also on more formal information such as the training documents provided by the health-care network that led the informatics researchers to define a functionality enabling users to mark the contents of the platform (documents, Q&A threads and members' stories) as 'useful tips' in order to help them browse easily among these precious contributions and retrieve them via a simple link.

To summarise, the data and results coming from the analyses conducted by researchers in psychology, conversational analysis and sociology were discussed with informatics researchers and not mechanically and simplistically translated into functionalities. Moreover, thanks to the conversational analysis of online social support exchanges, the medium into which social practices are being 'translated' is taken into account. Finally, the data taken from the interviews go beyond the design of a platform. For instance, they question the role of health-related websites, which are providing information to patients and by then change their relationships with their practitioner. One can also mention the implementation of 'respite care' services which is a matter for the public health policy. This study is then included into a broader process of intervention research.

9.4.3 Reflections

Dialogue between the social sciences and design is recognised as complex, and the implementation of the proposed approach is no exception. At the end of the second year of the research project described here, a collective return on the benefits and limitations encountered in this interdisciplinary activity was synthesised by the team. It was judged that cooperating in this project opened up exciting scientific thinking as working around shared concepts (i.e. social support, reciprocity) seen in the light of different disciplines, which then become boundary objects for research. The state of the art on the mobilised theories and objects has therefore been enriched by these interdisciplinary perspectives. Moreover, having to present his/her research to researchers from other disciplines facilitated clarification and explicitation and allows self-reflection on the limits of his/her own discipline.

With regard to the value of designing services on the part of human and social scientists, we noticed that this type of project permits us to identify more specifically the value of the human and social science research. Designing involves moving analyses and results outside their natural territory, particularly during the transition between describing the phenomena and prescribing the instrumentation of the activity. This is, in and of itself, a valuable experience for social and human researchers. In addition, the design can be seen as an opportunity to test research hypotheses.

For the informatics researchers in charge of the design, working with human and social scientists has permitted a better understanding of the activity and practices. A rich corpus of elements for design was made available, and dialogue with the colleagues mastering theoretical frameworks and analytical material to make sense of the activity has been a great help. Discussing how these elements have been translated into the services has improved the computer-based application and the understanding of the role of the tool for the designers.

However, the benefits of the interdisciplinary work itself was not seen as equal; informatics researchers found inspiration and valuable insights for the design, while the interest of human and social scientists for the computer-based application did not appear to be so obvious. A limit exists between the objectives for each of the researchers implied in the design project: designing a useful tool for practice – that satisfies users – is actually a quite distant and secondary research issue for sociology and conversational analysis. These disciplines are interested in describing and understanding social phenomena and practices but arguably less in the practical business of transformation. Building and deploying a tool, especially if it is supposed to be innovative and different from what may exist otherwise, disturb the 'natural' framework of actual practices in the field and make the study of this situation unattractive as it becomes local and specific. Unless being specifically interested in phenomena such as the appropriation of technology by a group, as it is the case for ergonomics or CSCW, the tool and its use are ultimately not much of interest to our colleagues.

A possible solution would be to see design as an opportunity for social and human researchers to theorise design choices in terms of potential effects in the field in relation to, for instance, social and cultural capital. This way of working seems promising but we were not able to work in this direction during this project. The expectations and assumptions of social and human researchers were not perceived or understood from the informatics side, while advancing the implementation of the application through mock-ups finally gave the impression to social scientists that the design was far away from them.

Each of the studies conducted during the MISS project is a research action in itself. This work led to publications in each discipline communities and led to questions that go beyond the issue of interdisciplinary design. Allowing the dissemination of work in each discipline without manipulation of one by the other appears to the participants as a prerequisite for cooperation between human and social sciences and informatics.

Several lessons can be learned from this interdisciplinary design cooperation: (1) more upstream work to identify and clarify the expectations of each stakeholder in relation to the design project is important so that each can be more responsive to the other and to some extent control the different interpretations that can be made of large initial objectives such as 'designing services to assist the social support activity'. (2) Being able to open the design to social and human researchers and to facilitate their participation is important. As such, we noticed that it is actually more important than ever that a mock-up looks like a mock-up (Erickson 1995), i.e. that it does not have the appearance of a finished product. In fact, the interactive mock-ups that we built have not been a very effective medium for discussion. Thus, the explanation of which has been translated, and the intended use seems to be an important complement support to the mock-ups to foster dialogue and improve translations. (3) In the context of interdisciplinary work, managing the time which is necessary for each of the disciplines to develop its analysis and its work is difficult to reconcile and could surely be better planned in advance. Following a development process with long iterations, as we did, devoting considerable time to studies during the first year of the project and to finally begin the design and implementation of a first prototype after two iterations may not be the best working solution. A more rapid prototyping option, with short iterations, as advocated by agile methods, would probably be more appropriate to facilitate the participation of all, giving a faster pace in the project and creating earlier links with the effective use of the system in the field.

Eventually, the MISS project we have reported here can be seen as the first step towards what Stokols (2006), in line with Kurt Lewin's analysis, conceptualised as a *transdisciplinary action research*, that is, an action research which entails transdisciplinary research and inter-sectoral partnership involving academics and representatives of community sectors. More precisely, Stokols mentions three types of collaboration in the context of a transdisciplinary action research: (1) collaboration among scholars from different disciplines; (2) collaboration among researchers and community practitioners; and (3) collaboration among agencies, organisations, institutions and communities. The MISS project is obviously an illustration of collaboration of the two first kinds, even though in our case we find more appropriate to speak about interdisciplinary than transdisciplinary research.

9.5   Conclusion

In this chapter, we briefly presented an approach that aims at conducting a research program that entails simultaneously a theoretical-empirical and a technological dimension. On one side the objective of this program is to contribute to the understanding of the socio-cognitive phenomena that underpins cooperation and collaboration in context. On the other side, it aims at contributing to a sustainable development of society by designing services that fulfil societal needs in a selected set of domains (risk and crisis management, social support for the disabled and the elderly, ecological sustainability and energy savings). As such, it can therefore be seen as a local contribution to a more general CSCW research program as depicted by Schmidt and Bannon (2013).

Applying such an approach is not always an easy nor a comfortable posture. As already pointed by other authors (Wulf et al. 2011), it is a continuous struggle to maintain a balance between contradictory stakes: short-term effective transformation of situations of activity and long-term immersion in real-world fields of cooperative practice, requirements from orthodox criteria of academic research and the distinctive features of the action-research approach and multidisciplinary investigation of transversal objects of shared interest and disciplinary-oriented valorisation of results.

Moreover, from an epistemological point of view, the real nature of the research program is highly problematic per se. First, if one considers the traditional definition of a research program (e.g. as defined in the tradition of Lakatos), it is obvious that our program starts from the traditional requirements: the definition of a strong core of hypotheses does not cope very well with the plurality of sometimes conflicting points of view applied to a single object. Similarly, the pragmatic use of theories seen as a toolbox to inform, inspire, anchor and design purposes/objectives may appear slightly suspect to the finicky.[9]

This can raise difficulties inside the team itself. The multiplication of ontological hypothesis inherited from different research traditions may eventually lead to tensions into the analytical scope. For example, psychologists may consider that each individual mentally constructs the world of experience through internal cognitive processes, while sociologists may favour a non-mentalist approach focused on social explanations of actions. Similarly, linguists may only consider interaction between agents rather than what occurs at individual level.

The fact is that until now, our approach is more a joint enterprise that aims at understanding a common object (cooperation) and (for some of us) designing situations of collective activity based on this plural rather than shared understanding. The multiplication of viewpoints obviously favours theoretical confrontation and is therefore an opportunity to enrich the design options. But it does not necessarily lead to substantial progress in the mutual elaboration of a body of knowledge in the context of a traditional research program, let alone the constitution of a transdisciplinary research which would ultimately aim at creating a new disciplinary field.

The risk here is to generate a sort of alliance of convenience that can be seen as a mutual instrumentalisation between human and social sciences on one side and informatics on the other side: informatics may use human and social sciences to inform the design in a more or less controlled way, and human and social sciences may utilise informatics to create artefacts that will allow them to explore phenomena of interest for their own purpose. A concerted commitment to design may not ultimately be realised. This issue is not new. Most research groups engaged in interdisciplinary work have to deal with it, and a huge amount of literature is devoted to this particular point. In the CSCW community, for example, since the seminal work conducted by the Lancaster team on studying air traffic controllers' practices and designing artefacts to support these practices, this tricky articulation between empirical data and design has been constantly questioned (see, e.g. Crabtree 2003; Hughes et al. 1993). The Situated Computing manifesto itself stresses the necessity to develop pluridisciplinary approaches to design but does not provide any method to proceed. The challenge remains still open to the EUSSET community.

---

[9]This point opens a traditionally much debated question: does design require any theoretical foundations to fulfil its instrumental goals? (see, e.g. Halverson 2002) in the context of CSCW).

Acknowledgements The MISS project was funded by UTT (strategic research program grant), with the support of Conseil Général de l'Aube for the doctoral work. Other mentioned projects benefited from various grants from the French National Research Agency (ANR) programs, Région Champagne-Ardennes, ANDRA, DGA, Orange Labs, France Telecom and EDF. We thank the anonymous reviewers for their helpful and insightful comments. We are also grateful to Jacques Theureau for his reading and comments on an early version of this paper.

References

Alaoui, M., & Lewkowicz, M. (2013). A living lab approach to involve elderly in the design of smart TV applications offering communication services. In A. Ant Ozok, & P. Zaphiris (Eds.), *Online communities and social computing* (Lecture notes in computer science, Ch. 37, Vol. 8029, pp. 325–334), Berlin/Heidelberg: Springer.

Atifi, H., & Marcoccia, M. (2003, July 13–18). *Cultural variation and standardization in CMC. A comparative analysis of French and Moroccan Newsgroups.* Paper presented at the 8th IPrA conference, Toronto.

Bardram, J. E., Bjorn, P., Glenstrup, A. J., & Pederson, T. (2011, 19–23 March). The global interaction research initiative at the IT University of Copenhagen, Denmark. *Proceedings of CSCW 2011* (pp. 489–495), Hangzhou, China.

Bourguin, G., Lewandowski, A., & Lewkowicz, M. (2013). Sharing experience around component compositions: Application to the eclipse ecosystem. *International Journal of Distributed Systems and Technologies (IJDST), 4*(4), 15–28.

Budweg, S., Lewkowicz, M., Müller, C., & Schering, S. (2012). Fostering social interaction in AAL: Methodological reflections on the coupling of real household Living Lab and SmartHome approaches. *i-com, 11*(3), 30–35.

Cahier, J.-P. (2009). *RCA-sos21: Serious Game pour les activités citoyennes liées au développement durable.* Paper presented at the Carrefour des Possibles FING (Fédération Internet de Nouvelle Génération), Rennes, France.

Cahier, J.-P., & Zacklad, M. (2001). Expérimentation d'une approche coopérative et multi points de vue de la construction et de l'exploitation de catalogues commerciaux "actifs". *Document Numérique, 5*(3–4), 45–64.

Cahier, J.-P., Ait-Said, A., & Zaher, L. (2008). Un Web 2.0 basé sur Hypertopic pour les initiatives de développement durable *Actes de la conférence IC 2008, Atelier spécial "IC 2.0", 17–19 Juin, Nancy.* 17–19 Juin, Nancy.

Cahier, J.-P., El Nawas, N., Zhou, C., & Benel, A. (2011, July 6–8). Web 2.0 & serious game: Structuring knowledge for participative and educative representations of the City. *Proceedings of the international conference on smart and sustainable city*, Shanghai.

Cahier, J.-P., Benel, A., & Salembier, P. (2013). Towards a "non-disposable" software infrastructure for participation. *Interaction Design and Architecture(s) Journal – IxD&A* (18), 68–83.

Cahour, B., & Salembier, P. (2012, 5–10 May). *The user phenomenological experience: Evoking the lived activity with "re-situating" interviews.* Paper presented at the workshop on theories behind UX research and how they are used in practice, CHI'2012, Austin, Texas.

Cahour, B., Salembier, P., Brassac, C., Bouraoui, J. L., Pachoud, B., Vermersch, P., et al. (2005). Methodologies for evaluating the affective experience of a mediated interaction *Workshop on Innovative Approaches to Evaluating Affective Interfaces, Proceedings of the CHI 2005 conference, April 2–7.* Portland, Oregon.

Caussanel, J., Cahier, J.-P., Zacklad, M., & Charlet, J. (2002). *Cognitive interactions in the semantic web.* Paper presented at the Semantic web workshop, Hawaii.

Crabtree, A. (2003). *Designing collaborative systems: A practical guide to ethnography.* London: Springer.

de Montmollin, M. (1984). *L'intelligence de la tâche.* Berne: Peter Lang.

DeMichelis, G., & Loregian, M. (2009). From CSCW to new workstations: The itsme project. *Proceedings of the 2009 International Symposium on Collaborative Technologies and Systems* (pp. xvii–xix). Washington, DC: IEEE Computer Society.

Dubois, E., Gauffre, G., Bach, C., & Salembier, P. (2006). Participatory design meets mixed reality design models – Implementation based on a formal instrumentation of an informal design approach. In G. Calvary, C. Pribeanu, G. Santucci & J. Vanderdonckt (Eds.), *"Computer-Aided Design of User Interfaces V", Procrrdings of the 6th International Conference on Computer-Aided Design of User Interfaces CADUI'2006 (Bucharest, 6–8 June)* (pp. 71–84). Berlin: Springer.

Erickson, T. (1995). Notes on design practice: Stories and prototypes as catalysts for communication. In J. Carroll (Ed.), *Scenario-based design: Envisioning work and technology in system development*. New York: Wiley.

EUSSET. (2012). *Situated computing – A proposal to explore and develop innovative socially embedded technologies*. From http://www.eusset.eu/index.php?id=5

Février, F., Gauducheau, N., Jamet, E., Rouxel, G., & Salembier, P. (2011). La prise en compte des affects dans le domaine des interactions homme-machines : quels modèles, quelles méthodes, quels bénéfices ? *Le Travail Humain, 74*(2), 183–201.

Gaglio, G., & Foli, O. (2011, September 7–10). *The organizational sense of internal communication practionners*. Paper presented at the ESA Congress (European Sociological Association), Genève.

Halverson, C. A. (2002). Activity theory and distributed cognition: Or what does CSCW need to do with theories ? *Computer Supported Cooperative Work (CSCW), 11*(1–2), 243–267.

Hughes, J. A., Randall, D., & Shapiro, D. (1993). From ethnographic record to system design. Some experiences from the field. *Computer Supported Cooperative Work (CSCW), 1*(1), 123–141.

Lacour, P., Freitas, A., Benel, A., Eyraud, F., & Zambon, D. (2013). Enhancing linguistic diversity through collaborative translation. In E. H. G. Jones & E. Uribe-Jongbloed (Eds.), *Minority languages and social media: Participation, policy and perspectives*. Bristol: Multilingual Matters.

Lewkowicz, M. Marcoccia, M., Atifi, H., Benel, A., Gaglio, G., Gauducheau, N., & Tixier, M. (2008, May 20–23). Online social support: Benefits of an interdisciplinary approach for studying and designing cooperative computer-mediated solutions. In P. Hassanaly et al. (Eds.), *Proceedings of COOP'08: 8th International Conference on the Design of Cooperative Systems* (pp. 144–155), Carry-Le-Rouet.

Matta, N., Loriette, S., Nigro, J.-M., Barloy, Y., Cahier, J.-P., & Sediri, M. (2012). Representing experience on Road accident Management. *Proceedings of WETICE, Track on Collaborative Technology for Coordinating Crisis Management, 25–27 Juin 2012*, Toulouse: IEEE.

Merle, F., Benel, A., Doyen, G., & Gaiti, D. (2012). Decentralized documents authoring system for decentralized teamwork: Matching architecture with organizational structure. *Proceedings of GROUP'2012, 27–31 October 2012, Sanibel Island* (pp. 27–31). Sanibel Island: ACM Press.

Palaci, F., Filippi, G., & Salembier, P. (2012). Coordination and artifacts in joint activity: the case of tagging in high-risk industries. *Work-A Journal of Prevention Assessment & Rehabilitation, 41*(Suppl 1), 69–75.

Reuter, C., Marx, A., & Pipek, V. (2012). Crisis management 2.0: Towards a systematization of social software use in crisis situations. *International Journal of Information Systems for Crisis Response and Management (IJISCRAM), 4*(1), 1–16.

Salembier, P. (2013, February 22). *A brief (and subjective) history of francophone ergonomics*. Paper presented at the workshop on Francophone ergonomics & CSCW, ECSCW 2013, Paphos, Cyprus.

Salembier, P., & Legout, M.-C. (2012, July 23–28). Analysing the design process of an interactive music installation in the urban space. *Proceedings of the ICMPC – ESCOM 2012 joint conference (12th International Conference on Music Perception and Cognition – 8th Triennial Conference of the European Society for the Cognitive Sciences of Music. Symposium on Cognition in Musical Composition: methodologies, results, challenges*. Thessaloniki, Greece.

Salembier, P., Dugdale, J., Frejus, M., & Haradji, Y. (2009, September 30–October 2). A descriptive model of contextual activities for the design of domestic situations. *Proceedings of ECCE 2009*. Helsinki: ACM.

Schmidt, K. (2011). *Cooperative work and coordinative practices – Contributions to the conceptual foundations of computer-supported cooperative work (CSCW)*. London: Springer.

Schmidt, K., & Bannon, L. (2013). Constructing CSCW: The first quarter century. *Computer Supported Cooperative Work – The Journal of Collaborative Computing and Work Practices, 22*(4–6), 345–372.

Schmidt, K., Bannon, L., & Wagner, I. (2011). Lest we forget – The European field study tradition and the issue of conditions of work in CSCW research. *ECSCW 2011: Proceedings of the 12th European Conference on Computer Supported Cooperative Work, 24–28 September 2011*, Aarhus, Denmark.

Soulier, E., & Caussanel, J. (2002, July 28). Narrative tools to improve collaborative sense-making. *Workshop on meaning negociation, held in conjunction with Eighteenth National Conference on Artificial Intelligence – AAAI'02*, Edmonton, Alberta, Canada.

Soulier, E., Rousseau, F., Bugeaud, F., Legrand, J., & Neffati, H. (2011). Modeling and simulation of new territories projects using agencements theory, mereological principles and simplicial complex tool. *Proceedings of the International Conference on Smart and Sustainable City (ICSSC), 06–08 Juillet 2011*, Shangai.

Soulier, E., Neffati, H., Rousseaux, F., Legrand, J., Bugeaud, F., Saurel, P., et al. (2012, July 4–6). Collective intelligence modeling throughout territorial agencements. *Proceedings of 2012 EcoMod*, Seville.

Stokols, D. (2006). Toward a science of transdisciplinary action research. *American Journal of Community Psychology, 38*(1–2), 63–77.

Theureau, J. (2006). *Cours d'action : Méthode développée*. Toulouse: Octares.

Tixier, M., & Lewkowicz, M. (2011). Design and evaluation of an online social support application for family caregivers. In A. Ant Ozok & P. Zaphiris (Eds.), *Proceedings of the 4th international conference on online communities and social computing (OCSC'11)*(pp. 267–276). Berlin/Heidelberg: Springer.

Tixier, M., Gaglio, G., & Lewkowicz, M. (2009, May 10–13). Translating social support practices into online services for family caregivers. *Proceedings of GROUP'2009*. Sanibel Island: ACM.

Tixier, M., Lewkowicz, M., Marcoccia, M., Atifi, H., Benel, A., & Gaglio, G. (2010). Practices analysis and digital platform design – An interdisciplinary study of social support. *Proceedings of COOP 2010 – 9th international conference on the design of cooperative systems, 19–21 May, Aix-en-Provence*. London: Springer.

Wulf, V., Rohde, M., Pipek, V., & Stevens, G. (2011, March 19–23). Engaging with practices: Design case studies as a research framework in CSCW. *Proceedings of CSCW 2011*(pp. 505–512). Hangzhou: ACM.

Zacklad, M. (2005). Introduction aux ontologies sémiotiques dans le Web Socio Sémantique. In M.-C. Jaulent (Ed.), *Actes des 16èmes journées francophones d'Ingénierie des Connaissances – IC'2005*. Grenoble: PUG.

Zhou, C., Bénel, A., & Lejeune, C. (2006). Towards a standard protocol for community-driven organizations of knowledge. *Proceedings of the thirteenth international conference on concurrent engineering. Frontiers in artificial intelligence and applications* (Vol. 143, pp. 438–449). Amsterdam: IOS Press.

Zouinar, M., Salembier, P., & Darcy, S. (2010). Etude exploratoire des usages d'une application mobile. *Proceedings of IHM 2010, Luxembourg, 20–23 Septembre*. New-York: ACM.

Part III
Design Issues

Chapter 10
Interaction Design at Itsme

Giorgio De Michelis

10.1 Introduction

After a 1 year long preparation, at April 1st 2008, we had the kickoff meeting of
itsme, a project with the ambition of designing and building an innovative front end
of Linux for workstations (De Michelis et al. 2009). The idea behind our project
was to go beyond the desktop metaphor shaping all existing operating systems for
workstations (Windows, MAC OS, Linux versions like Ubuntu, etc.) to create a new
system able to support the context awareness of its users.

Our project is still ongoing (after a radical stop, due to the end of the consumption
of the first round collected investment, we have slowly restarted to work in a two
persons' team, and we have completed in these days a first running prototype
exhibiting the main features of our system, and we are now planning to show it
to a new group of investors, to move toward the market), but it makes sense, I think,
to reflect and to discuss with a sensible audience what we have learned about how it
is possible to design a radical innovation in a crucial sector of ICT, where there is a
"de facto" standard and billions of people use it all over the world.

The issue I want to bring to the attention of the readers in this paper is how we
designed itsme, with a particular attention on how we inflected interaction design in
the process and on how we tried to interact with and get feedbacks from the users
even before they could test and evaluate our system. We have used in our project
unconventional versions of interaction and participatory design, but we did it paying
a constant attention on how we were working, and therefore, we learned a lot on
design of systems for the general public like an operating system for workstation (or
its front end). Our attention on how we were designing was motivated, not only by

G. De Michelis (✉)
DISCo, University of Milano – Bicocca, Milan, Italy
e-mail: gdemich@disco.unimib.it

© Springer-Verlag London 2015
V. Wulf et al. (eds.), *Designing Socially Embedded Technologies in the Real-World*,
Computer Supported Cooperative Work, DOI 10.1007/978-1-4471-6720-4_10

my academic interest on design but also and mainly by my awareness that designing a successful innovation, capable to substitute a widely diffused standard, needs a maximum of cure.

The paper is organized as follows: first, we shortly recall how we arrived to decide to try to design a radically innovative front end for the operating system of workstations, and then we discuss the main steps in our project. We will survey in particular: the composition of the itsme concept, the move from the concept to the software architecture, the interaction with the users, and the changes of the concept we did while design was still ongoing.

The last section will be dedicated to a discussion of our view on the couple "innovation-continuity," showing that, paradoxically, disruptiveness softens the opposition between them.

10.2   Beyond the Desktop Metaphor

In 1984, Apple, inspired by Alto and Star workstations of Xerox, presented Macintosh (in short, Mac) its innovative personal computer. The Mac had a great impact on the market and greater one on the companies producing personal computers and/or their operating systems, defining a "de facto" standard characterizing the features of all the workstations that would be offered on the IT market in the future. Graphic interfaces, mouse, windows, and icons can be considered the most innovative features characterizing the Mac, but what is mostly relevant is that all those features shaped the interaction with the machine on the basis of a simple and intuitive metaphor. As proposed by the Xerox PARC researchers, the workstation interface is based, in fact, on the "desktop metaphor" (Kay 1977), i.e., a replica of the surface on which users work: a plane supporting and containing several distinctive tools, documents, and objects of different types, a hierarchy of folders, a trash basket, etc. The success of the desktop metaphor stems from its ability to reproduce the arrangement of tangible things: if the personal computer is a multifunctional machine allowing to perform several distinct tasks, then users can easily do their tasks on it in the same way as they do on their desktops, without needing specific training and, even, without looking at their manuals.

As we have recalled above, in few years, all workstations adopted the same approach for their interfaces (Windows1 appeared at the end of 1985 with a limited success, but Windows2 that appeared at the end of 1987 gained in short time an immense popularity and a great share of the market), making the "desktop metaphor" the "de facto" standard for personal computers. However, the technological evolution of workstations after 1984 (always larger internal disks, e-mail becoming a universal medium, the World Wide Web with its growing information, services, and social interaction) has dramatically increased the number of tasks supported by PCs, adding, in particular, content and information management tasks to those that were already supported, and the digital contents and information accessible to their users grew even more rapidly (Eppler and Mengis 2006). Operating systems for workstations have tried to accompany these changes increasing the number of their functions and services, but this has made them always more complicated and difficult to use, while users have slightly changed their way of using personal computers in directions that are always more distant from their original nature of multitasking tools.

Surveying a literature dating back up to the early 1990s, Victor Kaptelinin and Mary Czerwinski, the editors of *Beyond the Desktop Metaphor* (2007), sum up that "the development of desktop systems over the last two decades has revealed limitations of the desktop metaphor. In particular, the metaphor does not provide adequate support for the access to information objects along with the display of the content of those objects, multitasking, dealing with multiple information hierarchies, communication and collaboration, and coordinated use of multiple technologies." (ibidem, 6).

It is difficult to dispute the above claim, since, even as users, most of us (I imagine to share with my readers a life of "knowledge worker"[1]) have experienced the limits listed there. The authors of the above quoted book continue their intellectual exercise giving form to what should substitute the current organization of personal computers claiming that metaphors themselves are inadequate for driving the design of new ways of interacting with digital devices and content (Freeman and Gelernter 2007, 23; "We prefer to approach software design not by metaphorics but by Nelson's concept of virtuality"). The limitations of the desktop metaphor appear to them as due to the increasing number of tasks supported by present-day personal computers, in particular on the content management side and to their inability to deal with the social dimension of human tasks.

When, on my side, in 2007, I begun to think how the limits of the desktop metaphor could be overcome, I agreed with the above critiques, but I was convinced that I needed also to go beyond the task-based view of personal computers to better capture what was happening in their use: users, more specifically some users, in fact, were changing what they were asking to ICT, from being supported in a large variety of tasks related with information management to having a companion in all the circumstances of their life. Instead of abandoning "metaphorics" for "virtuality," I tried, therefore, to look for a new metaphor capturing the changes undergoing in the way people use their PCs.

The distinction of some PC users among all that I did in the previous claim should not surprise the reader: in accordance with what has happened with other technological products (from pens to cars), becoming a universally usable machine has induced a differentiation process among its users. Even if a serious analysis of the emerging profiles of PC users has not yet been accomplished, we can recall that, today, users of personal computers encompass, on the one side, those using it, almost exclusively, to Skype with other people and for other simple tasks (e.g., the parents of sons and/or daughters studying away from home), on the other, people who are progressively becoming unable to do anything without the support of their

---

[1]In the next pages, we will come back to knowledge workers.

personal computer (e.g., knowledge workers). Without spending further words on the emergence of different user profiles, let us concentrate our attention on the people for which the PC is an unavoidable tool and on the way they use it.

As I have said above, I am thinking of active knowledge workers,[2] who are engaged in a variety of endeavors where they concur to create new knowledge and to publicize it in (multimedia) documents: for all of them, personal computers have become unavoidable, but always more inefficient, tools. The fact that today's personal computers contain a relevant part of the content and information they need and the tools for navigating and manipulating it, as well as almost all the knowledge they create (in the form of messages, posts, and multimedia documents) and the tools for creating it, modifies the way knowledge workers interact with their personal computers. It is not, generally, a matter of being supported in managing information, since searching, classifying, creating folders, etc., are time consuming and distracting tasks, with respect to the practice triggering them: what users want and need is having ready at hands, on the screen of their personal computer, all what is relevant for what they are currently doing. Combining the management of information with the execution of tasks, in fact, the way knowledge workers use their PC, is radically changing: most of them switch it on, as soon as they reach their workplace, because it has become an extension of their capability of acting and interacting, since, in most situations, only in accessing the information stored in the PC can they perform effectively. But while the task-oriented organization of their personal computers asks them to retrieve the content, using more or less sophisticated searching mechanisms, they need it immediately "present at hand," without distractions and losses of time. We, CSCW researchers and practitioners, know what this change in perspective means, because we have studied it from the very beginning of our common endeavor: recognizing the situatedness of our action and interaction in a context that is not only spatial and temporal, but, most importantly, social.[3] When we say that human action and interaction are situated in a context, in fact, we may refer to diverse dimensions of it: *spatial* context (where a person affects what she can do), *temporal* context (time is deeply affecting and/or conditioning what a person does), and, finally, *social* context (the people participating in a common experience share knowledge of their past,

---

[2] Knowledge workers (Blackler et al. 1993) have emerged as the most important category of workers within offices in the last 30 years. In the preface to *Knowledge workers in the Information Society*, Mosco and McKercher (2007) recall three main definitions of knowledge work. The first one, and most narrow, considers knowledge work any practice involving "the direct manipulation of symbols to create an original knowledge product or to add obvious value to an existing one." The second that extends sensibly the previous one considers knowledge work any practice involving the management and distribution of information. The third that is the broadest one considers knowledge work any practice involved in "the chain of producing and distributing knowledge products." People doing knowledge work under the broadest of these definitions correspond to our profile of PC users.

[3] Situatedness has been one major theme of research in CSCW from its very beginning. Without any aim of completeness, we can remember: Suchman 2007; Agostini et al. 1996; Schmidt 2002; De Michelis, Chap. 5, this book.

mutual commitments, and their potential for action and interaction). The social dimension of context is what matters in these pages, since it permeates any action and interaction of a person, imposing him/her to go beyond their tasks.

Without deepening the discussion on situatedness, I spend few lines for discussing the systems allowing people participating in common experiences to share knowledge. Early groupware systems – from the Coordinator (Winograd and Flores 1986) to Notes (Kawell et al. 1988) and beyond (e.g., Google Wave (Siegler 2009) and Google+ (Sanjay Kairam et al. 2012)) – cannot fully solve the situatedness problem, since they create and rely on spaces for collaboration among different users that are separate from their individual workspaces. Services like shared calendars and spaces, document management systems, networked repositories, co-browsing tools, and chats have all enriched what workstations offer to users, but none of them is able to take into account how the social experiences people are sharing influence their individual experiences, enriching and/or affecting them. This is visible only if we take into account that social contexts appear different from the viewpoints of their diverse individual participants, i.e., if we deal with them at the diverse individual workplaces of their participants.

It is the consideration of situatedness, or, in other words, context awareness, from an individual viewpoint, the issue that guided me toward inventing a new front end of a personal computer or, more precisely, of its operating system (called *itsme*). There is a growing evidence that the complexity users meet when trying to get rid of the large amount of objects stored in folders is not purely quantitative, since users at any moment need to access only those documents that constitute the pragmatic and semantic context of their current focus of attention. They have no ways to select what interests them in a given moment among all their objects. The context awareness provided by current workstations, let me repeat it here, is limited and partial: productivity tools (even if collected in suites) still have supremacy over the usage context of their objects, and, moreover, there is a clear-cut separation between them and communication and/or Web browsing packages, not allowing to organize all objects on the basis of their usage context.

10.3   The Itsme Project

The starting point of the itsme project has been the discovery that going beyond a task-based organization of ICT systems is not possible at the level of applications that are distinct and function-oriented pieces of software. Context awareness is not something users need while they are working with specific applications: on the contrary, they need it, irrespectively of the application they use, to articulate their work in relation with other people, to organize themselves, to access relevant pieces of knowledge, and to know what to do next. The services supporting context awareness should glue all the applications a person is using, so that all and only the knowledge related to a context are accessible altogether.

We need, therefore, to modify existing operating systems embedding in them context awareness services. This risks resulting in a greater complexity of workstations at the interface level, if we don't change them in a radical way, applying the simple rules governing contexts. As said in the previous section, contexts continuously form.

In order to provide users with an integrated experience of the services we have designed for context awareness in these years, we need to design a new (operating system for) workstation where, abandoning the desktop metaphor, what a user does is embedded in the context giving it sense.

Reflecting on the research done within the CSCW community, we conceived a new metaphor for the "look and feel" of a workstation, namely, that of *stories and venues* (please note the plural!). Everything users do is in the context of one of the diverse stories they live with other people. Any of these *stories* has created or imported during its evolution a large variety of things (digital and/or physical objects of different types, people's addresses, relevant URLs, exchanged messages, etc.), and, to perform adequately within that story, users need to have them, ready at hand, in a unique (physical and/or virtual, augmented) place, in a unique *venue*.

This requires, on the one hand, that the system goes beyond the distribution in different places of the things people need in their activities determined by the applications currently installed in a workstation (the documents created by the user are stored in the file system, the e-mail messages are inside the mail client, their attachments are in a particular folder of the file system, the bookmarked Web documents are elements of a list in the browser, etc.) putting them together.

On the other hand, stories are partially reflected in the threads generated by user interactions.[4] A story can, therefore, be seen as a bunch of threads of interrelated heterogeneous events (from the viewpoint of the applications supporting them: e-mail and chat conversations, RSS feeds, posts in a social computing platform, etc.). The creation and maintenance of the related venue can be straightforward and do not need user intervention, but corrections and refinements, if we let the system keep together its threads and add to a venue any new thread originating in it. By the way, it has to be underlined that this does not require that all the interacting users have workstations with the itsme operating system (i.e., based on the venues' metaphor), since itsme can locate objects in venues using only the information characterizing threads.

---

[4]After the coordinator, presented by Fernando Flores and Terry Winograd in 1986 (Winograd and Flores 1986), there has been a rich debate in the CSCW community following two different directions: on the one side, Lucy Suchman (1993) discussed it for its unnatural forcing human conversations within formalized patterns, allowing hierarchical control on it; on the other side, several authors paid a growing attention to conversations as threads of communication events underlining their switching among different media (Reder and Schwab 1988, 1990) and showing their relevance, beyond their reduction to illocutionary acts (Bullen and Bennett 1990; Winograd 1994; De Michelis and Grasso 1994). After a period where attention on them declined, threads have gained again attention with the Google Wave and Google+.

In our previous research, we revisited the language/action perspective (De Michelis and Grasso 1994) claiming the importance of threads, and these same concepts are now the bases of the new metaphor we are proposing:

- A thread contributes to constitute a context and its venue.
- Venues aggregate threads and the related objects.
- New venues are created as new threads begin, either from scratch (i.e., by reacting to an event) or spinning off existing ones (e.g., when the issue characterizing a thread changes or multiplies).
- Users can modify venues sorting the objects they contain, merging or splitting different venues, deleting them, and so on.
- Objects only exist within a venue or, when a venue has not yet been created, in a special space, called *limbo*, where all threads and objects not yet assigned to a venue are stored.
- A thread, and/or an object, can be stored, through replicated references, in several, diverse venues, if it contributes to constitute diverse contexts.

While the desktop metaphor does not preserve the individuality of different contexts, meaning that users can handle objects related to different contexts at the same time, in the venues' metaphor at any time, only one venue is open in front of the user. All venues are contained in the " home," where the user is brought when he/she switches on: the home is where he/she can browse all his/her venues and open any of them.

In itsme, I can, with few clicks, create a venue for each of my stories and manage them (with no constraints: I can create few – up to zero – or many stories, small or big stories; I can create them early or later, when they are well consolidated leaving the relative threads in the limbo; I can split a story in two, or merge two stories; I can move an object or a thread between two venues; etc.). Venues are self-updating, even if they are not "intelligent," because itsme uses metadata to keep threads together.

A quick example may help to put together the information presented above: like most of my peers, my life is complicated, due to my many commitments and engagements. During a typical working day, I switch from my lectures to the paper I am writing with two colleagues, from the master thesis in which I am advisor to a meeting of the foundation whose board I am a member of: all these are, in itsme terms, stories. Whenever I do a switch between two stories, I need to quickly situate myself in the new one, in order to be able to act and interact effectively in it: having a venue for each of my stories lets me have all what I need ready at hand. Consider the following case: while I am reading a paper, I receive a telephone call from my colleague Giuseppe asking me if I have read the document he sent me. He needs my comments, before going to the meeting where he will present his document. I received his document some weeks ago, and I have a vague recollection of it: it seems to me that I have read it, but I can't remember if I have some written notes on it or not. With itsme, I go to venue related with the story I share with Giuseppe, and there, I find his document and, if they exist, my written notes on it, so that I can almost immediately react to Giuseppe request; without itsme, I should search for Giuseppe's document and for my notes, if they exist, and it is not certain that this search will be straightforward. Itsme is not commenting Giuseppe's document for me, it is not doing my work, it only helps me to concentrate on my work without spending time in searching and recollecting!

Technically speaking, the starting point for itsme is the Linux operating system. In fact, itsme is going to be deployed as a Linux distribution with a peculiar front end that will exploit a set of characteristic services. Its novel graphical user interface relying on and illustrating the relationships between objects that characterize venues is supported by an intermediate stratus of software, allowing to associate to all the objects stored in the file system metadata and links and to manage them. The use of Linux will allow for the exploitation of all the available components, and itsme will represent a radical innovation and carry a significant contribution (in terms both of technology and of the presence of practitioners) to the existing community. However, the affiliation of itsme to the open source scene goes beyond the adoption of Linux development as a platform: one of the slogans with which the itsme concept has been demonstrated is *let's team up*, meaning that the involvement of people in the project is perceived to be essential. This idea basically translates to three aspects:

1. The constitution of a community following and providing directions for the project, implementing a form of participatory design; a great effort is being put in creating a "real-life" community of people meeting each other (through seminars and participation in public events), and also some of the so-called Web 2.0 services, such as social network sites, are being employed to make the community constantly grow and live.
2. The search for contributions from outside the company: new ideas, concepts, visual design components, and code. Community members are also being involved in the evaluation of ideas and the validation of design products.
3. Community members are helping us to generate hype on what we are doing and on the (long disregarded) issues that we are trying to solve. People are helping us to create the market before the real workstation is ready to be sold. In this way, itsme candidates itself to be the fulcrum for the innovation in consumer applications such as productivity tools and Web-based and e-mail-based applications.

The development of itsme has been carried on, up to now, in two phases. In the first one (2008–2011), a design and development team of almost 15 people worked full time on the itsme prototype. In 2011, the resources granted to itsme by its business angels came to an end, but the new resources we expected from private (venture capital) and public funding did not show up against our expectations. The project group was dissolved, and it started a new phase (2011–now) where the project continued with the aim to complete the first prototype release of itsme, even if I could only rely on one part-time developer (who was part of the team working on itsme during the first phase) and some students. The prototype, with an improved interface, has been completed in February 2014 together with a new release of the concept manual, and we make reference to the latter in our description of the system. We plan now to show the prototype to potential investors, to get new resources for the final steps toward the delivery of itsme to the market. During this third phase, we will reanimate the community supporting our project providing to its members a way to access and test the prototype. In this way, the development of the full version of itsme will reflect their critiques and suggestions.

10.4 The Team

The team engaged in the first phase of the itsme project merits some words. Besides me, there were 16 young people with different professional backgrounds: almost one half of them were software specialists, and their role was mainly to design and develop the software; 5 people were industrial and/or graphical designers, and their role was both interaction and interface design; the rest had different backgrounds (philosophy, business design, communication) and were managing the communication of the project (website, presence at fairs, relationships with the press, etc.). I paid a great cure to create out of them a well-amalgamated team, so that each of them felt to fully participate in the creation of an innovative piece of software with a potential great impact on the ICT sector. I tried to get this through different means: frequent meetings of the whole team to discuss design choices at any level, mixing people with different backgrounds in the small groups dealing with specific tasks or responsibilities, and seminars dedicated to reflect on the difficulties and risks of innovation design. Seminars have been dedicated to issues like how to find a balance between innovation and continuity, so that people who already use existing personal computers can move to itsme without effort, being prepared to redo all what we have done up to a certain moment, or a large part of it, when we discover that better choices are possible. They played a big role in creating an identity in the team.

I tried also to keep the team as open as possible, letting its members to participate in meeting with external people from the business, the technical and the design field, and constantly inviting them to discuss what they are doing with any person showing interest in the project.

Openness of the team is the first step toward being able to listen to users whenever it is possible. And users have been a constant concern during our project.

10.5 The Concept

When we did the kickoff meeting, at April 1st 2008, I had a clear idea of the "stories and venues" metaphor and of what itsme should be, but most of the team didn't know so much about it: they had only the vague idea of the new system they got from their conversations with me before being enrolled in the project. We decided to begin our work in accordance with two guidelines: (1) we wanted to adopt what could be considered, at best, an interaction design approach (De Michelis 2003), and (2) apart from the generic features of the system we had to design and develop (a Linux-based front end, the "stories and venues" metaphor, a system together with the services users could need for adopting it easily), nothing was fixed.

In few months, we came out with the first thing of our project: the concept manual. It was a rich description of the "look and feel" of the system and of the main features[5] characterizing it: the venues, the transit, the limbo, etc.

The effort we did for writing the first version of the concept manual involved mainly the designers of the team, but it was constantly widespread in the whole team, so that the concept became the document around which the object of design of our team was being created and shared and our communication policy was taking form. After the concept manual, we moved quickly away from the open brainstorming phase, to pass to a more focused design phase, where all what we did was put in relation with the concept. In particular, the concept was of paramount importance for both the first user participation phase and the design of the specs of the software we had to develop.

Our design process aimed at transposing the conceptual framework of itsme into proper design requirements and specifications for the operating system. It has to be underlined that the concept manual of itsme is not a full specification of the system, but the definition of what we are designing. The concept is continuously evolving in parallel with the design and development of the system without a strong alignment between them: in some sense, the differences between the concept and the system testify a design tension always present in the team and grant its openness to changes. The design activity has alternated phases dedicated to the investigation and development of specific design topics with phases dedicated to the refinement of itsme conceptual framework and assumptions and to the exploration of technical requirements and implications. More in detail, the process has followed a macro plan, starting with a problem setting phase, followed by the definition of an interaction design model and the exploration of interaction paradigms and a preliminary graphical user interface through schematic representations, to achieve a detailed design of the look and feel of the itsme visual interface. Given the complexity of the general task, the process has continuously evolved and adapted: a number of micro-activities and workshops involving both the design team, potential users, and the community of interest and stakeholders were organized in relation to the emergent needs.

From an interaction design perspective, itsme can be defined as a dynamic, adaptive, and supportive system whose dialogical qualities are emerging in relation to the interaction with, and by, its users.

While supporting the users in the creation and sedimentation of their personal stories, itsme manifests its own identity, acting more as a partner than as a tool, providing to the user both the context and the rationale for the management of documents, applications, and resources.

---

[5]We will give more details on the features of itsme in the next section.

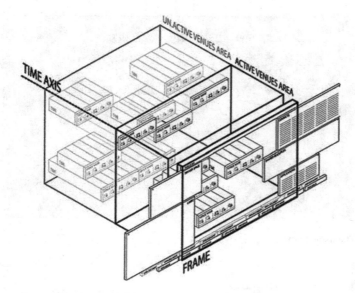

Fig. 10.1   The itsme interface architecture

From a structural point of view (Fig. 10.1), the interface of itsme is a continuous space where the x and y axes correspond to the visualization area of the screen, while the z axis corresponds to a timeline. Venues are automatically placed along the time axis, following their chronological order, but can be freely organized by the user on the screen surface that, as a sort of digital trompe-l'oeil, displays recent and active venues.

The *home* (Fig. 10.2) of itsme is, therefore, populated by the venues. In the home, venues may have two representations (Fig. 10.3): one, highly synthetic, is a stylized symbol with the short name and a number, indicating how many new objects are present in the venue, while the other, more detailed, indicates also, for each type of objects, the number of items and of new items contained in the venue. In the home, like in any other visualization of itsme, in the upper right angle, there is a button with a "plus" symbol, for the creation of a new venue.

From the interaction and interface point of view, *venues* represent the main contexts for personal information and content management: as said above, a venue (Fig. 10.4) is the place where the user finds all what is relevant within one of his/her stories and can manage his/her personal information and communication flow within it.

Within a venue, there are different channels, each represented by a specific tab. Each channel is both a way to easily access a specific category of objects and to quickly create new objects in that category: *messages* contains e-mails and chats, *documents* contains editable files, and *media* contains audio-visual read-only files. The right part of the venue contains the resources in use in the related story: *people*, *Web resources*, and *applications*. One of the main features within a venue, based on

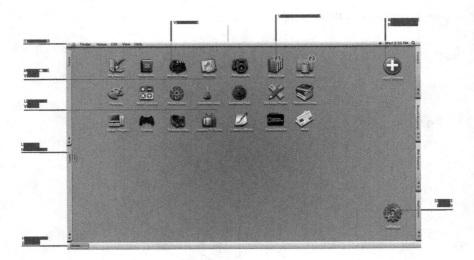

Fig. 10.2 The itsme home

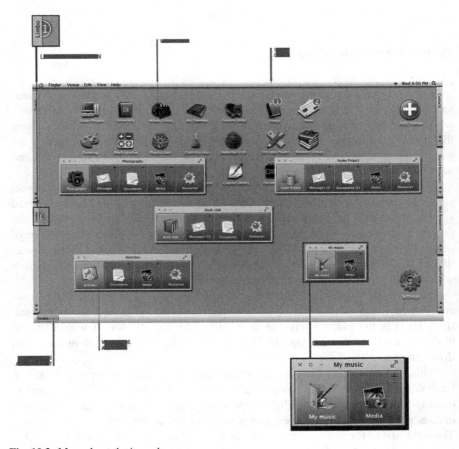

Fig. 10.3 More about the itsme home

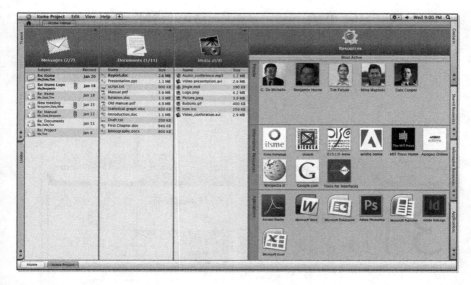

Fig. 10.4 A venue

the use of metadata, is the visualization of the correlations between different files activating a "highlight" mode that, starting from a specific object (e.g., an e-mail message), shows the whole thread containing it (e.g., the whole conversation, all its attachments, and the contacts to all the people participating in it as senders or recipients).

As underlined in Fig. 10.1, the frame surrounding what is displayed on the screen plays a relevant role from the interaction viewpoint.

Its vertical bars contain some sliding menus (Fig. 10.4). Those at the right bar allow a direct access to all the resources of the workstations: contacts, shared resource and web resources, and, finally, applications. More in detail:

- The *contacts* menu allows the access to the whole address book of the workstation.
- The *shared resources* menu allows access to both the *mail* (i.e., a standard e-mail client for Linux) and the *agenda* of the workstation (Fig. 10.5).
- The *Web resources* menu allows access to all the bookmarked informative resources.
- The *applications* menu allows access to all, local and remote, applications.

On the other hand, at the left bar, there are two sliding menus: transit and limbo:

- The *transit* menu allows the access to a buffer containing all the objects that are waiting for being located in a venue. There is a time limit for the permanence of these documents in the transit, after which they are moved to the limbo.
- The *limbo* menu allows the access to a space (resembling a venue) containing all those objects that are not located in a venue, i.e., that do not belong to a story, yet.

ITSME PROJECT VENUE AGENDA CONFIGURATION

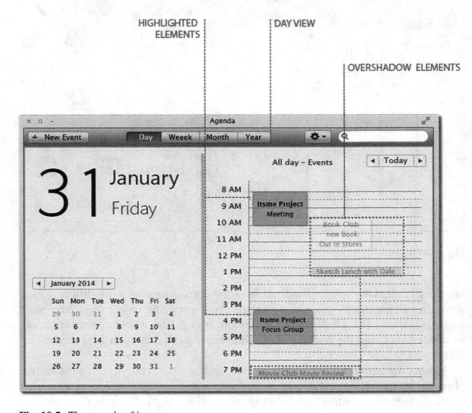

Fig. 10.5 The *agenda* of itsme

If and when a user has not yet created any venue, the limbo contains altogether all the objects of the workstation, avoiding their distribution in diverse places as with current operating systems (Fig. 10.6).

The two horizontal bars have been inspired by the interfaces characterizing most browsers (e.g., Firefox and Chrome) today: the upper bar contains the visualized venue, and the objects open in it; the lower one contains the home of itsme and the open venues.

This means that, if three documents are contemporarily open in a venue (Fig. 10.7), then they are also listed in the upper bar. If the user clicks on another venue in the lower bar, then the display substitutes the previous venue and its open documents with the newly selected one with its open documents, and the same does on the upper bar.

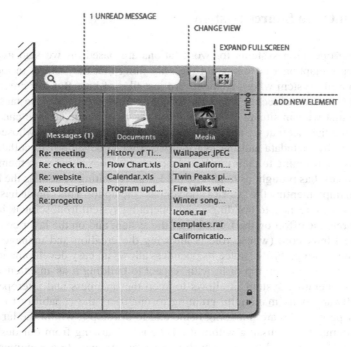

Fig. 10.6 The *limbo* menu

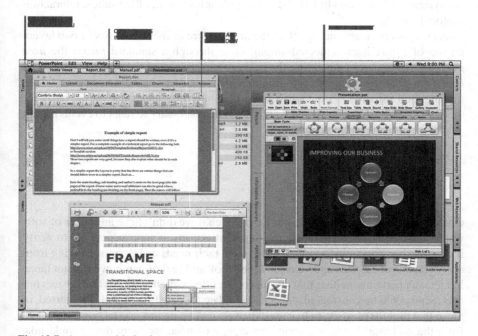

Fig. 10.7 A venue with the documents open in it

10.6 An Open Source System

All existing operating systems for workstations are based, as we said above, on the desktop metaphor. But this is not the only thing that they share: in fact, they share also a file system whose elements are just files of bits. But, for creating and managing venues, we need a smart file system whose objects can be tagged and linked, so that we can situate each of them in the right venue and we can browse threads. Both the fact that we are developing a new operating system whose objects are qualified by metadata and the fact that we want to develop it in collaboration with the users, listening to their needs and desires and conversing with them on our design choices, has brought us to choose the Linux operating system as the basis of the system implementing the "stories and venues" metaphor. This choice has several advantages: with respect to building a new operating system from scratch, it allows to concentrate the effort on the front end of the system and on the layer connecting it with the Linux core (whose role is allowing the creation and management of metadata decorating objects) since its openness allows an easy development of new features and functions on top of it; with respect to building it as an extension of a proprietary operating system, it allows to keep the openness and interoperability of our software at its maximum, granting to our users the capability to interact with other people who are not using itsme and to develop it within the large open source community, discussing within it all the issues arising from our design and development process and trying to push innovation in Linux (e.g., augmenting its file system with tags and links) and in its applications (e.g., office suites, interaction protocols, etc.).

As it appears clearly in Fig. 10.8, the architecture of itsme consists of two layers on top of Linux interconnected among them through a standard *proxy*: the *user interface* (in orange) embedding the desktop metaphor and the smart extension of Linux (in green) where the *logic* (the metadata and item managers, in particular), making the Linux file system smarter (its files have tags and links), is the basis for the *interface* (the event notifier and other modules necessary to react to events) being able to put objects in the venues.

10.7 Users Before Usage

Once the concept manual was in our hands, even if we didn't have any piece of software visible, we decided to interact with potential users as soon as possible to verify if what we had conceived was capable to meet their needs and desires. Moving from the metaphor of "stories and venues" to the look and feel of itsme, we did not have, in fact, any certainty neither that our discourse fitted with user needs and desires nor that itsme could be considered a decent candidate for satisfying them. We started, in those first months of work, to live the experience of being in a crystal bowl, detached from the real world, where internal coherency of what we were doing could take over dramatically on external valuation by the future (potential) users of the system.

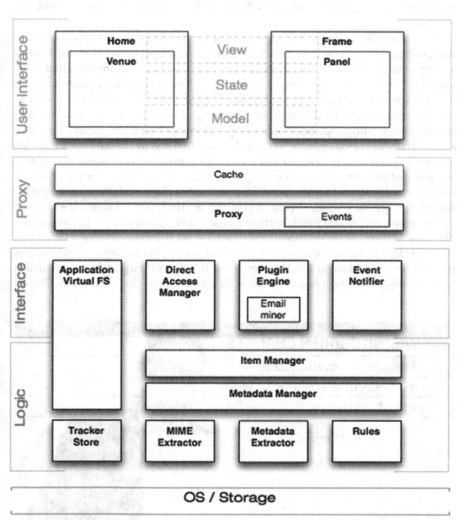

itsme OS architecture

as in the current prototype – November, 2009

Fig. 10.8 The architecture of itsme

I want to stress here that listening to users was an urgent need for orienting our design work, but also that there were no experiences that we could follow in order to do it effectively: participatory design, in fact, approaches have never been adopted for systems for the general public with the complexity of an operating system! Even if we adopted in some way the Apple approach (Isaacson 2011), sublimating the personal experience of the designers themselves and of their relatives and friends, enriched by the knowledge about cooperative work emerging from 20 years of research in the CSCW field, we were absolutely aware that the radical innovation, we wanted to bring forth, needed to rely on well-conducted experiments involving real users.

We decided therefore to do a large (at least for our dimensions) experiment with real people, representing a reasonable sample of our target users. With the help of a team from the University of Siena, lead by Patrizia Marti, we prepared four short videos presenting four users solving intricate problems with itsme: a journalist gathers in a new venue all that she needs (papers, documents, Web resources, contacts, etc.) to write an article; a researcher browses past venues for finding interesting people for the workshop she is organizing and invites them; the owner of a travel agency finds a previous plan of a trip to Norway to use it as the basis of a new one and discusses it with colleagues and customers; a manager rearranges his agenda, when one of his appointments is anticipated. After having seen one or more videos, participants answered to a questionnaire that combined the evaluation of the potential utility of itsme with the explanation of it (Fig. 10.9). This evaluation was made of two parts: on the one hand, participants selected a comment on the video in a predefined set and on the other associated to it a word, to be immersed in a tag cloud.

The videos were shown to some hundreds of people, in two large Autumn events in Italy: first, in Milano at SMAU (the largest ICT fair in Italy), where participants were mostly young people passionate with technologies, and second, in Firenze

Fig. 10.9 A screenshot of one of the videos

at Creativity Festival (a big event on arts, design, hi-tech, and social animation), where participants were mostly young creative people. Our sample was, therefore, made of people well oriented with respect to innovation but with heterogeneous backgrounds, being good representatives of what could be considered the target of early adopters of itsme. The answers of the participants were quite positive with respect to the "stories and venues" metaphor and gave us some interesting indications about the reasons why they considered a system based on it useful that confirmed the rationale of our project (among the most appreciated features of itsme, having all what is relevant in a story in a venue, the time bar, the previewing system, etc.). The tag cloud emerging from the survey underlined our intuition that stories were a quite natural concept for looking to personal social experiences and that navigating among stories was considered as a strong improvement with respect to navigating among messages or documents. Both the participation in two large public events with our stand and our t-shirts and the success of our testing experience gave to the whole team a greater awareness of what we had to design and develop.

While the team was developing the prototype of itsme, always in order to get new feedbacks from the users about its qualities, we decided to develop, in parallel, a Web-based emulator of it. It was a Web platform providing to its users a personalized space where all the actions and interactions constituting a story were put together. Its interface was replicating the design we had defined for itsme, and we thought that it allowed users to experience partially how they can use a system supporting their stories.

The first tests we did with the emulator were quite controversial, with severe negative outcomes and few interesting, positive comments. The messages we got were so strong that we did not go on with a larger experiment, and we immediately reviewed our project on their basis.

The first mistake we did, presenting the emulator of itsme to some people (mainly friends, already interested in our project), was to put them in front of a void system: they could see the structure of venue, but there was not anything inside it. This caused a dramatic paralysis in the users: they did not know what they had to do but also what they could do. So, instead of getting responses about the usability of venues, we got a strong negative feedback about its understandability. Reacting to this unforeseen impasse, we filled the emulator with some generic content, and we made some new experiments with users. This time, we had two different reactions: users with ICT competence could understand what the emulator offered, at a meta level (their behavior was in fact that of experimenting the potential for action and interaction of venues, without any reference to what they need and desire in their everyday life), but the same did not happen with users with no or little ICT competence. Again, we had a very negative feedback: people did not understand what the emulator of itsme was for. The reaction of non-ICT professional users to the emulator needed an explanation: we found it in the fact that filling a venue with generic content could not make visible to users what a venue was for – supporting a story they are living – but looked like a generic aggregation of content and services, whose sense was not clear. We decided, therefore, that the only way for presenting the emulator (and the same would become true for itsme, when ready for a beta test) was offering to users the possibility to access a story, corresponding to his/her habits, profession, and interests. We concentrated in professional stories that seemed to us having some "typical" features that could be embedded in a self-explaining story model: the main stories for general practitioners are those they live with their patients; the main story of a designer is his/her projects; the main stories of business angels are the start-ups on which they have invested; etc. We made, therefore, together with Carla Simone and Federico Cabitza of the University of Milano-Bicocca a study characterizing the care general practitioners give to their patients in terms of cure stories (Cabitza et al. 2014). It was surprising as, seeing the emulator embedding the stories of patients, even users not being in healthcare domain seemed to understand what stories and venues were. This had a relevant impact not only on the itsme emulator per se, as we will see later, but also on the services supporting the adopters of itsme we planned.

Some of the people who tested the emulator considered it, per se, as an interesting platform for Web services: when a service extends in time, they claimed its users live it as a story, and giving them a place where they can manage it efficiently may be an added value. These unexpected comments convinced us to start the development of a platform for Web services, called itsociety, whose prototype had positive evaluations.

It was a strong confirmation that our concept was opening a new perspective on the use of ICT, not only a new interface for personal computers.

10.8 Continuity and Innovation

But the problems users encountered with the itsme emulator brought to our attention a problem that we had not evaluated adequately. We were aware that, in order to convince users of existing personal computers to move to machine equipped with a radically new operating system, we needed to reduce the cost of this transition. For this reason, we had already planned to develop, together with itsme, a service supporting the transfer of their previous content to itsme. This service will grant that all transferred files will find applications for managing them on itsme (take into account that our system is Linux based) and will allow users to create their first venues, if they want. But this is not enough. The question is more serious. Itsme must be a system people can use without extra effort: this means that, when they access it, they must immediately understand what they have in front, what they can do, and, finally, how they can do what they want, even if what they want is doing as before! It seems a paradoxical requirement: itsme must be, at the same time, as any existing system and radically different from all of them. We can formulate this problem in terms of continuity and innovation: the stronger the innovation of your system, the stricter its continuity with respect to existing systems! We try to face this challenge offering to users a front end where they can behave like on a desktop, but they can also adopt venues, if they want and if they see that they offer better services. For this reason, what itsme does for all its users is creating a unique space where all objects (of any type) and resources (from tools to people and to information resources) are stored. Objects and resources related with a story can be moved in a venue, when the user decides it (and from that moment, all what is related with that venue goes directly to it). We are convinced that users, creating and using one venue, will discover its effectiveness and appreciate its services, so that they will move to venues more of their stories and of their content, but we avoid to force them toward venues: in some sense, itsme is an open arena where the user can choose among the desktop and the venues and any mix of the two. This choice characterizes itsme as an open tool where different users may adopt different ways of organizing their personal computers: they can choose when creating a venue (at the very beginning of a story or when it has consolidated), how many venues they create, conversely how much they leave in the limbo, how large is the span of a venue, etc., and they can change any of their choice, whenever they want.

A second choice that we did toward making migration from existing personal computers to itsme as smooth and easy as possible has been to use on itsme all applications available on Linux. This choice has also a technical justification: our software layers on top of Linux do not impact the applications, so that we need only to wrap applications in our middleware, without modifying them, containing our effort at software development, but have been reinforced and confirmed at the user side. The user who moves from his/her machine to itsme is not requested to learn to use new software packages, but he/she can continue to use the software he/she was using before or something quite similar to it (we must take into account that, in any case, if he/she must move from Mac OS or Windows to Linux, he/she finds an application only that is similar to some of the most popular ones he/she was using before).

It can also be interesting to recall that this choice convinced us to restart the design of the prototype. The latter was almost ready, when we thought that the choice of having light applications running on it, instead of some standard ones, would be unable to offer a clear experience of working with itsme. We decided, therefore, to restart our development with both a fully serviced suite of productivity tools and an e-mail client: in this way, interacting with our prototype will be a realistic example of what itsme will be and the user will be in the position to fully understand how much we were able to grant a good combination of continuity and innovation.

10.9   Conclusion: The Next Challenges

The prototype is currently ready, and we are now preparing ourselves to the next steps. These will be devoted to make the important move from the prototype to the system, even if in beta version. This requires evaluating the prototype to get clear guidelines for improving its usability, developing the services needed to support the transition to it by users of current personal computers, and, finally, defining a strategy for going to the market. Going to the market requires finding investors and/or partners to package our system in such a way that its potential users (in particular a first small group of them open to innovation) will be convinced to adopt it: we will live even conversations of this type as a step of our design process, because it will be a test-bed, from a particular angle, of the qualities of our system.

We move into this new phase of our project with an open mind and a lot of curiosity and, also, with a reasonable confidence that what we have done up to now has a value, but without any certainty that we will be successful.

We will get back with you after the beta test.

Acknowledgments The "stories and venues" metaphor and the itsme workstation project are indebted with many persons, even if the responsibility of what I have written is only mine, and it is not possible to list all of them. Let us recall at least, on the one hand, the itsme team (from the people who participated in the design of the prototype to the business angels that gave us the means for doing it and to the numerous people who expressed interest in what we are doing), who shared with me this unique experience and, on the other, the community of CSCW (computer-supported cooperative work) whose ideas and discussions constituted the basis of our work.

References

Agostini, A., De Michelis, G., Grasso, M. A., Prinz, W., & Syri, A. (1996). Contexts, work processes, and workspaces. *Computer Supported Cooperative Work, 5*(3), 223–250.

Blackler, F., Reed, M., & Whitaker, A. (1993). Editorial introduction: Knowledge workers and contemporary organizations. *Journal of Management Studies, 30*(6), 851–862.

Bullen, C. V., & Bennett, J. L. (1990). Learning from user experience with groupware. In *CSCW'90: Proceedings of the 1990 ACM conference on computer-supported cooperative work* (pp. 291–302). New York: ACM Press.

Cabitza, F., Simone, C., & De Michelis, G. (2014). User driven prioritization of features for a prospective inter-personal health record: Perceptions from the Italian context. *Computers in Biology and Medicine, 59*, 202–210.

De Michelis, G. (2003). The design of interactive applications: A different way. In P. Spirakis, A. Kameas, & S. Nikoletseas (Eds.), *Proceedings of the international workshop on ambient intelligence computing* (pp. 101–114). Athens: CTI Press.

De Michelis, G., & Grasso, M. A. (1994). Situating conversations within the language/action perspective: The Milan conversation model. In *CSCW'94: Proceedings of the 1994 ACM conference on computer supported cooperative work* (pp. 89–100). New York: ACM Press.

De Michelis, G., Loregian, M., & Moderini, C. (2009). itsme: Interaction design innovating workstations. *Knowledge, Technology & Policy, 22*(1), 71–78.

Eppler, M. J., & Mengis, J. (2006). The concept of information overload: A review of literature from organization science, accounting, marketing, MIS, and related disciplines. *The Information Society, 20*(5), 325–344.

Freeman, E., & Gelernter, D. (2007). Beyond lifestreams: The inevitable demise of the desktop metaphor. In V. Kaptelinin & M. Czerwinski (Eds.), *Beyond the Desktop Metaphor* (pp. 19–48).

Isaacson, W. (2011). *Steve Jobs: The exclusive biography*. New York: Simon and Schuster.

Kaptelinin, V., & Czerwinski, M. (Eds.). (2007). *Beyond the desktop metaphor*. Cambridge, MA: The MIT Press.

Kawell, L., Jr., Beckhardt, S., Halvorsen, T., Ozzie, R., & Greif, I. (1988). Replicated document management in a group communication system. In *CSCW '88: Proceedings of the 1988 ACM conference on computer-supported cooperative work* (pp. 395–404). New York: ACM Press.

Kay, A. (1977). Microelectronics and the personal computer. *Scientific American, 237*(3), 230–244.

Mosco, V., & McKercher, C. (2007). Introduction: Theorizing knowledge labor and the information society. In *Knowledge workers in the information society* (pp. vii–xxiv). Lanham: Lexington Books.

Reder, S., & Schwab, R. G. (1988). The communicative economy of the workgroup: Multi-channel genres of communication. In *CSCW'88: Proceedings of the 1988 ACM conference on computer-supported cooperative work* (pp. 354–368). New York: ACM Press.

Reder, S., & Schwab, R. G. (1990). The temporal structure of cooperative activity. In *CSCW'90: Proceedings of the 1990 ACM conference on computer-supported cooperative work* (pp. 303–316). New York: ACM Press.

Sanjay Kairam, S., Brzozowski, M., Huffaker, D., & Chi, E. (2012). Talking in circles: Selective sharing in Google+. In *CHI'12, Proceedings of the 2012 SIGCHI conference on human factors in computing systems* (pp. 1065–1074). New York: ACM Press.

Schmidt, K. (2002). The problem with 'awareness': Introductory remarks on 'Awareness in CSCW'. *Computer Supported Cooperative Work, 11*(3–4), 285–298.

Siegler, M. G. (2009). Google wave drips with ambition. A new communication platform for a new web. *Tech Crunch*. http://techcrunch.com/2009/05/28/google-wave-drips-with-ambition-can-it-fulfill-googles-grand-web-vision/

Suchman, L. A. (1993). Do categories have politics? *Computer Supported Cooperative Work, 2*(3), 177–190.

Suchman, L. A. (2007). *Human – Machine reconfigurations – Plans and situated actions* (2nd ed.). New York: Cambridge University Press.

Winograd, T. (1994). Categories, disciplines, and social coordination. *Computer Supported Cooperative Work, 2*(3), 191–197.

Winograd, T., & Flores, F. (1986). *Understanding computers and cognition: A new foundation for design*. Wilmington, DC: Intellect Books.

Chapter 11
Building Socially Embedded Technologies: Implications About Design

Federico Cabitza and Carla Simone

11.1 Motivations and Background(s)

It is something of an open secret that every now and then resonates with a tinge of disgruntled resignation in the specialist literature of the last 30 years or so and even more recently (e.g., Lyytinen and Robey 1999; Klein and Jiang 2001; Shapiro 2005; Pan et al. 2008; Warkentin et al. 2009): approximately half to two-thirds (if not more, in critical domains like healthcare; see Heeks 2006) of information systems (IS) projects fail. This fact strikes one even more in light of the almost universal recognition that the practice of information systems development has undergone a radical transformation in this period and has abandoned naive strictly structured life cycle methods of development in favor of more flexible, dynamic, and multidisciplinary approaches.[1]

Indeed, with the developing complexity of information systems, the tighter coupling of their components, and the increasing opacity of internal functioning, there is little wonder that a purposively contrarian theory like the "normal accident theory" by Perrow (1999) with respect to computer-supported organizations (Szewczak and Snodgrass 2002, p. 64) and their infrequent but potentially harmful technologically driven failures (see, e.g., Rochlin 1998; Ash et al. 2004) has continued to provoke until recently (Weick 2004) by stating: "failures are normal."

---

[1]If this is true, one could argue that it is probably also because some principles and sensibilities typical within the HCI, CSCW, and PD fields have so to say "trickled down" in the "consciousness" of IT practitioners in the "real" world (cf., e.g., Shapiro 2005; Fitzpatrick and Ellingsen 2012).

F. Cabitza (✉) • C. Simone
Dipartimento di Informatica, Sistemistica e Comunicazione, Universitá degli Studi di Milano-Bicocca, Milan, Italy
e-mail: federico.cabitza@disco.unimib.it

© Springer-Verlag London 2015
V. Wulf et al. (eds.), *Designing Socially Embedded Technologies in the Real-World*,
Computer Supported Cooperative Work, DOI 10.1007/978-1-4471-6720-4_11

A known essayist has even quite provocatively argued around the conjecture that digitizing (or informating) organizations and their work is of little or no use for their competitiveness and performance or even worse has a potential to corrode existing competitive advantages, for instance, by homogenizing complex business processes (Carr 2004).

Of course, there is little comfort in being aware, especially in the EUSSET community, that computing-related failures seem largely due to organizational and social rather than technical factors (Pan et al. 2008; Kaplan and Harris-Salamone 2009). Yet, even framing what "success" really is, how to detect it and gauge the extent a project is successful, can be seen as primarily a social and cultural effort rather than a merely technical one (Wilson and Howcroft 2002; Thomas and Fernández 2008): different approaches can focus more either on quantitative and economic indicators (e.g., DeLone and McLean 1992; Cooke-Davies 2002) or, at the opposite extreme, on users' perception and satisfaction (e.g., Myers 1995; Goodhue and Thompson 1995).[2]

Irrespective of our peculiar inclination to consider typical information systems as "good" or "bad" when such a computer-based system fails or, on a microscale, exhibits a relevant failure, two possible conjectures are likely to emerge, related to two opposite perspectives to the issue: what we denote as the Daedalus conjecture and the Icarus conjecture from the famous myth of the first manned flying machine. The former one is the attitude of who tends to speculate on users that misinterpreted or misused the system, assuming that the machine's design is proper and fit for intended use assuming correct operating procedures ("feather wings were not supposed to be used too close to the sun"). Conversely, the latter one is the attitude of one who fingers poor design and claims a right to pursue objectives also beyond the idea of "intended use," which he/she considers to be usually shortsighted and to limit real use excessively ("who the hell would employ mere wax to stick a pair of wings together?"). Whatever the cause anyway, Icarus comes to a bad end.

In this chapter, we argue in favor of a third approach toward technology's shortcomings, which we will articulate in what follows to scrape it off of its outward and possibly misleading nuances of provocativeness and end-unto-itself oddity: the perspective according to which computing tools cannot be really defined "a priori" and "in vitro" by someone external to their use, i.e., the "mighty designer," but only be iteratively constructed in the wet "mangle of practice" (Pickering 1995) by end users themselves. We propose this perspective to try to go beyond both the typical illuminist optimism of the "mighty designers" and the fatalistic attitudes of technological Cassandras in tackling the so-called software development crisis: a general condition that probably regards computer technology development since its beginnings that has been explicitly debated since the end of the sixties and said to

---

[2]This spectrum of utility evaluation seems to oscillate between the different stances of the philosophers who tried first to understand how to gauge usefulness and satisfaction, Jeremy Bentham and John Stuart Mill, respectively.

have in those years primed the so-called "software engineering" field (Haigh 2010) and its rational design-centered methods and methodologies to achieve IT success.

We like to characterize this approach in terms of a "contrarian and alternative mythology" with respect to the mainstream, design-centered mythology that has been dominant since the dawn of software engineering. We speak of mythology after Harris and Henderson (1999), who make the point that "while our hardware technology has improved by orders of magnitude, and our software has grown comparably more complex, the relationship between people (individually or in groups) and computers has only improved incrementally. In some cases, it has even *deteriorated*" (p. 88, our emphasis). The authors address the reason why it is so difficult "to translate [research insights] into comparable improvements in the usability (and more generally, the social integration) of computers" by advocating the adoption of a "better mythology for system design" in alternative to the standard mythology. This latter encompasses a set of "myths"[3] summarized in what follows:

- The parts of the system must interact according to a preestablished harmony defined during its design.
- The job of a designer is to discover, clarify, and when necessary invent the rules that define that harmony and then embed them into the computer system.
- The users must interact with the system in terms of the language or ontology that these rules create.

This mythology sustains the legitimacy of a process that is carried out by experts (in IT design) with the participation of experts (in their own practices) in order to represent and direct the unfolding of the production of computer-based information systems in an orderly manner in the face of chaos (AA 2001). The main merit of Harris and Henderson (1999) is to have shed light once again on some taken-for-granted assumptions. This is also our aim. In fact, only when "the limited and inaccurate perspective on work and technology imposed by the standard myths of both organization and system design [have been recognized], we can start to search for more effective approaches and write better myths around them" (ibid).

Although we also agree with the tenets Harris and Henderson (1999) proposed within their "mythology for the long term" almost 15 years ago,[4] in our little alter-

---

[3]Here and in the following, the word myth is not opposed to any truth fact, but it is rather used as synonym of "archetypical story" to indicate one possible stance, among many other ones as much as legitimate and reasonable. On the other hand, we keep using the term mythology for its powerful and evocative connotation, although probably the most indicated term would be "metanarrative," in the sense after Lyotard (1986), i.e., set of narratives that emphasize particular aspects of the practice of IT development and that, in doing so, do not drive practice in any strong sense but rather tell it, legitimate it, and "shape it by helping each participant construct and frame their account of their practice" (Harris and Henderson 1999, p. 89).

[4]Although the interested reader can refer to the original paper, we here summarize the main high-level recommendations contained in the mythology proposed by Harris and Henderson (1999): that we should i) honor every particularity, even those that do not fit the regularities imposed by the organizational rules; ii) honor accommodation, i.e., the "ad hoc elaboration of rules in use"; and iii) honor change, which is an intrinsic and unavoidable feature of a real world system.

native mythology, we will go a step further by arguing around the idea that the very conception of design that we are all well used to (and many of us also are fond of) should be challenged and indeed conjectured to be one of the most decisive factors leading to manifest failure.[5] A similar argument was put forward by Bryant (2000).

Our conjecture, while similar, limits itself to submitting that the main assumption underlying the modern idea of design, i.e., that it is proper and safe to distinguish between design and use, is too disconnected from practice, although it heavily relies on representations of the latter, and it is nourished as the central element of a reductionist framework where the process of system development is more or less rationally phased down into subcomponents that are ontologically distinct and where responsibilities are assigned on the basis of nominal competencies somehow reified in terms of specialized roles.

We are not saying a rational and engineering approach is bad per se, but we submit that it reflects conceptualizations of "what complex is" and "how to cope with complexity" (Cabitza and Simone 2012c) that are based on widespread misunderstandings of the complexity theory (Paley and Eva 2011; Maguire and McKelvey 1999)[6] and hence can bring unsubstantiated expectations and convictions.[7]

Thus, however radical this point may seem, we will take it seriously in order to justify the argument that such a conception (and the related professional activity) is not really necessary to build any successful computational, material artifact with which users have to interact to have their work done. We propose an alternative approach that manages without formal or conceptual design by which, as discussed in (Cabitza 2011), we contest the necessity and primacy of such kind of design in the development of computational interactive applications and information systems that are to be embedded in social cooperative settings. With "design," we here denote that specific phase of the larger development process in which professional analysts meet some (or many) user representatives and/or their managers to draw more or less formal models of how work is and should be accomplished (the "flow of work") and produce detailed specifications of the needs of the various stakeholders involved and of how the computational system will support work to fulfill needs and expectations. Thus, although we take the term to encompass business analysis, requirement elicitation, conceptual modeling, process (re)design, specification formalization,

---

[5]We will certainly not try to prove this conjecture, as we could never get over the causality fallacy that such a proof would entail (i.e., post hoc, propter hoc).

[6]For instance, Paley (2007) makes the point that many researches that declare a focus in complex systems do actually refer to the open systems thinking, which between the 1960s and the 1980s was aimed at replacing the Tayloristic organization-as-machine metaphor with the metaphor of organization-as-organism; more curtly, Maguire and McKelvey (1999) assert that most of the references to the complexity theory in the IT-oriented literature are not dissimilar from "mere retellings of old tales, [which use] complexity terminology tacked on retrospectively, gratuitously, and, in many cases, quite awkwardly."

[7]Moreover, Ivan Illich was among the first thinkers to denote a similar phenomenon as "principle of (paradoxically) counterproductivity": once most practices are institutionalized and engineered, they backfire on some of the stakeholders (Illich 1977).

and analysis, in what follows, we will use the general term "design" for brevity's sake. Other authors have cautioned against the fictional and ritualistic nature of this activity (e.g., Robey and Markus 1984; Robinson and Bannon 1991; Nandhakumar and Avison 1999). We contest the myths in which this ritual is considered necessary (see also, e.g., Shipman and Marshall 1999) and substantially unquestionable (see also Blackwell and Green 2008; Cabitza 2014a). Conversely, we will argue in favor of alternative myths according to which all the layers pertaining to human-computer interaction in the broadest sense – the model, the control, and the view – can be realized by the composition of elementary components without any "rational" design input and be put to work by end users alone, eventually (but not necessarily) flanked by IT professionals that are explicitly called to play the role of catalysts of a "reaction" that pertains to the dynamics of complex (socio-technical) systems in situ (Cabitza et al. 2014a, b).

We are aware that also our argumentation encompasses some myths, the most notable of which is that the "end user that can develop her own artifacts" somehow. Moreover, this alternative "mythology" is not "new" or "original" in any strong sense. It does however resonate with complementary recent discourses, as we shall see. We present these ideas again as a contribution of the foundation of an alternative way to build socially embedded systems.

The rest of chapter will be articulated as follows: in Sects. 11.2 and 11.3, we will briefly gather suggestions from two distinct discourses on which to ground our different mythologies: performativity thinking (see Sect. 11.2) will help us reappraise the value for IT development of the subterranean river that connects many influential thinkers from Nietzsche to Suchman and will provide us the conceptual space to think of system development differently. The metaphor of the *bricoleur* (see Sect. 11.3) will suggest to us a new strategy for building computer-based support in the wild. This pathway will lead us toward an alternative proposal in Sect. 11.4 discussed further in Sects. 11.5 and 11.6. Section 11.7 will look at a research agenda coherent with this alternative mythology for IT system development.

11.2   The Rediscovery of Performativity

Many things difficult to design prove easy to performance. (Samuel Johnson 1759)

In this section, we will first consider what we mean when we advocate that the alternative mythology we are envisioning should produce a "performative turn" in IT system development. Then, we will consider how the performative discourse has already come into design-related mythologies, in order to highlight the specific strand we aim to renovate with our proposal.

11.2.1 The Performative Turn

The expression "performative turn" is usually used to indicate two related aspects that we nevertheless prefer to distinguish for clarity's sake. On the one hand, it indicates a historically circumscribed research program, which has received an increasing interest in the last 15 years by researchers involved in cultural and social studies, like the science and technology studies field (notably Pickering and Latour) and related disciplines like ethnology, anthropology, sociology, and linguistics; in this former case, the term "turn" indicates the aim of this research endeavor to investigate an alternative way to look at how people interact, work, and share knowledge in social settings with respect to more mainstream strands like the pragmatic and realist paradigms, endorsing the claim that people create and recreate meaning and knowledge in social settings through performance (Van House 2009) and that even social reality itself is "created" while people "do things." As Law and Singleton (2003) put it:

The differences between realism and pragmatism are important, but neither share the performative assumption that reality is brought into being in the process of knowing. Or, to put it more precisely, neither would assume that the object that is known and the subject that does the knowing are co-produced in the same performance, or that the epistemological problem (what is true) and the ontological question (what is) are both resolved (or not) in the same moment.

The performative approach shared the critique of systemic, fully specified, and rationally conceived abstractions (e.g., with the nonrepresentational theorists[8]) and drew on the metaphor[9] of "performance" to reflect "a growing discontent with the traditional social sciences and their understanding of practices as texts or representations of genuinely symbolic concepts," to express "the reversion from systems of representations to processes of practice and performance," and to focus on "the active social construction of reality rather than its representation" (Dirksmeier and Helbrecht 2008).

In an attempt to summarize the recent, and quite protean, discourse about performativity in two lines, after Bramming et al (2012), we highlight three intertwined aspects: (i) reality is understood as incessant creation or practice; (ii) matter itself is understood as "entangled intra-relation"; and, of course, (iii) individuals do not preexist their interactions in any essentialist, objectivistic sense.

There is a second connotation of the expression "performative turn" that we now want to refer to. This latter, rather than a specific research program, can be better characterized as a sort of "sensitivity to specificities of materially heterogeneous

---

[8]It should be noted though that "a performative perspective does not delete the idea of representation, but rather views it as a specific aspect of performativity" (Jensen 2005), in that it focuses on the activity of representing, planning, and modeling rather than on the material outcome of those practices.

[9]Here and elsewhere, we use the term "metaphor" in the Nietzschean sense, as something that is used to impose order and intelligibility on a world that we cannot access directly.

events with special reference to differences and relations between performances" (Jensen 2002). This sensitivity has followed in the last century or so a peculiar karstic trend: it has recurred a number of times by different authors of different cultural milieus, and, although each time it was capable to gain a strong interest, this was never sufficient to establish itself as the mainstream thought in any of those milieus and somehow submerged until a next thinker contributed in its reappraisal.

In this sense, therefore, the idea of a "performative turn" evokes a more historical attitude, which was exhibited by individuals that have deliberatively turned away their focus from the allures of representationalism to embrace a more action-oriented and embodied perspective. The term "turn" thus indicates the will to reverse the ontological premises that the world is populated with particular objects, entities, and configurations that exist in and of themselves and that are endowed with particular essential qualities (Jensen 2002, p. 67) to consider objects, "not singular entities, but rather textures of partially coherent and partially co-ordinated performances" existing through multiple situated practices.

This sensitivity, or will, or discontent with representational/conceptual tenets indicates a sort of "fil rouge" that binds together thinkers like Nietzsche, Heidegger, Derrida, Pickering, and Latour[10] and some relevant feminist theorists (Bath 2009; Butler 1993) like Judith Butler, Karen Barad, and, especially for her involvement in the IT debate, Lucy Suchman (just to mention a few of those authors that influenced our understanding of the performative approach). A common trait among these thinkers seems then to be the need to find a viable alternative to representationalist tenets (i.e., stances that could be called as Cartesian or simply "modern"[11] (cf., e.g., Rorty 1991)), to shift the focus from questions of correspondence between models/representations and reality to matters of practices/doings/actions (Barad 2003).

In short, a performative approach asks us as observers of social settings to abandon the idea that these are sets of "object that are," to embrace the idea that they are made of "events that do." In doing so, it gives us a "resource to counter the positivist stance which essentializes categories and naturalizes the qualities of the entities whose stable existence it posits" (e.g., gender as a fixed attribute of a person) (Licoppe 2010). The concept of performativity therefore invites us to abandon the Kantian notion of "thing per se" (at least in system design) to recognize the relational and manifold nature of any perceived phenomenon, irrespective of its

---

[10]The fil rouge binds together unsuspected associates, like Pickering and Latour. One thing that unites these thinkers, for example, is that they are both "happy enough" to speak of material agency in nature without imputing any intentionality to the word "agency" (Pickering 1995, p. 6).

[11]Yet, we agree with Jensen (2002) when he points out that "the performative turn is a way to refuse the choice between the modern and the post-modern. The modern is about order purity. The post modern is a celebration of fragments and disorder. The performative turn is a series of claims and sensitivities that try to reach a fractional space in between. Something that is beyond the mono-dimensionality of modernity and beyond the free-floating multi-dimensionality of the post-modern. In this sense it has much in common with the parts of the Actor Network Theory tradition that claim to be non-modern."

seeming solidity,[12] as well as the co-constitutive entanglement of the social and the technological (i.e., material) and "the performance of the emergent sociomaterial assemblage" (Orlikowski 2007). According to this perspective, "meaning" is thus seen as an emergent phenomenon (or an epiphenomenon) of interaction (Hug 2010) but, even beyond this point, as a transient aspect of embodied interaction (Dourish 2001) that cannot be really decoupled from situated action (Suchman 2006) nor caught in abstract terms.

In this vein, researchers adopting a performative turn put first in their research agenda the study of the contingencies of time, space, technology, materiality, or discourse, "the heterogeneous sociomateriality and real-time contingency of performance," as Suchman (2006) calls them (p. xii): all things that the more classical "representational" model of thinking that is typical of "twentieth century technoscience" (Suchman 2004), i.e., the one assuming a detached observer that studies real objects and their essential properties in an objective world (or that designs and puts new objects into the world), escapes either consciously or unaware with profound consequences also on the conception of the role of technology in society and of its "designers" (Orlikowski 2007).

11.2.2 The Performativity Fil Rouge

In order to frame how the concept of performativity can influence IT system design in practical ways, we have to briefly outline the fil rouge mentioned above, which binds together influential thinkers of the last 150 years with the foundations of the CSCW approach to system design. To this aim, we have first to make a clear distinction between the discourse on performativity we are interested in and the so-called performance studies. These latter are usually at stake where scholars and researchers in the IT literature use expressions like "designing for performativity" (Morrison et al. 2010), "the role of performance in design research" (Jacucci et al. 2005), or "performing design." These expressions are more related to the traditional meaning of performance (Dirksmeier and Helbrecht 2008), as "showing of a doing" (cf. Grimes) or "activity before a particular set of observers" (cf. Goffman),[13] and they point all more or less to the "artistic" side of the discourse on performativity and as such they tend to "preserve," if not enhance, the creative role of designers instead of contributing in the overturn of the necessity of the idea of design.

---

[12]To support the legitimacy of the performative turn, we here recall that our ancestors (i.e., Latin, Greek, and Old English) used the words "res," "pragma," and "thing" (respectively) in order to denote an affair, a deed, a business, or an assembly (Telier 2011, p. 1), as well as the matters that were discussed and deliberated in such occasions and meetings. In other words, subject and object did not need to be disentangled on such occasions.

[13]It is nevertheless worthy of note that the meaning of performance as "performing a play" or "playing a drama" is much later than the more general meaning of "carrying out a promise" or "carrying in effect something" that dates from the sixteenth century.

Conversely, the concept of performativity we refer to is rooted in the Nietzsche's seminally deconstructive analysis of the relation between words and the world and in his powerful intuition according to which looking for a specific "doer" behind any action is recognized as an arbitrary and unnecessary (and indeed confounding) act.[14] This seminal contribution was then taken up by phenomenologist scholars, notably Heidegger, who further articulated the idea that the only way of being of human (i.e., Dasein) is engagement in practices (Existenz) (Riemer and Johnston 2012), that these latter depend on equipment[15] for their performance, and that the relationship between this latter and Dasein is fundamentally co-constitutive (Turner 2005). Many affinities can be then found between Heidegger and J. L. Austin (see, e.g., those discussed in Glendinning 1998), who introduced the concept of performative utterance to account for the capacity of human speech to act, i.e., have an effect in the material world, rather than just simply describe reality in terms of "true" and "false" statements; that notwithstanding, Law questioned the orderly taxonomy proposed by Austin and claimed that "all statements are in the slippery space between performative and constative," thus turning "the question of constative vs. performative [. . .] into an empirical question, and thus potentially an object for a sociology of performances" (Jensen 2002).

Years later, approximately at the same time as these concepts were taken up in the IT design arena by Winograd and Flores (1986) in their reappraisal of Austin's (and Searle's) elaboration of the so-called speech acts, the performative "fil rouge" unfolded again in the works of Andrew Pickering. We are referring to those contributions where this author made a clear distinction between a "representational idiom" and a "performative idiom" in scientific and technology-oriented discourses (Pickering 1995) and in particular for our design-related discourse, when Pickering (2008) contrasts the modern technoscientific approach to the design of things with the approach followed by British cyberneticians, like Beer, Ashby, and Pask, i.e., a hands-on experimental, performative, and non-representational one. At the same time, other authors drew upon the critical reinterpretation by Derrida (Simon 2010) of Austin's original differentiation between performatives and constatives, most notably Judith Butler and Karen Barad. These latter elaborated a complex concept of (posthumanist) performativity around the repetitive, or citational, aspects of performance, i.e., its ability to produce materiality. In this view, social structures, like rules and categories (such as gender), are not preexistent attributes of a given object or its behavior, but rather they are continuously produced through processes of repetition and social legitimization. This conviction echoes, but also in some way goes beyond, the views animated by Wittgensteinian philosophy that recognizes

---

[14]We are referring to the famous passage in *The Genealogy of Morals* where Nietzsche pointed out that "there is no 'being' behind doing, acting, becoming: 'the doer' is merely a fiction added to the 'doing'. Doing is all" (original: es giebt kein 'Sein' hinter dem Thun, Wirken, Werden; 'der Thaeter' ist zum Thun bloss hinzugedichtet, — das Thun ist Alles).

[15]Equipment can be seen as a term which denotes those things, or artifacts, that the Dasein encounters in fluent use, entangled and experienced in performance, when they are ready- to- hand (Zuhandenheit).

how, due to the intrinsic underspecification of human behaviors (Schmidt 2011a, b), it is the practice that determines the rule rather than the opposite and that invites us to abandon an "objectified and detached view of rules and procedures as external objects with fixed properties, to a performative view where rule following is characterized as a typically emergent, distributed and artifact-mediated activity" (D'Adderio 2008).

11.2.3 Performativity for IT System Development

All that said, one could rightly wonder what the performative turn, as it has been characterized above, has to do with the discourse regarding IT design in socio-technical settings and, above all, if there is anything new. We are aware that some of the performativity tenets like paying attention to "the negotiations between actors" (Wagner et al. 2010, p. 67) and the question of when design stops and use begins (cf., e.g., Brand 1995) "may seem old to people within the CSCW tradition" and related ones (i.e., HCI, PD, and the like).[16] That notwithstanding, we believe that this perspective can be fruitful along both the practical and conceptual dimension.

11.2.3.1 On the Practical Side: Toward New Meaningful Development Cycles

From the practical point of view, only a few contributions so far refer to the performative tenets explicitly with respect to design; for instance, Jensen (2008) advocates a reorientation of both the understanding and (less clearly) the practice of the process of IT design (or more specifically of CSCW design) as performativity; to this aim, he submits recommendations to keep in mind performative aspects in the design process, such as that "neither humans nor technologies determine each other" and that "materiality might trick us in practice." Unfortunately, the author falls short of clarifying how a performativity-aware disposition or "relativizing one's own ontology" (although certainly a useful exercise) could also "revitalize design" and really change the practice of IT design. With a more practical attitude, Danholt (2005) makes an argument about the performative nature of prototypes, by suggesting that prototypes "affect users in concrete, material, bodily ways in situ."

Recognizing the performative nature of prototyping is then related to recognizing that this way of designing artifacts is "mutually transformative for users as well as for the technology, a process of co-construction of humans and artifact"; if design

---

[16]This was honestly admitted by Jensen (2008), who has nevertheless advocated a better consideration of these ideas within those traditions. However, two years later, Bratteteig et al. (2010, p. 31) have conversely recognized that "the performative turn in post-structuralism is perhaps under-articulated in design research."

"is considered to be performative," it is recognized as "an emergent process where the end result is not predicated by either users or designers, but [is] an outcome of the process. [. . .] Performativity thus also means that the existing is continuously performed and reiterated in order to persist, which means that the existing is also always under construction and transformation. Slight changes in the way things are done lead to novel existences. Performativity thus implies a continuous possibility of transforming the existing."

While we would fully subscribe to these conclusions, we notice how user-centered, and even participatory design, approaches (let alone any approach within the more traditional, engineering mythology), in which users are considered to hold important knowledge on their practice and, *in virtue of this competence*, are involved in the design process (in some form), are nevertheless still considered to be end users and their practices as preexisting the design process and somehow invariant to the task, *in its essential traits*. Thus, while prototyping and participatory prototyping, especially when prototypes are not merely representational ones (i.e., mock-ups) but rather are working gears (like in the framework presented in Harel 2008), can make the distance between design and use (and hence designers and users) shorter, the co-construction of these prototypes usually takes place in a controlled and delimited environment ("in vitro" rather than "in vivo"). In so doing, the performative dimension of the development process is still kept at the margin of the real and never-ending (and very aptly depicted as loop-closed) process of the task-artifact cycle (Carroll et al. 1991), where both the task and the artifact coevolve as a whole and at a different pace.

Within a performative strand, such a cycle would likely resemble a more intertwined figure, where the task cannot be considered without the artifact with which it is accomplished and the artifact alone is just inert accoutrement outside the task. Taking seriously that "the social organization of work does not pre-exist in any precise or detailed way, but is constituted 'in the [artifact-mediated] doing' by practitioners" (Buescher et al. 2001) suggests then that tasks occur only when artifacts are used and artifacts make sense to practitioners only when these are put to work. In other words, there is no dualistic thing but situated action, which emerges from the indissoluble entanglement of tasks and artifacts, like in a variation of the widely known Taijitu symbol. It goes without saying that entanglements cannot really be designed, as "the take-up, modification and rejection of technology in a work setting, and the [consequent] accommodation of work practices that take place around a developing technology, are radically unknowable and unpredictable" (Buescher et al. 2001) till they actually occur.

11.2.3.2 On the Conceptual Side: Back to the Future

The conceptual contribution is no less important if we accept what Schmidt (1999) once pointed out, i.e., that "Lucy Suchman's radical critique of cognitive science and the 'situated action' perspective she proposed has played a significant role in defining the CSCW agenda and has become a shared frame of reference to many, perhaps most, of us." Since the publication of *Plans and Situated Action* (1987), the discourse around the concept of "situation" has become more prominent in system design and underlies the main tenets of the EUSSET's "Situated Computing Manifesto."[17] This focus on "situation," rather than on performativity, has resulted, we would suggest, in a certain ambiguity, perhaps due to its apparent roots in the concept of a (static) place (cf. Latin situatio, site).[18] As pointed out by Clancey (1997, p. 23), "the overwhelming use of the term situated [...] since the 1980s has reduced its meaning from something conceptual in form and social in content to merely 'interactive' or 'located in some time and place'." Suchman (2006) herself admitted that the passage where she had written that "the situation of action can be defined as the full range of resources that the actor has available to convey significance of his or her own actions and to interpret the actions of others" could be erroneously "taken to imply that 'the situation' exists somehow in advance of action and that it could at least in principle be fully enumerated and represented in the form of a model to be referenced" and therefore as something that can be drawn by some professional (i.e., the designer) before actually going "where the action is" (Dourish 2001). Conversely, "the sense of the situation [Suchman is] after is a *radically performative and interactional one*, such that action's situation is in significant respects constituted through, or stands in a reflexive relationship with, ongoing activity" (p. 125, our emphasis).

This remark cannot be underestimated. Indeed, when Suchman exposed the main themes pertaining to her decades-long research in the field of HCI in the preface of *Human-Machine Reconfigurations* (a reprint of *Plans and Situated Actions* that was enriched by new footnotes and additional chapters), she mentions: "the irreducibility of lived practice, embodied and enacted; the value of empirical investigation over categorical debate; the displacement of reason from a position of supremacy to one among many ways of knowing in acting; the heterogeneous socio-materiality and real-time contingency of performance; and the new agencies and accountabilities effected through reconfigured relations of human and machine" (Suchman 2006, p. xii). It is for us indicative that Suchman did not mention "situated action" nor situatedness. Here we briefly recall that the former concept was originally chosen "to underscore the view that every course of action[19] depends in essential ways on its material and social circumstances" (p. 70) and the latter term was not originally used by Suchman, although hundreds of scholarly papers associate it with her

---

[17]URL: http://www.thinkinnovation.org/eusset-has-just-engineered-the-manifesto-of-situated-computing/ (accessed 03-Sept-2014). Archived at WebCite on 03-Sept-2014 [http://www.webcitation.org/6SJclKI3B]

[18]This could have also laid the concept of situatedness open to some representationalist drifts: cf., e.g., the connotations acquired by the term "context," among which that of "container-like" (Suchman 2006, p. 19), in IT-related discourses about "context-aware systems."

[19]Including planning itself or "calling out a plan as a self-standing artifact": cf., respectively, p. 17 and 21

work[20] and has been the object of some criticisms,[21] among which we recall here the point by Ciborra (2006) regarding the paradoxical and somehow extraordinary lack in such concept of any affective, human, but we would also say performative, element.[22] In the same vein, also the current interests on either "situated software" (Balasubramaniam et al. 2008) or "situated computing" can be questioned. As Suchman put it:

> I believe that the argument made [in 1987] holds equally well today, across the many developments that have occurred since. The turn to so-called situated computing *notwith-standing*, the basic problems identified previously – briefly, the ways in which prescriptive representations presuppose contingent forms of action that they cannot fully specify, and the implications of that for the design of intelligent, interactive interfaces – continue to haunt contemporary projects in the design of the "smart" machine. (Suchman 2006, p. 3, our emphasis)

Thus, the IT system design discourse periodically contains terms and expressions that have the potential to overturn the traditional oppositions between abstraction vs. materiality, representation vs. performance, and between different kinds of design, e.g., the one that "solidifies and stabilizes procedures and classifications" (Orlikowski 1992a) and the one that "continues in use" (Carroll 2004): these terms and expressions nevertheless end up by getting like "muted," although they still remain as "sensitizing concepts [:::] which draw attention to important features of work and provide guidelines directing research in specific settings" (Crabtree et al. 2001). It is as if those "sensitizing concepts" were always put into a sort of seventh room of Bluebeard's castle, where they are seemingly kept alive, honored, and dolled up but actually in a state of harmless captivity, with no real influence on actual practices and on the inner convictions of the practitioners involved in design. This could be just the plain consequence of an "engineering education [which] had over-invested in analytical technique and scientific understanding at the expense of the practical, 'hands-on', the creative, the reflective, the social, the constructive, the ethical, the economic" (Bucciarelli 2003, p. 295).

In conclusion, we assert the topicality of the performative turn (especially in the sense of the intellectual legacy argued above) and advocate the concept of performativity to be taken more seriously in the future for at least two reasons: first it refers to a "doing" explicitly and in that it differs from the keywords like "situation," "situated(ness)," and "context" which all refer to a "state of being." Hopefully this could be enough to avoid falling victim to the Scylla

---

[20]In *Human-Machine Reconfigurations*, Suchman speaks of situatedness only once and only to challenge the meaning intended for such term by Rodney Brooks, the MIT engineer that questioned symbolic representational approaches in the field of robotics, as she found such meaning "evacuated of sociality."

[21]Including people, like Lave and Wenger (1991), who lament the vagueness of the definition itself of situatedness

[22]Ciborra (2006) writes: "'Situated' is the translation of the German 'befindlich'; situatedness is 'befindlichkeit'. [The former term] not only refers to the circumstances one finds himself or herself in, but also to his or her 'inner situation', disposition, mood, affectedness and emotion."

of essentialism/representationalism (Maturana and Varela 1992) and facilitate the reappropriation of Suchman's lesson, at least within the CSCW community.

Second, we believe that the performative view, in its nature anti-conceptual, anti-representational, and against the divide between design and use (i.e., practice), has a potential to bring us to the other side of the river (cf. the life-raft model mentioned by Buescher et al. 2001)) and let us assert that technology in practice (Orlikowski 2000) cannot really be "designed" but rather allowed to "emerge"[23] (Cabitza 2014). This would mark the shift with no regrets "from a focus on invention [we would say of design, Ed.], understood as a singular event, to an interest in ongoing practices of assembly, demonstration and performance. The shift from an analysis in terms of form and function to a performative account" (Suchman et al. 2002, p. 165). We re-propose this resolution within our alternative mythology as a way to bridge the literature contributions mentioned above and the following discourse on bricolage.

11.3   From Models to "Bricolages"

> I often try out little bits
> wheresoever they might fit.
> The sages call this bricolage,
> the promiscuous prefer menage . . . [24]

The discourse on the performative nature of socio-technical systems suggests we should recognize that designing for interaction and action is overambitious for its irreducible distance from the actual performance of the task. This would seem to cast a gloomy light on any constructive stance about computer-based support of complex human tasks. However, what gives us "some hope" is that an approach, if not a method, can be taken toward the actual realization of technological scaffoldings (Orlikowski 2006) for collaborative complex socio-technical systems: bricolage.

In the context of IT design-related research, we draw heavily on the concept of bricolage for its "overall generative effect [which] seems to be more dependent on interaction rather than on some overriding design rationale" (Lanzara 1999, p. 347) and because "bricolage privileges combinatory logics, loose coupling, and garbage can processes" (ibid) and minimizes the prospect that any designed thing, no matter how well conceived, will necessarily fall short of avoiding the "law of unintended consequences" (Mansfield 2010).

Early authors to use the concept of bricolage in relation to design (in a wide sense) were (almost independently) Weick (1993) and Ciborra (1992). These studies, although largely, provided the conceptual background for many subsequent contributions that leveraged, or simply were inspired by, this metaphor. Among

---

[23]Of course someone has still to develop the technological artifact, and someone else pays the bills.

[24]Thomas Erickson, 2000, allegedly written upon reading a commentary for a special issue of CSCW Journal on Theory

these, we also consider the contribution by Buescher et al. (2001), one of the first to provide some concreteness to the notion of bricolage within the actual process of the development of computer-based information systems in organizational settings. In their work, Buescher et al. (2001) suggest a "'life-raft' model of systems development – a continuously unfolding bricolage of technologies to hand, requiring much patching and baling, with an unknown destination" (p. 17). In this "overarching framework within which newly developed technologies are set in place and helped to 'work'," they argue that the design process had to become more "immediate and continuous" in order "to cope with the deeply built-in uncertainty of the relationship between technical systems and work practices" (p. 22). They provide a concrete definition of bricolage in a CSCW context:

> Bricolage can be described as 'designing immediately', using ready-at-hand materials, combinations of already existing pieces of technology – hardware, software and facilities (e.g., Internet providers) – as well as additional, mostly 'off-the-shelf' ones. It therefore also involves design as assembly [and] requires investigation of the process of assemblage as well as designing for it. (p. 23)

We substantially agree with the points regarding the idea of "design as assembly" and the immediacy of the bricolage-oriented approach. Yet, we interpret immediacy in terms of "unmediated spontaneity" rather than in terms of "ad hoc quickness" and therefore bricolage as an activity mainly accomplished without the mediation of designers or IT specialists. At the same time, asserting that bricolage is "a description of the existing context," the general activity of bricoleur as well as its "(unforeseeable) outcome" (i.e., an assemblage of "things that work," the solution coming out from a particular round of development), and even a (presumably context-independent) "method for design" is rather catchall.

We therefore prefer the more focused definition proposed by Hartswood et al. (2000):

> Users need the opportunity that only their work can offer to explore fully the possibilities for adopting, and adapting to, new systems and artefacts. When this is allowed to happen, and given the right choice of technologies, development work can assume the characteristics of 'bricolage' – i.e., the rapid assembly and configuration of 'bits and pieces' of software and hardware – led by users acting within their own work settings, with IT specialists taking on the role of facilitator.

In this light, we propose to dissolve the usual distinction between a passive end user and a more active end user (the latter idea has been called a variety of things in the literature; see, e.g., Cabitza et al. 2014a, b) and hence to consider all users as (at least potential) bricoleurs, i.e., who in different circumstances can play either the role of who constructs and assembles the pieces of technology (whom we denote as "bricolant" bricoleur) or who exploits those assembled pieces by actively using them according to the situation at hand (i.e., a sort of "actant" bricoleur). This is the twofold meaning of the term "bricoleur" that we submit for the IT discourse. This can be clearly traced back to the specific archetype of bricoleur that Levi-Strauss (1966) introduced to contrast with the opposite archetype of "engineer." In our view, then, the latter can personify the rational designer that builds systems from scratch after, and in virtue of, a conceptual effort, while the former denotes the user that fabricates her own tools from available resources, being immersed in situated performances and contingencies. In his words:

> The bricoleur is adept at performing a large number of diverse tasks; but, in contrast to the engineer, he does not subordinate each one of them to the acquisition of raw materials and tools conceived and procured for the project: his universe of tools is closed, and the rule of his game is to always make do with 'what's available', that is, a set, finite at each instance, of tools and materials, heterogeneous to the extreme, because the composition of the set is not related to the current project, or, in any case, to any particular project, but is the contingent result of all the occasions that have occurred to renew or enrich the stock, or to maintain it with the remains of previous constructions or destructions. (Levi-Strauss 1966, p. 17)

For our purposes, the key motivations for focusing on the active roles of the end users can be found in three statements by Levi-Strauss (1966). Firstly, objects "are not known as a result of their usefulness; they are deemed to be useful or interesting because they are first of all known" (p. 9). This means that what is "useful" or not cannot be predetermined in terms of functional requirements, irrespectively of the competence of the analyst/designer, as these are necessarily decoupled from the actual availability of the corresponding functionalities in the workspace of users. Conversely, each work item is perceived by users to be useful if they have already internalized its function, that is, if they already know it and have made sense of it. This means that the bricoleur is someone that uses the objects she can find around her, but it is also necessary that their meaningful arrangement entails that he/she has previously been involved in some sense in the creation of those objects. Thus, bricolage is seen as an arrangement of predefined objects, where predefined here just means "defined before" and not "from above by someone else."

Secondly, a distinction between the engineer/designer and the bricoleur is made in virtue of "the inverse functions which they assign to events and structures as ends and means, [the designer] creating events (changing the world) by means of structures and the 'bricoleur' creating structures by means of events." (p. 22). This point is particularly important in view of how the performative stance sees every event.[25] This cautions us against regarding any structure that the designer could conceive as either enabling or constraining action as these structures may be changed in the process of their enactment, even if such a change is unintentional and unacknowledged (Orlikowski 1996). It also relates to the more manifest feature of the activity of bricolage: as said above, not only to make things out of the materials one has lying about but also to make sense of those materials according to an interpretive act that reinvents the objects (at least their meaning, their function, and their value) anew in the face of change and that is hardly anticipatable and mostly unplannable as it is also deeply conditioned by past interactions (we would also say "situated" of course).

---

[25]That is, as "an autonomic and contingent occurrence with its own conditions and its own time-structure, [in respect to which] the meaning of the past for the present is not fixed but radically ambiguous" (Dirksmeier and Helbrecht 2008), i.e., inextricably intertwined with the given situation

Thirdly and importantly, "the engineer works by means of concepts, and the bricoleur by means of signs" (p. 20). This is meaningful in light of the fact that "signs can be opposed to concepts [in that] whereas concepts aim to be wholly transparent with respect to reality, signs allow and even require the interposing and incorporation of a certain amount of human culture into reality" (p. 20). The idea of transparency here hints at a clear development recommendation: whereas the engineer aims to hide information[26] and to make his idea of, say, patient into a number of attributes unambiguously codified in a relational DBMS, underneath the application logic, the bricoleur instead needs to pay attention to what fields will represent the patient in his/her artifacts, arrange them the way she needs, fill them in on the basis of informal conventions and customs, as well as disregard them and create some new attribute/field at need, irrespective of any ideal model of that disembodied entity. Users and designers own distinct perspectives but nevertheless they have to interact to make the technological artifact fully operational in the target environment. Their collaboration has to be sought at a level that is different from artifact construction, as will be discussed in Sect. 11.5.3.

Moreover, this third passage also clearly requires: first, that a second but by no means less important activity of the bricoleur consists in a continuous and seamless accumulation of any sign that could help her make sense of the bricolage in practice; in so doing the bricoleur can enrich the bricolage artifact, i.e., its content as well and any kind of meta-content attached, like comments, tags, and nested threads of conversations that unfold around and about the tangible artifact. In short, bricolage is a continuous and creative "playing with signs."[27] Second, this passage sheds light on the requirement that any computational support of the activity of the bricoleur must be oriented toward this continuous creative and interpretive activity, which, as we know (Berg 1999), can accumulate data as well as coordinate activities, toward the reconciliation of multiple, possibly diverging interpretations and above all toward the coexistence of these multiple and contextual incorporations, both in the local and in the global dimension.

This latter point is what makes us believe that the bricoleur-oriented mythology (as a specific kind of end user enabled by a specific kind of platform that we will outline in the next section) has the potential to oust the mythology oriented to the designer, i.e., the heroic and creative role that to some extent can be traced back up to the Renaissance imagination and that Hirschheim and Klein (1989) more prosaically denoted as the "systems expert." This stereotype still distorts in professional practice (and not only there) the fragile symmetry of the Janus-like relationship between users and designers (Bowers 1991). In the next sections, we

---

[26]cf. the principle of encapsulation, which is defined by Grady Booch as "the process of compartmentalizing the elements of an abstraction"

[27]This passage is strongly influenced by the reading of Nietzsche by Derrida in "Structure, Sign, and Play," where the Nietzschean perspective is related to "the joyous affirmation of the play of the world and of the innocence of becoming, the affirmation of a world of signs without fault, without truth, and without origin which is offered to an active interpretation." Bricolage itself is a concept that urges us considering system development as a game-related social undertaking.

will speak about how a "laissez faire les bricoleurs" method can be flanked by a specific "logic of bricolage," in order to empower end users and have them become the builders of their own artifacts within their daily practices.

11.4   Toward Environments Supporting Bricoleurs

Everything that can be said, can be said clearly. (Ludwig Wittgenstein 1922)[28]

In this section, we would like to address how the discourse that we have outlined above can converge into a coherent and practical proposal for the development of interactive and collaborative information systems whose related mythology of system development should situate itself among the research lines that are emerging within the HCI field. As also recently pointed out by Ardito et al. (2012), these lines focus on concepts such as:

- Appropriation: i.e., the process by which technologies are understood and used by users in their own ways, possibly subverting the designers' intentions (Orlikowski 1992b; Dix 2007)
- Meta-design (Fischer and Giaccardi 2006): also denoted as "design for designers," a design paradigm which allows various stakeholders, including end users, to act as co-designers even at use time. Accordingly, software engineers do not design the final application, as in traditional design, but create software environments through which different stakeholders can contribute to the design of the final application
- End-user development (EUD) (Lieberman et al. 2006): a paradigm that focuses on the capability of systems to offer support at run time to empower users to develop their applications, blurring the distinction between design time and run time

As we will argue, the alternative proposal we advocate builds on but is distinct from these approaches. The term "appropriation" can be read as implying taking as one's own, a "thing" that has been constructed by someone else. For instance, Carroll (2004) writes of "the crucial role played by users' actions in completing the design process" and that "[technology appropriation] is actually part of the design process. The design of a technology innovation is completed by users as they appropriate it." We find then that the notion of appropriation is deeply ingrained in the design-oriented rhetoric.

In the same mold, meta-design is a term that explicitly refers to a phase of design, one programmatically aimed at investigating "techniques and processes for creating environments that allow 'owners of problems' (or end users) *to act as designers*" (our emphasis, Fischer et al. 2004). The main contribution that we want to retain from this framework is then the idea of "underdesign"; this notion relates to design for purposely "incomplete" systems that, once deployed, would allow for important

---

[28]*Tractatus Logico-Philosophicus*, 4.116

modifications by end users themselves, in the face of unexpected and unanticipated needs that show up at use time. Underdesign hints at a conceptual design that does not have the ambition to fully set the system up for its "embedment" in a complex socio-technical system, but it also hints at a design for the "underlayers," i.e., aimed at the construction of environments where applications can be developed with a strong interaction (co-design) between users and professional designers. Fischer et al. (2004) use the term "seed" to denote an underspecified application that users can complete during its use; the authors of this work also report about the action research initiatives that led to the construction of such environments by means of specialized editors (e.g., a map editor). The term seed is fully coherent with the idea that applications grow (Truex et al. 1999) and evolve with their environments but, in some way, this latter idea seems to clash with the claim that end users have to *act as designers*, if this means to envisioning how the application ought to be and ought to behave in the unknown future, even if this activity is performed by end users who play the "designer" role.

EUD is the approach which has most clearly and explicitly stated in its agenda (as well as in its name) the involvement of users in the construction of their technology and without expecting them to act as designers. This shows a strong affinity with the approach we discuss, especially if the meaning at stake for the term "development" is the original one mentioned in Sect. 11.1: the notion of a continuous and indefinite "unfolding" over time, pruned of its abstraction and differentiation from the actual work practices. This is the point that resonates more with the passage by Levi-Strauss reported in Sect. 11.3 where the end user, the *bricolant* bricoleur of our mythology, is expected to "work with signs instead of with concepts." Thus, *constructing* (or modifying) the artifact should not be seen as radically different from *working with* the artifact. The constructs and structures with which end users work should be familiar, like blocks and parts of the artifact itself, and conceived to be rearranged or created by composition from smaller subcomponents that are not ontologically different from their compounds (e.g., big field sections in forms are made of smaller fields groups, and these in their turn are but data fields).

Adopting a fully and coherent EUD approach has a strong impact on what kind of system is supposed to support the continuous bricolage-based construction of *convivial tools.*[29]

11.4.1   *What Meta-system for End Users' Systems?*

It is possible to distinguish between two main ways a system can act as a sort of meta-system for the development of an application by end users or at least for its tight adaptation to their needs. On the one hand, we can consider systems

---

[29]This expression is taken from Illich. A convivial tool is defined as "that which gives each person who uses it the greatest opportunity to enrich the environment with the fruits of his or her labour" (Illich 1973).

that primarily (or exclusively) support configuration. This regards the so-called "flexibility through control" of systems that offer ways for people to adjust settings and reprogram the system or otherwise technically adjust it (Dourish 1999). Yet, allowing the setting of more or less articulated parameters that affect the application's behavior or its appearance at the interface level entails little room for intervention by end users, since the set of elements is taken from a predefined (at design time) set of values and corresponding effects on the application at run time; accordingly, such systems allow for an involvement that is, in our view, too superficial (also literally speaking) and is constrained by some model of feasible action or by some feasible pattern in the "fitness landscape" (Mansfield 2010, p. 50) that results from precise configurations in the "design space."

On the other hand, other kinds of systems offer an environment that is "flexible through openness" (Dourish 1999), that is, a sort of "meta-system" by which users are supported in the creation of new systems and applications of different complexity, according to their needs and competences: macro-programming, visual programming, and programming by demonstration are among the solutions that are given to users to "encourage their participation in the design process" (Dourish 2001, p. 170). Here the risk may arise that the motivations and purposes of EUD-oriented researchers may clash with the scope and aims of the actual tools that are made available to the end users: specific features of the environment (or their absence) can introduce, or even impose, rigid models of practice and affect how end users build and maintain their equipment. This latter point relates to an important feature that environments enabling EUD practices should possess: we call this quality, *universatility*, to hint at something in between the traditional qualities of generality, universality, and versatility. While generality is usually defined as "the degree to which a software product can perform a wide range of functions" (Khosravi and Gueheneuc 2004) and hence serve multiple purposes, universality and versatility (from which *universatility*) regard the quality of being both general purpose and easily tailorable to the needs of specific settings and thus able to fit local needs. In other words, where generality refers to the typical quality exhibited by Swiss Army knives, that is, to have multiple specific functions to serve distinct but anticipated purposes, *universatility* refers to the quality of a tool that offers affordances that allow an open-ended set of usages (De Michelis 2003). Thus, a powerful environment has to be universatile enough to avoid imposing restrictions on the applications that it allows the construction of. Here the core of the problem lies in how this quality is guaranteed and on what conceptual premises are grounded.

11.4.1.1 Universatility Based on an Ontological Approach

The first way to make an environment general enough to be applied to any cooperative setting but also versatile enough to fit any (in principle) of its situated tasks is what we call the "ontological approach." This is an expression of the representational and objectivistic approach we discussed in Sect. 11.2: the designer of the environment decides how to guarantee wide customization on the basis of a pre-understanding of how actors behave in a number of recurring situations in multiple domains; consequently, on the basis of this understanding (which is based on deep introspection or more interactive and qualitative techniques), the designer conceives a set of "labels" that identify the "things" that users will handle, associates that classification scheme with intended universal building blocks, and provides users with those elements, all together with specific rules for their composition, so that they can (acknowledge and) make value out of that given model. A paradigmatic example of this approach was the Coordinator (Flores et al. 1988) 25 years ago: there the ontological claim was that actors coordinate their actions in terms of negotiation of commitments, and according to this model, the technology offered a universal set of possible categories to characterize setting-specific behaviors and routines. The assumptions underlying this technological proposal have been widely discussed, and contrasted, since then (e.g., Suchman 1994) but other examples of this approach still abound, both in daily life, for example, where reference management software force us to univocally associate our academic works or books with a specific category and, in recent academic research, for example, when users are called to categorize others' comments in public discussion with a system like Reflect (Kriplean et al. 2012).

In addition to systems where the ontological approach is adopted in an explicit form, we notice that such an approach can also act within an IT system *implicitly* (if not surreptitiously), especially in all those systems that adopt a characteristic or strong metaphor representing "the" one way in which humans allegedly organize their world: this is the case of the most famous (and nowadays notorious) "desktop metaphor," as well of some recent alternatives, like the metaphor of "story" proposed by De Michelis et al. (2009b); in both cases, users are called to associate the objects they work with a concept (i.e., the notion of file or of resource) and characterize it in terms of a category – being it the name of the folder in which the file is virtually stored (as well as the location of this latter in the "file system") or the name of a sequence of interactions with someone or about something (i.e., the topic of a conversation). The same phenomenon occurs in the ambit of context-aware or situated computing where, as mentioned in Sect. 11.2, tools to characterize a context or a situation are part and parcel of the design of the application itself, and they are based, again, on a predefined domain model that the users can only customize (or appropriate); this seems in basic contrast with the idea of context as "embodied action" that we share with Dourish (2004).

All these approaches, either explicitly or implicitly ontological, are grounded in the hypothesis that things could be described univocally or, at least, that the "name for a thing" would mean *that* thing irrespective of the setting where such a name is used and for what aim (cf., e.g., Mark et al. 2002; Anderson et al. 2008): this is the essence of an ontological stance. However useful this approach may be for ordering and retrieval purposes, any more or less structured "ontology" (in the broadest sense of a taxonomy, classification scheme, interaction metaphor, and the like) is conceived at *design time* and it is given to the users so that they make sense of their world in a way that can make some tasks more orderly efficient; yet, this approach may also hinder the support of other, possibly more "hidden" tasks: this mirrors platforms that provide users with functionalities that allow for some degree of tailorability but, as the latter is constrained within the boundaries of the metaphor itself, do not encompass functionalities to let the application (and its underlying ontology) evolve toward and align with the idiosyncratic customs of the users. The availability of such functionalities, and their subsequent use, could seriously undermine the consistency of the overall model and hence the effectiveness of the former tasks (e.g., Peters 2006).

11.4.1.2 Universatility Based on a Performative Approach

The main tenet of EUD has to do with giving users a more substantial role in technology conception, development, and evolution. Component design is proposed as an approach that allows users to tailor their applications by enriching them with suitable components offering specific functionalities (Mørch et al. 2004). This would require the application to be open to this type of tailorization (Stevens et al. 2006). Moreover, while "component thinking" seems natural for the integration of preexisting applications or in the assemblage of computational materials – for example, by using Lego Mindstorm environments (Rusk et al. 2008), we also have observed (Locatelli and Simone 2010) that in the construction of applications from scratch, this could be perceived as difficult by users, who usually see their application in a more holistic way than the component-based approach would suggest. A more radical stance is taken by Fischer and Giaccardi (2006) and their notion of meta-design. We have already expressed some reservations, at least on a purely conceptual level, regarding those platforms that would be aimed at making users act as "designers," rather than allowing them to construct their tools much like they already do with their traditional artifacts: i.e., by individual or bottom-up organized initiatives, trials and errors, progressive amendments, and patchwork or bricolage attitudes. Indeed, we have observed that actors in their everyday (working) life do not follow a traditional design-based approach to solve their problems and to construct the tools they need (Cabitza et al. 2013); this perception finds confirmation in a number of field studies (e.g., Carstensen et al. 1995; Morrison and Blackwell 2009; Blackwell and Morrison 2010; Handel and Poltrock 2011; Morrison et al. 2011) that focus on not-yet-digitized settings and that show a continuity in work practice development and paper-based tool construction that current technology is still not able to reproduce or guarantee.

Indeed, if we agree that one of the main issues here at stake is the gap between users and designers (in the traditional sense) – which is grounded in a conceptualization of design that will always prevent users from taking full control and responsibility[30] of the development process – we believe that this gap can be bridged only if design and the conceptual modeling activity that design implies are

---

[30]Beath and Orlikowski (1994) show how most of the user-centered development methodologies that put a strong emphasis on user involvement (they make the case of information engineering) actually relegate users to playing a relatively passive role during development and, in virtue of this, ask for a more clear responsibility for project outcomes. We stress here the need to give full

simply avoided and if the approach toward "technology co-construction" takes work practices "seriously," by avoiding any sort of compromise at the application level and by deriving the related consequences at the technological infrastructure level. In this vein, taking work practices seriously means to conceive technology construction as part of *work and articulation work*, in the same way as paper-based artifacts are constructed by actors when they need and use them (e.g., Morrison and Blackwell 2009) or, more generally yet, in the same way as users use work-arounds when their applications cannot be tailored in any satisfactory way (Cabitza and Simone 2013b).

We then argue that the sort of universatility that platforms must guarantee should be based on a radical performative approach for two reasons: first, according to an ontological approach, specificity and situatedness are reached by having actors apply a universal model locally and such a model can be both *adopted* and *adapted*, but adaptation is here only a sort of extension of its basic assumptions and first-instance concepts; conversely, a performative approach guarantees such locality by delegating the users to create *their own* essentially open, underspecified, incomplete, and even ambiguous "models," by which they can make sense of their do-it-yourself tools (Cabitza et al. 2013; Cabitza and Simone 2012c).

Second, adopting a performative approach "seriously" calls for the requirement of an environment that limits itself to providing primitives by which users can build their application in a *bottom-up fashion*, that is, in an emergent process of trial and error, and *while they work*, as a way to improve the odds that the application will really reflect and support their situated practices: if this construction were "extracted" from those practices and moved to a controlled environment of introspection, modeling, and ontological representation, we believe that we would again tap into a less than effective ritual, which is stuck with the conviction that the task-artifact entanglement can be really untangled without losing both (see Sect. 11.2). As Lanzara put it: "systems do not only operate or change in time, but are literally 'made with time'." Within a performative approach, as we discussed in Sect. 11.2, end users can be seen as bricoleurs who build their digital tools tapping into their tacit knowledge and their creative skills to build the portion of the IT artifact that comes closest to their work practices.

11.5 Concrete Steps Toward a Logic of Bricolage

In order to make a contribution toward the conceptual foundation of environments supporting the practice of bricolage in EUD terms, we will take inspiration from the point that Lanzara (1999) made on the importance of "transient constructs and persistent structures" (p. 332), which are seen as the results of "a practical, situated, context-sensitive mode of design that feeds on the dynamic tension between the requirements of change and stability." We also think that what he called the "logic of bricolage" emerges from the intertwined interplay of structures and constructs,

---

control, rather than only responsibility, to the community of users that will host the information system.

transiency and permanency, and universality and locality. This requires that an environment supporting bricolage does not provide users with sophisticated (i.e., semantically rich) modeling tools that facilitate the top-down construction of the application: from the conception of the "entities" involved, their attributes, their mutual relationships, and of the "business processes" where all these latter interact; rather this logic is supposed to offer to the users a set of "bricks" that they can arrange and compose together in a bottom-up fashion within a conceptually consistent environment (i.e., the rules of composition).

In order to envision such an environment, we propose a multilayered architecture that is partly inspired by the research accomplished in the COMIC project.[31] In this architecture, the layers that are closer to the greater source of uncertainty and unpredictability, that is, the layers that are closer to the users and their environment, are those which can be changed faster and to a greater extent. With reference to Fig. 11.1, we distinguish between an infrastructure, a platform, and environments for editing and working. The infrastructure is the set of available services that are

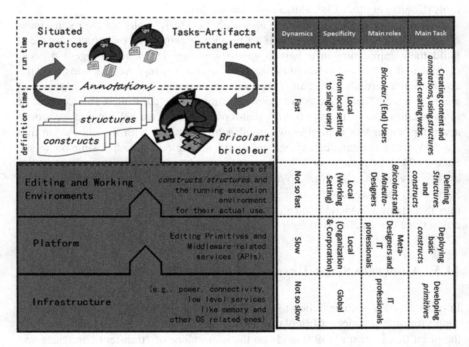

Fig. 11.1 A conceptual architecture for an environment supporting EUD bricolage (LOB keywords are in italics; each layer indicates its name and what it offers to the higher levels)

---

[31] The COmputer-based Mechanisms of Interaction in Cooperative work project was an EC-ESPRIT-funded basic research project No. 6225, from 1992 to 1995.

used by the computational platform that is specifically designed to support the bricoleurs in building and using their own tools.

This platform, in its turn, exposes specific services to make the bricolage-based information system possible and computationally augmented; with this aim, the platform instantiates a working environment where a persistent storage and a working memory, as well as an execution engine, are made available to the users, and it instantiates an EUD environment where users can create their building blocks and edit their tools; while working in this latter environment, users use specific visual editors to build both their constructs and their working structures that are put in operation when the working environment is "online."

The architecture outlined above sounds similar to the architectures usually proposed in literature to support modular approaches for application development, like the abovementioned component design or service orchestration (Papazoglou et al. 2007). In fact, although layers are actually common, what differs is their content. We aim at the definition of a platform implementing a general *generative* environment where bricoleurs can define, in principle, any sort of (collaborative) application, starting from elemental and universal building blocks and composing them according to universal composition rules. This idea is captured by the simplified "formal grammar" presented in Table 11.1. This is a first attempt to formalize the "logic of bricolage" toward its implementation.

Table 11.1 Generative productions of the logic of bricolage

<web-structure> ::= <layout-structure>+
<layout-structuree> ::= <topological-object>+
<topological-object> ::= <operand-construct> <coordinates >?
<operand-construct > ::= <constant> | <typed-variable> | <operator-construct>(<operand-construct >+)
<operator-construct> ::= <functional-operator-construct> | <actional-operator-construct>,
<annotation> ::= <style> <target-ref> + |<constant> <target-ref>+
< target-ref> ::= <functional-operator-construct> (<target>)
<constant> ::= <domain-values> | <multimedia-text>
<target> ::= <control-structure> | <topological-object> | <annotation>
<style> ::= <conventional-symbol> + | <operator-construct> (<target>)
<control-structure> ::= <rewriting-rule> | <connector>
<connector> ::= <functional-operator-construct> (<control-structure >+)
<rewriting-rule> ::= <condition> <action>+
<condition> : := <functional-operator-construct> (<state>)
<action> : := <operator-construct>(<state>)
<state> ::= <operand-construct>+

Legend: The LOB grammar is expressed in EBNF-like notation; therefore, the symbol "|" means "alternative," "<>" means "variable," "+" means "one or more occurrences," "_" means "zero or more occurrences," and "?" means "zero or one occurrences"; "domain values" are not specified and are the terminal symbols of the grammar (e.g., true and false).

In the following, we define the main elements of this grammar and illustrate them by means of the particular document-based information system environment that we have been developing in the last few years, called the web of active documents (WOAD, Cabitza and Simone 2010; Cabitza and Gesso 2011). The core concepts of WOAD can be summarized as follows: (i) the information system is parcellized in a set of hyperlinked active documents that can be annotated in all parts and sections and be associated with any other document, comment, and computational behavior; (ii) there is no rational and unified data model because users define their forms in a bottom-up manner and, in so doing, the platform instantiates the underlying flat data structures that are necessary to store the content that these forms will contain and to retrieve the full history of the process of filling in them; (iii) the presentation layer is in the full control of end users, who are called to both generate their own templates and specify how their appearance should change later in use under particular conditions (cf. the concept of affording mechanism proposed in Cabitza and Simone 2012b); and (iv) execution control is rule based. Users can define local rules that act on the documents' content and, as hinted above, change how documents look like (i.e., their physical affordances), to make themselves aware of pertinent conditions according to some cooperative convention or business rule like the need to revise the content of a form, or to consider it provisional, or to carefully consider some contextual condition (see, e.g., Cabitza et al (2009) for other examples of such conventions).

11.5.1 The Generative Environment

The grammar that supports the logic of bricolage (LOB) is based on the following first-class concepts or elements (see Table 11.1) where the technical terms *constructs* and *structures* are partly inspired by Lanzara's original contribution Lanzara (1999):

Constructing constructs. These are constructs that we denote as "constructing" because, first, they are *construct(ed)* during the inception phase of the platform within a cooperative setting, hopefully as result of a participatory design activity, and second because, once constructed, they are to be used as atomic "building blocks" by which the bricoleurs can create their working spaces and artifacts. We can further characterize these *constructing constructs*, distinguishing between *operand constructs* and *operator constructs*. Operators are all the feasible operations and micro-functions that users deem necessary to be performed over the operands; these latter are the most atomic data structures, components, and variables that the platform must make available in both the editing and working environments to be used in situated work practices. Both operands and operators are the "things" that are arranged and put together in the bricolage activity in order to, respectively, compose the artifacts and endow these of computational capabilities.

For example, in WOAD, the *operand constructs* are called *datoms* (document atom): these are any writable area with a unique name and a type (e.g., integer, string). A datom can recursively be a composition of one or more datoms: e.g., the "first name" datom (a string) and the "family name" one (also a string) can be combined into a "person name" datom that encompasses both. The *operator constructs* are a selection of atomic functions that include predicates and are denoted as *functional* in Table 11.1. For example, doctors from the medical setting described in Cabitza et al. (2009) required for their forms a construct to perform averaging and another one checking the occurrence of a value in a given set (i.e., the is-in construct), in addition to the standard arithmetic and Boolean operations. Operator constructs include also atomic functions that correspond to actions on specific operand constructs and are denoted as *actional* in Table 11.1. In the same vein as Simone and Schmidt (1993), we described a method to recognize and characterize these atomic components from the qualitative analysis of the paper-based artifacts used within a document-intensive work domain, i.e., two large hospitals (Cabitza 2011): in Table 11.2, we report the list of *actional operator constructs* that users agreed with us and they would need to apply to the "data fields" (i.e., *operand constructs*) of their documents. Not all of the constructs are easy to build. Indeed, as our subsequent studies show, while datoms can be created with a relatively simple editor (Cabitza et al. 2011b), which we realized to allow users to both create data fields and their templates, operations clearly need to be associated with specific behaviors exposed by the platform or the infrastructure (like printing or sending as a message).

The grammar allows more complex *operator constructs* to be recursively defined by composing more elemental ones by means of suitable *functional operator constructs* and their corresponding *primitives* (see below).

Structures. These are what any bricoleur creates by composing and arranging *constructing constructs* together. We distinguish between *layout structures*[32] and *control structures*. The former ones are sort of material (yet non-necessarily tangible) and symbolic work spaces that are recognized by members of a community of practitioners as the physically inscribed technological artifacts (Orlikowski 2000) with which to carry out their work. In document-based information systems, *layout structures* are the document templates of forms and charts that are to be used to both accumulate data and coordinate activities (Berg 1999), endowed with both physical properties (i.e., the topological arrangement of the constructs mentioned above, i.e., data fields and sections) and symbolic properties (the boilerplate texts, any iconic element and visual affordances conveyed through the graphical interface). For example, in WOAD, a *web structure* is a graph of hyperlinked templates (i.e., *layout structures*); these latter are a set of *didgets*: a didget is a *topological object*, i.e., a datom (see above) that is put in some place, i.e., is coupled to a set of *coordinates* (that in WOAD are represented as Cartesian pairs with respect to the

---

[32]We prefer the expression "layout structure" instead of "information structure" (or "data structure"), which would perhaps be the traditional mode to indicate those structures, as the latter term would have given the nod to the high-level, conceptual element those structures could be referred to by a human user. Conversely, we mean to hint at the material, spatial arrangement of meaningful signs that "act at the surface" in promoting cognitive processes of sense making and interpretation.

Table 11.2 Operator constructs identified in Cabitza (2011)

Document-based operations	
create	This operation is akin to picking a new empty sheet of a specific template to insert into the folder
retrieve	This operation is akin to picking a sheet from an archive and make it available for other operations
open/read	This operation is akin to getting explicit access to the content of a sheet or instance of artifact
write	This operation is akin to adding some new content to the artifact and accumulating new inscriptions on it
select	This operation is akin to pointing either an artifact (among others) or a specific portion of its content
copy	This operation is akin to putting some content into a buffer memory, like a little pocket sheet
correct	This operation is to be considered different from regular writing but rather similar to striking through some
transmit	This operation is akin to sending either the physical artifact or (part of) its content to an external party
print	This operation regards the physical printing, or copy, of part/whole content of an artifact
officialize	This operation regards the formalization/certification of part/whole content of an artifact
annotate	This operation differs from write in that it is aimed at adding informal or side content: it stands to writing as metadata stands to data
attach	This operation can encompass affixing an external resource to the artifact
cache	This operation regards the saving of part/whole content of an artifact for future use (modifications are still possible)
store	This operation regards the storing of the artifact in some repository, where only an operation of retrieve can take it from
protect	This operation regards the preservation of part/whole content of an artifact from further operations
delete	This operation regards the partial/complete elimination of either an artifact or parts of its content

origin of the template). In the domains of computer-aided design and collaborative drawing/editing, a layout structure can be considered the working space where users arrange command docking bars, symbol stencils, and predefined configurations of elements that must be set up before working on them.

On the other hand, *control structures* specify how the computational engine of the underlying layers of the architecture (see Fig. 11.1) reacts in response to events generated at artifact (interface) level, how this latter acts on the content inscribed therein, and how it interacts with the users during their use of the tool. On a formal level, *control structures* are compositions of *rewriting rules* (see the keyword connector in Table 11.1) that express rewriting systems, a general formalism that can be instantiated, e.g., as rule-based control systems, Petri nets, business process modeling language, or any sort of declarative control construct. In

WOAD, the control structures are called *mechanisms*, i.e., if-then rules whose if-part is a Boolean expression that is recursively defined using the predefined datom names as variables and the operators identified above, all together with the (obvious) constants of the basic types. The then part is a sequence of *operator constructs* that has to be executed on the template or on its inner components. In particular, these operators can change the affordances of an instantiated template to convey information to promote collaboration awareness according to its contents (Cabitza and Simone 2012a). Moreover, mechanisms are composed by the (implicit) OR *functional operator construct*.

More complex *control structures* can be obtained by composing more elemental ones by suitable *functional operator constructs* and their corresponding *primitives* (see below).

Annotations. We consider *annotations* as part of the first-class concepts of a logic of bricolage for their central role in work articulation, knowledge sharing, and mutual understanding (Luff et al. 1992; Cadiz et al. 2000; Bringay et al. 2006; Cabitza et al. 2013) yet at a more informal level with respect to institutionalized (layout) structures and to the official content that is accumulated therein during situated practice. To this respect, any form of annotation carried out by practitioners over and upon structures and their content can be seen as a more ephemeral, informal, and more user-driven piece of bricolage, which acts at a different layer with respect to primitives, structures, and content (see dynamics and specificity in Fig. 11.1) but that nevertheless plays an equally important role in making the artifacts in use flexible enough to support invisible work (Star and Strauss 1999). Annotations are then either stigmergic signs (Christensen 2014) and marks attached to the borders of documents, extempore comments, and semantic tags from either domain-specific taxonomies or setting-specific folksonomies or nested threads of both, as we described in Cabitza et al. (2012b): all pieces of a bricolage that hosts informal communication and handover between practitioners, their silent and ungoverned work of meaning reconciliation, and the sedimentations of habits and customs in effective (yet still unsupported computationally) conventions of cooperative work. For these reasons, we believe that any working environment aimed at enabling users to preserve (or even augment) their record-keeping conventions in the digitization of their traditional artifacts should support annotation as a first-class class activity of workers in their natural "ecosystem." In particular, then, also annotations should be referrable in control structures as we described in Cabitza and Simone (2012a, p. 232) and in Cabitza et al. (2012b).

Primitives. Primitives are basic operations that the platform makes available through the editing environment where the bricoleurs can create both their constructs and their structures. To adopt a pseudo-formal analogy, if constructs are the elements of an alphabet, the primitives can be seen as the composition rules of a grammar by which end users can generate meaningful sentences (i.e., structures). Specific primitives allow users to populate these structures with both content and meta-content, that is, any collaborative annotation.

The running environment executes *operator constructs* (both *functional* and *actional* ones) by interpreting them as more or less complex articulation of *primitives*; these latter, in their turn, are domain-independent functionalities exposed by the platform that have been expressed in terms of lower-level application programming interfaces by IT professionals. In particular, the platform conceives the following primitives (besides the usual arithmetic and logical operations like +, −, AND, OR, etc.): *read* and *write* that represent the conceptual operations at the basis of any computation; *bind*, which assigns constants to variables; *aggregate*, by which to build complex operands from simpler ones; *compose*, to build complex operators in terms of functional composition; and *place*, to associate an operand with some coordinates to create a topological object. Moreover, the *annotate* primitive allows us to associate a *domain value*, a *multimedia text*, or a *conventional symbol* (e.g., any character, word or iconic mark) to any construct or to an existing annotation. It is noteworthy that operator constructs can be just domain-specific specializations of *primitives*, like a user-defined procedure *sum()* that can specialize the + primitive of a programming language.

In WOAD, the basic operations conceived for the definition of both templates and mechanisms, i.e., *layout* and *control structures*, respectively, can be related to the *primitives* mentioned above especially *aggregate*, by which more complex datoms (as operand constructs) can be built from simpler ones, and *place*, by which users can associate a *didget* with a Cartesian coordinate with respect to the origin of a given template. A *mechanism* is a simple *control structure* made of a single rewriting rule while the *compose* primitive is a simple OR *functional operator construct*.

As mentioned in the previous section, the *primitives* are offered through an editing environment where *constructs* and *structures* can be defined. For example, in WOAD, this environment is constituted by two visual editors: one for the construction of mechanisms (Cabitza et al. 2012a) and one for the construction of datoms and, by arranging these latter topologically in terms of didgets, templates. The editing environment is associated with an execution environment that has been tested on realistic examples taken from the healthcare domain (Cabitza and Gesso 2012).

The conceptual architecture that is depicted in Fig. 11.1 incorporates that in complex socio-technical systems, change must be expected: indeed, it encompasses different layers that account for both different scopes (see Specificity), concerns (see Task), involved roles, and dynamics. We borrow again some terms from Lanzara's logic of bricolage to qualify the changing rate of the layers constituting the conceptual architecture. Any form of annotation carried out by practitioners over and upon structures and their content can be seen as a more transient, informal, and more user-driven piece of bricolage, which acts as a sort of different layer with respect to content, structures, constructs, and obviously the platform's primitives (see Fig. 11.1); nevertheless (or right in virtue of this complementarity), annotations play an equally important role in making the artifacts-in-use flexible enough to support also invisible work (Star and Strauss 1999) and hence fully appropriated by their users.

Layout structures are the immediately less transient components as they correspond to working spaces that users flexibly accommodate to their changing needs (Harris and Henderson 1999). Decoupling layouts, i.e., the data structures, from the logic acting upon them, i.e., the control structures, is a well-known engineering principle that the framework recognizes. However, although formally decoupled, control structures in practice follow and support the modifications of the objects/artifacts to which they are applied: therefore, they are at the same level of change rate.

On the other hand, constructs, especially the more basic and atomic ones, can be considered as changing at a slower pace than the structures they are part of, while the more complex ones can be revised (modified, deleted) more often but probably less frequently than the above mentioned structures. Primitives, conversely, are almost persistent: informally speaking, the composition rules must be more stable than the objects they apply to. Finally, the layers of the underlying technological infrastructure can be considered as almost permanent, in that changes can be planned, postponed, and made incrementally depending on the triggering technological evolution or organizational strategy. The emphasis on this aspect is motivated by the fact that IT professionals have to build the infrastructure and its relationships with constructs and primitives plastic enough to avoid any friction between the different layers that "drift" at different speed according to regular technological evolution and the users' needs.

11.5.2 Some First Implications for Research

The three-layered architecture described above is aimed at addressing the user-centered requirement to provide shop-floor practitioners involved in a digitization program with (at least) the same space of possibility they have when they work with non-digitized artifacts. In so doing, end users would get the opportunity to transition from their paper-based artifacts to computationally augmented ones by means of the editing and working environments, so that the layout structures that scaffold their activities (Orlikowski 2006) would change with the necessary gradualness (or do not differ at all) at least in theory.

To this aim, the grammar is left purposely flat, general, and simple: we do not want to introduce surreptitious entities, like the concept of artifact, activity, task, role, and the like, which traditional methods of software production may already employ as primitive elements for the phase of design. We have already recalled how any design of IT technologies either produces or adopts a model, sooner or later. These models, irrespective of the layers at which they manifest or are adopted, will necessarily end up by conflicting with work practices (for a recent account on this phenomenon see, e.g., Morrison et al. 2011). This is because these practices "by definition" change over time and make sense only in their doing (see Sect. 11.2), while models equally "by definition" introduce the level of representational rigidity that is necessary for their role in requirement elicitation and formal specifications (e.g., Bowers 1991; Robinson and Bannon 1991; Bannon 1994).

However, the architecture depicted in Fig. 11.1 requires a radical change of per-spective for all the stakeholders involved in technology conception and construction. In particular, this proposal requires us to focus on the idiosyncratic and fine grained ways in which users cope with unexpected change in their work environment (Bannon 1992). For IT professionals, this means focusing on how constraints have to be dynamically expressed to support the definition of the appropriate ordering of action and interaction in cooperative work in any circumstance (e.g., Pesic et al. 2007; van der Aalst et al. 2009), which pieces of information are used to support articulation and cooperative work, how these are arranged in suitable artifacts (e.g., Nemeth 2003; Cabitza 2011), and what habits, customs, and conventions are at stake and silently inform the exchange of information and the sense making occurring within and across communities of cooperating actors (Mark 2002; Cabitza et al. 2009). In sum, conceiving artifacts (and entangled tasks) as more or less transient "entities" emerging from the composition of constructs requires to understand what elementary bricks users *already* have on hand to flexibly compose their artifacts[33] and to conceive of ways to make those bricks computational, that is, associated with specific system behaviors (or functionalities), so that the performative and entangled nature of tasks and artifacts can be preserved and supported.

With respect to a research-oriented agenda, this requires further studies and meta-studies in the same vein of those by Martin and Sommerville (2004) and Cabitza (2011), which aim to identify recurring and "universal" elemental operations/behaviors. Their identification would facilitate the reuse of ways to map either domain- or setting-specific (operator) constructs with the APIs that the common platform has to expose to make the execution of *operator constructs* possible. These studies would share the assumption that leveraging general *operator constructs* will not impose users any specific practice or way to treat information (which is mainly represented in terms of *operand* constructs). This assumption seems reasonable first because the identified operations would be intended to be as "atomic" and therefore as elementary as possible and second because what could change in any specific setting would be the practices users are familiar with and hence the way users would make sense of and articulate together those basic elements within their work.

11.5.3 For Whom Tolls the Bell?

In the previous section, we hinted at the fact that an architecture that enables bricolage requires all the stakeholders to reconfigure their traditional roles to make the best use of it within the win-win game that motivates such reconfiguration. But who are the stakeholders that are involved on a practical level? In this section, we will just limit ourselves to the ones that are closer to the task-artifact entanglement[34]:

---

[33]We recall here the requirement that bricoleurs already *know* the available pieces (see Section 3).

[34]We are aware that buyers, top management executives, middle management officers, more or less official and institutionalized representatives of business units, and their employees have always been part and parcel of the development process of a corporate information system. However,

traditional frameworks usually denote these as end users, key users, and actors from one side of the divide and designers, analysts, programmers, and developers from the other.[35]

The former actors are those that are supposed to invest an important effort in bricolaging with the system, in the hope that this could pay off in terms of a better fit between the resulting system and their needs and of a smaller impact on their traditional coordinative practices and accepted power relationships. In this regard, it is often argued that one should distinguish at least between the regular end user and the so-called power user. This distinction, which can be of some value for purely analytical purposes, should yet be treated with caution if it is to drive the decision of "what to offer/allow to whom." The conventional label of power user, far from being used – as often is – to indicate a role having special rights in modifying the technology (like a sort of administrator, who is distinct from regular users for her "powers"), should be rather interpreted as originally intended by Bandini and Simone (2006), i.e., as an organizational or even more informal category that allows us to distinguish end users on the basis of their motivations in improving the artifacts *they also use* and for the competences they have acquired in understanding how things could be changed and why. In this light, power users are not the "chosen ones" that receive the right to modify the application from above but rather who, in virtue of their motivations and competencies, are either formally or informally delegated by their colleagues with the aim of taking personal care that the tool continuously evolves and fits the current needs of the community where it is put to work.

Therefore, within our perspective, the difference between power and regular user fades away in the notion of bricoleur: someone that can be factually involved in constructing and developing the bricolage or that anyway uses it and hence contributes in building and consolidating related habits and conventions of usage and interpretation. For this reason, access to the editing environment should be purposely left to be regulated according to social control and local and socially relevant conventions and initiatives that are just outside the scope of the technology itself.

In regard to the IT practitioners, obviously abandoning the traditional view of rational design does not entail getting rid of designers at all; besides being socially impossible, this sounds also undesirable. Rather, it requires designers, business analysts, and IT analysts to focus on different initial purposes and services to supply, as we hinted at in Sect. 11.5.2. In Sect. 11.3, we recalled the work by Hartswood et al. (2000) and hinted at the role of designers in terms of *facilitators* of the process of co-construction of both tasks and artifacts. A similar role has been identified by the approach that proposes participatory evolutionary design as a virtuous integration

---

articulating the reconfiguration of the larger actor network that encompasses all these levels of involvement and accountability would be out of the chapter's scope.

[35]Cabitza and Simone (2012c) show that this divide has historical roots, and hence it is contingent. In particular, the "divide" took place approximately in the second half of the 1950s when the computer, which had been thus far intended only as a mathematical instrument for which each of its users had to write his/her own code to be executed when it was his/her turn, became a full-fledged time-sharing equipment and established itself as a business machine or better yet an electronic data-processing machine (O'Neill 1992; Campbell-Kelly and Aspray 2004).

of EUD and participatory design (Sumner and Stolze 1997). The term "facilitator" yet must be taken more in the connotation first discussed by Hirschheim and Klein (1989), that is, more as that of a *catalyst* within a chemical reaction that really follows unpredictable and, above all, uncontrollable dynamics. Otherwise, the risk is to conceive them as professionals supposed to facilitate the process in which computer-based systems are finally accepted as "perfect bureaucratic tools" (Harris and Henderson 1999) and adopted within a community of practice or organizational setting.

In this view, we can detect two main roles involved in IT development from the IT perspective, which are characterized by specific and complementary competences. One, who acts as the catalyst/facilitator mentioned above, could be referred to as a *maieuta*-designer. Although such a word would be pronounced quite similarly to that of meta-designer,[36] its meaning would refer to a quite different thing. Maieuta is one who performs the art of maieutics, the Socratic approach where someone helps *bring out* implicit notions in the interlocutors' beliefs, mainly through a dialogic and narrative way encompassing a series of open questions that do not necessarily require an answer,[37] or just help them further refine their understanding and become more autonomous in their expression. Such a designer is primarily concerned with the front end of the enabling technology, i.e., with the graphical and semiotic aspects of the artifacts "to be built and to be used" through it. Also, the maieuta-designer is supposed to "close" the merely technological part of the design process and to *pass the baton* on the end users, i.e., (the bricoleurs), by helping them to find the means and motivations for the "in vivo" development of their artifacts on their own. As such, the maieuta-designer does not have to possess strong programming or architectural skills: rather he/she has to be a domain expert and a connoisseur of how the users of a particular domain (if not particular setting) are used to conceiving their tools and tinkering them over time (to what ends, on the basis of what political and cultural drives and constraints, and the like) in order to help users in exploiting the available editing environment in such a way that their bricolage does not become an erratic process but rather is *sustainable* over time.

Typical technology-oriented competencies must be conversely mastered by the IT professionals, or back-end designers, working on and developing the platform itself: these are called to the role of guaranteeing that the artifacts built on top of the platform can evolve over time, that is, that the enabling environments are easy to use for as many actual users as possible. This means guaranteeing that the best software engineering techniques (e.g., modularity, integration of data and routines) are employed to make the platform and exposed environments powerful and flexible enough to allow for the bricolage activities at the higher-level layers of the overall architecture, besides guaranteeing also that the platform is modular and robust enough to cope (and align) with (low rate) changes in the underlying infrastructure. We could say that "designing for unanticipated construction" could flank (or perhaps substitute) the old claim for "designing for unanticipated use" by Robinson (1993).

---

[36] And this is not completely by chance: mee'yootah vs. 'mee-tah.

[37] A list of this kind of questions can be found in Cabitza et al. (2014b).

11.5.4 What Is Outside Like This?

Our proposal tries to reinvigorate a discourse among the current mythologies of system design that conceives the progressive delegation of power and control to end users as a feasible way to cope with increasingly complex socio-technical systems, supported by increasing complicated IT systems (Latour 1996).

This goal can be achieved by supporting two dimensions of EUD: the collaboration among end users in the construction and tailoring of their applications and the technical aspects of the construction itself. The former dimension is captured by the notion of "use discourse" discussed in (Pipek and Wulf 2009): this concept has shaped the construction of environments that support users in negotiating the configuration of the software infrastructures and that are characterized by typical collaboration tools such as discussion forums, representation sharing (among which process diagrams) and annotation, and voting systems (Wulf et al. 2008; Stevens 2010).

As an alternative approach, in recent years, a small number of frameworks have been developed to support the end users as bricoleurs in the sense discussed in the previous sections. Among these, we obviously include WOAD, the document-based information system platform that we have introduced in Sect. 11.5.1. Although WOAD has been natively conceived to allow for the degree of flexibility and user autonomy, the specialist literature reports also other platforms and frameworks that exhibit similar features. For instance, placeless documents (Dourish et al. 2000) introduced the idea of document properties that are attached by single end users and, above all, properties that represent active ways to operate with documents (called active properties): users can add these properties to documents to make them carry executable code that can be invoked to control or augment their functionalities. This work, to our knowledge, was among the first to carry into the HCI arena notions from prototype-based object-oriented programming and operating system programming, like attaching code to documents as a means to control their behavior and the idea of letting users develop some bunches of runnable code to extend the system functionalities. WOAD decouples layout structures from control structures, although these can be related to each other by means of if-then mechanisms defined over the document's content.

Enabling end users to build their own documents is a common trait among recent initiatives on visual data-driven form generation; these projects are usually aimed at allowing users to generate even complex forms, intended as data-entry points to an underlying flat data structure, without particular programming skills, e.g., by means of a visual editor like Microsoft® InfoPath® as described in Mamlin et al. (2006) or by means of the layout mode in FileMaker Pro® as used in Chen and Akay (2011). This allows us to take "form design out of the programmers' hands and put it into the realm of content management, much as form-generation tools (like Ruby on Rails or Plone's Archetypes) aid the developer in rapidly generating forms" (Mamlin et al. 2006), and hence to address a specific need that so far has been raised by practitioners in the healthcare domain (e.g., Mamlin et al. 2006;

Morrison and Blackwell 2009; Chen and Akay 2011; Cabitza et al. 2011a). The system described by Mamlin et al (2006) presents also the feature to associate form elements with specific rules (expressed in the Arden syntax), making this similar to WOAD, although the editor defined in this latter framework allows for the reuse of form components (i.e., the datoms) and for the abovementioned decoupling between layout and the logic-based control flow of execution (datoms vs. mechanisms).

Finally, some effort has been paid by researchers to address the requirement of making the end user really autonomous in creating their document-specific rules, and this is usually enabled by means of visual and user-friendly tools (e.g., Cabitza and Gesso 2012; Krebs et al. 2012). An even more comprehensive approach to this general aim was proposed by Harel and Marelly (2003) in the Play framework: this latter allows users to build reactive systems by playing, so to speak, their specifications in a performative way, that is, through scenarios that are subsequently implemented by means of a Play-Engine that "plays out" the corresponding models of interaction; these are explicitly represented in terms of multistep control structures, what the authors call "live sequence charts." These are hence more complex and articulated interaction structures than simple rules are. Whether they cope well with unknown emergent behaviors is less certain. However, in Play, users can specify these models of human-computer interaction in a way that is innovative and peculiarly aligned with some of the tenets we discussed above: end users can interact with prototype user interfaces and have the system build the corresponding structures or write the intended behavior and its main exceptions handling procedures in brief sentences expressed in natural (yet structured) language or even tell it directly to the system, in a sort of versatile multimode way to teach the system what to do if some events occur (typically at interface level).

The Play framework has been specifically proposed as a concrete first step toward what Harel (2008) suggestively calls the *liberation of programming from its three straightjackets*: these are the "1) need to write down a program as a symbolic, textual, or graphical artifact; 2) the need to specify requirements (the what) separately from the program (the how) and to pit one against the other; 3) the need to structure behavior according to the system's structure, providing each piece or object with its full behavior" (p. 29). The aim of liberating programming from these representational straightjackets resonates in very close affinity with the tenets of an EUD approach and seems to go in the direction of drawing a common agenda where practitioners from different disciplines can perhaps meet together and inform their own research and development initiatives in a positive manner.

11.6   Some Final Remarks for Future Discussion

In this section, we will just outline two important aspects that should be the object of future research (or discussion) on the concrete applicability of the *laissez-faire* method and of the *logic of bricolage* in the development and evolution of socially embedded systems. These two topics relate to important strands of research that are receiving more interest from diverse communities of researchers involved in studying the impact of IT in social settings in the recent years. We broadly denote these two topics as "concerns about risk" and "concerns about interoperability" (and hence standardization).

11.6.1 How Risky Is a Different Development Strategy?

One could detect an irony in our advocacy of a *laissez-faire* approach for the construction of an efficient, effective, and safe technology, whereas it has been the need to guarantee such qualities that motivated the consolidation of engineering methods and methodology in IT system construction (Haigh 2010; Cabitza and Simone 2012c). This feeling could be reinforced by our explicit confidence that an environment enabling and supporting bricolage by end users could be a feasible alternative to any *-design of those systems. Indeed, in the specialist literature, there is a tendency to consider bricolage as akin to improvisation (Weick 1993; Lanzara 1999) and the bricoleur as someone, at best, who draws on the materials at hand to create a response to a task on the spot (Levi-Strauss 1966); in Lanzara's words: "in a broadly diffused engineering ideology, bricolage is usually associated with second- best solutions, maladaptation, imperfection, inefficiency, incompleteness, slowness." This prejudice is repeated several times within the system development discourse.

One reason for that is to be found in the misunderstanding coming from understating the radical novelty that the myth of the bricoleur carries. In fact, as long as bricolage is evoked in discourses that still refer to a traditional way to build computational artifacts or only moderate it (e.g., design with users, meta-design), that is, as long as bricolage is ingrained in a traditional way to think of IT design (even in the light of contributions coming from participatory design, action research, and ethnography), we will keep undermining the original sense of this concept in some (important) way and, worse yet for our aims, weakening its potential to move into a new and more useful mythology.

From what we have argued at length, it should be clear that we stress the ability of the bricoleur to "work and play with the stock [with] parts that are not standardized or invented, [but rather] appropriated for new uses" (Weinstein and Weinstein 1991, pp. 161–162) and that are taken from "an inventory of semi-defined elements [that] are at the same time abstract and concrete [and that] carry a meaning, given to them by their past uses and the bricoleur's experience, knowledge and skill, a meaning which can be modified, up to a point, by the requirements of the project and the bricoleur's intentions" (Louridas 1999): what we above called constructs. In this compositional mythology then, the concept of *bricolant* bricoleur should not be seen any longer as an "improviser," a tinker, hobbyist, or hacker in the negative connotation of these terms (e.g., Ciborra 2002, p. 47–48) but rather as a creative actor who is enabled by the sponsors of the digitization initiative to reach their purposes in the awareness that only end users are competent *enough* to reach a sustainable balance between effectiveness and efficiency in cooperative ambits and, above all, to meaningfully improvise in the face of the unexpected, in virtue of the fact that users, communities, and organizations *already* exist (i.e., they preexist digitization and informating initiatives) and *already* possess "a disposition towards their environment [...,] already [are] committed in a self-meaningful manner towards [their] own survival and prosperity" (Angell and Ilharco 2009).

Supporting bricolage then is not the slothful retreat of the blasé researcher that releases responsibility by advocating a more empowered and active role of end users in virtue of her democratic feelings. Rather it is the ultimate strategy to make the complex socio-technical systems that our IT solutions contribute more *resilient* in face of the *normality of accidents* (Perrow 1999). More than this, we submit that an architecture that adopts a *laissez-faire* method and the *logic of bricolage* described above could be said to be both intrinsically resilient and *evolutive*, two terms that are attracting more and more interest by researchers involved in the safety of IT systems (Hanseth and Ciborra 2007) especially in critical or delicate settings, like healthcare (Hollnagel et al. 2008). These two concepts engage the capability of a system to react or change to unexpected events, changes, or conditions at different time scales, respectively, short and long with respect to the occurrence of unexpected event. Being both resilient, that is, able to reach a stable and safe working state after that some unexpected event has occurred, and evolutive, that is, able to grow and increase one's own fit with respect to the surrounding environment, is a fundamental characteristic of socio-technical systems to properly face the increasing odds of failure of some of their multiple components that can result from the increasing complexity of their interrelated parts and corresponding links. This characteristic also constitutes progress with respect to the concept of robustness which refers to the capability of a system to resist and withstand adverse events and change, also in virtue of design and analysis phases usually aimed at identifying, prioritizing, and handling specific exceptions or at reducing the opportunity for their occurrence.

The architecture we envision above is intrinsically resilient as it, paradoxical as it may seem, delegates to end users the burden and responsibility of reacting to unexpected events by leveraging their innate creativity and the invaluable, and often irremediably tacit, knowledge of the overall system dynamics, sometimes much more based on intuition than on rationality (Mark and Semaan 2008) and because such an architecture purposely avoids providing users with information and execution structures that are constrained and articulated on the basis of strong assumptions on how the system will behave under certain conditions: a bricolage-based information system is just an environment for both the human and automated manipulation and processing of signs.[38] Moreover, interactive systems that are built on top of such an architecture are naturally and concretely open to evolution as they, differently from those systems that are built by someone else than their actual

---

[38]If the worst occurs, e.g., if power goes down, the overall socio-technical system is made more resilient simply by printing out some layout structures on paper and having the users work as usual, just without the computational augmentation of those structures.

users, are changed opportunistically by end users on their own when (or in a short time after that) they feel this necessary to accommodate their artifacts and tools to emerging conditions and newly recurring situations. Again in Lanzara's words:

[...], systems assembled by bricolage have an evolutionary advantage: being loosely connected and incoherent assemblies of mixed components, they can be partially reworked without much investment effort. Bricolage is a design strategy that makes sunk costs recoverable. In case of system's depletion, obsolescence or low performance, regeneration can be done without having to throw away the whole structure. [...] As a consequence, systems are persistent and robust because cannot be changed or moved easily, but at the same time keep structural plasticity and exhibit some self-correcting properties. Innovation can be accommodated locally. [...] As [bricolage] exploits the properties of existing structures for interactive and generative purposes, it successfully mediates the dilemmas of change and stability, innovation and conservation. On the one hand, by experimenting with transient constructs it allows for some variability and improvisation without incurring in the possible disruptions caused by excessive instability and radical change; on the other hand, by assembling robust but furtherly manipulable structures, it allows for some order and reliability without curbing the chances for system improvement and innovation. In short, it makes both radical innovation and complete unraveling unlikely. (p. 347)

We subscribe to this understanding of the role that an active, conscious, and responsible *bricoleur* can play in system development but also associate this with the awareness that new platforms must be built supporting this role and new professionals must be educated to mediate between the possibly conflicting stances of such an empowered actor and other roles that are in a hierarchical relationship with it.

11.6.2 Interoperability Concerns

The second issue we propose for future research and discussion regards the tension between the global dimension and the local one in the construction of a technology aimed at supporting whole organizations and/or networks. This is therefore the extension of what we have discussed so far in terms of collaboration within groups of limited size, what we call the local dimension, in the new terms of interoperability "in the large," i.e., across multiple settings and organizations. The separation between global and local has been already shown as illusory by who have recently proposed the concept of information infrastructure (e.g., Fitzpatrick and Ellingsen 2012), as it is recognized that any local event or practice can have the potential to affect the overall system, sooner or later.

In Sect. 11.3, we very briefly hinted at how this separation can be just seen as one way by which the interests of someone (typically institutional authorities of control and high-level regulatory bodies at regional or national level) are imposed on the practices of others (typically the producers of inscribed data and their first consumers for articulative reasons (Berg 1999; Winthereik and Vikkelso 2005)). Consequently, addressing the tension between local vs. global requirements means to also address one of the main root causes behind the pervasive (and still relatively neglected) phenomenon usually denoted as "work-around."[39] Such a circumvention of the system and its intended (and designed) uses that users perform to overcome the rigidity that the global view of IS imposes on their local practices can indeed undermine any serious attempt to engineer and deliver safe and robust technologies in socio-technical systems (Niazkhani et al. 2011; Handel and Poltrock 2011). In this section, we will outline how a laissez-faire method can be compatible with the increasing need for global interoperability between local systems and, in its little own, can contribute in going beyond the abovementioned tension by interpreting such seeming opposition in a more dialectical way toward the development of information systems that can be flexible enough to meet the local needs of data producers', i.e., the primary users of any information (Cabitza and Simone 2012c), as well as the needs/expectations of some relevant data consumers (i.e., secondary users) at the same time.

The relationship between the applications or functionalities that are developed by end users to respond to their local needs and the information systems that are conceived at the global level of the organizations has been investigated by Doerner et al. (2009) by leveraging the component-based approach (specifically an evolution of the service-oriented approach) and prefiguring an evolution of ERP systems that increases the role of end users as "prosumers" thanks to the transformation of the "cathedral" (i.e., ERP system) into a "bazaar" where end users can exploit the flexibility of SOA architectures and cloud computing. With a similar perspective, the contribution by Beringer and Latzina in this book illustrates the concept of transformative user experience (TUX) "as a design approach in order to dissolve the boundaries between applications and, to transform aspects of appropriation [...] into an intrinsic capability of the infrastructure rather than a post-design phenomenon inferred from observing how users interacted with the system. [...] One way to achieve this flexibility is to underspecify the user interface of an application to allow users to impose different meanings and usages on an IT-artifact at use time. [...] With a transformative user experience approach, we can overcome [the] concept of (unexpected) adaptation, and foresee ostensive usages by enabling transitions from one meaning to another in the system environment." With this aim, they introduce the notion of "elasticity" as a feature of both "containers" (that identify dynamic working spaces) and of the objects they contain: elasticity makes them able to take different meanings according to their dynamic contexts. On the one hand, this proposal aims to overcome the rigidity of the component-based approaches to EUD; however, on the other hand, it claims that "In a corporate work environment, those transitions happen most typically between process-oriented backends and task-oriented front ends," thus linking elasticity to a predefined set of contexts and therefore limiting the degree of tailorability of the resulting environment.

As aptly recalled by Lanzara (1999), "anthropologist Clifford Geertz has pointed out that the more we try to make the world 'global,' the more the world responds with the emergence of multiple 'local worlds' and identities that seem to be

---

[39] A short literature review of this concept can be found in (Cabitza and Simone 2013b).

irreducible to one another." In the same line but with a more technological perspective, Ciborra (1992) suggests that "Top management needs to appreciate local fluctuations in system practices as a repository of unique innovations and commit adequate resources to their development, even if the systems go against traditional approaches. Rather than looking for standard models in the business strategy literature, [strategic information systems] should be sought in the theory and practice of organizational learning and innovation, both incremental and radical." We believe that this passage offers an interesting stimulus to go beyond the way in which firms conceive their (strategic) information systems. Actually, letting information systems "[. . .] emerge from the grass roots of the organization, out of end user hacking, computing, and tinkering" asks for a significant change of perspective in IT design that is closely related to the performative and bricolage-oriented stance we advocated in this chapter. Since "organizational learning and innovation" occur where practices are and action is (Dourish 2001), we subscribe the suggestion by Ciborra (1992) and Lanzara (1999) to start from this "local dimension" to build a technological support that promotes firms' vitality not only for the sake of innovation but also for an effective every day performance. Moreover, since "learning and innovation" are "both incremental and radical," the requirement of having different layer dynamics (or change rate) that was discussed in Sect. 11.5 can be put in relation with the need to cope with incremental and radical changes in the organization itself and in the coevolving technology.

Our suggestion is to regard the "whole" not as a centralized and monolithic entity (to some extent) but rather as the composition of "small" entities, highly specialized to the local needs and highly connected in a web of loose connections linking "local spaces," i.e., peer nodes that are each characterized by local structure and semantics (Bandini et al. 2007) and that are easily adaptable to unexpected contingencies since they are concerned with (and hence control) a limited and well-known "piece" of the world. Obviously, a need to make this new kind of "whole" coherent and consistent with the overall good performance of the network would arise, which is the main concern of any higher-level management unit. However, instead of having the management promote (and enforce) coherence in terms of "obtrusive" control of local behaviors and top-down ontologies to order resources, the management unit itself might behave as a "local entity" with specific goals and expectations on data produced by other units, expressed in terms of its own local quality level constraints. These latter can be exposed as public expectations that other units can (or have to) comply with to interoperate, once either the producer or the consumer have selected what data structures are involved by these constraints and how these data have to be arranged and aggregated to respect the consumer's needs.

In this scenario, interoperability is achieved not by semantically enriching data on the producer's side, i.e., where those data are not natively attached with that semantics, but rather by having consumers pragmatically express what data they need, subscribe to a set of data that are exposed by producers, and, possibly, express also how they need those data be presented (i.e., reported, typically in aggregated form). In this view, the definition of "standard structures" (which play the role of boundary objects (Star and Bowker 1999)) end up by regarding much simpler pieces of information, i.e., a subset of the operand constructs of one unit that this latter exposes to the outside world (or to specific correspondent units, typically of higher level in a social hierarchy). As said above, these latter items can be considered as changing with a low speed rate, since they play a sort of minimum data set that characterizes the unit at hand, but they are in any case easily modifiable since they are not universally (and hence not rigidly) incorporated in more complex structures. In this view, consistency has to be obtained by an effective monitoring of the received structures, rather than by a prescriptive way on how to achieve interoperability about them.

11.7 Conclusions

Let every careful man be very far from writing about things truly worthy of care. (Plato, 352 BC, 7th letter)

The main claim of this chapter is that, in order to bridge the gap between what users need and what is given to them as solutions to those needs, the concept of design has to be substantially challenged and its role in IT development reformulated: in other words, that the IT systems should be at least partially *de-designed* (Cabitza 2014). To this aim, we submit that an old mythology of design, which is based on the separation between conceptual design and situated use and consequently on the modeling activity that entails this separation, should be abandoned in favor of a new mythology. We advocate this new mythology be grounded on both the notion of performativity, from the conceptual perspective, and on the notion of (bricolant/actant) bricoleur from the more practical perspective.

Reviewing the main tenets of this mythology has brought us to introducing a lean method for the development of socially embedded technologies, epitomized by the motto "*laissez faire les bricoleurs*" and the preliminary proposal of a "*logic of bricolage*" that specific environments should enact to empower end users in the process of development of their tools.

Quite distinct from those who welcome the increasing blurring of the roles of designers and users (e.g., Fischer et al. 2004; Johannessen et al. 2012), we do not advocate that users should increasingly "act as designers" (and researchers work to that aim). Rather, we rather believe that such an idea would foster an approach by which users adopt a spurious attitude. There is a danger that users become people who think to "design her own practices" as well (as claimed recently by Johannessen et al. 2012). Conversely, the role of IT professionals and of end users has to be characterized by a clear separation of concerns in the development of computer-based supports of cooperative, organizational work: hard engineering-based *design of meta-systems* for the former ones and *bricolaging* for the latter ones. Indeed, we submit that this separation is at least conceptually (if not also pragmatically) opposite to proposals that advocate a tight integration between, if not a unification of, conceptual design and end-user practices (e.g., the participatory design and the meta-design frameworks). This separation can have the advantage of making the relationships between these two roles not only less harmfully ambiguous but also and above all more productive with respect to the timely and effective deployment and maintenance of computational artifacts, since end users would be in full control of this process.

As we have mentioned in Sect. 11.4, there are examples of technologies that can be seen as steps toward the goal of letting users be in true control of the technology they need and wish to use. At a cursory glance, these technologies implement different kinds of platforms that enable users to perform bricolage-like activities in which the pieces that these platforms make available are composed and arranged in meaningful ways. However, there is still a long way to go in order to collect findings that would confirm that there is an alternative way to design than the conceptual and representational one that is currently ruling in our development methodologies and professional practices.

Apart from any technical consideration, this new approach would require a substantial change in the way young IT-related students are educated for information system design: this is traditionally based on a plethora of data models, from the business-oriented one (the conceptual model) up to the more machine-related one (the physical model), and on a collection of business process models and notations by which to describe how work is (or should be) carried out on those data. However, from a broader perspective, the main role that we have advocated for the development of collaborative applications and information systems, namely, the role of the facilitating *maieuta*-designer, would instead require an educational agenda that is quite different. This would encompass, for instance, teaching the basics of social informatics (Kling et al. 2005) and semiotics (de Souza and Leitao 2009; Beynon-Davies 2011), some qualitative research methods and techniques aptly adapted to the IT domain (Kling et al. 2005) and insights on current theories on IT impact on socio-technical systems and on both change and risk management (Hanseth and Ciborra 2007), as well as notions of socially informed history of technological evolution (Akera and Aspray 2004) and its interpretation from the humanities (Oudshoorn and Pinch 2005). The point is that all three of the roles we discussed in Sect. 11.5.3, namely, the user (as expert of the setting), the facilitator (as domain expert), and the IT developer (as expert of infrastructural concerns), should receive a newly formulated or seriously revisited educational program so that an effective way to take "human actors" seriously can be promoted again (Bannon 1992).

On the other hand, the layered conceptual architecture that we have illustrated has still to prove its practical value in a reasonable range of application domains (or settings) where legacy systems do exist and cannot be "obliterated"[40]: our personal research experience makes us confident that such an architecture is promising for the case of document-based, knowledge-intensive collaborative (information) systems; although many such systems can be found in the world out there, we are aware that this macroclass of applications simply does not cover all IT-based supports.

---

[40]To make a very long story short, legacy systems that automated data structures can – and should – be preserved and wrapped as new local nodes of the network described in Section 6.2; but what destiny to give to those legacy systems that once "automated" procedures and workflows . . . ?

In any case, in order to go a step further in this direction, better platforms and environments supporting an effective and reliable EUD approach are needed. We have proposed some basic principle on which these systems could all be based on: decoupled modularity of information and control structures, loose integration of the latter ones in terms of recomposition of elemental common constructs according to local needs (as opposed to the construction of unifying general schemes), full homogeneity across the layers for the construction of aggregated functionalities so that users can access them and operate with them with the same high-level language, and finally, tools supporting the technology development and managing its intrinsic complexity that are based on users' building practices (vs. the introduction of more or less "hard" engineering tools in EUD).

The two brief (and necessarily partial) outlines of the current discourses on performativity and bricolage, as well as our discourse, encompass notions like the *task-artifact entanglement*, the requirement of *universatility* for EUD environments, the concept of the *(bricolant and actant) bricoleur*, the foundation of a *logic of bricolage*, the distinction between *maieuta*-designers and traditional designers (also on an educational level), the *laissez-faire method* as a purposeful way to cope with the complexity of any socio-technical system and de-design its "technical" component, and even the scant peek to the *local/global illusion*; these are all notions provided as pieces of a bricolage. Like any bricolage, we do not see a particular truth in any of the pieces we brought together in this chapter; rather we have argued about the potential of the resulting jigsaw puzzle, in our opinion coherently kept together by the mythology of the performative end users, as a whole to come out being useful. Obviously our hope is that the EUSSET forum will host many similar discourses and give them some sort of legitimacy to inform common initiatives of research, education, and IT professional practice in the near future.

References

Akera, A., & Aspray, W. (Eds.). (2004). *Using history to teach computer science and related disciplines*. Washington, DC: Computing Research Association.

Anderson, S., Hardstone, G., Procter, R., & Williams, R. (2008). Down in the (Data)base(ment): Supporting configuration in organizational information systems. In *Resources, co-evolution and artifacts* (pp. 221–253). London: Springer. Retrieved from dx.doi.org/10.1007/978-1-84628-901-9_9

Angell, I., & Ilharco, F. (2009). Dispositioning IT all: A theory for thriving without models. In *Bricolage, care and information Claudio Ciborra's legacy in information systems research* (pp. 401–422). London: Palgrave Macmillan.

Ardito, C., Costabile, M. F., Matera, M., Piccinno, A., Desolda, G., & Picozzi, M. (2012). Composition of situational interactive spaces by end users. In *NordiCHI 2012: Proceedings of the 7th nordic conference on human-computer interaction: Making sense through design, October 14th–17th, Copenhagen, Denmark*. ACM Press.

Ash, J. S., Berg, M., & Coiera, E. (2004). Some unintended consequences of information technology in health care: The nature of patient care information system-related errors. *Journal of the American Medical Informatics Association, 11*(2), 104–112. doi:10.1197/jamia.M1471.

Balasubramaniam, S., Lewis, G. A., Simanta, S., & Smith, D. B. (2008). Situated software: Concepts, motivation, technology, and the future. *Software, 25*(6), 50–55. doi:10.1109/MS.2008.159.

Bandini, S., & Simone, C. (2006). EUD as integration of components off-the-shelf: The role of software professionals knowledge artifacts. In *End user development* (Vol. 9, pp. 347–369). Kluwer Academic Publishers.

Bandini, S., Sarini, M., Simone, C., & Vizzari, G. (2007). WWW in the small towards sustainable adaptivity. *World Wide Web, 10*(4), 471–501. doi:10.1007/s11280-007-0024-y.

Bannon, L. (1992). From human factors to human actors: The role of psychology and human-computer interaction studies in system design. In J. Greenbaum & M. Kyng (Eds.), *Design at work* (pp. 25–44). Hillsdale: L. Erlbaum Associates Inc. Retrieved from dl.acm.org/citation.cfm?id = 125470.125458

Bannon, L. (1994). CSCW, challenging perspectives on work and technology. In *Proceedings of the "Information Technology & Organisational Change" Nijenrode Business School, The Netherlands, 28–29 April, 1994.*

Barad, K. (2003). Posthumanist performativity: Toward an understanding of how matter comes to matter. *Signs: Journal of Women in Culture and Society, 28*(3), 801–831. doi:10.1086/345321.

Bath, C. (2009). Searching for methodology: Feminist technology design in computer science. In *Proceedings of the 5th European symposium on gender & ICT digital cultures: Participation - Empowerment - Diversity, March 5–7, 2009, University of Bremen, Bremen.*

Beath, C. M., & Orlikowski, W. J. (1994). The contradictory structure of systems development methodologies: Deconstructing the IS-user relationship in information engineering. *Information Systems Research, 5*(4), 350–377. doi:10.1287/isre.5.4.350.

Berg, M. (1999). Accumulating and coordinating: Occasions for information technologies in medical work. *Computer Supported Cooperative Work (CSCW), 8*(4), 373–401.

Beynon-Davies, P. (2011). *Significance: Exploring the nature of information, systems and technology*. New York: Palgrave Macmillan.

Blackwell, A. L., & Green, A. L. (2008). The abstract is "an enemy". Alternative perspectives to computational thinking. In *PPIG 08: Proceedings of the 20th workshop of the Psychology of Programming Interest Group*. 10–12 Sept 2008, Lancaster, UK.

Blackwell, A. F., & Morrison, C. (2010). A logical mind, not a programming mind: Psychology of a professional end user. In *PPIG 2010: Proceedings of the 22nd annual workshop of the psychology of programming interest group, September 19–22, 2010. Madrid, Spain*(pp. 175–184). University of Lancaster.

Bowers, J. M. (1991). The Janus faces of design: Some critical questions for CSCW. In J. M. Bowers & S. D. Benford (Eds.), *Studies in computer supported cooperative work* (pp. 333–350). Amsterdam, The Netherlands: North-Holland Publishing Co. Retrieved from dl.acm.org/citation.cfm?id = 117730.117753

Bramming, P., Hansen, B. G., Bojesen, A., & Olesen, K. G. (2012). (Im)perfect pictures: Snaplogs in performativity research. *Qualitative Research in Organizations and Management: An International Journal, 7*(1), 54–71. doi:10.1108/17465641211223465.

Brand, S. (1995). *How buildings learn: What happens after they're built*. New York: Penguin Books.

Bratteteig, T., Morrison, A., & Wagner, I. (2010). Research practices in digital design. In *Exploring digital design: Multi-disciplinary design practices* (pp. 17–54). Berlin: Springer.

Bringay, S., Barry, C., & Charlet, J. (2006). Annotations: A functionality to support cooperation, coordination and awareness in the electronic medical record. In *COOP'06: Proceedings of the 7th international conference on the design of cooperative systems*, France, Provence.

Bryant, A. (2000). It's engineering Jim ... but not as we know it: Software engineering; solution to the software crisis, or part of the problem? In *ICSE'00: Proceedings of the 22nd international conference on software engineering* (pp. 78–87). New York: ACM. doi:10.1145/337180.337191.

Bucciarelli, L. (2003). Designing and learning: A disjunction in contexts. *Design Studies, 24*(3), 295–311. doi:10.1016/S0142-694X(02)00057-1

Buescher, M., Gill, S., Mogensen, P., & Shapiro, D. (2001). Landscapes of practice: Bricolage as a method for situated design. *Computer Supported Cooperative Work (CSCW), 10*(1), 1–28. doi:10.1023/A:1011293210539.

Butler, J. (1993). *Bodies that matter: On the discursive limits of sex.* New York: Routledge.

Cabitza, F. (2011). "Remain Faithful to the Earth!": Reporting experiences of artifact-centered design in healthcare. *Computer Supported Cooperative Work (CSCW), 20*(4), 231–263. doi:10.1007/s10606-011-9143-1.

Cabitza, F. (2014). De-designing the IT artifact. Drafting small narratives for the coming of the Socio-Technical Artifact. In *ItAIS 2014, Proceedings of the 11th conference of the Italian chapter of AIS - Digital innovation and inclusive knowledge in times of change, track on design and re-design of socio-technical systems*, November 21–22, 2014, Genova, Italy.

Cabitza, F., & Gesso, I. (2011). Web of active documents: An architecture for flexible electronic patient records. In A. Fred, J. Filipe, & H. Gamboa (Eds.), *Biomedical engineering systems and technologies* (Vol. 127, pp. 44–56). IADIS, Berlin/Heidelberg: Springer.

Cabitza, F., & Gesso, I. (2012). Rule-based programming as easy as a child's play. A user study on active documents. In *IHCI'12: IADIS international conference interfaces and human computer interaction 2012 Lisbon, Portugal, 21–23 July 2012* (pp. 73–80). IADIS Press (online).

Cabitza, F., & Simone, C. (2010). WOAD: A framework to enable the end-user development of coordination oriented functionalities. *Journal of Organizational and End User Computing (JOEUC), 22*(2), 1–20. doi:10.4018/joeuc.2010101905.

Cabitza, F., & Simone, C. (2012a). "Whatever Works": Making sense of information quality on information system artifacts. In G. Viscusi, G. M. Campagnolo, & Y. Curzi (Eds.), *Phenomenology, organizational politics, and IT design: The social study of information systems* (pp. 79–110). IGI Global. Retrieved from 10.4018/978-1-4666-0303-5.ch006

Cabitza, F., & Simone, C. (2012b). Affording mechanisms: An integrated view of coordination and knowledge management. *Computer Supported Cooperative Work (CSCW), 21*(2), 227–260. doi:10.1007/s10606-011-9153-z.

Cabitza, F., & Simone, C. (2012c). Design Ltd.: Renovated Myths for the Development of Socially Embedded Technologies, arXiv:1211.5577v3 [cs.HC].

Cabitza, F., & Simone, C. (2013a). Computational coordination mechanisms: A tale of a struggle for flexibility. *Computer Supported Cooperative Work (CSCW), 22*(4–6), 475–529. doi:10.1007/s10606-013-9187-5.

Cabitza, F., & Simone, C. (2013b). "Drops hollowing the Stone". Workarounds as resources for better task-artifact fit. In L. Ciolfi, M. A. Grasso, & O. W. Bertelsen (Eds.), *ECSCW 2013: Proceedings of the 13th European conference on computer supported cooperative work. 21–25 September 2013, Paphos, Cyprus* (pp. 103–122). Berlin: Springer.

Cabitza, F., Simone, C., & Sarini, M. (2009). Leveraging coordinative conventions to promote collaboration awareness. *Computer Supported Cooperative Work (CSCW), 18*(4), 301–330.

Cabitza, F., Corna, S., Gesso, I., & Simone, C. (2011a). WOAD, a platform to deploy flexible EPRs in full control of end-users. In A. Blandford, G. De Pietro, L. Gallo, A. Gimblett, P. Oladimeji, & H. Thimbleby (Eds.), *EICS4Med 2011: Proceedings of the 1st international workshop on engineering interactive computing systems for medicine and health care, co-located with the ACM SIGCHI symposium on Engineering Interactive Computing Systems (EICS 2011) Pisa, Italy, June 13, 2011* (Vol. 727, pp. 7–12). CEUR-WS.org. New York: ACM Press.

Cabitza, F., Gesso, I., & Corna, S. (2011b). Tailorable flexibility: Making end-users autonomous in the design of active interfaces. In K. Blashki (Ed.), *MCCSIS 2011: IADIS multi conference on computer science and information systems, Rome, Italy, July 20–26, 2011* (pp. 20–26). IADIS.

Cabitza, F., Gesso, I., & Simone, C. (2012a). Providing end-users with a visual editor to make their electronic documents active. In *VL/HCC 2012: Proceedings of short papers of the IEEE symposium on visual languages and human-centric computing, September 30–October 4, 2012, Innsbruck, Austria* (pp. 171–174). Innsbruck: IEEE Computer Press. doi:10.1109/VLHCC.2012.6344509.

Cabitza, F., Simone, C., & Locatelli, M. P. (2012b). Supporting artifact-mediated discourses through a recursive annotation tool. In *GROUP'12: Proceedings of the 17th ACM international conference on Supporting group work* (pp. 253–262). New York: ACM. doi:10.1145/2389176.2389215.

Cabitza, F., Colombo, G., & Simone, C. (2013). Leveraging underspecification in knowledge artifacts to foster collaborative activities in professional communities. *International Journal of Human - Computer Studies, 71*(1), 24–45. doi:10.1016/j.ijhcs.2012.02.005.

Cabitza, F., Fogli, D., & Piccinno, A. (2014a). "Each to His Own": Distinguishing tasks, roles and artifacts in EUD practices. In L. Caporarello, B. Di Martino, & M. Martinez (Eds.), *Smart organizations and smart artifacts – Fostering interaction between people, technologies and processes* (Vol. 7, pp. 193–206). Berlin/Heidelberg: Springer.

Cabitza, F., Fogli, D., & Piccinno, A. (2014b). Fostering participation and co-evolution in sentient multimedia systems. *Journal of Visual Languages and Computing, 25*(6), 684–694.

Cadiz, J. J., Gupta, A., & Grudin, J. (2000). Using web annotations for asynchronous collaboration around documents. In *CSCW 2000: Proceedings of the 2000 ACM conference on Computer supported cooperative work* (pp. 309–318). New York: ACM Press. doi:10.1145/358916.359002.

Campbell-Kelly, M., & Aspray, W. (Eds.). (2004). *Computer: A history of the information machine*. Boulder, CO: Westview Press.

Carroll, J. (2004). Completing design in use: Closing the appropriation cycle. In *European conference on information systems* (paper 44). Association for Information Systems. http://aisel.aisnet.org/ecis2004/44

Carroll, J. M., Kellogg, W. A., & Rosson, M. B. (1991). The task-artifact cycle. In J. M. Carroll (Ed.), *Designing interaction: Psychology at the human-computer interface* (pp. 74–102). New York: Cambridge University Press.

Carstensen, P. H., Sorensen, C., & Borstrom, H. (1995). Two is fine, four is a mess: Reducing complexity of articulation work in manufacturing. In *COOP'95, proceedings of the international workshop on the design of cooperative systems* (pp. 314–333). Sophia Antipolis, FR: INRIA.

Carr, N. G. (2004). Does IT matter?: Information technology and the corrosion of competitive advantage. Boston: Harvard Business School Press.

Chen, W., & Akay, M. (2011). Developing EMRs in developing countries. *IEEE Transactions on Information Technology in Biomedicine, 15*(1), 62–65. doi:10.1109/TITB.2010.2091509.

Christensen, L. R. (2014). Practices of stigmergy in the building process. *Computer Supported Cooperative Work (CSCW), 23*(1), 1–19. doi:10.1007/s10606-012-9181-3.

Ciborra, C. U. (1992). From thinking to tinkering. *Information Society, 8*, 297–309.

Ciborra, C. (2002). *The labyrinths of Information challenging the wisdom of systems*. Oxford/New York: Oxford University Press.

Ciborra, C. (2006). The mind or the heart? It depends on the (definition of) situation. *Journal of Information Technology, 21*, 129–139.

Clancey, W. J. (1997). *Situated cognition: On human knowledge and computer representations*. Cambridge/New York: Cambridge University Press.

Cooke-Davies, T. (2002). The "real" success factors on projects. *International Journal of Project Management, 20*(3), 185–190. doi:10.1016/S0263-7863(01)00067-9.

Crabtree, A., Rodden, T., & Bb, N. N. (2001). *Wild sociology: Ethnography and design*. Lancaster: Department of Sociology for the Degree of Doctor of Philosophy, Lancaster University.

D'Adderio, L. (2008). The performativity of routines: Theorising the influence of artefacts and distributed agencies on routines dynamics. *Research Policy, 37*, 769–789. doi:10.1017/S174413741000024X.

Danholt, P. (2005). Prototypes as performative. In *CC'05: Proceedings of the 4th decennial conference on Critical computing, between sense and sensibility* (p. 1). New York: ACM Press. doi:10.1145/1094562.1094564.

De Michelis, G. (2003). The Swiss Pattada. *Interactions, 10*(3), 44–53. doi:10.1145/769759.769760.

De Michelis, G., Loregian, M., Moderini, C., Marti, P., Colombo, C., Bannon, L., Storni, C., & Susani, M. (2009a). Designing interaction for next generation personal computing. In T. Gross, J. Gulliksen, P. Kotzé, L. Oestreicher, P. Palanque, R. O. Prates, & M. Winckler (Eds.),

Human-computer interaction – INTERACT 2009 (Vol. 5727, pp. 926–927). Berlin/Heidelberg: Springer.

De Michelis, G., Loregian, M., & Moderini, C. (2009b). Itsme: Interaction design innovating workstations. *Knowledge, Technology & Policy, 22*(1), 71–78.

De Souza, C. S., & Leitao, C. F. (2009). Semiotic engineering methods for scientific research in HCI. *Synthesis Lectures on Human-Centered Informatics, 2*(1), 1–122. doi:10.2200/S00173ED1V01Y200901HCI002.

DeLone, W. H., & McLean, E. R. (1992). Information systems success: The quest for the dependent variable. *Information Systems Research, 3*(1), 60–95. doi:10.1287/isre.3.1.60.

Dirksmeier, P., & Helbrecht, I. (2008). Time, non-representational theory and the 'Performative Turn' – Towards a new methodology in qualitative social research. *Forum Qualitative Social Research, 9*(2), Art. 55.

Dix, A. (2007). Designing for appropriation. In *Proceedings of the 21st British HCI Group annual conference on people and computers: HCI… but not as we know it* (pp. 27–30). Swinton: British Computer Society. Retrieved from dl.acm.org/citation.cfm?id = 1531407.1531415

Doerner, C., Draxler, S., Pipek, V., & Wulf, V. (2009). End users at the bazaar: Designing next-generation enterprise- resource-planning systems. *IEEE Software, 26*(5), 45–51.

Dourish, P. (1999). Evolution in the adoption and use of collaborative technologies. In *Proceedings of the ECSCW'99 workshop on evolving use of groupware; 1999 September 16; Copenhagen, Denmark.*

Dourish, P. (2001). *Where the action is: The foundations of embodied interaction.* Cambridge, MA: MIT Press.

Dourish, P. (2004). What we talk about when we talk about context. *Personal and Ubiquitous Computing, 8*(1), 19–30.

Dourish, P., Edwards, W. K., LaMarca, A., Lamping, J., Petersen, K., Salisbury, M., Terry, D. B., & Thornton, J. (2000). Extending document management systems with user-specific active properties. *ACM Transactions on Information Systems, 18*(2), 140–170. doi:10.1145/348751.348758.

Fischer, G., & Giaccardi, E. (2006). Meta-design: A framework for the future of end-user development. In H. Lieberman (Ed.), *End user development – Empowering people to flexibly employ advanced information and communication technology* (pp. 427–457). Dordrecht: Kluwer Academic Publishers.

Fischer, G., Giaccardi, E., Ye, Y., Sutcliffe, A. G., & Mehandjiev, N. (2004). Meta-design: A manifesto for end-user development. *Communications of the ACM, 47*(9), 33–37. doi:10.1145/1015864.1015884.

Fitzpatrick, G., & Ellingsen, G. (2012). A review of 25 years of CSCW research in healthcare: Contributions, challenges and future agendas. *Computer Supported Cooperative Work (CSCW).* doi:10.1007/s10606-012-9168-0

Flores, F., Graves, M., Hartfield, B., & Winograd, T. (1988). Computer systems and the design of organizational interaction. *ACM Transactions on Information Systems, 6*(2), 153–172. doi:10.1145/45941.45943.

Glendinning, S. (1998). *On being with others Heidegger, Derrida, Wittgenstein.* London/New York: Routledge.

Goodhue, D. L., & Thompson, R. L. (1995). Task-technology fit and individual performance. *MIS Quarterly, 19*, 213–236.

Haigh, T. (2010). *Crisis what crisis? Reconsidering the software crisis of the 1960s and the origins of software engineering.* Milwaukee: School of Information Studies, University of Wisconsin.

Handel, M. J., & Poltrock, S. (2011). Working around official applications: Experiences from a large engineering project. In *CSCW'11: Proceedings of the ACM 2011 conference on computer supported cooperative work* (pp. 309–312). ACM. doi:10.1145/1958824.1958870.

Hanseth, O., & Ciborra, C. (2007). *Risk, complexity and ICT.* Cheltenham/Northampton: E. Elgar.

Harel, D. (2008). Can programming be liberated, period? *Computer, 41*(1), 28–37. doi:10.1109/MC.2008.10.

Harel, D., & Marelly, R. (2003). *Come, let's play: Scenario-based programming using LSCs and the play-engine*. Berlin/New York: Springer.

Harris, J., & Henderson, A. (1999). A better mythology for system design. In *CHI'99: Proceedings of the SIGCHI conference on human factors in computing systems: The CHI is the limit* (pp. 88–95). New York: ACM Press. doi:10.1145/302979.303003.

Hartswood, M., Procter, R., Rouncefield, M., & Slack, R. (2000). Being there and doing IT in the workplace: A case study of a co-development approach in healthcare. In T. Cherkasky (Ed.), *Proceedings of the CPSR/IFIP WG 9.1 participatory design conference* (pp. 96–105). New York: ACM Press.

Heeks, R. (2006). Health information systems: Failure, success and improvisation. *International Journal of Medical Informatics, 75*, 125–137.

Hirschheim, R., & Klein, H. K. (1989). Four paradigms of information systems development. *Communications of the ACM, 32*(10), 1199–1216. doi:10.1145/67933.67937.

Hollnagel, E., Nemeth, C. P., & Dekker, S. (2008). *Resilience engineering perspectives*. Aldershot/Burlington: Ashgate.

Hug, D. (2010). Performativity in design and evaluation of sounding interactive commodities. In *AM'10: Proceedings of the 5th audio mostly conference: A conference on interaction with sound* (pp. 1–8). New York: ACM Press. doi:10.1145/1859799.1859806.

Illich, I. (1973). *Tools for conviviality*. New York: Harper & Row.

Illich, I. (1977). *Disabling professions*. London: Marion Boyars.

Jacucci, C., Jacucci, G., Wagner, I., & Psik, T. (2005). A manifesto for the performative development of ubiquitous media. In *CC'05: Proceedings of the 4th decennial conference on Critical computing: Between sense and sensibility* (pp. 19–28). New York: ACM Press. doi:10.1145/1094562.1094566.

Jensen, T. E. (2002). *Performing social work, competence, orderings, spaces and objects* (PhD), University of Copenhagen, Department of Psychology.

Jensen, C. B. (2005). An experiment in performative history: The electronic patient record as a future-generating device. *Social Studies of Science, 25*(2), 241–267.

Jensen, C. B. (2008). CSCW design reconceptualized through science studies. In *Cognition, communication and interaction: Transdisciplinary perspectives on interactive technology* (pp. 132–148). London: Springer.

Johannessen, L. K., Gammon, D., & Ellingsen, G. (2012). Users as designers of information infrastructures and the role of generativity. *AIS Transactions on Human-Computer Interaction, 4*(2), 72–91.

Johnson, S. (1759). *The history of Rasselas. The Prince of Abyssinia*. London: R. and J. Dodsley, W. Johnston.

Kaplan, B., & Harris-Salamone, K. D. (2009). Health IT success and failure: Recommendations from literature and an AMIA workshop. *Journal of the American Medical Informatics Association, 16*(3), 291–299. doi:10.1197/jamia.M2997.

Khosravi, K., & Gueheneuc, Y. (2004). *A quality model for design patterns*. Montreal: Universite de Montreal.

Kling, R., Rosenbaum, H., & Sawyer, S. (2005). *Understanding and communicating social Informatics: A framework for studying and teaching the human contexts of information and communication technologies*. Medford, NJ.: Information Today, Inc.

Klein, G., & Jiang, J. J. (2001). Seeking consonance in information systems. *Journal of Systems and Software, 56*(2), 195–202. doi:10.1016/S0164-1212(00)00097-2.

Krebs, D., Conrad, A., & Wang, J. (2012). Combining visual block programming and graph manipulation for clinical alert rule building. In *Proceedings of the 2012 ACM annual conference extended abstracts on Human Factors in Computing Systems Extended Abstracts*(pp. 2453–2458). New York: ACM. doi:10.1145/2212776.2223818

Kriplean, T., Toomin, M., Morgan, J., Borming, A., & Ko, A. J. (2012). Is this what you meant? Promoting listening on the web with reflect. In *CHI 2012: Proceedings of the international conference on human computer interaction, May 5–10, 2012, Austin, Texas, USA*(pp. 1559–1568). New York: ACM Press.

Lanzara, G. F. (1999). Between transient constructs and persistent structures: Designing systems in action. *Journal of Strategic Information Systems, 8*, 331–349.

Latour, B. (1996). On interobjectivity. *Mind, Culture, and Activity, 3*(4), 228–245. doi:10.1207/s15327884mca0304_2.

Lave, J., & Wenger, E. (1991). *Situated learning: Legitimate peripheral participation.* Cambridge: Cambridge University Press.

Law, J., & Singleton, V. (2003). *This is not an object.* Centre for Science Studies, Lancaster University, Lancaster. Retrieved from www.comp.lancs.ac.uk/sociology/papers/Law-Singleton-This-is-Not-an-Object.pdf

Levi-Strauss, C. (1966). *The savage mind (La pensee suavage).* London: Weidenfeld and Nicolson.

Licoppe, C. (2010). The performative turn in science and technology studies. *Journal of Cultural Economy, 3*(2), 181–188. doi:10.1080/17530350.2010.494122.

Lieberman, H., Paternò, F., Klann, M., & Wulf, V. (2006). End-user development: An emerging paradigm. In *End user development* (Vol. 9, pp. 1–8). Amsterdam: Kluwer Academic Publishers.

Locatelli, M. P., & Simone, C. (2010). A community based metaphor supporting EUD within communities. In G. Santucci (Ed.), *Proceedings of the international conference on advanced visual interfaces, AVI 2010, Roma, Italy, May 26–28, 2010* (p. 406). New York: ACM Press.

Louridas, P. (1999). Design as bricolage: Anthropology meets design thinking. *Design Studies, 20*(6), 517–535. doi:10.1016/S0142-694X(98)00044-1.

Luff, P., Heath, C., & Greatbatch, D. (1992). Tasks-in-interaction: Paper and screen based documentation in collaborative activity. In *CSCW'92: Proceedings of the 1992 ACM conference on Computer-supported cooperative work* (pp. 163–170). New York: ACM Press. doi:10.1145/143457.143475.

Lyotard, J.-F. (1986). *The postmodern condition: A report on knowledge.* Manchester: Manchester University Press.

Lyytinen, K., & Robey, D. (1999). Learning failure in information systems development. *Information Systems Journal, 9*(2), 85–101. doi:10.1046/j.1365-2575.1999.00051.x.

Maguire, S., & McKelvey, B. (1999). Complexity and management: Moving from fad to firm foundations. *Emergence, 1*, 19–61.

Mamlin, B. W., Biondich, P. G., Wolfe, B. A., Fraser, H., Jazayeri, D., Allen, C., Miranda, J., Tierney, W. M. (2006). Cooking up an open source EMR for developing countries: OpenMRS - A recipe for successful collaboration. *AMIA Annual Symposium Proceedings, 2006*, 529. *Managing the human side of information technology: Challenges and solutions.* (2002). Hershey, PA: Idea Group Pub.

Mansfield, J. (2010). *The nature of change or the law of unintended consequences.* London: Imperial College Press.

Mark, G. (2002). Conventions and commitments in distributed CSCW Groups. *Computer Supported Cooperative Work (CSCW), 11*(3), 349–387.

Mark, G., & Semaan, B. (2008). Resilience in collaboration. In *CSCW'08: Proceedings of the 2008 ACM conference on Computer supported cooperative work* (pp. 137–146). New York: ACM Press. doi:10.1145/1460563.1460585.

Mark, G., Gonzalez, V. M., Sarini, M., & Simone, C. (2002). Reconciling different perspectives: An experiment on technology support for articulation. In *COOP'02: Proceedings of the international conference on the design of cooperative systems.* Saint Raphael (FR), 4–7 June (pp. 23–37). Amsterdam: IOS Press.

Martin, D., & Sommerville, I. (2004). Patterns of cooperative interaction: Linking ethnomethodology and design. *ACM Transactions on Computer-Human Interaction, 11*(1), 59–89. doi:10.1145/972648.972651.

Maturana, H. R., & Varela, F. J. (1992). *The tree of knowledge: The biological roots of human understanding.* Boston: Shambhala Publications.

Miller, R. G. (1995). Improving community service: Strategic cooperation through communication. *Communicating Organizational Change: A Management Perspective*, 65.

Mørch, A. I., Stevens, G., Won, M., Klann, M., Dittrich, Y., & Wulf, V. (2004). Component-based technologies for end-user development. *Communications of the ACM, 47*(9), 59–62.

Morrison, C., & Blackwell, A. (2009). Observing end-user customisation of electronic patient records. In V. Pipek, M. Rosson, B. de Ruyter, & V. Wulf (Eds.), *IS-EUD'09: Proceedings of the 2nd international symposium on end-user development* (Vol. 5435, pp. 275–284). Berlin/Heidelberg: Springer. doi:10.1007/978-3-642-00427-8_16.

Morrison, A., Westvang, E., & Skogsrud, S. S. (2010). Whisperings in the undergrowth: Communication design, online social networking and discursive performativity. In I. Wagner, T. Bratteteig, & D. Stuedahl (Eds.), *Exploring digital design: Multi-disciplinary design practices* (pp. 221–259). London: Springer.

Morrison, C., Fitzpatrick, G., & Blackwell, A. (2011). Multi-disciplinary collaboration during ward rounds: Embodied aspects of electronic medical record usage. *International Journal of Medical Informatics, 80*(8), e96–e111.

Myers, M. D. (1995). Dialectical hermeneutics: A theoretical framework for the implementation of information systems. *Information Systems Journal, 5*(1), 51–70. doi:10.1111/j.1365-2575.1995.tb00089.x.

Nandhakumar, J., & Avison, D. E. (1999). The fiction of methodological development: A field study of information systems development. *Information Technology & People, 12*(2), 176–191. doi:10.1108/09593849910267224.

Nemeth, C. (2003). *The master schedule how cognitive artifacts affect distributed cognition in acute care.* Cognitive Technologies Laboratory.

Niazkhani, Z., Pirnejad, H., van der Sijs, H., & Aarts, J. (2011). Evaluating the medication process in the context of CPOE use: The significance of working around the system. *International Journal of Medical Informatics, 80*(7), 490–506.

O'Neill, J. E. (1992). *The evolution of interactive computing through time-sharing and networking.* Ph.D. dissertation, University of Minnesota, USA.

Orlikowski, W. J. (1992a). The duality of technology: Rethinking the concept of technology in organizations. *Organization Science, 3*(3), 398–427. doi:10.1287/orsc.3.3.398.

Orlikowski, W. J. (1992b). Learning from notes: Organizational issues in groupware implementation. In *CSCW'92: Proceedings of the 1992 ACM conference on computer-supported cooperative work* (pp. 362–369). New York: ACM. doi:10.1145/143457.143549.

Orlikowski, W. J. (1996). Improvising organizational transformation over time: A situated change perspective. *Information Systems Research, 7*(1), 63–92. doi:10.1287/isre.7.1.63.

Orlikowski, W. J. (2000). Using technology and constituting structures: A practice lens for studying technology in organizations. *Organization Science, 11*(4), 404–428.

Orlikowski, W. J. (2006). Material knowing: The scaffolding of human knowledgeability. *European Journal of Information Systems, 15*(5), 460–466.

Orlikowski, W. J. (2007). Sociomaterial practices: Exploring technology at work. *Organization Studies, 28*(9), 1435–1448. doi:10.1177/0170840607081138.

Oudshoorn, N., & Pinch, T. (Eds.). (2005). *How users matter: The co-construction of users and technology.* Cambridge, MA/London: MIT Press.

Paley, J. (2007). Complex adaptive systems and nursing. *Nursing Inquiry, 14*(3), 233–242. doi:10.1111/j.1440-1800.2007.00359.x.

Paley, J., & Eva, G. (2011). Complexity theory as an approach to explanation in healthcare: A critical discussion. *International Journal of Nursing Studies, 48*(2), 269–279. doi:10.1016/j.ijnurstu.2010.09.012.

Pan, G., Hackney, R., & Pan, S. L. (2008). Information systems implementation failure: Insights from prism. *International Journal of Information Management, 28*(4), 259–269. doi:10.1016/j.ijinfomgt.2007.07.001.

Papazoglou, M. P., Traverso, P., Dustdar, S., & Leymann, F. (2007). Service-oriented computing: State of the art and research challenges. *Computer, 40*, 38–45.

Perrow, C. (1999). *Normal accidents: Living with high risk technologies*. Princeton, NJ: Princeton University Press.

Pesic, M., Schonenberg, M. H., Sidorova, N., & Van Der Aalst, W. M. P. (2007). Constraint-based workflow models: Change made easy. In *OTM'07: Proceedings of the 2007 OTM Confederated international conference on On the move to meaningful internet systems: CoopIS, DOA, ODBASE, GADA, and IS - Volume Part I* (pp. 77–94). Berlin/Heidelberg: Springer.

Peters, I. (2006). Against folksonomies - Indexing blogs and podcasts for corporate knowledge management. In *Proceedings of online information, London, UK* (pp. 93–97). London: Learned Information Europe.

Pickering, A. (1995). *The mangle of practice: Time, agency and science*. University of Chicago Press.

Pickering, A. (2008). Beyond design: Cybernetics, biological computers and hylozoism. *Synthese, 168*(3), 469–491. doi:10.1007/s11229-008-9446-z.

Pipek, V., & Wulf, V. (2009). Infrastructuring: Toward an integrated perspective on the design and use of information technology. *Journal of the Association for Information Systems, 10*(5), 1.

Riemer, K., & Johnston, R. B. (2012). What is IT in use and why does it matter for IS design? In *Proceedings of the IT Artefact Design & Workpractice Intervention, A Pre-ECIS and AIS SIG Prag Workshop, June 10, 2012, Barcelona, E*. Forskningsnaetverket VITS. Retrieved from www.vits.org/uploads/IT_Artifact/What_is_IT_and_why_does_it_matter.pdf

Robey, D., & Markus, M. L. (1984). Rituals in information system design. *MIS Quarterly, 8*(1), 5–15.

Robinson, M. (1993). Design for unanticipated use. In *Third European conference on computer-supported cooperative work* (pp. 187–202). Milano: Kluwer Academic Publishers.

Robinson, M., & Bannon, L. (1991). Questioning representations. In *ECSCW'91: Proceedings of the second European conference on computer-supported cooperative work*. Amsterdam, The Netherlands.

Rochlin, G. (1998). *Trapped in the net: The unanticipated consequences of computerization*. Princeton: Princeton University Press.

Rorty, R. (1991). *Objectivity, relativism, and truth*. Cambridge/New York: Cambridge University Press.

Rusk, N., Resnick, M., Berg, R., & Pezzalla-Grandlund, M. (2008). New pathways into robotics: Strategies for broadening participation. *Journal of Science Education and Technology, 17*(1), 59–69.

Schmidt, K. (1999). Of maps and scripts: The status of formal constructs in cooperative work. *Information and Software Technology, 41*(6), 319–329. doi:10.1016/S0950-5849(98)00065-2.

Schmidt, K. (2011a). *Cooperative work and coordinative practices: Contributions to the conceptual foundations of Computer-Supported Cooperative Work (CSCW)*. New York: Springer.

Schmidt, K. (2011b). Dispelling the mythology of computational artifacts. In *Cooperative work and coordinative practices contributions to the conceptual foundations of Computer-Supported Cooperative Work (CSCW)* (pp. 391–413). Berlin: Springer.

Shapiro, D. (2005). Participatory design: The will to succeed. In *CC'05: Proceedings of the 4th decennial conference on critical computing: Between sense and sensibility* (pp. 29–38). New York: ACM Press. doi:10.1145/1094562.1094567.

Shipman, F. M., & Marshall, C. C. (1999). Formality considered harmful: Experiences, emerging themes, and directions on the use of formal representations in interactive systems. *Computer Supported Cooperative Work, 8*(4), 333–352.

Simon, J. (2010). *Knowing together: A social epistemology for socio-technical epistemic systems* (PhD). Universitat Wien.

Simone, C., & Schmidt, K. (1993). *Computational mechanisms of interaction for CSCW, COMIC deliverable D3.1, Esprit basic research project*, Lancaster, U.K.

Star, S. L., & Bowker, G. C. (1999). *Sorting things out: Classification and its consequences*. London: MIT Press.

Star, S. L., & Strauss, A. (1999). Layers of silence, arenas of voice: The ecology of visible and invisible work. *Computer Supported Cooperative Work, 8*, 9–30.

Stevens, G. (2010). *Understanding and designing appropriation infrastructures: Artifacts as boundary objects in the continuous software development.* University of Siegen.

Stevens, G., Quaisser, G., & Klann, M. (2006). Breaking it up: An industrial case study of component-based tailorable software design. In H. Lieberman, F. Paternò, & V. Wulf (Eds.), *End user development* (Vol. 9, pp. 269–294). Springer: Dordrecht. Retrieved from dx.doi.org/10.1007/1-4020-5386-X_13

Suchman, L. A. (1987). *Plans and situated actions: The problem of human-machine communication.* Cambridge: Cambridge University Press.

Suchman, L. (1994). Do categories have politics? *Computer Supported Cooperative Work (CSCW), 2*(3), 177–190.

Suchman, L. A. (2004). *Figuring personhood in sciences of the artificial.* Department of Sociology, Lancaster University, Lancaster. Retrieved from www.comp.lancs.ac.uk/sociology/papers/suchman-figuring-personhood.pdf

Suchman, L. (2006). *Human-machine reconfigurations: Plans and situated actions.* Cambridge: Cambridge University Press.

Suchman, L., Trigg, R., & Blomberg, J. (2002). Working artefacts: Ethnomethods of the prototype. *British Journal of Sociology, 53*(2), 163–179. doi:10.1080/00071310220133287.

Sumner, T., & Stolze, M. (1997). Evolution, not revolution: Participatory Design in the Toolbelt Era. In M. Kyng & L. Mathiassen (Eds.), *Computers and design in context* (pp. 1–26). Cambridge, MA: MIT Press.

Szewczak, E., & Snodgress, C. (Eds.). (2002). Managing the human side of information technology: Challenges and solutions. Hershey, PA: Idea Group Publishing.

Telier, A. (2011). *Design things* (K. Friedman & E. Stolterman, Eds.). Cambridge, MA: The MIT Press.

Thomas, G., & Fernández, W. (2008). Success in IT projects: A matter of definition? *International Journal of Project Management, 26*(7), 733–742. doi:10.1016/j.ijproman.2008.06.003.

Truex, D. P., Baskerville, R., & Klein, H. K. (1999). Growing systems in emergent organizations. *Communications of ACM, 42*(8), 117–123.

Turner, P. (2005). Affordance as context. *Interacting with Computers, 17*(6), 787–800. doi:10.1016/j.intcom.2005.04.003.

Van der Aalst, W. M. P., Pesic, M., & Schonenberg, H. M. (2009). Declarative workflows: Balancing between flexibility and support. *Computer Science - Research and Development, 23*(2), 99–113. doi:10.1007/s00450-009-0057-9.

Van House, N. A. (2009). Collocated photo sharing, story-telling, and the performance of self. *International Journal of Human-Computer Studies, 67*(12), 1073–1086. doi:10.1016/j.ijhcs.2009.09.003.

VV. AA. (2001). *Extreme Chaos.* The Standish Group International, Inc. Retrieved from www.cin.ufpe.br/~gmp/docs/papers/extreme_chaos2001.pdf

Wagner, I., Stuedahl, D., & Bratteteig, T. (2010). *Exploring digital design: Multidisciplinary design practices.* London: Springer-Verlag London Limited. Retrieved from dx.doi.org/10.1007/978-1-84996-223-0

Warkentin, M., Moore, R. S., Bekkering, E., & Johnston, A. C. (2009). Analysis of systems development project risks: An integrative framework. *ACM SIGMIS Database, 40*(2), 8. doi:10.1145/1531817.1531821.

Weick, K. E. (1993). Organizational redesign as improvisation. In G. P. Huber & W. H. Glick (Eds.), *Organizational change and redesign: Ideas and insights for improving performance* (pp. 346–379). New York: Oxford University Press.

Weick, K. E. (2004). Normal accident theory as frame, link, and provocation. *Organization & Environment, 17*(1), 27–31. doi:10.1177/1086026603262031.

Weinstein, D., & Weinstein, M. (1991). Georg Simmel: Sociological flaneur bricoleur. *Theory, Culture Society, 8*, 151–168.

Wilson, M., & Howcroft, D. (2002). Re-conceptualising failure: Social shaping meets IS research. *European Journal of Information Systems, 11*(4), 236–250. doi:10.1057/palgrave.ejis.3000437.

Winograd, T., & Flores, F. (1986). *Understanding computers and cognition: A new foundation for design*. Reading: Addison Wesley.

Winthereik, B. R., & Vikkelso, S. (2005). ICT and integrated care: Some dilemmas of standardising inter-organisational communication. *Computer Supported Cooperative Work (CSCW), 14*(1), 43–67.

Wittgenstein, L. (1922). *Tractatus Logico-Philosophicus*. Cambridge: Dover Publications.

Wulf, V., Pipek, V., & Won, M. (2008). Component-based tailorability: Enabling highly flexible software applications. *International Journal of Human-Computer Studies, 66*(1), 1–22. doi:10.1016/j.ijhcs.2007.08.007.

Chapter 12
Exploring Challenging Environments: Contextual Research in the Car and the Factory Through an HCI Lens

Astrid Weiss, Alexander Meschtscherjakov, Roland Buchner, Ewald Strasser, Patricia M. Kluckner, Sebastian Osswald, Nicole Mirnig, David Wilfinger, Nicole Perterer, Petra Sundstroem, Arno Laminger, and Manfred Tscheligi

Nontraditional environments offer a variety of methodological challenges when exploring cooperation under very specific contextual conditions. We understand contexts as challenging when they exhibit very specific/unique characteristics that need to be explored beyond traditional and already better-understood working/office settings. Moreover, these challenging environments are contexts in which human-human interaction mediated by computing systems and human-machine collaboration is hard to observe. In this paper, we focus on two challenging environments: the highly context-dependent automotive environment and the complex context of a semiconductor factory. Both contexts offer potential in a variety of ways for novel computer-supported cooperative work research, such as driver/codriver cooperation and operator-robot cooperation. In this book chapter, two exemplary contexts "car" and "factory," will be characterized in terms of (1) research challenges posed by the context, (2) performed exploratory studies, and (3) methodological implications for the two exemplary contexts, as well as for CSCW and HCI research practices in general.

12.1 Introduction

Over the past years, the field of human-computer interaction (HCI) and computer-supported cooperative work has moved beyond the desktop and, by going into the field, has started to explore novel forms of interaction in different contexts. Various

A. Weiss • A. Meschtscherjakov • R. Buchner • E. Strasser • P.M. Kluckner • S. Osswald
N. Mirnig • D. Wilfinger • N. Perterer • P. Sundstroem • A. Laminger • M. Tscheligi (✉)
Centre for Human-Computer Interaction, Department of Computer Sciences, University of Salzburg, Salzburg, Austria
e-mail: manfred.tscheligi@sbg.ac.at

© Springer-Verlag London 2015
V. Wulf et al. (eds.), *Designing Socially Embedded Technologies in the Real-World*,
Computer Supported Cooperative Work, DOI 10.1007/978-1-4471-6720-4_12

theories and models to motivate context-oriented thinking have been proposed, such as approaches to "situated action," suggesting that the particular context determines how people behave in specific situations (Suchman 1987). The essence of situated action is that every experience is influenced by, and is constitutive of, the context in which it occurs. An in-depth understanding of context enables application designers to choose what context factors to consider in their applications (Dey 2001).

Since then, the research community became more and more interested in understanding not only the individual interacting with technology but the social context in which technology usage happens (Nardi 1992). Different social science methods (ethnographies, interviews, observations, etc.) and theories (distributed cognition, activity theory, situated action, etc.) entered HCI and CSCW and were used to gain knowledge about various domains. Enhancing the knowledge/understanding of specific contextual situations with deeper insights on user experience (UX) opens up new roads for research and challenges in all design and development phases. Notwithstanding this, however, Roto et al. stated that specific and comprehensive guidance for capturing data about the circumstances that affect user experience in "the wild" is missing (Roto et al. 2011).

By addressing the specific and challenging contexts of a semiconductor factory and a car as HCI research domains, we provide two examples how such contexts can be explored from an HCI perspective in order to enable cooperation between multiple users (as well as users and robotic systems in the factory). In this chapter, we follow an overview on HCI and CSCW approaches in various challenging contexts (e.g., the health sector and airplanes) by presenting the two specific contexts mentioned above. For both contexts, we will present our overall approach and our interpretation of the context with its potential to enable cooperative activities, followed by the research challenges these contexts offer. We will then describe, for both contexts, how we tried to explore them and what findings we could glean. Finally, we will present the specific methodological challenges we derived for both contexts and conclude with how these findings and implications can be of relevance for fellow HCI and CSCW researchers.

12.2 HCI Studies in Challenging Contexts

Several methodological approaches already exist in HCI and CSCW to explore contextual influences on workflows and interaction paradigms, which can build the empirical basis for design implications (Dourish 2006). Beyer and Holtzblatt, for instance, developed the methodological concept of contextual inquiry, which puts designers and engineers directly in the customers' work context, for gathering rich, in-depth data about working routines (Beyer and Holtzblatt 1998). Similar approaches used in HCI and CSCW are ethnographic studies, which are field research methods that combine several data-gathering methods such as participant observation, formal and informal interviewing, and the analysis of documentary sources (Powdermaker 1966; Wax 1971; Werner and Schoepfle 1987). Ethnography provides detailed insights into people's behavior, even if they themselves are unaware of it. Using ethnography (Fetterman 1998) has become increasingly prominent within HCI (e.g., Blomberg et al. 1993; Simonsen 1997; Crabtree 1998; Randall et al. 2007). The rapid ethnography method was subsequently developed for product development in order to close the gap between short design cycles and the long, complex nature of ethnographic research (Millen 2000). Originally, ethnography in HCI mainly focused on empirical studies of work routines in the setting for which a novel system should be developed. However, as Crabtree et al. phrase it, "the dominant concern for new approaches is to engage designers instead in a critical dialogue based on cultural interpretations of everyday settings, activities, and artefacts" (Crabtree et al. 2009). This also expresses our concern that we need to find new approaches for nontraditional environments (such as the car and the factory) to gain an understanding of the interplay of tasks, devices, and the (social) context.

As Magnusson et al. claim, there are contextual impact factors, which can only be identified through fieldwork of some kind and which need to be identified before designing a system (Magnusson et al. 2011). They suggest, for the development of mobile devices, to raise the understanding of such contextual constraints by conducting contextual walk-throughs, contextual trials, and key scenarios. They also argue that for a more accessible mobile device design, designers have to consider nonoptimal usage conditions, since mobile situations are very dynamic and change very quickly. Subsequently, usage scenarios for mobile phones should consist of nonoptimal lightning, noisy environment, cold hands (which reduce the touch-sense ability), and the context which requires attention (other people, traffic, etc.).

Two prominent challenging contexts, which have already been intensively investigated through an HCI lens, are the healthcare sector and airplanes. To gain deeper insights in the context of a Danish emergency medical service (EMS), different usability methods were applied to be able to build a set of designs for future EMS work (Kristensen et al. 2006). In total, 13 researchers took part in a 3-day training session, normally conducted with new personnel, to get a step-by-step introduction into the EMS. The interviews helped on the one hand to understand the end users' needs, as well as the use and usability of dictation solutions and electronic nursing documentation systems. On the other, however, researchers had to face similar challenges as in the factory context, such as privacy concerns, a wide variety of practices and contexts of technology usage, as well as the hectic nature of everyday work (Viitanen 2011). In the context of airplanes, one of the most well-known observational studies was conducted by Hutchins and Klausen. Based on the theory of distributed cognition (how information is propagated through a system in the form of representational states of mediating structures), they analyzed airline flight crews performing in a high-fidelity flight simulator (Hutchins and Klausen 1996). It was shown that the expertise of the systems resides as much in the organization of tools in the working environment as in the knowledge and skill of the humans. They also observed patterns of cooperation and coordination of actions within the crew, which could be identified as a structure of propagating and processing of information. On a different level, this structure appears as a system of activity where shared cognition comes forward as a system property. Ballas et al. investigated how to design an interface that supports smooth transition from automated to manual mode to control possibilities for pilots of an aircraft. They found out that intermittent operations of complex tasks in the cockpit are more effective using direct manipulation interface in a variety of dynamic, real-time systems. They showed that, when increasing the cognitive complexity of an interface, it adversely affects the resumption of its use after a period of time (Ballas et al. 1992).

Another challenging context, also explored through an CSCW lens, is that of fire fighting. Ramirez et al. describe how a combination of empirical work and prototyping in real fire fighters' training settings informed the design of the landmark concept to develop an indoor navigation system for fire fighters (Ramirez et al. 2012). Other difficult areas include the context of a paper mill. There, contextual research was conducted in order to understand work activities of production crews and the social and information infrastructure that support them (Auramäki et al. 1996; Robinson et al. 2000) and, subsequently, to inform the design of a collaborative interface. Furthermore, studies at several industrial assembly manufacturing units have been conducted to inform the design of a mobile support system for service technicians (Fallman 2003), ethnographic studies to understand working practices of print facility workers (Martin et al. 2007), and how a combination of ethnographic and human-centered design methods could inform the development of a CSCW system in a power tool organization (D'Souza and Greenstein 2003). More recent studies in the oil and gas industry were conducted to gain insights on the shift team of who is working in and across the industrial environment and the control room (Heyer et al. 2009; Heyer 2010).

Similarly, initial contextual studies have already been conducted in the car context through an HCI and CSCW lens. For instance, the contextual inquiry technique was used by Gellatly et al. to inform future automotive designs by the means of interviews which were conducted with the participants while driving (Gellatly et al. 2010). Another way to obtain naturalistic driving behavior is to make use of video data from vehicles in the field. An often cited example is "The 100-Car Naturalistic Driving Study" (Hanowski et al. 2006). Their goal was to obtain data on driver performance and behavior in the moments leading up to a crash. Therefore, they equipped 100 cars with video cameras over a span of 13 months. Their video analysis helped to understand crash causation and driver behavior. Brown and Laurier (Brown and Laurier 2012) use interactional analysis of video data from 15 naturalistically recorded journeys with GPS to understand the navigational practices deployed by drivers and passengers.

To summarize, challenging contexts beyond the office have already been investigated through an HCI lens by means of (observational) studies in the wild. However, to our knowledge, relatively little light has been shed on the factory and car context, especially in terms of identifying cooperation potential. In most of the cases in factories and in cars, the focus is on the individual user, namely, a single operator or the driver. However, as we will show in this chapter, cooperation happens in both contexts and could be additionally fostered by novel interface technology. In order to do so, we need to have an understanding of interaction paradigms in these contexts, and consequently there is a need for novel methodological approaches which allow us to capture the interplay of entities and factors in these contexts. In the following, we will present the semiconductor factory and the car as challenging contexts for HCI and CSCW research.

12.3   The Semiconductor Factory as Challenging Research Setting

The first exemplary nontraditional context we choose for HCI and CSCW research is the context of a semiconductor factory. The overall purpose of a semiconductor factory is to manufacture as many error-free integrated circuits as possible. A fundamental step during manufacturing is the processing of the wafers, which are thin slices of semiconductor material, such as silicon crystal. Wafers are typically combined into groups of 25 or 50 pieces and stored in plastic containers called "lot boxes." Each of these lot boxes has to complete a distinct path through the factory, during which it undergoes different processing steps (e.g., etching, exposure, etc.) performed on various equipment (i.e., the machines for processing the wafers). Many operators working on several different machines have to be coordinated to guarantee an efficient production process. From the point of view of single operators, it is not obvious what other colleagues work on and how the progress of the whole production process proceeds, as it is distributed over several halls and buildings. Understanding the factory as a collaborative socio-technical environment has the potential to develop new supportive interfaces that can enhance human-human cooperation but also human-machine cooperation, with a manufacturing robot. Thus, the overall aim of our research is to thoroughly analyze the semiconductor factory context to be able to redesign existing working routines and, therefore, develop novel contextual interfaces, which support cooperation between different (social) actors (e.g., operators, maintainers, shift leads, but also robots) over different departments, halls, and buildings. In order to gain this understanding, we need to apply and adapt methodologies from HCI and CSCW.

When researching the factory context, the biggest challenge we have to face is its complexity. Even though a semiconductor factory is a very controlled setting in terms of environment factors such as lighting conditions, dust particle control, and ambient noise, the interplay between the different actors and the working procedures is difficult to capture. At the factory with which we cooperate, the operators are relatively flexible in their activities, since they can decide which lot boxes to handle next.[1] This flexibility is often in contradiction to the normally high level of automation in a semiconductor factory. Therefore, a synergetic relationship between human operators and the surrounding technologies should be achieved by the means of "smart automation." A combination of different radio

---

[1]The company has directed its European subsidiaries towards the development and production of new technologies, which results in short production cycles and a high degree of flexibility within the whole production system, which increases its complexity for external observers.

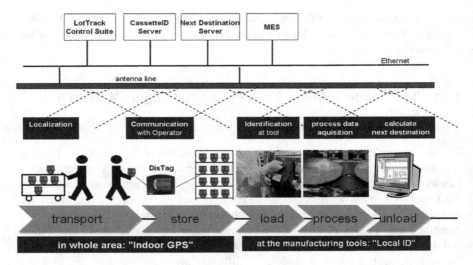

Fig. 12.1 Integration of smart automation technology in the production process in the factory

technologies with ultrasound technologies, innovative hardware (e.g., RFID), and software (e.g., message bus architectures) technologies have already been integrated in the production process to support operator coordination. Figure 12.1 gives an overview of how existing smart automation technologies are already implemented in the production process of the factory with which we cooperate.

Smart automation technology should enable that wafers run through the factory as fast as possible with little idle time, resulting in a maximized equipment load. As Fig. 12.1 shows, the general procedure is always the same in every section. (1) The wafers are stored in lot boxes in groups of 25 or 50 pieces and have to be transported to the right section. (2) They are then stored in the delivery rack where (3) an operator has to load the right equipment with the right wafer. (4) The wafer then gets processed, and (5) finally the equipment needs to be unloaded (afterwards the cycle starts again in the next section). Lot boxes are equipped with so-called DisTags. These DisTags are interfaces placed on each lot box providing several functions: identification, position tracking, announcement of the next production step, and error prevention by recognizing that a lot box was put into wrong equipment. The information provided by DisTags can, therefore, support the operators in their decisions, which tasks have to be conducted next and which processing steps should be applied to a lot box.

These production routines pose general challenges that come with the cleanroom environment. First, the factory is productive 24 h, 7 days a week, and 365 days a year. Second, various different tasks and tools implicate a high complexity. Third, special equipment such as cleanroom suits and cleanroom paper is required, and all electronic equipment (cameras, audio recorders, etc.) has to be carried in extra plastic bags. Exploratory research in the cleanroom is demanding, where work is conducted constantly in an air-conditioned area kept at 21 °C. There is only artificial yellow light, and operators are on their feet for 8 h, observing repetitive tasks. Researchers are also required (as all operators in the cleanroom) to wear the special cleanroom suit (see Fig. 12.3, second row, right corner), which makes it difficult to identify with whom one is speaking to. Acoustic quality is also limited, making it difficult to hear. Special paper and pens have to be used for documentation in the cleanroom, which are much smoother than conventional ones and produce fewer particles by friction while writing on the paper. Writing feels like using a thick ballpoint pen with waterproof ink.

These facts and the risk of industrial spying are the reason why only a few studies of exploratory nature exist in that area. Only a limited number of studies on HCI and user-centered design have been conducted in the context of the cleanroom so far (see, e.g., Lin et al. 2009; Mechtscherjakov et al. 2011). In these studies in which ethnographic and CI approaches were applied, only the working routines of operators were investigated. Other social actors in the cleanroom (e.g., shift leads, maintainers, or robots) were not at all considered. However, it proved to be useful for the requirement analysis phase of cleanroom prototyping to use observational methods to inform the design.

Another challenge is the size of the factory. As mentioned before, wafer production is separated into different processes, with the so-called recipe defining their sequence. In other words, different types of wafers follow a different path through the factory. The main standard processing procedures are conducted in the following different sections: chemical clean, photolithography, plasma/chemical etch, ion implant, and metal deposition/oxidation. Operators in these sections in general have to do the same basic tasks, but are specialized in the different processing steps. However, the sections themselves are again split into different subareas; for example, the lithography section is divided into coating and development, exposure, cluster, and photo-control. Photo-control in turn is a step which can only be performed by more experienced operators. In other words, the work in the factory is distributed over four halls (in total 19.282 m^2 cleanroom space), sections, and subareas, and the overall processing of wafers depends on the single steps performed by operators who are locally distributed over the cleanroom, and, therefore, the information is also distributed over various actors. This fact leads to special research challenges in every section, which again demonstrates the complexity of this research context and the necessity of becoming a domain expert before developing reasonable solutions for interfaces that can sustainably enhance cooperation between actors.

Subsequently, for our point of view, the semiconductor factory itself offers a huge potential for HCI and CSCW research to develop novel systems that foster cooperation between different social actors in the factory (operators, maintainers, shift leads, etc.) over different halls and buildings, such as intelligent guiding systems, feedback statistics which represent how single operator performance impacts the overall factory performance, and many more. However, we have to face several research and design challenges in order to gain sufficient domain understanding to develop useful systems for this difficult context and its actors

(Chamberlain et al. 2012). Therefore, we need to understand the semiconductor factory as a holistic concept, which is set up as a complex interplay between humans, interfaces, and (smart automation) technology.

12.3.1 The Holistic Factory as Cooperation Space

In contrast to offices where employees sit at a desk in front of a single computer, operators within a cleanroom have to move between several kinds of interfaces to gain all the information needed. This leads to the necessity of researching and developing communication interfaces, which accompany operators throughout the cleanroom and contain context-relevant information. From an HCI and CSCW perspective, the factory context can be considered as a triangle, which describes the potential interaction strategies in the cleanroom from an (1) equipment-specific view, (2) a unified interface view, and (3) a user-centered view.

The equipment-specific view is historically the first approach taken in the factory. In a semiconductor factory, there are five major process areas in wafer fabrication: chemical clean, photolithography, plasma/chemical etch, ion implant, and metal deposition/oxidation. Each of these areas consists of different machines with specific interfaces. Even within the areas, the different manufacturers use their own type of interface. This leads to a multitude of different interfaces in the cleanroom. As seen in Fig. 12.2, specific and inconsistent equipment interfaces can be identified within the factory with which we cooperate. From a user perspective, this leads to various problems. Users have to become experts in interacting with different interfaces and various interaction modalities. This leads to a reduction

Fig. 12.2 Equipment interfaces at the factory: the *first row* shows the heterogeneous signal lights of different equipment (depending on the manufacturer); the *second row* shows the heterogeneous interfaces, which can be used to control equipment

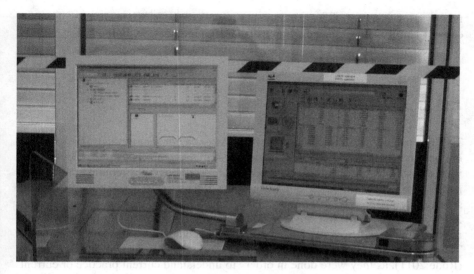

Fig. 12.3 The FabCockpit as unified interface for all kinds of equipment

in overall efficiency. An operator for the most part only knows the superficial commands and is unable to deal with difficulties or exceptions. Thus, specialists for each machine are required. New operators are confronted with a steep learning curve. To take up an analogy from computer science, this would resemble the era of mainframes, where only specialists are able to interact with computers.

The unified interface view is the next step in the development of the factory. The main idea is to unify the different interfaces of the equipment into one consistent interface. At the factory we cooperate with, this approach is partly already implemented. Every machine is coupled with a windows PC showing a program called FabCockpit (see Fig. 12.3). The FabCockpit looks exactly the same way for every machine. This leads to more flexibility, as operators can handle a wide range of machines. Also the ease of learning for new employees is improved. Yet this interface does not differentiate between the individual operators. At any time, all possible information is shown without taking into account either the interaction context or the user. Furthermore, the user only operates optimally on an individual level, not taking the entire factory into account, which is again a source of inefficiency.

The cooperative (but personalized) user-centered view is our future envisioned development for the factory. This view is focused on how a specific user and his working context can be linked with the working context of his/her co-workers (considering different roles, such as operators, maintainers, shift leads, etc.). The displayed information will be tailored for the individual within a specific situation taking contextual influence factors into account. We call this type of interface a "contextual interface," and its deployment in the factory should enhance zero-defect production by means of improved collaboration between the different actors in the factory. However, before we can develop these interfaces, we need to explore the context with suitable adapted methods from HCI and CSCW. In the following, we will present our approach.

12.3.2 Exploring the Factory

To gain insights into the context of the semiconductor factory and to establish a mutual understanding between university researchers and industrial practitioners, we used various observational methods, such as ethnography, contextual inquiry, participatory observation, and cultural probing. Intensive discussions about different styles of "ethnographic" research in HCI can be found elsewhere (e.g., Newman 2009; Dourish 2006) and are not in the focus of this chapter. In general, all methods presented here can be considered as "contextual" and "observational." They follow the most common HCI study design of "formative ethnographies" (Rode 2011), as they were done in order "to understand current practice or current practice surrounding technologies with an eye towards improving or creating new technologies." The different methods were intentionally chosen in order to suit the target group and the exploration aims. Overall, we explored four different main actors in the semiconductor factory:

1. Operators: the workers in the cleanroom who take care of processing the wafers
2. Maintainers: the workers in the cleanroom and the grayroom (i.e., the backstage of the cleanroom which has a higher particle rate allowed in which equipment can be repaired without disturbing the production line)
3. Shift leads: the workers who link production and maintenance work and structure the work of the shift cycles
4. Robots: they take over more and more routine tasks in the cleanroom and therefore change the working conditions for operators and maintainers in the factory. We took the view that they should be considered as acting entities in the cleanroom which, in some sense, collaborate with operators and so constitute a special artifact in the factory context

Table 12.1 shows an overview of the studies with their goals, applied methods, and their rational. As a detailed description of every methodology would extend the scope of this chapter, references to the relevant publications with details are added.

Studies researching the operators were conducted as ethnographies, where researchers actually worked like trainees in the factory to learn about existing systems and working routines in the etching and in the implantation department (Meschtscherjakov et al. 2010, 2011). Maintainers were in parallel studied with a contextual inquiry approach, as maintenance work is too complex to be understood in short-term ethnographic studies (Kluckner et al. 2012, 2013). In many cases, maintainers worked in production before they are skilled enough to change to maintenance work. We then decided to study shift leads, as we identified in our studies with operators and maintainers that shift leads often build the link between

Table 12.1 Factory study overview

Actor	Research goal	Method	Rationale	Reference
Operator	Understanding operators in terms of the interfaces, tools, and systems they use and the main tasks they perform	Three ethnographic studies	Three researchers worked as trainees in the etching, lithography, and implantation sector of the cleanroom. We decided that researchers are introduced to the work-life of an operator the same way as a new employee; however, co-workers were informed that the trainee is a researcher, who should explore the context in order to develop novel production interfaces	Mechtscherjakov et al. (2011)
Maintainers	Understanding maintainers in terms of the interfaces, tools, and systems they use and the main tasks they perform	Contextual inquiry	Two researchers accompanied 23 maintainers and observed and interviewed them in an apprentice/master constellation. As maintenance work is highly complex, and ethnographic approach would not have been the right choice for this group of actors. An inquiry with various maintainers, however, gave us the chance to learn about the reporting tool usage and the communication with other relevant actors in the factory	Kluckner et al. (2012) Kluckner et al. (2013)
Shift leads	Understanding shift leads, in terms of their main tasks and their quality, to link between different actors in the factory	Cultural probing	A creativity card booklet was distributed to 36 shift leads during job training. The booklet was filled in at home and returned by post. Our goal was to learn about the interplay between actors and overall procedures in the factory on a reflective level. Shift leads are the actors in the factory who could best provide an overview like that	Osswald et al. (2012)
Robots	Understanding robots: How are robots and automation technology experienced by the operators? Does experience change over time?	Participatory observation plus short questionnaire	One researcher observed the interaction of the operators with a robotic arm in the etching sector of the factory. Subsequently a short questionnaire on user acceptance aspects of the robots was distributed three times in order to observe a change in perception. As novel robotic systems are the most influential change for working routines in the production. It was relevant to understand on a behavioral and reflective level how the cooperation with these systems looks like	Buchner et al. (2012, 2013a)

operators and maintainers and are crucial for successful cooperation and production, but have very limited technology support for their work (Osswald et al. 2012). Finally, we explored human-robot collaboration in the factory in order to find out how the increasing deployment of robots in the factory is experienced by the operators and to identify possible changes in the cooperation between them (Buchner et al. 2012, 2013a). In the next sections, we will present an overview on our contextual findings followed by the overall methodological implications for the challenging factory context.

12.3.3 Special Context Findings

Besides developing redesigns for specific interactional problems and for specific actors in the cleanroom, our goal is to gain a thorough understanding of the semiconductor factory as a CSCW and HCI research context. This is of major importance for us, as we do not want to be caught in the trap of HCI research projects, which only "result in local solutions to local problems" (Hayes 2011); we want to build a descriptive model of the semiconductor factory from the empirical data gained in all our observational studies as "mosaic bricks" (see Fig. 12.4). We base our context model on the definition of Dey (2001), who coins context as "any information that can be used to characterize the situation of an entity. An entity is a person, place, or object that is considered relevant to the interaction between a user and an application, including the user and applications themselves." To narrow that definition, our understanding of context takes into any contextual information of the semiconductor factory in account, which is relevant for an "interactive task" (meaning a task in which the user has to interact with a computing system in order to achieve a specific work step). The overall context model consists of three main parts: the *user/personal context*, the *application* context, and the *real-world* context. All contextual factors we have identified so far in our observational studies can be mapped on this overall context model for the semiconductor factory (see Fig. 12.4).

This context model should contribute to the existing understanding of collaboration contexts in HCI and CSCW by identifying and describing all relevant influencing factors prior to developing novel "contextual interfaces" that should foster cooperation between workers. Interface developers should be aware of potential influence factors, which might serve as a key resource for identifying why a new interface is successful or not; the context model thus serves as an empirically grounded design space.

All environmental factors (e.g., lightning conditions, ambient noise, etc.) are mapped to the environmental/physical context that affects the perception of the user (1). Work conventions and the reliability of a user interface are considered as relevant information for the user to perform a job correctly and are, therefore, mapped to the information context (2). Attributes, which characterize our target groups (e.g., computer literacy, basic education, work experience, etc.), are mapped

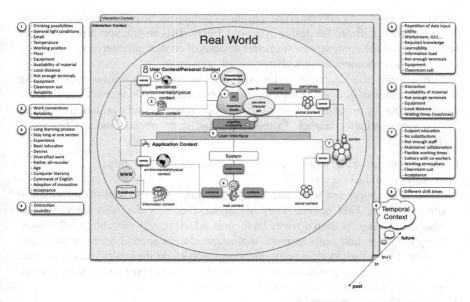

Fig. 12.4 Context model of the semiconductor factory through an HCI lens filled with mosaic bricks form the observational studies

to the personal knowledge and experiences of the user (3). Traditional usability aspects and distraction factors are mapped to the personal experience of the user (UX), as they influence how the user responds to a system (4). However, some of these aspects such as ease of learning, information load, and the heterogeneity of interfaces are also part of the user interface context (5). The architecture behind the interfaces and the core functionality of systems in the factory are mapped to the application context (6). The solidarity with co-workers and the working atmosphere are attributes of the group, which are mapped to the social context of the user and the other actors he/she has to work within the factory (7). Finally, regarding the temporal context, we have to consider the different shift times as well as that the perception and response towards a system might change over time (8).

Clearly, some factors have to be mapped into more than one group, as they have different specifications and influences. For instance, the cleanroom suit influences a series of context parts in this model. First of all, it has an impact on the way the environment is perceived (user/personal context (1)). The cleanroom suit also influences the social context, as it is hard to identify other people (real-world context (7)). Finally, it has an impact on the interaction with the user interface (e.g., reduced tactile feedback, limited field of view, etc., user interface (5)).

In general, the presented semiconductor factory context model does not aim for completeness; it should be considered as an abstraction of an interaction context through an HCI lens. We, thereby, follow the claim of Brooks, who argued that HCI specialists need to develop an appropriate abstraction that "discards irrelevant details while isolating and emphasizing those properties of artifacts and situations that are most significant for design" (Brooks 1991). This abstraction process shapes our thinking of the context, enables better designs of contextual interfaces for future, and eases the communication with our industrial partner.

Furthermore, the descriptive context model is added by relevant phenomena about the context derived from empirical observation, which builds our basic understanding for future HCI work in terms of prototyping and evaluation activities for the semiconductor factory. In the following, three phenomena are presented exemplarily.

1. Novice operators and expert operators perform tasks differently:
   (User/Personal Context)
   Novices are supposed to update equipment states and use tool-tip information offered in the FabCockpit. They are specialists only for selected tools and equipment. Experts train novices on the job, which is only possible in idle times. They consider their tasks as more sophisticated than general operator tasks and do not always trust system recommendations, but add their personal experience to decision-making processes. In other words, experts consider their experience as more effective than when slavishly following system advice.

2. Tasks differ in their complexity:
   (Application Context/Task Context)
   Lot delivery is a traditional task for novice operators, as it can be done correctly without support after approximately 1 week. Loading equipment with pre-assigned lots is also a classical novice operator task. Ambient distraction aspects (e.g., blinking equipment lights and equipment sounds) impact the task performance of novices during approx. the first 6 months.

3. Characteristics of human-human and human-system cooperation:
   (Social Context/User Interface Context)
   Shift groups first try to optimize their in-group performance and in a second step support other shifts. Training on the job is done by expert operators in idle times and is a key success element for overall productivity. Intelligent systems such as the DisTag are not considered to be fully trustworthy (a function of a more general distrust in the IT department). Operators with long experience often prefer established single systems as compared to novel integrated systems (e.g., configuring equipment directly over the equipment interface instead of using the FabCockpit).

Finally, the mapping of factors to the model helped us to identify knowledge gaps. As all our knowledge thus far was gathered through a user's viewpoint, we lacked knowledge on the application context. Knowledge in that area is of importance as it helps us to understand the constraints of prototyping interfaces better. This lack of knowledge needs to be filled by gaining insight in the system architecture of the interfaces, e.g., how the interplay between data basis work and where which information is stored. These are facts, which are important to know as they could affect the simulation of the context (e.g., in terms of timing aspects and information retrieval options) and the interfaces in the lab. Currently, we fill this gap with knowledge-transfer workshops with IT developers of the factory, in which the context model serves as communication basis. These workshops, moreover, give us insights into the historical development of existing systems and tools. Thereby we can close knowledge gaps, we are currently aware of in our semiconductor context model.

12.3.4   Methodological Implications

Our goal was to thoroughly analyze the semiconductor factory context to be able to redesign existing working routines and therefore develop novel contextual interfaces, which support cooperation between different social actors (e.g., operators, maintainers, and shift leads) over different departments, halls, and buildings. On spending time in the context as researchers, we found out that the "wilderness" of the factory is even more challenging than expected from a methodological point of view. Gathering data in the cleanroom turned out to be a challenge, as audio recordings can hardly be understood due to the ambient noise. Taking video footage is not allowed due to confidentiality agreements, and taking notes on cleanroom paper with cleanroom pens takes longer than normal handwriting. However, these are only the "practical" challenges. In the following, we will present our methodological lessons learned for all the studies listed in Table 12.1 above and, subsequently, describe our ideas as to how the next steps of iterative design (namely, evaluation of system and deployment in the cleanroom) could be conducted.

12.3.4.1   Gathering Observational Data in the Cleanroom: Lessons Learned

Several lessons are to be learned in relation to the efficacy of our enquiries. Clearly, we chose methods that we deemed best suited to achieving our exploration goals. However, each study method still involved advantages and disadvantages.

For the *ethnographic studies*, it turned out that the shift cycles are the biggest challenge, as the researchers could not adapt their day and night rhythm according to the shift cycles for just 1 or 2 weeks. However, seeing as many shift cycles as possible turned out to be important, as working routines change between shifts (e.g., the night shift is less stressful than the other shifts due to less work load and less operators in the halls) and as different operators work in different shifts (which implies an information loss, if one shift is missed out). The specific shift cycles our researchers were working in were the morning shift from 6:00 to 14:00 and the afternoon shift from 14:00 to 22:00. Additionally, it took the researchers 2–4 h to write down the notes for each day. Together with the 8-h shift work, this leads to a 10–12 h working day. We quickly recognized that this time schedule had a negative impact on the quality of the notes. First, shift work itself is already very demanding (constant concentration, high cognitive load, and unfamiliar cleanroom conditions), and second, there is too little time to take well-formulated notes. In other words, after a morning shift, the researcher has to write field notes after 8 h of demanding shift work. After an afternoon shift, the researcher was more likely to sleep and write the field notes the next morning.

Thus, in the second ethnography, we decided that researchers only work in the afternoon shift cycle, which was better suited in giving the researchers time for both working in the cleanroom and reflecting on it. In the first and second, ethnography limited themselves to keywords during the study and reworked them with the help of the audio records after every shift and after the completed field phase. This proved to be satisfactory, and the researchers had few if any problems of recall. The third ethnography completely waived field notes and only used the subjective memories combined with the audio files to fill identified knowledge gaps in the context model. The audio recordings, however, proved to be of utmost importance (despite their quality) as the work in production is characterized especially by monotonous and repetitive tasks, which are hard to remember. In order to respect privacy issues, the audio recorder was carried around visibly for everybody.

For future ethnographic studies, we plan to take into account the differences between the shift cycles (i.e., the different working routines for the operators and for the researchers). The ethnographic observations of the usage of our novel contextual interfaces in the actual cleanroom will be performed during the morning, afternoon, and night shift, whereas note-taking will be replaced completely by an audio diary, which will be transcribed and interpreted after the complete study.

Regarding the *contextual inquiry* with maintainers, it has to be mentioned that the work of maintainers is very different, depending on the department for which he/she is responsible and the functionality problems that can arise from different equipment types. Thus, it is difficult to explore "general" maintenance activities as these vary a lot between departments. Even for the departments in which we spent more time and accompanied several maintainers, a four-day contextual inquiry was not sufficient to come across all standard maintenance activities, and only a limited number of acute troubleshooting/fault repair activities could be observed. Moreover, maintainers are expert employees, important for keeping the 24/7/365 "zero-defect" production running; in other words, maintainers should not be distracted in their work and are only interviewed in idle times (which are very limited due to the requested standard maintenance activities). Subsequently, we did not get the chance to accompany maintainers with the highest skill level. We were, however, able to follow beginners and process managers, who have to use the same tools for reporting their work as maintainers. Our picture of all maintenance activities cannot be considered as 100 % thorough but provides a "good enough" insight into their usage of existing reporting tools (which are very similar over the different departments). We also conducted a reflection workshop with maintainers, managers, and process mangers, which allowed us to close knowledge gaps with experiences from different working groups. For future contextual inquiries with maintainers, we will more precisely specify the department of interest with our industry partner and, based on an expert interview with an experienced maintainer, define which main tasks need to be observed to gain a thorough understanding of the work routines.

Regarding the *cultural probing study* with shift leads, we learned a lot about the material we used. We intentionally developed a booklet with a large variety of probes and topics so every participating shift lead could find at least one topic of interest to fill in. However, we learned that not all of our probes could be filled in by every shift lead to the same degree, as not all of them have exactly the same work routines. Some shift leads are not working in production, but in the quality assurance or the laboratory. When we reported the results back to the shift leads, we got the feedback that the rather low response rate (only one third of the booklets were actually filled in and returned) can be explained by the fact that filling in the booklets at home was considered as an extension of the working day and that the very open format made it difficult to answer the questions. The shift leads preferred a short questionnaire (which we developed based on the probing results) in order to quantify the probing results. However, clearly this questionnaire could not have been developed without the probes, and we, as researchers, were satisfied with the quality of the data.

Regarding the *participatory observation* (i.e., the operators were aware that they are observed during their work) of operators interacting with the robots in the cleanroom, we learned about the necessity to have a technician accompanying us. Only with the additional comments and explanations of the technician was it possible for us to interpret the behavior of the operators (without disturbing them during their work) and also to understand the actions of the robot. However, the disadvantage was that operators felt even more observed during the work, as both a researcher and a company person "monitored" how they interacted with the robot. During the participatory observation, it became obvious that operators were not willing to discuss their real attitude about the increasing amount of robotic systems in the cleanroom (potentially due to the fact that they were afraid to be replaced by robots at some point). Therefore, we developed a supplementary questionnaire out of the observational data. The operators were willing to fill in this short questionnaire (with closed questions) that guaranteed them 100 % anonymity as it was directly sent back to the researchers and was not collected by the company. For future studies on robots in the cleanroom, we plan to keep this two-step approach of qualitative and quantitative data gathering. Currently, we are in discussions with the work council to collect video-data on how the operators interact with the robots over a longer period of time in order to have more observational data that can be quantified by the means of video annotation to explore usability issues of the operators when interacting with the robotic systems.

12.3.4.2 Evaluation of Cleanroom Redesigns: Field vs. Lab Trials

In addition to the methodological lessons learned from our requirement studies in the cleanroom, we had to make methodological considerations of how to evaluate novel contextual interfaces in terms of their ability to increase the cooperation between the various social actors in the factory. Clearly, natural interaction with our prototypes, such as an intelligent guiding system for the operators called "Operator

Guide" (Meschtscherjakov et al. 2010) and a mobile maintainer interface, which communicates the repair states of machines back to the operators, can only be evaluated in the "wild" and over a longer period of time to make ecologically valid statements. As it is understood by Rogers (2011), "in-the-wild" studies involve deploying new technologies in real-world situations and studying how they are actually used in this context, taking the fact into account that the physical and social context will have a critical effect on the usage. We aim to evaluate all our novel contextual interfaces at some point by the means of observational studies in the factory (taking into account the lessons learned, such as the need for expert discussions before the observation and the company of a technician to discuss behavior observations in parallel). A first "in-the-wild" study was already conducted to explore the actual usage of the Operator Guide and showed us unexpected usages and interpretations of the display (see Strasser et al. 2012).

However, we also want to evaluate the basic interaction concept and its iterations before we really enter the factory again (above all in order not to harm zero defect). Similarly, this poses a research challenge in itself, how to evaluate a semiconductor factory interface, without a factory. For basic concept evaluations, substitution tasks can be a reasonable approach (Osswald et al. 2012b), e.g., repetitive tasks, such as stapling chairs combined with cognitive tasks such as solving number puzzles can be used to "simulate" the working routines of an operator. However, substitution tasks can only help us to identify severe usability problems but cannot tell us anything about how the system supports actual operator tasks. Therefore, we needed to find a way to simulate the cleanroom in our laboratory. We reassembled equipment out of shelves (see Fig. 12.5/left) and

Fig. 12.5 Snapshot of the wizarding tool, which was used for the first lab-based cleanroom study; study participant loading equipment, reassembled out of shelves (*left*); cleanroom prompts and the Operator Guide display (*right*)

used real lot boxes as prompts. In combination with a self-developed Contextual Interaction Framework (based on the OSGi framework) for wizarding system states and logging performance data, we can simulate the working routines in the cleanroom (Zachhuber et al. 2012). Thereby, we built our own "HCI-semiconductor experience laboratory," which allows us to study redesigns before going back into the factory. By means of this system, we already successfully evaluated the Operator Guide in a laboratory setting (Strasser et al. 2012). However, another challenge that needed to be solved was the recruitment of representative study participants.

In the ideal case, study participants for our interface prototypes are trained cleanroom operators. However, as the cleanroom is not located at the same town of our research laboratory, it is difficult to recruit participants with this professional background. Thus, we developed the so-called proxy-operator concept as a methodological innovation for our interaction studies. Our understanding of proxy operators is a meso-level choice between people with no cleanroom experience at all (microlevel) and people who already have working experience in the cleanroom (macro-level).

In other words, the possible levels for interaction study participants could be summarized as follows:

1. Microlevel: Study setup uses elements of the cleanroom
2. Meso-level: Participants get introduced into the topic before every study
3. Meso-level: Panel participants (meaning a pool of participants who take part in several cleanroom studies over several years) take part in a cleanroom training before taking part in our studies
4. Macro-level: Participants who actually worked in the cleanroom before

We decided on the 3rd level and recruited a stock of 40 panel participants. Before their first study, participants got a training session about the tasks and behavior rules in the cleanroom. In every subsequent study they take part in, they have to fill in a questionnaire about their knowledge of the cleanroom and get an adapted training session before they take part in the study. Our long-term goal is to analyze this questionnaire material in order to assess the success of our proxy-operator concept. However, we are aware of the high degree of confounding variables in the approach due to the artificial setting in the laboratory, and therefore the results and its ecological validity need to be validated in comparative "in-the-wild" studies.

12.3.4.3   Integration into the Factory Software Architecture and Production Schedule

Another challenge for HCI and CSCW research in the factory is the integration in the production schedule and the existing software architecture of the factory (the manufacturing execution system (MES)). In phases of high-order volumes of wafers, novel systems clearly cannot be deployed in the cleanroom as this could negatively impact the "zero-defect" production rate. Due to the constantly high-order volume, novel systems can only be deployed during summer or Christmas time, when fewer operators are working in the cleanroom and fewer orders are taken by the company. However, the grayroom offers us a potential environment for "semi-wild" studies. The grayroom provides similar conditions as the cleanroom and is also used by the company to test novel equipment before being integrated in the production line. In other words, our novel contextual interfaces could be studied in the grayroom even under controlled experimental conditions with actual operators or maintainers without disturbing the "zero-defect" production. Another difficulty for us is that the company alone makes the decision as to whether one of our interface prototypes is robust enough to be rolled out in the factory, and we are obligated to follow their schedule. However, as soon as a system is deployed, valuable logging data is collected by the manufacturing execution system, which provides insights in how our systems change productivity in terms of quantitative data. Nevertheless, traditional usability testing or controlled experiments in the cleanroom will hardly ever be possible in this specific context. Therefore, we will explore the actual usage of the systems again by observational studies, such as ethnographies or contextual inquiries.

12.4 The Car as Challenging Research Setting

In addition to the factory, we have chosen the car as a challenging environment for HCI and CSCW researchers. Driving a car can be dangerous, and the driver must not be distracted – that is why collaborative aspects from other domains might bring fruitful ideas into the automotive context. So far advanced driver assistance systems (ADAS) are mainly technology driven and arguably fail to make use of social interaction in the car, and between different drivers. ADAS help us to keep within the lane (e.g., lane departure warning system) or even to change it (e.g., Lane change assistance); they assist us in dangerous satiations (e.g., blind spot detection, collision avoidance system), or they monitor our status (e.g., driver drowsiness detection). In addition, however, HCI research has recently started investigating the collaborative nature of driving (Forlizzi et al. 2010; Esbjörnsson et al. 2007; Inbar and Tractinsky 2011). Drivers are in a steady negotiation process with other car drivers, and traffic behavior is a social interaction (Juhlin 1999). Understanding the car as a collaborative social space has the potential to develop new ADAS, which support driver-driver collaboration, as well as driver-passenger collaboration. We need to understand ADAS as social embedded systems in order to increase acceptance and user experience. For exploring and understanding the automotive context in this sense, we need to apply and adapt HCI and CSCW methodologies.

When researching the car, apart from safe driving simulators with traditional HCI and CSCW methods such as ethnographies, researchers have to carefully reflect upon the dangers the research itself can have for the driving situation. Driving a car can be dangerous not only for the driver but also for passengers, the researcher included. Moreover, the research itself could potentially heighten risk for all parties. Car accidents can also be expensive. Questions such as "Who will pay for repair costs?" need to be discussed. Basically, the liability of the people involved needs to be specified. In addition, there might be regional legal differences that need to be considered. What makes interventions in the car dangerous, especially for the driver, is the fact that a driver always has a primary task: to drive the car safely from one place to another. Interventions in the car have to take into account that they compete with the primary driving task. This task is usually not interruptible.

At the same time, the car offers some methodological affordances. Cameras can be very easily mounted, and electricity for those and for potential systems can be pulled from the car itself. But again, the legal regulations/restrictions of the study location need to be considered. Also, power supply is often very instable in cars (e.g., the power supply is interrupted when the ignition is turned on or off). When mounting observation systems into the car, it has to be carefully checked that these are secured in a way that they become loose or detached when taking a sharp turn or when the car breaks. Similarly, they cannot be positioned in a way that they distract or impair the sight of the driver or act in the form of a safety hazard (e.g., obstruct the airbag).

In addition to safety and legal aspects, the effect of the presence of a researcher needs to be considered. It might be that we, as researchers, want to be present in the car during a study to take notes and interact with the driver or the passengers. In such cases, we also need to understand how the car in many ways offers a very limited space. In such limited spaces, we do not just affect the study from the official role researchers have. Researchers in the automotive domain can be seen as explainers, facilitators, encouragers, or mainly as technical support as discussed by Johnson et al. (2012). However, we can also affect the social space within the car during a ride. In order to reduce researcher participation, many studies use remote techniques such as video ethnography (e.g., Brown and Laurier 2012) to gain insights without being physically in the car.

In addition to these challenges, the car is typically a moving object. From a researcher's point of view, this can cause some practical problems, such as shakiness, constantly changing lighting conditions that may affect video and audio recordings, difficulties with note-taking, etc. When conducting studies in natural conditions (i.e., noncontrolled settings; journeys which would have taken even without the study), timing could also be challenging. When a researcher is present in the car, questions arise such as how will the researcher determine when and where the trip should start and end, how will the researcher get to the starting point in time and then back again, whether or not the start and end of the video recordings of a remote study should be automatic or done by the participant, and what should happen if the deployed prototype or the video system fails.

Another challenge of automotive studies is recruiting (appropriate) participants. If not investigating specific user groups, such as taxi drivers or other professional drivers, this can be tricky, as drivers are generally a very heterogeneous group. Researchers thus often use convenience samples that are reused several times, but do not represent the true characteristics of drivers. It is further not unusual to recruit students or people from the local area with specific characteristics (e.g., own a driving license for at least 3 years). Nevertheless, automotive studies often recruit from specific user groups who use their cars for business purposes such as commuters (Ben-Elia and Ettema 2011), taxi drivers (Phithakkitnukoon et al. 2010), and policemen (Hampton and Langham 2005). Thus, the pool of potential participants can be limited or untrained. Recruiting new drivers or older adults might be easier (since these are larger groups), but safety issues have to be handled since beginners have more cognitive overhead in operating the car, and older drivers are more likely to have restricted vision and longer reaction times. Some researchers have addressed this issue by conducting their studies with user groups that are easier to access, while still aiming at a generalization of their results (Esbjörnsson et al. 2007).

These challenges and opportunities make the car a challenging collaborative place to be studied in situ – where the action actually happens. This is why we need to tailor existing HCI and CSCW methods to this very specific context and develop new methods in order to understand user experience in the car. So far, we have been focusing – like most other research in automotive user interface design – on the driver. However, the car offers more than just driver interfaces. To fully understand the car as a design space, we need to look beyond the driver (e.g., the role of children in the car (Hoffman et al. 2013)). We need to see the car in a holistic way where collaboration and negotiation routinely happens. Inside the car, the driver often collaborates with passengers in operating the navigation system or handling the entertainment system. Outside the car, drivers are cooperating with each other to ensure a safe and smooth traffic. If this collaboration fails, accidents may occur.

12.4.1 The Holistic Car

In order to make technology in the car more controllable and to reduce workload and stress, while simultaneously enhancing user experience in the car, we have to understand the car in a holistic way (see Fig. 12.6). We need to understand how contextual influences are related to different user experience dimensions and how they influence the car design space. Additionally, we need to address both

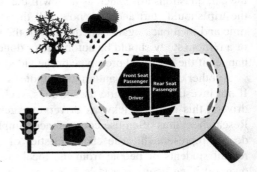

Fig. 12.6 The holistic car consists of three interconnected areas: the driver, the front seat passenger, and the rear seat passenger. These areas are again highly linked to the context they are currently in, shaped, for example, by other traffic participants and environmental characteristics

passengers and users outside of the vehicle. We need to understand the social nature of the car by identifying collaborative behavior inside the car as well as between drivers. To address the car more holistically, we propose two things.

First, we need to understand the interior. The car can be said to consist of three interrelated spaces: the driver's area, the front seat passenger area, and the back seat area. The last two areas, we suggest, have not yet been sufficiently researched from an HCI and CSCW perspective. Front seat passengers traditionally can be regarded as copilots. They help the driver in navigation tasks, and they can support the driver in operating navigation devices or the entertainment systems. They may even act as an additional pair of eyes in the primary task of driving. Passengers in the back seat are less likely to do so, for obvious reasons. Nonetheless, they interact with the driver to a certain extent. They might use smartphones to access information needed by the driver, or they may want the driver to perform certain tasks for them (e.g., switch the radio station). Collaboration and negotiation outside the car is done constantly and often implicitly. When the car in front of me brakes, I have to brake too. Indicator lights signal an intention. Horns call attention. These actions are highly collaborative. Thus, social systems, which are formed within the car and with its surrounding (e.g., other cars, other road users, surrounding infrastructure), cannot be left out when trying to understand how technology is used in the vehicle and how it should be designed in the future.

Second, we claim that, especially when focusing on contextual and cooperative user experiences, automotive interfaces have to be researched in the context, in which they will be used. While this also applies to other areas of HCI, context in the highly mobile automotive area is more unstable and dynamic than in other HCI domains due to the high speed with which vehicles are moving and the diversity of situations they are used in. In situ studies are the only way of allowing an investigation of how things happening around the car influence what happens in the car. At a first glance, it appears obvious that a vehicle is a very enclosed and private space that hosts interactions within. We are, nevertheless, convinced that the borders between interaction within the vehicle and interaction with the exterior are highly blurred. While simulator experiments have a high value when, for example, trying out prototypes of new interaction modalities, they often miss aspects of contextual influences as well as surprising and unexpected events.

Automotive research "in-the-wild" not only allows us to understand the influence of what we call "environmental" context but also the pre- and post-usage experiences that shape their goals and expectations towards technology. In one of our studies, for example, we came to a new understanding of the concept of distraction in the vehicle. Usually, efforts are taken to reduce distraction (from the road); however, we discovered distraction has a more ambivalent status and is often linked to events outside the immediate trip (e.g., angry discussions with the girlfriend). This richness of contextual aspects cannot be sufficiently represented in simulator experiments. Although context can also be prototyped in simulators, the diversity of situations is so high that sufficient representation in a simulator cannot be achieved. In conclusion, an in-depth understanding of users' experiences can only be achieved in the original context they evolve in (Law et al. 2008).

12.4.2 Exploring the Car

In order to grasp the car as a holistic space, we so far have conducted seven contextual studies in the car. They contribute to a broader understanding of the car as an interaction design space (see Table 12.2 for an overview). These seven studies focused on the driver, the front seat passenger, the rear seat passengers, and the interaction in between these spaces. For the studies, we used different methods with different degrees of researcher participation and technological support.

Studies researching the driver and driver-related tasks as well as driver user interfaces include three studies: a contextual inquiry with the focus on interaction with multifunctional rotary knobs (Neureiter et al. 2011), an ethnographic study experiencing drivers in traffic jams, and an adaption of the experience sampling method to gain insights on the relation between context and user experience factors (Meschtscherjakov et al. 2012). We conducted two studies focusing on front seat passengers: an ethnographic study observing the interaction between drivers and front seat passengers (Gridling et al. 2013) as well as a cultural probing study at the gas station to inform the design of the future front seat passenger design space. The rear seat space as third area was researched in two studies: a cultural probing studies utilizing a variety of probing materials to get inspiration for future interfaces in the backseat area of the car with a special focus on children as well as an exploratory study where we deployed and tested three prototypical games for children sitting in the back seat.

12.4.3 Special Context Findings

The in situ studies provided us with a huge amount of scientific findings, some of which are well known; others of which offered some deep insights into the nature of cooperative experiences in the car for drivers and passengers. The various studies provided us with inspiration for new ideas and novel prototypes. In this section, we present the most significant findings from our studies.

1. Primary tasks in the vehicle

Most research in the automotive domain still applies Geiser's distinction of tasks in the vehicle into primary, secondary, and tertiary tasks (Geiser 1985). Within our studies, we found a transition from the traditional sense of primary tasks (i.e., controlling a vehicle) to a more value-sensitive definition of primary tasks (e.g., staying in contact, having a good family time). While driving a vehicle should be the main focus of the driver, we as researchers have to be aware that it may not be the first priority for the person behind the wheel – at least not consciously. As our studies showed, drivers are often not aware of risky situations when being distracted from driving. In their mind, so-called secondary tasks (e.g., entering a destination into the navigation system, making a phone call, changing the radio station)

Table 12.2 Car study overview

Space	Research goal	Method	Rationale	Reference
Driver	Understand how driver uses central multifunctional systems and which contextual influences exist	Contextual inquiry (CI)	Participating in trips helped us to gain a first sense of drivers' tasks and contextual influences; a one-on-one observation and context-dependent inquiring was chosen to focus on the driver	Neureiter et al. (2011)
Driver	Investigate users' behavior and technology usage in rush hour traffic	Ethnographic study	Rush hour was a particularly interesting field identified in the CI, showing a highly diverse usage of technology and improvement potential; we used a video-supported ethnographic study to be part of peoples' daily commute	
Driver and passengers	Investigate the drivers' experiences and their relation to contextual parameters	Experience sampling method	The experiences and contextual influences that the CI had brought up were investigated in more detail collecting quantitative data more widespread; this was possible without researcher participation through experience samples	Meschtscherjakov et al. (2012)
Front seat	Investigate how an interactive system could support or substitute front seat passenger assistance	Ethnographic study	Finding that passengers are a main source of support and distraction, we collected assistance situations and the context in which they happened, as well as related aspects of user experience by taking part in trips with two or more passengers; we utilized a traditional ethnography (without technological equipment) to live the experience without distracting natural behavior	Gridling et al. (2013)
Front seat	Investigate front seat passenger experience with their space in the car to deduce design ideas for future interfaces in that area	Cultural probing	Based on the findings in the ethnographic study, we wanted front seat passengers to probe their view on their space, seeing how they could imagine interfaces in this space to be like; cultural probes were distributed at gas stations to get a broad range of inspirations	Osswald et al. (2013)
Rear seat	Identify technology usage on potentials for future technology in the rear seat	Cultural probing	The advantage that no researcher has to be present in a probing study was necessary to help us open the rear seat space for research. Including families as example user group, we investigated their use of the rear seat and related technology with a variety of different probing materials	Wilfinger et al. (2011)
Rear seat	Design mini games that make sitting still in the rear seat a fun activity	Explorative design study	Applying findings from the probing study; kids should be given tools for diversion that improve the situation of everyone in the car; game prototypes helped us exploring the	

becomes the primary task in terms of conscious relevance. Steering, accelerating, and breaking are often unconscious activities. This can be dangerous when the interaction with technologies in the car becomes too distracting. Acknowledging that modern vehicles are more than tools to get from one point to the other but tools to help users pursue their goals will support a less function-oriented design of technology in the vehicle.

2. Passenger-to-passenger interaction

Technology in the vehicle, to date, is very driver-centered. We believe that this is due to the high amount of trips with only the driver in the vehicle. Nevertheless, our experience sampling study showed an average of 1.52 people in the vehicle per trip, making the potential effect of passengers in the vehicle significant. Especially in the ethnographic study on front seat passengers, we found that they are a major source of assistance as well as distraction. We have investigated how front seat passengers do actually assist drivers (e.g., cleaning a steamed-up window) in a collaborative and cooperative way. Front seat passenger wants to be more involved in the driving task itself (e.g., monitoring the speed of the car or assisting with the navigation device). We have found that the balance between sharing information and being in control is crucial for a positive collaboration experience. Similarly, the rear seat cultural probing unveiled the positive and negative effects that the condition of passengers can have on everyone in the car. We, therefore, see the driver as administrator, being the most important user of the facilities in the car. The driver, for example, needs to be able to control technology usage in the rear seat while maintaining the driving task. The passengers, on the other hand, have a high amount of free resources they can use to assist the driver but which are also a source of boredom. We, therefore, see the necessity to include all passengers in the car into the driving task, based on their abilities and interests.

3. Context awareness

Context awareness has been a central concept in the efforts to improve in-car interfaces (see, for example, Bellotti et al. (2005)). Most approaches nevertheless aim at reducing cognitive workload by making systems context-aware, leading to less distraction and an increase in safety. While this is valuable, our results indicate that this approach does not go far enough. As in other areas of HCI, user experiences are very context-driven. In the vehicle, where contexts are highly dynamic, context-aware interfaces therefore also have to include the effect of changing context on UX. Driving through an unknown area in the dark, for example, can have a negative effect on perceived safety and cause anxiety. A navigation system should be aware of ambient lighting when guiding a driver through an unfamiliar part of the town during the night. Trip destinations and purposes have a major influence on how people perceive their trip. The studies conducted showed only a small fraction of possible contextual influences, but what we see is that strong efforts have to be taken in understanding the overall effect of context on the driver beyond distraction and workload. In a current study, we aim at investigating the effect of short-term pre-trip experiences on the perception of a trip in the vehicle.

4. Driving as a chain of plastic episodes

Based on the results of our studies, we propose a new perspective on interaction with automotive user interfaces, based on the "plastic" metaphor introduced by Rattenbury et al. (2008). Researching mobile computers, they refer to "plastic" as a term describing technology which allows users to fill opportunistic gaps, making the plastic time slots shrink and expand until interrupted. Interaction with in-vehicle systems have mainly been seen as continuous, having a constant level of distraction from the road. We found users to be highly flexible in how they interact with technology, routinely judging whether it is safe to interact with technology in a certain moment or not. Granted that these judgments were not always correct, it still shows the high potential of technology to support users in adopting a safer usage behavior based on "plastic" episodes, which allow a higher distraction from the road than others. Alt and colleagues (Alt et al. 2010), for example, propose to use contextual information to enable micro-entertainment in cars. They suggest anticipating how long a car has to wait in front of a red traffic light and fill this plastic time with entertainment snippets.

5. Smartphones on wheels

Many people are nowadays experienced with smooth interaction on smartphones and tablets. Multi-touch gestures and the immediate feedback of the device and high-resolution screens have, however, exaggerated expectations for these technologies. In the distraction study, we witnessed the negative effect on user experience of a resistive touch screen (no multi-touch, slow reaction time) when people expected the seamless interaction of a touch screen as used in most smartphones. In addition, people are used to being connected all the time via their smartphones to their social peers. They expect to be able to use text messages, Twitter, and Facebook, etc., all the time. They expect this connectedness also in their cars. Since production cycles for cars are significantly longer than for mobile phones, industry has to struggle with outdated technology in their cars. To enhance user experience beyond usability, these expectations have to be considered.

6. Make driving and riding more fun

Finally, we propose that both driving a car and riding in a car could be made more fun without making it more dangerous. Our explorative design study on making sitting still in a car for children more fun revealed significant potential. We experienced that sitting still could be actually fun when fostered through a playful design. This approach is not only true for children and/or the rear seat but for the whole car. We envision making driving safe or eco-friendly more fun and also enhancing passenger experiences. The driver's working place as well as the design space for front seat passengers and rear seat passengers offers huge potentials for future contextual "in-the-wild" studies.

12.4.4 Methodological Implications

Beside our empirical mosaic findings on the car context, we also recognized a number of methodological implications from our automotive "in-the-wild" studies. In this section, we summarize these implications and answer issues raised in Sect. 12.4.2.

12.4.4.1 Use the Automotive Context

In general, we found experiences in the vehicle to be a study topic that participants can easily relate to. People feel comfortable in sharing experiences with their car; it is something they use often, and it is easy to have an opinion or a good story about it. The same is true when communicating the study topics to the participants. Similarly, words that describe parts of cars, trips, and context (e.g., traffic) are often used in everyday language, making it easy for participants to express themselves. We also found the car to be a good space to work with children, since it is a familiar area (especially when the family car is used).

When studying interactions in the car, we found it to be beneficial to make use of what is imminent to making trips with a car. As with other researchers (Kern and Schmidt 2007), we, for example, found the break when filling up gas at the gas station to be an ideal moment for a survey, an interview, or the start of a probing study. We also found that other aspects of a trip might be utilized as new methods to research the automotive context. For example, when people take a trip (especially abroad), they may write a postcard to their family and friends at home. We suggest using this tradition for research purposes. In one of our probing studies, we asked participants to write a postcard "home" and express their experiences during this trip in relation to the car. When recruiting participants for automotive "in-the-wild" studies, we suggest being provocative and innovative. Gas station or garages are places where many car drivers can be easily observed or interviewed. Car retailers and online car sharing platforms also provide a pool of potential participants.

Although the car is restricted in some areas such as space, it also offers an infrastructure for studies "in-the-wild" that support research. The car itself provides a high amount of data that can be used for studies and prototypes. Speed, GPS, or throttle position provides rich input for interactive systems while allowing the recording of user behavior. Bringing cooperative technology into the car, however, is especially challenging, given potential drain on power and the possibility of, for instance, blown fuses. These potential breakdowns require at least an extra study assistant to be present, raising the effort that has to be invested.

In our studies, we found low-tech study materials, such as postcards and notebooks to be valuable. Cup holders are a well-suited place to store this kind of study material. Giving users the possibility to take the materials with them, nevertheless, did not prevent users from forgetting about the studies. We do not have any proof that this is a more severe problem in the car than in other spaces, but we certainly became aware of the need to remind participants of their study tasks.

12.4.4.2   Complexity of Automotive Studies

The car is a space eminently suitable for researcher involvement. The placement and position of participants in studies is very stable; it is, therefore, easy to conduct observations. Nevertheless, having a researcher taking part in trips requires some effort. On most occasions, researchers have to join at the beginning of the trip, travel with the participants, and, afterwards, make their return on their own. Research in the vehicle with participating researchers, therefore, creates a negative ratio of time in the study situation to time needed to travel there and back – an issue that technology-supported studies can solve. Unfortunately, the usage of recording equipment is challenging since lighting conditions rapidly change in the vehicle and the recording of sound is interfered by the ambient noise.

As well as the rapidly changing contextual factors influence research "in-the-wild"; interaction in the vehicle is also very season-dependent. Results of our rear seat probing study, for example, would have been different in the winter compared to the summer, where long vacation trips are made during hot weather. Both long-term and short-term contextual changes make conducting automotive "in-the-wild" studies a complex task – especially when researching the influence of context-dependent factors such as weather or traffic density.

Safety is a major concern in vehicles, making them a sensitive research environment. The main threat is that participating in any kind of study activity distracts the drivers from the road. One suggestion is to use spare time during driving when prompting drivers (e.g., during a traffic jam or in front of a red traffic light). Another possibility would be to use audible input and output for asking questions and gathering answers. Additionally, study equipment has to be secured and cannot be used if it causes a threat in case of a technology failure or obstructs safety measures (e.g., emergency braking). Researchers have to make sure that their equipment must not be the source of distraction or danger. It must be safely attached to the car and no equipment can be unsecured. Participants should be able to use the prototypes extensively prior to the ride.

Nevertheless, even when a high amount of countermeasures are taken, we are always alert to the possibility that we are creating difficulties in the automotive domain. Choosing the car as "wilderness" for research activities can be challenging, when safety has to be addressed without muting creative ideas that do not conform to current interface norms (Greenberg and Buxton 2008). Regarding liability and ethics, we suggest that participants should be made aware of the fact that safety is the most important aspect during an automotive in situ study and that all regulations must be complied with during the study, although an element of risk always remains. Researchers should be aware of this fact.

12.5 Conclusions

In this chapter, we presented two difficult and challenging research settings for HCI and CSCW, namely, a semiconductor factory and a car. We explained the general challenges which both contexts pose for exploratory research through an HCI and CSCW lens, such as environmental constraints (e.g., cleanroom conditions in the factory and limited space in the car). Then we presented our view on both contexts as cooperation spaces and how we tried to approach them with various different research policies. We used a set of different requirement methods (ethnography, contextual inquiry, cultural probing, and a participatory observation) in both contexts to gain an understanding of the different actors, their interplay and needs for cooperation, and the environmental conditions. Based on this contextual analysis, we derived empirical mosaic bricks with which we could describe both contexts in a holistic manner. These descriptive context models for the factory and the car should contribute to the existing understanding of collaboration contexts in HCI and CSCW by identifying and describing relevant factors prior to developing novel "contextual interfaces" that should foster cooperation in these contexts.

Moreover, we presented other salient issues in these challenging contexts, namely, the methodological lessons learned from the exploratory studies, as well as the challenges studies of future contextual interfaces will pose. This includes aspects such as lab-based studies within a "simulated" factory or car context and the integration of our work into the production cycle of the factory. Our implications have an influence on traditional contextual design and evaluation assumptions in HCI and CSCW. We suggest potential solutions that might also be used for other challenging domains, such as air planes, healthcare settings, public spaces, etc. We experience constraints in these contexts not only as a challenge but also as an opportunity to develop new interaction designs. Sometimes limitations can inspire through their challenging nature. The vision here is to better understand how to make use of the beneficial constraints for interaction design and how to cope with hindrances (Fuchsberger et al. 2014).

However, in these challenging contexts, close collaboration between HCI researchers and our industrial partners was crucial as they were the "context-holders." By this we mean that they provided us with knowledge about the context as well as access to it. For example, to study the factory context, a researcher needs to gain access to the cleanroom and actual operators. In the automotive context, it is crucial that a researcher gains access to the newest technologies in order to study them. We argue that the importance of a close collaboration between context-holders and researchers is important in most challenging contexts and the resulting collaboration could be beneficial for both partners. We explored two contexts, which have received only little attention from an HCI and CSCW perspective to date, with a view to the redesign of systems to optimize working routines for different actors. In other words, even if these observational studies in the wilderness of a semiconductor factory and a car denote a huge effort for both parties, its outcome justifies its effort.

Acknowledgments The authors would like to thank Martin Murer, Katja Neureiter, Axel Baumgartner, Wolfgang Reitberger, and Florian Pöhr for their contributions to the research presented in this paper. The financial support by the Federal Ministry of Economy, Family and Youth and the National Foundation for Research, Technology and Development is gratefully acknowledged (Christian Doppler Laboratory for "Contextual Interfaces").

References

Alt, F., Kern, D., Schulte, F., Pfleging, B., Shirazi, A. S., & Schmidt, A. (2010). Enabling micro-entertainment in vehicles based on context information. In *Proceedings of the 2nd international conference on automotive user interfaces and interactive vehicular applications, Automotive UI '10* (pp. 117–124). New York: ACM.

Auramäki, E., Robinson, M., Aaltonen, A., Kovalainen, M., Liinamaa, A., & Tuuna-Väiskä, T. (1996, November). Paperwork at 78kph. In *Proceedings of the 1996 ACM conference on computer supported cooperative work* (pp. 370–379). ACM.

Ballas, J., Heitmeyer, C., & Perez, M. (1992). *Direct manipulation and intermittent automation in advanced cockpits*. Technical report, DTIC Document.

Bellotti, F., Gloria, D., Montanari, R., Dosio, N., & Morreale, D. (2005). Comunicar: Designing a multimedia, context-aware human-machine interface for cars. *Cognition, Technology and Work, 7*(1), 36–45.

Ben-Elia, E., & Ettema, D. (2011). Changing commuters' behavior using rewards: A study of rush-hour avoidance. *Transportation Research Part F: Traffic Psychology and Behaviour, 14*(5), 354–368.

Beyer, H., & Holtzblatt, K. (1998). *Contextual design: Defining customer-centered systems*. San Francisco: Morgan Kaufmann Publishers. ISBN 1558604111.

Blomberg, J., Giacomi, J., Mosher, A., & Swenton-Wall, P. (1993). Ethnographic field methods and their relation to design. In D. Dchuler & A. Namioka (Eds.), *Participatory design: Principles and practices*. Hillsdale: Erlbaum.

Brooks, R. (1991). Comparative task analysis: An alternative direction for human-computer interaction science. In J. Carroll (Ed.), *Designing interaction: Psychology at the human computer interface*. Cambridge: Cambridge University Press.

Brown, B., & Laurier, E. (2012). The normal natural troubles of driving with GPS. In *Proceedings of CHI 2012* (pp. 1621–1630). New York: ACM.

Buchner, R., Wurhofer, D., Weiss, A., & Tscheligi, M. (2012). User experience of industrial robots over time. In *Proceedings of the seventh annual ACM/IEEE international conference on Human-Robot Interaction* (pp. 115–116). New York: ACM.

Buchner, R., Wurhofer, D., Weiss, A., & Tscheligi, M. (2013a). Robots in time: How user experience in human-robot interaction changes over time. In *Proceedings of international conference on social robotics* (pp. 138–147). Bristol: ICSR.

Buchner, R., Kluckner, P. K., Weiss, A., & Tscheligi, M. (2013b). Assisting maintainers in the semiconductor factory: Iterative co-design of a mobile interface and a situated display. In *Proceedings of the 12th international conference on mobile and Ubiquitous Multimedia (MUM '13)*. New York: ACM.

Chamberlain, A., Crabtree, A., Rodden, T., Jones, M., & Rogers, Y. (2012). Research in the wild: Understanding 'in the wild' approaches to design and development. In *Proceedings of the designing interactive systems conference, DIS '12* (pp. 795–796). New York: ACM.

Crabtree, A. (1998). Ethnography in participatory design. In *Proceedings of participatory design conference (PDC'98)* (pp. 93–105). Palo Alto: CPSR.

Crabtree, A., Rodden, T., Tolmie, P., & Button, G. (2009). Ethnography considered harmful. In *Proceedings of the 27th international conference on human factors in computing systems, CHI '09* (pp. 879–888). New York: ACM.

D'Souza, M., & Greenstein, J. S. (2003, October). Listening to users in a manufacturing organization: A context-based approach to the development of a computer-supported collaborative work system. *International Journal of Industrial Ergonomics, 32*(4), 251–264.

Dey, A. K. (2001, February). Understanding and using context. *Personal and Ubiquitous Computing, 5*(1), 4–7.

Dourish, P. (2006). Implications for design. In *Proceedings of CHI'06* (pp. 541–550). Montréal, Canada. New York: ACM Press.

Esbjörnsson, M., Juhlin, O., & Weilenmann, A. (2007). Drivers using mobile phones in traffic: An ethnographic study of interactional adaptation. *International Journal of Human-Computer Interaction, 22*(1–2), 37–58.

Fallman, D. (2003). Enabling physical collaboration in industrial settings by designing for embodied interaction CLIHC '03. In *Proceedings of the Latin American conference on human-computer interaction* (pp. 41–51). New York: ACM.

Fetterman, D. M. (1998). *Ethnography: Step by step* (2nd ed.). Thousand Oaks: Sage Publications.

Forlizzi, J., Barley, W. C., & Seder, T. (2010). Where should I turn: Moving from individual to collaborative navigation strategies to inform the interaction design of future navigation systems. In *Proceedings of CHI 2010* (pp. 1261–1270). New York: ACM.

Fuchsberger, V., Murer, M., Aslan, I., Meschtscherjakov, A., Tscheligi, M., Sundström, P., & Petrelli, D. (2014). Contextual constraints: Consequences for interaction design. *Workshop at DIS'14: Conference on designing interactive systems*, Vancouver.

Geiser, G. (1985). Man machine interaction in vehicles. *ATZ, 87*, 74–77.

Gellatly, A., Hansen, C., Highstorm, M., & Weiss, J. (2010). Journey: General motors' move to incorporate contextual design into its next generation of automotive HCI design. In *Proceedings of AUI 2010*. New York: ACM.

Greenberg, S., & Buxton, B. (2008). Usability evaluation considered harmful (some of the time). In *Proceedings of the twenty-sixth annual SIGCHI conference on human factors in computing systems* (pp. 111–120). New York: ACM.

Gridling, N., Sundstroem, P., Meschtscherjakov, A., Wilfinger, D., & Tscheligi, M. (2013). Come drive with me: An ethnographic study of driver-passenger pairs to inform future in-car assistance. In *CSCW '13 proceedings of the ACM 2013 conference on computer supported cooperative work companion*. New York: ACM.

Hampton, P., & Langham, M. (2005). A contextual study of police car telematics: The future of in-car information systems. *Ergonomics, 48*(2), 109–118.

Hanowski, R. J., Olson, R. L., Hickman, J. S., & Dingus, T. A. (2006). *The 100-car naturalistic driving study: A descriptive analysis of light vehicle-heavy vehicle interactions from the light vehicle driver's perspective*. Technical report, Virginia Tech Transportation Institute.

Hayes, G. R. (2011, July). The relationship of action research to human-computer interaction. *ACM Transactions on Computer-Human Interaction, 18*, 1–20.

Heyer, C. (2010). Investigations of Ubicomp in the oil and gas industry. In *Proceedings of the 12th ACM international conference on Ubiquitous computing* (pp. 61–64). New York: ACM.

Heyer, C., Wagner, I., Tellioglu, H., Balka, E., Simone, C., & Ciolfi, L. (Eds.). (2009). *High-Octane Work: The oil and gas workplace ECSCW 2009* (pp. 363–382). London: Springer.

Hoffman, G., Gal-Oz, A., Shlomi, D., & Zuckerman, O. (2013). In-car game design for children: Child vs. parent perspective. In *Proceedings of the 12th international conference on interaction design and children* (pp. 112–119). New York: ACM.

Hutchins, E., & Klausen, T. (1996). Distributed cognition in an airline cockpit. In *Cognition and communication at work* (pp. 15–34). New York: Cambridge University Press.

Inbar, O., & Tractinsky, N. (2011). Make a trip an experience: Sharing in-car information with passengers. In *Proceedings of CHI 2011* (pp. 1243–1248). New York: ACM.

Johnson, R., Rogers, Y., van der Linden, J., & Bianchi-Berthouze, N. (2012). Being in the thick of in-the-wild studies: The challenges and insights of researcher participation. In *Proceedings of the 2012 ACM annual conference on human factors in computing systems, CHI '12* (pp. 1135–1144). New York: ACM.

Juhlin, O. (1999). Traffic Behavior as social interaction – Implications for the design of the artificial driver. In *Proceedings of ITS 1999*. Crowthorne: Transport Research Laboratory.

Kern, D., & Schmidt, A. (2007). Gas station flash survey – A method for interviewing drivers. In T. Paul-Stueve (Ed.), *Mensch & Computer 2007 Workshopband*. Weimar: Verlag der Bauhaus-Universität Weimar.

Kluckner, P. M., Buchner, R., Weiss, A., & Tscheligi, M. (2012). Repair now: Collaboration between maintainers, operators and equipment in a cleanroom. In *Proceedings of the ACM conference on computer supported cooperative work, CSCW '12*. New York: ACM.

Kluckner, P. M., Buchner, R., Weiss, A., & Tscheligi, M. (2013). Collaborative reporting tools: An analysis of maintenance activities in a semiconductor factory. In *Proceedings of the 2013 international conference on collaboration technologies and systems (CTS)* (pp. 508–515). Piscataway: IEEE.

Kristensen, M., Kyng, M., & Palen, L. (2006). Participatory design in emergency medical service: Designing for future practice. In *Proceedings of the SIGCHI conference on human factors in computing systems, CHI '06* (pp. 161–170). New York: ACM.

Law, E. L.-C., Bevan, N., Christou, G., Springett, M., & Lárusdóttir, M. (Eds.). (2008). *Proceedings of the international workshop on meaningful measures: Valid user experience measurement (VUUM)*, Reykjavik.

Lin, C.-H., Hwang, S.-L., & Min-Yang Wang, E. (2009). Design for usability on supply chain management systems implementation. *Human Factors and Ergonomics in Manufacturing & Service Industries, 19*, 378–403.

Magnusson, C., Larsson, A., Warell, A., & Eftring, H. (2011). Key scenarios, contextual walk-through and context trails – Tools for better and more accessible mobile designs. In *Proceedings of the 13th IFIP TC13 conference on human-computer interaction, INTERACT 2011*, Workshop on Mobile Accessibility, Lisbon.

Martin, N., Sprague, M.A., Wall, P., Watts-Perotti, J. (2007). Giving voice to print production facility workers: Representing actual work practices in the streamlining of a labor intensive production print job. In *Ethnographic Praxis in industry conference proceedings 2007* (1), pp. 163–180. Keystone.

Mechtscherjakov, A., Kluckner, P., Pöhr, F., Reitberger, W., Weiss, A., Tscheligi, M., Hohenwarter, K., & Oswald, P. (2011). Ambient persuasion in the factory: The case of the operator guide. In *Advanced semiconductor manufacturing conference (ASMC), 2011 22nd annual IEEE/SEMI* (pp. 1–6). Piscataway: IEEE.

Meschtscherjakov, A., Reitberger, W., Poehr, F., & Tscheligi, M. (2010). The operator guide: An ambient persuasive interface in the factory. In *Proceedings of the AmI, 2010* (pp. 117–126). Berlin Heidelberg: Springer.

Meschtscherjakov, A., Wilfinger, D., Osswald, S., Gridling, N., & Tscheligi, M. (2012). Trip experience sampling: Assessing driver experience. In *The field. Proceedings of the 3rd international conference on automotive user interfaces and interactive vehicular applications. AutomotiveUI '12*. New York: ACM.

Millen, D. R. (2000, August). Rapid ethnography, time deepening strategies for HCI field research. In *Conference proceedings on designing interactive systems: Processes, practices, methods, and techniques* (pp. 280–286). New York: ACM.

Nardi, B. (1992, August 4–8). Studying context: A comparison of activity theory, situated action models and distributed cognition. In *Proceedings East–West conference on human-computer interaction* (pp. 352–359). St. Petersburg, Russia.

Neureiter, K., Meschtscherjakov, A., Wilfinger, D., & Tscheligi, M. (2011). Investigating the usage of multifunctional rotary knobs in the center stack with a contextual inquiry. In *Proceedings of EA AUI 2011*. New York: ACM.

Newman, W. (2009). The status of ethnography in systems design. In *Panel CHI'09* (Boston, MA). New York: ACM

Osswald, S., Buchner, R., Weiss, A. & Tscheligi, M. (2012). Using participatory design to investigate technology usage in the cleanroom of a semiconductor factory "The message in the bottle: Best practices for transferring the knowledge from qualitative user studies". Workshop at the *ACM conference on designing interactive systems*, Newcastle.

Osswald, S., Sundstroem, P., & Tscheligi, M. (2013). The front seat passenger: How to transfer qualitative findings into design. *International Journal of Vehicular Technology, 13*, 14.

Phithakkitnukoon, S., Veloso, M., Bento, C., Biderman, A., & Ratti, C. (2010). Taxi-aware map: Identifying and predicting vacant taxis in the city. In *Proceedings of AmI'10* (pp. 86–95). Berlin/Heidelberg: Springer.

Powdermaker, H. (1966). *Stranger and friend: The way of an anthropologist.* New York: W. W. Norton & Company Inc.

Ramirez, L., Dyrks, T., Gerwinski, J., Betz, M., Scholz, M., & Wulf, V. (2012). *Landmarke: An ad hoc deployable ubicomp infrastructure to support indoor navigation of firefighters personal and ubiquitous computing* (Vol. 16, pp. 1025–1038). London: Springer.

Randall, D. W., Harper, R. H. R., & Rouncefield, M. (2007). *Fieldwork for design – Theory and practice. Computer supported cooperative work* (pp. i–xi). New York: Springer, 1–330. ISBN 978-1-84628-767-1.

Rattenbury, T., Nafus, D., & Anderson, K. (2008). Plastic: A metaphor for integrated technologies. In *Proceedings of the 10th international conference on Ubiquitous computing* (pp. 232–241). New York: ACM.

Robinson, M., Kovalainen, M., & Auramäki, E. (2000, January). Diary as dialogue in papermill process control. *Communications of the ACM, 43*(1), 65–70.

Rode, J. A. (2011). Reflexivity in digital anthropology. In *Proceedings of CHI 2011* (pp. 123–132). New York: ACM.

Rogers, Y. (2011). Interaction design gone wild: Striving for wild theory. *Interactions, 18*(4), 58–62.

Roto, V., Väätäjä, H., Jumisko-Pyykkö, S., & Väänänen-Vainio-Mattila, K. (2011, September). Best practices for capturing context in user experience studies in the wild. In *Proceedings of the 15th international academic MindTrek conference: Envisioning future media environments* (pp. 91–98). ACM.

Simonsen, J., & Kensing, F. (1997). Using ethnography in contextural design. *Communications of the ACM, 40*(7), 82–88.

Strasser, E., Weiss, A., Osswald, S., Grill, T., & Tscheligi, M. (2012). Combining implicit and explicit methods for the evaluation of an ambient persuasive factory display. In *AmI2012: Proceedings of the 6th European conference on ambient intelligence.* Springer, Currently Submitted.

Suchman, L. A. (1987). *Plans and situated actions: The problem of human-machine communication.* Cambridge: Cambridge University Press.

Viitanen, J. (2011). Contextual inquiry method for user-centred clinical it system design. *Studies in Health Technology and Informatics, 169*, 965–969.

Wax, R. H. (1971). *Doing fieldwork: Warning and advice.* University of Chicago Press.

Werner, O., Schoepfle, G. M., & Ahern, J. (1987). *Systematic fieldwork* (Vol. 1). Newbury Park: Sage.

Wilfinger, D., Meschtscherjakov, A., Murer, M., Osswald, S., & Tscheligi, M. (2011). Are we there yet? A probing study to inform design for the rear seat of family cars. In *Proceedings of the 13th IFIP TC 13 international conference on human-computer interaction – Volume Part II* (pp. 657–674). Heidelberg/New York: Springer.

Zachhuber, D., Grill, T., & Tscheligi, M. (2012). Contextual Wizard of Oz – A framework combining contextual rapid prototyping and the Wizard of Oz method. In *Proceedings of AMI 2012.* New York: ACM.

Chapter 13
Design for Agency, Adaptivity and Reciprocity: Reimagining AAL and Telecare Agendas

Geraldine Fitzpatrick, Alina Huldtgren, Lone Malmborg, Dave Harley, and Wijnand Ijsselsteijn

It goes without saying that the developed world is facing significant challenges in dealing with the increasing demands of an ageing population, especially around health and care. It is also easy to understand why technology is seen as a key enabler for meeting this challenge. Application areas such as Ambient Assisted Living (AAL) and telecare are receiving increasing governmental, industry and research attention, taking advantage of maturing and increasingly ubiquitous wireless, mobile and sensor-based technologies. However, to date, many of these advances have been largely driven by technology-utopian visions without real understanding for how such technologies come to be situated in everyday life and healthcare practice and what their potential is for enhancing new ways of living into older age. Further, there is limited evidence of their effectiveness to date, and the problems with adoption from the patients' perspectives suggest it is timely to reflect on these experiences and reimagine new ways of approaching AAL/telecare from a broader socio-technical perspective. To this end, we propose AAL/telecare as modular infrastructures for the home that can be adapted and repurposed, starting with personal 'quality of life' and social needs (supporting peer care) and progressing to monitoring, physical and medical needs (supporting formal care) as relevant for

G. Fitzpatrick (✉)
Vienna University of Technology, TUWIEN, Vienna, Austria
e-mail: geraldine.fitzpatrick@tuwien.ac.at

A. Huldtgren
TU Delft, Delft, The Netherlands

L. Malmborg
IT University of Copenhagen, Copenhagen, Denmark

D. Harley
Brighton University, Brighton, UK

W. Ijsselsteijn
TU Eindhoven, Eindhoven, The Netherlands

© Springer-Verlag London 2015
V. Wulf et al. (eds.), *Designing Socially Embedded Technologies in the Real-World*,
Computer Supported Cooperative Work, DOI 10.1007/978-1-4471-6720-4_13

a person and as needs evolve. This extends the adoption path to supporting healthy ageing, taking notions of agency, adaptivity and social reciprocity as core principles. We illustrate this with some examples and identify some of the associated technical and methodological challenges.

13.1 Introduction

The challenge of caring for an ageing population, and an increasing 'burden' of care for associated chronic diseases, is now the *de rigueur* mantra (and as we will argue later, in agreement with Mort et al. (2012), a problematic rhetorical turn) to motivate the need for new technology-enabled models of care. As such it is both emblematic of and a model for a consideration of those issues which are discussed elsewhere in this book—notions of social engagement, value sensitivity, user involvement/codesign and so on. The key agenda of such models is to enable people to be looked after in their own homes, thus avoiding the costs and inconveniences of expensive institutionalised care. Such approaches are variously called Ambient Assisted Living (AAL), telecare, telehealth, telemonitoring and so on. Whilst the exact definition of many of these terms is still evolving (Greenhalgh et al. 2012) and the choice of label can depend on the cultural context (e.g. the term AAL is commonly used in Europe but not so much in the United States), we will use AAL/telecare as a placeholder here and focus on the European (EU) perspective.

Among AAL/telecare solutions and service offerings, there is a huge diversity in the different configurations of technologies and in the degree of involvement of healthcare professionals. However, they all tend to encompass some or all of the following features: monitoring of *safety and security*, e.g. to detect water left running, via sensors that operate in isolation and generate alerts when events are detected; monitoring of *activities of daily living (ADL) and lifestyle monitoring* via a network of sensors in the home, again with some alerting function, e.g. for fall detection; and *physiological monitoring*, which usually involves some direct participation of the users, e.g. in taking blood pressure measurements.

At its core then, the vision of AAL/telecare, as a solution for the 'burden of care for an ageing population', is based on some form of remote monitoring, exploiting the potential of wireless and sensor-based technologies to track aspects of concern and exploiting the potential of Internet connectivity to provide some form of communication back to a monitoring centre or care provider.

Buying into this vision and the associated rhetoric, there has been a substantial investment of funds and resources into AAL/telecare, both in supporting research programmes and in actual deployments. For example, the AAL Joint Programme of the European Union (EU) was started in 2008 with investments in the order of 600 million Euros. The aim is to specifically encourage cross-national collaboration of small- and medium-sized enterprises (SME), research organisations and user groups 'to create better condition of life for older adults and to strengthen the industrial opportunities in Europe through the use of Information and Communication Technology (ICT)'.[1]

Another example is the various initiatives funded by the UK Department of Health around long-term conditions, a recent high profile one being the Whole System Demonstrator (WSD) programme.[2] The cluster randomised control trial (RCT) for the WSD involved over 3,000 patients with diabetes, chronic obstructive pulmonary disease or heart failure, attending 179 general practices from three different areas in England. The expectations of governments for AAL/telecare are reflected in the stated aims of the WSD: 'to show just what telehealth and telecare is capable of, to provide a clear evidence base to support important investment decisions and show how the technology supports people to live independently, take control and be responsible for their own health and care'.[3]

However, evidence for the success or otherwise of such AAL/telecare systems is decidedly mixed and points to the 'current gap between policy enthusiasm for tele-monitoring and its more limited uptake and impact in practice' (Greenhalgh et al. 2012). Mort et al. (2012) also draw critical attention to the negative rhetorics around AAL/telecare, i.e. of 'threats', 'burden', 'age time bomb', 'silver tsunami' and so on, the 'stigmatising and ageist rhetoric forms' used to motivate the move to AAL/telecare.

The main focus of this paper is to argue for a different rhetorical and practical view of AAL/telecare as being socially embedded and practically situated in the everyday homes and lives of the people for whom they are intended and where the experiences to date with such systems suggest it is timely to reconsider the conceptualisation and design of AAL/telecare systems from a broader socio-technical perspective. A more detailed motivation for this shift is presented in the next section where we review reported experiences to date.

13.2   Mixed Outcomes from AAL/Telecare Experiences to Date

The outcomes reported from various studies paint a mixed picture of the evidence base for AAL/telecare (see, e.g. Barlow et al. 2007; Brownsell et al. 2011; DelliFrance and Dansky 2008; Hardisty et al. 2011; Steventon et al. 2012).

---

[1] http://www.aal-europe.eu/about/objectives/

[2] http://webarchive.nationalarchives.gov.uk/+/www.dh.gov.uk/en/Healthcare/Longtermconditions/wholesystemdemonstrators/DH_084255

[3] https://www.gov.uk/government/publications/whole-system-demonstrator-programme-headline-findings-december-2011

As will be seen below, studies of deployments of AAL/telecare solutions are most often based on smaller-scale pilot projects and tend to follow the medical model of randomised control trials (RCTs), relying on quantifiable measures; as such they tend to focus on aspects of efficiency and effectiveness, where evidence for the success or otherwise is usually reported in terms of health and cost outcomes oriented towards the medical system, such as the use of care services (admissions to the hospital, length of stay, etc.), patient compliance, etc. More recently, some qualitative studies are also starting to appear but are still relatively rare.

Across the various studies, there are some reports of positive outcomes. A 2012 report on the WSD trial indicated a reduction in mortality rates, admissions and patient bed days (Steventon et al. 2012). (Others have also critiqued the design of the WSD RCT studies, e.g. because the unit of randomisation was the general practice and no comparable interventions were offered (McCartney 2012), thus raising question marks about possible bias and how much the positive results really stand.) A systematic review by DelliFrance and Dansky (2008) reported an overall 'moderate, positive and significant effect' on clinical outcomes such as fewer visits to the emergency room, fewer admissions, etc., especially for heart disease and psychiatric conditions but not, for example, for diabetes. A different systematic review by Barlow et al. (2007) concluded that the most effective interventions were automated 'vital signs' monitoring and telephone follow-up by nurses, both resulting in reduced use of healthcare services, but there was insufficient evidence, for example, around effects of safety and security monitoring or about the effects of telecare for asthma, dementia and depression. Neither review found sufficient evidence to suggest cost advantages to date, and a recent report on the WSD project even found that the costs of the telehealth intervention were higher and thus not cost effective compared to 'usual care' (Daugaard 2013, Personal communication with Henning Daugaard, Director of Social, Health and Employment affairs, Frederiksberg Municipality 2013–07–15; Frederiksberg Municipality 2013, p. 82), especially as patients reported similar quality outcomes in both conditions (Henderson et al. 2013). In summary then, there are some positive effects to be found, but it is hard to compare such reviews and outcomes because of the range of different interventions and diseases included. Further, clinical outcomes do not always translate into cost savings.

On the other hand, there are also many other reports and systematic reviews that are less positive, pointing to a lack of supporting evidence and highlighting more complex issues that go beyond the technology to the broader clinical, organisational, legal and support structures and processes into which telecare needs to be embedded. For example, a systematic review of what the authors termed 'lifestyle monitoring technologies', i.e. called AAL/telecare here, concluded that in fact the 'evidence base for lifestyle monitoring is relatively weak, even though there are significant numbers of commercial installations around the world' (Brownsell et al. 2011). Hardisty et al. (2011) also point to broader issues with the implementation of AAL/telecare (using the language of 'telemonitoring'), concluding that 'attempts to use telemonitoring [...] over the last two decades have so far failed to lead to systems that are embedded in routine clinical practice' (p. 734).

Some of the reasons for the lack of embedding into actual practice might be found in Fitzsimmons et al. (2011) who report from their experience of trying to set up an RCT of a preventative telehealth service for chronic obstructive pulmonary disease (COPD) that 'whilst the need to improve care delivery modalities [. . .] is recognized, in reality, the shift to the primary sector is proving more difficult to enact than initially anticipated'. Their experiences highlight the complex service delivery issues entailed in telecare, that can challenge traditional boundaries between local authorities and healthcare providers and that can require significant changes to established roles and responsibilities, working patterns, data flows and so on.

However, even though one of the critical issues around AAL/telecare solutions is adoption from the seniors' perspectives, this tends to receive much less attention in evaluation studies and reviews. The studies included in the reports above, as previously stated, tend to frame the evaluation in terms of clinical and cost outcome measures and in doing so prioritise the perspective of the service delivery/medical system. It is also to be noted that these outcome studies, by definition, only involve patients who have agreed to use the system. Where 'patient' perspectives are included in evaluations, they are often noted in terms of some overall statement about usability and user acceptance, often based on survey data. Qualitative studies on actual user experiences are relatively rare.

It is these more qualitative studies though, foregrounding the processes and experiences of people actually using AAL/telecare or not, that we use as motivators to argue for a shift on our conceptualisation of AAL/telecare. Gale and Sultan (2013), for example, draw attention to the ways in which such technologies 'can modify emotional and bodily experiences' for the COPD patients they interviewed, who reported 'peace of mind', in part due to the way that telehealth legitimised contact with their health professionals and gave them increased confidence. Aarhus and Ballegaard (2010) conduct a more in-depth ethnographic work across a number of technologies and conditions for supporting care at home and unpack what they call the 'elaborate boundary work' that people engage in 'to maintain the order of the home when managing disease and adopting new healthcare technology'. Müller et al. (2010), in a study of the use of location monitoring for people with Alzheimer's disease, identify dilemmas between awareness vs. privacy and safety vs. autonomy. All these studies therefore point to the adoption of AAL/telecare into everyday life as a highly complex negotiated process, involving modifications, negotiations, integrations and segregations as people both deal with the disease issue and work out how to get on with life.

Studies of people who do not take up AAL/telecare are also instructive about what is important from patients' perspectives. Sanders et al. (2012), for example, also studied the WSD project but focused on people who rejected participation or who agreed to participate but later withdrew from the trial (i.e. unlike some of the people in Gale and Sultan's (2013) study, they did not experience 'peace of mind'). In a qualitative analysis of interviews with these people, the authors identified a number of barriers to the participation and adoption of telehealth and telecare from the patients' perspective. These

included (1) concerns about *technical competence* and the need for special skills
to operate the equipment, (2) concerns about 'threats to *identity* associated with
positive ageing and self-reliance' and to independence by undermining 'self-
care and coping' and (3) concerns about *disruptions* to existing services that
they valued (an interesting concern against Gale and Sultan (2013), pointing out
that the same technology can be experienced very differently by different people).

Other barriers identified in the literature around adoption of AAL/telecare are
a lack of perceived usefulness (Huang 2011), lack of face-to-face contact with
caregivers, poor usability, lack of trust, increased professional responsibility, lack
of organisational willingness to change and financial barriers like the absence
of reimbursement arrangements (Reginatto 2012). There is also a concern that
'monitoring [...] may also increase the amount of information which flows from
users to carers, which can result in a form of function-creep that actually undermines
independence [for older people]' (Draper and Sorell 2012) and that can reduce social
contact more generally (Mahood et al. 2008).

13.2.1 Motivating a Re-imagination of AAL/Telecare

In summary, what we are seeing across these different studies, reviews and
methodological approaches are what Greenhalgh et al. (2012) identify as different discourses around AAL/telecare. These are '*modernist* (technology focused,
futuristic, utopian), *humanist* (person centred, small scale, grounded in present
reality), *political economy* (critical, cautious) and *change management* (recognising
complicatedness but not conflict)' (Greenhalgh et al. 2012). The authors go on to
call for closer working across discourses, stakeholders and perspectives.

Hardisty et al. (2011) move in this direction, and whilst their systematic review
could be regarded as taking more of a modernist perspective, their conclusions
clearly point out the need to integrate more of a humanist and change management
perspective (to use the categories above): 'Attempts at implementation have paid
insufficient attention to understanding patient and clinical needs and the complex
dynamics and accountabilities that rise at the level of service models. A suggested
way ahead is to co-design technology and services collaboratively with all stakeholders' (p. 734). This is an important call and highlights the value of taking a
socio-technical practice-based perspective and involving all stakeholder concerns.

Roberts and Mort (2009), coming from a humanist perspective, characterise three
distinct areas of telecare discourses: monitoring, physical care and social–emotional
care. They argue that telecare only tends to deal with monitoring (that can be seen
as a modernist perspective) and that this 'fails to account for the complexities of
all kinds of care (physical, social-emotional and telecare)'. They go on to argue
that 'what counts as care needs to be rethought if telecare is to make a positive
contribution to the lives of older people and those who care for and about them'
(Roberts and Mort 2009) and that it is time for 're-imagining the aims of telecare

and redesigning systems to allow for creative engagement with technologies and the co-production of care relations' (Mort et al. 2012).

This is the call we take up in this chapter, to reimagine the aims of telecare and from this redesign such systems to allow for creative engagement and the co-production of care relations. Mort et al. (2012) started this re-imagination by reframing 'telecare users as embodied, located at home [. . . and care] as a temporal and negotiated achievement that requires shared work' (p. 11). We build on this to add a more practical design-oriented view. Significant in our reimagining of telecare is a decentring of the notion of 'practice' away from the formal care practices via the delivery of health and social *care* and towards the everyday lived experiences and practices of *ageing* (and later discussed in Sect. 13.6, as 'situated elderliness') as experienced by older people themselves. It is also informed by understanding some of the processual and experiential issues noted above and by considering how to address some of the barriers to adoption noted by Sanders et al. (2012).

The contribution of this chapter then is to add to this re-imagination of the design of AAL/telecare by focusing on the patients' perspectives. In saying this, it is also worth stating two aspects that are equally important for this re-imagination but beyond the scope of this chapter to address. Firstly, in an ultimate solution, the needs of both the clinicians/service organisations *and* the patients, and their family/friends, have to be considered, as argued by Hardisty et al. (2011); to manage scope here and to address what we see as a 'stakeholder' group that has received least attention, we put the focus first on older people. Future work will also need to reimagine, e.g. service delivery models from an organisational or clinical perspective. Secondly, a focus on the patient's perspective and on taking a more 'everyday ageing' practice-based view of AAL/telecare raises the challenge of finding evaluation methods that can account not just for the medical system-oriented outcomes, but also the practical everyday processes through which such outcomes are achieved by all participants, the older person, their peers/informal cares and the formal care system, as well as evaluating the lived experiences of such systems. Future work is needed to develop these new holistic methods of evaluation.

What we focus on here is a re-imagination of AAL/telecare that integrates both modernist and humanist perspectives and reframes the wireless- and sensor-based technologies of *AAL/telecare as modular infrastructures* for the home that can be *adapted and repurposed*. In this way the same base infrastructure can address personal quality of life and social needs in the first instance and can also involve monitoring for physical and social care needs as relevant for a person. It can make use of explicit communication channels and more implicit mutual awareness opportunities, e.g. by the appropriation of AAL-/telecare-type sensors in the person's home and providing engaging creative visualisations of the activities of others in the care network. That is, the same base infrastructure can be used for social interaction, preventative health/health promotion and more formal care and monitoring arrangements as needs evolve (illustrated in the 'future scenario' below and also later in Case 5).

Future scenario: adaptive solutions for AAL/telecare from peer care to healthcare

In our imagined future, social care and healthcare services offer an integrated support service. Mr. Jones and his neighbour had read about the range of community modules on offer by the service. After his neighbour's wife died, they discussed how they could keep a better eye on each other, so during their next annual 'health and well-being' check with the community care officer, they took up the offer of a base 'neighbour-aware' system. This involved having a video camera and video conferencing system installed in each of their homes that they could use to connect to each other by touching their photos. It also involved having some basic movement sensors installed in the living room. By giving permission for this information to be shared at a very simplified and privacy-preserving level, they can both see some abstract images that they have chosen to indicate a general sense of themselves and the other person. They use this as additional means to be in contact between their weekly card games and to keep an eye on each other.

Some time later, Mr. Jones has a cardiac episode, and on return from the hospital, the community nurse and his cardiologist suggest that he has some additional sensors installed in more rooms at home and that could detect if he falls. He thinks this is a good idea because he knows now how they work and discusses with the nurse exactly where they should be installed and who can see what level of information about him. He is also given a heart rate monitor to wear that communicates with his base station.

His neighbour still keeps a close eye on him with the very simple living room information and the video connection as before, but now, the data being collected by his additional sensors and the heart rate monitor are further processed and sent to his community nurse so that she can monitor his health status. Mr. Jones is also interested to see how his heart rate changes with different activity levels, and it helps him keep up with his activities at a more even pace.

This re-imagination reframes therefore *when* such technologies can be considered, creating an adoption path that can start with self-motivated social needs and opportunities, connecting with informal peer care networks, in a nonthreatening and noncritical context. The installation and use of these technologies also lay the foundation for people to gain familiarity and technical expertise in a relaxed way, hence addressing issues of self-efficacy; i.e. 'to develop training for users to use telecare, it is likely to be helpful to reduce users' anxiety and improve usage of telecare' as stated by Huang (2011). The goal then is that issues of acceptance can be dealt with via the motivation to accept the technologies because of their perceived social usefulness and providing an opportunity to contribute and that the subsequent familiarity with the technology will increase ongoing adoption (Mahmood et al. 2008) when more critical care needs arise.

In taking the patients' perspective for this re-imagination, we go back to the first principles and revisit notions of ageing, emphasising positive views of ageing as an adaptive developmental process and embedding the concerns about health conditions into an everyday life perspective (Sect. 13.3). This shifts the emphasis and language, from 'patients' to 'people'. We also use the terms 'seniors' and 'older people' interchangeably to reflect more positive stances on ageing.[4]

We then go on in Sect. 13.4 to explore new person-centred opportunities for AAL/telecare technologies as infrastructure, focusing particularly on notions of agency and reciprocity as key principles. Sections 13.5 and 13.6 then explore some of the technical and methodological challenges to designing reimagined AAL/telecare services.

13.3 Reconceptualising Ageing

A key starting point for this reimagining is a re-conceptualisation of the notion of ageing so that it can reflect the lived experiences of older people themselves and characterise them as active agents in their own care. We look at this issue from two different disciplinary perspectives, Gerontology and Psychology, where theories in both point to similar underlying phenomena of agency and adaptivity. This also means acknowledging the opportunities for social and self-development that persist as significant markers of well-being into advanced age alongside the more formal care demands that may develop and point to the opportunities around social connectivity and reciprocity.

13.3.1 Lived Experiences and a Turn to Agency and Adaptivity

A dominant focus on 'modernist' or monitoring approaches tends to conceptualise old age from an objective and deficit-driven perspective perpetuating a notion of ageing as an ongoing 'diminishment' of function. This can obscure older people's sense of agency in the context of care and undermine opportunities for ongoing development in other areas of life. Several theoretical notions have been put forward to support the view that significant development does continue in later life.[5] In particular here, we draw on theories of ageing that regard *ageing as a positive developmental lifespan process* (Tornstam 1989), which emphasises our

---

[4]We note that the use of language/terminology here is politically sensitive, but we also note that what is regarded as a more 'politically correct' term is often dependent on culture and context and that there is no universal agreement. In the end it is the attitudes, values and practices we bring as practitioners that will speak louder than words.

[5]We recognise too that there are many different theories of ageing and that there is no universal agreement across disciplines about how to conceptualise ageing. In presenting a range of different theorists' positions, our intention is not to advocate a particular one but rather to stimulate thinking differently about older people and to orient to more positive developmental notions of ageing.

focus on the relational and self-oriented aspects of daily life as significant in maintaining well-being. For example, Baltes and colleagues (Baltes 1993; Baltes and Baltes 1990; Baltes and Carstensen 1999) suggest that the developmental opportunities of 'successful ageing' take place when there is an awareness of ageing limitations married to *selectivity with optimisation and compensation*. This allows older people to maintain their quality of life by deliberately narrowing their life choices (selectivity) so that they can optimise existing capabilities (e.g. optimising arithmetic skills by doing Sudoku puzzles) and/or compensate for those that are in decline (e.g. compensating for poor memory by writing things down). Joyce and Loe (2010) extend a similar view of older adults as active adaptive agents to technology, arguing that 'far from passive consumers, elders are technogenarians, creatively utilizing and adapting technological artefacts such as walking aids and medications to fit their needs'.

Carstensen extends the selectivity model to include *socioemotional* goals highlighting the increasing significance of social connections as we age. Carstensen suggests we see, as a positive choice by older people, a deliberate narrowing of social connections in favour of longstanding intimate social ties in order to maintain ongoing activities, a sense of purpose in life and ultimately the integrity of the self in lieu of approaching death (Carstensen 1992, 2006; Carstensen et al. 1999). Others have suggested that advanced age may also invite a contemplative form of development through which an older person comes to reframe their relationship to themselves and others. Through this process of *gerotranscendence*, they may become more altruistic, lose their fear of death and learn to appreciate solitude and the mundane aspects of their life (Tornstam 2005).

Such theories of ageing show older people not as passive recipients of the physical ageing process (and the prescribed care that may accompany it) but as self-aware agents of change who are resourceful in dealing with the failings of their own body and adapting their behaviour, self-concept and relationships with others to maintain a quality of life. These adaptations are central to the lived experience of ageing and can be seen to constitute an individual's own particular 'practice' in relation to it. However, these can also be at odds with the practices of health and social care. Tornstam and Toernqvist (2000) found that gerotranscendent behaviours such as changes in the perception of time and the seeking of solitude were often interpreted as signs of dementia by care staff rather than as anything positive for that individual. Interestingly, the limiting of social contact described by socioemotional selectivity theory (Carstensen 1992) would similarly be deemed unhealthy by proponents of Active Aging,[6] an influential paradigm for health and social care throughout Europe and beyond (WHO 2002).

Self-determination theory (SDT) from Psychology also provides interesting perspectives to consider in reimagining AAL/telecare. Whilst not specifically targeted to older people, but in line with the fuller and more active characterisation of old

---

[6]Active Aging – a competing paradigm which suggests greater social involvement in society is always a good thing

age from above, SDT takes as a starting position that people have deep tendencies towards psychological growth and development, where well-being is defined as vital and full functioning (Ryan and Deci 2001). Self-determination theory postulates a number of key components for well-being: autonomy, competence and relatedness. First, *autonomy* refers to the universal urge to be the causal agent of one's own life. This does not imply, however, that one necessarily needs to be independent of others (Deci and Vansteenkiste 2004).

Second, *competence* refers to the extent to which an individual is effective in dealing with the environment in which one finds oneself. This is closely tied to concepts of *independence and self-efficacy*, which is of special relevance to the relationship seniors have with self-efficacy of care and their relation to modern technology in general. A necessary ingredient of satisfying interaction with technology is self-efficacy (Bessiere et al. 2006), defined as a person's belief about their own capabilities to produce designated levels of performance that exercise influence over events that affect their lives (Bandura 1977). Lack of self-efficacy can hinder adoption of new technology, as has been found in relation to the WSD discussed earlier. The level of self-efficacy is also related to stress. Increasing self-efficacy is associated with decreasing stress, and seniors in particular are more vulnerable to stress than younger adults (Hawkley and Cacioppo 2004), especially when stress affects, and is affected by, interface use (Hawthorn 2000). In particular older users could be negatively affected by stress during interaction with new media.

Finally, *relatedness* is the universal need to be socially connected to others in meaningful ways and involves both caring for others and having others care for you. Relatedness is experienced as a sense of communion/community through developing close and intimate relationships with others, and different people will have different needs for degrees of relatedness. Whilst SDT is largely defined with respect to the individual and to explore issues of motivation, the principles of SDT can also be practically interpreted as always being embedded in a social context and for older adults; such issues of relatedness can also be interpreted in relation to the socioemotional selectivity noted above.

When these three needs are supported and satisfied within a social context, people experience more vitality, self-motivation and well-being. In cases where such needs are systematically frustrated, this has been associated with psychopathology (Ryan et al. 2006). Hirsch et al. (2000) similarly point to the importance of independence (e.g. being able to care for oneself) and engagement (e.g. being able to participate in social activities) for quality of life and physical and cognitive health.

So what do these mean for the re-imagination of AAL/telecare? Overall, these theories point to the importance of *taking agency seriously* and raise challenges for how agency can be maintained and supported by new technologies. This can play out in a number of ways. Firstly, we suggest that the notions of active agency and autonomy provide arguments against system approaches that rely solely on passive monitoring or being surrogate data collectors for others' use. Currently, monitoring systems rarely give the seniors the chance to interact with and adjust the system; instead, the systems, and the data they collect, are mostly used by the service provider and/or informal carers to check on the seniors' situation.

This, as noted previously, 'actually undermines independence [for older people]' (Draper and Sorell 2012). Secondly, if we understand the importance of self-efficacy and competence, coupled with active agency, then strategies that enable people to develop skills and understandings around AAL/telecare in nonthreatening ways become important for adoption (Mahmood et al. 2008). Thirdly, if we understand the importance of 'selectivity with optimisation and compensation' as a positive adaptive strategy for maintaining a quality of life, it points to opportunities to further develop AAL/telecare as modular infrastructure that seniors can interact with to support their adaptation practices.

These theories also point to the importance of *meaningful social connectivity and relatedness*, with specific understandings of the need for more in-depth relationships (rather than many social ties, which seems to be the focus of Facebook and such) and the sense of purpose. We move on to discuss these social issues in more detail.

13.3.2   Social Connectivity and a Turn to Reciprocity

The importance of meaningful social connectivity and relatedness for well-being and quality of life is shown by studies of people who do not have the level of social contact that they want (as opposed to the positive sense of having fewer but more in-depth friendships noted above).

The experience of growing older in many societies is often associated with increasing levels of social isolation and reduced community involvement. This can be due, for example, to increased mobility and geographic distribution of families, to a decrease in physical mobility and ability on the part of the older person to engage in local communities and to their diminishing social networks due to bereavement and frailty (Lindley et al. 2008; Pedell et al. 2010). Social isolation, when experienced as loneliness, has been shown to negatively impact on emotional and psychological well-being, increasing an older person's susceptibility to depression (Choi and McDougall 2007), and cognitive decline (Zunzunegui et al. 2003), as well as being linked to poor functional health (Thomson and Heller 1990) and all causes of mortality and morbidity (House et al. 1988). Conversely, good social relationships have been identified as a key contributing factor to the quality of life for people over 65 (Gabriel and Bowling 2004, cited in Lindley et al. 2008).

However, such characterisations of social relationships tend to oversimplify the nature and complexity of relationships in later life, pointed to above in terms of expected and positively framed decreases in the size of social networks, but also in terms of differences in relationships with families versus friends/peers, and the more nuanced aspects of social interactions in terms of reciprocity, symmetry, dignity and self-worth, responsibilities, etc. (Lindley et al. 2008).

Reciprocity and symmetry, for example, are important aspects to draw attention to and highlight the two-way nature of social connectivity. This can be contrasted to the current framing of many AAL/telecare solutions which puts the person into a position of being a generator of signals to be sensed and a recipient of care, captured in the concerns above about loss of identity and independence. This in turn puts them in a disadvantaged position where systematically being in a receiving position may be associated with potential negative consequences such as mental distress and discontinuities or disruptions of relationships (Gregory 1994). An over-benefited status (receiving more than giving) typically undermines a person's sense of self-worth and independence, and seniors generally share a reluctance to accept 'charity', as this is closely associated with feelings of indebtedness, dependency, incompetence, shame and decreased self-worth. As DePaulo (1982) stated: 'In our eagerness to find ways to help needy populations (such as the elderly and the handicapped), perhaps we have too often overlooked one of the most genuinely rewarding and mutually satisfying arrangements- encouraging the "needy" to give useful help as well as to receive it'.

Moreover, current imagining of AAL/telecare may lead to further detachment from one's social network, as seniors generally find it more acceptable to give than to receive, causing a reluctance to seek help or maintain relationships where one is on the receiving end. This can further increase the level of social isolation and reduced community involvement that is associated with old age where social support networks tend to become smaller and less accessible. Both the decreased size of the social network as well as its reciprocal imbalance are known to have a negative impact on emotional and physical well-being (Choi and McDougall 2007; House et al. 1988). However, the impact of this imbalance can be dependent on the type of relationship, where, for example, parent/child relationships may tolerate a larger imbalance in reciprocity than relationships with friends, neighbours or more distant relations (James et al. 1984).

Therefore, central to our re-imagination of AAL/telecare is the concept of *reciprocity*: the process of 'give and take' that creates balance and stability in people's social relations. Reciprocity is one of the basic mechanisms underlying social relationships and is known to predict better mental health and life quality, than being in an over-benefited position (see Fyrand 2010 for a review). By taking this notion of reciprocity as a point of departure, our re-imagination moves AAL/telecare on from the current discourse around old age as primarily a period of loss, decline and consequent 'over-benefited' dependency through being 'done to' and 'monitored' by a formal care system: it moves it instead towards one of the continued engagements with an extended social network on the basis of continuous, mutual exchange of both instrumental and noninstrumental support, adapting to abilities and practicalities as the individual's issues and needs evolve. In so doing, it also mobilises an informal peer network in complement to, and parallel with, a formal care network.

In the following section, we move on to explore how such re-imaginations of AAL/telecare solutions might be realised, taking agency and reciprocity as core principles and embracing it as a socio-technical design challenge. A key element of the approach is the exploration of how sensors and devices that are part of AAL/telecare solutions can be taken as basic infrastructures to be repurposed to support other needs and so extend the adoption path back into healthier older age.

13.4 New Opportunities for Designing AAL/Telecare as Social Infrastructure

A number of authors, especially in the areas of human–computer interaction (HCI) and computer-supported cooperative work (CSCW), have started to draw attention to the design challenges associated with older people and the design of care technologies for the home (e.g. see Axelrod et al. 2009; Blythe et al. 2005; Fitzpatrick 2012; Grönvall and Kyng 2012). Blythe et al. (2005) point to the importance of considering a design perspective through understanding the 'users' and settings by labelling it as 'socially dependable design'. The home has also been identified as having very particular characteristics as a setting for care technologies (e.g. Aarhus and Ballegaard 2010; Axelrod et al. 2009; Blythe et al. 2005; Fitzpatrick 2012). This creates very specific design-related challenges, recognising that technologies designed to support a medicalised model of care in hospital need to be 'fit for care', but technologies designed for care at home need to be 'fit for life' and able 'to take account of the huge complexity and diversity of lived experiences at home' (Fitzpatrick 2012). Two general challenges arise then: design for integration, e.g. into everyday spaces, routines and practices and into the social context of the home, and design for active participation, e.g. via collaborative control and interpretation and active reflective engagement (Fitzpatrick 2012).

We take these challenges as given and go on to explore some specific examples showing how a person-centred socio-technical design orientation can open new types of functionalities and uses for AAL/telecare solutions for enabling peer networks and peer support. The cases paint a picture of a new path to adoption and show how sensors and devices can be repurposed to support other needs at an early stage of engagement, focusing on adaptive 'healthy ageing' and peer engagement, as a base for later moving to more supported ageing and professional care models, using the same core infrastructure.

13.4.1 Supporting Social Connectivity

An obvious and early 'repurpose' of AAL/telecare is the use of explicit communication channels. Many AAL/telecare solutions already include video conferencing capabilities and other communication channels such as email, chat, etc. To date, these have largely been thought about as supporting interaction with formal carers, as in doctors or nurses or a monitoring centre. However, these are *just* communication channels and form part of the communication infrastructure of the home.

Can we consider ways to install these channels earlier than just when a healthcare need arises? There is already increasing evidence about the uptake of video by seniors, especially in the form of 'Skype', 'YouTube' and similar products, motivated by a desire of seniors to keep in touch with remote family members, particularly grandchildren (Sayago et al 2011; Milliken et al 2012). There are also many prototype devices exploring such connectivity (e.g. Lindley 2011; Waycott et al 2013). The technology can just as well be used to communicate with friends and to expand into new social networks. However, these platforms are often independent from any broader notion of care infrastructure, and there are opportunities to better integrate these as first steps of an overall AAL/telecare solution. The case of 'geriatric1927' (Harley 2011; Harley and Fitzpatrick 2009) (Case 1) is useful to illustrate some of the benefit of such communications.

Case 1: geriatric1927 and reciprocal care via YouTube

Geriatric1927 (real name Peter Oakley) is an 86-year-old video blogger from the North of England who started posting videos onto the YouTube website in August 2006. Since then, he has become a hugely popular YouTuber posting 402 videos and having 41,074 subscribers to his channel (as of 12 June, 2013). Peter who lives on his own has found his involvement with the YouTube community to be a transformative experience in terms of social opportunities and his ongoing development of self. What started off as an opportunity to tell his life story to the younger generation (Harley and Fitzpatrick 2009) quickly developed into new roles for Peter with him acting as an informal advisor to troubled teenagers, older people's champion on the Internet, comedian and singer (Harley 2011).

Whilst these roles have come with a certain degree of responsibility, they have also provided Peter with an important opportunity for reciprocity, allowing him to give something back to this community and the younger generation. Peter's development of an online YouTube presence has also meant that the computer is now an ever-present source of social contact and companionship within his home. When sitting down to make a new video, he says, 'I sort of know who I'm talking to, not individually but we are back to this homogenous huggable community' (Harley 2011, p. 163). Some of Peter's YouTube friendships have also developed beyond YouTube with some making regular contact by email and Skype and others coming to visit him at his home.

13.4.2   Supporting Informal and Implicit Social Awareness

Whilst such social networking technologies provide opportunities for explicit interaction and communication, there are also ways to repurpose passively collected data to support implicit social awareness and peer interactions. This is data that can be captured from the embedded sensors, such as those used in AAL/telecare solutions, as well as data from smartphones if available and used (such as GPS location, accelerometer data and so on) and the data from social networking connectivity.

In a reimagined AAL/telecare scenario, peer networks can provide a first line of informal mutual care and support, where the participants' activity and lifestyle-based monitoring data can be represented in some lightweight and engaging way to be *reciprocally* shared with family and peers, as decided by the person who owns the data. For the people on the receiving end of this information, it is analogous to keeping an eye on your neighbour's curtains and getting to know their routines without needing to know the precise details of those routines (Riche and Mackay 2010). Neighbours do this for each other, hence promoting reciprocity.

Having such awareness can then trigger further opportunities to make personal contact, e.g. through visiting/meeting together or using the phone or some social networking platform for more explicit and active interactions. In this way, the opportunity for informal peer care by background awareness can also provide new non-threatening, non-stigmatising reasons to install AAL-/telecare-type activity sensors and puts in place the core monitoring technologies that can later be used for more formal care scenarios. It can also help build familiarity with those technologies.

Case 2: neighbours engaging in reciprocal peer care and the markerClock

In a study with 14 older participants, living independently in Paris, Riche (2008; see also Riche and Mackay 2010) explored the role of communication in maintaining independence and well-being. His results highlighted the key role of peer support in providing reciprocal care among friends and neighbours, their desire for nonintrusive means of communication and the ways they used an awareness of the other's rhythms and routines of daily life as a way of building awareness of each others' activities and well-being status.

Based on these insights, Riche (2008) developed the design concept of *PeerCare* and illustrated this with a *markerClock prototype* as an augmented clock representation with an ambient display. The display was based on implicitly collected motion data, reflecting people's home activities as if they had been sensed by AAL-/telecare-type sensors, and represented by symbolic codes to communicate status and routines. A study using the markerClock as a technology probe between friends 'confirmed the role of rhythm awareness in peer support and highlighted the need for value in direct communication'.

To date, AAL/telecare scenarios have largely interpreted the use of activity monitoring sensors as being embedded in the home, e.g. motion sensors in rooms, sensors to detect door openings, stove use, etc. This inadvertently frames daily life for older people as tethered to the home and does not recognise them as active participants in a broader community or indeed having mundane practices around the need to shop and so on within the limits of their abilities.

In a reimagined AAL/telecare scenario, there is also an opportunity to rethink where and how sensors are embedded, extending beyond the walls of the house or apartment, and to also embrace more everyday objects. Case 3, about Walky (Nazzi et al. 2012), illustrates this by combining an augmented walking aid and dedicated displays.

Case 3: Walky and instrumenting everyday objects for social awareness

The project SeniorInteraction (Brandt et al. 2010, 2012) introduced reciprocity in design for social interaction among senior citizens in two different living labs in urban neighbourhoods. Based on the idea of creating 'tickets to talk', everyday objects and everyday activities were augmented to establish an infrastructure for ad hoc meetings in the everyday life of senior citizens. One design concept of augmenting everyday objects with sensors is the Walky (Nazzi et al. 2012):

Danny lives in Bloomdale senior-housing and is 75 years old. He uses a walking aid to walk. He is a member of a shopping group that he initiated with five seniors in Bloomdale housing. Danny usually goes shopping twice a week. Whilst he uses his augmented walking aid, it broadcasts status notifications to his shopping friends.

During his breakfast, Peter, a member of Danny's shopping group, sees an update from his shopping friends on his tablet computer in the kitchen: 'Danny is out shopping'. Peter remembers the four bags of coffee discount offer in the supermarket and decides to ask Danny if he would like to share this offer.

Simultaneously, Danny's walking aid emits a mild vibration from its handles, making Danny notice that one of his friends has a shopping message. He calls Peter, and they decide to share the coffee offer.

Back at Bloomdale again, Peter – longing for company – invites Danny for a cup of coffee.

The general mechanism behind Walky is communicating by doing. A person, by simply using a walking aid, broadcasts activity clues to her specific community. At the same time, through feedback from her walking aid or from dedicated displays, a person can receive notifications from her community friends and notice their activity. Further, through very simple actuators, also walking aids themselves can become displays of what is happening in the specific community.

This scenario illustrates the role of everyday objects in mediating a situated human-to-human communication using a sensor-based infrastructure, the situatedness of the technology intended to facilitate seniors in the process of making their activity noticeable for others and to notice others' activity, the possibilities for social interactions opened up by simple reciprocal exchanges of clues and previous knowledge about each other's routines. The strategy of Walky for non-stigmatising social interaction is to enable senior citizens' act of sharing everyday activities for different purposes, without explicitly having to reveal what they are doing.

13.4.3 Supporting Self-Awareness and Reflection

In some cases, the collected sensor-based data could also be made available for the individual, whose data has been collected, for personal reflection and self-awareness.

Case 4: eHome project and data for self-reflection

The eHome project (Fitzpatrick 2012; Panek and Hlauschek 2011) involved a prototype AAL environment of an adaptive network of wireless sensors for activity monitoring where the system could learn and adapt to the behaviour patterns of the user. The prototype system was deployed in the homes of 11 people for a period of 3 months as part of a pilot study. To help researchers validate the sensor data (as this was a prototype), participants were asked to fill in a paper diary about their activities and movements.

One of the participants had always thought she cooked a lot for herself, but it wasn't until she looked back over the data she was recording about her actual cooking habits (used to check that the sensors on the stove top were working) that she realised she actually didn't cook very much at all for herself and that her diet was not good. She used this as a stimulus to change her habits towards better cooking and eating.

Whilst the data that prompted her to reflect on and change her behaviours was from a paper diary, it still points to the potential of having such data available from automatic sensor detection and being able to present it back in interesting ways, to the people about whom the data is being collected, for their own sensemaking purposes.

Working with the data in these ways could also help address self-efficacy and empowerment issues and lay the foundation for increased agency in more formal care scenarios. It can help educate the person about what sort of data can be collected by AAL/telecare infrastructures and empower them through knowledge to better engage in discussions about how and to whom to make such information available. When the technologies are installed by free choice for a positive self-benefit, rather than being framed as putting the person into an over-benefited needy position, it can also be envisaged that there would be higher acceptance and in the end greater self-efficacy through voluntary engagement.

In summary, there are many ways that AAL-type technologies can be repurposed to support earlier adoption in support of quality of life needs around social interaction, reciprocity and self-reflection. We emphasise here too that when we have talked about 'peer care', we have been talking about people caring for each other, supporting each other within a community and being complements to, rather than surrogates for, the formal healthcare system. The illustrative cases further show that the type of sensing that can be done (in AAL) is not only useful for seniors who are 'needy' in some way but to the whole community. In the YouTube case

(Case 1), the younger people benefited as much as Peter from their intergenerational engagement with him. The Walky example (Case 3) could also be used by younger or more mobile people in a community to optimise their shopping and time (e.g. by people who are very busy). The sensors could be in a shopping bag instead of a walker. For the reflection case (Case 4), again, learning about one's habits could be equally interesting for the old and young. An interesting aspect of this reimagined use of AAL/telecare is that it can help to significantly reduce the stigma if the solutions are not specifically for the older and less mobile people.

13.5 Open Technical Challenges for a Reimagined AAL/Telecare Agenda

In this chapter we have reconsidered AAL/telecare from a broader socio-technical perspective, taking the senior's perspective and their everyday practices as a point of departure. We have proposed that reimagining both the purposes of AAL/telecare technologies, and when and how they are implemented, might help also address some of the adoption challenges associated with current AAL/telecare deployments.

To realise such a vision, however, one of the key technical challenges to be addressed is how to personalise and visualise sensed data for non-professionals and for the purposes of peer awareness, peer care and self-reflection. Example questions include:

1. How to integrate heterogeneous sources of personal data for very different 'social' and personal purposes, compared to the precision and accuracy needed for formal care purposes:

   - From outside the home, e.g. using location and mobility data from smartphones/mobile devices
   - From inside the home, e.g. using home activity by repurposing data from AAL/telecare in-home sensors
   - From communication/social connectivity patterns, e.g. using network data from the above and perhaps from phones (calls made/received, etc.)

2. What are the new 'lightweight' ways of making this data available in different ways to peers and/or family, as chosen by the person, to support mutual awareness of each other's activities?

   - How to present creative/ambient visualisations of this data in a way that preserves privacy but gives a feel for general activity/well-being of the person?

3. How to give people control over their own data?

   - How to enable direct control by the person to configure what data is collected from which sensors?
   - How to enable adaptive personalisation of how that data is presented, so that the person is in control of who can see what at what level of granularity?

4. What sorts of display platforms can fit into the home and be easy to use (form, modalities of interaction, etc.)?
5. How can sensors be embedded into other everyday objects (similar to the Walky case) to support situated actions and keep the interaction with the sensors easy?

As an example, we go on here to discuss the visualisation of AAL/telecare data for non-professional uses in more detail.

13.5.1 Example Technical Challenge: Visualisation of Sensor Data for Non-professionals

Visualisation of sensor data in AAL/telecare more generally is an underexplored area (Cook 2012). Current approaches to personalising and visualising sensed data are mainly focused on the professional carer, where the focus is on the analysis and trend and/or event detection for raising alerts, not on the representation and particularly not on any representation for seniors and their peers and/or informal carers. Where representations of the data are used, they tend to be oriented to the monitoring service or to the system developers and take the form of complex visual/graphical interfaces with numerical data or of graphic renderings of the physical layout of sensors in space with annotations to indicate activities (Lotfi et al. 2012; Thomas and Crandall 2011). Some representational work is emerging to create visualisations of assistive smart home data for formal caregivers, e.g. using an Activity Dashboard (Cook 2012), reflecting more general trends in the use of clinical dashboards for healthcare data.

Other approaches to representing such data for the individual or carer are emerging, but these do not account for their personalisable use in a diverse peer network. Early examples of visualisations for informal carers include Digital Family Portraits (Mynatt et al. 2001) and Intel's CareNet Display (Consolvo et al. 2004), both using an image of the older person surrounded by a display indicating activity status. Whilst CareNet Display uses explicit icons to represent particular 'activities of daily living' (ADL) (e.g. knife and fork to represent a meal eaten), Digital Family Portraits uses a more abstract display of changing butterflies around the border to indicate general activity. We propose instead a more ambiguous lightweight display to indicate activity.

A key technical challenge then is exploring new 'lightweight' privacy-preserving ways of making data (from monitoring 'activities of daily living' from in-home sensors, social network activity, etc.) available to chosen peers/family to support reciprocal awareness of each other's activities. This provides a new dimension of support for peer communities, linking to AAL/telecare infrastructures and complementing formal support structures.

One approach to address this is to draw on the notion of 'ambiguity as a resource for design' (Gaver et al. 2003) and of representation 'as response rather than reality' (Boehner 2009). Presenting smart home data in an ambiguous form allows, on the one hand, the senior to preserve their privacy, and, on the other hand, it allows multiple interpretations (Aoki and Woodfruff 2005) by the receiver of the information, i.e. peers, informal or formal caregivers. The latter can interpret the visualised information openly and act according to their own interpretation.

This can in turn address an ethical concern with regard to AAL/telecare technology that allows informal caregivers to access monitoring data of the senior at all times and thereby putting new responsibility on them to act in case something is wrong. Informal caregivers with non-stop access to data could even be made accountable for threats to the health and well-being of their senior relative/patient and maybe, thereby, experience stress not to miss any crucial data. Ambiguous data displays could prevent such risks. It also addresses another concern about the imbalance in the care relationship by promoting mutual sharing and awareness between peers using the same system or between young and old family members.

There are some examples illustrating approaches to using ambiguity with sensor-based data that can be used as initial sources of design inspiration. One example is the Affective Diary (Ståhl et al. 2009), which focusses on an individual and is designed for self-reflection. Vibe Reflector (Boehner et al. 2003) does this similarly but for a group in a shared experience situation. Examples of ambiguous displays for home-based data include the work of Shankar et al. (2012) who have created alternative ambient displays using everyday objects such as a plant and clock, augmented with visual displays of activity data via lights, to give a remote carer a 'sense' of the presence of the remote person. However, these prototypes are focussed on one person and their carer, not a peer community, and on one-way monitoring though there would be no reason to expect, they could not also be used reciprocally.

The only work we are aware of to cater for shared ambiguous peer visualisations is the design concept of PeerCare with its markerClock prototype as previously described (Riche 2008; Riche and MacKay 2010), using a clock representation and imagining access to activity data to support 'awareness of rhythms and routines' between a pair of neighbours, but not implemented. This is further described in Case 5.

Case 5: markerClock revisited[7] and imagining evolving care need scenario

> Case 2 outlined the study that led to the design concept of *PeerCare* that was then illustrated in a *markerClock prototype* (Riche 2008). To provide more details, markerClock augments a familiar object in the home, a clock, and makes use of people's 'familiarity of the time/space mapping'. Awareness of routines is achieved using a trace of motion that is detected by a webcam in front of the markerClock, which is then represented as spiral traces in concentric rings showing the last 12 h of information for each person. There

(continued)

---

[7]http://www.yannriche.net/markerclock.php

are also symbolic codes to which the peers can assign their own meaning (e.g. 'I'm going to bed', 'It's time for our TV show') and then drop these onto the trace as a lightweight form of active communication.

The markerClock is displayed on a PC or tablet-sized screen, which each person locates in a central living area. Riche explicitly addresses the issues of negotiating privacy concerns by choosing not to do any aggregation or pre-interpretation of the data and using an ambiguous display. This then let the people themselves engage in the sensemaking and interpretation.

As an example of infrastructure that can evolve with care needs and creating different representations for different needs, one could imagine a situation when one of the participants later develops some healthcare needs that require more formal monitoring. The same activity data could still be collected and displayed as usual for their peer, and in parallel, the data could also be aggregated and processed to be presented in a more detailed and unambiguous way to the formal care provider, e.g. processed to look for deviations from usual patterns or indicators of decline. Additional symbolic codes could also be added in to enable the person to actively communicate their status to their formal care provider. The same familiar infrastructure evolved to meet changing needs.

13.6 Open Methodological Challenges

There are also methodological challenges relating to how to design reimagined AAL/telecare solutions in ways that can accommodate the lived experiences of older people themselves and the adaptations that accompany ageing, whilst maintaining an infrastructure that is suitable for health and social care needs. (There are also methodological challenges for evaluation more generally than we noted previously, but these are beyond the scope of this chapter.) This aligns with Hardisty et al. (2011) and their call for a codesign approach that would enlist older people as part of a design team. We extend this collaborative notion by building on the methodological experiences from CSCW and participatory design traditions. Following these traditions, we argue that there is a clear role for empirical and ethnographic studies, as also illustrated from many of the qualitative studies we referenced in Sect. 13.2. Here, we want to focus more on the design process itself. A central dilemma here is how best to involve older people in the design process in an empowering way so that their individual experiences of ageing are validated and remain central to design decisions. This is a particular challenge; based on reported experiences, 'design for and with the elderly carries with it some specific problems' (Müller et al. 2012).

One traditional approach to this has been participatory design (PD), but we suggest that with its democratic focus, unequal roles of users and designers can occur in these processes. According to Ertner et al. (2010), 'the PD researcher's practice is guided by unconscious assumptions and socially specific knowledge, which become reproduced and embedded in methods, categories and interpretations. By this the practitioner poses a risk of dominating the users, if they neglect to focus explicitly on deconstructing the tacit aspects of their own practice'. Similarly, Borning and Muller (2012), whilst discussing 'unintentional ventriloquism – i.e., stating the researcher's own views as if those views had been articulated by the informants' – suggest explicating the voice of the participants, e.g. through 'judicious verbatim quotation, with good contextualization, [as] is [already] the most frequent response to this problem in HCI and CSCW'. Equally, the voice of the researchers and designers needs to be explicated to clarify how their background impacts theory and method.

Instead, we explore codesign as an approach that might be particularly suited to accessing the lived experience of older people and that takes as its base the theoretical perspectives on the active agency of older people in shaping their own lives. Codesign is characterised by 'the creativity of designers and people not trained in design working together in the design development process' (Sanders and Stappers 2008). With a shift towards codesign, the roles of researchers, users and designers are shifting, too. The user who had the passive role of being observed or interviewed has to become a co-designer, and the researcher/designer will become a facilitator, providing guidance and tools to the user to make her a co-designer. These new roles can be challenging for everyone involved.

Below, we discuss three different codesign-related approaches, moving towards greater participation by older people: starting with concept-driven design, then value-sensitive design and finally a 'situated elderliness' approach. These approaches are all preoccupied with exploring new roles of the researchers, users and designers and in many ways can be seen to build on experiences with from a PD tradition.

13.6.1 Concept-Driven Design

One strategy that is about the researchers and designers rethinking how they engage in codesign has been a turn towards a *concept-driven design* approach (Stolterman and Wiberg 2010). This is a complementary approach to the user-centred approaches. Stolterman and Wiberg (2010) argue that much interaction design contains some new interactivity, whilst rarely contributing to the body of theoretical knowledge within interaction design research. Creating good concept designs aims at manifesting theoretical concepts in concrete designs, but still requires 'a good understanding of users, use contexts, and use' (Stolterman and Wiberg 2010, p. 5). Within the *concept-driven design* approach, methods have been developed that help put this design approach to practice. A recent example of such methods applied is found in the Walky design (Nazzi et al. 2012) mentioned in Sect. 4.2 in this chapter.

As Ertner and Malmborg (2012) point out, this concept-driven design approach involves a risk of establishing significant gaps between the way that AAL/telecare technology and services configure central concepts such as ageing, health and social interaction and the senior citizens' own accounts of this. This might have implications for both the effectiveness of services and technology developed and thus is an argument regarding the creation of better services and technologies that more people will use. However, it is also a moral and ethical argument, since by reproducing social norms, ideals and categories ascribed with certain stereotypes and values, there is a risk of reinforcing existing societal structures of in- and exclusion. This might particularly be relevant in terms of AAL/telecare scenarios, which operate with categories already embedded with stereotypes and moral judgements (as also noted earlier in the discussion about the negative rhetoric around motivations for AAL/telecare). Gaps between users' accounts and designers' visions of theoretical concepts may exist regardless of design approaches used, since design concepts, even though often invisible, also form the basis of most user-driven design approaches. Ertner and Malmborg (2012) emphasise the need for a more reflexive examination of AAL/telecare concepts and suggest the involvement of users as resource to reflect upon and challenge the imaginations and categories of 'elderliness' inscribed in design concepts and technological objects.

13.6.2 Value-Sensitive Design

Many of the ethical considerations raised in the previous discussion, in particular about the gap between designers' visions and users' account, point to the importance of foregrounding a 'value-sensitive design' (VSD) approach to designing AAL/telecare.

Many software requirements engineering methods include non-functional requirements, which deal with 'soft' characteristics of a system such as usability, flexibility and performance. However, in general, non-functional requirements differ from value considerations in that they are system specific (qualities *of a system*, reflecting more a modernist stance (Greenhalgh et al. 2012)), whereas values are primarily related to humans and human action, though they can be affected by systems. Values are more fundamental; consequences of not supporting them are worse, for example, when a person's dignity is undermined, when someone's personal autonomy is curtailed or when someone is suddenly held responsible for harm to others (examples that are prominent in systems supporting seniors and their caregivers through ICT).

The need to integrate values into design has by now been well-established within HCI (Cockton 2006; Flanagan et al. 2008; Friedman et al. 2006; Halloran et al. 2009; van den Hoven 2007). Several approaches have emerged to meet this need, of which value-sensitive design (VSD) (Friedman et al. 2006) is one of the most established. Over the last 20 years, VSD has been developed as a framework to systematically account for human values throughout the design process. VSD has been successful in accounting for stakeholder values in many research projects, for example, to improve the safety of homeless young people (Woelfer et al. 2011). Within the VSD framework, methods and models have been developed that help put VSD to practice. A recent contribution is the value-sensitive action–reflection model (Yoo et al. 2013), which introduces value-sensitive stakeholder and designer prompts to the codesign process to provide a means for bringing empirical data on values and to create a cycle of reflection on action. Such prompts can also be seen as creative triggers or boundary objects that support stakeholders and designers/researchers to be creative, to reflect on values and to communicate their perspectives.

The majority of VSD methods are focussed on conceptualising values and are most applicable earlier in the design process, for example, during the ideation phase. Methods (Friedman et al. 2011; Miller et al. 2007; Nathan et al. 2008) have been developed in order to elicit and make trade-offs between conflicting values. However, VSD currently lacks techniques to systematically translate values into technical designs. As a result, designers are forced to come up with ways of dealing with these unfamiliar concepts, and there is little guidance on dealing with these issues in design (see, e.g. Detweiler et al. 2012).

To date, there is little evidence of specifically labelled VSD approaches being used in the design of AAL/telecare solutions with seniors as participants. Within the domain of designing care robots, for example, a few researchers have recently advocated the use of VSD as a way to deal with ethical issues in the design process. For instance, van Wynsberghe (2013) points out the importance of 'rigorous ethical reflection to ensure [the robots] design and introduction do not impede the promotion of values and the dignity of patients at such a vulnerable and sensitive time in their lives'. She proposed a care-centred VSD framework. Sharkey and Sharkey (2012) stress the relevance of VSD approaches to handle the specific ethical issues arising due to the embodied and lifelike form of care robots. However, the works are limited to conceptual analysis and do not provide value-sensitive design cases. Such cases are still rare or in a very early stage of development, such as Fitirianie et al. (2013).

Hence, it remains an open research question how to contextualise VSD concepts and methods to an AAL/telecare context and link back to the notion of adaptivity in AAL in light of changing needs and where people might have a choice to adapt privacy levels. Values may mean very different things in different design contexts (for different individuals and also for the same individuals in different situations), as might happen over a longer adoption lifecycle in our reimagined AAL/telecare scenario.

13.6.3   A Situated Elderliness Approach

Whilst challenges with applying codesign methods and engaging stakeholders in creative activities are general, more specific challenges occur when dealing with senior citizens in codesign contexts. The first challenge is even identifying for whom we are designing. In codesign processes, designers and future users are carrying out design activities together. As designers we may have an initial idea of who these future users are, but users are never just 'out there'. People have to be recruited and mobilised to enact the roles of future users and to take on the membership in the 'group of users' that the design project enables.

Thus, applying a codesign approach addressing senior citizens creates a number of challenges related to identity, self-image and stigmatisation, when these senior citizens are to consider themselves potential co-designers. Östlund (2005) addresses this issue of stereotyping elderly in her discussion of design paradigms and senior citizens' ability to handle new technologies (Östlund 2005). When in a lifespan, do people consider themselves 'elderly', 'old' or as 'senior citizens'? And what does identification with such labels entail? Experience from codesign-oriented projects (Brandt et al. 2010) indicates that almost nobody among the group of people between 55 and 75 years old identifies themselves as 'elderly' or 'senior citizens'. Rather, they tend to refer to 'the others' or even to their own parents. These experiences are in line with Riche and Mackay observing 'that recruiting proved more difficult than anticipated, in part because people do not appreciate being stigmatized as 'elderly' and because they did not see a direct benefit for themselves' (Riche and Mackay 2010, p. 78).

One methodological strategy to approach recruitment of senior citizens for codesign, whilst avoiding the risk of reproducing existing norms and stereotypes, is the introduction of *situated elderliness* (Brandt et al. 2010), based on the idea that 'elderliness' is related to everyday practices and situations of 'feeling old' as opposed to 'being old', which refer to age as a defining position. The idea of 'situated elderliness' is inspired by the concept of *communities of practice* originally coined by Lave and Wenger (1991) and further expanded by Wenger (1998) in the field of work to capture the skills and competencies enacted by people engaged in a professional practice:

> In using the term community, we do not imply some primordial culture-sharing entity. We assume that members have different interests, make diverse contributions to activity, and hold varied viewpoints. In our view, participation at multiple levels is entailed in membership in a community of practice. Nor does the term community imply necessarily co-presence, a well-defined, identifiable group, or socially visible boundaries. It does imply participation in an activity system about which participants share understandings what they are doing and what that means in their lives and for their communities. (Lave and Wenger 1991, pp. 97–98)

When expanding this concept to include *everyday practices* outside work, it denotes *communities of everyday practice*, where senior citizens similarly are skilfully enacting everyday practices as seniors (reflecting the notions around adaptivity, selectivity and agency discussed in Sect. 13.3). Gradually, as they get older, they enact what is called *situated elderliness* (Brandt et al. 2010). Situated elderliness refers to specific practices and situations that involve activities that for some reason have become more challenging or perhaps even impossible to carry out. E-banking creates instances of situated elderliness when banks' new digital solutions create a group of senior citizens considered old as they are not able to handle their usual bank transactions due to lack of experience using the Internet. In these situations, in a contextual sense, they practice *situated elderliness*, whilst simultaneously being able to handle most other situations in their everyday life. (Interestingly, Vines et al. (2012) identified a similar situated elderliness scenario, using different languages, around the design of digital banking services, and coming up with a digital pen- and paper-based solution through a participatory design process with older people, a solution that would still afford some familiarity and fit into their everyday practices.)

This concept of situated elderliness, and communities of everyday practices, has been used as the basis for rethinking codesign workshops with older people, in particular highlighting the importance of artefacts for accessing lived experiences.

Whilst all people are commonly involved in some creative acts in their lives at some point, becoming co-designers requires a high level of passion and knowledge in a certain domain. Sanders and Westerlund (2011) pointed out that 'it can be difficult to get people to create ideas when they feel that they have insufficient knowledge and ... people who are brought into co-designing experiences may feel that they are not creative'. The authors suggest harnessing people's creativity with ambiguous visual and physical artefacts. Artefacts are not only important to trigger creativity for single participants, but serve as boundary objects supporting communication between participants with different backgrounds. An example is discussed in Case 6.

Case 6: situated elderliness and everyday practices as a codesign approach

The SeniorInteraction project (Foverskov and Binder 2011; Brandt et al. 2012; Malmborg and Yndigegn 2013) based on codesign through Living Labs focused on such communities of everyday practices and situated elderliness as an approach to engage senior citizens in design. Rather than introducing technological devices in ideation and early concept development, artefacts and props were introduced as a way to generate a shared language to address lived experience of ageing for further design collaboration.

Social media was made tangible through the design concept of Super Dots. Super Dots was not a conventional prototype, but a carefully crafted set of props aimed at facilitating dialogue on community building among senior citizens at a codesign workshop.

Probing into the everyday life of senior participants was combined with prototyping and scenario building involving both seniors and design researchers as well as public and private service providers. Unlike what is most often the case in user-centred design, prototyping and scenario building had an emphasis not on devices or appliances but on the social media infrastructure and how people establish, relate to and engage different media spaces of this infrastructure.

(continued)

> In this project the benefits of working with tangible scaffolding materials like props as a way to engage seniors in codesign based on their lived experience and the idea of situated elderliness were demonstrated. Social infrastructures and technological innovations seem to be more sustainable when grounded in lived experience of seniors' everyday life (Malmborg and Yndigegn 2013).

Across all these codesign approaches is a commitment to foreground the everyday practices of older people as active adapting agents in maintaining a quality of life that is meaningful for them. We recognise however that, in scoping this chapter to focus on the older perspective, there are still many open challenges to consider, in particular about how these approaches would scale up from smaller-scale applications at the early end of our reimagined AAL/telecare adoption path (that is more akin to everyday design, social support and informal peer care) to later on in the care path with whole-system design initiatives (involving formal care providers and diverse organisations) and where whole new models of care might be needed. Work is needed to consider how these approaches could be reinterpreted to engage all stakeholders and more importantly how to address the dependencies and complexities between these and develop the new models of care and infrastructures to support the reimagined AAL/telecare scenario. It is our hope that the methodological approaches presented here, along with the different theoretical approaches to ageing, might stimulate new thinking in these directions.

13.7 Conclusion

In this chapter, we have continued with Mort et al.'s (2012) challenge to reimagine AAL/telecare by taking a socio-technical design perspective that foregrounds the everyday life practices of people as they adapt to getting older. In so doing, we have provided a review of a specific domain, that of the elderly, which instantiates and evidences many of the conceptual, theoretical and methodological challenges reported in this book. Specifically, we have framed (as to Cabitza and Simone, Chap. 11) the discussion around challenges to the heroic modernist conception of the design process. We have suggested that the mixed reports on experiences with AAL/telecare to date, particularly around challenges of adoption, give cause to stop and reconceptualise when and how AAL/telecare is designed to be used. The foundation for this shift was taking a positive developmental approach to ageing and understanding the importance of agency, adaptivity and reciprocity as key elements of health and well-being for older people. We proposed that the devices and sensors of an AAL/telecare solution could be better thought of as an *infrastructure to be repurposed along a care spectrum, starting with active self-care and peer care and being adapted to the needs of formal care if and when care arises.*

The value of this approach is that it motivates uses of such technologies from a person-centred perspective, e.g. addressing social needs and providing opportunities to make meaningful contributions. At the same time, it provides nonthreatening opportunities for the person to develop expertise and competence with the technologies and empower them to actively engage in discussions of if and how these technologies are used in care and by whom. We gave examples to illustrate different uses for core sensing and communications infrastructures in this regard and also highlighted technical and methodological challenges that will need to be addressed to realise this scenario.

We have scoped this discussion deliberately around the perspectives of the older person. A challenge still remains though about how such an approach can gain broader acceptance within governmental and funding agencies, where modernist and change management discourses are more likely to dominate. Humanist and modernist approaches can, and indeed need to, coexist if this reimagined AAL/telecare is to be practically realised across the full adoption path. In particular, the same theoretical conceptualisations can be reinterpreted for all care providers and engaged stakeholders: as active agents, whose everyday practices and lived experiences matter and where codesign approaches can be used to find solutions to address these practices. We propose that it is critical to embrace this reimagining and its broader implications to properly address the challenges around adoption and delivering quality of life to the individual, not just cost savings to the system.

Acknowledgements The reflections and cases included in this paper were developed out of a number of diverse project experiences and deep interactions with our peer researchers and participants for each of the authors. Whilst we could never name all of them, we thank in particular Martijn Vastenburg, Nick Guldemond, Katarzyna Wac, Anna Pohlmeyer, Oezge Subasi and Wolfgang Reitberger.

References

Aarhus, R., & Ballegaard, S. (2010). Negotiating boundaries: Managing disease at home. In *Proceedings of the SIGCHI conference on human factors in computing systems (CHI '10)* (pp. 1223–1232). New York: ACM.

Aoki, P. M., & Woodruff, A. (2005). Making space for stories: Ambiguity in the design of personal communication systems. In *Proceedings of CHI'05* (pp. 181–190). New York: ACM.

Axelrod, L., Fitzpatrick, G., Burridge, J., Mawson, S., Probert Smith, P., Rodden, T., & Ricketts, I. (2009). The reality of homes fit for heroes: Design challenges for rehabilitation technology at home. *Journal of Assistive Technology, 3*(2), 35–43.

Baltes, P. B. (1993). The aging mind: Potential and limits. *Gerontologist, 33*, 580–594.

Baltes, P., & Baltes, M. (1990). *Successful aging*. Cambridge: Cambridge University Press.

Baltes, M. M., & Carstensen, L. L. (1999). Social-psychological theories and their applications to aging: From individual to collective. In V. L. Bengtson, J.-E. Ruth, & K. W. Schaie (Eds.), *Handbook of theories of aging* (pp. 209–226). New York: Springer.

Bandura, A. (1977). *Social learning theory*. New York: General Learning Press.

Barlow, J., Singh, D., Bayer, S., & Curry, R. (2007, June 1). A systematic review of the benefits of home telecare for frail elderly people and those with long-term conditions. *Journal of Telemedicine and Telecare, 13*, 172–179.

Bessière, K., Newhagen, J., Robinson, J. P., & Shneiderman, B. (2006). A model for computer frustration: The role of instrumental and dispositional factors on incident, session, and post-session frustration and mood. *Computers in Human Behavior, 22*, 941–961.

Blythe, M. A., Monk, A. F., & Doughty, K. (2005). Socially dependable design: The challenge of ageing populations for HCI. *Interacting with Computers, 17*(6), 672–689. doi:10.1016/j.intcom.2005.09.005.

Boehner, K. (2009, November). Reflections on representation as response. *Interactions, 16*(6), 28–32.

Boehner, K., Chen, M., & Liu, Z. (2003). The vibe reflector: An emergent impression of collective experience. In *Proceedings of CHI 2003 workshop on providing elegant peripheral awareness*. New York: ACM.

Borning, A., & Muller, M. (2012). Next steps for value sensitive design. In *Proceedings of the SIGCHI conference on human factors in computing systems (CHI'12)* (pp. 1125–1134). New York: ACM.

Brandt, E., Binder, T., Malmborg, L., & Sokoler, T. (2010). Communities of everyday practice and situated elderliness as an approach to co-design for senior interaction. In *OZCHI 2010 proceedings* (pp. 400–403). Brisbane, Australia.

Brandt, E., Mortensen, P. F., Malmborg, L., Binder, T., & Sokoler, T. (Eds.). (2012). *SeniorInteraktion – Innovation gennem dialog* [Eng: SeniorInteraction – Innovation through dialogue]. Copenhagen: The Royal Danish Academy of Fine Arts, School of Design.

Brownsell, S., Bradley, D., Blackburn, S., Cardinaux. F., & Hawley, M. (2011) A systematic review of lifestyle monitoring technologies. *Journal of Telemedicine and Telecare, 17*(4), 185–189. Publisher: Royal Society of Medicine.

Carstensen, L. L. (1992). Social and emotional patterns in adulthood: Support for socioemotional selectivity theory. *Psychology and Aging, 7*, 331–338.

Carstensen, L. L. (2006). The influence of a sense of time on human development. *Science, 312*, 1913–1915.

Carstensen, L. L., Isaacowitz, D. M., & Charles, S. T. (1999). Taking time seriously: A theory of socioemotional selectivity. *American Psychologist, 54*, 165–181.

Choi, N. G., & McDougall, G. J. (2007). Comparison of depressive symptoms between homebound older adults and ambulatory older adults. *Aging and Mental Health, 11*, 310–322.

Cockton, G. (2006). Designing worth is worth designing. In *Proceedings of the 4th Nordic conference on human-computer interaction: Changing roles (NordiCHI'06)* (pp. 165–174). New York: ACM.

Consolvo, S., Roessler, P., & Shelton, B. E., (2004, September) The CareNet display: Lessons learned from an In home evaluation of an ambient display. In *Proceedings of UbiComp'04* (pp. 1–17). Nottingham, UK.

Cook, D. (2012). *Bringing smart home data to caregivers*. Posted December 18 2012. http://www. igert.org/highlights/593

Deci, E. L., & Vansteenkiste, M. (2004). Self-determination theory and basic need satisfaction: Understanding human development in positive psychology. *Ricerche di Psichologia, 27*, 17–34.

DelliFrance, J., & Dansky, K. (2008, March). Home-based telehealth: A review and meta-analysis. *Journal of Telemed Telecare, 14*(2), 62–66.

DePaulo, B. M. (1982). Social-psychological processes in informal help-seeking. In T. A. Wills (Ed.), *Basic processes in helping relationship* (pp. 255–279). New York: Academic.

Detweiler, C. A., Dechesne, F., Hindriks, K. V., & Jonker, C. M. (2012). Ambient intelligence implies responsibility. In T. Bosse (Ed.), *Agents and ambient intelligence – Achievements and challenges in the intersection of agent technology and ambient intelligence* (pp. 33–61). Amsterdam/Washington, DC: Ios Press.

Draper, H., & Sorell, T. (2012). Telecare, remote monitoring and care. *Bioethics, 9702*, 195–200. doi:10.1111/j.1467-8519.2012.01961.x.

Ertner, M., & Malmborg, L. (2012, May 5–10). *Lost in translation: Inscriptions of the elderly in concept-driven design of welfare technology*. Position paper, CHI2012, Austin, TX, USA.

Ertner, M., Kragelund, A. M., & Malmborg, L. (2010, November). Five enunciations of empowerment in participatory design. In *Proceedings of PDC'10, Sydney, Australia* (pp. 191–194). New York: ACM Press.

Fitrianie, S., Huldtgren, A., Alers, H., & Guldemond, N. A. (2013). A smartTV platform for wellbeing, care and social support for elderly at home. In *Inclusive society: Health and wellbeing in the community, and care at home* (Lecture notes in computer science, Vol. 7910, pp. 94–101). Berlin/New York: Springer.

Fitzpatrick, G. (2012) New challenges for health IT – Design fit for life. In A. Yoxall (Ed.), *Proceedings of the design 4 health 2011* (pp. 121–135). Sheffield Hallam University, 13–15 July 2011. Available from http://research.shu.ac.uk/lab4living/design-4-health-2011-proceedings

Fitzsimmons, D. A., Thompson, J., Hawley, M., & Mountain, G. A. (2011, January 7). Preventative tele-health supported services for early stage chronic obstructive pulmonary disease: A protocol for a pragmatic randomized controlled trial pilot. *Trials, 12*, 6. doi:10.1186/1745-6215-12-6.

Flanagan, M., Howe, D., & Nissenbaum, H. (2008). Embodying values in technology: Theory and practice. In J. van den Hoven and J. Weckert (Eds.), *Information technology and moral philosophy*. Cambridge: Cambridge University Press.

Foverskov, M., & Binder, T. (2011). Super dots: Making social media tangible for senior citizens. In *Proceedings of the 2011 conference on designing pleasurable products and interfaces (DPPI'11)*. New York: ACM. doi:10.1145/2347504.2347575.

Frederiksberg Municipality. (2013). *Handleforslag 48: Plejebolig som kvalitetsforbedrende alternativ til omfattende hjemmehjælp* [in English: Activity proposal 48: Nursing home as quality improving alternative to extensive home care], 2013–04–21. Copenhagen, Denmark.

Friedman, B., Kahn, P., & Borning, A. (2006). Chapter 16: Value sensitive design and information systems. In *Human-computer interaction in management information systems: Foundations*. London: M.E. Sharpe, Inc.

Friedman, B., Nathan, L. P., Kane, S., & Lin, J. (2011). *Envisioning cards*. Seattle: University of Washington.

Fyrand, L. (2010). Reciprocity: A predictor of mental health and continuity in elderly people's relationships? A review. *Current Gerontology and Geriatrics Research*, Article ID 340161.

Gabriel, Z., & Bowling, A. (2004). Quality of life in old age from the perspectives of older people. In A. Walker & C. H. Hennessy (Eds.), *Growing older: Quality of life in old age* (pp. 14–34). Maidenhead/New York: Open University Press.

Gale, N., & Sultan, H. (2013). Telehealth as 'peace of mind': Embodiment, emotions and the home as the primary health space for people with chronic obstructive pulmonary disorder. *Health and Place, 21*, 140–147.

Gaver, W., Beaver, J., & Benford, S. (2003). Ambiguity as a resource for design. In *Proceedings of CHI'03* (pp. 233–240). New York: ACM.

Greenhalgh, T., Procter, R., Wherton, J., Sugarhood, P., & Shaw, S. (2012). The organising vision for telehealth and telecare: Discourse analysis. *BMJ Open, 2*(4), e001574. doi:10.1136/bmjopen-2012-001574.

Gregory, C. (1994). Exchange and reciprocity. In T. Ingold (Ed.), *Companion encyclopedia of anthropology* (pp. 911–939). London/New York: Routledge.

Grönvall, E., & Kyng, M. (2012). On participatory design of home-based healthcare. *Cognition, Technology & Work, 15*(4), 389–401. doi:10.1007/s10111-012-0226-7.

Halloran, J., Hornecker, E., Stringer, M., Harris, E., & Fitzpatrick, G. (2009). The value of values: Resourcing co-design of ubiquitous computing. *CoDesign: International Journal of Co-Creation in Design and the Arts, 5*(4), 245–273.

Hardisty, A., Peirce, S., Preece, A., Bolton, C., Conley, E., Gray, W., Rana, O., Yousef, Z., & Elwyn, G. (2011). Bridging two translation gaps: A new informatics research agenda for telemonitoring of chronic disease. *International Journal of Medical Informatics, 80*(10), 734–744. doi:10.1016/j.ijmedinf.2011.07.002.

Harley, D. (2011) *Older people's appropriation of computers and the internet*. Doctoral thesis, University of Sussex.

Harley, D., & Fitzpatrick, G. (2009). YouTube and intergenerational communication: The case of geriatric 1927. *Universal Access in the Information Society, 8*(1), 5–20.

Hawkley, L. C., & Cacioppo, J. T. (2004). Stress and the aging immune system. *Brain, Behavior, and Immunity, 18*, 114–119.

Hawthorn, D. (2000). Possible implications of aging for interface designers. *Interacting with Computers, 12*, 507–528.

Henderson, C., Knapp, M., Fernández, J.-L., Beecham, J., Hirani, S. P., Cartwright, M., Rixon, L., Beynon, M., Rogers, A., Bower, P., Doll, H., Fitzpatrick, R., Steventon, A., Bardsley, M., Hendy, J., & Newman, S. P. (2013). Cost effectiveness of telehealth for patients with long term conditions (Whole systems demonstrator telehealth questionnaire study): Nested economic evaluation in a pragmatic, cluster randomised controlled trial. *BMJ* (Online), *346*(7902).

Hirsch, T., Forlizzi, J., Hyder, E., Goetz, J., Kurtz, C., & Stroback, J. (2000). The elder project: Social, emotional, and environmental factors in the design of eldercare technologies. In *Proceedings conference on Universal Usability, CUU'00* (pp. 72–79). New York: ACM.

House, J. S., Landis, K. R., & Umberson, D. (1988). Social relationships and health. *Science, 241*(4865), 540.

Huang, J.-C. (2011). Exploring the acceptance of telecare among senior citizens: An application of back propagation network. *Telemedicine and e-Health, 17*(2), 111–117.

James, A., James, W. L., & Smith, H. L. (1984). Reciprocity as a coping strategy of the elderly: A rural Irish perspective. *Gerontologist, 24*(5), 483–489.

Joyce, K., & Loe, M. (2010). A sociological approach to ageing, technology and health. *Sociology of Health & Illness, 32*(2), 171–180. doi:10.1111/j.1467-9566.2009.01219.x.

Lave, J., & Wenger, E. (1991). *Situated learning: Legitimate peripheral participation*. New York: Cambridge University Press.

Lindley, S. E. (2011). Shades of lightweight: Supporting cross-generational communication through home messaging. *Universal Access in the Information Society, 11*(1), 31–43.

Lindley, S., et al. (2008). Designing for elders: Exploring the complexity of relationships in later life. In *Proceedings of BCS-HCI '08* (vol. 1, pp. 77–86). Liverpool, UK.

Lotfi, A., Langensiepen, C., Mahmoud, S., & Akhlaghinia, M. (2012). Smart homes for the elderly dementia sufferers: Identification and prediction of abnormal behaviour. *Journal of Ambient Intelligence and Humanized Computing, 3*(3), 205–218.

Mahmood, A., Yamamoto, T., Lee, M., & Steggell, C. (2008). Perceptions and use of gerotechnology: Implications for aging in place. *Journal of Housing for the Elderly, 22*(1–2), 104–126.

Malmborg, L., & Yndigegn, S. L. (2013, June 9–12). Sustainable infrastructure for ad hoc social interaction. In E. Brandt, P. Ehn, T. D. Johansson, M. H. Reimer, T. Markussen, A. Vallgårda (Eds.), *Experiments in design research. Proceedings of nordic design research conference 2013*, Copenhagen-Malmö.

McCartney, M. (2012). *Notes on the whole system demonstrator*. At http://www.margaretmccartney.com/blog/?p=1647

Miller, J. K., Friedman, B., Jancke, G., & Gill, B. (2007). Value tensions in design: The value sensitive design, development, and appropriation of a corporation's groupware system. In *Proceedings of GROUP 2007* (pp. 281–290). New York: ACM.

Milliken, M., O'Donnell, S., Gibson, K., & Daniels, B. (2012). Older adults and video communications: A case study. *The Journal of Community Informatics, 8*(1).

Mort, M., Roberts, C., & Callén, B. (2012). Ageing with telecare: Care or coercion in austerity? *Sociology of Health & Illness, XX*(X), 1–14. doi:10.1111/j.1467-9566.2012.01530.x.

Müller, C., Wan, L., & Hrg, D. (2010). Dealing with wandering: A case study on caregivers' attitudes towards privacy and autonomy when reflecting the use of LBS. In *Proceedings of Group 2010* (pp. 75–84). New York: ACM Press.

Müller, C., Neufeldt, C., Randall, D., & Wulf, W. (2012). ICT-development in residential care settings: Sensitizing design to the life circumstances of the residents of a care home. In *Proceedings of CHI2012* (pp. 2639–2648). New York: ACM Press.

Mynatt, E., Rowan, J., Craighill, S., & Jacobs, A. (2001). Digital family portraits: Supporting peace of mind for extended family members. In *Proceedings of CHI'01* (pp. 333–340). New York: ACM Press.

Nathan, L. P., Friedman, B., Klasjna, P. V., Kane, S. K., & Miller, J. K. (2008). Envisioning systemic effects on persons and society throughout interactive system design. In *Proceedings of ACM conference on designing interactive systems (DIS'08)* (pp. 1–10). New York: ACM.

Nazzi, E., Bagalkot, N. L., Nagargoje, A., & Sokoler, T. (2012). Concept-driven interaction design research in the domain of attractive aging: The example of walky. In P. Rodgers (Ed.), *Articulating design thinking* (pp. 227–245). Oxfordshire: Libri Publishing Ltd.

Östlund, B. (2005). Design paradigms and misunderstood technology: The case of older users. In B. Jæger (Ed.), *Young technologies in old hands* (pp. 25–39). Copenhagen: DJØF.

Panek, P., & Hlauschek, W. (2011). Experiences from user centric engineering of ambient assisted living technologies in the living lab schwechat. In *Proceedings of ICE, 2011* (pp. 1–8). http://ieeexplore.ieee.org/xpls/abs_all.jsp?arnumber=6041274

Pedell, S., Vetere, F., Kulik, L., Ozanne, E., & Gruner, A. (2010). Social isolation of older people: The role of domestic technologies. In *Proceedings of OZCHI'10* (pp. 164–167). New York: ACM.

Reginatto, B. (2012). Addressing barriers to wider adoption of telehealth in the homes of older people: An exploratory study in the Irish context. In *eTELEMED 2012: The fourth international conference on eHealth, telemedicine, and social medicine*. Red Hook: Curran.

Riche, Y. (2008). *Designing communication appliances to support aging in place*. Ph.D. thesis. INRIA/Universite Paris Sud.

Riche, Y., & MacKay, W. (2010). PeerCare: Supporting awareness of rhythms and routines for better aging in place. *Computer Supported Cooperative Work (CSCW), 19*(1), 73–104.

Roberts, C., & Mort, M. (2009). Reshaping what counts as care: Older people, work and new technologies. *ALTER – European Journal of Disability Research* [Revue Européenne de Recherche sur le Handicap], *3*(2), 138–158. doi:10.1016/j.alter.2009.01.004.

Ryan, R. M., & Deci, E. L. (2001). To be happy or to be self-fulfilled: A review of research on hedonic and eudaimonic well-being. In S. Fiske (Ed.), *Annual review of psychology* (Vol. 52, pp. 141–166). Palo Alto: Annual Reviews/Inc.

Ryan, R. M., Deci, E. L., Grolnick, W. S., & La Guardia, J. G. (2006). The significance of autonomy and autonomy support in psychological development and psychopathology. In D. Cicchetti & D. J. Cohen (Eds.), *Developmental psychopathology: Theory and method* (2nd ed., pp. 795–849). Hoboken: Wiley.

Sanders, E. B.-N., & Stappers, P. J. (2008). Co-creation and the new landscapes of design. *CoDesign: International Journal of CoCreation in Design and the Arts, 4*(1), 5–18.

Sanders, E.B.-N., & Westerlund, B. (2011, May). Experience, exploring and experimenting in and with co-design spaces. In *Proceedings of NORDES'11* (pp. 1–5), Helsinki, Finland.

Sanders, C., Rogers, A., Bowen, R., et al. (2012). Exploring barriers to participation and adoption of telehealth and telecare within the whole system demonstrator trial: A qualitative study. *BMC Health Services Research, 12*, 220.

Sayago, S., Sloan, D., & Blat, J. (2011). Everyday use of computer-mediated communication tools and its evolution over time: An ethnographical study with older people. *Interacting with Computers, 23*(5), 543–554.

Shankar, K., Camp, L., Connelly, K., & Huber, L. (2012). Aging, privacy, and home-based computing: Developing a design framework. *IEEE Pervasive Computing, 11*(4), 46–54.

Sharkey, A., & Sharkey, N. (2012). Granny and the robots: Ethical issues in robot care for the elderly. *Ethics and Information Technology, 14*(1), 27–40.

Ståhl, A., Höök, K., Svensson, M., Taylor, A., & Combetto, M. (2009, June). Experiencing the affective diary. *Personal and Ubiquitous Computing, 13*(5), 365–378.

Steventon, A., Bardsley, M., Billings, J., Dixon, J., Doll, H., Hirani, S., et al. (2012). Effect of telehealth on use of secondary care and mortality: Findings from the Whole System Demonstrator cluster randomised trial. *BMJ, 344*, e3874.

Stolterman, E., & Wiberg, M. (2010). Concept-driven interaction design research. *Human-Computer Interaction, 25*(2) 95–118.

Thomas, B., & Crandall, A. (2011). A demonstration of PyViz, a flexible smart home visualization tool. In *Proceedings of pervasive computing and communications workshops*. Piscataway: IEEE.

Thompson, M. G., & Heller, K. (1990). Facets of support related to well-being: Quantitative social isolation and perceived family support in a sample of elderly women. *Psychology and Aging, 5*(4), 535–544.

Tornstam, L. (1989). Gero-transcendence: A meta-theoretical reformulation of the disengagement theory. *Aging Clinical and Experimental Research, 1*(1), 55–63.

Tornstam, L. (2005). *Gerotranscendence. A developmental theory of positive aging*. New York: Springer.

Tornstam, L., & Toernqvist, M. (2000). Nursing staff's interpretations of "gerotanscendental behaviors" in the elderly. *Journal of Aging and Identity, 5*, 15–29.

van den Hoven, J. (2007). ICT and value sensitive design. In *The information society: Innovation, legitimacy, ethics and democracy* (pp. 67–72). Boston: Springer.

van Wynsberghe, A. (2013). Designing robots for care: Care centered value-sensitive design. *Science and Engineering Ethics, 19*(2), 407–433.

Vines, J., Blythe, M., Dunphy, P., Vlachokyriakos, V., Teece, I., Monk, A., & Olivier, P. (2012). Cheque mates: Participatory design of digital payments with eighty somethings. In *Proceedings of CHI'12* (pp. 1189–1198). New York: ACM Press.

Waycott, J., Vetere, F., Pedell, S., Kulik, L., Ozanne, E., Gruner, A., & Downs, J. (2013). Older adults as digital content producers. In *Proceedings of the SIGCHI conference on human factors in computing systems (CHI'13)* (pp. 39–48). New York: ACM Press.

Wenger, E. (1998). *Communities of practice: Learning, meaning, and identity*. Cambridge: Cambridge University Press.

Woelfer, J. P., Iverson, A., Hendry, D. G., Friedman, B., & Gill, B. (2011). Improving the safety of homeless young people with mobile phones: Values, form and function. In *Proceedings of CHI 2011* (pp. 1707–1716). New York: ACM Press.

World Health Organisation (WHO). (2002). *Active ageing: A policy framework*. Geneva: WHO.

Yoo, D., Huldtgren, A., Palzkill Woelfer, J., Hendry, D., & Friedman, B. (2013). A value sensitive action-reflection model: Evolving a co-design space with stakeholder and designer prompts. In *Proceedings of the SIGCHI conference on human factors in computing systems (CHI'13)* (pp. 419–428). New York: ACM Press.

Zunzunegui, M.-V., Alvarado, B. E., Del Ser, T., & Otero, A. (2003). Social networks, social integration, and social engagement determine cognitive decline in community-dwelling Spanish older adults. *The Journals of Gerontology Series B: Psychological Sciences and Social Sciences, 58*(2), 93–100.

Part IV
Social and Organisational Complexity

Chapter 14
Studying Technologies *in Practice*: "Bounding Practices" When Investigating Socially Embedded Technologies

Pernille Bjørn and Nina Boulus-Rødje

14.1 Introduction

The idea of socially embedded technologies (SET) constitutes a new approach into ICT research, one which has emerged from the European communities of research on computer-supported cooperative work (CSCW). SET is based upon the fundamental assumption that we need new ways to conceptualize research on design, which takes into account peoples' social practices without limiting the human interaction to an individual computer-user relation. People and practices are much more than their relationship with a technology, and thus the concept of "user" is problematic. We see ourselves as researchers who embrace the new agendas of SET, and in this chapter we will then explain approach and suggest ways for thinking differently about design. When studying *technologies in practice*, we ground our work within the CSCW tradition for workplace studies (Luff et al. 2000; Randall et al. 2007). In recent years, we have conducted research in the healthcare arena, studying patient tracking and triage systems in emergency departments (Bjørn and Balka 2007; Bjørn et al. 2009; Bjørn and Hertzum 2011), investigating the introduction of electronic medical records in primary and acute care settings (Boulus 2004, 2009, 2010; Boulus and Bjørn 2007, 2008), as well as studying the practices of monitoring patients with heart failure in a tele-monitoring setup (Andersen et al. 2010). We believe the healthcare arena to be a perspicuous setting for studying technology as socially embedded since it covers heterogeneous work practices, varying technical competencies and complex organizational arrangements. We have conducted both single-site and comparative studies (Boulus and Bjørn 2007; Balka

P. Bjørn (✉) • N. Boulus-Rødje
Technologies in Practice Research Group, IT University of Copenhagen, Copenhagen, Denmark
e-mail: pbra@itu.dk; nbou@itu.dk

© Springer-Verlag London 2015
V. Wulf et al. (eds.), *Designing Socially Embedded Technologies in the Real-World*,
Computer Supported Cooperative Work, DOI 10.1007/978-1-4471-6720-4_14

et al. 2008), and all of this work took place in Canada, Norway, or Denmark. In each of these studies, we applied ethnographic methods to examine the collaborative and complex practices of the particular site, with the aim of developing theoretical concepts useful for describing and articulating practices while informing the design of technologies that support the local and situated practices (Schmidt 1998). More recently, we have started to reflect on what these types of engagements mean for research and for practice, with the aim of continuously sharpening our research practices (Bjørn and Boulus 2011; Boulus-Rødje 2012).

One key challenge is that the "ethnography for design" approach embeds a sequential order to design procedure. We *first* study current practices and *then* design technology (Wulf et al. 2011). This sequential approach does not necessarily fit well with dynamic and constantly changing real-life practices, where technologies and practices are continuously redesigned and reorganized. To study technologies in practice, we have to reconsider how we think about our research approach, moving from a sequential ordering toward focusing on aspects of multiplicity (Law 2004) where technology and practices are dynamic and heterogeneous assemblages.

In this chapter, we explain how we can apply the focus on multiplicity when studying technologies in practice. We explore how this approach, foundationally, does not view technology design as sequential, and thus argue that it might be a way to move away from a linear design agenda toward an emergent perspective. We propose to take multiplicity as the starting point and to view practice and technology as intertwined. This means that when investigating the world, we must find a way to view the world as multiple, rather than consisting of dualities of practice and technology. We argue that to make sense of the world of technologies in practice, our work as researchers is to pull together and tease apart dynamic and multiple entities. We constantly create and recreate boundaries, "cutting" the world in the way that Barad (1996) suggests. We refer to this work as *bounding practices* (Bjørn 2012) and argue that the entities we study are dynamic, and we play an active part in shaping the entity under investigation. The boundaries of a technology are constituted in enactment. Enactment refers to "the claim that relations, and so realities and representations of realities…are being endlessly or chronically brought into being in a continuing process of production and reproduction, and have no status, standing, or reality outside those processes" (Law 2004, p. 159). In other words, we never simply observe an external reality that exists prior to or independent of its representations; rather, through engagement in representation, reality is performed—it is enacted (Law 2004). Thus, we cannot study technology independently of practices. The notion of enactment is used to emphasize that the world is performed through sociomaterial practices. In this chapter, we illustrate how this analytic lens can help us understand technology as a dynamic and multiple entity. We propose that to study design, we must take into account the sociomaterial practices that make the technology. Sociomateriality offers an analytical lens where neither artifacts nor people are single entities with inherent predefined properties. Instead, people and artifacts are made through relations: "[T]o be is to be related" (Mol 2002, p. 54).

We begin this chapter by introducing the ethnography for design approach and its related history. We then bring forward the sociomateriality approach, exploring how to comprehend technology and practices as multiple. Next we introduce the concept of *bounding practices* to describe the research activities required to study technologies in practice. We present one ongoing research project—technologies for democracy—to illustrate how bounding practices can help us to analytically understand what makes the technologies in this project. We then discuss the impact of this approach and where it might take us, and we finish by offering our conclusions.

14.2   Studying Technologies in Practice

When Schmidt and Bannon (1992) wrote what can be seen as the manifesto of CSCW research, the two prevailing issues within the CSCW community were (1) studying the basic nature of collaboration and (2) using this knowledge to design collaborative technologies (Schmidt and Bannon 1992). Back then the CSCW approach was challenging the dominance of office automation research by questioning basic fundamental assumptions about CSCW research. These led to the arguments that no formal description can fully capture collaborative work, that it is impossible to anticipate every contingency which might occur, that collaboration is open ended, that there will always be exception handling, and, finally, that plans are resources for work and that these are different from the actual work (Schmidt and Bannon 1992).

At this time the design community extended an invitation of collaboration to social scientists, and efforts were made to bring ethnographers into the field of computing. To acknowledge "the social" within technology design, the research agenda of CSCW was founded on interdisciplinarity. However, inviting ethnographers into the field of computing to learn from their methods also changed the field itself. Whereas ethnography is generally a descriptive discipline, the ethnographers entering the CSCW domain had to adjust their interests or, as Schmidt and Bannon put it, "enter, and you must change" (Schmidt and Bannon 1992, p. 11). Thus, although ethnography initially did not necessarily have an explicit change agenda, by entering the field of computing, the agenda was introduced. This new agenda for computing research as well as for ethnography became formulated in terms of ethnography for design (Bentley et al. 1992; Hughes et al. 1992, 1995), where the main interest is studying practices with the aim of supporting technology design (Blomberg et al. 1993). Over the years this agenda of bringing ethnography and design together has been discussed extensively (e.g., the Coordination Debate: Suchman 1994; Winograd 1994; Grudin and Grinter 1995), but arguably few ethnographic studies have succeeded in creating relevant design implications for technology innovation. Bridging between the two worlds of ethnography and design can also be referred to as the divide of CSCW (Schmidt 2009) or the problem of "implication for design" (Dourish 2006). From these debates we have learned, at the very least, that translating ethnographic findings into design implications is difficult and requires additional academic work from a diverse group of collaborators representing the different disciplines to bridge the gap. Often articles dedicated to discussing this transition focus on explaining ethnography while paying less attention to explaining the actual move from ethnography toward design. While there is a general agreement that we can extract requirement specifications and recommendations from ethnography for a particular user group, it is much more difficult to figure out how exactly ethnographic insights can add to design. This has led to several papers dedicated to producing findings in either one area (e.g., ethnography (Hartswood et al. 2003; Svensson et al. 2007; Møller and Bjørn 2011) or design (e.g., design (Dourish and Bly 1992; Gutwin and Greenberg 2002; Yamashita et al. 2008). However, it is not easy to find papers that aim to contribute to both fields. There are, of course, a few exceptions (Bardram and Bossen 2005; Bjørn et al. 2009; Wulf et al. 2011).

Although this divide is still a relevant issue for CSCW research, there is a distinct difference between the situation back in the 1980s–1990s and that of today and as we look toward the next decade, namely, the escalation of new technology inventions and their quick adaptation in the everyday lives of people. Today, we find the constant and rapid release of new technological devices (e.g., tablets and smartphones), new collaborative applications (e.g., Google Docs and Dropbox), and new apps (more than 100 new apps are released on a daily basis)—and people quickly adopt these devices and collaborative technologies into daily life. This offers a distinctly different situation from the studies of adaption of collaborative technologies back in 1992 (Orlikowski 1992).

In Orlikowski's (1992) study of Lotus Notes, she explained why collaborative technologies implemented in organizations did not lead to "instant collaboration" but instead required organizational implementation where people learned why they were using the technology, the basic nature of the technology, and then developed technology-in-use practices. There was a general consensus among researchers that collaborative technologies are more complex to handle than single-user systems, for example, in terms of adaptation, difficulties in evaluation and cost/benefits (Grudin 2004). However, in present-day western societies as well as in growing economies, ICT technology has become both mundane and ubiquitous. People are more likely to adopt new and unknown technologies with little hesitation. Thus, we might ask whether the time for CSCW researchers to conduct long-term, in-depth ethnographic studies in order to inform design is changing. By the time we complete our ethnographic study, new technological opportunities have already emerged, practices have already changed and so have the conditions surrounding these practices. Thus, we join other researchers (e.g., Pipek and Wulf 2009) in the attempt to remove the strict and simplistic separation between design and use, since the term "design" risk is misleading the focus to only concern the technological "artifact" while neglecting the surroundings by which the technology is to be enacted.

Therefore, as researchers who believe in designing high-quality collaborative technologies based upon an in-depth understanding of practices, we have to adjust to the contemporary changes around us and find new ways to study practices and technologies in a timely manner without abandoning a critical approach. The question then is how can we conduct solid academic research on socially embedded technologies when the social and the technical continuously and rapidly change?

14.3   Sociomateriality and Bounding Practices

If we are to redirect our research approach to the study of *technologies in practice* toward an approach, which takes into account the inseparability and multiplicity of the technology and the social, we first need to define what makes practice and technology. For this purpose, we to turn to sociomateriality (Leonardi et al. 2012; Jones 2013) as the theoretical foundation that can help expand our empirical views when studying technologies in practice. So what is practice? Applying the lens of sociomateriality, practice is the connections that hold together heterogeneous actors, artifacts, and activities (Orlikowski 2007). Practice is the entwined nature where neither artifacts nor people are single entities with predefined and inherent properties; instead the social and the material are inseparable and constitutively entangled (Haraway 1991; Barad 1996). Practice is a tangle of strings. Haraway (1987) uses the metaphor of a ball of yarn to explain practice. In the ball of yarn each string represents one cut down into reality. If we pull one string and follow it through the tangle of multiple strings, we learn how "this entity" is tangled into many other strings, each adding to the comprehension of the one string and the relations that make the string (Haraway 1987). Each string comprises the sociomaterial relations of technology and practice. The tangle is flexible, dynamic, and multiple. The strings can be pulled in different ways, bringing forward particular connections while moving others to the background. Each molding activity of the strings is part of what makes the entity of practice.

Applying the lens of sociomateriality, technology is never a stable entity; instead, it is always dynamic and multiple. Viewing technology as a dynamic entity is in line with the basic assumptions about collaborative technologies in CSCW, namely, that we cannot anticipate all contingencies, that collaboration is open ended, and that exception handling will always exist (Schmidt and Bannon 1992). However, in the early writings of CSCW, technology—which although could be technically reconfigured—was a relatively stable entity, while the social practices surrounding the technology were malleable. We propose in this chapter a different argument, namely, that technology is not simply a single entity. Instead technology is emergent in use—in the sociomaterial practices. This dynamic perspective on technology means that the boundaries for what makes the technology are not predefined by the technical artifact. Instead the boundaries for what makes the technological artifact come into being through the enactment of the sociomaterial relations which change over time. Technological artifacts can therefore be seen as a hyphenated structure of relations, where the relations are multiple and changing over time. The word processor that we are using to write this chapter is part of the technology relations that we are enacting. The entity might, at some point, emerge as [word processor-chapter-book-editors-coauthors-empirical work-literature] while at other times as [word processor-Internet-laptop-reference tool-reviewing chapter-book-editors]. Placing the social and the technical as "one entity", as one wholeness, "does not signify the dissolution of boundaries. Boundaries are necessary for making meaning" (Barad 1996, p. 182).

The sociomaterial perspective implies that all practices are part of the tangle of practices, which, in theory, are never ending and inclusive. However, not all relations are salient at all times. Those relations that act and are enacted create the boundaries for what is to be included or excluded from the unit of analysis. The question then becomes, how can we study something that does not have predefined boundaries? It means that studying technology in practice is not just about opening the black box of technology and retrospectively analyzing how it became stable (Latour 2005). Instead, opening the black box of technology requires us, the researchers, to search and identify the boundaries of that box at a particular point in time. Thus, the perspective on design of technology without predefined boundaries pays attention to the work of identifying boundaries over time as well as taking active part in changing these boundaries. In other words we, the researchers, and their methods, participate in the enactment of what makes the technology. "The argument is no longer that methods discover and depict realities. Instead, it is that they participate in the enactment of those realities" (Law 2004, p. 45).

The world is composed of entangled, complex, and multiple relations of technologies and practices. This makes the work of the researcher attempting to access, map, and analyze these relations more challenging, since there is no one set of relations existing out there ready to be mapped. Instead, when studying technologies, we at all times have partial access to part of what makes the technology. The critical question then becomes, how do we know that these are the relevant relations for our purpose? When we study and design technologies without predefined boundaries, we need analytical tools and instruments that can help us comprehend the world (the tangle) not simply as an untangled complexity but as an investigation of where the important enacted relations become visible, available, and salient. We refer to this work as *bounding practices* (Bjørn and Østerlund 2014). Bounding practices is work required to zoom in on a technology—a particular interest—and investigate all relations that are part of the technology while creating the boundaries for what makes the technology. Bounding practices is the work required to pick and pull the strings in the entangled yarn in order to identify the different relations and decide how to draw the boundaries around the entity being studied. Bounding practices "has a double meaning – namely to bind together, as in hyphenated-structures, *and* to set the boundaries for what makes the entity, as in [bracketing structures]" (Bjørn 2012). Thus, the work we, the researchers, have when we study technologies and practices as dynamic and ever-changing phenomena includes the work of identifying and deciding how to pull out strings within the practice—strings which are critical to understanding the object of interest and reveal interesting and relevant sociomaterial relations in the hyphenated structure. We will now illustrate the application of this approach.

14.4   The Democratic Technologies Project

The second author is currently involved in a large research project called *DemTech* (2011–2016), studying democratic technologies. The project brings together computer scientists and social scientists with the aim of studying the design and implementation of electronic voting technologies. DemTech is a strategic research project where one key goal is collaboration between researchers and industry. Therefore, the project has different partners, including two IT vendors[1] and the three biggest municipalities in Denmark. The project started in July 2011, with ethnographic observations of the parliamentary election in Denmark, including following closely the planning, implementation, and evaluation phases of the election. The research team conducted formal and informal interviews with different policy makers and municipal employees. Furthermore, the team attended seminars for municipal employees (one that prepared staff for the upcoming election and one that evaluated the election), conducted and participated in several meetings with different stakeholders, organized a public event at the parliament and workshops with both academic and nonacademic audiences, and participated in various public debates in the media.

What is particularly interesting in the DemTech project is that it illustrates how the technology in question is a dynamic entity that is changing over time and where the researchers are actively taking part in (re)defining what makes the technology. Furthermore, the role that the ethnographic observations play in this research project is quite different from merely providing requirement specifications for a prototype. In this way, the conventional sequential process of first ethnography and then design is not appropriate for this kind of research.

14.5   Democratic Technologies as a Sociomaterial Entity

In this section, we will demonstrate how the technology in the DemTech research project took different forms over the period of the project. In particular, we will pull different strings in the ball of yarn which makes "democratic technologies" and explore the sociomaterial matters at different points in time. Each time we pull a string, we bound the technology in particular ways, and it is within these bounding practices that the technical artifact emerges as an enacted sociomaterial artifact. We will present three concrete parts of the DemTech project and pull out how the "democratic technologies" were bounded at that time. The examples we chose all relate to the early stages of the research project and as such reflect upon the initial grant proposal and to how it was forced into a "traditional" sequential understanding of *first* conducting ethnography and *then* designing. However, in practice, this approach sets constraints for what actually turns out to be the important

---

[1]This was the case at the time of writing this chapter; however, the project no longer has the two IT vendors as partners.

research findings for such projects relevant for both research and society. Thus, our argument concerns how some of the funding agencies tend to perceive ICT research in an old-fashioned perspective and a suggestion into how we can conceive optimal opportunities for future ICT research.

14.5.1   Grant Proposal

When the DemTech grant application was originally submitted to the Danish strategic research council, the argument was that although computers have already began replacing different parts of the democratic process (e.g., calculating seat assignments in parliament), and although this technological change has often been ascribed different advantages (e.g., in terms of efficiency and finance), it also brings about different risks. Therefore, the aim of the project was to provide insights into ways to modernize the elections without jeopardizing fundamental and crucial principles upon which democratic elections rest. It is important to keep in mind that while many countries across North America and Europe have been suffering from declining voter turnout, Denmark has had one of the most stable trends with an average voter turnout of approximately 85 % for parliamentary elections.[2] Danes are generally perceived to have a relatively strong trust in their electoral system and in democracy. What is at stake here—democracy—is thus a very precious and well-oiled machine that has been built through many generations. It is, therefore, of utmost importance to make sure that digitalizing elections is done in a manner that it preserves the strong tradition of democracy in Denmark. The DemTech funding proposal reflects on some of the views that claim that the digitalization process of elections is inevitable and the question is thus not if this will happen but rather how and when this will happen. These views see technologies in an almost wholly positive way, increasing voter participation and making elections more inclusive by encouraging the youth, the elderly, and the people with disabilities. The question that remains is, how can the elections be modernized without jeopardizing its trustworthiness and the trust of the voters? Research in the DemTech project is expected to explore this question by studying existing election practices in order to ultimately propose and experiment with different technological innovations. In a way, it can be said that the project mimics to some extent the way in which ethnography for design has been portrayed since the beginning of the CSCW field.

14.5.2   Parliamentary Election 2011

Three months after the official launch of the DemTech research project, the prime minister of Denmark called for parliamentary elections in June 2011. While in many countries parliamentary elections take place every 4 years, this is not the case in

---

[2]http://archive.idea.int/press/pr20011120.htm (27 May 2011).

Denmark where these elections can take place any time before the maximum length of parliament, if the prime minister decides to call for such an election. The research team was thus thrown out into the field to conduct preliminary ethnographies of the election practices. "Democratic technologies" initially concerned "e-voting" machines and the focus was on how these machines could replace the actual processes which are part of elections (e.g., ballot casting, ballot counting, etc.). The preliminary ethnographic observations brought to the foreground the various artifacts that emerged as relevant and crucial for making the election process democratic.

When we lift the curtain and look inside election practices, we see that these practices stretch beyond election day. For instance, election practices are enacted not only on the day of election; they exist also during several months of preparation where election officials (i.e., municipal workers) work long days in order to be able to get everything ready. Furthermore, election does not end on election day; various election officials continue to work weeks after the election, reporting summaries to the different authorities, evaluating the election, etc. It becomes quickly clear that the actual ballot casting is only a very small part of the large sociomaterial machinery which makes "technology for democracy." Observations of the election revealed the importance of the different artifacts which are part of what makes "technologies for democracy." This included, for example, the ballot boxes at the election locations, the curtains and the voting booths, the ballots and the voters cards, the lists of political candidates, the many rubber bands and Post-It notes, the pencils used for marking the ballots, the local volunteers and municipal workers, the laws and regulations for tallying and for ensuring the presence of representatives from political parties, etc. All these are sociomaterial components, which are a critical part of what contributes to the relatively high trust in elections in Denmark. While giving a complete description of all the sociomaterial practices involved in elections is not the intention of this chapter, our main point is that the "democratic technologies" were clearly much more than "e-voting machines"; these include complex practices where artifacts and people engage in particular ways to ensure the trustworthiness of the election. Exploring the different bounding of what makes "technology for democracy" over time from the grant proposal toward the different activities conducted as part of the research project, interesting transformations emerge. What is part of "technology for democracy" initially is changed over the period of the project. The entity "technology for democracy" becomes inclusive of new relations while excluding other relations. One can say that particular aspects of the entities are bracketed out, while other aspects become bracketed in. As can be seen from the above, the "technology for democracy" as a sociomaterial entity has thus changed since writing the research proposal.

14.5.3 Political Agency

During the DemTech project, the research team received several invitations from the different partners, which gave the project the opportunity to have political agency. However, each opportunity constituted invitations into supporting the different political agendas of a diverse set of people.

A workshop was organized by the Ministry of Finance and Interior in order to initiate a debate about e-voting technologies. The research team was invited to assist with organizing and holding the workshop in collaboration with the Danish Board of Technology (Teknologirådet). The research team accepted the invitation which was seen as a way to facilitate and participate in the political discourse around e-voting technologies in Denmark. Different social groups were invited to participate in the workshop, including municipal employees, different kinds of experts (IT, law, etc.), technology critics, hackers, and activists, all with different perspectives on "democratic technologies." The activists and technology critics were questioning the municipalities' interest in e-voting and asked whether there was any solid business case behind the wish to implement e-voting technologies. Questions were raised about the cost of e-voting technologies and about whether there was any solid and scientific evidence backing up the expected benefits of these technologies. Furthermore, the IT and security experts expressed their concerns while explaining that none of the technologies available today were secure enough against tampering and hacking attempts. Thus, during the workshop, the "technology for democracy" was constantly redefined.

In general, it can be said that the workshop led to questioning several basic, yet taken for granted, assumptions, for example, that the implementation of e-voting technologies will inevitably happen as part of the modernization process and that this will lead to cost reductions, increased efficiency, etc. Although e-voting technologies were at the center of the debate, the workshop also invited municipal employees in order to include their insight about the current work practices, procedures, and traditions surrounding elections. This was followed by a presentation by the second author summarizing the insights from the preliminary ethnography during the 2011 election. This presentation focused on lifting the curtains behind elections and unpacking the various organizational processes and sociomaterial practices that take place when organizing elections. It became evident that a greater understanding of the current paper-based system would be beneficial, if not necessary, before considering any e-voting technology. In other words, before discussing the requirement specifications for the new electronic system, we needed to investigate in greater depth the current practices, regulations, and traditions surrounding elections.

This workshop can, to some extent, be conceptualized as a design workshop where the space for design extended the boundaries of the technical artifact. The "technology for democracy" was no longer a simple and clear black box of e-voting technology that *must* come into existence. Instead the construction and existence of the technology were questioned by some of the workshop participants. In this particular case, the role of the researchers was not merely to identify requirement specifications (which in and of itself is a difficult task requiring in-depth understandings of technological opportunities) but rather to facilitate a critical discussion about e-voting technologies and enroll the different actors and voices that are relevant. Thus, the researchers' contribution was participating in and influencing the discourse on what constitutes the technology, rather than merely listing requirement specifications.

During the short period of the research project, the team received various invitations from different stakeholders. Initially the research team collaborated with two smaller municipalities, but during the project they received requests from other municipalities who wished to join the project. In another incident, the municipalities invited the research team to *join the effort to change the law* in Denmark that does not permit experimenting with e-voting technologies. The municipalities invited the researchers to study their work practices and help them *showcase the need* for e-voting technologies. In a difference incident, one of the vendors invited the researchers to conduct experiments and test his e-voting machines with real voters. In this case, the researchers did not accept this invitation. They feared that participating in the vendor's experiments might risk their position as it was important for them to protect their independent academic and scientific voice. Finally, the researchers were invited to meet other stakeholders and businesses involved in elections in different countries (i.e., Africa, the Philippines, and Egypt). In November 2011, after the popular uprising, some of the team members who went to Egypt to participate in initial discussions were interested in e-voting technologies.

Around the same period, the research team was also invited to work with the ministry. Thus, part of the research team's activities became to advise and guide the ministry about the topic of e-voting. These engagements and relations with the municipalities, the vendors, and, not least, the ministry have given the researchers a unique opportunity to participate in influencing policy and the debates about e-voting technologies in Denmark. At the same time, it has been immensely important for the researchers to preserve their independence and critical academic role.

14.5.4   Societal Impact

As can be seen from the above examples, during the relatively short period of the research project, the research team has been drawn in different directions, invited to take different roles and to create different sociomaterial relations with various stakeholders. These different invitations and roles change depending on the contextual circumstance as well as the political context at particular points in time. For instance, at the outset of the research project, the prime minister announced parliamentary elections in Denmark. This meant that the research team did not have as much time as they initially assumed and they were rushed into the field. During this election, one of the vendors demonstrated their e-voting machines. Thus, although the research team was cautious and avoided introducing any technology at that point in time, the vendors have already moved ahead and demonstrated their e-voting machines. Not too long after, a letter was written by several municipalities and was quickly submitted to the ministry requesting to change the law. The municipalities have already attempted to change the law a few years ago but with no luck. The newly elected government seemed initially more welcoming; however, the situation changed and the government turned down the second request to change the law. These are some of the changes in the local conditions that influenced the research agenda and activities.

It is worth noting that the pressure initiated by the municipalities to change the law was partially influenced by the fact that Norway had initiated a new pilot project testing Internet voting. The context surrounding the DemTech project has been continuously and rapidly changing, influencing the opportunities and types of roles and interventions that the research team received at different moments in time. What is critical here is that at no time was it relevant for the researchers to contribute by identifying requirement specifications or evaluating the technology. Instead, the main contribution from the researchers has been in the form of shaping the discourse and practice which makes "technology for democracy" while at all times keeping track of this dynamic entity by binding together new and bracketing out other sociomaterial relations.

14.6 Socially Embedded Technologies

Studying technologies in practice while acknowledging that we cannot make a separation between the social and the technical brings particular research agendas to the table and changes the focus for what the researchers have to do when engaging with practice. We propose the concept of bounding practices to describe the work the researchers do when studying technologies in practice as sociomaterial dynamic entities.

We presented examples from the DemTech project to illustrate how different boundings of technology are created and changed over time. The example of the ministry workshop to which bloggers, hackers, and activists were invited illustrates very clearly the bounding practices, which took form during the research project. That is, the relations toward the requirement specification were cut, while new relations were created, for instance, by inviting activists and technology critics. This illustrates how the role of ethnography for design has to expand when we study such dynamic and multiple entities. We are no longer simply identifying requirements or evaluating technology use; instead we are part of creating the technology and conceptualizing the sociomaterial relations that make the technology. While this role is not limited to ethnographers, it includes all the different kinds of research practices engaging in projects similar to DemTech. What this finding points to is that funding for ICT research has a clear tendency toward a particular type of research, namely, technological deterministic research, where the center of attention is the creation of a technological artifact. It can be said that it is not entirely a coincidence that the original agenda in the DemTech research proposal pays great attention to the technical artifact. Reviewing funding calls for ICT research in, for example, the European Horizon 2020, the types of projects which can be funded are typically centered on the construction of a technological artifact, which is expected to improve practices. Even though we ICT researchers are well aware that the technical artifact does not automatically lead to improved and successful new practices and that research opening up and critically examining such technologies serve a valid and important ICT research topic, we still find ourselves in situations where we have to adopt the technologically deterministic rhetoric of the funding agencies when writing research proposals. The rhetoric of research proposals obviously does not imply a complete adherence to the actual research practice. As we saw in the DemTech project, the researchers took upon themselves the role of participation and letting the empirical field guide what made the entity "technologies for democracy." This investigation includes political, technological, and commercial environments and all important information infrastructures constituting the practice of democracy.

What is important to note here is that in most cases, the ostensible purpose of ethnography in strategic technology project grant applications is formulated as providing requirement specifications for the future design of a technology. ICT funding is directed toward the design of technical artifacts, and the role of other disciplinary engagements in design is often seen as supportive. The sequential order between first studying practice and then designing technologies remains dominating in the nature of ICT funding structures, a sequential ordering which does not take into account the complex sociomaterial practices which shapes technology in a modern society. Technologies are not stable singular objects; instead they only come into being when enacted in the practices by which they are part.

"Democratic technologies" were enacted in multiple different ways along the DemTech project, and these became different things at different points in time. What made the "democratic technologies" in the interactions with vendors and commercial interests was different than what made the "democratic technologies" when the researchers interacted with technology critics. But rather than referring to these differences in terms of different perspectives, we argue that the unit of analysis—"democratic technologies"—was made in different ways, and thus the boundaries for what makes this unit were dynamic and constantly changing. The entity "democratic technologies" is both a commercial interest and a possible engine for trust in democracy. This entity is bounded continually and over time it takes multiple forms. If we are to design "technologies for democracies," we have to take a diverse set of boundings into considerations, which only appears to us if we pay analytical attention and expand our notions for what makes the boundaries of technology design.

In this chapter we propose that socially embedded technology research is a promising opportunity for dismissing the current technological deterministic perspectives on ICT research, and we propose that one possible replacement is the sociomaterial-design approach (Bjørn and Østerlund, in progress), where we attempt to design technical artifact without predetermined boundaries. This approach suggests that researchers should pay critical attention while participating actively in the bounding practices making the technology.

14.7 Final Remarks

We argue that the sequential order of first conducting ethnography and then designing technology no longer holds because technology today is dynamic and ever changing, and by the time we complete our ethnography, both practice and technology are already evolving, sometimes dramatically so. Therefore, we recommend rethinking the role of research in such situations, and, in particular, we suggest thinking about the researchers' role as creating and managing the boundaries for what makes the technology. The boundaries for what makes the technology are no longer simply predefined; instead they are created and recreated when people enact technology, and they are continuously changing and being bound in different ways.

We cannot study the technology without the social, and as such the social becomes constitutive part of what makes the technology. Socially embedded technologies form an overall umbrella of different approaches for ICT research. In this chapter we have proposed a way to conceptualize the practices of SET research, namely, in terms of designing technological artifact without predetermined boundaries by investigating, experimenting, and participating in the bounding practices which make the technology. Our role as researchers is thus to engage with relevant groups and communities with invested interests in the ICT topic and to study how technology becomes bounded in practice. This includes identifying relations in a hyphenated structure as well as [bracketing] the entity by distinguishing what makes the boundaries for the black box of technology.

Acknowledgment We highly appreciate the discussions we have had on our work with the great researchers within the EUSSET community including Dave Randall, Myriam Lewkowicz, Volker Wulf, and Kjeld Schmidt as well as many others. We would also like to acknowledge Carsten Schürmann, the principle investigator of the DemTech project, for his comments on the final draft of this chapter. This work was supported in part by grant 10-092309 from the Danish Council for Strategic Research, Programme Commission on Strategic Growth Technologies.

References

Andersen, T., Bjørn, P., et al. (2010). Designing for collaborative interpretation in telemonitoring: Re-introducing patients as diagnostic agents. *International Journal of Medical Informatics, 80*(8), e112. doi:10.1016/j.ijmedinf.2010.09.010.

Balka, E., Bjørn, P., et al. (2008). Steps towards a typology for health informatics. In *Computer supported cooperative work (CSCW)*. San Diego: ACM.

Barad, K. (1996). Meeting the universe halfway: Realism and social constructivism without contradiction. In *Feminism, science, and the philosophy of science* (pp. 161–194). Dordrecht: Kluwer.

Bardram, J., & Bossen, C. (2005). *A web of coordinative artefacts: Collaborative work in a hospital ward*. Sanible Island: ACM Group.

Bentley, R., Hughes, J., et al. (1992). Ethnographically-informed system design for air traffic control. In *Computer supported cooperative work (CSCW)*. New York: ACM Press.

Bjørn, P. (2012). Bounding practice: How people act in sociomaterial practices. *Scandinavian Journal of Information Systems, 24*(2), 97–104.

Bjørn, P., & Balka, E. (2007). Health care categories have politics too: Unpacking the managerial agendas of electronic triage systems. In *ECSCW 2007: Proceedings of the tenth European conference on computer supported cooperative work*. Limerick: Springer.

Bjørn, P., & Boulus, N. (2011). Dissenting in reflective conversations: Critical components of doing action research. *Action Research Journal, 9*(3), 282–302.

Bjørn, P., & Hertzum, M. (2011). Artefactual multiplicity: A study of emergency-department whiteboards. *Computer Supported Cooperative Work (CSCW): An International Journal, 20*(1), 93.

Bjørn, P., & Østerlund, C. (2014). *Sociomaterial-design: Bounding technologies in practice*. Cham: Springer.

Bjørn, P., Burgoyne, S., et al. (2009). Boundary factors and contextual contingencies: Configuring electronic templates for health care professionals. *European Journal of Information Systems, 18*, 428–441.

Blomberg, J., Giacomi, J., et al. (1993). Ethnographic field methods and their relation to design. In D. Schuler & A. Namioka (Eds.), *Participatory design: Principles and practices* (pp. 123–155). London: Lawrence Erlbaum Associates Publisher.

Boulus, N. (2004). *Managing the gradual transition from paper to electronic patient records (EPR)*. Master, University of Oslo.

Boulus, N. (2009). Sociotechnical changes brought about by electronic medical record. In *Americas conference on information systems*, San Francisco, CA, USA.

Boulus, N. (2010). *A journey into the hidden lives of electronic medical records (EMRs): Action research in the making*. Vancouver: School of Communication, Simon Fraser University.

Boulus, N., & Bjørn, P. (2007). Constructing technology-in-use practices: EPR-adaptation in Canada and Norway. In *Third international conference information technology in health care: Socio-technical approaches*. Sidney: IOS Press.

Boulus, N., & Bjørn, P. (2008). A cross-case analysis of technology-in-use practices: EPR-adaptation in Canada and Norway. *International Journal of Medical Informatics, 79*(6), 97–108.

Boulus-Rødje, N. (2012). Action research as a network: Collective production of roles and interventions. In *Proceedings of the 20th European conference on information systems (ECIS)*. Barcelona: ESADE.

Dourish, P. (2006). Implications for design. In *Computer human interaction (CHI)* (pp. 541–550). Montreal: ACM.

Dourish, P., & Bly, S. (1992). Portholes: Supporting awareness in a distributed work group. In *Computer human interaction (CHI)* (pp. 541–547). New York: ACM Press.

Grudin, J., & Grinter, R. (1995). Ethnography and design. *Computer Supported Cooperative Work (CSCW): An International Journal, 3*, 55–59.

Grudin, J. (2004). *Crossing the divide. ACM transactions on human-computer interaction*. New York: ACM Press.

Gutwin, C., & Greenberg, S. (2002). A descriptive framework of workspace awareness for real-time groupware. *Computer Supported Cooperative Work (CSCW): An International Journal, 11*, 411–446.

Haraway, D. (1987). *Donna Haraway reads "the national geographic" on primates*. youTube video. http://www.youtube.com/watch?v=eLN2ToEIlwM

Haraway, D. (1991). *Simians, cyborgs and women: The reinvention of nature*. London: Free Associations Books.

Hartswood, M., Proctor, R., et al. (2003). Making a case in medical work: Implications for electronic medical record. *Computer Supported Cooperative Work (CSCW): An International Journal, 12*(3), 241–266.

Hughes, J., Randall, D., et al. (1992). Faltering from ethnography to design. In *Computer supported cooperative work (CSCW)* (pp. 115–122). New York: ACM Press.

Hughes, J., King, V., et al. (1995). The role of ethnography in interactive system design. *Interactions, 2*(2), 57–65.

Jones, M. (2013). A matter of life and death: Exploring conceptualizations of sociomateriality in the context of critical care. *MIS Quarterly Special Issue on Sociomateriality, 38*(3), 895–925.

Latour, B. (2005). *Reassembling the social: An introduction to actor-network-theory*. Oxford: Oxford University Press.

Law, J. (2004). *After method: Mess is social science research*. London/New York: Routledge.

Leonardi, P., Nardi, B., et al. (2012). *Materiality and organizing: Social interaction in a technological world*. Oxford: Oxford University Press.

Luff, P., Hindmarch, J., et al. (Eds.). (2000). *Workplace studies: Recovering work practice and informing system design*. Cambridge: Cambridge University Press.

Mol, A. (2002). *The body multiple: Ontology in medical practice*. London: Duke University Press.

Møller, N. H., & Bjørn, P. (2011). Layers in sorting practices: Sorting out patients with potential cancer. *Computer Supported Cooperative Work (CSCW): An International Journal, 20*, 123–153.

Orlikowski, W. (1992). Learning from notes: Organizational issues in groupware implementation. In *Conference on computer supported cooperative work*. New York: ACM.

Orlikowski, W. (2007). Sociomaterial practices: Exploring technology at work. *Organization Studies, 28*(9), 1435–1448.

Pipek, V., & Wulf, V. (2009). Infrastructuring: Toward an integrated perspective on the design and use of information technology. *Journal of the Association for Information Systems, 10*(Special Issue), 447–473.

Randall, D., Harper, R., et al. (2007). *Fieldwork for design: Theory and practice*. London: Springer.

Schmidt, K. (1998). The critical role of workplace studies in CSCW. In C. Heath, J. Hindmarsh, & P. Luff (Eds.), *Workplace studies: Recovering work practice and informing design*. Cambridge: Cambridge University Press.

Schmidt, K. (2009). *Divided by a common acronym: On the fragmentation of CSCW* (European conference on computer supported cooperative work (ECSCW)). Vienna: Springer.

Schmidt, K., & Bannon, L. (1992). Taking CSCW seriously: Supporting articulation work. *Computer Supported Cooperative Work (CSCW): An International Journal, 1*(1–2), 7–40.

Suchman, L. (1994). Do categories have politics? The language/action perspective reconsidered. *Computer Supported Cooperative Work (CSCW): An International Journal, 2*, 177–190.

Svensson, M. S., Heath, C., et al. (2007). Instrumental action: The timely exchange of implements during surgical operation. In *European conference on computer-supported cooperative work (ECSCW)*. Limerick: Springer.

Winograd, T. (1994). Categories, disciplines, and social coordination. *Computer Supported Cooperative Work (CSCW): An International Journal, 2*, 191–197.

Wulf, V., Rohde, M., et al. (2011). Engaging with practices: Design case studies as a research framework in CSCW. In *Computer supported cooperative work CSCW* (pp. 505–512). Hangzhou: ACM.

Yamashita, N., Hirata, K., et al. (2008). Impact of seating positions on group video communication. In *Computer supported cooperative work (CSCW) conference* (pp. 177–186). San Diego: ACM.

Chapter 15
Designing for Lived Health: A Practice-Based Approach for Person-Centered Health Information Technologies

Elizabeth Kaziunas and Mark S. Ackerman

15.1 Introduction

Health is almost always a deeply *personal* issue. As individuals, people struggle to maintain and enhance their health within their own "messiness"—their values, practices, and beliefs.

At the same time, a person's health is always *social*. It is arranged against and in conjunction with medical practices and institutions. Health is also engaged often within a family and almost always within a community context (e.g., with a person's lifeworld and set of social worlds).[1]

Systems that incorporate both a deeply personal view of one's health and at the same a nuanced understanding of its social contexts would be—in keeping with the arguments in the rest of this book—the most helpful and usable. Currently, a medicalized viewpoint limits system designs to narrowly prescribed forms of activity, almost always within the hierarchical relationship of doctor and "patient." (Indeed, in US medicine, there is currently no vocabulary for "person" outside of "patient" and "consumer.") While the Human-ComputerInteraction (HCI) and

---

[1]In this paper we use "community" in the common usage to refer to a group of people living in the same place (e.g., Flint community) or having common characteristics (e.g., medical informatics community). We use the technical term "lifeworld" to talk about an individual's view of their lives and social contexts. For a fuller discussion of the "lifeworld," see Luckmann (1970), Shutz and Luckmann (1973), and Schutz (1967). We will use the term "social world" to talk about specific collectivities that form and encapsulate social contexts. For a fuller discussion of "social world," see Strauss (1991, 1993).

E. Kaziunas (✉) • M.S. Ackerman
School of Information, University of Michigan, Ann Arbor, MI, USA
e-mail: eskaziu@umich.edu

© Springer-Verlag London 2015
V. Wulf et al. (eds.), *Designing Socially Embedded Technologies in the Real-World*,
Computer Supported Cooperative Work, DOI 10.1007/978-1-4471-6720-4_15

Computer-Supported Cooperative Work (CSCW) research communities have a more nuanced view of the "personal," designs are arguably still limited in their adoption of social context.

This chapter examines what sets of social relations "person centered" has and might include, based on theoretical grounds and grounded in a field study in Flint, Michigan (a city in the American Midwest). We wish to ask how relationships among family, friends, caretakers, and community health workers can be reflected in healthcare designs. Below, we first examine the history of the "personal health record" (PHR) and find that the design of PHRs has swung toward an individualized view of the patient mirroring that of institutionally controlled electronic health records. It has become, over time, limited in its view of the "personal." We then proceed to extend the PHR's view of the "personal" based on recent social-theoretical frameworks and show that this extension is in line with recent HCI and CSCW personal health application designs.

We argue for a new approach to healthcare systems—oriented toward *lived health*—that supports the social richness of people's practices. As a part of this wider design space, we call our socially enhanced vision for the PHR a "person-centered health technology" or PcHIT. (We use the "PcHIT" term primarily for expository clarity here; it can also be seen as a general extension of the personal health record or of personal health applications.) The chapter then demonstrates the analytical power of this extension by showing that it fits the findings from a study of people with chronic diseases in Flint.

We begin with a brief history of work in medical informatics that involves "personal" health information.

15.2 Framings of the *Personal* in PHRs

One place where conceptions of the "personal" have most prominently played a role in medical informatics is personal health records (PHRs), of growing interest to a wide range of academic disciplines. PHRs have optimistically been lauded by many as ushering in a new age of patient-empowered medicine. As Sittig (2001) writes, "Internet-based, personal health records have the potential to profoundly influence the delivery of health care in the twenty-first century."

It has often been remarked upon, however, that "PHR" as a concept and technology includes a range of definitions and designs (Angst et al. 2006; Archer et al. 2011; Gearson 2007; Kaelber et al. 2008; Osterlund et al. 2011). Over its relatively brief history, the "P" in PHR has stood for personal, patient, parent, and patient controlled and patient held (Kim et al. 2011). The medical informatics literature has increasingly come to see PHRs as various arrangements of information, architectures, and tools focused on supporting the institutional role of the patient and the work practices of clinicians; yet, other less bounded interpretations of PHRs have been voiced. A widely cited report released by theMarkle Foundation, for instance, broadly defines the PHR as "a single, *person-centered* system designed to track and support health activities across one's entire life experience" (original emphasis, Markle 2003).

This section surveys how medical informatics has come to adopt a particular viewpoint toward the "personal." In short, a set of institutional imperatives— including fixing a dysfunctional and fragmented healthcare system in the United States—have pushed toward conceptualizing the PHR as a unified data set for an individual that can be shared across organizational boundaries. In this way, the "P" in PHR has become more specifically framed around the medicalized role of the *patient*.

15.2.1 PHRs: A History

The personal health record is far from a new concept in that people have long maintained paper-based health records, be it a notation of births and deaths inscribed in a family bible or a list of medications hastily scribbled on the back of an envelope. Community health studies in the 1970s and 1980s focused on the use of paper health records in specific populations. This research—grounded in the theoretical discourse of medical anthropology and medical sociology—acknowledged that meanings of health varied widely among groups of people. This understanding of health provided the starting point for research on health records driven by social interests.

Kim et al. (2011) note that the first appearance to a PHR in an academic journal came in 1969, a brief allusion to a "personal record linkage." Studies on the history of personal health records show that there was a steady number of references to PHRs in the medical informatics literature through the 1990s and a dramatic increase in PHR references around 2005. During this period of heighted attention, a number of publications engage specifically with the challenges of classification as researchers within medical informatics set themselves the daunting task of "defining" the PHR. (For a complete review of the PHR literature, see Jones et al. 2010, Kim et al. 2011, and Archer et al. 2011.)

In the 1990s, the "P" in the acronym of PHR held a number of interpretations. Kim et al. (2011) point out, for example, how the terms "*parent held* record" and "*patient-held* health records" were both introduced to the medical informatics literature in 1993. Many of these early descriptions of PHRs offer inclusive understandings of the personal. Such a viewpoint can be found in Iakovidis' (1998) article on the adoption of electronic health records in Europe that heralds the emergence of personal health records. Iakovidis describes PHRs as a "new generation" of electronic healthcare records that would be connected to "virtual healthcare centers." PHRs are positioned as tools for patient empowerment that will support people in taking a more active role in managing their health information and making decisions about personal health-related activities.

Although "patient" is referenced heavily in Iakovidis' design narrative, several of his design specifications demonstrate a nuanced understanding of the personal that extends beyond a strictly biomedical framing.

The electronic healthcare record will not only be accessible to the patients but it will also incorporate their views and notes resulting from self-monitoring of chronic illness, to make dietary notes, monitor sport and exercise performance, behavioral activities and moods etc. We could see in the near future the development of personal health status monitoring and support systems at home that interact with personal health records and complete the picture in the continuity of care scenario. (Iakovidis 1998)

Iakovidis' vision of self-monitoring and data tracking, interoperable home health technologies, and emphasis on health and wellness can be seen in the current Health Information Technology (HIT) landscape of endless mobile health applications, biosensing technologies, and the popularity of the Quantified Self movement whose participants enthusiastically record, track, and share a variety of biometric data from sleep patterns to heart rate fluctuations. This early PHR vision is additionally compelling in that Iakovidis also suggests people will "incorporate their views and notes" on diet and health conditions. This wording implies that PHRs have the potential to extend beyond a strictly medical framing to include reflective activities that engage individuals in sensemaking.

Despite an early openness in the medical informatics community to explore alternative framings, the personal became increasingly conceptualized in a way that was synonymous with that of patient. In what Kim et al. (2011) describe as "a shift to patient centeredness," the conflation of the term personal with that of patient was directly linked to the development of EHR systems in the 1990s. In particular, the Institute of Medicine's 1991 report, *The Computer-Based Patient Record, an Essential Technology for Healthcare*, played an influential role in helping shape the boundaries of the electronic health records movement in the United States. This document includes directives for digitizing provider-controlled patient records (what would become known as EHRs) in order to lower the rate of medical errors (Gearson 2007). Although the report does not specifically mention personal health records, the concept of EHRs provided an intellectual template for PHRs that framed the personal in terms of an individual's interaction with various clinicians and relationship to professional medical work. An emphasis on "patient needs" in this literature details concerns about an individual's access and ownership to their health information in the context of the healthcare system. Some researchers in the medical informatics community have suggested the term "*patient-controlled* health records" as a way of championing patient rights (Kim et al. 2011, emphasis added), and advocacy for more patient control continues to be heavily reflected in recent definitions of PHRs.

The role of the patient in managing their health information was also being explored through commercial designs as well as policy reports. Gearson (2007) describes the impetus for Internet health start-ups in the late 1990s like Followme.com and WellMed.com as increasing patient safety in the healthcare system by bridging an increasingly fragmented healthcare system. Echoing similar concerns, recent corporate entrants to the web-based PHR market such as Microsoft's Health Vault in 2007 and Google Health in 2008 proposed to entice people to use PHRs by giving users the option of sharing their health information with other health information systems. Despite these efforts, the use of PHRs by the general public has remained low (Nazi 2013). Citing lack of widespread PHR adoption, Google discontinued Google Health in 2012 and gave users until January 2013 to download their personal health data. Google Health's early demise reflects a general tempering of earlier rhetoric in media and the academy that PHRs would "revolutionize" healthcare.

The conversation, then, has turned to how to unify patient data through the connection of PHRs, EHRs, and other sources of electronic health data (Gearson 2007), instead of discussing PHRs as distinct systems for patient empowerment. Healthcare providers like hospitals, insurers, and employers have offered "tethered" PHRs that are integrated or connected with the organization's information system. One such example of this architecture model is Dossia founded by a consortium of corporations including Wal-Mart and Intel. These integrated health systems often give people access to their medical information through a "patient web portal" that has an array of functions and tools. People can view an abstract of their health record or parts of their clinical record, have their prescriptions filled, and make clinical appointments. In some of these designs, patients also have the ability to add specific types of information about their health status through journals/diary applications or communicate to healthcare providers through secure messaging tools.

In 2003, the highly influential Markle Foundation report (2003), "Connecting for Health," reconceptualized the PHR as a "single, *person-centered* system" (original emphasis). Unlike earlier views, the Markle report highlights the role of the individual. This point is made again through the use of bold underlined text, with the firmly worded statement: "The *individual person* is the primary user of the PHR." Tang et al. (2006) build on the Markle report detailing a spectrum of designs from stand-alone applications to PHRs that are fully integrated with the healthcare provider's EHR system. While the authors note a PHR "includes information managed by the *individual*" (original emphasis), they also acknowledge that PHRs may contain data about other family members and even nonmedical settings such as home and work environments. These nonmedical social contexts, however, are not fully explored.

Defining the personal health record in relation to other electronic patient records like the EMR and EHR has now become a common framing device in much of the medical informatics literature. In 2008, the (US) National Alliance for Health Information Technology published a report called "Defining Key Health Information Technology Terms" that defined EMRs, EHRs, and PHRs (emphasis added):

- An electronic record of health-related information on an individual that can be created, gathered, managed, and consulted *by authorized clinicians and staff within one healthcare organization*
- An electronic record of health-related information on an individual that conforms to nationally recognized interoperability standards and that can be created, managed, and consulted *by authorized clinicians and staff across more than one healthcare organization*

- An electronic record of health-related information on an individual that conforms to nationally recognized interoperability standards and that can be drawn from multiple sources while being managed, shared, and controlled *by the individual*

These definitions categorize records as different types of collaborations between people, standards, and data. The EMR is coordinated by clinicians and staff using the standards of a single organization, the EHR is coordinated through national standards by clinicians and staff across multiple healthcare organizations, and the PHR utilizes information based on national standards but is coordinated by the individual. Accordingly, the EMR, EHR, and PHR—if fully integrated in an ideal manner—work together to comprehensively aggregate health information for each individual.

The report notes that given the sharing of data, it is often difficult to distinguish between an EHR and PHR. The authors argue for a PHR that is defined primarily in terms of information access in which the individual has "control" of their health information. How this control actually works in relation to practicalities of system architecture and the power dynamics of the healthcare industry, however, is less clear. The report states, for example, that information found in the "patient portal" interface of a typical PHR are also maintained by the healthcare provider.

> Through various technological means, selected content in an EHR can be made available for individuals to view and use in guiding activities of health and wellness through what is called a "patient portal." The health care provider operating the EHR system typically controls the patient portal. Many of these portals are given the name PHR, but the source of control of the information is important to determining whether this model is a PHR or remains within the scope of an EHR. To be a PHR, access to the record must be managed and controlled by the individual. Information that passes from an EHR to a PHR transfers to the control of the individual. (National Alliance for Health Information Technology (U.S.) 2008)

The report also acknowledges that current PHRs allow individuals to enter only limited forms of information; yet they optimistically maintain that "PHRs have the potential to be a robust, better-assembled and more organized source of both clinical and wellness information." This robustness would come through the addition of new sources of health information that extend beyond the patient-physician-pharmacy configuration currently available in most PHRs. The report suggests that in the future, PHRs will connect healthcare providers, healthcare clinicians, medical devices, wellness promoters, individuals, health insurers, public health officials, and research institutions promoting medical studies and recent publications.

It is worth pointing out that the report does not provide a discrete category for an individual's family and friends, at least those who are not formally designated as "proxies" or "agents." It is puzzling that the people often most intimately involved in a person's health—a sister, a close friend with a similar health condition—are absent from this lengthy list of health information collaborators that includes everyone from insurance agents to academics running clinical trials.

Finally, a recent article, by Jones et al. (2010), confirms a wider trend toward data integration in the vision of PHRs. After discussing several conceptualizations of PHRs, they offer up a working definition:

Electronic personal health record (PHR): a private, secure application through which an individual many access, manage, and share his or her health information. The PHR can include information that is entered by the consumer and/or from other sources such as pharmacies, labs, and healthcare providers. (Jones et al. 2010)

To summarize, personal health records are defined as containing a variety of health information, types of users, and technological tools that allow for the collection, sharing, and maintenance of health-related data. In addition, these definitions discuss the aims of PHRs as primarily supporting the communication practices between health professionals and patients and the integration of health information systems. PHR models range from a data set controlled by an individual on a personal computer to information shared between a variety of systems and organizations; however, the definitions found within the medical informatics literature appear to increasingly support a vision of data integration between PHRs and EHRs. The current state of the literature emphasizes a medicalized perspective of health information in which the personal understood primarily in terms of a patient's role and rights in a wider healthcare context. Hence follows the general preoccupation in these publications with issues of information "access" and "control."

The consequence of the *personal* being increasingly understood in terms of the *patient*, we argue, was the loss of original concern around social context and personal reflection. Interpretations of the personal grounded in family and community life were sidelined; the pressing needs to integrate data across healthcare providers and implement working health and medical systems, especially in the United States, became the focus instead.

Recently, there appears to be a renewed interest in social contexts. Recent position papers outlining future research directions, for example, indicate a need to study PHR use in diverse populations such as "people with chronic conditions, individuals with disabilities, parents with small children, people with a strong interest in maintaining health lifestyles, and the elderly or their caregivers" (Archer et al. 2011) and nonmedical settings like the home (Tang et al. 2006). Furthermore, it is acknowledged that long-term sustainability issues around design and the ways in which people might use PHRs at different periods in their lives are still not well understood (Archer et al. 2011). In the next section, we examine an alternative framing for the PHR that positions *the personal* as inherently *social* and grounded in a diverse range of contextualized practices. This framing both revisits an earlier conceptualization of the personal that guided prior studies on paper-based personal health records and also introduces some new considerations on personhood in an age of digital health technologies.

15.3 Theoretical (Re)Framings

We believe a more compelling framing for PcHITs can be found in theoretical work that allows for a richer understanding of social complexity. Taken together as a theoretical (re)framing of the personal, it challenges the idea of the personal represented in PHR definitions as an individual, unified patient and takes instead social arrangements as a starting point for understanding how bodies and selves are situated, enmeshed in local contexts. This alternative understanding of person-centeredness is furthermore explored through attending to *practices*.[2] These practices might include patient work but also consist of a variety of other non-biomedical activities that are a part of people's everyday life and located within a range of social contexts.

15.3.1   The Role of the Lifeworld in Healthcare

Medical sociologists studying doctor-patient communication have long discussed the need to understand how the richness of people's lives might be more meaningfully integrated with professional healthcare work (Rodin et al. 2009; Barry et al. 2001; Mishler 1984). It has often been noted, for instance, that the patient's "voice of the lifeworld" (e.g., contextually grounded experiences) is held in tension with the physician's "voice of medicine" (e.g., technical information) (Scambler and Britten 2001).

The need for health professionals to relate clinical information to the lifeworld is especially important in treating people with chronic illnesses as these health conditions are inextricably woven into the fabric of daily life. For example, Barry et al. (2001) writes:

> As the role of the GP [general practitioner] changes with the rise of chronic illness in an aging population GPs may have to change their notions of success from purely technical considerations to include their patients feeling understood, listened to and treated like whole and unique human beings. (Barry et al. 2001)

Studies detailing the patient's lifeworld present a sociological critique of professional medical practice by arguing that institutionalized healthcare too often ignores social context, dehumanizes the patient, and "depersonalizes" health information. Although the literature on medical sociology demonstrates a need to think holistically about health, the ways in which medical information might be integrated with patient lifeworlds are still not well understood (Waizkin 1989, 1991).

It is worth considering then how people's lifeworlds might be better integrated into the design of PcHITs. Envisioning users strictly in terms of *individuals*, for instance, might not resonate with people for whom *the family* is the most important social unit. Designs that seek to be "person centered" rather than simply "patient centered" would benefit from future research that investigates the important sets of social relationships found in people's lifeworlds.

---

[2]Practices here focus on human action (e.g., *what people do*). Health practices refer to the ways that people manage their health through specific, situated actions. For example, a person organizing their prescriptions on the kitchen counter in order to remember taking their daily medications.

While drawing attention to the social context of health, the medical sociology literature on the lifeworld is limited in its theoretical scope as it does not fully grapple with the complexity of a person being a part of multiple lifeworlds; nor does it offer a nuanced understanding of the role technological artifacts play in shaping the personal. To do this, we turn to social analyses that offer a critique of the self as a unified individual and suggest how PcHITs might support socially richer conceptualizations of the personal.

15.3.2 The Personal as Practice: Embodiment, Emerging Selves, and Health Records

Drawing from theoretical traditions across the humanities and social sciences, academic fields like science and technology studies (STS) articulate a conceptualization of personhood that is inextricably entwined with the cultural and material worlds. Posthumanist theorists like Haraway, for instance, attempt to disrupt and subvert an understanding of the body as singularly human: "Why should our bodies end at the skin?" (Haraway 1991). People and technology are in a constant state of flux, shaping and (re)shaping one another through a variety of interactions with different social contexts. This theoretical position implies an inherent multiplicity in a person's lived experience as different arrangements of technologies, processes, and people perform new self/selves. Furthermore, a growing collection of work has turned to practices as a theoretical lens and design methodology in which to understand and engage with this multiplicity (Orlikowski 2000; Schatzki et al. 2001; Suchman 2007; Danholt 2008).

In *The Body Multiple* (2002), a study of atherosclerosis, Mol conceptualizes the lived experience of a disease as "multiplicities of realities" made visible through the relations between practices of knowledge systems, the human body, and technologies. Information is not neutral but presents a version of reality that is always intertwined with practice (Mol 2002, p. 171). The patient record as an information technology includes an array of discrete logics (and realities) such as images of blood vessels, clinician notes, patient complaints, and numerical lab results that all perform a person's blood sugar levels. Although this information does not neatly align, Mol maintains that the patient record holds together as a form of coordination across the organizational contexts of healthcare institutions. In *The Logic of Care* (2008), Mol further argues that for healthcare to be person centered, policy-makers and practitioners need to grapple with contextual multiplicity by attending to localized health practices found both within and beyond the world of medicine.

Understanding the ways in which medical and health systems, especially PcHITs, are related to embodiment—how the personal is digitally performed—is also a matter of design. Berg and Harterink (2004) trace the history of medical records from the early twentieth century and demonstrate how the medical record has long conceptualized the patient as a singular, independent, and rational subject. They further argue that emerging technologies have the potential to shift our understanding of personhood to be "decentered, dispersed, and multiplied subjects" (Berg and Harterink 2004). Current PHRs, however, still largely design for a patient in isolation and apart from "the mess[3]" that is a part of contextual specificity: the localized practices found in particular communities, family situations, and geographies. If one accepts Berg and Harterink's (2004) postulation that digital patient records can help shape and support new forms of embodiment, then one must also think constructively about how to incorporate the contextual multiplicity of lived experience.

Suchman (2007) presents a practice theory approach that closely examines people's behavior in a specific context as the starting point for design work. Understanding people's practices—or in Suchman's terminology *situated actions*—helps articulate the complicated arrangements of people, social processes, and artifacts. As with Berg's (1999) "sociotechnical" approach, Suchman holds that good designs should embrace, rather than dismiss, the "mess" found in people's everyday actions be they in the home, workplace, hospital, or an online forum.

The notion of the postmodern/posthuman self as an assemblage of decentered and dispersed subjects argues for future design directions to help people manage a multiplicity of healthcare practices around different contexts such as family life, religious organizations, illness support groups, and local communities. That different types of personal health information may overlap, conflict, or coexist does not necessarily have to lead to technical chaos or poorer health outcomes. Disparate but meaningfully connected health information might open up new design trajectories that enable a holistic vision of health information technology that is integrated into people's everyday practices and lifeworlds.

15.4   HCI/CSCW Design Approaches Toward *Personal* Health

As discussed above, the vision of an "ideal" PHR underlying many of definitions in the medical informatics community has come to a view of the "personal" that is based primarily on the idea of a "modern self": unified, individual, and governed primarily by reason. This view of the personal is translated into the medicalized

---

[3]In earlier work (1999), Berg outlined a "sociotechnical" approach to designing health information technology. This framework, he writes, "overtly critical of approaches that denounce the 'messy' and 'ad hoc' nature of health care work, and that attempt to structure this work through the formal, standardized and 'rational' nature of IT systems. [. . .] It engages in constructive critique rather than in delivering yet another set of guidelines for design and implementation." For Berg, design work should start with a nuanced understanding of health practices, where practices include networks of people, tools, organizational routines, and documents. For another interpretation of "mess" in design, see Dourish and Bell (2011).

PHR as a well-managed data repository and coordination tool between an individual and their healthcare team. On the other hand, the concepts of the lifeworld and posthuman assemblages present a more nuanced understanding of the "personal" that engages with multiplicity, temporality, materiality, and "the messiness" of everyday life. This viewpoint reframes the personal in terms of fully contextualized social arrangements. This would be difficult, at best, to fully incorporate in technical systems.

The HCI/CSCW literature offers a middle ground by considering some, but not all, contexts for situated health practices in technological designs. That is, context is a necessary, albeit imperfect, part of the design process or is to be incorporated partially in the design itself. HCI/CSCW prototypes that have been commonly labeled as personal health applications (PHAs), although differing in key respects from the PHR definitions above (and from one another as well), are aligned in their approach to design. In attending closely to social contexts, they are representative of HCI/CSCW research that has focused on designing health technology in "complex, diverse, and locally situated" settings (Fitzpatrick and Ellingsen 2012).

In the following, we note two studies we believe exemplify the HCI/CSCW approach toward a personal health record. We necessarily privilege some HCI/CSCW studies in the following. There are many more that could have been included (e.g., Bardram et al. 2013; Caine et al. 2010; Kientz et al. 2009; Klasnja et al. 2010; Mynatt et al. 2001; Mamykina et al. 2008) but we did not do so for lack of space.

Enquist and Tollmar's (2008) *Memory Stone* is a record-keeping system designed to support pregnant women, their families, and health providers in Denmark. Their prototype both explores the personal in the context of family as well as highlights the multiplicity of social roles such patient, parent, and caregiver that are performed at different points in a person's life. The design specifically engages the issues of temporality and materiality and demonstrates how health technologies might support a range of social "selves."

In their study, the authors found that during pregnancy women are in contact with multiple healthcare professionals including physicians, nurses, and midwives. Heath data is thus distributed between many parties and contexts; furthermore, it is both health related and social (Enquist and Tollmar 2008). One information artifact of particular importance in Denmark is a pregnancy journal kept by women and used as a coordinating device for health information. This journal served as the inspiration for the design of *Memory Stone*, as a communication and coordination artifact that supports the collection, annotation, and sharing of information related to pregnancy and maternity (Figs. 15.1 and 15.2).

Enquist and Tollmar emphasize a lifeworld framing in their design work. "In Denmark," they write, "pregnancy is not considered a medical condition, but rather a psychological, social and biophysical one. The pregnant woman is not a patient; she is not ill in the medical sense and hence is not treated." Furthermore, the authors express a clear intention to engage with the theoretical notion of assemblages in their design objective and ask: "How do we design devices/systems that can be

Fig. 15.1 *Memory Stone*
prototype

Fig. 15.2 Social context of *Memory Stone* users (Enquist and Tollmar 2008)

manipulated and configured to work as resources in changing settings?" (Enquist and Tollmar 2008).

Memory Stone is designed to support the integration of sentimental/biographical and clinical information. Parents can add personal notations and notes, images, videos, and sound recordings to the medical information that is stored on the device. Different types of health information can inclûde experience-based narratives on what to expect at different stages of pregnancy, media files of the fetus and its mother like ultrasounds and images of a woman's growing stomach, and more clinical information like logs of blood sugar levels for woman with gestational diabetes (Enquist and Tollmar 2008).

Although *Memory Stone* is built as stand-alone device that can currently integrate with only one other healthcare information system (an electronic patient journal used by nurses), the authors imagine a software architecture that makes it possible to run the *Memory Stone* on a variety of technological platforms such as mobile devices or PCs.

> The woman should thus be able to construct and deconstruct assemblies, for example, between her *Memory Stone* and other devices with medical record systems at the general practitioner's office, and with different types of displays. Similarly, she should be able to construct connections between her *Memory Stone* and other devices providing services, e.g. biosensors or ultrasound scan machines. (Enquist and Tollmar 2008)

Fig. 15.3 Example of a *Media Biography*

A second study, Crete-Nishihata et al. (2012), describes a series of designs to support older adults with Alzheimer's disease (AD) and mild cognitive impairment (MCI). The intended system users included these adults and their caregivers, such as partners, siblings, and children.

Over the course of three related studies, the authors worked to collaboratively produce *Media Biographies* that "told the life story of patients through various personal media such as photos, home movies, documents, music and audio narration" (Crete-Nishihata et al. 2012). *Media Biographies* were then shown on ambient displays in people's kitchens to provide ongoing memory support of adults with AD and MCI. The authors also designed narrative slideshows comprised of curated selections of SenseCam images for people with AD or MCI and their caregivers (Figs. 15.3 and 15.4).

Crete-Nishihata et al. (2012) reported a positive reception of the designs from both adults with AD and MCI and their caregivers. They note, "family members believed that viewing *Media Biographies* helped third-party caregivers learn about their loved one's history and enabled them to better empathize with them and care for them." On the use of *Media Biographies* with ambient displays in the home and its impact on older adults, the authors found that the use of digital narratives improves positive self-image and a reduction of apathy, even though there was no accompanying improvement in people's memory abilities.

Crete-Nishihata et al. (2012) offer important design implications for PcHITs. The designs in the paper point to a type of personal information management that is narrative based and interwoven with issues of health and emotional well-being in a family setting. These prototypes also provide insight into the management of personal health information as people age. As well, the importance of multiple stakeholders and the psychosocial impacts of health more broadly suggest that all PcHIT designs carefully consider the integration of "nonclinical" framings around memory, identity, and family dynamics. Crete-Nishihata et al.'s (2012) work

Fig. 15.4 Display in kitchen (Crete-Nishihata et al. 2012)

suggests that designing PcHIT systems to support storytelling activities might make biomedical data more valuable for many of the people who use them.

The implication of these two systems is that health applications should consider framing the personal in terms of non-patient specific roles, such as that of a parent. Parenthood might involve patient work if a child is sick or if a woman experiences complications with pregnancy such as with gestational diabetes. It also encompasses other types of social relations and activities that are grounded in the lifeworld. A mother, for example, is also a daughter, friend, and partner. As seen in *Memory Stone*, these roles are inextricably tied to parental activities such as sharing a child's photographs with grandparents, discussing concerns about a child with a partner, or debating the benefits of vaccinations with other young parents. Furthermore, these relationships are fluid across a person's lifespan. As seen with *Media Biographies*, a caregiver's role can switch between parent and child later in life. Both of these systems also point to the importance of biographical work that is deeply connected to family life and health.

15.4.1 Community-Based Explorations of "Person-Centered" Health

This chapter so far has been guided by several interconnected inquiries around person-centered health: What sets of social relationships should "person centered" include and exclude? How might family, friends, and caretakers potentially be reflected in PcHIT designs? What types of cultural framings might be important to contextualize health data in different communities? Answering these questions has to be grounded in a thorough examination of people's practices, so as understand what *they* want and need. These concerns have informed our research on designing technology to manage and document chronic illness.

Our field-based research extends current HCI/CSCW arguments that argue for contextually grounded health and medical systems design by focusing on the local needs and values of a *community*. In our research on managing chronic illness in Flint, Michigan, we observed the informational and social complexity of community-based health practices. We present a selection of these practices to help broaden the design space around person-centered health records and suggest socially rich design trajectories around the notion of *lived health*.

15.4.1.1 Living with Chronic Illness in Flint

We have conducted a series of interpretivist-based studies on managing chronic illness in Flint, Michigan (in the American Midwest), a community with significant health disparities. The studies have been interview and focus group based, and our participants have included people living with diabetes, hypertension, and/or kidney disease in Flint. We also spoke with numerous local clinicians, including nurses, physicians, and certified diabetes educators, as well as community health workers active in city churches and "block club" members representing particular neighborhoods.

Flint's history is closely tied to the US automotive industry, and significant layoffs and plant closures over the last 20 years have left the city in deep economic and social turmoil. Flint's neighborhoods vary greatly: There are areas of large houses, well-kept lawns, and an air of prosperity. There are also areas of middle-class and working-class families. The downtown area has been the recipient of recent revitalization efforts, and Flint's Cultural Center boasts museums and a symphony orchestra. Here, we focus on describing the experiences of people living among the "northside" neighborhoods of Flint. A historically African-American community, longtime residents remember it as a swath of once flourishing neighborhoods with many family homes, schools, and parks. The area, however, has changed drastically in the last 10–15 years as a population of less economically stable residents moved in. A rise in violent crime and drug use spurred many remaining families who had the financial means to relocate to safer areas. As the population decreased, abandoned and boarded-up houses began sprouting up and local schools were closed. City services— already limited due to a budget crisis— were further reduced; for instance, our participants mentioned darkened street lights, limited garbage removal, and bus routes that have stopped running. Indeed, there are some sections of the city that participants described as forgotten, a kind of no-man's land where vacated houses are set on fire by bored teenagers.

Healthcare in Flint can be problematic as participants reported a number of challenges when interacting with the local healthcare system. Participants, especially those with marginal health insurance, spoke of difficulties finding doctors who were accepting new patients and often relied upon free healthcare clinics at different points in their lives. The crowded conditions at these facilities resulted in difficulties getting appointments and long waits to see clinicians. Participants reported extremely rushed consultations, as brief as 5 min in some cases. From the perspective of our participants, this did not leave time for them to find out why medications were being prescribed, let alone have a meaningful dialogue with healthcare providers about treatment plans and healthcare options.

In addition, participants described many interactions with what they called "bad doctors," doctors who failed to adequately inform them or to inquire about their health and well-being. From our participants' perspectives, bad doctors spoke too quickly, appeared dismissive or even insulted when a patient asked questions, and didn't ask questions of the patient. "Good doctors," on the other hand, were described with deep respect by participants; in fact, some participants worried about losing their physician and expressed concern about disappointing him or her when they did not strictly follow their treatment plans. Sometimes a reluctance to be "fired" by a doctor led to the participants withholding information that would cast them in a negative light during their clinical visits.

At times, participants felt their clinicians gave conflicting advice, which led to feelings of confusion and mistrust. Participants with diabetes recounted that their primary physicians told them to stop eating all "white foods" while diabetes educators taught them it was safe to eat rice and potatoes in moderation. More common during consultations was the experience of receiving generic advice of the "eat better, exercise more" variety that required participants to puzzle out ways to turn clinical information into meaningful practices.

> Even when participants were able to discuss their health conditions with medical professionals, they indicated they were often skeptical about the information received. Mistrust stemmed from the lack of time clinicians spent diagnosing patients during clinic visits, personal experiences of medical negligence or malpractice, and a long history of civil rights abuses against the African American community. (Veinot et al. 2013)

Accordingly, community-based health information was especially important in Flint. In past work (Kaziunas et al. 2013), we have detailed the ways in which health information is intertwined with highly situated everyday activities and concerns such as finding affordable, healthy food, exercising in safety, or coping with high levels of stress. We found that people living with chronic illness have numerous strategies for "localizing" health information from clinicians and other sources like the Internet to make it meaningful and actionable in their community context. In the absence of fresh fruits and vegetables at a local grocery store, for example, participants rinsed salt from canned beans and ate frozen fruit. If participants could not afford their prescription medication that month, blood pressure pills were rationed and diabetes test strips could be shared among friends. Many people living with hypertension in Flint turned to alternative, "homemade" remedies passed down in their families such as drinking vinegar to lower blood pressure. Other participants spoke about turning to religious rituals such as prayer to reduce anxiety and stabilize blood sugar levels. While these local health practices can be viewed in part as a pragmatic response to living with chronic illness in a community with few resources—indeed, many participants in our study are currently or in the recent past without health insurance—our participants also continuously expressed how these practices were personally meaningful, intimately bound up with their family relationships, church life, and even city history.

15.4.1.2 Navigating Multiple Health Viewpoints

Our work in Flint shows that participants drew upon multiple social worlds to fashion their health practices. Two notable social worlds for people managing chronic illness in Flint are local churches and diabetes clinics. Grounded in different perspectives of health (e.g., religious faith and medicine respectably), sometimes faith-based practices clashed with medical treatment plans. Institutional medicine was not necessarily viewed by participants as the most useful or meaningful, an insight recognized by the majority of diabetes educators we interviewed. As people with chronic illness and clinicians navigated these differing viewpoints, the routine overlapping of their social worlds created new sets of health practices that would not have been anticipated—or appreciated—in a medicalized PHR. However, understanding these practices is essential to properly designing a useful and usable PcHIT. We now turn to examining health practices in which people engaged diabetes in the church and faith in the clinic.

15.4.2 *"Not Claiming" and Faith Healing Practices in Flint*

The vast majority our participants spoke of the important role churches had in their community. Along with religious activities like prayer and worship on Sunday, active members of local churches routinely ate and hung out together during the week, and members and nonmembers alike utilized church services such as food giveaways, van rides, and shelter. It was not uncommon for participants to speak warmly of their "church family." As explained by one man:

> At church it is nothing for them to come over and take you to the doctor or the grocery store, or to take you to pay bills. We had one lady who used to come over and help my wife wash when she was sick, brush the kids' hair, make sure of this or that. [...] She was like a mother to my kids. Her kids use to spend the weekends with my kids, and my kids would spend the weekends with hers. It was a family-oriented thing.

Health is often discussed at church. People with diabetes might trade tips about what foods to eat, discuss medication side effects, and pray for one another's health. Additionally, many Flint churches have dedicated health team ministries and offer support groups for people living with chronic illness. Healthcare teams at churches often run health fairs or screenings for the community and organize walking programs to help community members get physical activity safely.

While representing a diversity of Protestant denominations, many African-American churches in Flint practice charismatic forms of faith healing in which the body is healed through spiritual means. In some variations of the faith healing tradition, physical health is an outward manifestation of one's spiritual well-being, and to be ill is to not be well spiritually. Being spiritually strong in one's faith is often seen as the most important part of life (Bowler 2013). We heard reoccurring stories from our participants about people who would "not claim" their diabetes; among certain church congregations in Flint "not claiming" an illness is a respected act of faith. "Claiming" diabetes implies that a person has a distressing lack of faith, and many who would "not claim" their illness believe instead that God can supernaturally heal the sick through devout faith and rituals like prayer or the laying on of hands. A person with this viewpoint may refuse to take medication or go to the doctor to get a medical diagnosis.

While widespread in the community, particularly among the older generation of residents, we found "not claiming" was a contested practice in many churches. Congregations with active healthcare teams, often composed of volunteers from the church who have formal medical training, often seek to help people navigate the biomedical and faith-based worldviews. One man with diabetes shared that people in his church will often go to church leaders such as the pastor or health team for counsel when first confronted with a health concern. They would pray about the health issue together and then the pastor would offer to take them to the doctor. He expressed his view on faith and health:

> Faith first, but He [God] wants you to go check out the doctors. That's what He gives us a mind for. I'll never knock faith, but He's showing you that you need to go to the doctor too.

Another man spoke about his wife, a trained nurse, and how she shares nutritional information in a way that helps people at their church connect religious teachings to the traditions of southern soul food cooking.

> My wife tried to bring some of these things [health information] to the church to help people understand what is going on with them and connect those to the Bible where God say[s], "Everything is good for you." But we have to do that in moderation, don't be a glutton with it.

For our participants, the boundaries between biomedicine and religion are often fluid in daily life, and participants who practice forms of faith healing draw upon multiple meanings of health. Biomedicine for many people does not hold a place of uncontested authority whether in the church or in the clinic.

This issue was also reflected in the practices of local diabetes educators (both nurses and dieticians) in Flint, since they had also to navigate between these overlapping social worlds. The interviewed diabetes educators we spoke with in Flint were highly aware of the influential role churches had in community life.

While there were diabetes educators who dismissed practices of "not claiming" as a form of denial, many clinicians developed practices around exploring the intersections of faith, diabetes, and medical information so as to move people toward the recommended biomedical treatment plan. One diabetes educator, who described herself as a "faith-based person," often draws upon theological concepts or Biblical references with patients when talking about diabetes. For example, she explains to her religious patients that "high blood sugar itself begets higher blood sugar" (where "beget" is a term from the Bible creation story). She explains her approach to those who practice faith healing forms of "not claiming":

> I'm not going to argue with them about their claiming, I'm going to try and help them meld both their faith and health. So I do a lot of talking about how the body is created; how it functions. I won't necessarily use the word "created." I'll say "designed" a lot. "The body was designed to function in this way, and so when we honor how the body was designed . . . "

Those diabetes educators who themselves frame issues of religion in strictly medical terms, such as coping with diabetes-related distress, are careful to open up space for alternative meanings. Group classes on diabetes, for example, allow time for people to talk about faith with one another. Diabetes educators less comfortable about drawing on the language of faith themselves facilitate this discussion by asking questions.

> We'll ask, "How does your faith play into your diabetes?" We just ask the question. [. . .] I open it up because I think we often ignore those things and yet you are missing some richness in the conversation. You are missing understanding how people are actually coping with all of this.

In summary, practices around faith healing in Flint demonstrate the necessity for researchers and designers to grapple with the richness of health information in all its varied meanings. In melding blood sugar with scripture, the work of local diabetes educators and community health workers highlights the intersections among social worlds. To be clear, while a lack of resources makes the socially contextualized meaning and significance of health practices stand out more sharply in Flint, the issues and the importance of social context, we believe, are present in all communities. In this regard, our study points to a very different conceptualization of personal health information than what is currently being supported by PHR systems, and we argue that our findings demonstrate how important this difference is in properly constructing useful and meaningful PcHITs. In the next section, we articulate a design space that we call *lived health*. It is a conception of the personal that uses practices to critically and generatively engage social complexity in healthcare settings and to imagine technological designs that allow for heterogeneous health information to overlap, collide, and coexist in meaningful ways.

15.4.2.1 Designing PcHITs to Support *Lived Health*

We believe our findings fruitfully extend other current work in CSCW and HCI, some of which were highlighted in Sect. 15.3 of this chapter. As with many CSCW studies, we found that it is necessary to contend with social context. Our findings from the Flint studies demonstrate, however, that there is not one predominant social context, but rather an array of social contexts around health. They also show that the boundaries of these social contexts are fluid and shifting. As Mol (2002) points out, chronic conditions are seldom one integrated conceptual entity or activity; instead, people's perceptions of their chronic conditions change in varying social contexts. Current health systems are brittle and limited, compared to the vast flexibility and nuance that people actually need in their daily lives (Ackerman 2000). Many CSCW systems provide for greater social context but still are largely limited to specific contexts.

Indeed, our findings argue for a different kind of health technologies that extend beyond the PHR. Such a health technology, which we term a PcHIT (a person-centered health technology), would allow a heterogeneity of personal health meanings to exist simultaneously. Furthermore, it would allow interpretations to change over time, as one goes through life, based on the negotiated order and (re)ordering one comes to with medical institutions, other healthcare providers, family, community, and the full range of social contexts. Current HIT is unnecessarily narrow in conceptualizing the social. We recognize that we are limited in our abilities to design systems with this capability; nonetheless, it does not mean that people's practices do not argue for it. A PcHIT is not likely to be unified and completely coherent, but neither are people's practices.

Finally, our findings argue for adopting a stance where people's—not just clinicians'—viewpoints are recognized and respected. This is a strong stance in CSCW, and we reiterate its importance here. A flexible, reinterpretable set of records would appear to better suit people's activities, especially in their social contexts, allowing people to highlight the important characteristics, norms, and values that they carry through their everyday lives. The current health record suggests the rationality of the medicalized viewpoint and the apparent nonrationality of people's everyday health practices. While we recognize the importance of medical knowledge and action based on that knowledge, people's practices still argue for not diminishing their meanings and emotive underpinnings.

Focusing on health as a set of practices interwoven with other aspects of the personal highlights the everyday interplay between institutions and people, memories and things, and inspiration and information. There is a rich and relatively unexplored design space that exists between the rigidity of clinical medicine and individual, idiosyncratic health practices, a design space we think of as *lived health*. We take as inspiration the framing of "lived religion" as described by Robert Orsi whose work details the everyday practices of spiritual life, such as urban shrines and religious street festivals. Orsi (2002) argues that the study of lived religion goes beyond formal theology to understand "how the dead are buried, children disciplined, the past and present imagined, moral boundaries established and challenged, home constructed, maintained and destroyed, the gods and spirits worshiped and importuned" (Orsi 2002, xxxi). Scholars of lived religion are thus critical of hierarchy in terms of understanding beliefs and practices, viewing theological teachings and institutional rituals as intertwined with—rather than in opposition to—people's everyday spiritual activities. Adopting this framework for health contexts calls us to attend to how people use glucometers, pray for healing, cook for their families, and organize prescription medications.

Lived health focuses on how people deal with health as situated in particular social worlds and as negotiated across the boundaries of multiple social worlds.

These practices are often messy and contested. Professional medical recommen-dations do not always sit easily with everyday constraints, let alone cultural expressions of religious piety. Practices such as enjoying traditional food culture and being a "happy diabetic" or "not claiming" diabetes can be seen to subvert the carefully medicalized boundaries of illness and disease. Lived health encompasses such tensions, bearing what religious historian David Hall refers to as the marks of both regulation and resistance (Hall 1997). In this way, lived health does not displace institutional or normative perspectives on health and medicine but looks to include multiple, overlapping, and even contradictory meanings embodied in health practices.

There are several ways in which a lived health approach can help us aesthetically and technically design a suitable PcHIT (or rethink the PHR). First, lived health opens up the design space to consider different configurations of data sharing among family, clinicians, and community members. For instance, how might we visualize relationships between biomedicine and alternative health framings? While boundaries between social worlds were not neatly drawn by the Flint participants, health technologies do not often help people meaningfully engage with heterogeneous, and potentially conflicting, health information. One might imagine a person-centered health record being able to support expertise sharing from a range of divergent perspectives. We are currently exploring how diverse viewpoints, both medical and community based, might be incorporated within a health application. In our FIT (Flint Information Translations) application, users can see a variety of "officially sanctioned" medical views of illnesses and health conditions, as well as the ones offered by community members. In addition, users can see translations of those medical views into practices grounded in their everyday contexts. Figure 15.5 shows the current FIT prototype, although we expect it to change as we codesign it with our participants.

Additionally, lived health expands the design space of "health information" to consider what Orsi (2002) refers to the "the density of practices" that make up social worlds such as objects, gestures, and ideas. Studies of health practices in CSCW have been quick to point to the materiality of health artifacts and the embodied nature of illness, but have less often engaged explicitly with the practices around ideas. What would it look like to engage people's health imagination through technology? One design trajectory worth exploring, we believe, is the design space around health memory. Viewing health as a form of cultural work means that practices are historically situated and time bound. What health memories are personally and collectively meaningful? How might PcHITs help support the long-term sharing of health information across generations? What role does forgetting play in designing for health memories? Furthermore, how do you support people in reflecting on important health information that is often wrapped up in the mundane, everyday elements of life?

In summary, a practice lens has led us to a very different place in considering PHR design and health information in general. Only by examining people's practices could we understand how people use glucometers, pray for healing, cook for their families, and organize prescription medications. Our work in Flint follows

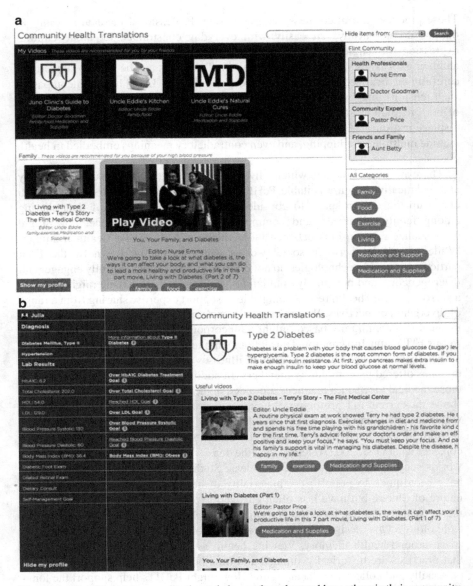

Fig. 15.5 The FIT prototype application to help people understand how others in their community understand and live with a chronic disease condition: (**a**) A user can see videos describing a condition, showing sample recipes, or strategies for coping. (**b**) A user can see health information, tailored for him/her by a community member, explaining medical test values and medical instructions as well as videos further explaining what to do

others (e.g., Mol 2002, 2008; Danholt 2008; etc.) who have documented practices around chronic health conditions like diabetes and found that health practices are dynamic, shaping, and shaped by a multitude of social dimensions, including family arrangements, locality, healthcare organizations, and personal beliefs.

In this chapter, we argue for the centrality of a "lived health" viewpoint, which incorporates how health practices must be considered in the full range of people's lives. People, in the lived health framework, are cast as narrators and (re)interpreters of their own health experiences. We have also argued here that lived health leads to a better design perspective on personal health systems, one that places the design firmly in the social and incorporates how people actually view their health.

Acknowledgments The first author was funded by a National Science Foundation IGERT fellowship (0903629, Open Data). The work was also funded, in part, by the School of Information, the US Institute of Museum and Library Services (LG-52-11-0212-11), and the National Science Foundation (0903629). Any views, findings, conclusions, or recommendations expressed in this publication do not necessarily represent those of IMLS or the NSF. The authors want to thank our study participants and also Tiffany Veinot, Myriam Lewkowicz, Hilda Tellogiu, Volker Wulf, Melissa Chalmers, Pedja Klasnja, Kai Zheng, Charles Senteio, Chris Wolf, Ayse Buyuktur, Tao Dong, Jasmine Jones, and Pei-Yao Hung for their insights and comments. We also thank Angus Lo for the FIT prototype.

References

Ackerman, M. S. (2000). The intellectual challenge of CSCW: The gap between social requirements and technical feasibility. *Human-Computer Interaction, 15*(2–3), 179–203.

Angst, C., Agarwal, R., & Downing, J. (2006). *An empirical examination of the importance of defining the PHR for research and for practice.* Retrieved September 28, 2013, from http://ssrn.com/abstract=904611

Archer, N., Fevrier-Thomas, U., & Lokker, C. (2011). Personal health records: A scoping review. *Journal of the American Medical Informatics Association, 18*, 515–522.

Bardram, J., Frost, M., Szanto, K., Faurholt-Jepsen, M., Vinberg, M., & Kessing, L. (2013). Designing mobile health technology for bipolar disorder: A field trial of the MONARCA system. In *Proceedings of CHI 2013* (pp. 2627–2636). New York: ACM Press.

Barry, C., Stevenson, F., Britten, N., Barber, N., & Bradley, C. (2001). Giving voice to the lifeworld. More humane, more effective medical care? A qualitative study of doctor-patient communication in general practice. *Social Science & Medicine, 53*, 487–505.

Berg, M. (1999). Patient care information systems and health care work: A sociotechnical approach. *International Journal of Medical Informatics, 55*, 87–101.

Berg, M., & Harterink, P. (2004). Embodying the patient: Records and bodies in early 20th century US medical practice. *Body and Society, 10*, 13–41.

Bowler, K. (2013). *Blessed: A history of the American prosperity gospel.* New York: Oxford University Press.

Caine, K., Zimmerman, C., Hazlewood, W., Schall-Zimmerman, Z., Sulgrove, A., Camp, L. J., Connelly, K., Lorenzen-Huber, L., & Shankar, K. (2010). DigiSwitch: Design and evaluation of a device for older adults to preserve privacy while monitoring health at home. In *Proceedings of the 1st ACM international health informatics symposium (IHI'10)* (pp. 153–162). New York: ACM.

Crete-Nishihata, M., Baecker, R., Massimi, M., Ptak, D., Campigotto, R., Kaufman, L., Brickman, A., Turner, G., Steinerman, J., & Black, S. (2012). Reconstructing the past: Personal memory technologies are not just personal and not just for memory. *Human-Computer Interaction, 27*(1–2), 92–123.

Danholt, P. (2008). *Interacting bodies: Posthuman enactments of the problem of diabetes: Relating science, technology and society-studies, user-centered design and diabetes practices* (Datalogiske Skrifter; No.120). Roskilde: Roskilde Universitet.

Dourish, P., & Bell, G. (2011). *Divining a digital future: Mess and mythology in Ubiquitous computing.* Cambridge, MA: MIT.

Enquist, H., & Tollmar, K. (2008). The memory stone: A personal ICT device in health care. In *Proceedings of the 5th nordic conference on human-computer interaction-NordiCHI'08* (pp. 103–112). New York: ACM Press.

Fitzpatrick, G., & Ellingsen, G. (2012). A review of 25 years of CSCW research in healthcare: Contributions, challenges and future agendas. *Computer Supported Cooperative Work, 22,* 609–665.

Gearson, C. (2007). *Perspectives on the future of personal health records.* Report prepared for California HealthCare Foundation. Retrieved August 27, 2013, from http://www.chcf.org/publications/2007/06/perspectives-on-the-future-of-personal-health-records

Hall, D. (1997). Introduction. In D. D. Hall (Ed.), *Lived religion in America: Toward a history of practice.* Princeton: Princeton University Press.

Haraway, D. (1991). A cyborg manifesto: Science, technology, and socialist feminism in the late twentieth century. In D. J. Haraway (Ed.), *Simians, cyborgs, and women: The reinvention of nature.* New York: Routledge.

Iakovidis, I. (1998). Towards personal health record: Current situation, obstacles and trends implementation of electronic healthcare record in Europe. *International Journal of Medical Informatics, 52*(1), 105–115.

Jones, D. A., Shipman, J. P., Plaut, D. A., & Selden, C. R. (2010). Characteristics of personal health records: Findings of the medical library association/national library of medicine joint electronic task force. *Journal of the Medical Library Association, 98,* 243–249.

Kaelber, D. C., Jha, A. K., Johnston, D., Middleton, B., & Bates, D. W. (2008). A research agenda for personal health records (PHRs). *Journal of the American Medical Informatics Association, 15*(6), 729–736.

Kaziunas, E., Ackerman, M. S., & Veinot, T. C. E. (2013). Localizing chronic disease management: Information work and health translations. In *Proceedings from ASIST 2013*, Montreal, Quebec, Canada.

Kientz, J. A., Arriaga, R. I., & Abowd, G. D. (2009). Baby steps: Evaluation of a system to support record-keeping for parents of young children. In *Proceedings of the conference on human factors in computing systems-CHI 2009* (pp. 1713–1722). New York: ACM Press.

Kim, J., Jung, H., & Bates, D. (2011). History and trends of "personal health record" research in PubMed. *Healthcare Informatics Research, 17*(1), 3–17.

Klasnja, P., Hartzler, A., Powell, C., Phan, G., & Pratt, W. (2010). HealthWeaver mobile: Designing a mobile tool for managing personal health information during cancer care. In *AMIA 2010 symposium proceedings* (pp. 392–396). New York: ACM Press.

Luckmann, B. (1970). The small life-worlds of modern man. *Social Research, 37,* 580–596.

Mamykina, L., Mynatt, E., Davidson, P., & Greenblatt, D. (2008). MAHI: Investigation of social scaffolding for reflective thinking in diabetes management. In *Proceedings of CHI'08*, Florence, Italy (pp. 477–486). New York: ACM Press.

Markle Foundation. (2003). *Connecting for health: The personal health working group final report.* Retrieved June 13, 2013, from http://www.connectingforhealth.org/resources/final_phwg_report1.pdf

Mishler, E. G. (1984). *The discourse of medicine: The dialectics of medical interviews.* Norwood: Ablex.

Mol, A. (2002). *The body multiple: Ontology in medical practice.* Durham/London: Duke University Press.

Mol, A. (2008). *The logic of care*. New York: Routledge.

Mynatt, E., Rowan, J., Jacobs, A., & Craighill, S. (2001). Digital family portraits: Supporting peace of mind for extended family members. In *Proceedings of CHI'01* (pp. 333–340). New York: ACM Press.

National Alliance for Health Information Technology (U.S.). (2008). *Report to the Office of the National Coordinator for Health Information Technology on Defining Key Health Information Technology Terms*. Released by the United States Department of Health & Human Services. Retrieved March 14, 2014, from http://cdm16064.contentdm.oclc.org/cdm/singleitem/collection/p266901coll4/id/2086/rec/10

Nazi, K. (2013). The personal health record paradox: Health care professionals' perspectives and the Information ecology of personal health record systems in organizational and clinical settings. *Journal of Medical Internet Research, 15*(4), e70.

Orlikowski, W. J. (2000). Using technology and constituting structures: A practice lens for studying technology in organizations. *Organization Science, 11*(4), 404–428.

Orsi, R. (2002). *The Madonna of 115th street: Faith and community in Italian Harlem, 1880–1950*. New Haven: Yale University Press.

Osterlund, C., Kensing, F., & Davidson, E. J. (2011, June 24). Personal health records in the US and Denmark: From visions to versions? In *The third international workshop: Infrastructures for healthcare*. University of Copenhagen.

Rodin, G., Mackay, J. A., Zimmermann, C., Mayer, C., Howell, D., Katz, M., Sussman, J., & Brouwers, M. (2009). Clinician patient communication: A systematic review (Supportive care in cancer, Vol. 17, pp. 627–644). Berlin: Springer.

Scambler, G., & Britten, N. (2001). System, lifeworld and doctor-patient interaction: Issues of trust in a changing world. In G. Scambler (Ed.), *Habermas, critical theory and health* (pp. 45–67). London/New York: Routledge.

Schatzki, T., Knorr Cetina, K., & von Savigny, E. (Eds.). (2001). *The practice turn in contemporary theory*. London: Routledge.

Schutz, A. (1967). *The phenomenology of the social world*. Evanston: Northwestern University Press.

Shutz, A., & Luckmann, T. (1973). *Structures of the life-world* (Vol. 1). Evanston: Northwestern University Press.

Sittig, D. (2001). Personal health records on the internet: A snapshot of the pioneers at the end of 20th century. *International Journal of Medical Informatics, 65*, 1–6.

Strauss, A. L. (1991). *Creating sociological awareness: Collective images and symbolic representations*. New Brunswick: Transaction Publishers.

Strauss, A. L. (1993). *Continual permutations of action*. New Brunswick: Transaction Publishers.

Suchman, L. (2007). *Human-machine reconfigurations: Plans and situated actions* (2nd ed.). New York: Cambridge University Press.

Tang, P., Ash, J., Bates, D., Overhage, J. M., & Sands, D. (2006). Personal health records: Definitions, benefits, and strategies for overcoming barriers to adoption. *Journal of the American Medical Informatics Association, 13*, 121–126.

Veinot, T. C., Campbell, T. R., Kruger, D. J., & Grodzinski, A. (2013). A question of trust: User-centered design requirements for an informatics intervention to promote the sexual health of African-American youth. *Journal of the American Medical Informatics Association, 20*(4), 758–765.

Waizkin, H. (1989). A critical theory of medical discourse: Ideology, social control, and the processing of social context in medical encounters. *Journal of Health and Social Behavior, 30*(2), 220–239.

Waizkin, H. (1991). *The politics of medical encounters: How patients and doctors deal with social problems*. New Haven: Yale University Press.

Chapter 16
Organisational IT Managed from the Shop Floor: Developing Participatory Design on the Organisational Arena

Johan Bolmsten and Yvonne Dittrich

16.1 Introduction

Modern organisations need to be able to adjust to changes in the environment, changes which are ever more rapid, and in doing so capitalise on the creativity and innovations of their employees. As suggested by Boulus-Rødje and Bjørn (Chap. 14), information technology (IT) applications today are likely to take the form of complex, integrated infrastructures, supporting collaboration within and across organisations. This places requirements on the IT infrastructure. As the work practices within an organisation change, the supporting infrastructure also needs to evolve.

This chapter presents an action research study of infrastructure development at the World Maritime University (WMU) in Malmö, Sweden, a UN-based university with a strong tradition of delegating responsibility and the commitment of the personnel to develop both work practices and supportive organisational and technical structures. The research question thus became: How can the development of an organisational IT management be based on a shop floor development strategy?

The first author is employed as an in-house IT professional at WMU and had the possibility to use his everyday work as an empirical basis for his research. The 'native' shop floor development approach of IT support, which was in place

J. Bolmsten (✉)
IT University of Copenhagen, Rued Langgaards Vej 7, 2300 Copenhagen, Denmark

Academic Information Manager, World Maritime University, Citadellsvägen 29,
21118 Malmö, Sweden
e-mail: jb@wmu.se

Y. Dittrich
Software and System Section, IT University of Copenhagen, Rued Langgaards Vej 7,
2300 Copenhagen, Denmark
e-mail: ydi@itu.dk

© Springer-Verlag London 2015
V. Wulf et al. (eds.), *Designing Socially Embedded Technologies in the Real-World*,
Computer Supported Cooperative Work, DOI 10.1007/978-1-4471-6720-4_16

before the research started, has been used as a base for action research to support an evolving organisational IT management. Improved IT management in the organisational arena has been deliberated on by, and developed together with, the users and IT professionals of the organisation and answered the need to coordinate isolated projects in order to take advantage of the synergies of a shared technical and organisational infrastructure.

The empirical challenge formulated in the research question implicates the challenge to incorporate participatory design (PD), infrastructure 'design in use' (Hanseth and Braa 2001; Star and Ruhleder 1996) and even end-user development (Paternó et al.). Similar complexities of interlaced heterogeneous design and use activities have been documented and discussed by Dittrich et al. (2002) and Pipek and Wulf (2009). Unlike more orthodox PD contributions (see, e.g. Bødker et al. 2004) that tend to focus on design preceding implementation, this research study relates to design that covers use, process and technology (Floyd et al. 1989, 1992; Wulf and Rohde 1995), a theme that resonates throughout this book.

Such dynamics are not reflected in prevalent information management (IS) approaches. Ciborra (2000) scrutinises a number of cases from a technical and organisational infrastructure development perspective and finds practices that at times 'substantially diverge from the wisdom contained in the management and IS literature' of today. Understanding organisational IT management as a process of infrastructure development is a notion that was useful also in this research study. It essentially turns prevalent IS management conceptualisations upside down; the question becomes how shop floor development constituencies can continuously deliberate on and iterate a technical and organisational infrastructure to support them, as compared to having one imposed on them. In other words, how can the type of 'shop floor IT management' as identified and discussed by Eriksén (1998) be supported with organisational structures and processes that allow the coordination of the dispersed developments and support them with an adequate technical base? Organisational IT management as a process of infrastructure development can, in this sense, be understood as providing 'plans as resources for situated [design] action' that are initiated from shop floor development constituencies (Suchman 1987, 2007).

The implemented approach extends recent contributions about process-oriented infrastructure development (see, e.g. the special issue on infrastructure in the Journal of the Association for Information Systems, Volume 10, Issue 5) by supporting organisational IT management that derives from self-organising 'management' on the shop floor. It provides an example of how shop floor workers can participate in the co-evolution of a decentralised organisational IT management. Cooperative decision structures and processes can be integrated with an approach based on PD that makes it possible to involve workers on the shop floor in a meaningful way in organisational IT management.

The next section introduces the prevalent approach to IS management with relevant literature from the PD discourse in order to outline the basis for a PD way to organisational IT management. Section 16.3 presents the action research approach. Sections 16.4, 16.5 and 16.6 report the research results. Section 16.4 presents the shop floor IT development tradition of WMU that the researchers encountered when the project started. Section 16.5 presents the stepwise deliberation of the organisational structures, processes, and methods towards participatory IT management. Section 16.6 describes and evaluates the introduced changes. In Sect. 16.7, we discuss the results, and Sect. 16.8 concludes the chapter.

16.2 Related Work

In this section, we first summarise prevalent approaches to organisational IT management in the IS field. The following section then presents research results from the PD discourse that indicate the necessity to think of PD not only as a way of design before implementation but to extend the participatory approach to include 'design in use', end-user development (EUD) and evolution of both individual programs as well as the infrastructure. Combining the arguments for 'sustained PD' (Simonsen and Hertzum 2012) with the criticism of the prevalent IT management approaches, we develop a base for a 'PD way of organisational IT management'.

16.2.1 Prevalent Organisational IT Management Approach

IS management approaches are commonly denoted by management and documentation frameworks intended to establish comprehensive plans to be communicated top-down throughout the different levels of the organisation. It is argued that by establishing such focus, it is possible to develop explicit and purposeful plans on how to achieve the desired results in regard to organisational IT management. Strategy formulation and implementation is translated into plans for IT infrastructure development that often results in major projects spanning over substantial periods of time. Such planning is predominately seen as the responsibility of management, whose decisions are rolled out through the organisational hierarchy. Effectiveness criteria stem from control over the environment. Consequences of applying action strategies can be comprehended through conscious comparisons, which then can be used to further refine and structure an overall guiding strategy (Hedman and Kalling 2002). One such approach that is currently in the spotlight, both from a research and industry perspective, is enterprise architecture (EA) (Bernard 2005). The aim of EA, like other mainstream IS management approaches, is to improve the governance of software development processes in the organisational arena in a disciplined and consistent way. The overall goal is to institutionalise best practices throughout the organisation through a standardisation process.

Figure 16.1 visualises the philosophy behind EA. On the one hand, EA integrates with organisational IT governance through established channels to strategic, workplace, and capital planning. On the other hand, EA integrates with project-specific approaches such as a business process re-engineering (BPR). Together, this is intended to give a complete approach to manage IT development on all levels of the organisation.

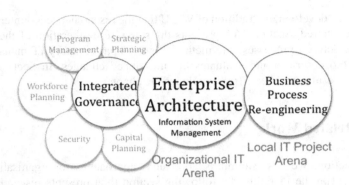

Fig. 16.1 IS management (Based on Bernard's (2005) EA IT governance framework)

16.2.2 Participatory Design

PD, in contrast to top-down approach of IS management, is fundamentally defined by taking a bottom-up starting point. PD describes a set of methodologies to support the collaboration between IT professionals and domain experts to codevelop work practices and the technologies supporting them (Greenbaum and Kyng 1992). As the technology and its usage evolve, PD needs to evolve as well. Kensing and Blomberg (1998), for instance, indicate that PD projects have been 'focused on the individual project arena where specific systems are designed'. More recently, Bødker et al. have produced what can be seen as an exemplary collection of methods, tools and techniques to support participation (2004). Emphasis has been put on how to foster a 'direct and unmediated partnership between designers and the users of systems' (Gärtner and Wagner 1996). A challenge which remains, however, is to move PD into those organisationally complex arenas that we are dealing with. Both Clement and van den Besselaar (1993) and Gärtner and Wagner (1996a, b) have, for instance, indicated the challenge for PD to deal with the broader organisational arena 'on which PD initiatives depend for their long-term survival'.

Empirically, organisational IT management from the shop floor and the need to support the participation of domain experts in its evolution has been addressed by Eriksén (1998). Development takes place in interlaced shop floor design constituencies (Wessels et al. 2008), i.e. assemblies of different stakeholders who are entitled – through their interest, role or expertise – to contribute to specific design and development activities.[1] Both the design constituencies and the organisational affiliation of specific participants are subject to situated negotiations and decisions. People participating in shop floor IT management are in this study referred to as workers on the shop floor, users or domain experts depending on their role and

---

[1]In this study, the notion of shop floor development constituencies is used to highlight the inclusion of both design and implementation.

the context. To conceptualise shop floor IT management from an organisational perspective and to challenge PD to move 'beyond the project', Dittrich et al. (2002) propose the notion 'PD in the wild'.

To this end, Karasti and Syrjänen (2004) make use of the notions of 'artful integration' (Suchman 2007) and process-oriented infrastructure development, sometimes referred to as 'infrastructuring' (Star and Ruhleder 1996), to focus attention on multifarious relations and processes in two particular cases of community PD. In IT infrastructures, PD – or rather evolution – needs to take a starting point in the existing 'working relationships of technology production and use' (Suchman 1994, 2007). 'Artful integration' (Suchman 2007) aims at understanding the ongoing dialectics between design and the use of software support from both a 'use in design' and 'design in use' perspective and how this results in a 'located accountability' of design. Along the same lines, Pipek and Wulf (2009) use the term 'infrastructuring' (Star and Ruhleder 1996) to relate the preparatory design of new parts of an infrastructure to the ongoing design in use and to recognise both professional and EUD (Lieberman et al. 2006) as contributing to the continuous shaping of the infrastructure in use.

16.2.3   Towards a Participatory Design Approach to Organisational IT Management

Already in 1996, Andreu and Ciborra (1996) articulated a general critique of prevalent IS management assumptions (see above). They argued that the overall view of organisational IT management has been biased towards the analytical, the conscious, top-down, control and simplicity, structure and the separation of action and structure. According to Andreu and Ciborra (1996), this view is incomplete and incorrect, because it does not take into account the difficulty with these projects as they progress. Instead, IT projects are often nurtured and developed at operational levels in bottom-up processes. They depend in part on unplanned, local and competence-based approaches, and they rely as much on preexisting cognitive frameworks as on the organisational context. The notions of bricolage and radical learning are used to conceptualise learning, knowledge creation and change through bottom-up processes in the organisation – from the development of local work practices to strategic core capabilities. Organisations need to accommodate these practices in order to cope with new and emerging challenges (Andreu and Ciborra, 1996).

This opposition to dominant IS management approaches is referred to by Ciborra (2000) and others as process-oriented technical and organisational infrastructure development. Based on their empirical findings, Hanseth and Braa (2001), for example, find that defining a top-down infrastructure in prevalent IS management approaches is like 'hunting for the treasure at the end of the rainbow'. Similarly, several contributions in a recent special issue on infrastructure in the Journal of

Fig. 16.2 Ciborra's (2000)
'control to drift' interpreted
in the context of an integrated
management scheme

Local IT Project
Arena

the Association for Information Systems (Volume 10, Issue 5) use the notion of 'infrastructuring' (Star & Ruhleder, ibid.) to target the technical and organisational process of a locally accountable (Suchman, ibid.) infrastructure development. In reviewing the dynamics of infrastructure development in a number of large multinationals, Ciborra (2000) elaborates on an answer to this end under the heading 'from control to drift'. The notion of 'drift' is put forward as a raison d'etre to denote the nature of modern corporate infrastructure development as opposed to control-oriented IS management approaches. 'Drift' in this sense is argued to be a type of organisational IT un-management with regard to infrastructure development (see Fig. 16.2). Ciborra (2000) asks 'why not play with the idea of a different partition between the limited scope of our management of infrastructure and the scope for the infrastructure itself to manage us?' (p. 40) and questions the development of more elaborated control structures such as 'meta-decision-making forums' (p 39; also see Peppard 1999). In a similar way, research on infrastructuring today can be seen to focus on highlighting how 'situated action' in individual shop floor development constituencies denotes technical and organisational infrastructure development and not an alternative form of organisational IT management planning.

Along with Ciborra and others, this chapter acknowledges 'drift' as a feature of bricolage and radical learning in the process of infrastructuring. However, in understanding the issues and opportunities of the existing shop floor IT management approach at WMU as a base for research (Sect. 16.4), 'drift' does not become positioned as an end but rather as a foundational assumption denoting the characteristics of infrastructure development. The challenge entails involving users in the development of the very meta-design, where a bricolage and radical learning capability deriving from the shop floor can continue in a landscape of increasingly complex technologies and a larger number of workers participating in projects. In this sense, the action research reported is not an effort to abandon the existing shop floor management – in favor of, for example, EA – but to nurture its core qualities such as a locally anchored development that gains its momentum from the domain experts themselves. This ties back to extending the 'located accountability' of Suchman's (1994, 2007) artful integration on an organisational IT management level. However, it implies the extension of the project-centred PD methods and tools with concepts, methods and tools supporting the interlacing of heterogeneous design and use activities (Dittrich et al. 2002) that is the integration of parallel activities of users, end-user developers and professional designers that together comprise the continuous IT infrastructuring (Pipek and Wulf 2009) of an organisation.

16.3   Research Approach

Researching 'infrastructuring' for a PD approach to organisational IT management demanded a participatory approach to the research itself. It was important to work with the workers on the shop floor themselves. To this end, we adapted the Cooperative Method Development (CMD) approach – developed by Dittrich et al. (2008) for software engineering – to develop organisational IT management structures and processes together with the involved organisational actors and IT professionals. In addition, the main researcher combined his employment as an IT professional at WMU with his PhD research. This provided both opportunities and challenges. Below, we first introduce the research approach, then describe its implementation and finally discuss the trustworthiness and limitations of the results. The following section presents the research results.

16.3.1   Cooperative Method Development

The objective of action research is to expand scientific knowledge while at the same time solving practical problems (Baskerville and Myers 2004). Given that the main author was working as an embedded researcher and that the empirical research targeted both 'use in design' confined to a defined project and continuous 'design in use', a robust methodological framework that allows to plan, implement and document the action of the researcher in a scientifically accountable way was called for.

Dittrich et al.'s (2008) Cooperative Method Development (CMD) approach as a methodological framework was used to guide both the action and the ethnographic research. CMD uses a cyclic and iterative research approach that combines ethnographically inspired empirical research with selection, appropriation and development of methods, tools and techniques. This is based on Checkland and Holwell's (1998) cyclic process guideline for action research: movement between observation, planning of the action to be taken, and implementation of the action. Five guidelines are used to structure the research:

1. An action research cycle consisting of three phases: *(CMD 1)* understanding, *(CMD 2)* deliberating and implementing change and *(CMD 3)* evaluating improvements
2. Ethnographically inspired research complemented by other methods if suitable

3. A focus on shop floor software development practices
4. Taking the practitioners' perspective when evaluating the empirical research and deliberating improvements
5. Deliberating improvements with the involved practitioners

The presentation of the results in Sects. 16.4, 16.5 and 16.6 is structured in accordance to the three phases of the CMD and accounts for the application of the guidelines.

16.3.2 Data Collection and Analysis

To provide a sound basis for the empirical results, the first author took care to document both relevant parts of his everyday work as well as all the actions explicitly taken in relation to the research. Primary vehicles for documentation of the research were a research diary and audio recordings. When completing the empirical work, the research diary contained 1,500+ entries. The research diary has been used to document the day-to-day work process and interactions with organisational actors and to link to organisational and project process documentation. Development interactions during formal and informal meetings, workshops, and participatory observations were audio recorded.

The in situ empirical data collection was complemented with interviews – partly by the second author – and document analysis. In conjunction with the formal start of the research in 2008, a number of semi-structured interviews were, for example, carried out based on already conducted development work with faculty stakeholders to establish a situated account. In a similar way, to provide a scientific account for the practices of the end-user developers presented in Sect. 16.4.2, the participatory observation was complemented with semi-structured interviews.

Deliberations of changes were both of informal and of formal nature. Informal discussions would typically take place in the different offices of people participating in the research and deal with matters of relevance for ongoing projects. These meetings could also be scheduled and structured by a set agenda. More formal meetings took place in connection with project events where the proposed methods, tools and techniques were used and focussed on the discussions of implications of decisions made. Collages and sketches on whiteboards, notes, mock-ups made in PowerPoint and Photoshop and horizontal and vertical prototypes are examples of artefacts for the collaboration used. Other primary arenas for ongoing reflection were the meetings of an IT-coordination group and an IT-steering committee. These meetings were both used for informal reflection –similar to the above description of the local project context – and for more structured deliberations in prepared workshops dealing with, for example, decisions in regard to the proposed project model.

To gather heterogeneous perspectives of the change process and the implemented structures, methods and tools, reflective interviews and workshops were conducted:

- To zoom out and reconstruct how IT professionals collaborated with workers on the shop floor to develop software support, interviews were used to reconstruct the timeline of the events and evaluate the actions taken.
- A series of e-mail interviews were conducted with stakeholders that had left the organisation.
- A workshop was carried out with the IT professionals and the Head of IT coordination as members of the IT-coordination group to evaluate on the organisational IT management changes.
- A semi-structured interview was conducted with the chair of the computer committee to understand how he worked to improve the committee's work and to understand his view of the results.

Section 16.6 is based both on the observation of the changes and the analysis of these evaluative interviews.

After an initial analysis, a set of audio recordings of particular relevance were selected and transcribed. These were then analysed together with the field notes using the qualitative research tool HyperRESEARCH. The analysis started with identifying codes in the transcribed material. Based on this open coding, a number of categories were developed that were used for axial coding, relating the different transcripts and field notes. Code maps were also developed to cluster different categories in relation to each other (see Figs. 16.3 and 16.4 for examples). Offsite debriefing sessions involving the first and second authors also took place regularly. Contextual specificities thus were elaborated throughout the research process. The second author joined the evaluation of the interview transcriptions and the identification of the discussion themes of Sect. 16.7. Where meaningful,

	JB: men det är så man jobbar för att få det operativt
	AI: ja precis
PSA - situated also on traditional strategic PSA - internalizing PSA - craftmanship	AI: man får det, man har ju hela den här mänskliga ä börjar tänka på det här sättet, dom börjar internalise arbetet och börjar tänka vi ska ju pusha dom här str hantverk, sen så, och det var ju mycket såna här kor det kan vara modeller, fyr fems matriser som man ar
	[00:15:20.000]
PSA - knowing the trait PSA - top down creativity in managing the	AI: tänkande och så, sen så flyttade jag till asien till I där hade vi redan börjat med i zurich, vi använde de implementeringen av den strategiska planen spegla väldigt konkret,
	JB: ja

Fig. 16.3 Codes in the context of the empirical material

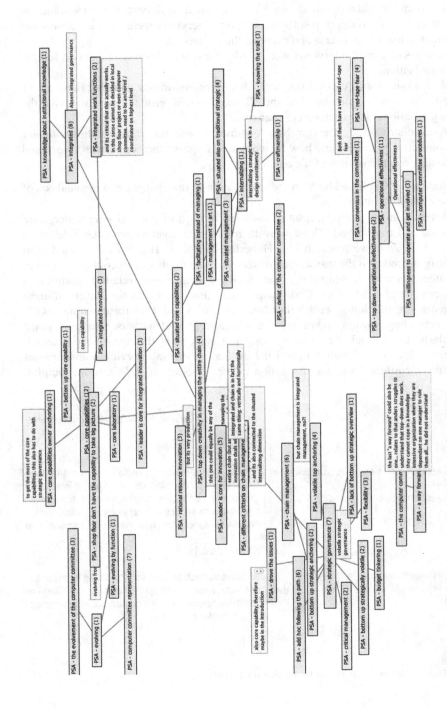

Fig. 16.4 A code map clustering and relating code categories with notes

analysis and interpretation of the research has been discussed with the members of the organisation involved in the research to make sure that our interpretations match the members' perception.

16.3.3   The Trustworthiness of the Empirical Research

As described in the subsection above, the authors took care to create a scientifically valid account of both the events and their own action in the organisation. Specifically, (1) we provided an as complete as possible account of the empirical research and its analysis (traceability); (2) where possible the participatory observations were complemented with other data sources like recordings of meetings, interviews and document and artefact analysis (data triangulation); (3) the second author has continuously provided support for reflection on the social constructions of the research material through off-site debriefing sessions and implemented complementary interviews (researcher triangulation); and (4) the implemented changes as well as parts of the analysis have been evaluated and discussed with the relevant members of the organisation (member checking). Based on these grounds, we are confident that we can provide a trustworthy account of the research process and results below.

As with all qualitative research, our results might not be easily transferable to other organisations. We discuss the related limitations in the final section. The following three sections present the empirical research implemented following the phases of the CMD approach.

16.4   CMD 1: Understand Existing Shop Floor Development Practices in Their Historical and Situational Context

One of the motivations for starting a research project at WMU was its long tradition of a 'native' shop floor development approach; people working together for specific tasks – like the administration and implementation of courses – were accustomed to taking charge and building shop floor development constituencies for the related IT support. Two such shop floor development practices at WMU are described below to provide the situational context within which the action research set out to deliberate on and to improve organisational IT management.

16.4.1   Shop Floor Development With IT Professionals

The course administration shop floor development constituency was the first that the main author encountered and became part of when he was employed as an IT professional at WMU in 2005. In an interview, the Vice-President (academic) described the benefit in having faculty assistants and IT professionals working closely together and sharing work assignments and even offices:

> I wanted, this online marking...I just want[ed] this, but he came up with a product which goes beyond my expectations [...] he then worked out [how] to give the individual marks to the students individually, this I didn't think, but he made it, he showed it is possible, because he saw our three secretaries, every week busy to type one small piece of paper.

In this way, a long-term ambition of the development of the technical base of the course administration was to both improve 'use in design' in the daily collaboration between IT-professionals and shop floor workers and further enable 'design in use' for faculty assistants to carry out development and configurations themselves.

16.4.2 Shop Floor Development Without IT Professionals

Besides collaborating with IT professionals, members of WMU configured and customised their own tools. In some cases, shop floor workers took on technical infrastructure development themselves without any primary dependence on IT professionals.

Starting in 1993, the Registrar gradually began to construct an accountable registry management system that included computerised support together with his staff. The rationale for this approach to software development was to get useful software support. In this way, a Registry Assistant exemplified the nature of the day-to-day development collaboration in regard to an issue with menu tabs being divided into different databases in her interface: 'You can always call him, go in to him, and he listens [...] it is not like it is [too] small [for him], he does do, writes it down on his little notepad. I have not thought about it before, but now when we are talking about it, it is pretty great [...]'.

In a similar manner, an Administrative Assistant manages the technical development of electronic forms and a contact database and describes herself as 'sort of a spider in the net', both in regard to working with users and IT professionals. For both the electronic forms and the contact database, she gradually developed a model for user involvement. Acknowledging a wide range of competences, she, for example, developed an implicit ranking of users from computer illiterate to technical experts for the purposes of prototype testing. Her rationale for user collaboration was that she is one of the first to get notified if her development ventures do not work: 'I end up with more questions then, and if there are more questions, I end up with people who don't use it'. And people 'who don't use it' means more work for herself.

These two complementary accounts of how development of software support practically takes place by users themselves give an indication of what the organisational IT management has to cope with.

16.4.3 Defining the Need for Organisational IT Management Deliberations

The motivation to improve the organisational IT management came with a need for better integrated technical and organisational infrastructure. While people working on the shop floor were satisfied with the existing local development practices, they also recognised opportunities (as well as challenges) of synergies in terms of improved quality and efficiency if different local software systems were integrated. In reference to the examples in the previous sections, a lot of cumbersome manual work had to be carried out to transfer marks between the faculty and registry system, which not only took up time but also caused mistakes.

To this end, a number of organisational IT management structures already existed that later came to underpin the action research deliberations:

- The IT-coordination group: At the time of the first author's employment in 2005, an IT-coordination group was initiated. The three IT professionals at WMU were formally sorted under the management of different individual departments. To this end, the IT-coordination group provided an IT-professional forum for coordination, chaired by a 'Head of Information'.
- The IT-steering committee: The IT-steering committee gathers user, IT professionals and management representatives from the different shop floor development constituencies. This was one of the earliest committees at WMU with a history dating back to 1983. In realising a need for organisational IT management, the committee was initiated by user and domain expert representatives from the shop floor development constituencies themselves. The development of software support such as the course administration, the registry system and the electronic forms and contact database have all been reported to the IT-steering committee. Representatives from the shop floor development constituencies and IT professionals at WMU have served as committee members in accordance to a rotating scheme.
- The management committee: The management committee is chaired by the president of the university and gathers heads of the different departments such as administration, faculty, finance and registry. The IT-steering committee's formal function is to act as a subcommittee to the management committee, providing advice on hardware and software capacity and maintenance as well as advising on present and future demands for information technology provision and its coordination within the university. In practice the IT-steering committee, however, operated with relative freedom and also managed the annual computer budget.

In their functioning at the time, these organisational IT management structures were not suited to take on the increasing coordination needs for technical and organisational infrastructure. A Head of Information reflected in the following regarding the challenges in integrating the development going on in the different shop floor development constituencies: 'IT R&D priorities are intimately linked to organisation requirements. Strong personalities can and do skew the ranking of such priorities as everyone is number one in line when it comes to an expressed need'.

16.4.4 A (Failed) Top-Down Organisational IT Management

The first organisational response to the above challenges was to hire an outside IT manager to implement a 'best-practice' type of IS management. The account of these efforts contextualises the following action research deliberations reported in Sect. 16.5.

To this end, during 2007 and 2008, an attempt was made to put a traditional IS management in place at WMU. An 'Integrated Information Services Strategic Plan' (ISS) was defined that detailed a standardised and comprehensive IS management scheme. One of its main paragraphs was that the management was to define a number of 'realistic, obtainable, sustainable and measurable' service-level agreements that would define the organisational IT management. These would then be implemented across the local shop floor development constituencies through a set of predefined maturity stages.

This also strategically implicated a new take on the functioning of the organisational structures in place: (1) the shop floor IT management model would be reduced to primarily adaptation of implemented software, (2) the role of the IT-steering committee would be reduced to an advisory/announcement forum and (3) the IT professionals would formally sort under the IT-coordination group who would assume an extended organisational IT management role over software support development.

Once implemented, this was intended to result in local development requests being made to the IT-coordination group that would, in turn, be vetted and prioritised against service-level agreements and preset quality goals defined by the management body and then announced in the IT-steering committee. According to the plan, this would step-by-step enable an integrated infrastructure both on a technical and organisational level.

The core objectives and strategy of the ISS plan were established with the president to secure a change mandate. Following this, 3 months were spent on conducting interviews to identify, analyse and concretise service-level agreements of how existing work processes and IT systems on an operational level could achieve their strategic potential through the established framework.

The result, however, was not what was intended. The ISS plan was rejected by the workers in the shop floor development constituencies. Upon launch, in regard to a concrete development instance, the ISS plan proposed that on a technical infrastructure level, all local databases would be exchanged to a common database format. To this end, users, domain experts and managers stepped up their critique, both inside and outside the IT-steering committee. The Registrar, for example, vocally complained that his local needs and those of other individual departments were not sufficiently understood and that the route for change defined could not cater for the future needs of the departments. It also resulted in friction between the representatives from the shop floor development constituencies to the point that the IT-steering committee was temporarily taken out of operation. This course of events contributed to the responsible IT manager leaving WMU in early 2009.

16.5   CMD 2: Deliberating and Implementing a New Organisational IT Management

The failed nature of the ISS plan created a mandate for organisational IT management from the shop floor supported by action research deliberations between 2009 and 2011. As a member in the shop floor development constituency managing the course administration development put it: *'The message is not that the current situation can't be improved. We clearly need a better software organisation. But let's implement one that fits with the activities and nature of the organisation'.*

The deliberations were based on an evolutionary approach that intended to cultivate the intended function of the original structures and processes: the shop floor development model and the empowered function of the IT-steering committee in relation to the management body and the IT-coordination group as a supporting function. The deliberations entailed the following measures to further collaboration amongst an increasing number of participants in projects and between local projects and the coordination structures. The intention was to make IT professionals available as resources for local shop floor development constituencies, rather than steering them:

- *Story cards to improve coordination in growing local development*: A practice of story cards was decided as a mean to enable more shop floor workers to participate in evolutionary development in the local development projects as well as to create a foundation for a linkage between the local development and organisational IT management and infrastructure development. The original 'native' shop floor development model, described in Sect. 16.4, did not necessarily depend on any formal project management framework or documentation of the development. The challenge that the story cards targeted was to support the original shop floor development model as much as possible but enable more workers to participate in project planning. The development of the story cards was based on Beck and Andres (2004) and Kyng (1995). The intention was to remind (not define) participants of current work situations in need of change and present a vision for overall change entailing both new system design and work practice design. As Fig. 16.5 illustrates, the first part of a story card gave an overview of a concrete area in need of change. The second part of the story card then presented a vision for overall change, both regarding technical functionality as well as user interfaces and work organisation. The final part of the story card detailed a technical and organisational implementation. As is also visible in Fig. 16.5, the story cards represent both the system being designed

Story Card 2.1 – Assessment schedule

1. Overview

This story card describes the design of a new intranet assessment schedule that replaces the current excel based version (see figure 1). This development is part of implementation priority 2 in the in-depth analysis and relates to streamlining the work around assessments both from a staff and student perspective (3.2.3 and 3.2.4). The new user interface is based on the newly updated "subject and schedule" page design and should thereby be intuitive to use.

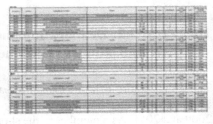

2. Visions For Overall change

2.1 Functions and user interfaces

2.1.2 Academic and registry staff interface
The new intranet assessment schedule design (figure 2) revises and extends the current excel based assessment schedule:

1. By using the top menu items it is possible to define the assessment schedule view. The choices available are the same as in the "subjects and schedules" interface with the addition of the "Assessment Type" options.

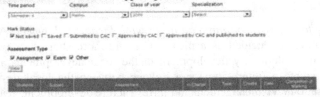

1

2.2 Work organization

Examples of usage:
1. CAC members may use the new interface to get an overview of the configuration of defined assessments for a given time period.

3. Implementation strategy and Plan

3.1 Technical

3.2 Organizational

2

Fig. 16.5 *Top left.* Example of story card (course administration)

and the work situations. An extended use of representational means was another change meant to support the involvement of increasing number of users in design and implementation projects. See examples of representational means used in projects in Figs. 16.6 and 16.7.

- *Customised MUST approach to connect local development to organisational IT management*: The second deliberation concerned the adaptation and use of the MUST approach (Bødker et al. 2004) as a local project management framework. The MUST approach was proposed as it is a coherent user-centred design project management framework that builds on core PD principles such as a coherent vision for change between IT systems and work practices, genuine user participation in IT-design, IT-designers having firsthand experiences with work practices and anchoring visions for change with affected user constituencies. The MUST project management framework, however, needed to be customised to include not only the design but also the implementation project. As Fig. 16.6 shows, the guidelines for developing a project charter were used to define the premise of a project, including assignment and objective, financial and technical framework and key critical factors. The second phase of the MUST guidelines is an in-line analysis to connect to strategic organisational IT management considerations. To support this function, the in-line analysis was expanded to connect to the business plans described below that allow discussing the relation and dependencies between different projects. The third phase of the MUST guidelines concerns an in-depth analysis to understand the particulars of a work domain in need of change. In the adaption of MUST, the in-depth analysis was customised to describe current work procedures and problems, needs and ideas for solutions to provide a context for the story cards. Finally, instead of ending with a design proposal (preceding a later implementation project) in the original MUST model, the last phase of MUST was extended to detail an evolutionary implementation process of the story cards.
- *Business plans to coordinate organisational IT management*: To create an organisational IT management anchoring of the MUST project management framework and to link local development projects, a notion of 'business plans' was developed. The business plans were created annually and positioned in upcoming and ongoing development projects. They connected to the in-line analysis of the MUST approach and were used to create accountability of how the IT professionals could be used as resources for development projects to the IT-steering committee and management committee.
- *Improved procedures in the IT-steering committee*: The final deliberation concerned improved procedures in the IT-steering committee. The procedures included: how agenda items were to be prepared in making use of the story cards, MUST project planning and business plans; improved decision procedures to ensure that representatives from the shop floor development constituencies had a saying in the matters discussed; and how minutes and follow-up action are to be defined.

Project Charter – Course Administration

1. Premise

1.1 Background

One of the main sets of components on the intranet is the course administration. These components consist of a large and diverse body of functionality, including the definition and

1.2 Assignment and objective

This project takes a broad stance where usability and usefulness concerns are put in the centre. Targeted areas include:

1.3 Financial and technical framework

- As we are using our existing web-based technical platform DotNetNuke, the main costs relate to the work time of the project members.

1

1.4 Inline analysis considerations

Although the intranet (or any other of the WMU portals) does not have any written down organizational mandate, it has continuously been developed to function as a primary ICT

1.5 Key critical factors

- As already stated, usability and usefulness concerns are put in the centre. It is therefore critical to satisfactory anchor a new design in the work practices of:
  o Administrative staffs (Malmö and China)

2. Organization

2.1 Project Organization

2

3.3 Plan

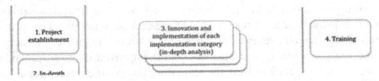

Fig. 16.6 *Top right.* Example of project charter (course administration)

Course Administration – In-Depth Analysis

This document aims to establish a common understanding of present work practices and the rationales determining their form around the main activities connected to course administration on the intranet. In addition, overall problems, needs, and ideas for solutions are identified.

1. Backdrop and focus

Overall, this project strives to incrementally improve work connected to course administration on the intranet. In addition to the course and subject professors, SI is thereby a main stakeholder when it comes to proposed changes. The intention of the proposed changes, taken together, is to not increase SI's overall workload.

1

2. Overview of existing course administration functionality on the intranet

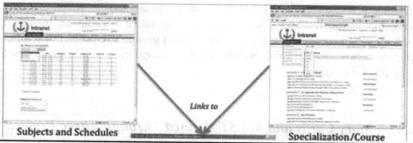

Subjects and Schedules   *Links to*   Specialization/Course

2.1 description of current work procedures and intranet functionality

2.1.1 Subject page
Each subject has a subject page. The subject pages are intended to be the main hub of information resources for each subject and by the default contains the functionality items: subject information, schedule, e-learning material, syllabus, and assessments.

2

2.2 Problem, Needs, and Ideas for Solutions

An overall identified issue with the course administration functionality is a perceived lack of simplicity and clarity. Even though a major revision was made to make the dispersed course administration functionality of the old intranet more homogeneous when the "new" intranet was launched in 2008, it still does not appear to be fully anchored in organizational practices.

Readiness for change: medium

3

Fig. 16.7 *Bottom left.* Example of in-depth analysis (course administration)

The improved processes and procedures for organisational IT management planning were discussed and implemented in a bottom-up manner.

An early approach of boundary objects that the first author worked with in the beginning of the action research deliberations was referred to as 'reflection papers'. These were intended to enable reflection on infrastructure matters between workers at the shop floor users, the IT-coordination group, the IT-steering committee and the management committee. They described a concrete technical and organisational infrastructure issue from the perspective of a shop floor user. One reflection paper, for example, used a concrete example of course administration to illustrate that changes to the technical infrastructure were not enough and used the current shop floor development model as a base to illustrate how better management needed to be developed on both the local project and organisational arena.

Throughout the action research, the usefulness of the story cards and MUST project management framework was tried out in local shop floor projects. The progress would then be discussed in weekly IT-coordination group meetings. In addition, the IT-coordination group carried out two workshops where the MUST framework was discussed, adapted and extended. On a continuous basis, the IT-coordination group would report the progress to the IT-steering committee where further deliberations would take place in refining the story cards, MUST project management framework as well as the business plans and improved procedures. During the action research, the IT-steering committee became an increasingly important venue compared to the IT-coordination group. The project development examples below illustrate the evolution and appropriation of the processes and procedures for planning.

16.5.1 Story Cards and MUST Refined Through Three Projects

In a first workshop, the main author presented the original MUST framework (Bødker et al. 2004) and early ideas about how it could be appropriated together with the story cards. In addition, a first discussion of business plans proposed by the Head of Information took place. The presentation was later repeated for the IT-steering committee and the management committee. The outcome was a conceptual understanding of what using new planning methods would entail. The importance of not adding 'bureaucratic red tape' (IT-steering committee member) to shop floor development and implementation projects was highlighted.

16.5.1.1 External Website

When the changes to the organisational IT management were discussed, an *external website* project had already been initiated. The project's strategic mandate had been decided, problems as well as potential solutions for a new design had been isolated and the current technical solution and work processes had been identified. The old external website carried an outdated interface design and could only be updated by one person. The solution was a new design with a new technical platform and a distributed organisational work arrangement to update the website. It was, therefore, considered 'red tape' to halt the ongoing development process to conduct a new in-line and in-depth analysis and write story cards. However, a first MUST project charter was defined to coordinate the ongoing development between users and IT professionals. In addition, new PD tools and techniques as positioned by the MUST framework were used to involve more workers in the design process. As Fig. 16.8 illustrates, picture mock-ups were used to support design between users bringing different ideas to the table. The top picture shows early design sketches by one of the IT-designers and members of the original shop floor development constituency. The bottom picture shows how the Administrative Assistant – who had previously not been involved in the external website development – was able to contribute to the final design with ideas picked up from Stanford's external website.

16.5.1.2 Electronic Forms

The second project also involved the Administrative Assistant and concerned the design of new electronic forms. As also presented in Sect. 16.4.2, she had over a long period of time designed WMU's internal forms, for example, concerning leave of absence for both staff and students. For this purpose, she had used Microsoft Word. The question now was whether she could design the forms using a new technical system that connected to a shared database developed by the first author. In total, about 20 different forms existed. In this case, a project charter was developed, containing an in-line analysis that was vetted with the IT-steering committee. Following this, the first author sought to acquire an in-depth understanding of White's current design procedures through a number of participatory observation sessions. A report of the in-depth analysis was published to the IT-steering committee. The new design of the forms was based on a number of mock-ups, where design ideas were solicited from different stakeholders. Figure 16.9 shows an example of a design proposal with revision notes from a faculty professor.

16.5.1.3 Course Administration

The most comprehensive example in utilising the story cards and the MUST project management framework was a revision of course administration functionality. Figures 16.5, 16.6 and 16.7 show how the course administration project made use of the MUST guidelines: project charter, in-line analysis and in-depth analysis. Seven main story cards were positioned that detailed a revision of subject, schedule and assessment administration in the university's online academic portal. The understanding of current problems and ideas for solutions was developed through day-to-day interaction between users and IT professionals. In addition, three

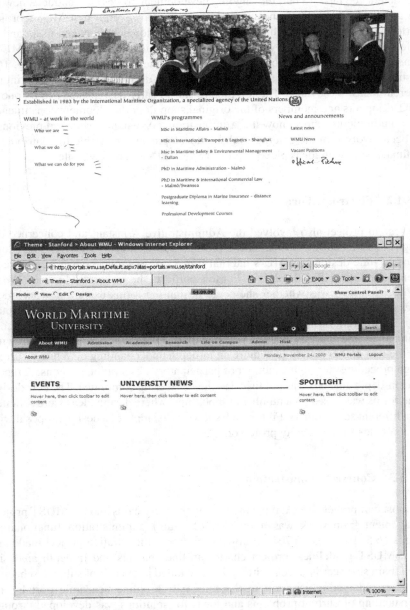

Fig. 16.8 Picture mock-ups of external website design

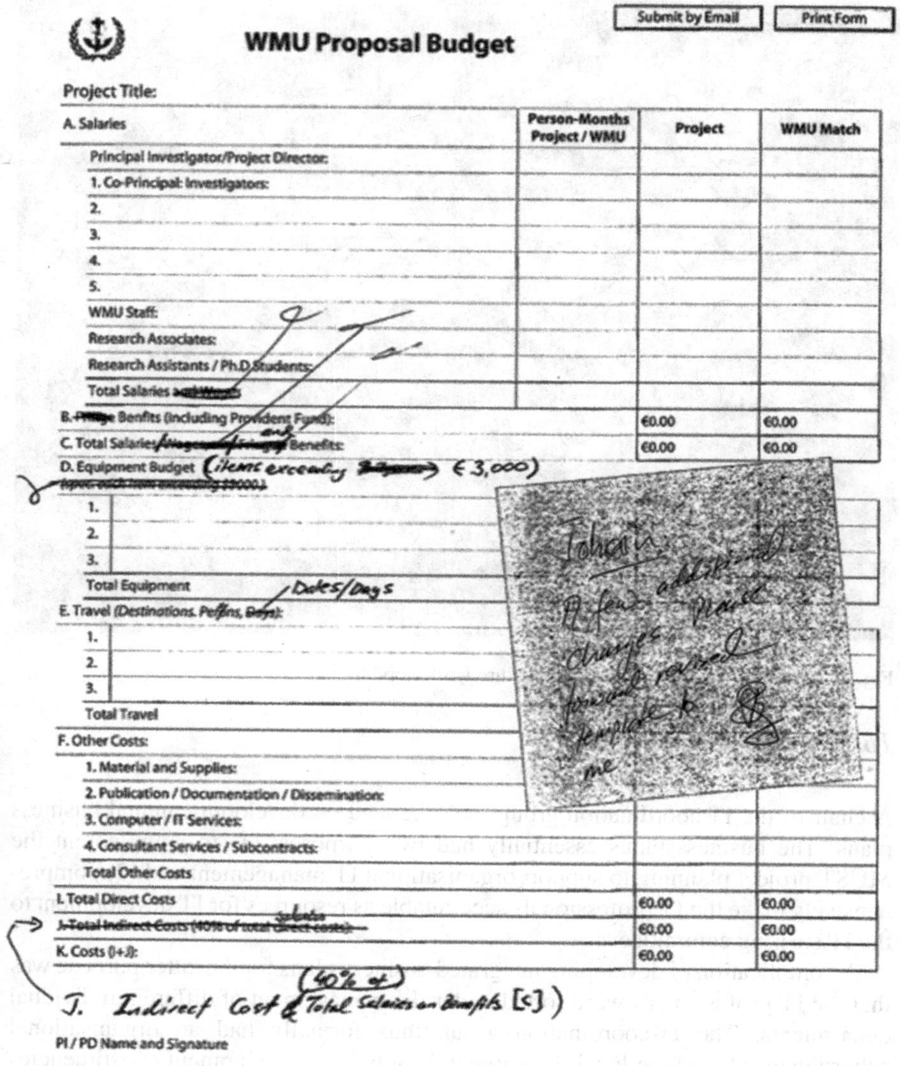
Submit by Email | Print Form

WMU Proposal Budget

Project Title:

A. Salaries	Person-Months Project / WMU	Project	WMU Match
Principal Investigator/Project Director:			
1. Co-Principal: Investigators:			
2.			
3.			
4.			
5.			
WMU Staff:			
Research Associates:			
Research Assistants / Ph.D Students:			
Total Salaries and Wages			
B. Fringe Benfits (including Provident Fund):		€0.00	€0.00
C. Total Salaries/Wages and Fringe Benefits:		€0.00	€0.00

D. Equipment Budget (items exceeding € 3,000)

1.	
2.	
3.	
Total Equipment	

E. Travel (Destinations. Persons, Dates/Days):

1.	
2.	
3.	
Total Travel	

F. Other Costs:			
1. Material and Supplies:			
2. Publication / Documentation / Dissemination:			
3. Computer / IT Services:			
4. Consultant Services / Subcontracts:			
Total Other Costs			
I. Total Direct Costs		€0.00	€0.00
J. Total Indirect Costs (40% of total direct costs):		€0.00	€0.00
K. Costs (I+J):		€0.00	€0.00

J. Indirect Cost (40% of Total Salaries an Benefits [€])

PI / PD Name and Signature

Fig. 16.9 Electronic forms mock-up with revision notes

workshops were conducted with different constellations of faculty (Fig. 16.10 shows one of the rich pictures that were constructed during these workshops), student representatives were consulted and starting ideas of faculty and registry integration were envisioned with the registry staff.

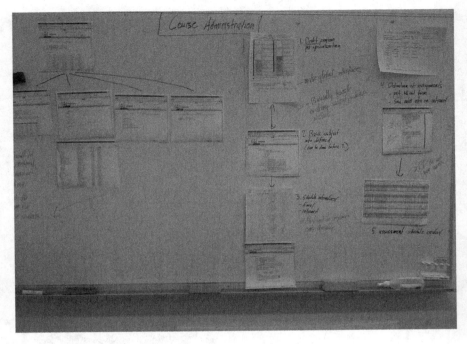

Fig. 16.10 Course administration rich picture workshop

16.5.2 Business Plans

A chair of the IT-coordination group took the lead on developing annual business plans. The business plans essentially had two purposes: (1) to complement the MUST project planning to support organisational IT management and (2) comprehensively make the IT professionals accountable as resources for IT development to the IT-steering committee.

A complication of developing integrated business plans for the latter purpose was that the IT professionals were sorted under the management of different individual departments. The IT-coordination group thus formally had an organisational subordinate role, where local departmental shop floor development constituencies had precedence. For this purpose, the business plan procedure was gradually evolved during the course of 2 years. Starting 2009, a trial version of a business plan was defined that compiled ongoing and upcoming project work, including the three projects accounted for above. This version was used to test the concept of using business plans for coordination between the IT-coordination group, the IT-steering committee, the management committee and the management of the respective departments. In addition, as described above, some of the projects did not have a fully defined project scoping using the MUST framework. The following year, a version of the business plan was defined that utilised the strategic in-line analysis definition of the MUST project management framework to coordinate ongoing and upcoming projects.

The coordination of the IT development by the IT-steering committee using the business plans required the individual shop floor development constituencies to give up the dispersed management of the IT professionals. This became a success indicator for the new bottom-up approach for organisational IT management. In 2010 the change was implemented, where the IT professionals became common resources for the IT-steering committee.

16.5.3 New IT-Steering Committee Procedures

The above account of the implementation of the business plan, the MUST framework and story cards provides a picture of how local project development continuously interacted with the IT-steering committee. The improved IT-steering committee agenda and decision processes were initially prompted by the turmoil of the failing ISS plan accounted for in Sect. 16.4. Further changes were implemented following the first business plan, usage of the story cards and the appropriation of MUST procedures through the three IT development projects presented above. A chair of the IT-steering committee described (1) how the new processes enabled the committee to focus on the 'subject matters' and (2) how they contributed to the existing procedures that were based on the university's rules and regulations' framework and consolidation of best practices from other committees:

> if we are going to work with this, we are going to work with the subject matters, ... What I essentially was after also in the computer committee, and we have it partly built into the system, it is in the rules and regulations, there is a standard for how protocols should be written, and that is the beginning, because then everybody can understand, it is easy to comprehend information in a way.

16.6 CMD3: Observation and Evaluation of Changes, A Locally Accountable Organisational IT Management

As the changes described above were implemented to address the need of the shop floor development constituencies for coordinating IT development on an organisational level, the evaluation is based on the perspectives of the different stakeholders voiced in workshops and interviews.

16.6.1 Power from and to the Workers on the Shop Floor

The changes to the organisational IT management kept the competence of the management of the infrastructure with the shop floor development constituencies and cultivated their capabilities in also addressing the infrastructure's technical and organisational integration. The recognition that the design of organisational IT management needs to take its starting point with the workers on the shop floor was an at times difficult but necessary lesson to learn.

The cancellation of the efforts to implement a top-down approach to IT management described in Sect. 16.4.4 is the most prominent example of the power of the shop floor development constituencies. The shop floor development constituencies gradually withdrew their support, and as a consequence it failed.

Another example concerns the Administrative Assistant that was developing the electronic forms and the database and her membership in the IT-steering committee:

> *Second Author: They have something like where they coordinate. Johan [Bolmsten] told me about it. He told me first of all the steering or the coordination group and then he told me also there is a computer committee?*
> Adm Ass: *Why do they have a steering group and a computer committee; what is the difference between the two?*
> *Second Author: I don't know.*
> Adm Ass: *Me neither. I have no idea, I don't know about that.*
> *[. . .]*
> *Second Author: And the computer committee and that is still to coordinate the?*
> Adm Ass: *Yeah, infrastructure, yes, and the budget [. . .] but bugger that*
> *[. . .]*
> Adm Ass: *They have minutes of meetings, which I haven't seen very often I must say.*

For a while the Administrative Assistant was replaced in the IT-steering committee, as she was not recognised as an IT professional. This was not only a vulnerability for the EUD that she carried out but, by extension, for the organisation, as her expletive, 'bugger that', indicated her indifference to bureaucratic formality and she continued with her development – anyway – to the best of her capabilities.

Her example illustrates an important dimension in how the situational and historical setting at WMU of shop floor development constituencies interplayed with the development of organisational IT management. The power in managing the development of software support was not *given* to the shop floor workers by management or by IT professionals but developed over time based on experience and competencies.

16.6.2 The Only Partial Reach of Organisational IT Management by IT Professionals

The analysis of our empirical material consistently shows that the reach and mandate of the IT professionals to manage the technical infrastructure development were only partial. Especially, the two cases of EUD reported in Sect. 16.4.2 indicate that shop floor workers might not even depend on IT professionals to develop their IT infrastructures. With the availability of more and more EUD-friendly development tools, the viability of shop floor workers to develop their own technical infrastructure can be expected to increase. Organisational IT management today and tomorrow cannot assume that IT professionals will own the technical infrastructure development agenda.

16.6.3   A Deliberate Work in Progress

The organisational IT management's use of the extended MUST approach and its linkage with the story cards, the business plans and the improved procedures in the IT-steering committee came about in an evolutionary manner. This evolution used local projects as probes to gradually understand the different needs of organisational IT management. Different shop floor development constituencies also had different needs with respect to organisational IT management.

The further development of the course administration right from the start needed better IT management. The development was growing to include an increasing number of workers across different departments. To answer this need, the business plans from the beginning entailed a comparably extensive use of the MUST approach and coordination with the IT-steering committee. In total, the new organisational IT management coordinated seven in-depth analysis workshops with eight faculty stakeholders that included professors, lectures and faculty assistants; the in-depth analysis was then used as an input to eight overall story cards that each evolved the EUD functionality of the course administration support. The story cards were created together with workers on the shop floor in agile design and implementation phases and included both technological and work process changes.

At the same time, the current state of the development of the electronic forms required a different type of attention in the early business plans. The shop floor development by the Administrative Assistant that was already taking place was now to be supported by an IT professional. Here, it became important to properly recognise her development efforts and competencies in the business plan, rather than to implement the full MUST framework.

The organisational IT management needs to maintain flexibility in order to accommodate the needs of different projects. This kind of 'tinkering' and radical learning, where the organisational IT management evolves together with and based on the experiences gained with software development ventures, allows to keep the organisational IT management in sync with the needs of the organisation.

16.6.4   Organisational IT Management with Workers
on the Shop Floor

With the IT-steering committee, a partial organisational IT management based on representative management principles already existed. However, there was a need for process and procedure improvements to make it work in a landscape of increasingly complex technical and organisational infrastructure development. In a retrospective interview, the chair of the IT-steering committee described how the improvements resulted in an organised and constructive approach to planning by focusing on the 'subject matter':

> "then one hase the subject matter, one has a presentation, the one who has prepared the case then has to focus on what is suggested[. . .] it is important that opinions can be put forward, subject matter arguments, and that it is documented, then that goes a long way[. . .] if one can come to a clear concrete decision, and if I then don't get a hearing for my view then one kind of has to accept, there has been a forum, I have put forward the arguments, and they were not approved, then one has to accept the vote of the majority.

It is important to recognise that negotiations of weighting, for example, different interests against each other in the business plans, were sometimes difficult. From time to time, as further described by the chair of the IT-steering committee, the discussions in the IT-steering committee were heated:

> The first indication of personal attacks amongst the committee members there will be a yellow card, I took [sic] out a yellow card, the first indication of a personal attack on me, there will be red card.

Although there was never any football type of referee cards used, the citation illustrates that the decisions in WMU's IT-steering committee are actually important. It also shows that its procedures need to be carefully designed in order to support the development in the local projects.

16.6.5 Meaningful Artefacts

One of the challenges of implementing a participatory approach to organisational IT management is the need to represent complex technical and organisational dependencies in an understandable way for shop floor development constituencies. This is still an area that needs further experimentation.

Early inspiration came from the reflection papers used to discuss the situational context of infrastructure issues. They were based on a concrete issue experienced by workers on the shop floor and intended to present relevant issues that needed to be taken into account when designing for the local projects. This idea was then comprehensively extended during the action research by using the story cards integrated with the MUST framework and the business plans.

This type of representations can be contrasted with the ones provided in the cancelled ISS plan (Sect. 16.4.4), where there were no meaningful representations for deliberations available to shop floor development constituencies.

Though the representations developed for the organisational IT management are to be regarded as work in progress, they have proven to provide a basis to discuss and decide difficult design questions involving both IT professionals and domain experts.

16.6.6   Trusted Representation

It is important that members of the organisation informally and formally can trust the people that are representing them. Mutual trust underpinned the research from the beginning but only became a central topic in a retrospective interview with the Senior Registry Assistant and a Student Social Officer.

Especially in comprehensive developments of new software support, it is important to recognise that normal day-to-day work does not stop just because an IT development project commences. A busy period when handling a new student intake was used to exemplify how it was not possible for all registry staff to attend vendor presentations and workshops concerning a new part of the infrastructure. However, as the Student Social Officer noted, she felt well represented with respect to her needs:

> So in a way, I felt comfortable that [the Registrar] went to this presentations, because he would be able to represent us.

In a comprehensive project, staff in a particular domain need to be able to trust their co-workers to represent their interests, in this case in the IT-steering committee. As there are other tasks to do as well, the whole development constituency cannot participate all the time.

Based on the empirical material, we can observe that (1) this trust is often built up over time through the joint work in shop floor development constituencies and (2) workers on the shop floor need to be able to influence those who represent them. Although the latter was understood in the action research, representations were one of the dimensions that were not explicitly discussed.

16.7   Discussion and Concluding Remarks

The research reported above underlines the importance of taking the contribution of both IT professionals and shop floor users to the design and evolution of an organisation's infrastructure. This research study has reported on how shop floor development is put in the centre in deliberation on an organisational IT management initiative. The structures and processes of organisational IT management can be regarded as an infrastructure for the local development activities. The shop floor development constituencies themselves asked for a more structured organisational IT management to take advantage of synergies in coordinating a shared technical infrastructure.

With the empirical outcome of the action research, a new alternative to the organisational IT management outlined in Sect. 16.2 is emerging (see Fig. 16.11). The first one is constituted by the current predominately top-down control-oriented IS management approaches; the second one is Ciborra's (2000) bottom-up process-oriented 'control to drift' approach – that basically argues for an organisational IT un-management. This study introduces a third alternative that makes use of local

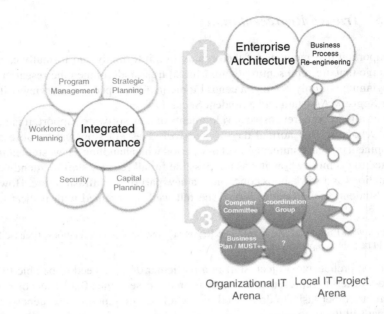

Fig. 16.11 Three alternatives to organisational IT management: (*1*) IS management, (*2*) process-oriented 'from control to drift' and (*3*) the empirical results of this study

creativity but allows for coordination across different contexts where beneficial. The organisational IT management plans are seen as resources for the situated development. In the research presented above, the Computer Committee, the Coordination Group and the extended MUST are all part of this cross organisational coordination. The question mark in the figure indicates the need to appropriate and extend these measures. The following five subsections discuss the empirical results in the context of existing related work: Sect. 16.7.1 confirms shop floor management as a core capability; Sects. 16.7.2 and 16.7.3 deal with how the implemented organisational IT management makes a difference; and Sects. 16.7.4 and 16.7.5 deal with how it was deliberated as organisational IT change management.

16.7.1   Shop Floor Development as a Core Capability

The empirical results of this study confirm that shop floor development can be regarded as a core capability in the organisation. Dittrich et al. (2002), where shop floor development is identified 'in the wild', also describe such cases. More and more examples of similar types of development, where 'design in use' complements 'use in design', can also be found in the emerging interlinkage between PD and EUD – see, for example, the book on EUD edited by Lieberman et al. (2006) and the proceedings of the international symposium of EUD (Costabile et al. 2011).

The prime contribution of this study is to show how a local shop floor IT management model develops to extend to technical and organisational infrastructure development. For this purpose, the work by Ciborra and Andreu (Ciborra 2000; Andreu and Ciborra 1998) has been conceptually important to understand how shop floor IT management 'in the wild' interlinks to the development of core capabilities in an organisation. Ciborra's understanding is also recognised in mainstream IS management literature: Hedman and Kalling (2002), for example, reference Andrew and Ciborra's bottom-up organisational knowledge creation and innovation cycle that is based on bricolage and radical learning. This is the foundation for understanding the unfolding of the empirical results in this research and constitutes a fundamental stance against mainstream IS management approaches.

16.7.2 A Call for (a Different) Organisational IT Management

In the case presented here, the workers on the shop floor were not content with an un-managed IT infrastructure as implied by Ciborra (2000). This was one of the motivations of this action research study and was accounted for already in the understanding of the existing practices preceding the research (Sect. 16.4). To this end, the IT-steering committee was, for example, not instigated by the research project. It had been established as one of the earliest committees at the university as a forum for organisational IT management.

The third way of organisational IT management put forward here essentially deals with a type of meta-decision-making that provides a frame and structure for the bottom-up 'drifting' nature of technical infrastructure. The deliberations at WMU show that users and IT professionals can, on an equal footing, develop frames and structures to discuss, design and coordinate the organisational IT infrastructure in their organisations. This can be referred to as triple loop or deutero-learning (Georges et al. 1999). It becomes an additional learning cycle of single- and double-loop learning (Argyris and Schon 1974) implied by the tinkering with current work practices of bricolage and radical learning that entails stepping out to expose different and conflicting perspectives against each other in order to innovate in a new manner.

16.7.3 Extending Local Project PD

Our empirical results extend the predominate application of PD tools and techniques on the individual project arena. Bødker's et al. (2004) MUST framework has been of practical importance to our study. In its original design, MUST limits itself to the local project arena and only reaches out to the organisational IT management arena through the in-line analysis. A question remaining is what the local project should reach out to.

Our extension of MUST and the business plans sets out to provide this anchoring. In prevalent IS management, project management approaches enjoy comparably established interfaces to organisational IT management such as EA (Bernard 2005). In our research, these had to be invented in situ as well.

16.7.4 Expanding Circles of Located Accountability

Our empirical results not only show that a different IT management on the organisational arena is called for but provide a lead-in to the process of how it might come about. A foundation to understand the 'how' of a PD-prone organisational IT management becomes the located accountability of Suchman's (1994) artful integration where plans become 'resources for action' put in the context of specific infrastructure development. For this purpose, our study features two qualities that can be referred to as expanding circles of located accountability:

- Grounded: The study shows that the structures and planning entities of organisational IT management put forward are grounded in the situated contingencies and needs of the organisation.
- Evolving: Grounded entities push for evolution. The IT-coordination group needed to relate to usage in a better way; therefore, the interest in developing the agenda of the IT-steering committee, the IT-steering committee and the IT-coordination group did not operate effectively, hence the need for the MUST framework and the business plans. Though here framed within a research process, it is a feature of continuous action pushed by the evolution of the organisation and its technical and organisational infrastructure.

Together, these two qualities provide a 'located accountability' of the organisational IT management that takes its stance in expanding circles of meaningful user engagement from the shop floor.

References that we have found that can be related to the expanding circles of local accountability of creating a meta-design on the organisational management arena include the (Georges et al. 1999; Romme 1996; Romme and Dillen 1997) circular organisation approach where users strategically are collaborating on the organisational arena. However, although these types of references point in the right direction, they primarily present a structure and do not account for the grounded and evolving process that substantially contributed to progress in our case.

16.7.5 Emerging Useful Representations

The usage of 'reflection papers' in the discussion and design of the technical side of IT infrastructures illustrates how representations enable users as well as IT professionals to take part in these deliberations in a meaningful way. Their character stands in stark contrast to the top-down controlled nature of, for example, Bernard's (2005) EA documentation framework. In line with the representational qualities argued for by Kyng (1995), their story card character intended (successfully) to prompt reflection through reminding, rather than comprehensively defining, actors of relevant factors for infrastructure reflection.

Using, for example, one of the faculty assistant's experiences of the technical infrastructure as an intentional base for deliberations, the reflection papers worked in accordance with the guidelines of the CMD approach in regard to (1) a focus on shop floor software development practices taking the practitioners' perspective and (2) deliberating change together with involved practitioners.

At this point, our representations for organisational IT change management were a situated response to supporting reflection, but they do not constitute a finished concept. However, they do set a focus on how a different type of representation for deliberations can be developed.

16.8 Conclusion and Future Research

The action research project presented in this chapter resulted in (1) an IT-steering committee deciding on and designing organisational IT infrastructure development between management, users and IT professionals; (2) business plans that relate individual projects to the overall development of the organisational IT infrastructure, a project model based on a PD method (MUST) extended to comprise the implementation as well; (3) and an IT-coordination group coordinating development from a technical perspective showing that it is possible to involve users in a meaningful way in complex organisational IT management.

As discussed in relation to the related work, the contribution of this study confirms that shop floor development can remain a core capability given increasingly complex technical and organisational infrastructure development. However, as the workers on the shop floor themselves called for, meaningful shop floor governed organisational IT management is necessary. Organisational IT management itself needs to come about through a grounded and evolving process of expanding circles of located accountability that takes its stance in shop floor development. Our results constitute a third way compared to both the mainstream IS management and the infrastructure development as the 'drifting' argued by Ciborra (2000).

This study is exploratory in the sense that it does not put forward a complete and packaged framework. However, although more can be done to specify the type of meta-decision-making body argued for, the outcome can never be a comprehensive control-oriented framework such as EA. The grounded and evolving nature that comes with a 'located accountability' demands 'non-programmatic solutions' (Clement and van den Besselaar 1993) that are situated in the work realities at hand. This strength also indicates the major limitation of the study: the developed participatory approach to organisational IT management clearly depended on a culture of shop floor development by faculty members and administrative personnel and a management that embraced heterogeneity. Whether, how and what kind of participatory organisational IT management can be developed in other kinds of organisations remains a research challenge for future work.

References

Andreu, R., & Ciborra, C. (1996). Core capabilities and information technology: An organisational learning approach. *The Journal of Strategic Information Systems, 5*(2), 111–127.

Andreu, R., & Ciborra, C. (1998). *Organisational learning and core capabilities. Information technology and organisational transformation.* Chichester: Wiley.

Argyris, C., & Schon, D. A. (1974). *Theory in practice: Increasing professional effectiveness.* San Francisco: Jossey-Bass Publishers.

Baskerville, R., & Myers, M. (2004). Special issue on action research in information systems: Making IS research relevant to practice-foreword. *MIS Quarterly, 28,* 329–336.

Beck, K., & Andres, C. (2004). *Extreme programming explained: Embrace change.* Reading: Addison-Wesley.

Bernard, S. A. (2005). *An introduction to enterprise architecture.* Bloomington: AuthorHouse.

Bødker, K., Kensing, F., & Simonsen, J. (2004). *Participatory IT design. Designing for business and workplace realities.* Cambridge, MA/London: MIT Press.

Checkland, P., & Holwell, S. (1998). Action research: Its nature and validity. *System Practice and Action Research, 11*(1), 9–21.

Ciborra, C. (2000). *From control to drift: The dynamics of corporate information infrastructures.* New York: Oxford University Press.

Clement, A., & van den Besselaar, P. (1993). A retrospective look at PD projects. *Communications of the ACM, 36*(6), 29–37.

Costabile, M. F., Dittrich, Y., Fischer, G., & Piccinno, A. (2011, June 7–10). End-user development – Third international symposium, IS-EUD 2011, Torre Canne, Italy, Proceedings. Berlin/Heidelberg: Springer.

Dittrich, Y., Eriksén, S., & Hansson, C. (2002). PD in the wild; evolving practices of design in use. In *Proceedings of the participatory design conference*, Malmo, Sweden. Computer professionals for social responsibility, pp. 124–134.

Dittrich, Y., Rönkkö, K., Eriksson, J., Hansson, C., & Lindeberg, O. (2008). Cooperative method development. *Empirical Software Engineering, 13*(3), 231–260.

Eriksén, S. (1998, September 30). *Knowing and the art of IT management: An inquiry into work practices in one-stop shops.* Lund: Lund University.

Floyd, C., Reisin, F., & Schmidt, G. (1989). STEPS to software development with users. *ESEC, 89,* 48–64.

Floyd, C., Züllighoven, H., & Budde, R. (1992). *Software development and reality construction.* Berlin: Springer.

Gärtner, J., & Wagner, I. (1996a). Systems as intermediaries political frameworks of design & participation. *Human-Computer Interaction,* 1–11.

Gärtner, J., & Wagner, I. (1996b). Mapping actors and agendas: Political frameworks of systems design and participation. *Human-computer interaction, proceedings of PDC.* Computer professionals for social responsibility, pp. 37–46.

Georges, L., Romme, A., & Van Witteloostuijn, A. (1999). Circular organising and triple loop learning. *Journal of Organisational Change Management, 12*(5), 439–454.

Greenbaum, J., & Kyng, M. (1992). *Design at work: Cooperative design of computer systems.* Hillsdale, NJ: Lawrence Erlbaum Associates. pp. 169–196.

Hanseth, O., & Braa, K. (2001). Hunting for the treasure at the end of the rainbow: Standardizing corporate IT infrastructure. *Computer Supported Cooperative Work (CSCW), 10*(3), 261–292.

Hedman, J., & Kalling, T. (2002). IT and business models: Concepts and theories. *Recherche, 67,* 02.

Karasti, H., & Syrjänen, A.-L. (2004). Artful infrastructuring in two cases of community PD (Vol. 1). *Presented at the PDC 04: Proceedings of the eighth conference on participatory design: Artful integration: Interweaving media, materials and practices* (Vol 1, pp. 20–30). New York: ACM.

Kensing, F., & Blomberg, J. (1998). Participatory design: Issues and concerns. *Computer Supported Cooperative Work (CSCW), 7*(3–4), 167–185.

Kyng, M. (1995). Making representations work. *Communications of the ACM, 38*(9), 46–55.

Lieberman, H., Paternò, F., Klann, M., & Wulf, V. (Eds.). (2006). *End-user development: An emerging paradigm.* Berlin: Springer.

Peppard, J. (1999). Information management in the global enterprise: An organising framework. *European Journal of Information Systems, 8*, 77–94.

Pipek, V., & Wulf, V. (2009). Infrastructuring: Towards an integrated perspective on the design and use of Information technology. *Journal of the Association for Information Systems, 10*(5), 447–473.

Romme, G. (1996). A note on the hierarchy-team debate. *Strategic Management Journal, 17*(5), 411–417.

Romme, G., & Dillen, R. (1997). Mapping the landscape of organisational learning. *European Management Journal, 15*(1), 68–78.

Simonsen, J., & Hertzum, M. (2012). Sustained participatory design: Extending the iterative approach. *Design Issues, 28*(3), 10–21.

Star, S., & Ruhleder, K. (1996). Steps toward an ecology of infrastructure: Design and access for large information spaces. *Information Systems Research, 7*(1), 111–134.

Suchman, L. A. (1987). *Plans and situated actions: The problem of human-machine communication (Learning in doing: Social, cognitive and computational perspectives).* New York: Cambridge University Press.

Suchman, L. (1994). Working relations of technology production and use. *Computer Supported Cooperative Work (CSCW), 2*(1), 21–39.

Suchman, L. A. (2007). *Human-machine reconfigurations: Plans and situated actions.* New York: Cambridge University Press.

Wessels, B., Walsh, S., & Adam, E. (2008). Mediating voices: Community participation in the design of E-enabled community care services. *The Information Society, 24*, 30–39.

Wulf, V., & Rohde, M. (1995). Towards an integrated organisation and technology development. In *Proceedings of the 1st International Conference on Designing Interactive Systems: Processes, practices, methods and techniques* (pp. 55–64). New York: ACM Press.

Chapter 17
Concluding Remarks: New Pathways

Volker Wulf, Kjeld Schmidt, and David Randall

It is perhaps stating the blindingly obvious when we say that technologically, organisationally, and socially, we are experiencing rapid change. Whether, however, our analytic approaches have kept up is an open question. In these concluding remarks, we examine the changing face of social, organisational, and work practice as a dynamic sociotechnical phenomenon and present an argument for a modest and productive approach to generalisation which will allow us to bridge the gap between, on the one hand, case studies which can be narrowly focused and short-term and, on the other, decisions about the appropriate level of generality which might allow us to transfer insights and be a basis for technological design. We use the word 'modest' advisedly here for some part of what we have to say will be avowedly polemic. Many of the problems we discuss are not new. Issues around participation, the politics of design, the role of the reflexive researcher, and so on have been discussed ad nauseam. Our main contention, however, is that we have yet to provide a systematic alternative to more conventional approaches to the investigation and design relationship. We see this to be the focus of an emerging

V. Wulf (✉)
School of Media and Information, University of Siegen, Siegen, Germany

Fraunhofer FIT, St. Augustin, Germany
e-mail: volker.wulf@unisiegen.de

K. Schmidt
Department of Organization, Copenhagen Business School, Kilevej 14A, Frederiksberg, Denmark

School of Media and Information, University of Siegen, Siegen, Germany
e-mail: schmidt@cscw.d

D. Randall
School of Media and Information, University of Siegen, Siegen, Germany
e-mail: D.Randall@mmu.ac.uk

© Springer-Verlag London 2015

V. Wulf et al. (eds.), *Designing Socially Embedded Technologies in the Real-World*,
Computer Supported Cooperative Work, DOI 10.1007/978-1-4471-6720-4_17

discourse on socially embedded technologies. In the following, we will elaborate on such a research agenda, developing it out of a critical evaluation of the state of the art in the CSCW discourse.

At the outset, the CSCW community was founded on the recognition of a number of inadequacies in traditional computer science, cognitive science, and social psychology thinking which had to do both with understandings of the nature of design processes and assumptions about how to best gather and analyse information relevant to the direction of technology design. (What will it be used for? By whom? What practical problems are people encountering and will the technology resolve them? Will it create unanticipated problems? How will it impact the balance of skills, expertises, and formal organisational processes? What impact has the new technology had?) Equally, CSCW asked conceptual questions which we can gloss as having variously to do with 'interaction', 'work', 'practice', 'community', and admixtures thereof. These broad interests have scarcely changed and have had, in some sense, an enormous impact. They may well constitute, by analogy, what Imre Lakatos called the 'hard core' of any given science. These central commitments remain, despite the fact that the range of topics under investigation under the CSCW umbrella has developed quite considerably in recent years and now includes questions around mobile devices and their use in work and play, gaming, identity work, new technology and development, the various social media and their uses, and so on. However, and despite this 'hard core', the methods and conceptual formulations of the CSCW community remain eclectic. There is, and never has been, any overall agreement as to whether we should have a preference for the various qualitative methods associated with those of a broad sociological/anthropological persuasion or for laboratory studies/experimental approaches largely associated with cognitive and social psychology. Now, it is not part of our project here to legislate the topical directions we might take or the methods we should adopt. All these topics are legitimate and the way they interact with each other raises new challenges. All methods might be appropriate, depending on the purposes they serve and the analytic claims made on the back of them. Even so, and this would be our main point, some at least of the ambitions associated with the (more or less radical) positioning of CSCW against design orthodoxies remain largely unfulfilled.

Before we discuss why this might be, we should at least note that the problem of analysing the interrelationship between work, technology, and organisation goes back a long way and is subject to constant reinvention. We can certainly trace this set of interests back to the scientific management approach of Frederick Taylor and others, the human relations school in sociology (see, e.g. Whyte 1948), the sociotechnical systems approach of institutions such as the Tavistock Institute (e.g. Emery and Trist 1973), and the early work of Enid Mumford (1981, 1995; Mumford and Henshall 1983), along with German and Swedish work science (see Bannon et al. 2011, for a review). More recently, approaches from HCI, participatory design, CSCW, business process modelling, interaction design, UX modelling, and design research, to name a few, have had their turn in the spotlight. These approaches compete with each other in respect of a number of questions. These include how best to describe these interrelationships, to what degree we can provide for some general conclusions about them and what kind of generalisations they might be, whether and to what extent the current situation contains problems which are in need of solution (and who gets to define them), what might be done to effect some changes, what these changes should be, and who should be involved in making decisions about them.

At the risk of oversimplifying, one central fault line runs through all these competing perspectives, and that has to do with the degree to which answers to the above questions can be provided by something that looks like a 'science'. Now, it is no part of our purpose to engage in a philosophical debate about the nature of science (see Okasha 2003 for background). Rather, we provide a rough characterisation (something of a caricature) of it as follows. Scientific commitments, as we see them, for the most involve the assumption that description can be done objectively (founded in empiricist or realist epistemologies). They involve the view that the concepts that the science has evolved can be deployed for the analysis of any relevant problem (a more or less reductionist position). They lastly entail the proposition that problems and solutions are causally related. Put simply, once a precise statement of the problem(s) is obtained, it can be decomposed and associated with specific kinds of solution. Well-defined problems will lead to specifiable solution paths.

Arguably, the most recent example of this apparent precision is design science. We also discuss these themes in a proliferating discourse about the 'scientific' basis of design. Recent years have, for instance, seen appeals to 'design science' as providing a more rigorous approach to design problems (see, e.g. Hevner et al. 2004). Hevner and Chatterjee (2010:5) argue:

> Design science research is a research paradigm in which a designer answers questions relevant to human problems via the creation of innovative artifacts, thereby contributing new knowledge to the body of scientific evidence. The designed artifacts are both useful and fundamental in understanding that problem.

Of course, the science in question does not have to be physics. Hevner and Chatterjee (2010: 5) go on to distinguish design science from the natural sciences:

> Behavioral science which draws its origins from natural science paradigm seeks to find the truth. It starts with a hypothesis, then researchers collect data, and either prove or disprove the hypothesis. Eventually a theory develops. Design science on the other hand is fundamentally a problem-solving paradigm whose end goal is to produce an artifact which must be built and then evaluated. (ibid: 5)

Leaving aside the utter naivety of statements about 'behavioural science', one wonders on the basis of the above two statements exactly what is notable about design science. Elaboration brings no clarity:

> One source of confusion to novice design science researchers is to understand the subtle difference between conducting DSR versus practicing routine design. Is the iPod a good design or is it an example of design science research? ... Perhaps yes or perhaps no. It depends on whether the designers at Apple had actually invented something new with the compact design, the easy-to-use dial interface, or produced better sound clarity. They may have. In that case, if the team documents that their new 'artifact' is better, faster, or more optimal through *rigorous evaluation methods and comparison with similar artifacts*, then new knowledge is indeed created. (ibid p7. Our emphasis)

Clearly, some kind of comparison is involved from the outset. Indeed, Bonsiepe (2007: 27) make this explicit:

First, complex design problems can no longer be solved without prior or parallel research. It should be noted that design research cannot be equated with consumer research or variations of it that take the form of ethnomethodology, i.e. an empirical science that examines the behaviour of consumers in their everyday environments and thus refrains from carrying out laboratory research.

Quite why ethnomethodology should be equated with consumer research escapes us, but, again, the implications of claims of this kind are obvious. Mere description, of whatever kind, is not enough. The basis of this 'science' as with any other, is its 'rigorous' approach to comparison (and subsequently evaluation) which – here – is associated with laboratory work. We would not be the first to comment on the fact that problems can easily be described as if they are solutions. Our point, simply, is that finding an appropriate basis for description, comparison, deciding what to build, or evaluation is precisely the problem (see Rohde et al. 2009 for a more systematic critique of design science). The disputes between CSCW (in its original form) and the more 'scientific' views of the design problem are precisely disputes about whether anything like 'rigour' is, or can be, achieved.

17.1   The Challenge in, and for, CSCW

Now, it can be argued that design science, like any other approach to the problem of design, is predicated on some simple propositions. These would include:

- Identifying methods of discovery. How do we best, in as accurate a way as possible, characterise what we know about an application domain?
- From this, how do we go about identifying a problem, a lack, or a need (or a want)?
- How do we then identify its scope – roughly speaking, how much of a problem is it, where does it exist, and how serious is it (the comparison or generalisation problem)?
- How do we go about identifying a design solution?

All the arguments, of course, are about how we move from description to design. At the outset, CSCW provided a challenge to orthodoxy. This was embedded in the claims of DCog (see, e.g. Hutchins 1995), activity theory (see, e.g. Kaptilinen and Nardi 2012), participatory design (see, e.g. Greenbaum and Kyng 1991; Simonsen and Robertson 2013), ethnomethodology (see Garfinkel 1967; Suchman 2007), grounded theory (Glaser and Strauss 1967; Corbin and Strauss 1998; Corbin and Strauss 2008), and so on. These were important and necessary. They drew attention to problems inherent in the supposed rigours of (some) cognitive and social psychology, where generalisation on the back of limited experimental evidence seemed to take place with no reference to the contexts in which these experiments took place and where an emphasis on usability arguably meant that relatively little attention was paid to whether technologies were useful or usable in a much wider sense.

Moreover, at least in some views, such perspectives entailed a deductive 'scientism'. That is, they seemed on the face of it to provide a precision which, in the context of useful computing applications, turned out to be not very precise at all. In the case of cognitive science, this precision relied on the statistical method, such that the application of confidence limits to small numbers of experimental subjects was enough to generate 'objectivity'. The fact was, and is, that relatively few results were ever replicated and that, unlike the natural sciences, nothing like an accretion of knowledge about experimental behaviours has ever been established (a brief review of Solomon Asch's famous work on 'conformity', as an example, demonstrates the instability of even the best- known conclusions (see, for instance, Perrin and Spencer 1980, 1981; LaLancette and Standing 1990; Hodges and Geyer 2006). A similar critique was applied, in the case of structured design, to the logical decomposition of design phases. Here, the early phase of 'requirements analysis' would, if robust enough, allow for a logical decomposition which eventually would produce the necessary and appropriate hardware and software. This was, of course, what is conventionally known as the waterfall method, although it came with many variants. Again, the fact that the use of such methodologies has produced a huge catalogue of failure in one context after another is less often acknowledged (and certainly outside of CSCW) than it should be.[1] In the UK and elsewhere, for instance, we have seen the ambitions associated with electronic patient records largely scaled down and in some cases more or less abandoned. In the UK, at a cost of some £10 billion, the Lorenzo system was abandoned and subsequently described by a House of Commons committee as the 'biggest waste of public money ever' (see the Guardian online, September, 2013). By 2008, half of the main contractors had withdrawn, or had been dismissed, from the project. Similar experiences have been reported in the USA (see, for instance, the Washington Post 2013/01/11)

The critique further gave rise to a new emphasis on investigation in situ – what is sometimes termed 'ethnography', sometimes 'fieldwork' (see Randall et al. 2007, for discussion of this distinction). Arguably more importantly, they entailed various commitments to 'the point of view of the actor' (see, e.g. Dourish 2004). This, of course, turned out to have a number of different meanings, including a political/moral commitment to a particular set of interests; a recognition that human beings are embedded in networks, communities, or cultures which affect the nature of local behaviours; and the view that understanding 'practice' was critical to design ('practice' itself has been subject to a number of interpretations; see Reckwitz 2002;

---

[1]This is not to argue that decomposition is unnecessary or irrelevant. Large-scale design problems more or less necessitate a common approach to documentation and the language used within it. The point is rather that decompositional strategies rely utterly on the quality of the initial steps, and the CSCW position has been that 'requirements' analysis has been relatively neglected as a problem (see Jirotka and Goguen).

Wulf 2009; Wulf et al. 2011; Kuutti and Bannon 2014; Schmidt 2014). Behind these commitments lie one or more epistemologies which exist in contradistinction to the more or less 'scientific' principles we outline above, predicated instead on induction (or abduction), interpretivism, or (in the case of ethnomethodology) common-sense understanding. The starting point here is that people usually have good grounds for doing things the way they do, that through observation, we can identify regularities in what they do and categorise them in some 'grounded' fashion, identify sometimes highly local and specific factors which underpin what they do, and – depending on one's stance – perhaps represent their interests and/or mediate their participation in the design process. So far, so good. It is difficult to see how anyone in the CSCW community could or would object to these outline principles.

Nevertheless, it seems to us that (to a certain degree) CSCW has found itself 'going up a blind alley'. This, we feel, is a product of a number of factors. The first is an understandable but quasi-obsessional focus on problems of 'method'. Thus and for instance, a surge in the use of 'grounded theory' in recent years has led, more than anything else, to a series of arguments about the coding process that later versions tended to emphasise (see Charmaz 2006). This position ignores two rather important features of the grounded theoretical process. The first, as Strauss and Corbin (1990) pointed out, is that it is inevitably 'messy'. Real-world research does not, and cannot, fit neatly into a set of coding proposals. The second, and much more importantly, is that in origin it was *a defence of the case study in respect of generalisation*. Put simply, it was intended to provide a basis for comparing one set of data with another, most often when looking at a number of different settings within a single 'domain'. Domain at that time tended to be narrowly assumed. An obvious example is the work of Glaser and Strauss on dying across various ward settings in the medical domain (in a single hospital). It was not intended to be a vehicle for justifying or validating conceptual choices on a single data set, and a moment's thought tells us that, without access to the data set itself, it is impossible to judge the merits of the coding choices made. This is not intended to be a critique of grounded theory for we find exactly the same debates about the role of ethnography, about participative techniques, about interviewing, and so on. However, we would suggest that the later interpretations of grounded theory (e.g. Charmaz 2006) tend towards a position whereby the spurious precisions we associate with deductivist positions are replaced with an attempt to provide the same (spurious) precisions using inductivist (or abductivist) methods. Again, it is all too often forgotten that Glaser and Strauss were insistent that 'plausibility' was the standard by which case study data was to be assessed. What was espoused as a fairly radical epistemological position has regressed to a debate about the rigours of method. There is a very important but largely neglected point to be made here, and that is that the limits and purposes of acceptable comparison have never really been established. It is one thing to look at responses to mortality across different wards in a single hospital and quite another, as Kashimura et al. attempt to do (Chap. 4, this volume), establish points of comparison across a whole domain which they refer to as 'construction and maintenance'. It is one thing to compare because the appropriate level of generic technology is being sought and quite another to compare because there is a sociological demand for theories which emanate from case studies.

A second possible explanation for this overall lack of progress might lie in the problem of interdisciplinarity or rather the lack of it. Most academics shaping the CSCW discourse still do this from their disciplinary perspectives, commitments, and epistemologies. While high-level statements about conceptual relationships are of decreasing value, it has been our position for a long time now that the absence of a corpus of studies (in any useful sense) continues to limit the work that the CSCW community carried out over the last 25 years. These may seem contradictory statements, but they are not. The commitment to common concepts which we lack in CSCW as a research field results in a nonexistence of relevant corpora.

Our point is that comparison across a corpus of different studies needs to be at an appropriate level of generality. A corpus must be more than simply a collection of studies, for without some kind of conceptual framework, comparison of the studies within the corpus is difficult, to say the least (see for a first attempt Chap. 7, Wulf et al., in this volume). At the same time, one-size-fits-all theoretical statements are of such generality they have little practical value. What is needed, we would suggest, are frameworks which recognise some degree of domain specificity or at least provide us with some means to compare the usefulness of tools and technologies from one setting (and possibly domain) to another. Why do such conceptual frameworks not exist? A possibility is that candidate alternative approaches seem vested in defensive positions where, other than vacuous claims about the superiority of one perspective over another (vacuous given that we have no means to measure competing theoretical claims in relation to the success or failure of designs), the dominant tendency is simply to ignore the competition. Why might this be? One reason is that they remain mired in their original disciplinary concerns. All are imagined to be universal acids, in which *all* design problems can be dissolved, independent of any domain specificities and, more often than not, independent of any sense that analytic choices might depend to a degree on the specific nature of the design problems we deem to be relevant. Discussion, where it takes place at all, continues to take place at the level of professional privileging (why ethnographies need to be done by anthropologists, why the rigours of the experimental method conducted with small numbers of undergraduate students are deemed relevant to the kinds of problem we describe, why social psychological concepts of dubious provenance (see Brannigan 2004) continue to be used largely uncritically, and so on).

A third factor may be that the number of serious, long-term studies of organisational life and its relationship to new technology is not increasing, while the number of short-term, narrowly focused studies of matters relating to mobile phone use, game playing and new technology, the different (and sometimes surprisingly ephemeral) social media, and so on most certainly is. If this seems like a complaint about topic, it is not. Some of the editors, at least, have been involved in studies of this kind. Indeed, such topical studies might teach us a lesson. It is quite likely that qualitative studies in focused areas such as game playing might well provide for generalities precisely because they cover a relatively homogeneous set of cases.

The homogeneity in question is not difficult to identify, given that there will be some natural limit to the number of ways one can usefully categorise the differences between one game and another. Our complaint is of a quite different kind. It is that we pay progressively less attention to 'difficult' cases, cases where precisely what the hugely complex arrangements to be found in any organisational context tell us about the introduction and use of technologies designed to support those arrangements. Our (unoriginal) insistence on practice-based computing is aimed at reminding us that many of these problems remain obdurate.

In the following, we want to line out some of the research challenges when taking a practice-based perspective on socially embedded technologies seriously.

17.2 Time, Distance, and Heterogeneity

'Practice', put simply, must involve some notion of endurance. Practices can only be recognised as practices if they have a degree of regularity and persistence. At the same time, as long ago as 1965, Emery and Trist noted that organisations vary in their capacity to respond to rapid change in their external environment. Design of the kind we are interested in, that is, needs to reflect not only practices in the organisation but also changes which impact on them. Practices clearly do change as a result of the introduction of new technologies and/or changes in organisational rules brought about by external pressures. The first challenge, then, is to make sense of how the passage of time affects our analysis. Technological innovation can, and frequently does, move very fast indeed. If practices are embedded in routines, skills, and material artefacts, then changes in that artefactual ecology will inevitably have effects.

A second challenge is to assess the importance of the way in which new technology and new organisational forms have affected practice. They have evidently enabled new forms of geographic mobility and dispersal. Colocation cannot now be assumed. It is now possible for bank clerks sitting in processing centres in one part of a country to deal with customers dispersed right across that country as data about those customers is shared. It is now possible for work to be done as one sits at an airport gate waiting for a plane to take one home late on a Friday night. It is now possible for business and commercial interests to collect and use data directly from a range of online behaviours associated with, for instance, the social media.

The third challenge lies in the so-called knowledge economy. There can be little doubt that we are situated in a rapidly evolving information landscape. While we do not completely buy such conceptions of late capitalism in all their detail, especially given that an increasing number of people seem to be working in low-paid, low-skill jobs, it is nevertheless the case that one category of skilled worker – call them 'knowledge workers' – is engaged in aggregating and deploying a range of heterogeneous skills that we need to understand better. If there is any substance to the concept of 'knowledge economy', it is safe to assume that role flexibility is associated with it. As Beringer and Latzina put it in Chaps. 1 and 2, new industrial and commercial demands have developed as a result of mobile technology, Web 2.0 networked solutions, semantic technology, and so on, and, in turn, this is producing a new generation of knowledge workers for whom 'context of use' might mean something quite different.

Of course, *that* these changes have taken and are taking place is not the point. Any sociologist with ten minutes to spare can generate arguments to this effect. The problem is to understand *how* these effects are working through. These sources of complexity mean that the self-contained ethnographic study is going to have limited effect. Not least, technological development of a significant kind often takes place as enquiries are taking place into practices in a given setting. The kind of 'design case study' approach advocated by Wulf et al. or Lewkowitz and Salembier (Chaps. 6 and 8) provides at the very least lineaments of the discussions we need to have.

17.3 Participation

The word, 'participation' is so value laden that it is hard to imagine anyone in our design community wanting to argue against it. It is, effectively, a sine qua non. Of course, when it comes to participation by whom, for how long, for what purpose, and with what degree of power or control, that apparent consensus quickly vanishes. We should point out here that some kind of orientation to participation is fundamental to the CSCW perspective we avow, in the sense that the rejection of 'scientism' necessarily entails a recognition of a reflexive relationship between the person doing the studying and his/her subjects. Sociologists have long recognised that all observation is participant observation (see Gold 1958). The simple business of asking questions, for instance, entails the soliciting of relevant responses. Participation can, at its simplest, mean nothing more than the gathering of information. Ceding some degree of power or control, a much stronger vision of the role of the user, has long been the objective of the participatory design community. A number of our contributors examine the issue of participation and in particular the point at which participation might start or stop (or much more radically, whether it ever should – see Chap. 11, Simone and Cabitza in this volume). A developing theme, in their work, in the work of people concerned with 'Living Lab' research, and indeed others (see in particular Fischer and Hermann on metadesign), is how we deal with the ethics of participation and how the participatory relationship can be made 'sustainable'. Academic projects, in particular, tend to have clear start and end point kinds of setting, and as various authors have reported (see Lancaster/Siegen comparison), this creates dilemmas all of its own, especially given the different expectations of various partners. Organisational complexity and the attendant heterogeneities already mentioned mean that the problem of participation can no longer be conceived of as a discussion about the relationship between the researcher and the researched, important though that is. It becomes, as much, a discussion about the various communities of interest that constitute the 'researched' in the first place.

17.4   Transferability

Much of the work in the chapters above engages with the kind of conceptual problem entailed in comparing one setting with another. Our authors, in their different ways, are attempting to find a means to engage with conceptual issues such that the concepts in question do not evolve from, say, sociological truisms about the nature of 'identity', 'community', and so on but instead reflect the fact that work practices are complexly constructed in domain-specific ways. Of course, saying this is easy. Identifying these specific modalities and relating them to the applicability that technologies must have are not. A moment's thought will tell us that understanding the specificities of a setting alone is of variable value in a design-related context. Such analysis may repay substantially in poorly understood domains, of course, but is less likely to be of value – on its own – where applications are intended to be of use across a variety of settings. What matters is the degree to which these settings are or are not similar to each other. Design by definition entails some level of generality.[2] And, of course, it is true that comparison of a kind is always taking place at the level of the literature review. Nevertheless, the tendency in the qualitative CSCW literature, we would suggest (often for reasons of publication need), is to emphasise the differences between what is discovered in the setting in question and what might be true elsewhere (there are some exceptions, e.g. Chap. 14, Bjørn and Boulus-Rødje, this volume). There are good reasons for this as well, since we know from a variety of evaluation studies that what works in one setting may not necessarily work so well in another. At the same time, we also know that certain kinds of devices work extremely well in a wide range of contexts. Our problem is that we cannot know for sure which situation will pertain in advance to enquiry, installation, and evaluation – as the very substantial literature on electronic patient record systems indicates. Our point is precisely that an adequate examination of similarities and differences can only be done with a careful and consistent application of relevant concepts, grounded in the comparison of different settings within comparable domains. Of course, the issue is what kind of comparison is likely to prove useful for design-related purposes. One might reasonably expect, therefore, to find that over time, a set of concepts which range from the low-level and specific up to some appropriate mid-level concepts develop which are precisely a basis for comparison across settings.

It is clear that if our chosen topic is the complexity of various interwoven practices in complex organisational and work settings, then we need to find more convincing ways of dealing with the similarities and differences we find across the various settings which we can characterise as being part of a domain. Domains, we will stipulate, are characterised by more or less common objectives. That is, they are defined by *what* needs to be done. We can speak of transportation as a domain because there is a common purpose in getting people from A to B. Retail sales,

---

[2]We are only too aware that even the most narrowly construed qualitative study will produce some kind of generalisation – to the effect that, for instance, respondents 'typically' report X or Y. That isn't the point, of course. Comparison from one setting to another is.

financial services, construction and repair, and so on can be thought of as domains in that sense. Nevertheless, selling shoes may not be exactly like selling food, and if we are to understand why some kinds of online sales appear to be more successful than others, it may be worth understanding why. After all, if it turns out to be the case that people are reluctant to buy fruit and vegetables online because they are uncertain about freshness, it might be difficult to transfer that to an understanding of what motivates people (or not) to shop for shoes online. The work of a hedge fund may not be exactly like the work of a retail bank (at least, we earnestly hope it is not). Treating an acute cancer patient may entail very different practices from treating children with long-term chronic illnesses. Treating chronic illness in a hospital may be different from managing chronic illness at home (see Chap. 15, Katzianis and Ackerman in this volume). A 'setting' in this context, then, we can characterise as a set of practices bounded by common organisational and/or normative rules, by more or less stable or routine 'ways of getting things done' and by common technological/material features supporting those ways. There are a number of reasons why consideration of the setting is important. In the first instance, we need to pay attention to the precise way in which any given set of technological artefacts is designed such that it does not unnecessarily disrupt existing practices. Equally, we need to be sure that benefits do accrue after the introduction of new technology, and efficiencies are not the product of people producing 'workarounds'. We also need a 'situated' form of evaluation that allows us to compare the different ways in which new technologies are appropriated in different settings.

It is not difficult to see, in principle, how settings within a domain can share common features while at the same time exhibiting specific elements. Certain systematic themes play out in the various contributions to this book which relate to this problem of usefully relating similarities and differences. We begin to see this in the chapters above which concern themselves with different kinds of healthcare (Fitzpatrick; Katzianis and Ackerman). This, we argue, is essential if a CSCW perspective is to continue to mount a coherent challenge to the orthodoxies we recount above. The task, put simply, is to find useful ways of dealing with similarity and difference.

The editors have argued, jointly and independently, over a number of years that the benefits of a 'CSCW' perspective will be seen to accrue when a corpus of studies has evolved, and, moreover, the corpus in question needs to evolve from a 'practice-based' approach of the kind we support. A corpus, however, requires a great deal more than merely assembling a large number of studies. No corpus can exist, as we have suggested, without some sort of conceptual, methodological, and domain-relevant procedure which renders it readable across cases. Some degree of systematicity is evidently needed. Again, we recognise that this is easy to say, not so easy to do. It is our contention that the chapters in this book in their different ways all implicate a view of 'practice-based' computing which might allow for transferability from one setting to another. What that may entail, we now discuss.

Our approach favours the abandonment of high-level visions of ICT development, necessitates reflection on the inadequacies of the 'situated' approach to computing (treated alone), and looks for a mesa-level form of analysis that affords work, business, and other environments real and practical methods for developing, understanding, and progressing design. In this way, we hope to address the three problems that constitute the main themes of the book. These are, in turn, the continued domination of large-scale, generic application development in the European context, the challenge of and the need to move beyond some naive versions of the 'situated'.

We have alluded to the fact that the generic applicability of computer systems has not, in CSCW, been accompanied by a level of generalisation which matches it. It would be a mistake, however, to see generality as being only a matter of concept formation. Just as much, it is a matter of the artefacts themselves.

17.5 Supporting Appropriation and End-User Development

As already mentioned, the transferability of insights in our academic community does not only happen by means of concept building but also via the appropriation of appropriately designed IT artefacts. In this sense, the transferability of insights happens when a specifically designed IT artefact is appropriated in a new domain of social practice. Findings about the context-specific applicability of IT artefacts have, therefore, a high level of design relevance.

The transferability of IT artefacts always requires the user community to incorporate the IT artefact into their social practices (and develop their practices in that way) (Pipek and Wulf 2009). We can basically distinguish two cases (Wulf 1999):

- The IT artefact is sufficiently generic to allow for appropriation in new domains of application.
- The IT artefact requires modifications, extensions, or tailoring to support (and develop) the necessary practices in a new domain of application.

Both cases may require technical support for the appropriation work of a user community, e.g. via communication channels within the user community or via the exchange of best practices concerning the appropriation of the IT artefacts (Pipek 2005; Stevens 2010; Stevens et al. 2011). The second case requires additionally that its functionality can be modified fast and with little efforts inside the domain of application. To minimise efforts necessary to modify an artefact, one may combine approaches of end-user development (Lieberman et al. 2006; Beringer and Latzina, and Dittrich, in this volume) with evolutionary approaches in software engineering. In situations where the given functionality does not support the development of the relevant social practices, options to tailor the groupware should be explored. This has clear implications not only for end-user development but also for the kinds of system we envisage. Thus, the system's software architecture, its user interface, and its support for appropriation work should offer enough technical flexibility to enable the transferability of IT artefacts.

In conclusion, we have laid out a position which will be familiar to many qualitative researchers working in HCI and CSCW, but our view, remember, is that despite the vaunted ambition of early CSCW position papers, rather less has actually been achieved than we might have hoped for. The contributions in this book, we hope, go some way towards explaining why this might be and making recommendations as to how progress might be made.

References

Bannon, L., Schmidt, K., & Wagner, I. (2011). Lest we forget. In *Proceedings of ECSCW'12*. Seattle: Springer.

Bonsiepe, G. (2007). The uneasy relationship between design and design research. In R. Michel (Ed.), *Design research now*. Basel: Birkhauser.

Brannigan, A. (2004). *The rise and fall of social psychology: The use and misuse of the experimental method*. New York: Aldine de Gruyter.

Charmaz, K. (2006). *Constructing grounded theory: A practical guide through qualitative analysis*. London: Sage.

Corbin, J. M., & Strauss, A. (1998). *Basics of qualitative research: Techniques and procedures for developing grounded theory*. Thousand Oaks, CA: Sage.

Corbin, J., & Strauss, A. (2008). *The basics of qualitative research: Grounded theory procedures and techniques* (3rd ed.). London: Sage.

Dourish, P. (2004). *Where the action is : The foundations of embodied interaction*. Cambridge, MA: MIT Press.

Emery, F. E., & Trist, E. (1965). The causal texture of organizational environments. *Human Relations, 18*(1), 12–32.

Emery, F. E., & Trist, E. L. (1973). *Towards a social ecology: Contextual appreciation of the future in the present*. London: Plenum Press.

Garfinkel, H. (1967). *Studies in ethnomethodology*. Cambridge: Polity Press.

Glaser, B., & Strauss, A. (1967). *The discovery of grounded theory: Strategies for qualitative research*. Chicago: Aldine.

Gold, R. (1958). Roles in sociological field observations. *Social Forces, 36*, 217–223.

Greenbaum, J., & Kyng, M. (1991). *Design at work: Cooperative design of computer systems*. Hillsdale: Lawrence Erlbaum.

Hevner, A. R., & Chatterjee, S. (2010). *Design research in information systems: Theory and practice*. New York: Springer.

Hevner, A. R., March, S. T., Park, J., & Ram, S. (2004). Design science in information systems research. *MIS Quarterly, 28*(1), 75–105.

Hodges, B., & Geyer, A. (2006). A nonconformist account of the Asch experiments: Values, pragmatics and moral dilemmas. *Personality and Social Psychology Review, 10*(1), 2–19.

Hutchins, E. (1995). *Cognition in the wild*. Cambridge, MA: MIT Press.

Kaptilinen, V., & Nardi, B. (2012). *Activity theory in HCI: Fundamentals and reflections*. San Rafael: Morgan and Claypool.

Kuutti, K., & Bannon, L. (2014). The turn to practice in HCI: Towards a research agenda. In *CHI'14 proceedings of the SIGCHI conference on human factors in computing systems*. Paris: ACM Press.

LaLancette, M.-F., & Standing, L. (1990). Asch fails again. *Social Behavior and Personality: An International Journal, 18*(1), 7–12.

Lieberman, H., Paterno, F., & Wulf, V. (2006). *End user development*. Berlin: Springer.

Mumford, E. (1981). Participative systems design: Structure and method. *System Objectives, Solutions, 1*(1), 5–19.

Mumford, E. (1995). *Effective systems design and requirements analysis: The ETHICS approach.* Basingstoke: Macmillan.

Mumford, E., & Henshall, D. (1983). *Designing participatively: A participative approach to computer systems design: A case study of the introduction of a new computer system.* Manchester: Manchester Business School.

Okasha, S. (2003). *Philosophy of science: A very short introduction.* Oxford: Oxford University Press.

Perrin, S., & Spencer, C. (1980). The Asch experiment: A child of its time. *Bulletin of the British Psychological Society, 32,* 405–406.

Perrin, S., & Spencer, C. (1981). Independence or conformity in the Asch experiment as a reflection of cultural and situational factors. *British Journal of Social Psychology, 20,* 205–210.

Pipek, V. (2005). *From tailoring to appropriation support: Negotiating groupware usage.* PhD thesis, Faculty of Science, Department of Information Processing Science, University of Oulu, Oulu, Finland.

Pipek, V., & Wulf, V. (2009). Infrastructuring: Toward an integrated perspective on the design and use of information technology. *Journal of the Association for Information Systems, 10*(5), 1.

Randall, D., Harper, R., & Rouncefield, M. (2007). *Fieldwork for design.* London: Springer.

Reckwitz, A. (2002). Toward a theory of social practices: A development in culturalist theorizing. *European Journal of Social Theory, 5*(2), 243–263.

Rohde, M., Stevens, G., Brödner, P., & Wulf, V. (2009). Towards a paradigmatic shift in is: Designing for social practice. In *DESRIST 09.* Malvern: ACM Press.

Schmidt, K. (2014). The concept of practice. *Proceedings of COOP,* Nice, France.

Simonsen, J., & Robertson, T. (2013). *Routledge international handbook of participatory design.* New York: Routledge.

Stevens, G. (2010). *Understanding and designing appropriation infrastructures: Artifacts as boundary objects in the continuous software development.* PhD thesis, University of Siegen.

Stevens, G., Pipek, V., & Wulf, V. (2011). Appropriation infrastructure: Mediating appropriation and production work. *Journal of Organizational and End User Computing (JOEUC), 22*(2), 58–81.

Strauss, A., & Corbin, J. (1990). *Basics of qualitative research: Grounded theory procedures and techniques.* Thousand Oaks: Sage.

Suchman, L. (2007). *Human-machine reconfigurations: Plans and situated actions.* Cambridge: Cambridge University Press.

Whyte, W. F. (1948). *Human relations in the restaurant industry.* Oxford: Mcgraw-Hill.

Wulf, V. (1999). Evolving cooperation when introducing groupware: A self-organization perspective. *Cybernetics & Human Knowing, 6*(2), 55–74.

Wulf, V. (2009). Theorien sozialer Praktiken zur Fundierung der Wirtschaftsinformatik. In J. Becker, H. Krcmar, & B. Niehaves (Eds.), *Wissenschaftstheorie und Gestaltungsorientierte Wirtschaftsinformatik* (pp. 211–224). Heidelberg: Springer/Physika.

Wulf, V., Rohde, M., Pipek, V., & Stevens, G. (2011). Engaging with practices: Design case studies as a research framework in CSCW. In: *Proceedings of ACM Conference on Computer Supported Cooperative Work (CSCW 2011)* (pp. 505–512). New York: ACM Press. http://www.theguardian.com/society/2013/sep/18/nhs-records-system-10bn. http://www.washingtonpost.com/blogs/wonkblog/wp/2013/01/11/why-electronic-health-records-failed/